Founding Fathers

A Captivating Guide to Benjamin Franklin, George Washington, John Adams, Thomas Jefferson, John Jay, James Madison, Alexander Hamilton, and James Monroe

Free Bonus from Captivating History (Available for a Limited time)

Hi History Lovers!

Now you have a chance to join our exclusive history list so you can get your first history ebook for free as well as discounts and a potential to get more history books for free! Simply visit the link below to join.

Captivatinghistory.com/ebook

Also, make sure to follow us on Facebook, Twitter and Youtube by searching for Captivating History.

Contents

Introduction

They came from all walks of life, all social classes, and all religions, but they were united by their unquenchable thirst for freedom. Armed with unwavering courage, they first came to a new country, faced a raw, rugged land, and saw a vision of a new world after the eclipse of tyranny. The Founding Fathers parented a nation that dared to be different from all that had come before it. Because of the courage of the Founding Fathers, America was no longer an experiment but instead a never-ending process renewed throughout the generations.

The Founding Fathers lived and worked during the most tumultuous and exhilarating times of a new nation conceived in liberty. These men were all different from each other, but they forged America into a harmonious collage of strength and individualism.

The first and perhaps most well-known Founding Father was George Washington. As a young man, he surveyed the untamed lands of the Ohio Valley and was the first to see the Shenandoah River carving its way through the Blue Ridge Mountains.

They used to say that George Washington was destined to be a wealthy planter, but he spent seven years fighting a war instead— the American Revolution. In 1776, Washington arrived outside of

Boston in an old and tattered uniform from his early military days to lead a motley group of volunteers. They were dressed in britches and toted worn muskets. None of them had learned how to fight professionally; this group was made of backwoodsmen, tailors, and farmers, to name a few. As Washington's eyes darted back and forth over them, he saw the light of liberty glowing in their eyes and sensed that these scruffy warriors could win against all the odds. But quoting the immortal words of the philosopher, Thomas Paine, George Washington said, "The harder the conflict, the greater the triumph."

His soldiers were fiercely loyal as he was to them. Throughout the bitter winter at Valley Forge, Washington begged for clothing, ammunition, and supplies. The most illustrious and well-loved nobleman of France, the Marquis de Lafayette, was at his side. Lafayette had arrived early to help with the fight, as it wasn't until America had won the Battle of Saratoga in 1777 that France officially allied with America. This alliance was sought and obtained through the undying efforts of the elder statesman and Founding Father Benjamin Franklin.

In Philadelphia, two other Founding Fathers—John Adams and Thomas Jefferson—worked with Franklin to hammer out the principles that culminated in the Declaration of Independence in 1776. John Adams was initially drafted to write the declaration, but he humbly declined, telling Jefferson, "You can write ten times better than I can."

John Adams' practicality was always apparent and engendered gratitude. When the Continental forces were forming, Adams saw to it that they would be paid for their courage and their efforts during the war. After being appointed to head up the Board of War, Adams recognized the pressing need for foreign support because the colonists had no navy nor sufficient arms to fight a long-term war for independence. He thus went to France to present an appeal, taking Benjamin Franklin with him. As a result, the

Marquis de Lafayette and a skilled military soldier, Baron von Steuben, crossed the mighty Atlantic with some ships and arms.

John Adams didn't rest; he worked behind the scenes. He made arrangements for arms and military equipment from Spain through a shell company and even convinced the Dutch to support the War of Independence and secured a two-million-dollar loan from them to fund the war effort.

In 1783, Benjamin Franklin, John Adams, and a young statesman and future Founding Father from New York, John Jay, formulated the details of the Treaty of Paris, thus ending the war.

After the Revolution, it wasn't yet time for George Washington to lead the life of a gentleman farmer at his plantation in Mount Vernon. He had inspired a generation of future Americans through his selfless efforts during the War of Independence and was elected the first president of the new nation in 1789. Washington served in that office for eight years. John Adams was his vice president for both terms.

During his presidency, George Washington heavily consulted his Cabinet as he wanted all sides of an issue to be represented. Partisan politics was abhorrent to him because of the relative youth of the nation. He selected young Thomas Jefferson and Alexander Hamilton to serve even though they were usually on opposite sides of most issues. Jefferson, a planter from Virginia, was one of the Founding Fathers who eventually became the third president of the country. Washington knew Hamilton, another Founding Father, as his aide-de-camp during most of the war. Hamilton also fought under Washington at White Plains, Brooklyn Heights, Trenton, and Princeton. Hamilton was one of the soldiers present at Cornwallis' surrender at Yorktown and was the artillery captain responsible for the unexpected fate of the headless horseman whose story is still told today in the "Legend of Sleepy Hollow."

After he retired from the presidency in 1797, George Washington was followed in office by his vice president, John Adams.

Although he reached his adulthood during a time of crisis in the British colonies, Adams was a man of peace. He knew the value of compromise more than the fiery Patriots around him who had impulsively resorted to violence to express their anger toward Great Britain. Adams was perhaps the first American to promote the effectiveness of passive resistance

In 1796, John Adams ran against the very popular Thomas Jefferson and won in 1797. One of the reasons that happened was due to the fact that the French Revolution exploded and not only in France, as it spread to other European countries as well. The United States was in its infancy stage and forging out its own future, different from that of France. It was Jefferson who had supported France and lost many votes because of that.

Early in his administration, John Adams was confronted with the challenge of keeping peace with France and Britain, particularly against the pressures emanating from one article from the Treaty of Amity and Alliance. It stipulated that America would join France in case of an attack. In 1793, Britain had declared war against France, meaning that the United States should now declare war on Britain. To avoid war, Adams sent a secret peace commission to Paris led by three men under the code names "X," "Y," and "Z." This meeting and its aftermath was called the "XYZ Affair" after their code names. When the commission failed, Adams was highly criticized until it was revealed that the foreign minister of France, Charles Talleyrand, tried bribing the United States into giving him a hefty amount of money. Suddenly, John Adams was heralded in the streets as a hero who stood his ground and as a man who stood for truth and justice the American way.

France hadn't reconsidered its stance since the XYZ Affair, and in 1798, France sent ships into American waters, confiscating men and vessels from the nascent American navy. On the high seas, French warships like *Le Croyable*, *L'Magicienne*, *Bonaparte 7*, *Cere*, *La Vengeance*, and others harassed American ships, sinking some of them in the process. Adams retaliated by commissioning the building of 45 United States warships like the *USS Constellation* and the *USS Merrimack* to protect and defend American shipping lanes. These naval engagements never reached the level of becoming a declared war, so the action was called the "Quasi-War."

Although Adams was preparing his ground troops against a potential invasion from France, a ground war never happened. Napoleon Bonaparte had ousted the outdated and overspent National Assembly and seized power over all of France. He had no interest in engaging in conflict with America. So, in 1800, the Treaty of Mortefontaine put an end to the Quasi-War.

Also in the year 1800, John Adams ran for reelection, along with another Federalist, Charles Pinkney, whom everyone liked. Partisan politics, however, had reared its ugly head. John Adams ran for a second term, but he discovered that Alexander Hamilton had slammed his reputation. Others picked up on Hamilton's verbal assault and began to mock Adams. Because Adams was short and portly, his decriers called the president "His rotundity!" Because of the blatant negativity, he didn't win the reelection. From that point on, Adams realized he had political enemies even in his own party.

Jefferson had by this point in time solidified a unified base called the Democratic-Republicans, and Hamilton tried to influence the next election by promoting John Adams' running mate, Charles Pinckney, rather than John Adams. Insane rumors flew around about Adams, one of which stated that his young son, John Quincy, planned on marrying the daughter of King George III of England!

In 1800, Thomas Jefferson became the third president of the United States, and Hamilton's nemesis, Aaron Burr, became the vice president. Adams had been stung badly by the strident partisan politics and retired to his farm at Peacefield where he had a blended family composed of his own children and his deceased son's children. He was frequently visited by his married son, John Quincy Adams, and their delightful family as well.

John Adams' political opponent in the 1800 campaign for president, Alexander Hamilton, had been born in the West Indies and knew a great deal of hardship as a boy and an adult. The tyranny he had witnessed sensitized him to the necessity of guiding America during its nascent stages. Hamilton realized early on that he could assess people and—coupled with his interest in politics—he knew he could influence and persuade people. He was an extraordinary political power broker of his age. For a man who was born into a dysfunctional family and left penniless while young, this was an invigorating experience. For once, he found that people judged him not for his wealth but for his mind and heart.

One wonders how it was that he was able to place the country on such solid financial footing, considering that he grew up in poverty. After the American Revolution, the country owed about 54 million dollars, mostly to foreign governments. Because Hamilton had bounced from poverty to a secure financial status in his own life, he felt that nothing was impossible for anyone who was determined. As secretary of the Treasury under Washington, Hamilton established the First National Bank and braved the criticism of the populace who called him the "bastard of eastern speculators." The plan worked until a few corrupt speculators connived a scheme and wasted the funds in 1792. However, Hamilton was unafraid of taking up the gauntlet and corrected the situation.

Hamilton was also a "charmer." Tall, good-looking, and suave, he attracted women to him. Of course, that pleased him immensely, but it caused problems as well. While he was juggling with finances, a beautiful woman and her estranged husband lured him into a madcap scheme that resulted in an illicit love affair. Once that came to light, it was fodder for the gossip-mongers in the capital, and Hamilton was forced to reveal the embarrassing details of the whole episode.

During his role as a campaigner, Hamilton gained as many friends as enemies. He ran into severe political differences with other Founding Fathers, including James Madison, Thomas Jefferson, and James Monroe. They were all Democratic-Republicans while Hamilton was on the other side, being a Federalist. One of the individuals whom Hamilton considered "dangerous" was Aaron Burr. For fifteen years, Hamilton followed Burr's career in politics and tried to wield his influence against him. What's more, Hamilton supported his own relatives when they ran for office against Burr, and it was Hamilton's opposition that led to Burr's defeat in his gubernatorial election. Aaron Burr never handled political enmity well, so he challenged Alexander Hamilton to a duel. Hamilton had to respond for the sake of his honor and was gunned down by Burr in 1804 in Weehawken, New Jersey.

Like Hamilton, the elder statesman Benjamin Franklin was also a "ladies' man." One of his favorite female admirers used to call him *"Mon cher Papa."* When George Washington tried to send Franklin secretly to France for aid, the women and the people organized a parade in Nantes. His likeness was even printed on snuff boxes, rings, and medallions!

When John Adams was in France, he was told he lacked the "social graces and the ornaments" that would make for a proper courtier at the "Court of Saint James." Yet this older gentleman by the name of Benjamin Franklin, who wore spectacles and a fur hat tied at his chin, was a hit, especially among the women. Like Thomas Jefferson, he was a masterful conversationalist and had a delightful wit. As a young man, Franklin was naïve and took a risk when he ran away from home. He trudged through miles of mud in New Jersey with two loaves of bread stuffed into his pockets, engendering laughter wherever he went. Was it not for the brilliance he imparted when he spoke with clerics and storeowners upon his arrival in Pennsylvania, he could have been thrown into jail for vagrancy.

Armed with the support of more well-off patrons, Franklin set up his own print shop. He also bought a newspaper, *The Pennsylvania Gazette*, and became the most popular printer in the northern colonies. He was even hired to print the first Continental dollar bills.

In 1733, he published *Poor Richard's Almanac*, a journal of witticisms and wisdom that was snapped off the racks as soon it was published. Were it not for Franklin, there would be no fire stations in the early colonies, no insurance, and no libraries. Without him, there would be no mail.

Franklin's true avocation was that of an inventor. In 1744, he invented the Franklin stove and the lightning rod in 1751. Not only that, but he invented swim fins, the whale-oil lamp, a flexible catheter, the bifocal lens, a new odometer, and the "Armonica," a delightful musical instrument that the women loved. Franklin was so well known in the early colonies that Pennsylvania sent him to England to represent the state in resolving a financial dispute between the very powerful Penn family and Great Britain. By 1762, he impressed even the most powerful nobles in the king's court, including the prime minister, Lord Bute, and Dr. Joseph Priestley, a respected scientist who supported equal rights to the colonists, as well as William Strahan of British Parliament.

In 1765, when the colonists were burdened with the unfair imposition of the Stamp Act, Franklin was asked to intercede and went to heroic efforts to do so. Due to his connections at the higher levels of government there, he was heard by the highest commission in Great Britain—the Privy Council itself. They put him through a humiliating procedure, but he convinced them that it was unwise to enforce the Stamp Act as it would compel the colonists to boycott English goods. In 1766, Franklin finally did get England to repeal the Stamp Act. Even King George complimented him when he quipped to his council, "That crafty American is more than a match for you all!"

When the Second Continental Congress met in Philadelphia in 1775, many of the Founding Fathers, including John Adams, John Jay, and Thomas Jefferson, wrote the Olive Branch Petition and sent it to Franklin in England. Upon reading it, Franklin rapidly added his signature and presented it. When Franklin discovered that the petition was unilaterally rejected by the king, Franklin told the colonists. Therefore, they reached the conclusion that all attempts at a peaceable settlement wouldn't be reached, and war (the American Revolution) would be the inevitable result.

John Jay, another one of the illustrious Founding Fathers of the United States, met Benjamin Franklin in England. He loved Franklin for his creative mind and raised money for two colleges Franklin promoted—King's College (now known as Columbia University) and the University of Philadelphia.

Because of his astute mind, John Jay embraced the study of law. In his work, he was meticulous and always planned on being crystal clear when expressing himself. The passage of the burdensome Stamp Act of 1765 abruptly interrupted his legal work as it made the paper used for legal documents more expensive. More unreasonable taxes were passed by Great Britain following that, and John Jay was incensed. He then became a motivating member of the Committee of Correspondence, which was designed to create a shadow government that could be the basis for a new union.

Jay married Sarah Livingston, but the young couple was forced to cut their honeymoon short when his country called for his participation in the Second Continental Congress. His life as a father and husband were trying, as he had a son who died of smallpox and a daughter who was blinded by the same disease. His eldest son had a learning disability, and another daughter, Eva, had emotional difficulties.

During the American Revolution, John Jay set up the first spy network to investigate and defeat conspiracies against the country by British loyalists and agents. Therefore, he was considered the first head of counterintelligence in the country. Today, the proud New York institution, John Jay College of Criminal Justice, stands as a testimony to John Jay.

When the Second Continental Congress created the Articles of Confederation, John Jay, Alexander Hamilton, and a fellow Founding Father, James Madison, wrote some *The Federalist Papers*, which advocated for the passing of a U.S. Constitution that provided more flexibility to conduct national and foreign affairs. The essays were printed in 1788 under the shared pseudonym "Publius."

John Jay had a predilection for the study of law, and he was one of the most famous lawyers who lived in colonial America. In 1789, he became the first chief justice of the United States. John Jay, it can be said with certainty, was a "lawyer's lawyer." Because of Jay, justices are required to be unbiased and neutral, thus fulfilling the principle cited in the Declaration of Independence that everyone is entitled to equality under the law.

Even though he wasn't noted for his physical prowess, that didn't stop Jay from being courageous in the face of adversity. For instance, he was knocked off a roof when quelling a campus insurrection and bravely withstood mockery and sarcasm when he was burned in effigy for having formulated the Jay Treaty in 1794. Instead of complaining, he remarked that the light cast by the fires made his walking easier at night!

John Jay became the governor of New York in 1795, and he was still in office when the Quasi-War broke out at sea in 1798 under John Adams' administration. Jay then battled for the funding to restore a ruined fort on today's Governor's Island in New York Harbor. It is an unusual star-shaped fort meant to defend New York and the northeastern coast from a naval attack. Today, that fort is called Fort Jay and is a national historic site.

In the 1800 election, Jay surprisingly only won one electoral vote. Partisan politics was then at a fever pitch due to the momentum created by Alexander Hamilton and Thomas Jefferson. That was an uncomfortable atmosphere for John Jay, so he retired from politics.

Thomas Jefferson, as a young statesman, was highly respected among his contemporaries for his verbal and writing skills. Close to his heart were the issues of the planters and the farmers in the South. He felt that all too often they were overlooked when bureaucrats lobbied for the passage of bills in Congress which often favored the merchant classes who never had to deal with the financial setbacks of drought or floods. The Democratic-Republican Party was his and James Madison's contribution to the political backdrop that flavored the elections. Jefferson's party favored the inalienable rights of the individual over the all-encompassing rights of the state. Because of his propensity for elegance in the written word, he was chosen to write the Declaration of Independence, which helped to set off the American Revolution. Every time there was need of a bright and eager delegate, Jefferson was the first to come to mind.

Jefferson was delighted when his country called upon him to serve as minister to France in 1785. Jefferson loved the French and fostered an ongoing commercial and cultural relationship with that country. Washington liked him for his level-headed leadership abilities and the fact that he could speak five languages, so he appointed him secretary of foreign affairs—a position that was later called secretary of state.

As a Cabinet member, Jefferson doggedly defended his political agenda and engaged in arguments with Alexander Hamilton, the secretary of the Treasury. It was said that he had relations with his household slave, Sally Hemings. That was considered to be a forbidden practice at the time, but some historians doubt it even occurred. However, evidence has been found recently that may substantiate that claim when a basement room was discovered at his plantation.

Thomas Jefferson was enormously popular and became the third president of the United States in the year 1801. He was the president who dealt with Emperor Napoleon Bonaparte, and in 1803, he leaped at the opportunity of making the famous Louisiana Purchase. This vast territory consisted of 827,987 square miles and secured America's access to the mighty Mississippi River. The American people wanted to know what geographical wonders lay in that huge tract of land, so Jefferson commissioned Meriwether Lewis and William Clark to embark on a two-year journey.

Although he wasn't known as an architect, Jefferson was highly skilled in that profession. He designed his home, Monticello, a building at the College of William and Mary in Williamsburg, and the Rotunda at the University of Virginia, which he founded. He also drew out a design of the campus. The North had fine educational institutions, and Jefferson wanted an American-built college in the South. So, after leaving public office, Jefferson received a donation of land from another Founding Father, James Monroe.

Although he looked like a healthy man, Jefferson suffered from stomach ailments and migraine headaches all of his adult life. His close friend and riding companion, James Madison, used to tease him unmercifully about that as it was usually a disorder that inflicted women.

During the American Revolution, Madison's capital city of Richmond was invaded by the British. He, his staff, and the people had to evacuate hurriedly. The state of Virginia was ravaged by the war, but George Washington responded by leading his highly motivated troops over 800 miles from New Jersey to Yorktown, Virginia, which is where the battle that marked the end of the War of Independence took place.

Madison wasn't healthy as a young man either. He tended to repress his feelings, so when he was overly concerned about his performance, his small, fragile body reacted to that. All young men alive during the onset of the American Revolution enlisted in the military to serve the country. It was expected. Upon his recruitment, however, he fainted during the exercises! Seeing that he didn't have the vigor or the stamina to serve, he was drummed out of the military.

Madison felt the urge to make his contribution toward laying the foundation for the new nation instead. He was just 25 years old when he went to Williamsburg to help inaugurate the movement toward independence. As a Southerner, he was especially sympathetic to individual rights and very much opposed to a strong central authority that had no sensitivity toward people in the interest of equal and uniform treatment.

Madison, unfortunately, was a purist and believed that people impassionedly chose their representatives. Of course, the power of persuasion needs the crutches of pleasure to boost itself. His opponents would throw parties and offer free drinks to potential voters. Due to his incredible naiveté, he lost the 1777 election of the Virginia House of Delegates.

His friends and family didn't want Madison's skills to go untapped though, so he was placed on the Governor's Council in Virginia. The council placed him on the Committee of Public Safety, and it was his responsibility to provide uniforms and weapons to the Continental Army led by George Washington.

After having learned to be a more hospitable host for voters, Virginia finally elected him to serve on the Second Continental Congress. While there, he resurrected his objections to some of the aspects of the Articles of Confederation, the first laws of the country. Because so many of those precepts were weak, Madison encouraged the assembly to develop a whole new body of legislation.

Many of the members of the Second Continental Congress were otherwise engaged in farming or fighting in the Revolution, so James Madison assumed the singular responsibility of shepherding the Constitution toward ratification. For that reason, he earned the title "Father of the Constitution."

Alexander Hamilton and Madison didn't see eye to eye on a number of issues, especially regarding Hamilton's establishment of the national bank. Madison had seen the banks foreclose on property loans on his neighbors in Virginia. Banks were heavily supported by the Federalist Party, which consisted mostly of Northerners who had never used a hoe. Madison then sought out Thomas Jefferson, and the two of them founded the Democratic-Republican Party. That party provided some healthy competition for the policies supported by those who favored a strong central government.

Madison considered the John Jay Treaty harmful as it gave a "most favored nation" status in commerce to Great Britain. Like Jefferson, Madison favored France as they had been so vital to the success of the American Revolution. In fact, when George Washington heavily promoted the John Jay Treaty in 1794, Madison vociferously objected. Washington had a very warm relationship with Madison up until that point. After that, neither of them communicated again.

Madison's clear support of preference for France led him to oppose John Adams, the second president of the United States who favored Great Britain as a primary trading partner. Madison then drew even closer politically to Thomas Jefferson. When Jefferson succeeded Adams and became the third president of the country in 1801, he selected James Madison as his secretary of state.

As secretary of state, Madison was extremely busy during the second term of Thomas Jefferson's presidency. Tensions between Britain and, surprisingly, France kept rising related to American commerce. In 1807, Britain's warship, the *HMS Leopold*, and the *USS Chesapeake* engaged in a naval battle fought mostly in the dark off the coast of Virginia. It was a British victory, and that gave Britain an appetite for more. France also joined in the fray by confiscating American vessels. Great Britain was often at war with France throughout the years, and this antipathy grew even stronger during Jefferson's second term. As in the years before, those two countries tried to suck America into their own battles. That hostility set the stage for the next president who was James Madison himself. He was elected in 1808 and served until 1817.

James Madison spent the early years of his administration enveloped in foreign affairs. International commerce, monarchical England, Napoleonic France, and the delineation of the Canadian border in the Northwest Territory served as the backdrop for America's involvement in the War of 1812. Even though the stage was set for this during Jefferson's administration, perhaps even prior to that, it was still known as "Mr. Madison's War." It was a vengeful war, resulting in the burning of the capital, Washington D.C., which was reduced to crumbled stone and smoldering ruins. Madison barely escaped alive. Another Founding Father, James Monroe, who was serving as Madison's secretary of war, came through for Madison during those brutal engagements. In September 1814, the Battle of Baltimore ended the war in an American victory. When Madison left the office of president, the United States had definitively proven that it was willing and able to fight for its rights.

James Madison's Secretary of War James Monroe served in the dual role as secretary of state. Upon Madison's retirement, Monroe was elected as the fifth president. Monroe had the good fortune of being president during a time known as the "Era of Good Feelings" (1817 to 1825). This was a casual American term that marked the whimpering collapse of the Federalist Party and was a period when the ferocity of partisan politics was at a low ebb.

Monroe's history in American affairs started during the American Revolution. When George Washington made his momentous crossing of the Delaware River at night to invade the British and attack their Hessian mercenaries, young Lieutenant James Monroe was already across the shore, establishing the route the Continental Army would take. He and his small vanguard regiment proceeded to McConkey's Ferry just a mile from Trenton. Their function was to cut off any escape route for the British and secure the road to Princeton, which was northeast of there. In relating the events of that night, Monroe said, "The drums were beat to arms, and two cannons were placed in the main street to bear upon the head of our column as we entered." It was shortly thereafter that Monroe was shot in the chest and shoulder and carried off the field of battle.

It was James Monroe's goal as president to make the entire United States free from foreign aggression and colonization. One of the most troublesome areas was the current state of Florida. In northwest Florida and Georgia, farmers and planters were subjected to raids from the Seminoles and the Creeks, Native American tribes who dwelled there. During the administration of James Madison, Monroe, as secretary of state, had unsuccessfully attempted to gain possession of the sunny state, which was owned by Spain at the time. Once he was president, Monroe tasked General Andrew Jackson with securing all of Florida. In 1819, Jackson was successful. By then, America controlled the land from the eastern coast to the borders of Idaho, Wyoming, eastern Colorado, and Texas.

The most significant feature of the Monroe presidency was what is called the Monroe Doctrine of 1823. For years, the settlers of the nascent United States were besieged by greedy foreign powers, anxious to nibble off sections of the new country for their own colonization. In addition, some of the European countries even wanted to regain control of the former colonies in British America. To put a final stop to this interference and their incursions, James Monroe, in no uncertain words, announced, "The American continents are henceforth not to be considered as subjects for future colonization by any European powers." By "American continents," he meant the Western Hemisphere. In exchange, he agreed that the United States would refrain from involvement in European conflicts. Like all Americans during the 18th century, Monroe firmly believed in the country of "the liberty of conscience in matters of religious faith, of speech and of the right to trial by jury," adding that, "if these rights are secured against encroachments, it is impossible that the government would ever degenerate into tyranny." James Monroe, along with Jefferson and Adams before him, was the third president to die on Independence Day—July 4th.

What can be said about the Founding Fathers of America? Their own ancestors came from lands across the sea to immerse themselves in the freedom of a new country. Some, like John Jay, were brought to the new world by their parents or ancestors because of the lack of religious freedom in their home countries. The ancestors of other early American settlers escaped their countries to attain political freedom. George Washington's great-grandfather lost his position during the English Civil War in 1643, and he came to America to support himself and his family. Hamilton came to the United States alone, seeking better opportunities in a land that promoted the ideals of freedom.

What all of them had in common, though, was their desperate human need for liberty and the pursuit of happiness. The evils of tyranny drove all of the Founding Fathers to create a nation and a society where there were no longer castes polluted by the whims of nobles and the greediness of kings. They pushed and pulled during painful political processes in order to create a future for their children and descendants, a future inundated with purpose, meaning, and the freedom of choice. The Founding Fathers established a foundation that would work for the future and for people whom they would never meet—even those who would follow them in the 21st century.

Part 1: Benjamin Franklin

A Captivating Guide to an American Polymath and a Founding Father of the United States of America

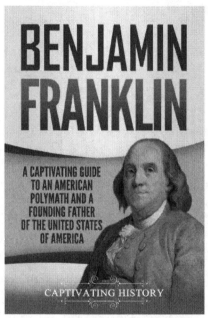

Introduction

Benjamin Franklin was a Founding Father of America and had an enormous impact on America as it is today. In addition to that, there are many little-known facts about the man who was Benjamin Franklin. Unlike many of the other Founding Fathers, he started out in humble circumstances. Franklin never finished college because his parents couldn't afford it. He hated his first job, and when he did get another one, he left without notice. He also took off from home without a word to his parents. Yes, Ben Franklin had money, but that ran out, and he wandered the streets of New Jersey and Pennsylvania broke and homeless. He, who once had pipe dreams of becoming a sailor, was shipwrecked near the coast of New York. Franklin was incredibly naïve as a young man. He could be easily fooled and was—on more than one occasion.

As an adult, he captivated the intellectuals of the day. His best friends were doctors, noted chemists, professors, philosophers, scientists, inventors, politicians, and authors. Benjamin Franklin's name is recorded in the National Archives of Great Britain and France as well as in the Library of Congress in the United States. He was a polymath with remarkable skills. Franklin was a writer, a scientist, a postmaster, a printer, a diplomat, and an inventor. One of his well-known inventions was the lightning rod, but the governor of Pennsylvania refused to install it. His mansion was in fact later struck by lightning!

There are plenty of rumors about him in the history books, and some are true. In 1998, skeletons were found buried in his basement! No, he wasn't a deranged murderer, but there was a sane and logical explanation for it. There were always logical reasons for his every action, but Benjamin Franklin was a unique person who was lost in the beginning but found himself and fulfilled his destiny.

From a young age, Benjamin Franklin fought for the rights of America at home and abroad. Yet, he bore the burdens of leadership and never shirked nor faltered in his mission. His greatest asset was his charm and friendliness, but he had his detractors as well, and felt the emotional impact of that.

Benjamin Franklin had enormous psychological and intellectual energy and worked every day until a week before he died at the age of 84. His impact on the future of America was unparalleled.

Chapter 1 – Young, Earnest, and Foolhardy

The Early Years 1713-1723

As a young boy, Benjamin reported every day to an odoriferous little shop run by his father, Josiah Franklin, at the corner of Hanover and Union Streets in colonial Boston. There, he made soap and candles. Carefully, he poured the hot fat of slaughtered sheep into narrow wooden molds and placed a frame on top with wicks he had made. Even in winter, the shop was hot and smoky. As he worked at the family trade, Ben's gaze strayed outside and he dreamed of traveling in those grand clipper ships across the ocean like his older half-brother, Josiah Jr., a sailor for the British Navy.

If he ran off to sea like Josiah Jr., Benjamin could climb up to a position on the topgallant yardarm and check out the horizon for miles and miles around. Instead of smelling putrid animal fat melting in his father's shop, he could smell the cool salt air and test the wind direction—oh, if only he was a sailor!

When he was 11 years old, Franklin had become an avid swimmer and wanted to design something that would help him move along faster in the water. He then created a pair of swim fins. They weren't used on one's feet, however; they were designed to be attached to the hands. This was his first real invention. In his autobiography of 1773, he wrote: "When a youth, I made two oval pallets, each about ten inches long, and six broad, with a hole for the thumb, in order to retain it fast in the palm of my hand."

A sailor's life would release him from a family where he had to live with fourteen other siblings still at home. Fortunately, the members of the Franklin household related well to each other. Of his early childhood upbringing, Benjamin once wrote:

> It was indeed a lowly dwelling that we were brought up in, but we were fed plentifully, made comfortable with fire and clothing, had seldom any contention among us, but all was harmonious, especially between the heads (parents), and they were universally respected—and the most of the family in good reputation—this is still happier than multitudes enjoy.

The house was small, so it was an overcrowded and noisy home. Benjamin was nearing the age that he could enroll in the British Navy, but his parents wanted a better life for him. Most young boys at sea were abused by the other sailors, and many of them were orphans or delinquents. Benjamin was smart and thought independently. Both his mother, Abiah, and his father knew he was unhappy in the candle and soap-making business.

His parents thought that Benjamin would make a fine minister. Toward that end, they had him enrolled in the Boston Latin School, but he didn't finish because they didn't have the money to keep paying his tuition, and Benjamin didn't show any interest in life as a clergyman anyway. In lieu of that, Josiah realized that Benjamin must have a trade to pursue. So, he took him to his Uncle Samuel's shop. Samuel was a cutler who made knives and other fine-edged tools. Franklin showed some interest in this, but Sam wanted Josiah to pay a fee for his apprenticeship. Ben could have become indentured instead, but that would bind him under contract, and Josiah felt that there might be better opportunities for him. Besides, Ben hadn't demonstrated any extraordinary ability in working with his hands.

Benjamin's half-brother, Josiah Jr., was lost at sea in the year 1715, so perhaps that wiped out any future consideration of such a dangerous career. Ben never brought up joining the navy again. Fortuitously, his other older brother, James, had recently returned from England where he had learned the printing business. Upon his return, James got a printing press and typesetting trays, and set up a print shop. He published a newspaper there called the *New England Courant*. Benjamin was a voracious reader by nature, having read every book in his father's small library, though many of them, in Ben's words, "were dry-as-dust religious texts except for Rev. Cotton Mather's *Essays to Do Good*." While a boy, he read *Plutarch's Lives* and John Bunyan's collection, which he purchased after reading *Pilgrim's Progress*. Ben was a lover of history as well and also bought Clarence Burton's *Historical Collection*.

When Ben saw the print shop and its newspaper, he was very interested, and his father was pleased. Because Josiah couldn't afford to pay for an apprenticeship, he indentured Benjamin to James. Benjamin would have to work for a number of years at the print shop, but it afforded him the chance to learn the trade from his brother.

This also meant Ben would get a stipend. He temporarily became a vegetarian at that time and discovered that the elimination of meat from his diet left him enough money to rent a room over the shop. There, he set up a library of his own, which grew very large in time.

Alias Silence Dogood

Twenty-two-year-old James was like most young lads at that age, headstrong and opinionated. To James, Benjamin was a mere child, dependent and devoid of ideas. That wasn't true, however.

Even as a young adolescent, Benjamin had ambitions of his own, and he was passionate about writing. So, Benjamin went to work for James but had to start out at the entry level and work as a "printer's devil." In time, Ben hoped to have his own byline.

Benjamin was a great help to his brother, but, according to historians, James was very demanding and unreasonable. Consequently, they had a lot of arguments. On a number of occasions, Benjamin's father even had to referee their disputes when they became overheated. Usually, Josiah took Benjamin's side in the frequent arguments.

While he worked at the print shop, Ben borrowed books from his other friends in the printing business, but had to return them rapidly because the books were intended for delivery to a third party. There was no such thing as a lending library in those days. Benjamin was always punctual in returning books and that added incentive made him a speed reader.

Benjamin really wanted to try his hand at writing some letters to be included in James' *New England Courant*. When he asked his brother if he could, James adamantly refused. Still determined to get his work in print and read the readers' reactions, he started mailing a series of letters to the paper in 1722 under the pseudonym "Silence Dogood," a fabricated widow. Ben was extremely prolific and sent in other letters under the amusing pseudonyms, "Anthony Afterwit" and "The Busy Body." People loved them, and the circulation of the *New England Courant* soared. When Ben proudly announced his authorship, James was furious and seething with jealousy. James himself then anonymously wrote editorials that occasionally criticized the English authorities in the colonies. In one reflection about problems with the Indian population in Canada, the paper criticized the way in which the English authorities there were handling the matter. In the *Courant*, it said:

> If Almighty God will have Canada subdued without the
> assistance of those miserable savages, in whom we have

too much confidence, we shall be glad that there will be no sacrifices offered up to the devil upon the occasion, God alone will have the glory.

Editorials were James' forte, and the *New England Courant* became one of the most read papers in Boston. Then, the governor of Massachusetts Bay Colony, Samuel Shute, found out about the editorials. He vehemently objected to some of those opinion pieces and the matter was referred to the Massachusetts General Court. As a result, poor James and even Benjamin were arrested. Because the Court indicated that the editorials cited some references in the Bible, they labeled them a perversion of the Holy Scriptures. It was suspected that the real reason for the governor's vindictiveness stemmed from the governor's disagreements with the colony and other British officials. Governor Shute was known to have many arguments with the Massachusetts Assembly and frequently suspended their sessions without just cause. He was also negligent in providing for the defense of the colony, which was a requirement he was supposed to fulfill, and the colonists were angry about that.

As a result of the case, James was sentenced to a month in jail, but the Court let Benjamin—who was only 16—get off with a stern warning. To make matters worse, the court also declared that James could no longer run the *New England Courant*, so Benjamin stepped in while his brother was incarcerated. In his own fashion, Benjamin wrote his Silence Dogood pieces and other articles that asserted the colonists' rights to free speech. In one of those Dogood letters, he stated:

Men ought to speak well of their Governors is true, while their Governors deserve to be well spoken of; but to do public mischief without hearing of it, is only the prerogative and felicity of tyranny: A free people will be showing that they are so, by their freedom of speech.

After James returned, he met with his friends regarding the future of the *New England Courant*. He and they decided to have

Benjamin remain on as the new editor, but wanted to draw up a new indenture for him. So, James took back the old indenture and had Benjamin sign a new one for another four years. Soon afterward, Benjamin and James had another dispute, and Ben's father disagreed with Ben this time.

Benjamin didn't want another term of indenture and was growing weary of their frequent bickering, so he permitted his emotions to overcome his judgment and left the print shop without notice. James was incensed and black-balled him all over the area so that Benjamin had difficulty finding new work in Boston. In the British colonies in the 18th century, it was considered a crime to escape one's indenture, so Benjamin's father became enraged about his departure and even put a notice in the *New England Courant* calling for his apprehension and return.

Because his brother had besmirched his reputation in town, Ben decided to go to New York. Surely, he could find work there. With the help of a friend, he sold a lot of his books to finance the journey. In New York, he scouted around for work in the printing business but found none. However, he met a printer named William Bradford who referred him to his son, also a printer, who needed a new employee. Bradford's son worked in Philadelphia, and that meant Franklin would have to travel by sea around the coastline and up the Delaware River. Shortly after he left in a sloop, a storm blew in. After being tossed and turned about, his boat was hung up on some rocks off the coast of Long Island. People tried to help, but nothing could be done until the storm had passed. So, he anchored the boat and tried to sleep. On the following day, he trudged ashore, soaked and filthy. After taking shelter, he grabbed his bag and changed his clothes. The next day, the water was calm, so he sailed for Amboy in New Jersey.

The rest of the journey was made by trudging across acres and acres of land in the incessant rain that haunted him as he crossed New Jersey. Painfully, he had learned that impulsive decisions such as the one that incited him to abandon the security of his print job with James had turned him into a hapless vagabond. He was wet and dirty and must have aroused suspicion among the people who saw him in this sad and sorry state. In his memoirs, he said, "I was thoroughly soaked, and by noon a good deal tired, so I stopped at a poor inn, where I stayed all night beginning now to wish that I had never left home."

Rather than being arrested for being a runaway servant, he discovered the charity of people to whom he was a stranger—and a miserable-looking one at that. The people he met took pity on him. What's more, Franklin discovered the rewards of being friendly and sharing his knowledge with other learned men. At the tavern where he stayed, he befriended the owner, a Dr. Brown. The doctor was fascinated with his superior knowledge, and they conversed many hours. In fact, Franklin maintained that friendship for the rest of his days.

After walking many miles, and paddling rented canoes, 17-year-old Benjamin Franklin arrived in Philadelphia.

Chapter 2 – Naiveté Collides with Reality

In 1723, Franklin pulled up to the Market Street Wharf. It had rained again, and he was soaked and hungry. Ben had only a few pence left and asked a boy to tell him where he might find some bread. After hearing that there was bread at the shop near the shore, he bought what he could for three cents. Again, his friendliness and pitiable innocence appealed to others, and he was given puffy rolls and a lot of copper and silver coins. After buying more bread, he stuffed his pockets with the loaves and strolled along the street munching. A young woman laughed at his comical appearance. She became Franklin's future wife a number of years later.

At long last, he met Andrew, the son of William Bradford, the New York printer who referred him. Unfortunately, Benjamin arrived too late because Bradford had already hired a new apprentice. However, Andrew was generous and offered to introduce him to another in the same trade, but only after he had a tasty breakfast.

His reference, a Mr. Samuel Keimer, was a scholarly man but not an excellent writer. Keimer was the publisher of the *Pennsylvania Gazette*. He also fancied himself a gifted poet and wanted Franklin to publish some elegies he had composed. Keimer knew nothing about repairing and setting up the old printing press which he had purchased at a discount, so Franklin employed his skills to help him. This was just part-time work, but Bradford offered to board Franklin there in a small room above the shop. It was a dismal room, but served his needs for the time being.

Later on, Andrew Bradford also stopped by, indicating he had occasional need of help at his print shop as well. The printed word barely reached the level of literacy between these two editors. Bradford, unfortunately, was functionally illiterate and Keimer— while somewhat more scholarly—didn't have a feel for journalism. Thus, Franklin survived for a time at these part-time endeavors.

Every once in a while, Benjamin became homesick—in a sense. He had given up living with his family and the securities of home. However, he had been gravely offended by his brother's retributions. Recognizing that he himself bore some responsibility in the private feud and the subsequent abandonment of his own family, he felt both guilt and a sense of pride because he wasn't going to return like the prodigal son. He was determined to be independent and self-sustaining. This was a turning point in his life.

To fight off the feelings of homesickness that crept in on him, Franklin befriended a lot of people in Philadelphia. He was a friendly and lively conversationalist especially at the print shops of Bradford's and Keimer's. When Keimer learned about his homely quarters at Bradford's house, he put Benjamin in touch with the nicer boarding house offered by a Mr. Read. Much to his surprise, Read's daughter was the same young woman who laughed at him with his bread-stuffed pockets wandering the streets. She was a lovely person, and Ben was enamored. He and Deborah dated, and they grew quite fond of each other. As he became more comfortable in his new city, Benjamin met more people there. Discovering that many were educated, Franklin and his new friends engaged in vivacious conversations. As a result of his friendly nature, word traveled, and he was no longer a "stranger" in town. News has a quick way of circulating, and Benjamin's presence became known to the captain of a sloop, Captain Robert Holmes. Coincidentally, Holmes was married to Ben's half-sister, Mary. Holmes regularly sailed a sloop between Boston and Newcastle, which was just south of Philadelphia. He later had a letter delivered to Benjamin, explaining that his family missed him and all would be forgiven if he returned home. Benjamin replied in a carefully worded and discreet letter about his reasons for leaving and his intentions to remain in Philadelphia.

Ben then showed the letter to his brother-in-law, Captain Holmes. Impressed with the composition of the letter, Holmes showed it to his passenger, Sir William Keith, the lieutenant-governor of Pennsylvania. Keith was amazed at the literacy of this young man and commented that the two Philadelphia printers Ben knew were lacking in literary skills. Keith was then determined to help Franklin get a good start in the printing and publishing business by providing him with material to print. Perhaps this would be a stroke of good luck.

The Governor's Surprise Visit

Without notice, Governor Keith and his companion, Colonel French, arrived at Keimer's humble shop. Keimer rushed downstairs to greet them but was astonished when the Governor inquired about Franklin instead of himself. When Franklin came in, Keith complimented him for his skills and suggested that the three of them retire to the local tavern to talk business. Keith had long desired a means by which he could reliably and professionally deliver the news to the colonists about the public businesses of both the governments of Philadelphia and Delaware. Keith then proposed that Benjamin's own father could fund him and set him up in a printing business of his own, where the governor would provide plenty of material to print. Keith promised to give Benjamin a letter to that effect, which would convince Josiah,

Ben's father, that the resulting publication would be successful. He then told Franklin to keep this matter private for the time being.

Benjamin's Disappointment

Benjamin made arrangements to go with Captain Holmes to Boston, and the captain eagerly told the Franklin family in advance about his upcoming visit home. By way of a preamble to Benjamin's arrival home, Captain Holmes mentioned to Josiah Franklin that the governor was very impressed with the boy. However, Josiah was a cautious man and asked Holmes many questions about the governor.

Captain Holmes took Benjamin back to Boston and wished him luck. Benjamin arrived at the harbor in a new suit, looking very businesslike and successful. Unlike his arrival in Philadelphia, he now had some silver coins in his pockets and little gifts for his mother and siblings at home. James wasn't there, as he was working at his print shop, and Josiah was out too. Franklin's sisters and mother were delighted when he gave them the gifts. Everyone talked for several hours. They inquired about his well-being and asked him about all of his undertakings since he left. Excitedly, he told them about his experiences in the print shops and his work on the *Pennsylvania Gazette*. His sister, Jane, was particularly delighted to see him, as they had always been very close. In fact, Jane and Benjamin kept up a very close relationship throughout life, and Benjamin was happy to have some time to speak with her.

Franklin then went to visit his brother's printing house. The employees there were very impressed with his fine suit, but James treated Ben in a very curt manner. Benjamin did, however, make it a point to meet with Collins, his dear friend, who was very excited and thrilled to see him. As they talked, Collins entertained the idea of leaving his dreary job at the Boston Post Office and even proposed that he and Benjamin could go to New York to create a new business for themselves that could be more lucrative. Collins was a learned young man, who had studied mathematics and philosophy, and was very interested when Ben talked about his career plans.

Josiah, on the other hand, showed little excitement about the governor's letter, saying that he and Benjamin would discuss it later. When Josiah finally made his opinion known, he told Benjamin that he was pleased the governor took such an interest in his son but felt he was still too young to undertake such a project. Benjamin was just eighteen years old at the time. Josiah then wrote a reply to the governor, indicating he wouldn't fund such an endeavor. Josiah told Benjamin that he might be willing to help set him up in business, but only when he was older and more experienced. Of course, Benjamin was very disappointed.

When he returned to Philadelphia, Franklin heard from Governor Keith again. Keith was dismayed that Josiah Franklin wouldn't help set the boy up in business, so he said,

> Since your father will not set you up, I will do it myself. Give me an inventory of the things necessary to be had from England and I will send for them. You shall repay me when you are able; I am resolved to have a good printer here, and I am sure you will succeed.

Keith then told Franklin to travel to England, and he would give him letters to carry directly to English suppliers. He said he would send a large packet of letters to the ship, several of which would be for Franklin. These, Keith informed him, were letters of credit so that Benjamin could purchase printing equipment and ship it back to Philadelphia. However, the matter must be kept secret, Keith added. On the pretext he was visiting home, Franklin took some time off from the employ of Keimer and Bradford.

Trip to London

Benjamin was scheduled to leave for England in 1724. Before his departure, he proposed to his dear Deborah. However, her mother wouldn't consent to the marriage because he hadn't shown her that he had a visible means of supporting her. The two were crestfallen but agreed to keep in touch. Benjamin felt he could reestablish the relationship when he returned to set up his new print shop.

When he spoke of his upcoming trip to some friends, Benjamin came upon another friend of his, James Ralph, who had also booked passage to London. On board, they met an older gentleman by the name of Thomas Denham, a Quaker merchant. Their friendship was a delightful one, and Denham even had him visit in his spacious cabin aboard ship. When he heard that poor Franklin and Ralph could only afford to travel in steerage, Denham made arrangements for them to stay at a cabin originally intended for his wealthy friend, Andrew Hamilton, who had to cancel at the last moment. What luck!

When he was arriving near the English Channel, Benjamin inquired about the letters that were carried aboard from Governor Keith. The captain, Colonel French, let Benjamin go through his packet of mail in search of Keith's letters for him. There were other letters in the pouch, but none for Franklin...none at all! Benjamin was deeply distressed over that and rushed over to Denham telling him of this. Denham replied he wasn't surprised at all, because he knew that Governor Keith was very unreliable. As for letters of credit, Denham indicated that Keith didn't even have sufficient capital to give anyone a letter of credit. Benjamin was gullible and incredibly naïve, even after having had experiences in life which should have precluded such an occurrence. Denham told Benjamin that he was going to be in Bristol for a while, should he ever have need to visit him, and suggested that Benjamin and his friend look for work in that city where there might be more opportunities.

It was now Christmas Day, 1724, and there they were in London. Ralph had no work prospects there. He was actually deserting his wife, whom he had left in the colonies, and planned on becoming an actor. Now, both were unemployed. When Ralph didn't find an acting job, he moved to Berkshire. So, there was Benjamin going door-to-door at Christmastime in search of work. Much to his surprise, he secured a job at Palmer's small print shop. Palmer didn't publish a newspaper. He published some ads about new stores opening up and printed some material for other customers, so there wouldn't be any opportunities for Franklin to start writing again. After a year had passed, he secured a better job at Watt's print company, but there was no option there for upward mobility. His friend, James Ralph, also occasionally visited, but mostly for the purpose of borrowing money rather than visiting. Benjamin was generous and always tried to help him out, but Ralph kept it up until Franklin himself was nearly out of money. Benjamin became depressed and was afraid he might have to stay there for the rest of his life.

While he was in London, he made it a point to visit with Thomas Denham from time to time. Two years later, Denham offered Benjamin a job when he returned to Philadelphia. Denham was a merchant and tradesmen in the dry goods business. This wasn't a job in publishing or printing, but Franklin could handle being a bookkeeper, an inventory clerk, and storekeeper if he could move back home. Denham even said he'd be willing to finance Benjamin's trip, and Franklin graciously accepted the offer. They departed for the shores of America and arrived in the summer of 1726. Shortly after he had worked with Thomas Denham, Benjamin developed pleurisy and was sick for some time. As soon as he recovered, however, he returned and assiduously applied himself to his tasks.

Chapter 3 – "B. Franklin, Printer"

Benjamin Franklin liked to sign his writings with the modest credit, "B. Franklin, Printer." When he first started out in Philadelphia, people knew him by that. Even though he had been away for a while, he was still no stranger in town.

When he was back in Philadelphia, he discovered that Deborah Read had married another man in 1725. Unfortunately, her new husband, John Rodgers, greedily grabbed her dowry and disappeared somewhere on the island of Barbados. Because of the bigamy laws, it would be illegal for Franklin to marry Deborah, but it made him heartsick to think that she had been abandoned and was virtually poverty-stricken as a result.

That wasn't the only misfortune of fate to befall him upon his return. Three years later—in 1728—his good friend, Thomas Denham, died of distemper, and his business folded. Franklin was now alone and jobless. There was no one in whom he could confide. These were not good times.

Printing had been his first trade, so he returned to Keimer's print shop. Keimer welcomed him warmly and gave him an even higher position than he originally held. Keimer knew Franklin was experienced in the use of the mechanics of the press and would be a great asset to his business, which had now expanded. Everything there went well until Keimer started arguing with Benjamin frequently. He seemed to find fault with Franklin's work and was often in a bad frame of mind. This reminded Franklin of the abuse of his brother, James, and he became disillusioned, even to the point of questioning his own competence. One day, however, Benjamin discovered that Keimer was heavily in debt. Distraught about this change of circumstance, Benjamin knew that the business might soon fail and was insecure about having to go through the drudgery of finding yet another job. Then, a regular customer came in, a Mr. Hugh Meredith, who was a well-to-do gentleman in Philadelphia. Meredith was in the business of sales and merchandising, and had a constant need of printers. Meredith was also well-aware of Keimer's financial situation and suggested that Franklin go into his own printing business. After Franklin indicated he had no money to do that, Meredith said he would partner with him.

Unlike the unfortunate experience with Governor Keith, Meredith was a responsible man and shipped in equipment from England. Franklin then set it up and hired some men. In 1729, Franklin purchased the *Pennsylvania Gazette* from his former employer, Keimer. Fortunately, Keimer had recovered a little from his financial woes but was still struggling. Keimer had started a new weekly paper, called *Instructor*, but it only had ninety subscribers.

Under Ben Franklin, the *Pennsylvania Gazette* soon became very popular. In order to spice it up a tad, Benjamin published wise adages in it. In addition, he discovered he was a talented advertiser and placed ads in it for Hugh Meredith and other people who wanted to sell goods. He then expanded it to include personal ads but kept certain standards by refusing to print defamatory or libelous articles written by private people. The quality of the print surpassed that of Keimer's paper. In 1730, the colony of New Jersey wanted paper money printed. They compared the quality of the three printers—Bradford, Keimer, and Franklin—and chose Franklin to print the first paper currency in New Jersey. He went to Burlington, New Jersey, with his aide to do that. It was quite a profitable job for Meredith and Franklin, and the extra funds provided capital to widen the circulation of the *Gazette*. After seeing the quality of Franklin's work on the New Jersey currency, Delaware also contracted him to print their money. The fortunes of fate were turning around.

Marriage to Deborah Read

Now that he had met with some success, Benjamin rekindled his relationship with Deborah Read. In 1730, he established a common-law marriage with her. Franklin then acknowledged that he had an illegitimate son, William. Franklin never revealed the identity of William's mother, but Deborah welcomed William into their home anyway and treated him as her own son. They had two more children of their own though, Francis and Sarah.

Deborah was a skillful seamstress and made all of Benjamin's clothes. Years later, he once said, "It was a comfort to me to recollect that I had once been clothed from head to foot in woolen and linen of my wife's manufacture, and that I never was prouder of any dress in my life."

Francis was born in 1732, and they called him "Franky." It is said he was a precocious child and it seemed clear that he was intelligent due to his alertness to all the stimuli around him. Franklin said of him that he was "a golden child, his smiles brighter, his babblings more telling and his tricks more magical than all the other infants in the colonies combined." The smallpox vaccine had been developed by then, but James, Ben's brother, argued against it, believing that it wasn't safe enough. Franklin was in favor of the inoculation, having had one himself. However,

Franky was ill for some time with influenza, so he and Deborah delayed, thinking they might wait until he recovered from that. Unfortunately, that took too long, and Francis contracted smallpox. He died in 1736. Benjamin and Deborah were devastated. Following that tragedy, Franklin wrote, "In 1736, I lost one of my sons, a fine boy of four years old, by the smallpox taken in the common way. I long regretted bitterly and still regret it."

The Junto and the First Library

Franklin's relationship with Hugh Meredith became stronger when the two of them started engaging in scholarly conversations. Meredith introduced him to some friends of his—Stephen Potts, George Webb, and a number of others. They had a study club and discussion group which they called "The Leather Apron Club," which was later called the "Junto." Topics were presented in the form of questions, and every time they met, they opined on the subjects. Many of these questions gave Franklin the ability to investigate many areas of science, religion, and politics, which he pursued later on in life.

The Age of Enlightenment, or Age of Reason, was an intellectual movement that arose during the 18th century, which provided the impetus for the Junto. The famous thinkers of that age included John Locke, Isaac Newton, and Voltaire. Thomas Paine and Benjamin Franklin were considered prominent American figures typifying the ideals of that age. The Junto applied logical, philosophical, and scientific approaches to the questions they pondered.

Below are some examples of questions posed at the Junto meetings which Franklin recorded in his diary:

"Can any one particular of government suit all mankind?

"Why does the flame of a candle tend to go upwards in a spire?"

"Should it be the aim of philosophy to eradicate the passions?

"Whence comes the dew that stands on the outside of a tankard that has cold water in it in the summer time?"

"Would not an office of insurance for servants be of service?

The members of the Junto then decided to set up a common library that might benefit others. Franklin organized it and charged a subscription rate. Scholarship in the colonies needed to be encouraged and not all could afford to buy printed books. From the funds, members of the Junto purchased books, and people could go to the building they leased in Philadelphia, as it was open to the general public. The facility was called the "Library Company of Philadelphia." A reader would leave some money down, borrow the book, and the money was returned when the reader returned the book. Lewis Timothy was the first head librarian, and his wife succeeded him in running the library after Peter's death a year later.

His Own Shop

In 1730, Meredith wanted to relocate, so he and Franklin dissolved their partnership under amicable circumstances. Franklin gave him his share of the profits, and Meredith left Benjamin with the ownership of the printing press and equipment. Meredith wanted to establish a company in a Welsh settlement farther south because there were sales opportunities in that area.

By 1731, there were six pages in the bi-weekly *Pennsylvania Gazette*. That was a lot for a newspaper in the early 18th century. It was sold not only in Philadelphia but parts of Delaware as well. Politically, the newspaper took a neutral stance. It contained essays and humorous anecdotes which Franklin himself wrote. One of its distinguishing features was the advertising. Many of the ads had to do with runaway slaves, business, real estate, auctions, and personals. Some were extremely personal, and Franklin eased up on his former principles by printing ads that may have harmed reputations. For example, Mr. Michael McKeel's wife had apparently deserted him, and he wanted to publicly embarrass her and take no responsibility for her:

> Without any just cause of complaint, Mrs. Mary McKeel hath eloped from my bed and board, all persons are therefore desired not to trust her on my account, as I am determined not to pay any debt she may contract after this date unless she returns to her good behavior. All persons are forewarned, at their peril, (for) harboring her.

Poor Richard's Almanac

Franklin had a great sense of humor and common sense as well. To please the readers' palates, he started publishing *Poor Richard's Almanac* in 1733 and continued publishing it until 1758. The *Almanac* sold about 10,000 copies per year. In addition, he also published the quotations anonymously. Some pithy examples:

1. He's gone, and forgot nothing but to say Farewell to his creditors.

2. He that lies down with dogs, shall rise up with fleas.

3. Better slip with foot than tongue.

4. He that cannot obey, cannot command.

5. Onions can make even heirs and widows weep.

6. Fools make feasts and wise men eat them.

7. A plowman on his legs is higher than a gentleman on his knees.

8. Creditors are a superstitious set, great observers of set days and times.

9. Remember that time is money.

10. God helps them that help themselves.

Franklin initially published *Poor Richard's Almanac* under the pseudonym, "Richard Saunders." In an effort at humor, Franklin falsely foretold the deaths of astrologers of the day. It was in jest, and they understood that.

Later, Franklin changed "Richard Saunders" into "Poor Richard." Poor Richard was based on "Isaac Bickerstaff," a character from Jonathan Swift's writings. Franklin also used *Poor Richard's Almanac* as a vehicle for his own political philosophy and scientific discussions. Franklin was clever, too. As a teaser, he published many stories in serial form, so he was able to sell the *Almanac* year after year.

Freemasonry

In 1731, Benjamin Franklin joined the Freemasons. Freemasonry is an outgrowth of the Middle Age system of the guilds formed by the cathedral builders and masons. After the Middle Ages were over, the Freemasons found themselves in a membership decline, so they expanded their membership by converting the organization to include social, political, and charitable functions. Freemasonry then became basically a fraternal organization. Members kept the old rituals and symbolism of the 15th century, and it was a secret organization, meaning one would have to apply and may or may not be accepted into a Lodge. Franklin rose quickly into prominence and became a Grand Master in Pennsylvania. In 1734, he edited and reprinted the organization's constitution originally written in 1723.

He also wrote articles about Freemasonry, saying, "I assure you that they are in general a very harmless sort of people, and have no principles or practices that are inconsistent with religion and good manners."

Freemasons take an oath to a set of moral conduct related to the practice of non-sectarianism in religion, obedience to legal, civic authorities, and the application of one's energies toward his respective occupation. Gluttony and drunkenness were forbidden (although members were permitted to drink). Quarreling was discouraged, and members were expected to help each other in times of need—financially and otherwise. Promotion within the society was based solely on merit, not seniority or social status.

Franklin attended the meetings of the Masonic Lodges while he was in England and France in later years. Franklin saw this participation as a means by which he could befriend the nobles and people in those countries, which constituted part of his diplomatic missions.

Chapter 4 – Philosopher, Inventor, and Public Servant

Ideas that were discussed at his Junto meetings planted the seed for new ideas and solutions. Franklin applied his inventive skills toward developing devices and systems that could help everyone in the future. They talked about the most effective plans for recruiting men to the colony militias, along with techniques for fundraising to set up new hospitals, universities, and institutions for the public. One of the topics occasionally discussed at his Junto meetings was the idea of creating a company that could resolve the need for protection for people from the disastrous effects of fire, and at least help them recover after their loss.

The Union Fire Company and Fire Insurance

In 1736, Franklin incorporated the Union Fire Company, modeled after one established in Boston. For a fee, members would join and be required to help other members who might be trapped in their homes; they were also required to furnish six buckets each to the houses belonging to the members. Linen cloths were provided for carrying what goods and valuables they could retrieve from the homes. The service wasn't extended to non-members, however, so more and more fire companies opened up all over Philadelphia to meet the need. Engines with pumps were purchased. Later on, in 1752, a large bell was purchased to be rung in case of fire. In his newspaper, Franklin published articles related to fire prevention. One of the problems he noted was the fact that many people were careless when carrying hot coals from one fireplace to another.

Franklin was also well aware that people lost valuable property due to fire and suffered financially because of that. To answer the need, Franklin set up the country's first insurance company, called The Philadelphia Contributionship for the Insuring of Houses from Loss by Fire. It was incorporated in 1753, and Franklin was named "The Father of American Insurance." During its first year, the company wrote policies for 143 members.

The American Philosophical Society

In 1743, Franklin founded the American Philosophical Society. It was an outgrowth of his fondness for the Junto group that he and a number of friends established to discuss questions about nature and beliefs about morals, natural phenomena, and physics. A friend of his in Philadelphia was a botanist and talked to Franklin about setting up a society that could ponder scientific and philosophical issues and write about them. Some of the themes they discussed were farm production, grain importation, mining techniques, mapmaking, the study of fossils, and mapmaking.

This society remains active, but its membership fell off during the 1760s. At that time, it was reinvigorated by Charles Tomson, who altered the themes to include medicine, chemistry, trade, commerce, and other pursuits.

Retirement from Printing

Franklin's interest in inventing and science was growing so he reassessed his financial situation and his print shops, which were now well-established. There were shops not only in Philadelphia and its environs but in New York and the West Indies. He also contemplated one in Jamaica that he hoped two of his nephews would run. His plan for his nephews required six-year apprenticeships under a journeyman Franklin would hire. If the businesses did well, his nephews could buy the press and continue on their own. That way, they could support themselves.

David Hall was his journeyman at his main shop. Hall was very skilled, and Franklin implicitly trusted him. In 1748, Franklin made Hall a partner, and drew up a contract by which Hall would have full use of the equipment and Franklin would receive a regular payment. This contract called for Franklin to receive a portion of the profits for about twenty years.

The Franklin Whale-Oil Lamp

In the very early days of colonial America, the settlers used what was called the "Betty Lamp." The earliest versions used animal fat that was melted and poured into a metal canister with a wick in it, after which it cooled and hardened. The canister was held up by a hook, and the people would light the wick, which would burn like a candle emitting light. The Betty lamp could then be carried from room to room in order to see at night. Later on, whale oil or fish oil could be used which gave better light.

In 1740, there were some improvements on that model, one of which was invented by Benjamin Franklin. It consisted of two wick tubes spaced just one tube-space apart. It was discovered that Franklin's lamp gave off three times as much light as the other one and even the two-wick models developed before that. In the 1860s, Abraham Lincoln used the Franklin version of the lamp in his Illinois law office.

The Franklin Stove

In 1742, Ben Franklin noted, "It is strange, methinks, that though chimneys have been for so long in use, the construction should be so little understood till lately that no workman pretended to make one which would carry off the smoke." He also complained that traditional fireplaces drew cold air into the room and sometimes the cold air hit one's back while keeping the front of them warm. He then designed a stove, the function of which was to radiate heat. His first stove consisted of iron sides and a top and back with an opening in the front, like a fireplace. The stovepipe was exposed until it joined the chimney, which would help radiate heat. He called his first invention "The Pennsylvania Stove." He later improved it by adding a hollow baffle that acted as a reverse siphon, drawing some of the excess loss of heat downwards to add to the temperature. It didn't sell that well, as he had made an error in the placement of the flue. Much later, a scientist, David Rittenhouse, solved that problem, but the credit for the idea was Franklin's.

Franklin's Electrostatic Machine

Since he was a child, Franklin noticed static electricity, which is when a spark flies out from a person's finger after they rub it on a piece of wool or something similar. He wanted to explore the concept further, so he attended some lectures by Ebenezer Kinnersley in Philadelphia. Franklin then purchased Kinnersley's equipment and took it home for further experimentation. Many of the electrical experiments performed at the time utilized a glass tube for the generation of electrical charges. Franklin increased the intensity of these charges by rotating a glass globe instead, which was rotated by hand with a crank. At the base of the sphere, he mounted a swatch of leather on which it would rub with every turn. Just outside the globe, he positioned vertical metal needles. As the globe turned, sparks flew out and made contact with the needles, creating a mini-bolt. Franklin called this "electrical fire," and published a paper on it called "Electrical Minutes," which has since been lost.

Using a beaded iron chain, Franklin collected the electricity generated and fed it into a Leyden jar. The early Leyden jars were glass bottles lined with thin metal, and each contained a metal rod attached to it leading upwards. The Leyden jar is an early version of a capacitor, which stores potential electricity. The final outcome was the 18th-century version of a battery. Franklin sensed that, if he combined the principles demonstrated in these experiments, he could develop a practical use for it.

Despite the success of this invention, there was still superstition among some people. A Boston minister called Franklin a blasphemous meddler by "tampering with the battery of heaven!"

Invention of the Lightning Rod

Franklin was aware of the dangers of coming into direct contact with a lightning bolt. He also understood the concept of insulators which wouldn't conduct electricity and preserve one from being electrocuted. In 1751, he constructed a silk kite, as paper could easily be burned by a lightning strike. The current would be conducted through the twine tied to the kite. The lower part of the twine was held inside so as to remain dry because water conducts electricity. To that twine, Franklin attached a key. Then he and his son, William, went out during a thunderstorm and flew the kite into a storm cloud. When a bolt hit it, Franklin noticed that the bristles of the twine hemp stood on end. As he moved his finger very close to the key, a spark flew. From what he learned from his kite experiments, he designed the first lightning rod.

Success in any scientific endeavor depends upon the universality of the concepts and formulas theorized, and as scientists were able to duplicate these experiments, they approved of the usefulness of the lightning rod, and many were manufactured. Some of the less enlightened preachers of the day mocked his kite experiments and said Franklin was "flying in the face of Providence."

The Single Fluid Theory

From his experiments with electricity, Franklin theorized that electricity flowed from a single "fluid," which would explain its passage from one person or conductive object to another. He recognized the charges as being positive or negative. The current runs from the positive to the negative charge such as what happens in a battery.

In 1753, Franklin was awarded the Copley Medal from the Royal Society of London for his "curious experiments and observations on electricity." Later on, in 1759, the University of St. Andrews awarded him *in absentia* with an honorary degree of Doctor of Laws. It was said that Professors David Gregory, David Young, and/or Thomas Simson might have made the proposal that he be so honored. In 1762, Oxford University also gave him an honorary doctoral degree for his contributions to science.

The Bifocal Lens

Although Franklin didn't even complete college, he constantly queried about everyday items with a view to improve them. He was what one might call an "idea man." Franklin found it annoying to constantly change his spectacles, as he had to use one pair to look ahead and the other to read. To resolve the nuisance of switching frequently from one to the other, he had bifocals made. The optometrist, John Isaac Hawkins, inventor of the trifocal lens, credited Ben Franklin with the invention of bifocal glasses, and publicized it. He knew Franklin was a humble man, but Hawkins wanted him to receive credit for it, as it was well-deserved.

Academy and College of Philadelphia

Back in 1739, Benjamin Franklin came across an Anglican preacher by the name of George Whitefield. He wanted to open what he called a "charity school" in Georgia and traveled to some of the colonies conducting revivalist meetings. Rev. Whitefield held some of these revivalist meetings in Philadelphia to raise funds for his proposed charity school. Franklin's wife attended one meeting and encouraged Franklin to do so as well. Franklin went and was impressed with Rev. Whitefield's powerful voice and speaking style. About his speaking style, Franklin said:

His delivery of the sermon was so improved by frequent repetition that every accent, every emphasis, every modulation of voice, was so perfectly well turned and well placed that without being interested, I, the subject, could not help being pleased with the discourse.

Although Franklin wasn't an Anglican, he became friends with this itinerant preacher and helped him build an establishment in Philadelphia. Franklin and Whitefield had jocular debates, and the preacher often tried to convert Franklin. Franklin, on the other hand, encouraged Whitefield to include a larger primary school as well. To help in fundraising, Franklin even printed some of his sermons. Franklin felt that preachers of any religious persuasion should be allowed to preach in Pennsylvania and around the country. The school was built, but due to Whitefield's increasing popularity, it needed to be expanded. Franklin then proposed that more subjects be added and a larger school be established.

In 1749, Franklin and some other notables talked about including a more advanced curriculum and the addition of a secondary school. Many schools at the time followed the English model and taught Anglicanism to the exclusion of other religions. During his upbringing, Franklin was taught Presbyterianism based on the dogmas of John Calvin. He rebelled against that when older, and likewise wasn't heavily committed to Anglicanism, although he didn't reject it either. He was a Deist, as he believed in God as a creator who occasionally intervened in the world and aided mankind. He did believe in prayer and once said, "Without the belief of a Providence that takes cognizance of, guards and guides, and may favor particular persons, there is no motive to worship or fear its displeasure, or to pray for its protection." Franklin was impatient with religious debates because he felt that no one could have a full comprehension of a divinity that is unseen but only can be understood in terms of creation. He felt that religion was important because it was needed to prevent people from becoming wicked. However, he didn't see the value in enforcing one particular religion over another. Through his experiences in Pennsylvania, he developed an admiration for Quakers and ministers whom he came to admire. He disagreed with other ministers, not in terms of their beliefs, but because of their vigorous evangelism. Franklin therefore insisted that the school be non-sectarian. He said,

> Both the house and ground were vested in trustees, expressly for the use of any preacher of any religious persuasion who might desire to say something to the people at Philadelphia; the design in building not being to accommodate any particular sect, but the inhabitants in general; so that even if the Mufti of Constantinople were to send a missionary to preach Mohammedanism to us, he would find a pulpit at his service.

A new building was proposed and partially planned, but Rev. Whitefield, who really preferred to be an itinerant preacher, returned to the South. In 1751, Franklin and a few notables in the area aspired to create a college. Franklin then selected Rev. William Smith to be the provost. Fortunately, Smith agreed with Franklin's non-sectarian approach, so that made it easier. Franklin also preferred that the sciences be taught along with the classics and mathematics, instead of Greek and Latin. This institution focused on preparing students for business, rather than for the clergy like the traditional universities: Yale, Harvard, William and Mary College, and Princeton. Later on, in 1755, it was granted a charter and became the College of Philadelphia. After the American Revolution started, the college became a hotbed of politics, and a plethora of Loyalist pamphlets was issued from there. In 1779, the colonial government took it over. This upset Franklin, who had intended the college to be an institution of learning, not an organ of politics. After the war was over, it was reopened. The college was re-chartered, and a year after Franklin's death, it became the prestigious University of Pennsylvania, as it is known today.

From Clerk to Delegate

Since 1736, Franklin had been serving as a clerk to the Philadelphia City Council under Patrick Gordon, the deputy governor. In 1753, Franklin was elected to the Pennsylvania Assembly and was also appointed Postmaster General of the British colonies by England. The postal service prior to that only used older horses, and mail delivery was usually very slow. He introduced the use of a "stage wagon," which could carry more mail and move faster because there was a team of horses pulling it. He then introduced a "fast-mail" service that promised quicker delivery. It was remarkably successful, especially because a lot of business was conducted that way.

On the following year, seven of the British colonies—Maryland, Connecticut, New Hampshire, Massachusetts, New York, Rhode Island, and Pennsylvania—held a meeting at Albany, New York. It seems the French were willfully building forts in Pennsylvania and New York. Borders of these colonies had been established earlier, and the British colonies were becoming concerned about this intrusion. In addition, the French were making strides in allying themselves with some of the tribes in those regions, mostly those known to the French fur trappers who had been living and working in those areas for years before. One of the purposes of the Albany conference was to cement an alliance with the Iroquois nation, also known as the Six Nations. These tribes were also asked to send representatives to the Albany meeting. To this day, the Six Nations still exists as a united confederation whose headquarters is on the Native American territory of the Onondaga tribe (south of the city of Syracuse).

The other purpose for the Albany meeting was presented by Benjamin Franklin and was called the "Plan of Union." This plan called for the levying of taxes to finance any possible hostile actions and for the defense in this contested region. It was passed by the colonial delegates but wasn't approved by the English authorities, who were anxious that the colonists be prevented from the right to levy taxes.

Political Life and Foreign Affairs

In 1754, the French and Indian War broke out. It took place mostly in northern Pennsylvania, which was part of the Ohio River Valley. Troops were led by General Edward Braddock. George Washington, a colonel and later the first president of the United States, was one of the commanders of that expedition.

Franklin worked for the Philadelphia Militia by helping to create a system to finance Pennsylvania's portion of the expenses for carriages, horses, and food for the soldiers who were serving in the French and Indian War. Many of his meetings were held at the Tun Tavern in Philadelphia. Franklin frequented the tavern from which he made a number of recruitment efforts. This tavern became the birthplace of the Marines, which was first authorized in 1775, and it served as a base for recruitment for the new Continental Army during the American Revolution. A replica of the tavern exists at the Marine base in Quantico, Virginia.

Chapter 5 – Benjamin Franklin: England 1757-1762

Ben Franklin, the Penn Family, and Great Britain

As heirs, the Penn family owned a great deal of territory in Pennsylvania by virtue of a land grant by Charles II. They arbitrarily announced that they weren't responsible for any taxes at all and overturned the colonial legislation requiring them to do so. That meant that very little money was going into the treasury of Pennsylvania. The colony also needed the money to defend its unsettled regions. Because the monies collected from Pennsylvania wouldn't be sufficient in the short-term, the Assembly proposed a twelve-year plan to pay for it. Deputy governor Robert Morris refused to sign it, insisting upon a term of five years. It was impossible for Pennsylvania to meet that goal.

The contentious issue went back and forth between the governor and the assembly. William Penn's son then appointed William Denny as the new deputy governor. Because of a last-minute proposal with Deputy Governor William Denny, a ten-year property tax by the Pennsylvania Assembly included the Penn properties. Denny refused to sign that. To appeal the matter, Ben Franklin himself wrote to the very influential English lord, Robert Charles, complaining about it. There was no response. As a result, the colonists and Denny came to a less than ideal agreement, so the funds were exhausted rapidly. Now, more funds were needed.

In 1757, in his capacity as a delegate to the Pennsylvania Assembly, Benjamin Franklin was asked to go to London to represent the colonists of Pennsylvania against the overwhelming power of William Penn's descendants. Franklin arrived in London and took his son, William, with him.

First of all, Benjamin Franklin met with the hostility of some of the British noblemen including Thomas Fermor, the Earl of Pomfret. William Penn's son, Thomas, had married Fermor's daughter and together they lived in Pennsylvania. However, Thomas Penn was in England at that time, along with his younger brother Richard. Franklin contacted them there with regard to the grievances of the Pennsylvania colony. Penn, of course, was adamantly opposed to Franklin's entreaty, even though Franklin brought up the issue of the hardships it would create if he opposed. Instead of addressing the matter with Franklin directly, Thomas Penn sent Franklin's letter to the King's Council, noting that Franklin wasn't respectful because he hadn't used the proper salutation mentioning Penn's official titles. Franklin intended his missive to be an informal request, though, but Penn chose to overlook that. The matter dragged on unresolved for months. John Paris, Penn's attorney and solicitor general, was handling the case and he delayed his work on it. Finally, Paris completed his phase of the case and forwarded it to the attorney general, Charles Pratt. Pratt repudiated Franklin's appeal. However, the matter still needed to be reviewed by the Privy Council so there might still be a chance.

To tarnish Franklin's reputation, Thomas Penn also sent a haughty letter to the Pennsylvania Assembly saying that Franklin lacked candor and was disrespectful. Penn's attorney then followed up with a similar letter. In defense of Franklin, two members of the Pennsylvania Assembly spoke up and called the actions of the Penn family tyrannical.

While he was awaiting the ruling from the Privy Council, Franklin used the time to establish amicable relations with other English officials. His friendly manner and cordiality resulted in good contacts there that could be used in the future to improve the relations between England and the colonists. Franklin made the acquaintance of Lord Bute, the prime minister, and prevailed upon him to appoint his son, William Franklin, to the governorship of New Jersey. Other notables in England he contacted included Dr. Joseph Priestley, physicist and philosopher; Richard Jackson, the counsel for the Trade Commission; Dr. Joseph Hadley, scientist; Lord Kames, a Scottish lawyer, judge, and philosopher; and William Strahan, a member of Parliament. Franklin took this opportunity and sent Kames his 1755 publication on population studies because it had political implications. The publication had already been republished in England and was a topic of discussion by politicians and philosophers as well.

While Franklin was waiting, he continually made contacts within the English government. He also spoke with many of the British about the colonies and conversed with interested parties about his own writings.

Population Studies

Intellectuals in Great Britain asked Franklin about his study on population, which was called "Observations Concerning the Increase of Mankind." Some were distressed because of the increase in population growth in the colonies and feared that the American population might soon be larger than that in England. If the population in the colonies was to surpass that of Britain, they thought it might be necessary to place restrictions upon British America so it could still be controlled. Addressing those concerns, Franklin pointed out that population growth could be a boon for

Great Britain because of the increase in trade. He presented solid rationale for his premise in terms of the vast amount of unsettled land available. That land, he indicated, could be used to construct manufacturing plants and expand farming, plantations, and animal husbandry. He stated, "Land being thus plenty in America, and so cheap that a laboring man who understands husbandry can in a short time save money enough to purchase a piece of new land sufficient for a plantation." He went on further to say that it will take many ages to fully settle the land and would represent new opportunities for a long time.

When England annexed Quebec, Franklin also registered his approval because the population of British America would be increased and help make both the colonies and Quebec stronger on the world stage. He wrote to Lord Kames in 1760 saying, "I have long been of the opinion that the foundations of the future grandeur and stability of the British Empire lie in America," and commented that he needed to append his publication on population growth due to the British annexation of Quebec.

Benjamin Franklin and Joseph Priestley

Both Dr. Joseph Priestley and Ben Franklin studied the politics of England firsthand and came to the realization that King George III and his immediate advisors were feeding into English hostility toward the colonies. Priestley was a supporter of equal rights and religious tolerance, as well as a noted scientist.

As they spoke with each other, Franklin found out that Priestley was experimenting with electricity and gases. Franklin then collaborated with Priestley in the writing of his essay, "History and Present State of Electricity." First, Franklin and Priestley duplicated an experiment with gases attributed to the chemist, Antoine Lavoisier. Franklin worked with Priestley and varied the procedure, which led to the discovery of a substance they called "dephlogisticated air." Priestley and Franklin applied it to the biological process of promoting better respiration. Priestley later improved the procedure and is credited with the discovery and isolation of oxygen as a pure element.

Benjamin Franklin and Dr. John Hadley

In 1758, when he visited Cambridge University, Franklin contacted Dr. John Hadley, a professor of chemistry. Together they conducted experiments by dipping a thermometer into a vial of ether and discovered that, when they removed it, the thermometer dropped several degrees. They repeated this over and over again until finally the thermometer registered a temperature that was below freezing. The both of them then concluded that evaporation was a useful tool to cool an object down. Franklin later said that a man could freeze to death on a summer day by applying this principle. This is an innovation later used to make air conditioners.

While he was studying this, Franklin also observed that black clothing is warmer than white clothing in the summer heat. However, he didn't delineate the property of the pigments which contributes to that effect.

Benjamin Franklin was constantly alert to phenomena around him, even the most trivial. On occasion, he would develop a new invention, and at other times, propose a series of questions for scientists and thinkers to ponder and answer. About eight years prior to his arrival in England, Franklin reflected on the function of sweat on the human body and noted that it cooled his body to some extent. At that time, he noted that sweat was essential to protecting a human being during excessively hot weather, but the essential benefits of sweat weren't long-lasting. He then discovered that adding some diluted liquor to water and applying it to the body slowed the cooling effect so that it lasted longer.

Invention of the New Odometer

Franklin was forever thinking and developing mechanical solutions for everyday situations. In 1760, in England, the British tapped into his illustrious mind regarding ways to make postal delivery systems more efficient. The odometer came into being in ancient times, but it wasn't that precise in its measurements. While at home, Franklin had toyed with many ideas as to how to create one that was more accurate. He compared the distances traveled with how many revolutions a wagon wheel would make to reach one mile. He discovered that the wheel would make 400 revolutions to cover a distance of one mile, or 1.6 kilometers, and suggested that the English work on a device that could use that data.

Invention of the Armonica

In 1761, Franklin watched a demonstration of the glass harmonica in Cambridge. He then improved on the design and invented a more mechanical apparatus to yield clearer tones from the glass structure. He worked with a London glassblower, Charles James, to build it. Because it used a keyboard, variations in the sound could be made. Franklin's version used 37 glass bowls and chords that could be played—an impossibility with the original design. This instrument Franklin called the "Armonica." Franz Mesmer, who developed the technique of hypnosis called "mesmerism" in the later 18th century, used Franklin's Armonica as an integral part of his procedure. Beethoven also used it to produce his melodrama, *Leonore Prohaska*. A replica of the instrument has been utilized by the current performing dance company, the Joffrey Ballet.

Ruling of the Privy Council

After waiting for so long, Franklin received the ruling of the Privy Council on his presentations regarding the collection of taxes from the Penn family. In their ruling, the Privy Council stated that Pennsylvania had the right to charge and collect taxes from the Penn family. However, there were a lot of caveats to that which diluted that right in the form of six amendments. The colonists were furious and refused to sign the amendments. Deputy Governor Hamilton, the new governor of Pennsylvania, had been in league with Thomas Penn and continued to pressure the

Assembly in Pennsylvania to sign the amendments, but they would only sign a few.

Pennsylvania's Reaction

In the colonies, Franklin's political enemies made fodder of his failure. A cartoon even appeared in a circulation that had a caricature of the devil with Franklin saying, "Thee shall be my agent, Ben, for all my dominions."

It should be pointed out that many of those people had connections to the Penn family, who spread their hostility far and wide. Even though some of the Pennsylvanians were irate about Franklin's less than stellar performance, the Pennsylvania Assembly considered it at least mildly successful because Pennsylvania was able to levy some taxes on the Penn family properties. Nevertheless, because Pennsylvania didn't want to continue to pay Franklin a salary, they called him home. Franklin himself also knew he had a lot of work to do with the Assembly in terms of dealing with England. In 1762, he arrived in Philadelphia. Much to his shock, Franklin witnessed angry mobs from all over the colonies, and many people were hostile toward him.

To make an attempt at amends, he turned over his earned salary of $15,000 back to the colony. He still felt, though, that it would be in Pennsylvania's best interest to continue working on a positive relationship with England.

Chapter 6 – Benjamin Franklin in London: 1764-1769

In 1764, Great Britain passed a tax on sugar. Many of the taxes were hardships for the colonists who had already raised a great deal of money to supply the troops during the French and Indian War. In addition, the farmers experienced some downturns in their profits due to the weather. The colonists also underwent a crisis because gold and silver became scarce. Landowners and others had the resources, but without the precious metals, they were unable to conduct business. To resolve the problem, the colonies issued their own currency called "Bills of Credit," but there was an uneven system for providing security to back up the bills. Some banks based it on the value of land alone. Other banks charged interest, but some didn't. Certain "Bills of Credit" were only targeted to pay a debt, but not for buying and selling.

British merchants were also very uneasy about accepting the new unstandardized paper currency. So, in 1764, Parliament passed the Currency Act which prohibited the colonies from issuing their own paper currency and presented them with one-pound British notes to use. This created confusion. As a result of this new act, the British government was controlling currency in the colonies, and there was an uproar. The Pennsylvania Assembly then quickly sent Franklin to England again. The colonies of New Jersey, Georgia, and Massachusetts also appointed him as their agent in London. They recognized that Franklin was a successful businessman in his own right, and that was an important asset.

Financial Burdens on the Colonies

Shortly after his arrival, Franklin contacted influential figures in England. Regarding the Sugar Act and Currency Act, he spoke to Richard Jackson of the House of Commons, whom he had met on his earlier trip. Jackson was in charge of trade and commodities in England. Franklin told Jackson that the sugar came from the British West Indies and shouldn't be taxed as a British product. In addition, he intimated that America might resort to buying sugar from Native Americans who could grow it in and near the Spanish territories in Florida. Franklin also presented a case for allowing the colonists to trade lumber and iron directly with Ireland.

The Stamp Act of 1765

In 1765, the Stamp Act was passed. It wasn't a tax on stamps, per se; it was a tax on the embossed paper the colonists needed to draw up legal papers, newspapers, and the like. Franklin voiced his opposition to it on the basis that the British colonies had no representation in the English Parliament and mentioned that to Jackson as well. Franklin also wanted to contact Lord Bute, who was the prime minister in England during Franklin's last visit, but, unfortunately, Bute had been replaced by George Grenville. Grenville usually catered to the whims of the king. Because of the attitudes of the new prime minister, he was unable to make any headway. Franklin then continually tried to meet with Parliament. He was well-versed and versatile, and used his interpersonal skills to glean influence in the political sphere. One gentleman, by the name of William Strahan, was a printer Franklin met twenty years earlier. During this visit, he and Strahan often chatted about print styles, formats, and fonts. When Strahan was elected to Parliament, Franklin was thrilled because he needed supporters there. Strahan made attempts on behalf of Franklin but had little success getting a hearing because Prime Minister Grenville continued to defend the tax strenuously. Franklin soon concluded that the passage of the Stamp Act was inevitable. In a letter to a friend just a few weeks later, Franklin wrote, "We might as well have hindered the sun setting."

In 1765, Franklin's wife wrote to him, saying that she and the children had to flee to Burlington, New Jersey in order to escape the wrath of the mobs who were harassing them in Philadelphia. People blamed Franklin for the failure to get the Stamp Act repealed. In the streets, more protests erupted. A secret organization, the Sons of Liberty, formed in Massachusetts to devise methods to fight taxation. Prominent members were Samuel Adams, Patrick Henry, and two of Franklin's fellow Pennsylvanian statesmen, John Hancock and Paul Revere. The situation was becoming dire.

The Quartering Act of 1765

Great Britain then passed the Quartering Act, which required that the colonists financially provide for the housing of British soldiers in the colonies who couldn't secure rooms in colonial rooming houses and hotels. That meant that barns, stables, taverns, and storehouses belonging to the colonists had to be used to house these soldiers. This was an intrusion on the privacy of the colonists and effectively substituted for another tax by requiring them to pay for this housing. Even Prime Minister Grenville was somewhat uncomfortable about it. Franklin took advantage of that and worked out a compromise by communicating with his friend, Thomas Pownall of Massachusetts. The both of them developed the Pownall-Franklin Compromise, which denied entry onto private property but provided housing in empty buildings and had the colonial governments foot the costs of some basic provisions for the soldiers. Grenville approved of this and signed the compromise. While the colonists objected to the Quartering Act, the impetus of their protests turned back to the hated Stamp Act. In fact, the colonists started finding clever ways of avoiding it by using old paper and even smuggling some paper from willing merchants. As these actions increased, England's profit from the Stamp Act decreased substantially. As a result, England started sending over more British troops in order to attempt to enforce the act, but that wasn't successful. British officials were harassed on the streets and at their offices, with some vandalism occurring as well.

Rotating Prime Ministers

Grenville developed personal disputes with King George because he was forced to reduce the personal allowance for the king, who was an extravagant spender. The king had also been subject to a barrage of complaints from the colonies and was pummeled with letters from the more influential colonists who said that they needed representation in the English Parliament. In 1765, the king dismissed Grenville from office and replaced him with Charles, the Marquess of Rockingham. Rockingham was much more interested in horse racing than in the ministry and lasted only thirteen months! William Pitt "The Elder" replaced him. Pitt was more sympathetic to the American cause, and the king hoped that Pitt could resolve the matter peaceably. Pitt, however, was getting very ill and appointed Charles Townshend, the exchequer, to step into his role. Because of his accounting skills, Townshend realized that the English war debt from the Seven Years' War was depleting the treasury of England and looked toward the colonies as a fresh source of revenue. In 1767, he persuaded Parliament to pass the Townshend Acts which was a series of five taxes in the form of import taxes, excise taxes, and the like. Knowing that America had been starting to manufacture its own goods, Townshend selected items he suspected the colonies couldn't easily manufacture like lead, paint, china, and glass, taxing those as well. Then Townshend suddenly died. William Pitt had, by then, become so ill that he had to retire from office and was succeeded by Augustus Fitzroy, the Duke of Grafton, who preferred to humor the king rather than get the job done. He served as prime minister for two years and was succeeded by Frederick Lord North in 1770. Franklin had a good relationship with William Pitt, but all of the others were Tories or under the thumb of the king and supported the excessive taxation.

This excessive taxation forced the colonists to initiate a boycott against British goods. "Save your money and save your country" was the popular slogan the Patriots used to fuel their campaign.

The American Boycott and Repeal of the Stamp Act

Ben Franklin wasted no time and spread the word around England that the colonies would manufacture their own goods and boycott English imports. Even though some items were difficult to manufacture in the colonies, a boycott would still have a heavy impact on trade. Patriots in the colonies also vandalized some of the retail stores selling British products. As this protest continued, the English merchants complained bitterly. The British government wasn't able to collect taxes on their exports that remained unsold. The king himself soon realized that his trade with the colonies was being affected. In addition, the Whig Party in England lent some support to the American cause. The Marquess of Rockingham, who served just a short time as prime minister, supported the repeal of the Stamp Act in particular, although he did nothing about it while in office. The powerful political philosopher and orator, Edmund Burke, understood the motive behind the boycott, and eloquently spoke up about the injustice.

In 1766, the House of Commons asked Franklin to appear to answer questions concerning the Stamp Act, other taxes, and the boycott. They asked, "Are not all the people very able to pay those taxes?" Franklin replied, "No. The frontier counties, all along the continent, having been frequently ravaged by the enemy (Native American tribes) and greatly impoverished. They are able to pay very little tax." The term "frontier" referred to large rural areas such as western Pennsylvania, New York, southern New Jersey, and other outlying districts.

When asked, "Do you think it right that America should be protected by this country and pay no part of the expense?" he answered, "That is not the case. The colonies raised, clothed and paid during the last war (the Seven Years' War), provided near twenty-five thousand men and spent many millions." The British had promised to reimburse the colonists for such expenditures, so they asked Franklin about that. Franklin responded to that concern by saying that the British reimbursement to the colonies amounted to only 40% of their expenses. He also added that the colonies had no representation in Parliament so they couldn't vote on the laws that affected them.

The House of Commons then directly addressed the issue brought up by Franklin himself related to his population studies. They asked how much the population of America had increased since it became British America. He said,

> I think the inhabitants of all the provinces together, taken at a medium, will double in about twenty-five years. But their demand for British manufactures will increase much faster...but (only) grows with the growing abilities of the same numbers to pay for them.

That clever answer informed the British that it would be to their advantage if they made concessions. Franklin also dovetailed into that response the implication that high taxes would only serve to reduce the colonists' ability to pay for goods sent from Great Britain.

During his appearance, Franklin also addressed the hardships caused by the Currency Act of 1764. He told Richard Jackson of the Trade Commission that the Currency Act would cause the colonists to hoard what legal tender they already had. When asked about the colonists' attitudes toward Parliament, he said they no longer had much respect for Parliament because of its severe restrictions related to currency.

One of the most repeated questions had to do with the quality of British goods. Franklin politely answered that British goods were of excellent quality, but the colonists were now making their own clothes and goods and would continue to do so if the excessive taxes continued to be levied. Franklin was amazingly calm when he said that, making it a point to omit any hostile statements, although he must have felt that way.

The House then presented Franklin with the key question, "Do you not think the people of America would submit to pay the stamp duty, if it was moderated?" Franklin firmly responded, "No, never, unless compelled by force of arms."

William Pitt, who was now serving in the House of Commons after his prolonged illness, asserted England's right to tax the colonists but felt that the difficulties imposed by the Stamp Act were far too burdensome. He had a strong voice in the House, and his address helped Franklin a great deal. He said that "...the Stamp Act should be repealed absolutely, totally and immediately; that the reason for the repeal...was founded on an erroneous principle." He also likened it to "taking money out of the colonists' pockets without their consent."

Edmund Burke said of Franklin's appearance, "Dr. Franklin, as he stood before the bar of Parliament, presented such an aspect of dignity and intellectual superiority as to remind me of a schoolmaster questioned by schoolboys." In 1766, the notorious Stamp Act was repealed. The highest tribute came from the lips of King George himself when he uttered, "That crafty American is more than a match for you all!"

News traveled rapidly in the colonies. Astonishingly, even Lieutenant-Governor Penn entertained several hundred distinctive guests in the state house, and they all drank to the health of Dr. Franklin. A banquet was held in his honor on a barge named

"Franklin" in the Schuylkill River. After that, the merchants from the colonies of Georgia, Massachusetts, and New Jersey appointed him as their agent in London, and he was paid handsomely to serve in that capacity. However, in Massachusetts, there was opposition to his appointment by the eminent politician, Samuel Adams. Adams felt that Ben Franklin was well-meaning but too passionate and easy-going. Franklin always spoke in a calm and rational manner, but Adams had been raised in a very restricted puritanical household and was much more reserved than Franklin.

The Townshend Acts

In 1767, Great Britain had passed the Townshend Acts that imposed excise taxes on items exported to the colonies, including glass, paper, and tea. It even required that shipments made from other European countries go to England first and be taxed before being forwarded to America. John Dickinson, a colonial patriot, had his "Farmer's Letters" published in the colonies in 1767 to protest the Townshend Acts. He sent a copy to Ben Franklin, who added a preface to the piece and had it published not only in England but in Ireland and France as well.

Franklin also fought back in the most powerful of media—the printed word. He masqueraded as an anonymous Englishman and published letters under various pseudonyms in the *London Chronicle* and other widely-read publications in England. He interspersed his remarks with wit and a sense of humor. This attracted a wide readership, and some of his letters were even republished in Paris.

Franklin Alters His Opinion

Up until that point, Ben Franklin had been lobbying for a compromise between Great Britain and the colonies, as he felt that the English were intelligent men and could be reasonable, given a little persuasion. However, he witnessed first-hand the hostility and close-mindedness in Great Britain. He was confronted by the stubbornness of the prime ministers, with the exception of William

Pitt. They had overwhelming power over King George III and the House of Burgesses in Parliament. The colonists' angry reactions, which Franklin knew were justified, was rising to a fever pitch. He then started to reverse his opinion about England. Every time America forged a compromise about legislation passed in England, another tax or burden was imposed. The relationship between America and England was deteriorating. Events happened with alarming rapidity. Franklin observed, "Things daily wear a worse aspect, and tend more and more to a breach and final separation."

Chapter 7 – Benjamin Franklin in London: 1769-1775

Repeal of the Townshend Acts

In 1769, British trade with America was half that of 1768. What's more, many of the colonies united in their efforts to resist the taxes on British goods. Some British vessels were even turned back from American ports. The merchants in England formed an association and complained incessantly to Parliament and the new prime minister, Lord North. The merchants even resorted to trickery to get their goods sold in America but met with little success. Finally, in 1770, Lord North and Parliament repealed all but one of the Townshend Acts because of Franklin's efforts. The one remaining act was the tax on tea.

The *Craven Street Gazette*

In 1770, Franklin purchased a printing press and started his own publication in London called the *Craven Street Gazette*. In terms of politics, Franklin responded to his newspaper correspondents. In one letter to a prominent businessman of England, he said:

I see with pleasure, that we think pretty much alike on the subject of English America. We of the colonies have never insisted that we ought to be exempt from contributing to the common expenses necessary to support the prosperity of the empire. We only assert that, having parliaments (assemblies) of our own, and not having representatives in that of Great Britain, our parliaments are the only judges of what we can and what we ought to contribute in this case; and that the English Parliament has no right to take our money without our consent.

One of the intents of the *Craven Street Gazette* was also to create a release for Franklin's penchant for light sarcasm and humor as well as political issues. An article he published in 1770 was a fictional piece about the depressing effects of the absence of Queen Margaret on the population when she was away and the mischief it caused. In the article, he wrote, "It is remarked that the skies have wept every day in Craven Street because of the absence of the Queen." He then wrote a facetious letter to the "publisher," that a "great person" had been half-starved by a "set of the most careless, blundering, foolish, crafty and knavish ministers that ever got in a house." The subtle references to ministers were deliberate. Franklin signed the article "Indignation."

In one small section of the *Gazette*, Franklin had a humorous stock report and death notice:

Stocks – Biscuits – very low

Buckwheat and Indian meal – both sour

Deaths – In the back closet and elsewhere, many poor mice

The Hutchinson Letters Scandal

In 1772, Benjamin Franklin obtained about ten letters written by Thomas Hutchinson, a Loyalist and the colonial governor of Massachusetts Bay Colony. The letters were written to several people in the ministry in England, primarily Thomas Whately, who was an advisor to England's prime minister. In the letters, Hutchinson grossly exaggerated the hostility of the colonists and included suggestions by his secretary, Andrew Oliver, that the Massachusetts colonists be more vigorously regulated by England. The purpose of these letters was to inflame tensions between England and the colonies. Franklin wisely realized that these letters represented deliberate mischaracterizations and were sent to selected members of the Parliament intended to bias them against the colonies. In one letter, Hutchinson said:

> There must be an abridgement of what are called English liberties…I doubt whether it is possible to project a system of government in which a colony, 3,000 miles distant from the parent state, shall enjoy all the liberty of the parent state…There must be a great restraint of natural liberty.

Franklin became alarmed by that and knew that the deeply incendiary nature of these letters could trigger a violent reaction on the part of Great Britain. Nevertheless, he felt it his duty to inform the colonial authorities of the treasonous nature of the writer's words but advised that the contents of these packets be kept private. He then sent the letters to the head of the colonial assembly in Massachusetts, Thomas Cushing.

Although the Hutchinson letters came to the attention of Samuel Adams of Boston, he kept them private but orchestrated a propaganda war against Hutchinson and Oliver. At that time, Samuel Adams was a member of the radical but clandestine Committees of Correspondence which held chapters in Massachusetts, Connecticut, New Hampshire, Rhode Island, and South Carolina, and which called for more forceful but non-violent resistance to English domination.

What made matters worse was the fact that portions of these letters were leaked to the press and published in the *Boston Gazette*. The colonists were furious. Effigies of Hutchinson and Oliver were burned in the streets of Boston and there were many demonstrations there. As knowledge of this betrayal by the colonial representatives spread around Boston, other uprisings occurred.

The Boston Tea Party and The Siege of Boston Harbor

In 1773, colonists, disguised as Native Americans, dumped over three hundred chests of tea leaves off a British vessel in Boston Harbor. This event stunned the seamen on the ship, most of whom had never seen a Native American before. Benjamin Franklin still had the mindset that he could placate the British and persuade them to see the relationship between the hostilities of the colonists and the excessive taxes that the king and Parliament were charging. In an attempt to appeal to their common sense and intelligence, he contacted Parliament with regard to the incident. First, he said that compensation would be made for the destruction of the tea, but balanced that comment with further qualifications. To reiterate what he had been telling them, Franklin issued a publication called "Hints for Conversation upon the Subject of Terms that might probably produce a Durable Union between Great Britain and the Colonies," in which he indicated that the tea tax and other taxes levied on trade with the colonies should all be repealed. After that, the colonies could reenact them if they wished, but the tax money should go into colonial treasuries, and its distribution should be controlled by colonial authorities, not British officials. Furthermore, Franklin stated that Parliament should have no control over the internal affairs of the colonies and should place no restrictions on the manufacture of goods in the colonies.

Following that, England blockaded the port of Boston. Instead of the regular English regimental units, the English hired Hessian mercenaries to execute the blockade. When William Pitt found out about that, he realized the injustice, not only because of the blockade but also the use of foreign mercenaries to do it. He was incensed at the behavior of the king and the Tories, saying, "If I were an American, as I am an Englishman, while a foreign troop was landed in my country, I would never lay down my arms—

never! *Never!* NEVER!" Franklin and his friend, William Pitt, then discussed the matter of the Boston Tea Party and the groundswell of animosity growing in the colonies. Pitt said that the colonies did, indeed, have the right to defend their rights, and he himself was making a strenuous effort in Parliament to alter the British stance on the dilemma. Franklin then delineated the grounds for colonial complaints and told Pitt that the injustices might even lead to open resistance; he basically predicted the Revolutionary War.

William Pitt asked Franklin to accompany him to a meeting of the House of Commons in the British Parliament. He and William Pitt approached the doorkeepers of the House, who graciously admitted them. Franklin, undergoing an attack of gout, limped in alongside Pitt. Pitt introduced a motion that the English vessels be withdrawn from Boston. There was a heated debate following that, but the majority of the members in the House voted against it. Pitt then worked on a draft of a compromise plan and conferred with Franklin about it. Franklin noted that there were so many caveats in the proposal that he rejected it. Pitt then redrafted it and returned. This plan would, in effect, represent an agreement between Britain and the colonies that—it was hoped—would bring about a reconciliation between the two parties. This time, Franklin approved it, and Pitt brought him back into the House where it would be analyzed. Franklin and Pitt had support from some of the members. However, Edward Montagu rose up and became belligerent. He loudly accused Franklin of writing the proposal himself, saying the American had written it and he was a "bitter and mischievous enemy." Pitt calmly assured the assembly that he himself had written the proposal. The House retorted that it was "weak" and "bad." Montagu and Pitt argued vehemently, and the whole assembly joined in. Everyone in the room was shouting. In the end, the House of Commons laid the proposal aside and tabled the motion. Pitt sensed that this whole episode would have explosive consequences and warned everyone against harassing the colonists. He also approached the monarch about it, but King George ignored him.

Franklin was astounded. In his memoirs, he wrote:

> To hear so many of the hereditary legislators declaiming so vehemently against, not adopting merely, but even the consideration of a proposal so important in its nature, offered by a person of so weighty a character ... gave me an exceeding mean opinion of their abilities, and made their claim of sovereignty over three millions of virtuous sensible people in America, seem the greatest of absurdities, since they appeared to have scarce discretion enough to govern a herd of swine.

Appearance Before the Privy Council in England

Benjamin Franklin was called before the Privy Council around March of 1774, once they were informed about the Hutchinson letters. Franklin's friend, Dr. Priestley, through the intercession of Edmund Burke, gained admission to the meeting.

In the initial introductory session, the speaker of the Council, Solicitor General Alexander Wedderburn, defended England's approval of Hutchinson as colonial governor by pointing out his virtues:

> His Majesty's choice followed the wishes of his people; and no other man could have been named whom so many favorable circumstances concurred to recommend. A native the country (of America), whose ancestors were among its first settlers.

Wedderburn characterized the affair as being a misunderstanding and that the collection consisted of private letters "stolen by Dr. Franklin," whose motive was to become governor of Massachusetts. Then they intimated that Franklin himself contrived against the governor and Oliver. Next, the Council spent its follow-up interrogation trying to ferret out the identity of the person who gave Franklin the letters. Throughout the entire proceedings, Franklin never revealed the name of the person who gave him those letters. To this day, no one knows who that person was.

At the close of the meeting, Wedderburn upheld the innocence of Hutchinson and Oliver and went on a tireless harangue against the character of Franklin. An observer at the meeting said that Benjamin Franklin stood like a rock "abiding the pelting of a pitiless storm." The Privy Council admitted that there were no grounds to bring any charges against Dr. Franklin but did see to it that he was dismissed from his position as postmaster general of the colonies. Fortunately, his son-in-law, Richard Bache, had been working under him as secretary and comptroller and took over the position.

Word about these disdainful proceedings circulated in the colonies. The colonists felt immediate sympathy for Franklin and admired him for the courage it took to face the Privy Council itself and emerge unscathed. He was now 68 years old and had stood for nearly three hours in the Council's chambers because no one offered him a chair. The citizens of Philadelphia burned both Hutchinson and Wedderburn in effigy. After that, Hutchinson moved to England and faded into history. Wedderburn initially was celebrated, but later historians dismissed him as being superficial and even vulgar.

After spending nearly seventeen years representing the colonies in England, Franklin realized he must leave. He had done all he could to prevent the relationship between America and England from accelerating into war. After hearing the attitudes of King George III and his supporters, he became wholly committed to the cause for freedom.

In 1774, the colonists held their second meeting of the Continental Congress. Fifty-one of the colonial delegates to this Congress signed a petition addressed to King George III of Britain, listing a number of their grievances. In the petition, they asked the king directly to exert all efforts to address these issues. They sent a copy of it to Franklin along with an attached cover letter to him from Charles Thomson, the secretary of the Congress. It was signed by John Dickinson, who wrote the final draft, and John Hancock, Roger Sherman, Charles Thomson, John Adams, John Jay, and Thomas Jefferson. Franklin read it and added his signature to it. This document became known as the Olive Branch Petition. The king himself, however, had already declared that the colonies were in open rebellion, and refused to read it!

Unfortunately, Franklin found himself firmly opposing those Englishmen who were once his supporters and friends. Franklin's friend, William Strahan, developed a more hostile attitude toward Franklin and the patriotic cause. Now disillusioned with Strahan's sudden lack of empathy for the American position, Franklin wrote to Strahan in 1775 saying that he, as a member of Parliament, was one of the majority who doomed America to destruction. Franklin said, "You have begun to burn our towns and murder our people...You and I were long friends; you are now my enemy, and I am yours."

Welcome Worn Out

The Massachusetts patriot, Samuel Adams, had the impression that Franklin wasn't really committed to the principles of liberty that the colonies were promoting. That wasn't true. While in England, Franklin spoke up to justify reasons for the behavior of the colonists who were reacting, sometimes violently, to the domination of England. Nevertheless, in America, Franklin was considered "too English," and in England, he was considered "too American." The atmosphere was getting much too controversial in England. Franklin knew that he had done his utmost to mend the breach between Great Britain and the colonies, but no longer felt he could do anything more there. Franklin also desperately wanted to return home.

His children were so much older now. His daughter, Sally, had married and had two children of her own. He dearly missed his wife and felt guilty for having left her for so long—eleven years altogether. They did correspond, and he often sent her gifts. In 1772, he was concerned because she had some health concerns and gave her some advice in terms of certain foods to avoid. Historians have presented two theories about why Deborah didn't accompany him to England. One is that she was afraid of traveling across the ocean, and the other one, taken from her own words, indicates that she feared she wouldn't look that presentable to the fashionable English ladies and would embarrass Benjamin.

As he was preparing to leave for America, Franklin received word that she died. Friends said that he was extremely upset about the loss, which he hadn't anticipated. There was no prolonged illness on her part, and it was later reported that she died suddenly of a massive stroke.

In December 1774, Franklin left Great Britain. While he was at sea, the American Revolution broke out. It was triggered by the Battles of Lexington and Concord in 1775. Franklin wrote to Edmund Burke about the event and described the frenzied retreat of the English commander, General Gage: "General Gage's troops made a most vigorous retreat—twenty miles in three hours!—scarcely to be paralleled in history."

Bones in the Basement

While living on Craven Street in London, Ben Franklin took in a lodger by the name of William Hewson who was a surgeon. In his lodging in the basement, he taught anatomy and held laboratory classes. The practice of grave-robbing and human dissection was deemed criminal in the 18th century. Because medical students sorely needed to learn firsthand about anatomy, the practice continued but was performed under the cover of darkness. Men would creep around the graveyards disinterring corpses or snatching bodies from the gallows. Then they squirreled them away to sell to clandestine labs like Hewson's. In 1998, when the residence was being restored for museum purposes, the skeletons of four adults and six children were discovered buried under Franklin's house. Colin Schultze reported in the *Smithsonian*: "From a one-metre-wide, one-metre-deep pit, over 1200 pieces of bone were retrieved." The historians of the Ben Franklin House there, which eventually became a museum, indicated that Franklin most likely knew that this activity was being conducted.

Chapter 8 – Home and on to France

Franklin was home briefly and stayed with his grown daughter, Sarah, whom he called "Sally," and her husband, Richard Bache, along with their child, Benjamin. However, Benjamin startled them one day by bringing with him William Tempe Franklin, the illegitimate son of his eldest son.

Ben was pleased to discover that Sally was contributing to the Revolutionary War efforts by sewing uniforms for the troops. Not only that, but she motivated a number of Quaker women in Pennsylvania to help. Quakers, by virtue of their religious beliefs, weren't permitted to enlist in the military, but a family friend said that Sarah showed great persuasiveness and "… courage in asking, which surpassed even the obstinate reluctance of the Quakers in refusing."

Richard Bache had a grocery store and also served on the Pennsylvania Board of War. He also functioned as the head of the new political group, the Republican Society in Pennsylvania.

Franklin's Break with His Son

With great disappointment, Franklin discovered that his son, William, who had accompanied him to England, was a committed Loyalist. With Franklin's help, William was installed as governor of New Jersey, but William spent his time vigorously working against American interests for freedom. In 1776, William was arrested by the Provincial Congress of New Jersey for treasonous behavior and placed under the custody of an American merchant. However, while there, William continued to send information about American troops to the British. Once that was discovered in 1777, Pennsylvania transferred him to a dismal jail in Litchfield, Connecticut. When the sheriff, Lynde Lord, arrived to oversee the jail, he then moved the young man into solitary confinement. The cell had no furniture or toilet facilities. Reportedly, Ben Franklin didn't intervene to help. While William was there, his wife died.

Next, Governor Trumbull of Connecticut transferred him to East Windsor, Connecticut. He became ill while there. After a long period in recovery, a prisoner exchange was arranged, and he was released. Soon afterward, William emigrated to England where he spent the remainder of his life. When Ben Franklin was much older, he wrote to William expressing his extreme disappointment saying, "Nothing has ever hurt me so much and affected me with such keen sensations as to find myself deserted in my old age by my only son, and not only deserted, but to find him taking up arms against me, in a cause wherein my good fame, fortune and life were all at stake." Franklin had now lost his wife and his son, too, in a sense. When he rewrote his will, Benjamin left nothing to William.

The Declaration of Independence

In 1775, Dr. Franklin was elected as a delegate to the Second Continental Congress. Franklin, now 69 years old, did attend a few of the initial sessions for the drafting of the Declaration of Independence. However, he was ill during much of that time with gout and didn't attend too many of the early sessions. When he returned in better health, Franklin, Thomas Jefferson, Robert Livingston, John Adams, and Robert Sherman were selected to help draft the document. Jefferson was an eloquent young statesman and writer, and he wrote the Declaration, asking Franklin to advise him at times. Benjamin Franklin signed it, along with the other delegates, but it needed to be ratified by all of the colonies. With the Declaration of Independence, the colonies would then be enabled to attempt to get military and logistical support from other countries because the document was a definitive declaration of war.

Pennsylvania Constitution

In 1776, immediately after the Continental Congress, Franklin was elected to the presidency of the Pennsylvania Assembly that was tasked with drawing up its own constitution. The colonial charter set up while England controlled America was abrogated. During the discussions about the new Pennsylvanian constitution, Franklin especially campaigned for its declaration of rights. This was a plainly worded but forceful statement that "all men have a natural right to worship Almighty God according to the dictates of their own consciences and understanding, and that no man ought to or be compelled to attend any religious worship." Franklin was very firm on that issue throughout life.

America's Ambassador to France

In October of 1776, Ben Franklin was appointed ambassador to France and was sent there on a confidential mission to secure their support for the American Revolution. America had no navy and lacked sufficient military equipment. Franklin left immediately and took his two grandsons, William Temple Franklin and Benjamin Franklin Bache. During their trip across the Atlantic, they underwent a number of frightening storms and were even attacked by English vessels on the way.

Maintaining the secrecy of the trip proved to be impossible. Franklin's experiments with electricity and his invention of the lightning rod had already reached France and stunned the French community. Already the invention of the Armonica was known there, and the French queen had entertained her friends with the instrument at their dinners.

One of the reasons Franklin hoped to maintain secrecy was the fact that the French foreign minister, Comte de Vergennes, had been smuggling French-made weapons to America in violation of the export ban in place at the time. In 1779, Franklin had also secretly obtained funds from France to have some ships built to be used for privateering. Captain Paul Jones was in command of that fleet and called his flagship the *Bonhomme Richard*, meaning a "sugar baby," which was a play on the words *Poor Richard's Almanac*. Furthermore, France didn't want to trigger a conflict between themselves and England if they found out about Benjamin Franklin's visit prior to any potential agreement.

Unfortunately, the merchant Silas Deane, who was involved with the secret shipment of arms to the colonies, wasted no time at all in telling other colleagues that Franklin was in France, and gossip raced all over Paris. Although Franklin sneaked down the Seine in a simple rowboat, he was met with crowds of well-wishers, and a welcome dinner was held for him in Nantes.

After the affair, he was brought by coach to his hotel. Again, he was greeted by cheering crowds along the streets. Shortly thereafter, Count Jacques-Donatien de Chaumont invited Franklin and his grandsons to stay at his chateau instead. De Chaumont was a noble who was a firm supporter of the American Revolution and often aided support to the American colonies.

After his arrival at the Chateau de Chaumont, Franklin sent his youngest grandchild to a French school, Le Coeur's, that taught English-speaking students from the colonies. As for his 15-year-old grandchild, William, Franklin sent him to Geneva where he could gain experience in a foreign country.

Franklin was a charismatic and ingenious character. His remarkable uniqueness made him a curiosity, and the French people admired him for his individuality. Instead of the traditional powdered wig and elaborate coiffure typical of political leaders, Franklin wore a fur cap and dressed plainly. The French were intrigued by him. In fact, he became so popular there that his likeness appeared on snuffboxes, medallions, watches, and rings!

After reporting to his office at the Chateau, Franklin found out that Prime Minister North discovered he was in France. North made a desperate attempt to stop the Revolutionary War. No more were there any delays in communications. North contacted Franklin promising that England would stop taxing the colonists altogether, adding that the Americans would no longer be considered "rebels," but "His Majesty's faithful subjects." Franklin didn't respond. Revolutions cannot suddenly reverse themselves.

The nobleman and military strategist, the Marquis de Lafayette, was already committed to the American cause before there was any alliance established between America and France. Without securing official permission, Lafayette sailed for America having financed his own voyage. He accompanied George Washington early in the war. When Lafayette returned to France, he met the eloquent Ben Franklin. Together they worked to secure full French support.

In 1777, the colonists prevailed over General Burgoyne at the battlefields in Saratoga, New York. This was a decisive victory and was the turning point in the American Revolution. General Burgoyne was considered by both the English and the French as one of the most capable military commanders of England, and the Saratoga victory demonstrated the depth of the American commitment to the cause of freedom. The French court took notice of this success, giving them the confidence they needed to enter the war as America's ally.

In the meantime, the British ambassador to France, Lord Stormont, spread false rumors throughout France that the initial battles of the

American Revolution were resulting in loss after loss. When visitors asked Franklin about whether or not that was true, Franklin replied, "Oh no, it is not the truth. It is only a *Stormont*." The term "Stormont" became a synonym for lying, and the French people loved to laugh at it.

The drafts of two treaties were drawn up by Franklin, Silas Deane, and Arthur Lee, an agent sent along later from the colonies. The first was the Treaty of Alliance, by which each party agreed to defend the other if either was attacked by the British. An offer was also extended to other interested nations to join with America in its fight for independence; Spain and the Dutch Republic responded that they were indeed interested in assisting the cause. The second draft was the Treaty of Amity and Commerce. By virtue of the amity treaty, France recognized America as an independent nation and was granted certain exclusive shipping and trading rights. Franklin then obtained a copy of the constitution of each colony. After gathering all these documents, Franklin sent a message to the court at Versailles, asking to see King Louis XVI. The king responded, saying the parties could meet at the Hotel de Crillon in Paris.

In 1778, the treaties were signed. France made the Comte de Rochambeau the commander of an expeditionary force, and he proceeded requisitioning men, equipment, and supplies. With him, he brought Lafayette and several ships containing over 6,000 French soldiers, supplies, and armaments. Lafayette excitedly contacted George Washington, saying,

> There is nothing to be found in France which might offer to me so delightful a prospect as those ships and troops. Everything will be soon provided for and we shall be able within these few days to set off at a moment's warning so that our expeditions will go very well.

A famous English author and historian, Edward Gibbon, often visited France and dined at the French cafes there. Franklin's time-tested technique consisted of contacting well-known men and establishing relationships with them. One time, when Franklin spotted him at a cafe, he slipped Gibbon a note inviting him for a drink. It was intended as a simple gesture of cordiality and a matter of intellectual curiosity. Gibbon sent him back a note with a haughty response saying that he wouldn't speak to a "rebel." Franklin sarcastically responded in a follow-up note suggesting that Gibbon's next book should be the "Decline and Fall of the British Empire!" a play on Gibbon's famous book *The Decline and Fall of the Roman Empire.*

The Troublesome John Adams

The Continental Congress appointed the well-known patriot, John Adams, as a commissioner to France. He arrived in France several months after the Treaty of Alliance and the Treaty of Amity and Commerce were signed. Adams met with Franklin and Lee but disapproved of both of them. In addition, he harbored a distrust of France. Adams felt France had a greedy self-interest in the trade and commerce treaty. Lee, Franklin, and Adams had a number of arguments about it as a result of Adams' pessimism. Adams then drafted a letter to the Comte de Vergennes, demanding more naval vessels. After Franklin read it, he toned down the emotional language and sent it on. De Vergennes responded indicating that their fleet was also engaged in the West Indies, one of their territories. He also communicated with Adams and the Continental Congress regarding their full commitment to support the cause of America's freedom. In America, the French Navy later sent Admiral de Barras north from the West Indies to America to rendezvous with George Washington, Lafayette, and Rochambeau in Virginia. It is unknown as to whether or not Adams was instrumental in bringing that about, or if it was Lafayette's intervention.

In 1780, the Continental dollar was devalued, and Adams was summoned to see de Vergennes. The French were concerned that this currency downturn would upset trade relations with France if America won the war. De Vergennes asked Adams to make an exception for the French merchants. Adams adamantly refused and defended the congressional decision regarding the currency. However, he didn't stop there. He followed up with a diatribe listing his other grievances about France and objected to any exclusive trading rights with France. This alarmed de Vergennes, who felt that any subsequent American trade agreement with England would threaten France. Historically, John Adams was a very outspoken man, who often spoke before he considered what another's response might be. Many of his written contributions to the Continental Congress were strongly worded, and fellow members frequently had to soften the wording in those documents.

In fact, de Vergennes himself personally disliked Adams and even wrote to the Continental Congress stating that he would only deal with Franklin and requested that the Congress appoint Benjamin Franklin as the sole plenipotentiary minister to France. Congress did so, and Adams was transferred to the Dutch Republic to talk about its interest in supporting America. The Continental Congress transferred Arthur Lee to Spain because that country was also interested in joining the war effort.

The Troubles Continue

Adams' foreign policy was influenced by a pamphlet by Thomas Pownall, the former lieutenant-governor of New Jersey. In it, Pownall indicated that it was essential that the Revolutionary War be concluded as soon as possible so that Great Britain and America could reestablish trade with each other. The war wasn't yet over, but Adams impatiently made incessant efforts to have England draw up a peace treaty with America. In 1780, Adams wrote a letter saying that America should also be allowed to conduct trade with Great Britain, saying "...no other nation would be able to rival England in those manufactures which we most want in America."

There were a number of letters exchanged between Adams and some of the colonists having to do with Adams' concerns about the trade agreement. After that, Adams published his letter, along with other related ones. Fortunately, they weren't printed until 1782 just before the war ended. Had the French read Adams' publication earlier, it is quite possible that they would have pulled out of the treaties of alliance.

In the year 1781, the theater of operations in the American Revolution switched from the Northern to the Southern colonies. General de Rochambeau, who had been dispatched from France, was instrumental in working with George Washington as the commander-in-chief. Rochambeau and Washington focused their attention on the English threat in Yorktown and fought to expel the British. Due to the overwhelming support that came from the French Navy, Washington and the French allies ended the American Revolution in victory.

When Prime Minister North got word of the momentous victory of America at Yorktown and the surrender of their lieutenant-general, Charles Cornwallis, he shouted, "O God! It is all over!"

Benjamin Franklin: A Faux Pas

In 1782, Comte de Vergennes, the foreign minister of France, proposed the culminating treaty between England and America. Together they drew up a document called the Peace of Paris, which determined the borders of America and granted fishing rights off of Newfoundland to France. Great Britain made concessions to France by granting it control of the islands of Tobago and Senegal, two tropical colonies that France always craved possession of. Franklin then secured the agreement of the Comte de Vergennes for the Peace of Paris. De Vergennes was delighted that he could be included in the settlement, signed it, and moved the process along rapidly through the legal process. This treaty wasn't destined to go into effect until it was signed by both the Americans and Great Britain, however.

Back home, America didn't approve of the Peace of Paris. For one thing, America wanted to cut Comte de Vergennes out of the negotiations. To resolve what they saw as weaknesses in the Franklin-Vergennes peace treaty, they sent John Adams back to France, along with John Jay and Henry Laurens, to work with Franklin on drawing up a revised treaty. America also felt that separate negotiations should be set up with England as well as Spain. To accomplish that, John Jay traveled to England and contacted its prime minister, Lord Shelburne. The existence of two possible treaties was a political embarrassment, especially in view of the fact that the Comte de Vergennes wasn't going to be included in the final settlement, which left Franklin in an awkward situation. Franklin was then ordered to offer an apology to de Vergennes for the confusion.

The Treaty of Paris

Problems often happen when treaties are negotiated, especially when various diplomats compete in order to receive the credit for negotiating. John Jay and Shelburne set up a treaty more favorable to England than to France in terms of trading rights, but it acknowledged American independence. This treaty granted America the right to occupy all of the land east of the Mississippi River up to the southern border of Canada. America would have the right to fish off the waters of Canada. In addition, any property confiscated from legal British owners would be returned to them.

Spain received Florida, with the exception of some smaller territories north and northwest of there, and Menorca. Grenada and Montserrat in the West Indies had been conquered by the Spanish and French but were returned to England as a result of the treaty.

France was granted rights to Tobago and Senegal, which is something de Vergennes had wanted when he and Franklin had worked out the defunct Peace of Paris. France also was given the right to fish off the coast of Newfoundland.

In 1783, the Treaty of Paris was signed by David Hartley and Richard Oswald representing King George III of England, and Franklin, Jay, Laurens, and Adams on behalf of America.

After the signing of the Treaty of Paris, a story circulated around Paris about a dinner that was held with the English ambassador, David Hartley, Richard Oswald, the French king's minister, and Ben Franklin. Hartley offered a toast to the king whom he said was like the sun at midday. Oswald drank to the health of King Louis XVI of France. Franklin lifted his glass very high and toasted George Washington, adding that the commander-in-chief was like Joshua in the Bible who made the sun and moon stand still, and "...they obeyed him!"

When Thomas Jefferson was sent to France as the next ambassador in 1784, the Comte de Vergennes asked him if he was going to replace Franklin. Jefferson, who admired Franklin immensely, replied, "No one can replace him, sir; I am only his successor."

Relationship with John Adams

John Adams was always annoyed by Franklin's casual manner and off-handed remarks, and never fully trusted him. When Franklin made the mistake of introducing Adams to one of his French female friends, he was scandalized by the woman's seductive appearance. Abigail Adams, John Adams' wife, was horrified when the Frenchwoman kissed Franklin, although she merely kissed him on the cheek. In a couple of her letters to friends, Abigail said that the woman threw her arms around Franklin, and appeared rather unkempt and slovenly in appearance—thoroughly lacking in manners. She and her husband had been raised in a strict Puritan household, where they were taught that people should be very restrained and proper. In addition, Adams—who was much more formal in his communication with foreign dignitaries—was taken aback by Franklin's use of French vocabulary. Franklin had taught himself French, but Adams was educated in the use of the language. In addition, there are pronunciations of French which are considered more proper and is referred to as the "Parisian dialect." According to French contemporaries, Franklin's use of French was considered adequate, although he made grammatical errors. Even though Adams was formerly educated in French and thought he spoke it fluently, the French people themselves criticized him, saying that he often had to search for words.

The enmity of Lee, Adams, and Jay for Franklin grew, but Franklin adroitly avoided any outward show of hostility. Thomas Jefferson, the rising statesman and Virginia delegate, expressed concern about the comportment of Adams as a negotiator at all. He is recorded to have said that Adams "hates John Jay, hates the French and hates the English."

The French respected Franklin more than they did Adams, and Adams appeared to be jealous of Franklin's ability as a diplomat, although he did recognize it. Adams once said about Franklin that he "…is always an honest man, often a wise one, but sometimes in some things, absolutely out of his senses." It is unfortunate that personal feelings interfered with foreign relations.

Franklin's "Women"

Even though he was 70 years old, Franklin was what is called a "ladies' man." His wit and charm attracted a number of women, and he didn't resist their charms either. Upper-class women used to crowd around him and engage in light-hearted conversations and jokes.

Elisabeth, Countess d'Houdetot, and her husband had what one might call an "open relationship," and the countess often had affairs with other men. When Franklin was in France, he was entertained at her house. Reportedly, she wasn't very good-looking but was a quick wit. That drew Franklin to her, and they exchanged sarcastic and amusing barbs.

Another woman that Franklin met was Madame Helvetius, the widow of Claude Helvetius, a philosopher. She once was offended that Franklin didn't ask to spend a night together with her. To that, he replied, "Madame, I am waiting until the nights are longer." Franklin visited her often, as he enjoyed her sense of humor and her intelligence as well as her affection. It was said that Franklin did actually propose to her and bemoaned the fact that she wouldn't marry him. Franklin even wrote a somewhat suggestive letter to her couched within a facetious analogy which he told about a fictitious dream in which Socrates spoke to him about Helvetius. In the story, Socrates said, "I will confess to you that I loved her extremely, but she was cruel to me, and rejected me."

Franklin's mind then wandered to thoughts about his deceased wife and continued his stream of consciousness:

> ...Then I saw Mrs. Franklin. I reclaimed her, but she answered me coldly and said "I have been a good wife to you for forty-nine years and four months, nearly half a century; let that content you. I have formed a new connection here which will last to eternity."

Perhaps that sprang from guilt because Franklin was away from her for so long.

Although it was a platonic relationship, he and Madame Brillon de Jouy, who was married, often associated with each other. She called Ben Franklin "*Mon Cher Papa*," that is, "My Dear Papa." Once when he passed her house while Mme. Brillon was away for a prolonged period, Franklin wrote to her saying,

> I often pass your house; it appears desolate now to me...I find the Commandments very inconvenient and I am sorry they were made. If, in your travels, you happen to see the Holy Father, you might ask him to repeal them, as having been given only to Jews and too hard for good Christians to keep.

It was said that she responded to Franklin, saying she absolved him of all sin, "present, past and future." Franklin even shared stories about his relationship with Madame Helvetius with Madame Brillon. She then quipped, "Give this evening to my amiable rival, Madame Helvetius, kiss her for yourself and for another...and I grant you the power of attorney to visit my neighbor, Mademoiselle Le Veillard."

Franklin actually did try to visit Mademoiselle Le Veillard, but she wasn't in when he arrived. When she heard about this visit, the mademoiselle went to Franklin's house who funnily enough wasn't in at the time. She then left a note on Franklin's door saying, "Mademoiselle Le Veillard came by to have the honor to be kissed by Monsieur Franklin."

Madame Brillon's husband—dismayed by Franklin's frequent appearances—wanted to keep Franklin from seeing his wife in case the liaison escalated. So, he introduced Franklin to Madame Foucault, saying, "She is marvelously plump once again and has just acquired new curves. Very round curves, very white, they seem to have a quality most essential in the eyes of amateurs such as you. It would be possible, I bet, to kill a flea on them."

King Louis XVI knew of Franklin's attraction to women, and theirs for him. He then saw it for himself at a celebration in his court. The women fawned all over him to the point that the king considered it quite inappropriate. He then had a chamber pot designed and sent to a high-ranking French countess, Diane de Polignac. The chamber pot had Franklin's likeness in the bottom of it!

Franklin didn't shy away from his experience and knowledge of women, and once wrote a letter entitled, "Advice to a Young Man on the Choice of a Mistress." In it, he advised the man to select an older woman because there would be no danger in having children, and she would most likely be discreet about an affair, an affair which would prevent a man from "…ruining his health and fortune among mercenary prostitutes." Curiously enough, however, publication of that letter wasn't released until the 19th century and has been used as a rationale for repealing obscenity laws.

His Farewell to France

Dr. Franklin was now 79 years old and rather infirm. Joseph Bentham, a printer for the University of Cambridge, was a witness during Franklin's appearance before the Privy Council in England. He said that Dr. Franklin was very debilitated by some respiratory ailments and said that, "…even his voice was so husky and choked with phlegm, that it refused utterance to the sentiments which were directed by his superior intelligence." Franklin's respiratory condition grew worse with time, and he was occasionally bedridden while in France.

When he was preparing to leave France, Franklin wanted to personally bid farewell to the Comte de Vergennes but was prevented from doing so because of his increasing debility. Instead, he sent a letter to him saying:

> May I beg the favor of you, Sir, to express respectfully for me to His Majesty, the deep sense I have for all the inestimable benefits his goodness has conferred on my country; a sentiment that it will be the business of the little remainder of the life now left to me, to impress equally on the minds of all my countrymen.

Accompanying a letter of gratitude, the king sent Franklin a portrait of himself embedded with jewels, mostly diamonds. It is still very valuable and is located in the Smithsonian National Portrait Gallery in Washington, D.C.

Chapter 9 – Benjamin Franklin's Last Years

In 1785, Franklin returned home. The people of Philadelphia crowded the wharf on Market Street to greet him. A great cannon was fired and bells rang from all the churches. His son-in-law, Richard, was there with the throngs of people who cheered and followed his coach as he went home to see the rest of his family.

His status as a statesman and Founding Father was appreciated, and he was called upon in 1787 to serve in the Pennsylvania Assembly once again. He was also unanimously elected as president of the Supreme Executive Council of Pennsylvania and served in that capacity until 1788. The prestige and weight of that appointment was as important as the position of governor. The Supreme Council formulated the constitution of the Commonwealth of Pennsylvania. Franklin contributed to that formulation, and the finalized constitution was passed in 1790. He served for three years, but was becoming more ill and had to retire.

Later in 1787, Franklin was called upon to participate in the Constitutional Convention. Because he was in his 80s and very frail, he didn't speak often during those sessions. Occasionally, he had another Pennsylvanian delegate, James Wilson, read some of his contributions aloud for the assembly.

The Constitutional Convention

When he attended the Constitutional Convention, Franklin was seated next to George Washington, who sat in a chair with the picture of a sun on the back of it. The Convention argued about boundary lines, and the colonies broke out in arguments over trade and the payment of war debt. Washington became frustrated that his new nation already seemed to be breaking into fragments. He stood up and boldly and said to the assembly, "We are one nation today. Will we be thirteen tomorrow?"

The members of the Convention wrestled with its wording, and the process dragged on for a month. Franklin didn't entirely approve of the final draft of the Constitution, due to his concerns with some of the issues about trade, slavery, taxes, and foreign affairs. He felt, and history bore him out, that those factors would cause contention in the future. However, he saw a great deal of quality within the new Constitution, saying that it was near perfection. He also felt that members of the Convention should approve of it in its current form, but remain open to making some changes in the future due to changing circumstances. He said, "I doubt whether any other convention we can obtain may be able to make a better Constitution." Some people wanted to put it off until Washington rushed forward and signed it. Once Washington signed, the others signed in quick succession.

After the signatories signed the Constitution, Franklin glanced at the sun painted on the back of Washington's chair and said:

> I have often and often in the course of the session…looked at the sun behind the president (George Washington, president of the assembly), without being able to tell whether or not it was rising or setting. But now, at length, I have the happiness to know that it is a rising and not a setting sun.

Franklin and Paper Currency

During the sessions of the Constitutional Convention, the issue of the payment of war debt also arose. This reawakened Franklin's earlier views on the advantages of using paper money, rather than relying on gold and silver to pay debts.

Franklin wrote essays fostering the use of paper currency in 1740 and defended its usage. Gold and silver could only be procured through foreign trade for the most part, and that had created difficulties in the past. If there were shortages of these metals, it would stifle trade, even that between the colonies. Needless to say, carrying sacks of coins in order to purchase items was clumsy and cumbersome. In his treatise, "A Modest Enquiry into the Nature and Necessity of Paper Money," he said, "Money as a currency has additional value by so much time and labor as it saves in the exchange of commodities." He also pointed out the fact that, if there was a scarcity of gold and silver, people might have to resort to bartering in order to purchase goods. Wisely, he pointed out that the precious metals tend to vary in value.

He further cautioned that the amount of paper currency issued must be limited by assets that could be designated to maintain its assessed valuation, or inflation would occur. As a backup asset, Franklin proposed land. Later on, he altered that notion by indicating that silver be used instead of land as security.

Banks, he said, would be well situated to stabilize quantities of currency in circulation. Today, economists use the term "money in circulation," or "M1." Franklin indicated that a well-run bank would never loan more money than its landed securities allowed for. In recent years, that principle he advocated has been violated, causing bank failures and the depreciation of a country's currency in the global market. Actually, that happened in America following the American Revolution when banks paid for war debts in the hopes that they could later charge taxes to cover the costs.

During the American Revolution, Continental currency was counterfeited by the British and its usage was suspended. That caused some disastrous results when George Washington's troops refused to continue in their march through New Jersey because the currency that was used for their wages was valueless. He was then forced to borrow gold and silver from one of his allies during the war. A standardized system was needed that was less vulnerable to counterfeiting and fully secured by collateral in the banks. This would build confidence and help with getting the currency accepted by all parties.

Franklin had plans to wrestle with the problem of counterfeiting, which he indicated could be resolved in the printing process. When he had a contract to print money for New Jersey in 1730, it was said that it didn't easily lend itself to counterfeiting.

It is unknown as to how he weighed in on the issue of paper currency at the Constitutional Convention. However, in view of Franklin's general attitude toward the use of paper currency, it would be safe to conclude that he was in favor of it, but with the caveat that the monetary system be handled responsibly.

Benjamin Franklin and Slavery

When Benjamin Franklin was a young man, he held prejudicial views about Black people. In 1730, he compared "the sauciness of a Negro" to the "prattle of a child." He also wrote about African Americans in economic terms when he estimated the cost of losing slaves to smallpox. In the *Pennsylvania Gazette*, he continually published advertisements for slave owners who were trying to recover their runaway slaves. While he wasn't a slave trader, one could say that he was a broker—an intermediary between sellers and buyers of slaves, which led to a conclusion by some historians that he was a slave trader, even if in a limited sense.

For example, he advertised the sale of "A likely young Negro fellow, about twenty-six years of age, suitable for any farming or plantation business, having been long accustomed to it and has had the smallpox." And, "To be sold. A prime able young Negro man, fit for laborious work in town or country, that has had the smallpox. As also a middle-aged Negro man that has likewise had the smallpox. Inquire of the printer hereof, or otherwise they will be exposed to sale by public venue." When Franklin went to England, he brought his slave, Peter, with him. Later, he complained about Peter's behavior saying that he was "of little use and often in mischief," but he did add that they had a good relationship. Sometimes he spoke about Black people saying that they "misbehave," a term used when speaking of a disobedient child rather than an adult. He even put an advertisement in his *Pennsylvania Gazette* for Peter when he ran away. Yet, if he felt that Peter wasn't useful, why did he bother?

Like other colonists, he thought that Black people were inherently inferior to Caucasians. In his "Observations on the Increase of Mankind" published in 1755, there was a section on nonwhites, with the exception of the tribal people who were the first natives of America. In the essay, he asked, "Why increase the sons of Africa by planting them in America, where we have so fair an opportunity, by excluding all Black people and Tawneys, of increasing the lovely white and red?" However, he later remarked that he was "partial to the complexion of my country." Some elements of white supremacy do appear to be present.

Besides the ads about the sale of slaves, Franklin also printed letters from those who were promoting the cause of abolitionism in the colonies. In 1740, he informed the public that Reverend George Whitefield was seeking to build a "Negro school" in the colony, and included a solicitation for donations that could be sent to the "printer" of the newspaper for that purpose. Due to the fact that America was beginning to espouse equality for all men, Franklin realized that he had to reexamine his own beliefs.

In the early 1760s, Franklin met Thomas Bray, an Anglican minister in England, who contacted him in regards to sending out missionaries to convert Black people and building schools for them in the colonies. Franklin was enthusiastic and encouraged him to do so. In 1758, Bray set up a small school in Pennsylvania, which was successful. Prior to her death, Franklin's wife wrote to him in England praising the effort after she herself had attended some classes that Bray already had opened. During that year, Franklin visited some of the schools he had a hand in establishing and wrote,

> I have conceived a higher opinion of the natural capacities of the black race than I had ever before entertained. Their apprehension seems as quick, their memory as strong, and their docility in every respect equal to that of white children.

After that, Franklin started altering his opinion and wrote that these perceived negative characteristics he and others had stemmed not from race, but from poor education, negative environments, and the institution of slavery itself. In 1760, Franklin was appointed chairman of Bray's Associates. He also recommended that William Dawson, the president of the College of William and Mary, open a school in Virginia for Black people. According to his correspondence, Franklin became more active in promoting education for Black people in Rhode Island in 1763.

He joined the Pennsylvania Society Promoting the Abolition of Slavery and the Relief of Free Negroes Unlawfully Held in Bondage in the 1780s. When he was elected president of the society, he appended their charter and outlined procedures he deemed appropriate before anyone freed their slaves. This Franklin called the "Plan for Improving the Condition of the Free Blacks, 1789." Then he set up 24 subcommittees to the task of providing apprenticeships for them. It should be noted that the thesis Franklin wrote was about only those who were free Black people.

He also supported the Quaker abolitionist, Anthony Benezet, in his founding of a school for Black people in Philadelphia. In 1758, Franklin opened several free schools for Black people and financially gave them support.

In 1787, he was elected the president of the Abolitionist Society, and published letters to the public on behalf of the group and sent a petition to Congress to promote the cause of abolishing slavery altogether. One of the questionable issues that he cited at the Constitutional Convention had to do with slavery. Insightfully, he realized that simply freeing slaves would be a disservice if it wasn't accompanied with providing them with skills related to education and the tools they would need to secure gainful employment, as well as some financial support to start out.

Just three months before his death in 1790, Franklin sent an official petition to Congress which stated:

> From a persuasion that equal liberty was originally the portion, it is still the birthright of all men, and influenced by the strong ties of humanity and the principles of their institution, your memorialists conceive themselves bound to use all justifiable endeavors to loosen the bounds of slavery and promote a general enjoyment of the blessings of freedom.

There are no consistent records as to what actually happened to Franklin's slaves in the 1780s. He did have a clause in his 1757 will for the freeing of his two slaves upon death. While Franklin supported the abolition movement and education of Black people, he wasn't ever outspoken about it. His stance on the issue would seem to be ambiguous.

Contrary View

In his book, *Runaway America: Benjamin Franklin, Slavery, and the American Revolution*, Dr. Waldstreicher of Temple University indicated that Franklin may not have been as heavily subscribed to the abolition of slavery as it seems. He did promote the abolitionist cause, it's true, but only after other Founding Fathers did, and only after it became the more prevalent trend in the colonies after the ratification of the Declaration of Independence. In 2004, Waldstreicher said, "Events after 1776, of course, do matter, as do the final acts of great lives. Franklin lived just long enough for his slaves to run away and die off, and for antislavery to become politically safe in his home state."

Quakers were more numerous in Pennsylvania than in any other state or commonwealth. Because they were committed abolitionists, it was politically expedient for Franklin to come out as a leader who likewise opposed slavery.

In addition, the other Founding Fathers, like Washington and even Thomas Jefferson, were softening their support of slavery. When focusing upon the factual lives of these men and their views about slavery, one cannot help but note a contradiction between their words and their acts.

The Gulf Stream Project

Franklin was a communicator and would engage nearly anyone in a conversation. In 1768, when he had been postmaster, he once asked a captain why packets mailed from Great Britain seemed to take longer to arrive than those shipped via other merchant ships. The captain told him that the maps of the Gulf Stream, a massive ocean current in the Atlantic Ocean, had been printed in America, and the British tended to ignore them because of their prejudice against the colonies. Therefore, the British often sailed straight across the Gulf Stream, rather than taking advantage of the west to east current it generates. During the American Revolution, Franklin had maps printed, and distributed them to France, the American ally, for navigational purposes.

In 1786, Franklin consulted with navigators and revised the original maps of the Gulf Stream. Today's experts have examined the revised map that Franklin developed and discovered that it is remarkably accurate.

Unpublicized Inventions

Franklin created a number of devices which he used for his businesses and at home. In 1787, George Washington wrote about a visit he made to Franklin's residence and noticed a machine that Franklin had constructed for ironing flat cloth, rather than using irons. It consisted of a large heated metal plate that was lowered upon another, used for pressing tablecloths and other flat fabrics used for dinner napkins and handkerchiefs.

Another invention occurred when Benjamin Franklin's brother, John, who was sixteen years older than he, developed bladder stones and had to insert a catheter daily to urinate. In those days, they used a rigid metal tube. John found the insertion to be painful and mentioned it to Benjamin. After researching it, Franklin went to a local silversmith and designed a tube made of tiny segments. Historians have credited him with having developed a flexible catheter that would be less painful to insert. However, Franklin was a humble man and indicated that it was invented in 1720, possibly by Francesco Roncelli-Pardino. John indicated that the device was far less painful, and Franklin was pleased.

Another invention was created when Franklin realized the disadvantage of his height. Franklin was less than six feet tall and often had difficulty reaching books on higher shelves. So, he altered a chair using a reversible seat, converting it into a small stepladder. In addition, he also designed an extension arm with two prongs on the end. The prongs could be opened and closed by pulling on a cord. This gadget is similar to the grabbers used today. Franklin used to take one or another of those inventions with him when he went to his library in Philadelphia. No doubt it must have been amusing to the other library patrons to see this older gentleman carrying one of these items on his visits there.

When he went to the downtown library at night, Franklin noticed that the street lights were much dimmer on his way home. These lamps had to be lit each night by the lamplighter, who also needed to clean them. The lights consisted of glass globes equipped with a wick that was fed by a container of whale oil. As the hours passed, the globe would become darker, as it filled with the carbon residue from the burning. In order to resolve the problem, Franklin ventilated the lamp by placing a long glass funnel in it that could channel the smoke upwards. Then he inserted crevices into the bottom to provide a more efficient air flow. They used some in Philadelphia, and those lights stayed bright until morning. In addition, Franklin also praised the use of permanent lights at the base of outside steps.

After pondering the subject of night lighting, it occurred to him that there would be less need for that during the summer when dawn came earlier. In an essay called "An Economic Project," Franklin suggested setting the clocks one hour back to take advantage of the extra daylight. Today, many countries use Daylight Savings Time for that very purpose.

He also theorized the design of a clock that is simpler. The clockworks on this "Benjamin Franklin Clock" ran on the rotation of three interior wheels with teeth. It quite accurately measured the quarter-hour, the half-hour, and full hour. It measured the minutes as well. Although Franklin never actually wrote about it, he discussed it with a Dutch physiologist, Jan Ingenhousz, and another friend from England, James Ferguson. Ferguson designed the clock according to Franklin's discussion and later improved it, much to Franklin's delight.

While living in London, Franklin was astounded by the number of misspellings that occurred in written material. So, he felt that a spelling reform was needed. Seeing that certain letters can sound differently, he created a phonetic alphabet. It had lowercase letters, but he eliminated the consonants c, j, q, x, w, and y. His difficulty with those letters was the fact that there were various ways of pronouncing them and were redundant. For example, hard "c" could sound like a "k," and the soft "c" sounded like an "s." To those, he added six letters and even had typesets manufactured showing what they looked like.

For the vowels, he used a double vowel to signify long vowels. For example, "remeen" meant "remain." Linguists have examined Franklin's proposals but found some inconsistencies in it. In 1789, Franklin wrote to Noah Webster regarding it. Webster was already in the process of updating the English language and spoke to Franklin who was attending some of his lectures. The greatest stumbling block to the promulgation of Franklin's new alphabet was the unavailability of the types needed to print the written pieces. In time, Franklin lost interest in the project because of its inconvenience.

The Death of Benjamin Franklin

In his declining years, Benjamin Franklin was somewhat hunched over and dressed very plainly. He was mostly bald and wore no hat. Walking or standing for any period of time was painful for him. Franklin had the property around his house redesigned with a number of winding gravel walkways interspersed with flowering bushes and trees. Under the shade, there were tea tables at which he entertained friends. Many of his friends were those he knew from the Philadelphia or Constitutional Convention. Franklin and they played cards, chess, and cribbage. Sarah Franklin Bache, his only daughter, lived there with him along with three of her children, and they enjoyed plenty of family time together.

Besides spending time with friends and family, Franklin also enjoyed bathing and felt it was healthy for him. It was because it relieves the symptoms of gout which he had for many years. Although he was corpulent, he also admitted that he was indolent. Toward his later years, he made it a point to walk around his rooms for nearly an hour if possible. Unfortunately, the pain and swelling from his gout often made him stop, and those episodes could last up to a full week, making Franklin occasionally bedridden.

Gout is caused by an excessive accumulation of uric acid that isn't efficiently excreted. It can be caused by eating too much red meat, seafood, or organ meat. Obesity intensifies it. As he aged, he developed boils. Most likely, they came about due to a build-up of uric acid from gout, although he attributed it to "dropsy." Nevertheless, he continued to read avidly and frequently wrote letters to the authors, who were pleased to hear from this well-known man. When he was on his deathbed in 1790, George Washington sent him a letter. In it, he said, in part:

> You have the pleasing consolation to know that you have not lived in vain...Be assured that, so long as I retain my memory, you will be thought of with respect, veneration and affection by your sincere friend, George Washington.

When Franklin became more debilitated from his illness and infirmity, he started developing sore throats, had trouble talking, and could only eat barley. While he attended the conventions, he fell several times trying to keep up with the younger men. However, his call to duty was something he felt compelled to do for his country.

About three weeks before his death, Dr. John Jones presented a report on the failing health of Benjamin Franklin in the *Pennsylvania Gazette*. In his report, he said that Franklin had an extremely high fever, a persistent pain in his chest, a chronic cough, and had difficulty breathing.

Like his brother John, Franklin developed stones in his bladder. Surgeons of the 18th century were able to perform procedures to remedy that, but Franklin felt that he was too old and it wasn't worth the cost of having the surgery performed. He had frequent colds and fits of vomiting. An abscess developed in one of his lungs and burst, causing excruciating pain. Afterward, his pain thankfully left him. He was exhausted and became extremely lethargic. The clinicians today indicate that he most likely suffered from pleurisy and empyema, which is caused by an increase of pus in the lungs and also caused by a bacterial infection, probably due to the burst abscess. His last words were, "A dying man can do nothing easily."

On April 17, 1790, he died quietly.

The *Pennsylvania Gazette* and many other national and overseas publications carried his obituary:

> Died on Saturday night in the 85th year of his age, the illustrious BENJAMIN FRANKLIN. The world has been so long in possession of such extraordinary proofs of the singular abilities and virtues of this FRIEND OF MANKIND that it is impossible for a newspaper to increase his fame, or to convey his name to a part of the civilized globe where it is not already known and admired.

In 1728, Franklin actually wrote his own epitaph which read:

> The body of B. Franklin, Printer, like the cover of an old book, its contents torn out, and script of its lettering and gilding lies here, food for worms. But the work shall not be wholly lost; for it will, as he believ'd, appear once more in a new and more prefect edition, corrected and amended by the author.

The House of Representatives adopted the suggestions of young James Madison to wear symbols of mourning for one month. However, the Senate did not, due to the influence of John Adams and Arthur Lee, who still harbored antipathy toward him. Both Adams and Lee had often spread negative sentiments about him particularly after they were in France with him to negotiate the formulation of the Treaty of Paris. They had been disedified by his lack of eloquence in dress later in life and his casual manners, as well as being morally offended by his comradery with women. They were likewise offended by the political stance of his grandson, Benjamin Franklin Bache, who was a staunch anti-Federalist.

Upon hearing about Franklin's death, the French National Assembly announced a month of mourning in honor of Benjamin Franklin, calling him "the genius who freed America and shed torrents of light on Europe." Count Mirabeau, a French member of the Assemblies in France and supporter of the French Revolution, knew of Franklin through the Marquis de Lafayette. About Franklin, Mirabeau said, "He was able to restrain thunderbolts and tyrants."

After Franklin's death, there was a massive crowd of 20,000 who came to the funeral. That was an astounding number of people in those early days.

Legacy

Benjamin Franklin lived his life openly. He was vulnerable, but his vulnerability was his strength. He had the courage of a warrior who needed no shield. In his autobiography, he listed the principles by which he always wanted to live. These he called the Thirteen Necessary Virtues:

> 1. TEMPERANCE. Drink not to indulgence; drink not to elevation.

> There were never any reports of Ben Franklin being drunk, but he did enjoy wine. In 1779, he said, "Behold the rain which descends from heaven and is incorporated into grapes to be changed into wine; a constant proof the God loves us and loves to see us happy."

> 2. SILENCE. Speak not but what may benefit others or yourself; avoid trifling conversation

> When Franklin was pondering political and scientific issues, he was absolutely silent, but shared his views freely with those whom he knew would be affected by following the suggestions that he thought might be beneficial to others. Despite the fact that he wrote and designed numerous inventions, Franklin never took out any patents

on them. He said, "…as we enjoy great advantages from the inventions of others, we should be glad of an opportunity to serve others by any invention of ours; and this we should do freely and generously."

3. ORDER. Let all things have their places; let each part of your business have its time.

Franklin kept meticulous records of everything he did. He could produce documentation for all the logistical proposals that he made and accompanied his actions with a written record of it.

4. RESOLUTION. Resolve to perform what you ought; perform without fail what you resolve.

Franklin's entire life was directed toward a goal. When he was sent as a troubleshooter and an ambassador to England and France, he worked feverishly toward accomplishing his goals. When he had to appear before the Privy Council in England, he was nearly 70 years old, but stood up the entire time and persevered throughout the lengthy procedure like a 20-year-old, because that was his job.

5. FRUGALITY. Make no expense but to do good to others or yourself; waste nothing.

During the boycott of British goods prior to the American Revolution, Franklin instructed all Americans to manufacture their own goods. He also canceled his own personal orders for English goods and instructed his own staff to manage with what they had on hand or create a substitute.

6. INDUSTRY. Lose no time; be always employed in something useful; but off all unnecessary actions.

Benjamin Franklin lived until he was 84. During his lifetime, he did thousands of useful things to the point that records of his work fill volumes. He never stopped. For example, when he went to the Tun Tavern in Philadelphia, he made it a point to combine business with pleasure. He used the tavern as a place where he could hold meetings and recruit troops, as well as enjoy the company of others.

7. SINCERITY. Use no hurtful deceit; think innocently and justly, and, if you speak, speak accordingly.

In the annals of history, there is no record of Franklin ever making false claims about another person. In fact, he was so straightforward that some of his detractors were taken back by his "plain speech."

8. JUSTICE. Wrong none by doing injuries, or omitting the benefits that are your duty.

When he objected to someone's view, Franklin always gave the other the benefit of the doubt.

9. MODERATION. Avoid extremes; forbear resenting injuries so much as you think they deserve.

Franklin was never considered to be a hostile man. In responding to a politician who disagreed with him, he always addressed the issue without resorting to personal insult.

10. CLEANLINESS. Tolerate no uncleanliness in body, clothes or habitation.

Although there's no record of his habits related to cleanliness, no comment was ever made about him to the effect that he was sloppy. However, when he crossed New Jersey to get to Philadelphia, the rain was so constant that, no doubt, he arrived disheveled and soaked!

11. TRANQUILITY. Be not disturbed at trifles, or at accidents common or unavoidable.

During his experiments, Franklin made many errors, like shocking himself when he flew his famous kite with the key. That never stopped him. It was his sense of tranquility that gave him persistence.

12. CHASTITY. Rarely use venery but for health or offspring, never to dullness, weakness, or injury of your own or another's reputation.

Franklin was a "ladies' man," and rumors abounded about his promiscuity, although not all of his relationships were sexual, and perhaps none were.

13. HUMILITY. Imitate Jesus and Socrates.

It is difficult to compare Franklin to Jesus, but he was just as deep a thinker as Socrates and tried to imitate the qualities of Jesus.

His Will

Benjamin Franklin owned a great deal of land which he divided up and bequeathed to his family. In addition, he divided up his buildings and wealth at the time of his death among his survivors with the exception of his eldest son William, with whom he had a serious falling out late in life. William already owned some land in Pennsylvania, which—of course—was rightfully his. He restricted his will to the forgiveness of any outstanding debts William owed and gave him the papers and books William already had possession of.

Franklin was particularly fond of a portrait given to him by King Louis XVI of France, containing 100 precious diamonds. That he gave to his daughter, Sarah Franklin Bache. In his will, it was clear he tried not to forget anyone. That even included some of the people who worked for him in the printing and publishing business.

To his grandchild, Benjamin Franklin Bache, he bequeathed his printing press and equipment. His grandson had pursued printing as a career and was already publishing a newspaper, the

Philadelphia Aurora. He was a writer, too, who wrote about politics like his grandfather and even tried his hand at poetry.

Benjamin Franklin bequeathed to Boston and Philadelphia 1,000 pounds to be placed in a 200-year trust fund. More than $2,000,000 had been collected in the Philadelphia trust by 1990. It loaned money to the people of Philadelphia and was used to finance their mortgage loans as well. The Boston trust fund had accumulated about $5,000,000, which was used to finance the Franklin Institute of Boston, and what remained was used to maintain the institution.

The most precious item that he gave was invisible to the eye but known to every living American. It was his ceaseless effort to assure that America will remain free.

Conclusion

Benjamin Franklin was, by far, one of the most versatile polymaths the world has ever known. He wasn't a "generalist" or a "jack of all trades," in the sense that he knew a little bit about everything. He knew a *great deal* about a wide variety of fields—science, philosophy, medicine, politics, finances, human relations, chemistry, religion, physical science, publishing, humor, writing, printing, and even candle making! Franklin was the Leonardo da Vinci of his day, although he never considered himself to be a genius (though he probably was). Franklin simply exploded with boundless curiosity.

He lived during one of the most tumultuous periods of America. Not only was he instrumental in bringing about freedom and liberty for the United States, but he assisted in the birth of a new nation. When there were difficulties, he didn't fret; he dealt with them. This was a surprising characteristic, given the fact that he demonstrated all the traits of an average—but rather wild—adolescent. His incessant addiction to knowledge motivated him to become self-taught in many subjects.

Unlike other thinkers, he believed in testing out his beliefs and theories in a practical setting. At a time when there was no such thing as mass communication, his viewpoints spread across Europe at a breathtaking pace. In his roles as ambassador, emissary, and agent, he spent over twenty years abroad, but frequently arrived overseas only to find out that the people in Europe were already knowledgeable about his accomplishments. While in England and France, he promoted and publicized the values of the American Enlightenment way of thinking.

Benjamin Franklin was one of the most versatile and productive Americans of the 18th century. As a Founding Father of the United States and political theorist, he helped formulate a framework for a democratic republic and guided a new nation toward becoming a bulwark of freedom. In addition, he stimulated scientific curiosity to the point that it fostered the proliferation of invention and innovation. Franklin is still important today because he showed generations to come that curiosity and freedom of thought has everlasting rewards.

If you enjoyed this book, a review on Amazon would be greatly appreciated because it helps me to create more books that people want.

Thanks for your support!

Part 2: George Washington

A Captivating Guide to an American Founding Father Who Served as the First President of the United States of America

Introduction

One day at Mount Vernon, a young boy climbed into a window, fell, and hurt himself. George Washington, who had advanced rheumatism then, called for his servant to help. When the boy recovered, Washington asked why the boy had come in. The servant told him the boy wanted to get a look at the president. Washington then asked to see the boy.

"You wanted to see the president, did you? Well, I am George Washington."

"No!" retorted the boy, "You are only just a man. I want to see the President!"

This is the history of George Washington who was a president, a general and a Founding Father of a new nation. But, most of all, it is the story of George Washington the man. Many of the anecdotes related herein are true stories told by the people who were his own family and friends.

Washington was a tough disciplinarian, but even more disciplined with himself. He knew he had remarkable leadership abilities, but also knew it was his duty and destiny to lead a new nation and help it reap the rewards of the freedom and liberty it espoused. Many criticized him for being a wealthy aristocrat, which he was. Yet, it wasn't gold or glory he sought; it was the courage to face the truth that freedom is bonded to sacrifice. George Washington deeply understood he needed to give back what he had received. He was a highly skilled warrior as seen in his magnificent job as the first commander-in-chief during the American Revolution. He was a man who was like a father leading his child safely through the growing pains endured in the interest of self-determination, independence, and liberty.

Washington was a warrior, but one who never drew his sword except for a just cause. He never killed for fanfare or fame. Yet, it was his destiny to become celebrated and famous. George Washington believed that people must make the best of everything, including their own misfortunes—a rare quality in a man.

Most people don't realize that George Washington never got a full college education, although he got a license in land surveying from William and Mary College. Later in life, he was awarded an honorary doctor's degree from Harvard, but admitted he was rather embarrassed about it because he didn't feel he deserved it.

As his eulogy, one of his officers during the American Revolution, Colonel Henry "Light-Horse" Lee, said Washington was "First in war, first in peace, and first in the hearts of his countrymen."

Chapter 1 – She Was Horrified!

George's mother, Mary Washington, was horrified when he boldly announced he was going to join the British Navy. His mother's stepson, Lawrence, was in the British Navy and George admired him. What's more, George wanted to be independent and away from home. In 1746, George was fourteen, which was considered an appropriate age to enlist. He felt that the navy would give him the opportunity to go into a career and give him a chance to make money on his own. However, George was very mature for his age, and his mother depended upon him. Concerned about his possible departure, she anxiously wrote to her brother regarding the British Navy. When her brother responded, Mary Washington became alarmed, so she showed the letter to George. In part, it said:

> "…a common sailor before the mast has by no means the common liberty of the subject, for they will press him from ship to ship, where he has fifteen shillings a month, and then they will cut and slash his pay and use him like a dog."

George, on the other hand, was stubborn and didn't want to believe that piece of news. Optimistically, he felt he could get a post as an officer. He and his mother argued and argued. When George insisted, 18th Century historians said she cried incessantly. George had never seen this strong woman in such a vulnerable state so he reluctantly relented.

Although it was said that George's mother was strict and firm, she had the daunting task of caring for her daughter and four sons. As a member of the aristocracy in Virginia, it was essential that the children be mannered and poised, so Mary raised them with determination. George's grand-stepson once described her as a "parental authority which commanded obedience."

Mary also needed to plan for their future. Her oldest stepson, Lawrence, would receive the 2,000-acre plantation on the Potomac River when he came of age. When he did obtain legal age in 1743, he renamed it "Mount Vernon" after a British commander under whom he served—Vice Admiral Edward Vernon. Mary's second eldest son, Augustine Jr., would inherit his father's property at Pope's Creek along with the money his father earned in his partnership at the iron works nearby. George, when he was 21 years old, would inherit Ferry Farm. His father, Augustine Washington Sr., also bequeathed smaller lots of land to his other sons. According to Augustine's will, Mary was the manager of Ferry Farm until George reached the age of 21.

Ferry Farm

"Ferry Farm" in Fredericksburg, Virginia was called that because it was near a ferry crossing on the Rappahannock River. The Rappahannock was a wide and wild river that ebbed and flowed with the tides of the Chesapeake Bay. It was alongside that river that George Washington spent his early days. The river was red due to the iron ore in the region. There they raised flax, corn, tobacco, and a flock of sheep for wool.

Two legends were told throughout history about George as a boy. One was the story of him chopping down his father's cherry tree and telling the truth when confronted with by his father. The story appeared in *McGuffey's Second Reader* in 1836 and is believed by historians to have been more of a moral tale related by

Washington's first pastor, Mason Locke Weems. Weems also told the story of how George threw a silver dollar across the Rappahannock River. Interestingly enough, George had unusually large and long arms, and because that river recedes at low tide, that may have been possible.

Augustine's sons by a prior marriage, Lawrence and Augustine Washington Jr., were at school in England when George was just a boy. After the death of his father in 1743 and Lawrence had returned from school, he oversaw the management of his father's plantation on the Potomac River. Then he joined the British military in the Virginia Colony and shipped off to Jamaica. When Augustine Jr. returned, he managed his father's other plantation on Pope's Creek until he married and inherited his wife's estate. Even though Augustine Sr. had three estates to leave, there still wouldn't be enough money available to send George to school in England as was customary for the landed gentry. In addition, it was now up to Mary Washington to raise George and the younger children.

George's Early Education

George received his basic education at Rev. Mayre's Anglican school in Fredericksburg under a variety of tutors. He felt frustrated at home as an adolescent and used to feel oppressed by the confinement of domestic life. His stepbrother, Augustine Jr., knew that and had him move in with him and his wife, Anne Aylett, at Pope's Creek and attend school under a Mr. Williams. There Washington learned geography, history, and mathematics. Williams was fond of George and introduced him to James Genn, a land surveyor. Genn noted Washington's intellectual curiosity and took George with him when he went out on assignments. George liked the work. After he completed his studies at Mr. Williams' school, George returned home and occasionally visited with his other stepbrother, Lawrence. George always came to Lawrence for advice and support. At that time, George was restless and again felt an intense desire for independence and the need to break out on his own. When he told Lawrence about their mother's reaction when he tried to join the British Navy, Lawrence responded by saying that there would be many more opportunities besides the British Navy. After George mentioned that he had explored land surveying under a mentor, Lawrence suggested that he make the acquaintance of his wife's cousin, the elderly Lord William Fairfax of England, who was a land investor in the colonies. Fairfax was due to arrive shortly for a visit.

Fairfax liked George because he was a soft-spoken and polite boy, and they went hunting together. Lord Fairfax told Washington he had recently purchased a number of land tracts in the Blue Ridge Mountains and wanted the land surveyed. That rekindled George's interest in surveying, and he talked excitedly with Fairfax about his experiences doing surveys while at Mr. Williams' school. George really loved the wild, unharnessed land. When he discussed this with his stepbrother, Lawrence suggested that he pursue surveying professionally.

Through Fairfax's connections, George attended the College of William and Mary in Williamsburg and obtained a license to conduct surveys in the county. It was a short course, and by the year 1749, he had his license. Then he reached out to Lord Fairfax regarding his land tracts.

Washington – A Land Surveyor

Lord Fairfax hired George after he obtained his license. Washington, recruited his former mentor, John Genn to assist in the expedition. Then George, Lord Fairfax, and James Genn set out, first to a valley where the Shenandoah River cuts through. "Shenandoah" was a name by the local Native Americans which means "Daughter of the Stars." In the Shenandoah region, they met a number of Native Americans. John Genn could speak their tongue somewhat, and the tribe befriended them. One time, the surveying party even joined in one of the tribal celebrations during which there was a great fire and a lot of dancing. George described it, saying, "...the best dancer jumps about the ring in a most comical manner and is followed by the rest...Then the musicians play music with rattles and a half pot water with deerskin stretched over it which they beat with sticks." That was an 18th-century version of a drum.

In 1752, after completing his task in the Blue Ridge Mountains, Washington secured temporary work for the Ohio Company, which was funded by English land investors who were interested in expanding the British American colonies. The Ohio Company had made an arrangement with five nations of Native Americans to take possession of some parcels of land in the Ohio Valley and planned to establish new colonies there. However, the French also wanted to create their own colonies along the Mississippi and the Ohio River. France already had possession of Louisiana at that time, and new French colonies would represent a northward expansion to the Canadian border. To bolster support, France made arrangements with local tribes there. Washington noted that England and France were reaching a crisis point over control of the area.

Death of His Brother

In the same year, 1752, Washington's stepbrother, Lawrence, developed tuberculosis, which was called "consumption" in those days. For health reasons, George took Lawrence to Barbados, since the warmer climate might help cure him. The journey eased his symptoms but only to a limited degree. Shortly after his return, Lawrence became much more ill, and within three months he died.

After Lawrence died, his widow, Anne, took over the estate at Mount Vernon. She had lifetime rights to the plantation, and upon her death, George was entitled by his father's will to assume ownership. When Anne remarried, she and her new husband moved and leased the property to George. He then moved there and his mother remained in Fredericksburg.

Shortly after arriving, Washington developed smallpox. Although smallpox claimed many victims, George Washington was strong and survived. He spent time during his recovery sitting on the terrace at the mansion that overlooked the Potomac.

After his brother Lawrence died, that also left his position of adjutant of the Virginia Militia open. Washington still had an intense interest in military service, so he lobbied for the post, was accepted, and appointed a major after his training. His mother realized how strongly he wanted this, so she didn't object this time. When it was discovered that George was familiar with the Ohio Valley, he was promoted to lieutenant colonel and sent to the region by General Dinwiddie as a scout to protect the interests of Great Britain. He was given a regiment of troops, whom he led into the Ohio Valley.

In the Ohio Valley – 1753

Once Washington reached the Ohio Valley, he made contact with the tribes there, as he had done before on his land surveying missions. Just east of the Ohio River, Washington introduced himself to the Seneca tribal chieftain, Tanacharison, a spokesman for the Seneca, Iroquois, and other tribal nations. Tanacharison responded well to this respectful and friendly man, and Washington was able to earn his interest in dealing with the English.

While exploring the mountainous regions in the valley, Washington noted that the French had started building forts in the area, including a huge fort at two tributaries of the Ohio River named Fort Duquesne. Upon his return, Washington reported information about the French forts back to Dinwiddie. Dinwiddie then related that to his superiors in England. In the hopes of drawing up an agreement, England told the French that Great Britain also had interests in the Ohio Valley. French officials made numerous excuses and deliberately delayed any proposed meetings. England sent follow-up messages, but those letters were ignored. The crisis was coming to a head.

The French and Indian War

In 1754, Dinwiddie sent Washington back to the Ohio Valley with more troops and orders to expel the French. Washington took the same route as he had done before and was met by his Native American friend, Tanacharison. Tanacharison warned Washington about a large French military scouting party at a glen east of the Ohio River. In exchange for exclusive trading rights with the British, Tanacharison agreed to rally his warriors in support of Washington.

Washington's forces were relatively small because the British were having difficulty enticing many colonies in British America to send militias into the Ohio Valley. Virginia, however, did send some troops (about 150), along with a colonel by the name of Joshua Fry, some British regulars, and a small contingent from the North Carolina Militia. In the meantime, Tanacharison attempted to get the support of more tribes, specifically the Delaware and Shawnee tribes, and he was successful to a limited degree. Washington, his militia, and his new tribal allies started to build a fortification which he called "Fort Necessity." It took a month to construct. During this period, the colonel from Virginia, Joshua Fry, was suddenly killed in a fall from his horse. Dinwiddie then promoted Washington to full colonel.

Battle of de Jumonville Glen

When the mixed troops arrived at the glen, Washington noted that the French scouting unit was vulnerable, so he and his men ambushed them. During the onslaught, the French-Canadian general, Joseph de Jumonville, was slain. This battle, it is said, only lasted about fifteen minutes, but was a victory for the English forces under Washington.

In May of 1754, the French poured out from Fort Duquesne under the command of Joseph de Jumonville and descended upon

Washington and his men before the completion of Fort Necessity was accomplished. De Jumonville was killed in that encounter, and the French surrendered.

Soon after Fort Necessity was finished, the French forces poured out again from Fort Duquesne and proceeded toward Fort Necessity under the command of Colonel Louis de Jumonville, the half-brother of the colonel who was killed at the glen during the first battle led by George Washington. Louis de Jumonville was determined to avenge his brother's death.

Along the way to Fort Necessity, de Jumonville spotted scalps the tribes had nailed to trees as a kind of psychological warfare. De Jumonville was immediately repulsed, so he stopped to bury them and whatever bodily remains his men could find.

Back at Fort Necessity, Washington had his men build more entrenchments near the local woods, and his tribal allies arrived to help. However, the area was muddy and soaked from a sudden and prolonged downpour. He was also concerned because the provisions at Fort Necessity were sparse and much of the gunpowder was wet from unrelenting rain.

Battle of Fort Necessity

Before Washington was able to obtain sufficient supplies and replace his gunpowder, Louis de Jumonville's forces descended upon them. Washington's forces were outnumbered by the French and were forced to fight on the open field outside the fort. Washington was also hampered by the poor aim of some of the British regulars assigned to him. After engaging the French, he was forced to retreat back to his fort. Although Washington's men fought courageously, he had to accept surrender. However, Washington wasn't familiar with the French language, and the surrender terms indicated that he had "assassinated" Louis' brother at the prior battle at the glen.

When his commanding officer noted the so-called assassination, he questioned Washington. Although Washington explained the error, indicating that Louis de Jumonville's brother died during battle, they were ambivalent about trusting young George Washington. This error disparaged his future reputation. The date was July 3, 1754.

Battle of Fort Duquesne

Great Britain had lost confidence in George Washington due to the mistranslation error. So this time, they sent in Major General Edward Braddock from Great Britain, and appointed him the head of the French and Indian War in British America. Washington was then instructed to join him along with Lieutenant Colonel Thomas Gage at the Monongahela River. Daniel Boone, the famous frontiersman, was among Braddock's troops, having been hired on as a wagoner.

General Braddock was accustomed to the block formations of the British military. Washington advised him against that, indicating that the enemy tribes allied with the French would fight from the woods and shrubbery, rather than in traditional formations. Braddock chose to ignore Washington's advice and set up the troops into rigid formations consisting of two lines and had Colonel Gage split off to his flank. Washington held up the rear guard. Like Washington, Daniel Boone also felt that Braddock's formations would make them vulnerable to guerrilla-style tactics.

The French and their tribal allies fired from the woods and forced the British to engage them there. That confused the British so they shot without aiming and even ended up killing some of their own men. Many retreated when they saw the marauding tribesmen, including Boone who was disgusted at the military ignorance displayed by the British.

During the encounter, Braddock was seriously injured, so Washington rode to the head of the remaining troops then rode back and forth in the battlefield and gathered his soldiers together. He also had Braddock and the other wounded men carried away from the battlefield. There weren't enough able-bodied British soldiers left, so that made a counter-attack infeasible. This was a significant defeat. As for Braddock, he later died of his wounds. The year was 1758.

Operation at Fort Duquesne

Washington couldn't obtain a higher commission in the British military because he didn't get a recommendation from General Braddock before his death. Washington knew the region and he knew the fighting style of the French Canadians and their tribal allies, so he felt frustrated.

Washington and his men were then relegated to work on a road nearby that would give the new British commander, General John Forbes, access to Fort Duquesne in order to attack it again. After a crucial section of that road was finished, Forbes marched toward the fort. However, he neglected to send out scouting parties to gather intelligence, so he was handily defeated by the French before reaching the fort.

Forbes was puzzled when he saw no activity there and asked Washington to inspect it. Washington discovered that the fort was burned by the French after they abandoned it. There was little left of the structure but broken wood and smoldering debris. The tribal warriors had also beheaded some of the British soldiers from Scotland and displayed their kilts above them. Washington had seen that type of brutality before, but many of his soldiers had not and were utterly shocked and disgusted.

Later it was discovered that the French had abandoned the fort for two reasons: 1) their supply lines had been cut, and 2) they had lost the support of the native tribes. So, the French forces made their way toward another fort they held, Fort Legonier.

The British decided to send in some fresh forces to construct a new fort near the site called Fort Pitt, named after the English secretary of state, William Pitt. As for Washington, the British generals still didn't trust him to be in command. He was sent back to Virginia, to be on-call with the Virginia Militia.

Chapter 2 – From Tranquility to Turmoil

After he left the Ohio Valley area, George returned home to the tranquility of Mount Vernon. He envisioned his future as a Southern planter, earning his living in the agrarian lifestyle among his family and friends. He also associated with the landed gentry of the area and kept pace with current events.

Mount Vernon: Plantation and Manufacturing

The main family crop on the Mount Vernon plantation was tobacco. Unlike other landowners in Virginia, Washington assumed a lot of the duties of management on the plantation and adjoining farm. He rose early, patrolled his estate, and even broke in new horses himself. In addition, he was his own clerk and carefully kept track of supplies and expenditures needed to run Mount Vernon. In the interest of frugality, he established some manufacturing on site. When he made his rounds, Washington firmly advised his workers that they shouldn't buy anything they could make themselves. There was a blacksmith shop on premises for the horses, and the blacksmith sold services to neighboring farms as well. Washington also built a small four mill. He also had a specially fashioned wood-burner built for the making of charcoal to heat the house. Washington employed the services of a number of carpenters whom he hired out to frame houses near Alexandria. A staff of weavers produced linen from wool he purchased from England. What they couldn't manufacture at Mount Vernon was ordered from England.

Near the river, Washington had a fishery. In his writings, Washington reported, "This river is well-supplied with various kinds of fish at all seasons of the year...shad, bass, herrings, perch, carp and sturgeon." The staff, as well as Washington and his family, ate fish for their main meals.

Marriage to Sweet Martha

After his return from the French and Indian War in 1758, Washington was elected to the House of Burgesses, which represented Virginia in British America. In that capacity, he met Francis Fauquier, the lieutenant governor of the colony in Williamsburg. It was there that George met a lovely widow named Martha Custis. The two shared a mutual interest in agrarian life, as she had helped her late husband manage their property. She also had children by her former marriage. Washington fell madly in love with this kind and attractive woman, and they courted briefly.

In 1759, they married. At the wedding, Martha was clad in silk and satin while George wore silver and blue trimmed with scarlet. Martha then moved to Mount Vernon with her two children, Martha Parke Custis, or "Patsy," and Daniel Parke Custis, or "Jacky." Young Martha was four and Jacky two. George adopted them immediately.

Because his bout with smallpox left Washington sterile, he was delighted to have a "ready-made" family with children. Unfortunately, little Patsy Custis was inflicted with epilepsy. George and Martha did what they could for her during her seizures, but there was no medication for epilepsy in those days.

Washington dearly loved little Martha and Jacky. As a matter of fact, his first order from England that year was:

10 shillings' worth of toys

6 little books for young children

1 fashionably-dressed baby doll

a box of Gingerbread toys

It was his nature to care. As he looked upon his loving family, he decided to take them camping in the woods of Virginia. When they were enjoying the woods during the birth of spring in 1773, poor little Patsy had a serious epileptic fit. Although George and Martha tried to assist her as best they could, she died. He held her and rocked her tender, ravished body in his arms. In a later letter written to his friend, Burwell Bassett, he said,

> "It is easier to conceive, than to describe, the distress of this family, especially that of the unhappy parent of our dear Patsy Custis, when I inform you that yesterday removed the sweet innocent girl to a happy and peaceful abode than any she was met with, and the inflicted path she hitherto has trod."

He then spent three months with his wife while both them and Jacky mourned the passing of Patsy.

Washington: Wealthy Landowner

Martha's late husband died intestate, so his estate was divided into three segments: 1/3 to Martha, 1/3 to Patsy, and 1/3 to Jacky. The estate took several years to settle, but in the end, the Washington's had 5,000 more acres and 84 slaves. Balancing the finances for managing the acreage was sometimes burdensome for Washington and was sometimes very profitable. It all depended mostly upon the tobacco harvest.

George Washington was very familiar with the lifestyle of being a wealthy landowner, so of course his favorite activities included dancing, the theater, fox hunting, and parties with the upper echelon in the colony. He and Martha occasionally went to parties held on his festive barge and those of other planters in the area, including the Fairfaxes. The two of them would also attend balls in Richmond when the House of Burgesses was in session.

At this point in his life, Washington assumed that he could basically be a planter and a member of the Virginia aristocracy and that the rest of his life would be spent in those pursuits. As a landowner, it was essential that he continue his involvement in politics because it affected him financially and socially. In the year 1761, he ran for re-election in the House of Burgesses and was voted in by a large margin. George was one of the younger members; he was 29 years old at the time. However, he made a commanding appearance at 6'2" with wide, strong shoulders. His arms and legs were muscular, and he was impeccably dressed.

Oppression from England

During the mid-18th Century, the colonists felt that the British king was becoming more autocratic and tyrannical. New taxes were being levied upon them, and tax collectors were sent over to collect the funds, which were shipped back to England. There were steep import duties charged on products shipped from England.

British soldiers were continually present in the thirteen colonies, patrolling the streets and frequenting the bars and hotels. They often stopped people to question them, and the English governor and other officials from England often made it a point to meddle in colonial affairs. The colonists became alarmed with this encroachment upon their freedom and rights, as well as the growing presence of troops.

The Quartering Act of 1765

As the number of British soldiers grew, the public houses (hotels) were filled. As a result of this lack of lodging, England passed the Quartering Act. That act permitted the soldiers to move into colonists' buildings and even their homes on occasion. According to this new precept, no notification was needed, so British soldiers could enter at any time. They took full advantage of this and sometimes even demanded that the colonists provide food.

If the colonists didn't comply with the Quartering Act, the royal governor in the colony wouldn't sign any local ordinances passed by the local assemblies or Houses of Burgesses which performed functions in the community, including the organization of local militias. In some of the colonies, they closed down the Houses of Burgesses for indefinite periods of time.

The Stamp Act of 1765

England had been burdened by tremendous war debt after its involvement in the European theater of the Seven Years' War (1756-1763). That war awakened hostilities among nearly all the countries in Europe over their territories and mercantile rights. The French and Indian War, in which Washington served, is considered part of that war. In order to pay for that debt, Prime Minister George Grenville suggested to King George III that he place a new tax on the colonies in British America. When the news hit the colonies, Patrick Henry, the fiery orator, leaped up on the floor of the House of Burgesses and shouted, "Caesar had his Brutus, Charles the First his Cromwell and George the Third may profit from their example…If this be treason, make the most of it."

The people in the colonies were furious about the stamp tax. They already had to pay import duties on goods shipped in from England. Washington also had to pay those duties, as he was accustomed to ordering many items from Great Britain.

This approved stamp was placed upon all shipments of paper from England once the tax was remitted, and this was the paper the colonists needed. After the Stamp Act was passed, few bought the paper and developed crude ways of making their own or reusing paper they already had. They also harassed the British tax collectors. Those who were more devious made deals with English merchants to smuggle in paper.

Washington himself spoke to other people in the area who frequently bought goods from England and suggested that they also refrain from buying English products as much as possible, and even refuse to sell tobacco to the English if they could afford to. He instructed his merchants in England to hold back shipments to Mount Vernon until that deplorable act was repealed. He once said in a letter to a Virginian:

> "I am convinced, as much as I am of my own existence, that there is no relief for us but in their distress; and I think, at least I hope, that there is public virtue enough left among us to deny ourselves everything but the bare necessaries of life to accomplish this end."

When the anger of the colonists reached a fever pitch, an activist group called "The Sons of Liberty" broke into the mansion of the English governor, Thomas Hutchinson, and sacked it. According to an eyewitness, there was nothing left except the walls and the wooden floor. In addition, the Sons of Liberty did the same to Hutchinson's brother-in-law's house. He was the despised stamp tax administrator in Massachusetts.

Through Washington's efforts and that of many of the colonists, during the following year, 1766, the Stamp Act was repealed.

The Declaratory Act of 1766

Despite their concession by repeal of the Stamp Act, the haughty British Parliament and its King said that they had "…the full power and authority to make laws and statutes of sufficient force and validity to bind the colonies and people of America in all cases whatsoever." Then they passed the "Declaratory Act." In essence, it gave England the overarching right to do anything it pleased to the thirteen colonies.

The famous statesman from Pennsylvania, Benjamin Franklin, went over to London in 1766, indicating that the colonists already contributed substantially to England in its war against its primary foe, France. Even though the colonists were paying import duties and other taxes, they had no voting power in the English Parliament and no voice in Great Britain with regard to legislation that affected the British colonies. James Otis, Jr., a member of the Massachusetts Provincial Assembly and a pamphleteer, coined the well-known phrase: "Taxation without representation is tyranny."

Actions and reactions between the colonies and Great Britain continued and fomented hatred between the two in a war of words and deeds. Then, the colonists were further assaulted by the passage of the Townsend Acts the following year.

The Townsend Acts of 1767

These acts placed taxes on paint, glass, paper, and tea. British tax collectors often intimidated the colonists to be sure the taxes were paid. In the port of Boston, regiments of British soldiers stood on guard to prevent smuggling and remind the colonists that they were subservient to Great Britain. Again, many of the colonists boycotted English products and England was barraged by letters from irate colonists. In 1770, Britain repealed all those taxes except for the tax on tea.

Sporadic Violence in Boston 1770

Within the colonies antipathy arose regarding the loyalties of the colonists; some segregation occurred based on those loyalties. Establishments were identified as having owners who felt that Great Britain was well within its rights to enforce the taxes, even though they were harsh at times. Those colonists felt that some of their neighbors were like insolent children who must be disciplined and regulated. Gradually, those people, their homes, their stores and establishments were known as "Tory- affiliated." Another term they used was "loyalist."

Other colonists looked upon themselves as builders of a new country forged out of open vacant land and developed an economy where there was none before. Their greatest loyalty resided within the sphere of the thirteen colonies, not with a distant country in which they had no voting rights and no means to recommend legislation that would aid the colonies. They were incensed when England kept charging new taxes and emphasizing their own domination. Also, the poorer colonists and agrarian workers who were afflicted by poor harvests found those taxes especially oppressive. They called themselves "patriots."

As tempers flared, some colonists took out their hostilities on each other. Occasionally there were violent incidents. In February of 1770, patriots threw rocks through the window of a store operated by a loyalist in Boston. When the British official, Ebenezer Richardson, attempted to intervene by firing his gun to break up the crowd, he accidentally killed a child. The colonists were shocked and enraged.

Other incidents occurred, particularly with regard to British tax officials. In March, violence erupted between a British soldier guarding a custom house. When the official called for back-up, more British soldiers arrived and fights broke out on the streets. Suddenly, bells rang out in Boston, and a number of patriots toting sticks and clubs descended upon the scene. Unexpectedly, a British soldier yelled "Fire," and the other soldiers began shooting. Five colonists were killed and six wounded.

As result of this, the acting British governor, Thomas Hutchinson, arrested eight soldiers. Six were acquitted, and two were convicted of manslaughter. Those two were sentenced to branding on their hands – a deplorable practice by today's standards – and were given short sentences. Ironically, their defense counsel was John Adams who later became an American president.

The Boston Tea Party 1773

The English imported Chinese tea from the British East India Company. The people in England paid no tax on it at all because the East India Company was owned by the British. However, they taxed the colonists on that very same tea! One night, a huge group, mostly made up of members of the Sons of Liberty, dressed themselves in the garb of Native Americans, boldly boarded the ships, and dumped the contents of 343 chests loaded with tea leaves. The frightened British sailors had never seen Native Americans before and made no attempts to intervene.

The Coercive Acts 1774

King George and his vengeful Parliament decided to "punish" the people of Boston and their colony. They passed the Coercive Acts, which the colonists dubbed "The Intolerable Acts." Some of its precepts: were:

- The Boston Port Act – by which the British closed the port of Boston, shutting off all imports and exports until such times as the colonies could pay back the British for the tea theft

- The Massachusetts Government Act – which forbade all local town meetings and restricted the Governor's Council to appointed members only

- The Administration of Justice Act – granting all British officials immunity from prosecution under local Massachusetts law

- The Quebec Act – permitted Catholics to practice their religion right on the Canadian borders of the people in the colonies, most of who were Protestants

At his next meeting of the House of Burgesses in Williamsburg, Washington leaped up and complained bitterly of the atrocities at Boston. He said, "I will raise a thousand men, subsist them at my own expense, and march them to the relief of Boston."

Chapter 3 – Two If by Sea!

Signs of the Times

George Washington's young son, John Custis, married and moved away. He and Martha were lonely, so they began inviting neighbors to Mount Vernon. The mood in all of the colonies differed, and visitors to his home at Mount Vernon had long and loud discussions about the issues. Washington's brother-in-law, Rev. Bryan Fairfax, told George that he had wanted to go to England to have an audience with King George about the colonies. However, when he was asked to take a loyalty oath, he declined.

Other Loyalist visitors took the opposite position and complained about the colonists. One particularly haughty gentleman, a Mr. C. Etherington who did business in London, said, "I have served the king as well as I know how and I trust I shall have the pleasure to aid in the punishment of some of those insolent rebels."

For one of these visits, Washington invited the wealthiest planter in the area, George Mason from Fairfax County. George Mason had a 5,500-acre estate near the Potomac River and raised a diversity of crops. Patrick Henry, who owned a small plantation in Virginia, also stopped by on this occasion. All three often became involved in heated discussions about the situation with Great Britain, the taxes, and the lack of representation in the British parliament. They felt that something needed to be done. While much was going on in Massachusetts, Virginia also needed to formulate a response.

The Fairfax Resolves – July 1774

The official meetings of the House of Burgesses had been suspended by the English governor due to the Boston Tea Party, so the Virginians decided to meet informally at the Fairfax courthouse. Members elected Washington to chair the meeting, and under his chairmanship, influential Virginians discussed the status and position they felt the colonies should adopt. As a result of this meeting, Mason wrote up a document they felt would help the colonies become a unified force in their efforts to rectify the injustices. Mason then asked Washington to edit the document.

In the document, they insisted that the colonies had all the rights of a British subject and should be able to elect and hold their own legislative assemblies. Likewise, they indicated that they had a right to representation to decide on any action emanating from England involving the British colonies. Nowhere in the document did it state that armed conflict should take place, however. They had all hoped that England and the colonies could resolve the matter without bloodshed, such as that which took place in Boston.

Usually, the House of Burgesses provided the upkeep of a militia to protect the colony, which was also left undone when the House was suspended. The colony had no means to protect itself from outside intruders or maintain law and order within. At the close of the meeting, the members realized that they needed to form their own militia, so they planned on soliciting funds from the various counties in Virginia for a militia and train it in the art of war. Such a force wasn't only done in anticipation of a war with England, but to defend the colony from Native American tribes and any other hostile threats.

The First Continental Congress – September 1774

The First Continental Congress was formed when Washington circulated a proposal to all the colonies calling for each one of them to elect representatives. Those men would then attend a meeting in order to develop some strategies as to how to deal with their grievances against Great Britain. Twelve of the thirteen colonies sent delegates to Philadelphia where the first meeting was to take place. Although the colony of Georgia agreed with the main goal of this Congress, they refrained from electing representatives, as they were having serious problems from the Creek tribes in the area and needed British troops to help.

Peyton Randolph, the attorney general of Virginia, was elected to be the president of the 1774 Continental Congress. He had attended Oxford where he was licensed as a lawyer. Virginian delegates circulated the *Fairfax Resolves* that George Mason wrote. Another set of resolves was also distributed – the *Suffolk Resolves* – written by Joseph Warren, a physician and patriot from Boston. The *Suffolk Resolves* were carried into the Congress by the famous silversmith and patriot, Paul Revere.

The *Suffolk Resolves* included the following resolutions:

1. A proclamation that indicated the Coercive Acts were void, and any official that attempted their enforcement should be asked to resign

2. A statement to the effect that Massachusetts would consider itself a free and independent state until the Coercive Acts were repealed

3. A declaration that future tax collections for England be retained by Massachusetts

4. A recommendation that a boycott of British goods should take place

5. A decision that Massachusetts should appoint and arm its own militia

6. A warning to the British general, Thomas Gage, that any attempts to arrest citizens on political charges will result in the detention of the arresting officials

The most significant accomplishment of this Congress was the *Declaration of Colonial Rights,* which combined elements from the Fairfax and Suffolk Resolves. The first precept of that declaration stated that the colonists were entitled to life, liberty, and property, and would never cede those rights to any sovereign power without the colonists' consent.

The Virginia Convention – March 1775

Because of the alarming events that continued to escalate, there was a decision to call a convention in Virginia. This assembly met at St. John's Episcopal Church near Jamestown, Virginia. Peyton Randolph was elected president of the convention, and he distributed notes about the proceedings of the First Continental Congress to the attendees. Among those in attendance were George Washington, Patrick Henry, and Richard Lee, a statesman from Stratford, Virginia.

Patrick Henry arose and presented three resolutions for consideration, mostly having to do with procedures it should adopt for forming armed militias:

1. Militias should be formed in the colony and composed of able-bodied men for the defense of freedom.

2. The need for establishment of such militias is imperative because England has suspended the House of Burgesses which normally provides forces for Virginia's protection.

3. Virginia's position is one of defense and its soldiers must be numerous enough for that. They need to be trained, disciplined, and armed so as not to give England the impression that the colony isn't able or willing to defend itself.

Randolph indicated that the members should weigh their decisions carefully, realizing that the presence of armed colonial troops would be seen by England as an act of hostility and prelude to war. However, Patrick Henry argued that the war had actually begun in a way, and it was unlikely that there would be any reconciliation.

Henry's third resolution touched off a number of debates, as there were some more conservative members present who felt that a solution to resolve the differences between the colonies and England might still be possible.

It is interesting to note that in his speech, Henry also followed up by alluding to the problems encountered by the Bostonians. He stated: "The next gale that sweeps from the North will bring to our ears the clash of resounding arms."

Patrick Henry then concluded with the most notable oration of his career:

> "Is life so dear, or peace so sweet, as to be purchased at the price of chains and slavery? Forbid it, Almighty God! I know not what course others may take; but, as for me, give me liberty or give me death!"

Although the vote was close, all three of Henry's resolutions were passed by this assembly. George Washington was placed on a committee to prepare a workable plan for the embodiment of forming and training the militias recommended.

Just one short month later, Patrick Henry's prediction about the conflict starting in the North came true. The British were concerned about the possibility of a rebellion in Massachusetts, and wanted to remove weapons from the arsenals and other storage sites. On April 14, 1775, Colonel Gage mustered his British troops at Boston Harbor with the intention of going to Concord, where they knew there was a store of weapons in the armory. However, Paul Revere had secret sources in London who told him that ahead of time. After Revere sent word to the Sons of Liberty, they moved the weapons out of the arsenals at Concord and hid them in farms and villages around the area.

Revere was also charged with notifying the militia in Massachusetts as to where the British soldiers would enter. He then set up a system at the Old North Church overlooking the harbor in Boston. Two lanterns in the church tower meant the British were coming by sea; one lantern signified that they would invade by land. On the night of April 18th, two lanterns swung from the belfry of the Old North Church. The British were going to cross the Charles River and march westward through Lexington, which was along the road that led to Concord.

Paul Revere and William Dawes rode on ahead to warn all the citizens in the area, especially John Hancock, a noted Boston merchant and influential patriot. Through his investigations, Revere had discovered that Hancock was going to be targeted by the English because he was president of the Massachusetts Provincial Congress, which was operating without English oversight. Revere and Dawes rode up to Hancock's childhood home in Lexington where he had been staying, warning him not to return to Boston. Hancock shouted out the window that his place was with the Minutemen, who were the local militia group. They were going to gather on Lexington Common. Revere and Dawes told Hancock that he would be much more valuable as a leader of the patriots' cause and should hold back. He did so.

Chapter 4 – One Shot Starts the Revolution

Lexington

As soon as they heard the news about the British arriving, the minutemen rushed out of their homes and taverns and nervously assembled at Lexington Common. They had weapons, but most lacked musket balls and had only gunpowder in their weapons. Only 77 Minutemen were there when the British soldiers brashly arrived in tight formation. "Throw down your arms! You villains…you rebels!" shouted the British major, John Pitcairn.

A shot rang out. No one knows who fired it, but it was the "shot heard 'round the world," as it says in the famous verse from Emerson's poem, *The Concord Hymn*. The date was April 19, 1775.

Not hearing any orders from their English commanders, the British frantically fired a volley…then another and another. The Minutemen tried to retaliate. Because of the large amount of gunpowder, the whole area was consumed in smoke. Those who had balls in the muskets shot wildly at the British. The Redcoats then rushed at them with bayonets, running several through. Bodies fell, bleeding out upon the flattened grasses. The wounded were rushed to the safety of nearby buildings. One man died on the doorstep of his own home. The British commander called for a last-minute volley of gunfire. After that, Major Pitcairn was hit by a musket and blood oozed from his thigh. He then called for a retreat. Nine colonists had died, but of the British, only Pitcairn was wounded.

Concord

By that time, many more Minutemen had arrived and collected themselves on top of the high grounds near the North Bridge east of Concord. Hidden in the shrubbery, they watched the British troops march irresolutely toward Concord. There were nearly 400 Minutemen against a much smaller company of Redcoats in the vanguard. When he spotted some of the Minutemen, the British colonel anxiously sent word for reinforcements just in case there was a problem. Loyalist spies had informed the English that the arsenal was empty, but a huge cache of weapons was at Barrett's farm beyond the North Bridge. Then they marched toward the farm. In the meantime, more British arrived from behind, then fanned out and searched the nearby farmhouses for muskets and artillery pieces. They set fire to buildings, forced their way into local taverns to search the cellars, and beat down the doors of the farmhouses. From the hill, the Minutemen saw smoke rising and raced down from the ridges to help put out the fires.

By then, thousands of Minutemen rushed in from neighboring towns. Within a matter of hours, there were about 3,000 colonists gathered at the town center. As per orders, the British continued searching through the alleys, buildings, and streets. Finding a few gunning trunnions at Barrett's farm, they destroyed them.

Colonel Barrett, the owner of Barrett Farm was in charge of the colonial forces at Concord, had given his men orders not to fire unless fired upon. So, the Minutemen followed the British soldiers, carefully watching them from behind stone walls and bushes. As a small contingent of British tried marching back across the North Bridge, they spotted more Minutemen and pandemonium broke out. The Redcoats then raced away from the bridge. In a panic, they turned around, aimed at the Minutemen nearby, and shot into the crowd wildly. Then Colonel Barrett hollered out, "Fire, for God's sake, fellow soldiers, fire!" The Colonials then fired a volley. Totally outmaneuvered and outmanned, the British fled back toward the center of the town, colliding with their own force of grenadiers who were also leaving. The whole contingent frantically headed back east toward Lexington, relentlessly pursued by the colonists. At every bluff and hill, the British were besieged by musket fire from the colonials. The English were very unaccustomed to these kinds of scattered volleys from the woods and walls that separated the farms. Frantically, the exhausted British made their way back to Boston Harbor.

At the North Bridge, the British had left their own dead behind, and the colonists buried them as a courtesy. In the end, there were 73 British killed, and the colonists lost 29.

George Washington was alerted at Mount Vernon about Lexington and Concord. The war had started! Word then arrived that the Continental Congress must meet again quickly. Washington donned his militia uniform and headed back to Philadelphia.

The Second Continental Congress 1775

George Washington was greeted by Samuel and John Adams, two of the Massachusetts delegates, who were pacing outside. They indicated that a colonial army must be mustered. John told Washington firmly that he would nominate him, and Samuel said he would second that motion.

John Hancock was elected president of the proceedings. When the floor was open for discussion, John Adams arose and said, "Gentlemen, if this Congress will not adopt the army before ten moons have set, New England will adopt it, and she will undertake the struggle alone!" Some of the conservatives among them who wanted to make further overtures toward peace triggered a debate. However, the debate was cut off when John Adams again stood up and announced loudly:

> "Gentlemen, I know the qualifications of a commander are high...Does anyone say they are not to be obtained in this country? In reply, I have to say they are; they reside in our body, and he is the man whom I now nominate – George Washington of Virginia."

A vote was taken and George Washington was appointed "General and Commander-in-Chief of the Army of the United Colonies and of all the forces raised by them." Washington accepted and asked in return only that he be reimbursed for his expenses.

On June 18th, Washington wrote to his dear Martha explaining to her that he was now Commander-in-Chief and must rush to Boston to take on his duties. He wrote, "It has been determined in Congress, that the whole army raised for the defense of the American cause shall be put under my care, and that it is necessary for me to proceed immediately to Boston to take command of it."

The Congress took more actions. Because the situation was in crisis mode, they decided not to go through the long and tedious process of getting all the legislative authorizations needed from all the colonies to proceed. In effect, they were now functioning as the new government of the colonies. Delegates were informed that they needed to issue a financial appeal to their colonies and must firmly urge that each colony should choose independence from Great Britain. In addition, the delegates were aware that the war had already begun in Lexington and Concord, and British warships were lurking in Boston Harbor.

Because time was of the essence, the Continental Congress assumed the right to raise armies, sign treaties, appoint military officials and ambassadors, and secure loans from Europe.

Furthermore, they agreed to issue paper currency, called "Continentals," and disburse funds for military action and supplies.

The First Flag

To clarify the identity of the colonies and bolster patriotism, it was ordered at that meeting that Betsy Ross of Philadelphia sew a flag to represent the thirteen colonies. Although there have been some controversies about the flag designer, it is commonly agreed that Francis Hopkinson developed the design. Hopkinson also designed the first Continental currency and US coin.

Several men from the Congress, including Washington, met in a committee and submitted the proposed flag design to the Congress. After some minor alterations in the design were made, the flag had thirteen alternating red and white stripes and a blue oblong on which were to be placed thirteen 5-pointed stars in a circular pattern. The flag was later approved in the year 1777.

Battle of Bunker Hill – June 1775

The colonists in Massachusetts had been watching the harbor of Boston carefully since the British siege. They knew war was coming and had been surreptitiously planning for it for a year. In the effort to give notice to other colonies, the editors of the *Virginia Gazette* printed a notice to motivate able-bodied men to make preparations. The notice stated, "The province of Massachusetts Bay, it is said, when occasion requires, can raise 80,000 effective men." Although it is doubtful that eighty-thousand could be enrolled in the militia in 1775, the piece was intended to arouse attention.

The British had hidden themselves in Boston and didn't immediately realize the amount of progress the colonists had made. While the British hesitated, the patriots fortified Bunker Hill which overlooked the Boston Harbor and its environs. General Howe instructed his English soldiers to disembark on the inner harbor shores and they marched up to a place called "Breed's Hill." Seeing that, the colonists relocated there.

Rapidly the patriots pieced together barriers made of fencing, stone, and earth in order to strengthen their positions. As expected, the English formations were broken up by the impromptu obstacles as they marched forward. When the English were within 50 yards of the colonists, the patriots opened fire. The British fell back, leaving piles of their dead behind them. Relentlessly, the patriots continued to fire their muskets. The Redcoats retaliated, and it was a bloody battle. After being pounded in three separate assaults, the colonists ran out of ammunition. Regardless, they then resorted to hand-to-hand combat before retreating. Cleverly, the two commanders, John Stark and Israel Putnam, organized an orderly exit, avoided more gunfire from the British, and prevented the English from circling the hill. At the end of the day, unfortunately, thousands of more English soldiers penetrated the city of Charleston, which was on one of the southern peninsulas. They burned buildings all over Charleston, as the militias hadn't yet organized in that city. Although the Battle of Bunker Hill was considered a British victory, the Redcoats suffered the loss of over 1,000 men. The patriots walked away with less than half of that, about 450 men.

Washington on the Way

Washington had left Philadelphia with a large troop of horsemen moving at a quick pace northwards, until a messenger boy met him and told him about Bunker and Breed's Hill. Washington asked, "Did they stand the fire of the regular (British) troops?" The boy indicated that they did until they ran out of ammunition. To that response, Washington exclaimed, "Then the liberties of the country are safe!"

Mustering the Troops

George Washington made an impressive appearance as an advocate for liberty. He and his small band of troops were greeted by an enthusiastic crowd of cheering people from the Massachusetts Colony under the old elm tree at Cambridge Common. His brown hair was drawn back and fastened at his neck. He had rosy cheeks and bright eyes which darted back and forth upon the faces of an anxious crowd. His sword hung at his side as he sat erect upon his fine mount. Alongside him was Colonel Henry Lee whom Washington knew from the French and Indian War. The colonel was nicknamed "Light-Horse Harry" because of his fame as an expert horseman and leader of cavalry forces. Lee was a scruffy warrior, familiar with the hit-and-duck colonial warfare techniques; in other words, a perfect choice for training new recruits. Immediately, Washington instructed Lee and his junior commanders to train the new recruits and volunteers. Washington and his other men occupied part of their days erecting fortifications and encampments all over Cambridge and the burned-out ruins of Charleston. Empty fields were cut up into entrenchments. Tents were set up between the horses and herds of cattle. Some redoubts were brick; others were made of stone or wood.

Washington was grateful when more men from Northern New England flooded into the region and signed up. By the time he had organized the chain of command, Commander Washington had very experienced military men as chief commanders—Generals Morgan, Lee, Ward, Putnam, Knox, and Hamilton. Ward and Putnam served during the French and Indian War, and Knox had just come in from the Battle of Bunker Hill along with Morgan, who was an expert rifleman. The infamous Benedict Arnold was also one of the generals Washington appointed. Prior to his notorious betrayal, he was a wise and capable officer.

Washington's first encumbrance was a lack of gunpowder and weapons. General Knox and his troops quickly left for Fort Ticonderoga in New York and secured cannons, artillery, and ammunition. Washington's second problem was how to tackle the disciplinary problems and even some corruption among the untrained recruits. The Commander-in-Chief was a stern disciplinarian and spared no one from penalties for their misbehaviors. He knew that the survival of the newly emerging country was at stake, so he needed obedient men.

Washington then moved his men toward Boston and encamped all over the area. A large contingent of colonials fortified Dorchester Heights. Upon seeing large numbers of colonial troops around Boston, the British general, William Howe, took 10,000 of his troops and marched them North. Little by little, the British vessels in the harbor were met by more English warships, but most of the ships had already left Boston Harbor. Where were they going?

Chapter 5 – Canada to New Jersey

George Washington was a brilliant military strategist and studied the hand-drawn maps from his surveys. Through his vast experience in the Ohio Valley, he had an idea of the layout of a land. As he studied the maps, he felt that the English warships would sail out toward other navigable harbors—Quebec in Canada and New York Harbor.

Canada 1775

In those days, the British occupied Canada. That massive territory provided them with an opportunity to attack the colonial troops in the North. To counter that, Washington dispatched General Richard Montgomery toward Montreal and General Benedict Arnold to Quebec.

Battle of Montreal

River vessels were built at the New Hampshire town of St Johns for the Continental troops. General Montgomery and 1,200 men left Fort Ticonderoga, New York, then headed through New

Hampshire where they were met by more colonial recruits from both New Hampshire and Connecticut. The total of fighting men was now about 2,800. Montgomery had the support of some Native Americans, primarily the Oneida tribe. Proceeding northeast on the St. Lawrence River, the colonial force confronted the British outside the city of Montreal. The English were supported by Canadian tribes, however, and Montgomery's advance troops were defeated. Montgomery's backup troops came from behind to stage a counterattack. Luckily for the Continental troops, the English lost their own tribal support when they were persuaded by the colonial-allied Oneida tribe to desert. General Carleton and his British regiments were now weakened. To make matters worse, some of his own men deserted Carleton. Montgomery then sent a message to Carleton claiming there were more gun batteries further east on the St. Lawrence River ready to assault them. Carleton believed him, even though it was a fabrication, and the British surrendered. Afterward, the Continentals occupied Montreal, but the British went on to Quebec.

Battle of Quebec

Benedict Arnold had left Cambridge, Massachusetts with General Morgan's rifle squad and was headed through Maine on the Kennebec and Chaudiere Rivers. Travel was difficult, as the rivers had rapids in some areas and his troops were encumbered with algae and seaweed. During the river journey, the weather turned bad. Rain and snow pelted their boats, which were flimsily constructed. Consequently, much of the gunpowder got wet. Their food was also running out, and Arnold had to send some of his men back. Fortunately, they were able to secure more gunpowder and ammunition from a supportive Frenchman who owned an iron works facility in the area.

General Montgomery had now moved Northeast from Montreal with a force and joined Arnold. The combined force then attacked Quebec. Carleton was there with his English regiments, and the two sides engaged in a long, cold conflict. Unfortunately, the colonial forces were significantly outnumbered forced to surrender. Arnold was wounded, Montgomery had been killed, and General Morgan was taken prisoner. Following that, the Continental Army was afflicted with smallpox and deemed unfit for service.

More Recruitment Plans

It was now 1776. The British at that point were inflicted with smallpox. With his more capable troops, General Howe regrouped and sent word to England that he needed more reinforcements to replace the sick and dead among his troops.

In the meantime, Washington had the same problem. He needed not only reinforcements, but new recruits from the colonies. He sensed that Howe would be targeting New York next and sent out General Henry Lee to raise and organize new military contingents from New York. Washington then pulled his forces out of Boston and had them march to New York. There he had fortifications built on South Manhattan Island and a few on Western Long Island. While doing that, he had his generals and officers train new recruits.

When General Howe and his British reinforcements arrived, they had as many as 32,000 Redcoats. By the time Washington had his troops trained, he had 23,000 soldiers in the area—ten thousand less than the British.

Meeting of the Continental Congress 1776

In the spring, Washington was called to another session of the Continental Congress in Philadelphia. To demonstrate the military's progress, General Washington arrived, accompanied by four battalions, a rifle battalion, a light horse brigade, and three artillery companies. Washington hoped that his showing would motivate new recruits to join up. The members of the Congress had many questions, but were extremely impressed with the rapidity of his response and the disciplined appearance of these troops.

Declaration of Independence

During the first months of 1776, the Continental Congress drew up a rough draft for a *Declaration of Independence*. However, this initial document was weakly worded and came across like a declaration of colonial rights. Many delegates noted that, and had the delegate, Richard Lee, add a resolution announcing in very clear terms that the colonies were going to declare full independence from England. Without that, they would not be able to get foreign assistance. The new resolution was strongly-worded and meant that the colonists' armed conflict wasn't merely a rebellion. Predictably, Lee's Resolution met with opposition. After much debate, it was approved, and a revised draft of the declaration of independence was approved. Young Thomas Jefferson had shown such elegance of pen that he was recruited to write the final document. He had to rush his task and it took just seventeen days for him to complete the *Declaration of Independence.*

The delegates at the Congress needed authorization from their colonial assemblies to vote upon the declaration. By July, the delegates were given the authorization to vote. It took a while for all the colonies to agree to it. The colonies who hesitated were pressured by others to sign it, and by July, the vote was 12 to 1 in favor of independence, with New York abstaining. Although the Declaration of Independence wasn't signed by 12 colonies at the same time, July 4, 1776, was the date designated as the final date of its signing.

The reason for New York's abstention was the fact that all the delegates of New York's colonial government weren't present. The city was suddenly under British attack.

George Washington Rapidly Leaves

When he heard that the British had entered New York, George Washington rushed out of the meeting hall. He had fortified New York already and left his capable commanders there to man the fortifications, but needed to develop a strategy. Most of those fortifications were in Manhattan because it was the primary entrance to the two deep rivers, the Hudson and the East Rivers. Those waterways could handle many ships with deep keels. Washington was shocked when he arrived when he discovered that the British had attacked Long Island instead of Manhattan because most of his fortifications were in Manhattan. Nevertheless, he moved his troops over there to confront them.

Battle of Long Island 1776

Unfortunately, Washington was misinformed about the massive numbers of British troops that General Howe had under his command. Howe had around 20,000 troops, but Washington had thought he only had 8,500. From the Brooklyn Heights at the western end of Long Island, the Continental forces had armaments in place. There were several passes there that led through the Heights that provided access to the East River. The colonial troops on the island were able to block entry to all but one pass—Jamaica Pass. They didn't have sufficient forces available to protect that one. In need of a guide, the British commander held a rifle to the head of a resident and threatened his family unless the man would lead them through Jamaica Pass. Fearing for his family, William Howard reluctantly cooperated. After the British moved through the pass, they penetrated the colonial forces and gunfire erupted. With their superior numbers, the British defeated the colonists. The Continental Army lost about 300 men, but the British only lost 64.

Washington realized that his losses were building up and assigned one of his generals to lead boats from the North Shore of Long

Island back to Manhattan, hoping to prevent the British from entering the East River. It was the middle of the night, but his general was able to evacuate the survivors from Long Island and escort them safely into Manhattan totally unobserved. Historians consider that nighttime action one of Washington's most remarkable strategies. That whole expanse of water is very visible from the shore, even today.

Assassination Conspiracy!

New York was inundated with Tories who supported Britain. On Long Island and particularly in Manhattan, they met at taverns and even dispatched men into Manhattan and Long Island to prevent the progress of Washington and his men. These taverns were usually in the basements of hotels. The walls were made of darkened stones, and the rooms were dark and dank. Into the night, they crouched together and muttered their conspiratorial plots and plans. One of the plots was hatched by Thomas Hickey, an Irish recruit who guarded Washington himself. Hickey had secured money from the former British governor and bought weapons and ammunition from a Tory-affiliated gunsmith. The colonials, however, heard about this nefarious plot. The New York Militia arrested Hickey and delivered him into the hands of Continental officials. Hickey was court-martialed and convicted on charges of mutiny, sedition and correspondence with the enemy. They sentenced Hickey to be hanged, and Washington approved of the sentence. The execution took place at the Bowery on the tip of Manhattan.

Washington's Informant

It was now December, 1776 and was one of the coldest winters on record. General Washington's troops had suffered demoralizing failures in New York, and his troops were weary. Washington stopped at Fort Lee which stands on the New Jersey side just across from upper Manhattan in northern New Jersey. He had come there specifically to see a man by the name of John

Honeyman, whom he met in Philadelphia while attending one of the sessions of the Continental Congress. Honeyman had served on the British side in actions near the St. Lawrence River but was no longer loyal to the British. He told Washington that he moved to Pennsylvania and now stood firmly with the colonists in their struggle for independence.

At Fort Lee, Washington proposed to Honeyman that he act as a "double-agent" for the colonies. Honeyman readily agreed. He had the perfect cover for the ploy, because he was discharged from the British military in good standing. When he returned to his home in Griggstown, New Jersey, Honeyman spread the story that he favored the Tories. It wasn't unusual to find many Tory supporters in New Jersey, but Honeyman made his position well-known. His openness about his political leanings made him sound sincere when he met Englishmen and colonial Tories in the course of his occupation as a weaver. Because of his political leanings, though, patriots raided his house, and he was forced to flee to New Brunswick, New Jersey.

At his new shop, John Honeyman continued to trade with the English and ferreted out what information he could from them about the British actions in New Jersey. He discovered that they had set up a garrison in Trenton manned by the Hessians, who were British mercenaries. Honeyman then traveled west, made his way across the Delaware River, and relayed his report to Washington who was then in Pennsylvania. In a ruse, Washington had him imprisoned at his headquarters as a "Tory," and later let him "escape." The plan was for Honeyman to provide the British Hessians with misinformation. After pretending he escaped from Washington, Honeyman went to Trenton and told the Hessians that the Continental Army was totally demoralized and had no plans to attack Trenton. Honeyman also related the story about his imprisonment which provided him with a cover story. Washington then planned a surprise attack on the garrison.

Honeyman was instructed to continue with his charade, and maintain the appearance of being a Tory to prevent any recriminations against his family in Great Britain. It worked well. Historians have debated the veracity of the story, but there is some evidence that it might be true.

Winter Encampment

There was much sickness among Washington's men, and the brutality of winter was very trying. After establishing some redoubts and more small bases along the Pennsylvania shores of the Delaware River, he and his men encamped there. General Howe, in command of the British units, held fortresses and small bases on the New Jersey side of the Delaware.

Battle of Trenton

Plans for the attack were top-secret. Washington planned on sailing over the river just north of Trenton at twilight and create a three-pronged attack: 1) One division would attack Trenton from the Northeast led by Sullivan and Washington; 2) a second division led by Greene would attack Trenton from the Northwest; and 3) a diversionary force led by Cadwalader would move South, cross the Delaware River, and move toward Bordentown. In Washington's papers, there's a letter written to Cadwalader which says, "Christmas day at night, one hour before day, is the time fixed for our attempt on Trenton. For Heaven's sake keep this to yourself, as the discovery of it may prove fatal to us."

The crossing was difficult because it was sleeting heavily and the river was icy. Ice on the Delaware is deceiving, as it isn't always as thick as it appears. Upon his arrival, Cadwalader discovered that he had to delay until the ice was thicker. The river needed to be frozen over so his men could drag the heavy artillery pieces across it without mishap.

It was now December 26, 1776, and the Hessian officers were still frolicking at their Christmas festivities at the house of Sir Hunt when a messenger arrived and raced in to give the note to Colonel Rahl. The message contained vital information about Washington's unexpected arrival. Instead of reading it, however, Rahl foolishly thrust the letter into his pocket.

One of Washington's smaller units attacked Rahl and his men at the Hunt house where he was dining. Most of the Hessians were drunk, and they were all shot, including Colonel Rahl. At their garrison nearby, the Americans led by Greene stormed in, alarming the rest of the Hessians. After engaging them, the colonial forces drove the soldiers up against the walls with their bayonets, while Washington placed a cannon on the street outside to discourage escape. Thousands were taken prisoner. Washington always tried to treat prisoners of war fairly. With reference to Washington, one of those prisoners later said, "There was a smiling expression on his countenance when he spoke and that won our affection and respect."

The Letter from the Continental Congress, December 27, 1776

A committee of the Congress met to discuss the progress of the war. They were thrilled to hear of Washington's success at Trenton and endowed him with military powers that seemed almost tyrannical. Although he was flattered with their well-intended comments, he responded:

> "I find Congress has done me the honor to entrust me with powers in my military capacity of the highest nature and almost unlimited extent. Instead of thinking of myself freed from all civil obligations by this mark of their confidence, I shall constantly bear in mind that, as the sword was the last resort for the preservation of our liberties, so it ought to be the first thing laid aside when those liberties are firmly established."

Chapter 6 – A Year of Hardship

The year was now 1777. Many hardships were endured by Washington and the Continental Army. Although some of the delegates at the Continental Congress were wavering in their support, there was still much support for the Revolution among many patriots. This was a year of many changes, but marked the turning point in the American Revolution.

Battle of Princeton

The English had a massive garrison at Princeton, which Washington knew had to be attacked. There were also regiments of British troops under General Charles Mawhood along the Post Road that leads to Princeton. From Bordentown, Cadwalader needed to move his forces and artillery Northward toward Princeton. The ground was now quite hard in January of 1777, and the heavy equipment could easily be moved, even through the woods. Washington was closer to Princeton and needed to have his troops move in a Northeastern direction. Another colonial battalion was already near Princeton under Hugh Mercer.

The English under General Cornwallis were further South on the Post Road between Trenton and Princeton. However, like an old fox, Washington stealthily bypassed Cornwallis and then planned to join up with Mercer at Princeton. Cadwalader would be there slightly behind Washington. His instructions were to cross a small bridge at Stony Point and destroy it after he passed over in order to prevent Cornwallis from getting there.

Mawhood then attacked Brigadier General Hugh Mercer and decided to engage him. Mercer moved in, but the British overran Mercer's smaller unit. Mercer was fatally wounded in the attack. Many of his men were new recruits and tried to flee.

Washington then arrived and rushed in to help. Seeing Mercer's fleeing troops, he rode back and forth in front of the frightened soldiers, encouraging them to fight. When Cadwalader arrived shortly thereafter, he rounded up the stragglers. The combined Continental forces were then able to repel the British at Princeton.

Washington and his men chased the British into the downtown area of Princeton, and found the British soldiers holed up in Nassau Hall just off the campus grounds of the University of New Jersey (later called Princeton University). General Sullivan, who had helped Washington at Trenton, later arrived. He was a very persuasive man and told the frightened English soldiers at Nassau Hall that no one was coming to reinforce them. The British at Nassau Hall then surrendered.

Washington had originally planned to move on New Brunswick next. However, he saw that his men were hungry and weary, so decided to move them to higher ground further North where they could rest and recover.

Need Supplies! Need Inoculations!

Washington moved his troops to winter at Morristown, New Jersey, and set up a fortification on a grassy knoll overlooking acres of territory where he could watch out for British troops. He called it "Fort Nonsense." While in Morristown, Washington stayed at the Ford Mansion. His wife, Martha, actually traveled up there to join him. Five aides-de-camp stayed there also. Those men included Alexander Hamilton, who helped Washington draft documents for military purposes and for communication with the Continental Congress, of which Hamilton himself was a delegate.

Washington's men camped on the grounds. Many of them were very ill from smallpox. Although the smallpox vaccine wasn't fully developed until 1793, there was a more primitive method available. After watching so many of his soldiers suffer and many die, Washington insisted on having mass inoculations for his armies. He frantically sent out messages to his commanding officers to send doctors into Morristown and into Philadelphia where other Continental troops were encamped. The program was successfully executed. Consequently, there were as many as 11 hospitals constructed in the Northeast to not only inoculate the troops, but also to care for the injured.

Although Washington was able to inaugurate a program of inoculations, his men were suffering from the cold of the winter and their clothing was in ragged condition. During the earlier years of the American Revolution, an enormously wealthy man from Philadelphia, Robert Morris, was providing a great deal of financing for the war efforts. Washington himself planned to move his troops back into Pennsylvania and he made it a point to meet with Robert Morris, whom he knew personally.

Washington Weeps

Washington entered Morris' study and asked Morris if he could borrow some money for the war effort. Morris was very upset when he heard that plea because he wanted to help, but couldn't. He had used up all his credit and could do nothing at that point in time.

According to an account related in a letter from a cleric in 1777, it said that Washington covered his face with his hands and "...burst into an abandon of weeping, and as he sat there sobbing, the tears trickled through his fingers and dropped down to his wrists."

Battle of Brandywine

In September, 1777, while in the Brandywine Valley in the Southern area of Pennsylvania, Washington was informed by the colonists that General Howe was in the area. Washington then designated that valley for his next encounter. Washington knew he needed to continue the war, after having had substantial victories in Trenton and Princeton.

Altogether, the troops under Washington, Knox, Stirling and Greene numbered about 14,000 and the British under Howe and Cornwallis had 15,000 men. Washington and his Continental forces marched toward the wide, rapidly flowing Brandywine Creek. In an ambitious move, General Cornwallis and Howe marched Eastward to meet them head-on.

Cornwallis attacked the right flank of Sullivan's troops, then circled around and caught the other Continental troops by surprise. The Continentals didn't have enough time to rally and counterattack. Knox and Greene's forces were bombarded by the British grenadiers. The Continental forces consistently shot into the British divisions, but the action proved to be too weak.

Outmaneuvered near Philadelphia

General Howe regularly tried to deceive Washington as to where he and his troops were destined. Howe had moved his vessels out of New York Harbor and had them sail South to the port city of Perth Amboy. His ground troops moved Westward on land toward Edison in central New Jersey. Unbeknown to Washington, Howe also moved some of his naval vessels south along the New Jersey coast. Some British vessels circled around the tip of New Jersey and headed North on the Delaware River. He then sent the remaining vessels Southward along the Atlantic Coast. By the end of the summer, George Washington wasn't sure exactly where Howe planned on going.

Howe, a very optimistically ambitious military commander, set up confusing and elaborate plans to control:

1. Philadelphia, Pennsylvania

2. Albany, New York, and its environs

3. The Hudson River outlet from Manhattan

4. Newport, Rhode Island

5. Virginia and South Carolina

When Washington heard from his spies that Howe was at sea off the southern tip of New Jersey, it was too late for him to get there on time.

Capture of Philadelphia

The Continental Congress became alarmed when they saw the proximity of the British troops, and rapidly relocated further west to York, Pennsylvania. Many of the colonists fled Philadelphia. In July of 1777, Howe sent two divisions up the Delaware River and marched into Philadelphia unopposed and was greeted by the Tory-leaning Pennsylvanians. While there, the British were short of supplies, so they stole cattle, horses, wood, clothing, and food. There was looting everywhere, and the British wounded were housed in the homes of the colonists. Patriots were thrown in jail. Soon, the colonists had little food and clothing.

There were two small Continental forts on the Delaware River and they attempted to dislodge the British. However, they didn't have enough men available and lost control of those forts.

While Washington was on his way, he and the Continental troops were out of food and supplies as well. He sent an urgent message to the Continental Congress saying, "…three days successively we have been destitute of bread. Two days we have been entirely without meat. The men must be supplied or they cannot be commanded." Because of that, Washington couldn't do much at the time to repel the British from the city.

After the humiliation of having lost Philadelphia, some of the colonists lost their faith in Washington. Divisions and jealousy erupted within the governments of each state. An early historian, Wayne Whipple, wrote that in the winter of 1777,

> "There were thirteen States, and each of these States sent troops into the field, but all the States were jealous of one another...the members of Congress agreed on only one thing – that it was not prudent to give the army too much power. It is true that they had once given Washington large authority, but they were very much afraid that somehow the army would rule the country."

A Pseudo-Conspiracy

After the capture of Philadelphia, several officers in the Continental Army attempted to have Washington removed as Commander-in-Chief. History has labeled this act as the "Conway Cabal," as it was masterminded by General Thomas Conway. He conspired with several other men including Thomas Mifflin, a congressional aide, and General Horatio Gates.

They wrote a letter to the Continental Congress. After some debates among members of the Congress, the members ultimately refused to remove Washington from his command. Gates apologized for his role in the affair. Mifflin was later accused of embezzlement and resigned in shame.

Washington's loyal general, General John Cadwalader, was so furious about Conway that he challenged him to a duel. Although Conway was shot, he recovered and fled to France where he spent the remainder of his life.

Battle of Saratoga

While Howe was attempting to play a "cat-and-mouse" chase with Washington, the British General John Burgoyne was steadily marching South from Quebec in the Fall of 1777. Howe had planned that Burgoyne would take control of New York. Burgoyne had about 7,000 men, but called for reinforcements when he discovered that Washington was moving North to meet him with 13,000 men. Although the soldiers were tired and hungry, they maintained their steadfast loyalty to Washington and the cause of independence.

As for the British, Howe was supposed to reinforce General Burgoyne, but neglected to do so. Instead, General Howe joined his troops in Philadelphia and never sent any aid. Howe spent a couple of months there, before withdrawing his forces from Philadelphia.

The British lost a lot of men at Saratoga. Burgoyne was then forced to move back and encamped at Bemis Heights nearby. The Continental forces then closed into Bemis Heights under the command of Benedict Arnold, the man who later betrayed the American cause. He excelled in his actions there. After the Continental troops destroyed or captured the redoubts and defenses at Bemis Heights and in Saratoga proper, General Burgoyne had no choice but to surrender. Saratoga represented the turning point in the American Revolution. General Howe resigned shortly after the episode at Saratoga.

The Wicked Winter at Valley Forge

Washington encamped with his troops for the winter of 1777 at Valley Forge, just Northwest of Philadelphia. He had his men build a village of small log cabins. Every cabin had a fireplace in the back of it. For supplies, he sent out his men who scoured the countryside, begging people for blankets, food, and clothing.

Disease spread among the men and some died there. Washington himself lived in the same kind of quarters his soldiers had and shared all their hardships. He kept encouraging them and complimented them for their heroism.

One of Washington's generals, "Light-Horse Harry" Lee and his men were encamped at an outpost in the distance. One night, he sneaked into a small enemy encampment nearby, harassed their foraging party, and raided the British storehouse. Then he raced back to Valley Forge with arms, supplies, and clothing. It was a godsend.

In later years, Washington wrote Lee a letter in which he said, "I offer my sincere thanks to the whole of your gallant party and assure them that no one felt pleasure more sensibly, or rejoiced more sincerely than your affectionate G. Washington."

Training

Baron von Steuben was a Prussian who moved to the colonies and volunteered for service in the Revolution. He had extensive military experience and initiated a training program for the troops at Valley Forge. This was not only extremely helpful, but also gave the men an opportunity to warm their bodies through exercise. It increased their confidence significantly and boosted their morale. Even though he spoke very poor English, von Steuben knew how to swear. This amused the troops greatly and he became very popular. Today, an annual parade is held in his honor in New York, and there are numerous statues of him in the city and the surrounding metropolitan area. His home was in River Edge, New Jersey and is a historic site today.

The Marquis de Lafayette

In 1776, the elderly statesman, Benjamin Franklin, had been sent to France to attempt to get their assistance in the American Revolution. That was one issue that Patrick Henry presented to the

Continental Congress, and it proved to be a helpful contribution to the Revolutionary War.

During Franklin's visit, the well-known French Marquis de Lafayette, was alerted about the struggles of the new nation. He became a staunch supporter of the Revolution. Even before France concluded their debate about Franklin's appeal, Lafayette left there with funds and supplies to sail for America. He joined George Washington at Valley Forge. Washington was extremely fond of him, and Lafayette became his confidante throughout his life. The Marquis de Lafayette had vast military experience and was an invaluable addition, and boosted morale at Valley Forge.

This encampment lasted a total of six months. The year 1778 was a disruptive year in terms of political divisions due to the Conway Cabal and the political infighting on the part of delegates to the Continental Congress. In addition, the country's financial resources were deleteriously affected by an unexpected devaluation of the Continental currency. There was also mismanagement—deliberate and otherwise—among some of the colonists who were in charge of providing provisions for the Continental Army. In addition, at Valley Forge some of Washington's own officers were disruptive. One of Washington's generals, Charles Lee, even argued openly with Washington and sometimes even disobeyed orders.

Chapter 7 – Victory

Official Entry of France into the American Revolution

France was particularly impressed with Washington's stunning victory at Saratoga against the formidable General Burgoyne. Many of the French looked upon the American struggle as a mirror of their own conflicts to achieve more representation in the workings of their own government. In 1778, France and America signed the Treaty of Alliance. They immediately sent ships, soldiers, and a number of capable admirals to help.

Battle of Monmouth 1778

This was the last battle of the Northern campaign in the American Revolution, and it took place in Monmouth County in the approximate center of the colony. Washington appointed General Charles Lee to command the advance forces to make a stand against the British troops in the area. Lee, however, refused the command saying that he felt the battle plans Washington drew up wouldn't be successful. Washington then planned on giving the assignment to Lafayette. Once Lee heard that, he changed his mind and assumed command. When Lee reached Monmouth, he organized a haphazard formation. After just fighting several hours in the heat of June, Lee called for a retreat. General Nathaniel Greene and Washington were close by. As he was approaching the area, Washington came upon Lee and his men fleeing from the English. He was furious. Washington had been having trouble with the argumentative Lee before, but when Lee heatedly argued with Washington about the retreat, he was relieved of command.

Washington then took over Lee's troops and called out to the soldiers, "Stand fast, my boys, and receive the enemy. The Southern troops are advancing to support you." There was a sound of courage and determination in Washington's voice, and the Continental soldiers rallied. Washington was then joined from the south by Lord Stirling, Anthony Wayne, Henry Knox, and Lafayette.

The British and Americans fought in the hot summer sun for an entire day. Wayne's regimental division was defeated, and the British under Cornwallis attempted twice to assault the other American forces but were repelled. Then night fell. Washington wanted to resume the battle the following day, but the British had retreated in order to move South. Although it appeared to be a victory for the Continental troops, historians indicate it was a "tactical draw," most likely due to the fact that the reported casualties were about equal.

Because Washington had so few provisions, Lafayette returned to France to secure more money, ships, supplies and equipment to help out.

New York Frozen

During the winter of 1778-1779, the entire harbor of New York was frozen over. The British who had left Philadelphia moved back into New York City. General Benedict Arnold was then put in charge of defending Philadelphia in case the British returned.

The Continental troops wintered in Valley Forge again, but Washington made plans to move some troops down south when he got word that the British General Charles Cornwallis was nearing Charleston, South Carolina. There were also British naval forces offshore which he needed to watch. Washington felt he had to remain near New York to deal with British regiments under Sir Henry Clinton while he waited for Lafayette's return with reinforcements. What he did not know was the fact that Clinton had gone down South, leaving a garrison in New York under the control of Hessian commander, Wilhelm von Knyphausen.

When more supplies arrived, Washington had to send some of his troops down South to deal with the British troops under Cornwallis. Having already arrived from New York, though, General Henry Clinton and his English troops were entering Charleston. Benjamin Lincoln, a North Carolina Militia officer, presented a courageous defense. However, he was unable to expel them because he only had 6,000 troops. The English had more than double that amount. Following Lincoln's defeat, the British troops laid siege to Charleston.

Lafayette Returns 1780

Washington, who had been stymied due to the serious lack of provisions, was delighted upon Lafayette's return. Lafayette brought back a lot of supplies, along with naval forces and artillery. He then conferred with Washington, who was anxious to move toward New York but was likewise concerned about the British down South.

Lafayette now had the command of the French Navy and told Washington he would have Admiral De Barras sail down the East Coast from Newport, Rhode Island. Washington met with Lafayette and one of his French Commanders, Comte Jean-Baptiste de Rochambeau, to discuss his plans. Rochambeau suggested that Lafayette, Washington and he attack the British down South instead of in New York, because the French had ships under Admiral de Grasse in the West Indies and could be called upon to assist. De Grasse could bring 24 warships, 3,200 soldiers, siege equipment and a substantial amount of money. He only had a limited amount of time, though, as he had to return to the West Indies.

Washington agreed and it was also decided that Yorktown, Virginia would be the best area to engage Cornwallis because of its more accessible harbor. He then appointed one of his other commanders to man a garrison in New York.

Intelligence Operations

In late 1778, Washington formed the "Culper Ring," which was commissioned as an intelligence operation. It was under the leadership of Colonel Benjamin Talmadge. Under his command, the Culper intelligence ring discovered several pending plots over two years' time:

1. A plan to thwart the French General de Rochambeau as he was taking his forces south

   Outcome: De Rochambeau circumvented the British forces along the route.

2. A plot concocted by the British spy, Major André, to help the British take control of West Point

   Outcome: Major André was arrested in New York.

3. The treachery of the American, General Benedict Arnold who had left his post in Philadelphia, betrayed the American cause, and had plans to seize West Point for the British

   Outcome: An interstate hunt was initiated to locate and arrest him.

4. A plot to divide Washington's forces in Connecticut

   Outcome: The Connecticut Regiments were reorganized and placed in a defensive position around New York.

5. A plan to counterfeit Continental currency

   Outcome: The Continental Congress discontinued the use of Continental dollars.

Loyal Soldier, Montagnie

Just prior to moving south, Washington leaked some misinformation to the enemy indicating that the Franco-American forces intended to attack at the New York Harbor. Washington contacted a Baptist clergyman, Mr. Montagnie, a militia volunteer who was in Northern New Jersey and ordered him to deliver a letter to the colonial troops who manned Fort Nonsense in Morristown. Washington instructed the young soldier to travel through the pass in the Ramapo Mountains at New Jersey's Northern border and take that route to Morristown. "But I shall be taken if I go through that pass," he told Washington. Washington stamped his foot emphatically and firmly said to him, "Your duty, young man, is not to talk, but to obey."

Montagnie did as he was told but, as he predicted, was captured by a British patrol. Once he was jailed in New York, he realized the purpose for Washington's orders. In that missive was a fictional plan for a Continental Army attack at New York. The ruse worked well. Once the English came into possession of that letter, they reinforced their troops in the North and stayed there, unaware that Washington, Lafayette, and de Rochambeau along with the French fleets were going to Yorktown in Virginia.

Generally, the British treated colonial prisoners humanely, so Washington sent a letter later on, stressing the fact that his messenger, Montagnie, should be treated decently. Montagnie was released the following year and lived to tell his story.

Siege of Yorktown: British Surrender 1780-1781

The notorious American traitor, Benedict Arnold, suddenly showed up in Virginia and raided the port city of Richmond. He was going to receive more British reinforcements, a fact that alarmed Washington. Washington knew Arnold had been an excellent strategist, so he attempted to get some French naval forces to relocate to Richmond and relieve that port. When he couldn't get any naval forces to intervene, Washington asked Lafayette to interfere. Once Benedict Arnold heard that the mighty Lafayette was approaching with a Franco-American army, he and his accompanying general, William Phillips, withdrew.

General Cornwallis was in South Carolina at that point. At the Battle of Guilford Court House in Greensboro, he defeated the American forces under Nathanael Greene. However, it was a pyrrhic victory. The British lost nearly 100 men, and 400 were wounded. Fever raged through the British forces, and reduced Cornwallis's overall effective fighting force to slightly more than 1,000. So, he was delayed as he had to await reinforcements from the English allies.

In the meantime, Rochambeau with his troops of over 5,000 men and Washington's men marched 680 miles from New Jersey to Yorktown in 1781. When the American soldiers reached Maryland, there was a problem. The colonial forces halted their march and demanded to be paid in gold or silver. The Continental dollar had collapsed because of the British counterfeiting scheme discovered by Washington's intelligence unit in 1779. Unfortunately, the Congress had failed to rectify the situation right away.

Washington understood the dilemma felt by the soldiers whose service he respected and admired. De Rochambeau then generously extended a loan to Washington consisting of a huge cache of Spanish gold coins. Washington graciously accepted it and paid his soldiers. Seeing this remarkable demonstration of fairness on Washington's part, both the French and American troops respected Washington even more.

As the naval plan unfolded, Admiral de Grasse and his French fleet were already arriving from the West Indies. At the end of the summer of 1781, he reached the Chesapeake Bay with his equipment and troops. The French fleet under Admiral de Barras was speedily heading south from Rhode Island as planned. Once the British got word of that move, they suddenly realized that the theater of operation wasn't New York, but down South. In a panic, they sent Admiral Graves and his British fleet there, but was it too late for their ground troops to go to Virginia. Washington, de Rochambeau, Lafayette, and the naval forces were too far ahead.

Once Graves' fleet reached Chesapeake Bay, he found de Grasse's French fleet blockading the harbor. In a fruitless effort, he attempted to break the blockade, but was outnumbered and outgunned.

General Cornwallis called upon his military leaders in the South to join his troops at Yorktown. By the time the two enemy forces met, Cornwallis had 9,000 troops and Washington had about 18,000.

Both sides feverishly built trenches and redoubts all over the area and put their artillery in place. Most of the American fortifications were built on a moonless night, much to the surprise of British troops at daylight. The British tended to expect action during the daytime only. Gunfire erupted on both sides. The Continental troops were in trenches, on the ground, and on the hills. Cannon fire thundered across all of the farms and hills outside Yorktown. By the evening of October 14, the Americans launched a full-scale attack on the hastily constructed British garrison there. The commander of the garrison, Major Campbell, was forced to surrender this initial engagement when he lost most of his men.

The English were getting desperate and sabotaged the American cannons. However, these guns were repaired at a rapid pace. Cornwallis was almost successful at one of the redoubts until Lafayette's French forces rushed in. In the meantime, Admiral de Grasse had arrived and unloaded his guns and French troops. Quickly putting the fresh artillery in place, the Americans beat back the Cornwallis' and the other English forces. The English admiral, Thomas Graves, was blocked in at the harbor by de Grasse's vessels. Then de Barras' ships arrived and prevented any outlying vessels from sailing back out to sea.

Heavily outnumbered and incurring the losses of men and equipment, Cornwallis attempted to evacuate his troops. He wanted to move North and board the smaller English boats waiting at a small inner cape at Gloucester Point. There he planned to board the sloops and cross the James River in order to attack Maryland. However, a squall hit, making that impossible.

On October 19, 1781, the British surrendered.

The Treaty of Paris

After the surrender, official terms needed to be formulated between the Americans and Great Britain in order to state that the victory in the American Revolution would result in the British recognition of the sovereignty of the states. Known as the *Treaty of Paris of 1783*, its key points included:

1. Great Britain acknowledges the independence of the Thirteen Colonies, now called "states."

2. Great Britain honors the fishing rights of America to the waters off Newfoundland and the Gulf of the St. Lawrence River.

3. Recognition that debts are owed by the thirteen states and Great Britain.

4. The states will pay restitution for confiscated lands legally owned by the British in America.

5. All prisoners of war will be released, and non-landed property, including slaves, will remain in the hands of America.

6. Great Britain and America will have full access to the Mississippi River.

7. Boundaries of the US will include the Northwest Territory, specifically Ohio, Michigan, Indiana, Wisconsin, and parts of Minnesota.

An Honorable and Humorous Dinner

Even though the British had lost the war, George Washington maintained respect for their loyalty and honor in the service of their country. Likewise, he was grateful to the French. One evening, Washington invited de Rochambeau, Lafayette, and even Cornwallis to his headquarters for dinner. As they began, de Rochambeau offered a toast to the United States. Washington offered one to the king of France, and Cornwallis offered one to the king of England, after which Washington quipped, "And may he stay there!" All of them laughed. From that point on, Cornwallis and Washington became friends.

Chapter 8 – George Washington, The First President

Washington Thought He Was Home

George Washington was pleased the war was over and returned home to his dear Mount Vernon and his loving wife Martha. He loved the plantation and he loved riding his horses. Nelson was his trusty sorrel, and he liked to take him out daily to inspect the plantation and farms. It was lovely and tranquil. There was no more pounding of mortar shells and no more cries from desperate dying men who had served him and the country to their last breath of life.

Washington followed the political events of the day including the *Articles of Confederation* that had been passed in 1781 by what was called the Confederation Congress, that had replaced the Continental Congress. After reading the Articles, Washington felt they were a "rope made of sand." The Articles were not only weak, but they left the matter of paying the provisions for the military, paying the salaries of soldiers and paying war debt practically unenforceable. Washington keenly remembered how often he had to beg the Congress for money to support the war effort. He remembered the 680-mile march down the East Coast when his soldiers needed to be paid. Throughout the war, Washington had to borrow money from de Rochambeau, the French general, and even financed part of the war himself when he could. He wrote to a number of statesmen regarding his opinions about weaknesses in the *Articles of Confederation.*

However, Washington knew he alone couldn't build the new nation. He was in his mid-50's, had a perennial battle with rheumatism and was war-weary. Regardless, letters poured in from the most influential statesmen of the time, including James Madison, the young delegate from Virginia, asking that Washington attend a convention in Philadelphia. Washington knew Madison personally, as he lived nearby and occasionally visited him at Mount Vernon.

Decision Year 1787

Washington felt a sense of melancholy about the thought of breaking off his cherished retirement and politely refused the invitations. Despite that, he was elected as a delegate of Virginia. He knew he had the ability to guide this new nation, but also knew that others must carry the torch after him. Then he read the reports about a rebellion started by Daniel Shays, a Revolutionary soldier who hadn't been paid, and Washington was upset by that. Washington began to fear that the nation might tear itself apart due to the inequities. He then sent a letter to the members stating:

> "I shall remain but a few days here, and shall proceed to Philadelphia, when I shall attempt to stimulate Congress to the best improvement of our late success, by taking the most vigorous and effectual measures to be ready for an early and decisive campaign the next year. My greatest fear is that Congress, viewing this stroke in too important a point of light, may think or work too nearly closed, and will fall into a state of languor and relaxation. To prevent

this error, I shall employ every means in my power, and if unhappily we sink into that fatal mistake, no part of the blame shall be mine."

The Philadelphia Convention 1787

It was summertime when the delegates met in Philadelphia. As their first act, they unanimously elected Washington president of the assembly, and he accepted.

Prior to this meeting, many of the statesmen discussed the issues related to the structure of the new nation. In one of his letters addressed to James Madison, Washington said, "We are either a united people or we are not. If the former, let us in all matters of general concern act as a nation…If we are not, let us no longer act a farce by pretending to it."

One of the weaknesses the Confederation noted was the same that Washington did, that is that the Articles of Confederation weren't strong enough to unite the nation. It was then decided that they wouldn't simply modify the Articles; they would discard them altogether and draw up a new document. In order to avoid alarming the States, they agreed to secrecy, even to the point of shutting all the windows and pulling down the shades in the sweltering heat.

George Washington was fairly quiet during the initial sessions of the convention, as he wanted this new document to represent the opinions of its members, not merely his own. The assembly basically agreed from the onset that the new government would be split into executive, legislative, and judicial departments. The most heavily debated issues on the open floor revolved around:

- How proportional representation of each state was going to be achieved

- Whether to put the executive department under the leadership of one or three persons

- Terms and process of elections

- Impeachable offenses
- The right to levy taxes
- The slavery issue
- The process for the appointment of judges

After that, the convention split up into various committees of state delegates charged with discussing those issues, and scheduled to return to the general floor later to make decisions. A number of plans were created, most of which had strong similarities.

When they reassembled, the convention favored two plans: *The Virginia Plan* and the *New Jersey Plan*. *The Virginia Plan* rose in popularity, but rebuttals occurred when the members noted that it discriminated against smaller states. It was then decided that each state should have two senators in a bicameral congress. Roger Sherman from Connecticut forged a document that combined the most favored elements in the New Jersey and Virginia Plans and was met with overall approval in its final form.

Slavery Issue at the Convention

Nearly one-third of the delegate states had slaves. The Northern states, for the most part, had eliminated slavery, but the South had many of them. In the South, nearly one-fifth of the population was slaves. Yet, these states were among the wealthiest in the nation and provided food for all the states. In fact, the entire economy of the Southern states depended upon slavery. Therefore, the assembly was unwilling to eliminate the institution of slavery.

One of the contentious issues with slavery was whether or not slaves should be considered to be property or part of the populations of states who had slaves. If they were part of the population, that would mean that Southern representation in Congress would be higher. What wasn't discussed, however, was whether or not slaves would be given the right to vote. It was simply assumed they didn't have that right.

The delegate from Pennsylvania, James Wilson, proposed that a slave be counted as three-fifths of a person for the purpose of proportional representation of populations. This was accepted by the convention. This was called "The Three-Fifths Compromise."

The Constitution of the U.S.

James Madison was appointed to write the initial draft of the Constitution. After much discussion and contentious debates, he made the recommended modifications. In addition, he also wrote the Bill of Rights. The convention then accepted the final document, with George Washington being the very first man to sign it. The states took a year to ratify it, and the final date attributed to the creation of the first US Constitution was 1789. From that time on, this Philadelphia Convention was later known as the 1st Constitutional Convention.

George Washington returned to his beloved Mount Vernon following the convention, yet he knew that the nation still had need of him. The states each called upon their electoral delegates, and in March of 1789, George Washington was elected president. John Adams from Massachusetts was elected his vice-president.

In his personal diary, he wrote, "I bid adieu to Mount Vernon, to private life, and to domestic felicity."

He then stopped at Fredericksburg where his terminally ill mother was residing. It was a tearful farewell, as both knew they would never see each other again. She said to him, "George, fulfill the high destinies which Heaven has appeared to have intended for you...and a mother's blessing be with you always."

During the same year he had assumed the office of the presidency, his mother died and was buried just outside her house in Fredericksburg, Virginia.

The First President of the United States

New York was the first capital of the United States under the Constitution. When Washington arrived, he was accompanied by a military and civilian parade. Thousands of people were lined up along the way, including cheering Revolutionary War veterans. The route was strewn with flowers and banners. When he reached Federal Hall in Manhattan, there was a 21-gun salute.

Washington took the oath of office on April 30, 1789.

His first responsibility was to set up a cabinet. He chose:

1. General Henry Knox – Secretary of War

2. Alexander Hamilton – Secretary of the Treasury

3. Edmund Randolph – Attorney General

4. Thomas Jefferson – Secretary of Foreign Affairs (position later called Secretary of State)

Washington was a firm believer in a strong central government. So was John Jay, Edmund Randolph, and Alexander Hamilton. Knox was a soldier who believed in the rights of the soldiers, but not to the degree that would advocate the overthrow of those in command. Both Knox and Hamilton fought alongside Washington in the Revolution.

Historians have always wondered about Washington's selection of Thomas Jefferson, who tended to prefer the rights of the people above those of the central government. However, Washington truly believed that all voices in the country needed to be heard and likewise knew that the power of compromise was greater than a betrayal of true liberty and freedom.

Dispute over War Debt

Hamilton's first assignment was to develop a plan to pay the war debt. After the Revolution, the country owed $54 million dollars, including interest. The debt was owed to foreign governments as well as to the states, and it was the obligation of Congress to impose taxes in order to pay it. However, the issue of the responsibility of the states to assume part of that debt was hotly debated. Hamilton's plan was to establish a borrowing mechanism by which the government could pay back debt at lower interest rates. Because part of that debt was due to investors, mostly Northerners, those people would stand to make a tremendous profit, as they had bought government bonds at 15 cents on the dollar.

Other states like Pennsylvania, North Carolina, and Virginia had already paid off their war debts and didn't want to be taxed again to help pay. Jefferson led the opposition and loudly argued with Hamilton. For as long as six months, this dispute raged. Finally, James Madison interceded and proposed a compromise. It stated that in exchange for a promise of Southern votes, Hamilton would agree to transfer the nation's capital to the South along the Potomac River. Prior to constructing a new building, it was decided that Philadelphia would serve as an interim capital.

For his entire term as president, Washington had to referee debates between Hamilton and Jefferson. It was a matter that caused him much concern, but he also understood that all sides of an issue should be considered in the interest of independence and freedom.

Washington Gravely Ill

During his first year as president, Washington suffered two physical ailments. The first one was caused by a virulent attack of anthrax. It was very painful, and Washington felt he was going to die. His doctor indicated he could recover but recovery might take a while. For over six weeks, he had to retire to his bedchamber and left the running of the country in the hands of John Jay, as there was no set procedure for choosing someone as a replacement at the time. Washington did finally recover but was very weakened.

Shortly after that, he was alerted by his doctor that he needed surgery. The historical records don't indicate the nature of the illness other than to indicate it was a cyst. The nation was informed of the procedure and the citizens were extremely concerned. The operation was considered risky, but Washington survived. He was in an even weaker state when he returned to his office during the summer of 1789.

The Tariff Act of 1789

At that time, Congress had drawn up a method to protect trade and charge taxes on the goods brought into the country. The federal government was in need of revenue, and this Act was seen as a fair way to collect it without further burdening the states.

George Washington signed the Tariff Act in July. The additional benefit of this law was the fact that it would boost domestic manufacturing, a point made clear by Alexander Hamilton. By buying US-made products, merchants could then resell the goods at high prices.

Chapter 9 – The New Capital

In 1790, the new capital was moved to Independence Hall in Philadelphia. It was deemed more appropriate than New York for the meetings of the new congress and the quarters and office of the president. While his new quarters were under construction, George Washington stayed at a house owned by Robert Morris of Pennsylvania, the well-known financier.

Rent in the city soared at that time, much to the annoyance of the congressmen who needed to relocate there. Construction workers rushed there in order to build new buildings for housing and government purposes. Philadelphia was a center for social activities, so many of the wealthy flocked to the area, adding to its population.

Whenever Washington arrived in his carriage at Independence Hall, young boys used to crowd around the carriage waving. The president loved children and used to tip his hat to them, after which they cheered. When he held state dinners, he told his steward to call in the children of the neighborhood and feed them the leftovers as well as cakes, raisins, and nuts.

The First Bank

In his position as the first treasurer of the United States, Hamilton supported the establishment of a bank that serviced the nation. Among its powers would be the management of the excise taxes charged to non-American vessels for goods shipped from other countries. It also provided a system of credit for the national government and the establishment of a mint.

Funding

The Bank was funded by a sale of $10 million in stock, and the Bank itself would own $2 million of the shares. Those shares could be paid back in installments. The public could buy $8 million worth of shares, but one-fourth had to be paid back in gold or silver. There was a mandatory rotation of directors of the Bank to avoid any impropriety. In addition, the government was prohibited from making loans that weren't fully capitalized.

Washington was hesitant to sign the bank bill into law when James Madison and Thomas Jefferson objected to the constitutionality of the bill. Madison and Jefferson indicated that the Constitution didn't extend the power to establish a federal bank to the government, and Washington was inclined to agree. However, Hamilton indicated that the bank shouldn't be considered a part of the federal government itself, but as privately owned and operated by people who weren't elected or appointed by the government. Hamilton's argument convinced Washington. Congress likewise supported it, and the bill was signed into law.

Jefferson vs. Hamilton Dispute

The Jefferson-Hamilton feud continued during the rest of Washington's first term. Although Washington attempted to get Jefferson and Hamilton to resolve their differences, he was unable to do so. After that, their hostility became known to the public.

The early 20th-century historian, Wayne Whipple, described this feud saying, "These wise men...were almost evenly balanced in idiocy about things that they did not understand."

In 1792, Jefferson and Hamilton again erupted into fiery debates when the Bank went into crisis causing a bank run. To remain afloat, the Bank demanded that their debtors make full payment on all open loans, which, of course, they couldn't. Historians indicate that the crisis was caused by unscrupulous speculation.

Jefferson and Madison were quick to point out the perceived error of permitting the establishment of a national bank. However, Hamilton was a very capable financial manager and was finally able to restore the stability of the Bank through the sale of securities. In addition, he insisted that the Bank put in safeguards to avoid this in the future.

Political Parties 1792

Besides their marked differences regarding the establishment of a national bank, other political differences continued to divide Thomas Jefferson and Alexander Hamilton. James Madison tended to agree with Jefferson's point of view and joined with him to found the Democratic-Republican Party. Hamilton's faction became known as the Federalists. Most of the supporters of the Democratic-Republicans were slave-owning Southerners while the businessmen of the North were usually Federalists.

Washington himself detested political parties, as this was just a young nation and he felt that political parties tended to polarize the people. When asked, he refused to be identified with either party.

The Federalists published the *Gazette of the United States* to promote their partisan views and circulated it on a bi-weekly basis. To counter-balance that, Jefferson and Madison hired Philip Freneau, a noted editorialist and poet, to write and edit the *National Gazette.*

Freneau knew Washington's stance on political parties. Nevertheless, he sent not just one, but three copies of the *National Gazette* to Washington every time it was issued. When Washington read them, he lost his temper. Usually the president kept his temper under check, but considered the impudence of Freneau a personal insult. Throwing down that newspaper one day, he called Freneau an "impudent rascal" at the top of his voice.

In addition to the *National Gazette*, Jefferson and Madison encouraged others of like mind to establish Democratic-Republican Societies in the various states. They held monthly meetings and discussed issues regarding what they considered to be excessive power in the hands of the central government.

The Whiskey Rebellion 1791-1794

The Constitution gave Congress the right to levy import taxes. In 1791, Hamilton proposed that an additional tax be passed on the sale of distilled spirits. All of the states produced spirits and sold them to other states, with whiskey being the most popular. This tax became more popularly known as the "Whiskey Tax." The tax adversely affected Pennsylvania, and to some degree Maryland, North Carolina, South Carolina, Kentucky, and Georgia. Northeastern farmers could ship whiskey to other states more economically because Hamilton gave quantity discounts to farmers who were major distillers, and most of them resided in the North. Because of the disparity, small farmers in Pennsylvania and Kentucky, for example, were paying 9 cents per gallon in tax, while the Northeastern farmers were paying only 6 cents.

The people in Pennsylvania sent a petition through the US House of Representatives in Philadelphia to change that system. As result of that, the federal government reduced the tax by 1 cent per gallon. It wasn't enough to satisfy the farmers. These people had been through a Revolution meant to bring them liberty and freedom from tyranny. They keenly remembered the efforts of the English monarch to charge outrageous taxes, and they felt like that extortive behavior had arisen again. These were people who knew battle and learned that armed resistance was one of the most effective and practical solutions to injustice. Tax collectors were tarred and feathered, and militia officers who were sent out to issue warrants to the attackers were likewise harassed. Tax officials who tried to intimidate the locals had their houses burned. As a result of this widespread insurrection, the whiskey tax was becoming unenforceable. Battles broke out, the US Mail was robbed and houses of wealthy landowners were destroyed and their families threatened.

As result of those acts, the Pennsylvania State Militia was sent out to quell the rebellion, but it only served to accelerate the violence. There was talk in Pennsylvania about ceding from the union and even bringing in the guillotine to execute tax officials!

Washington's Response

Washington perceived the Whiskey Rebellion as a significant threat to a national government that was essentially just three years old. However, he wanted to handle the matter as delicately and wisely as possible before creating a federal force. Although he eschewed the use of force inside his own country, the rebellion grew in strength. Washington deemed that it may be needed to suppress the mob violence, so he decided that a mechanism was needed for its establishment.

The Militia Acts of 1792

Washington proposed to Congress that they pass the Militia Acts to address that issue. These acts provided the federal government with the power to take command of state militias if needed. The Militia Acts also raised the pay of soldiers and conscripted every able-bodied man between the ages of 18-45 to serve in their state militias for three years.

Still hoping that reconciliation might be possible, Washington sent in commissioners to peaceably meet with representatives. He also sent in a large federal militia to accompany them. The added benefit of this action was the fact that the people would see that the federal government had tangible power and was willing to enforce the law.

Knowing that he was popular among the people, Washington used that to his own advantage. He traveled to Pennsylvania with General "Light-Horse Harry" Lee to head up the federal force. The militia marched into Philadelphia, and the tremendous force of about 12,000 men put an immediate end to the rebellion. No shots were fired. The militia officers then attempted to arrest a number of the instigators, but most fled to the Pocono Mountains. Only ten men were apprehended. Of those, only two were convicted and sentenced to be hanged for treason. However, a short time later Washington pardoned them.

The Northwest Indian War 1785-1795

As result of the *Treaty of Paris,* Great Britain granted the United States control over the lands lying northwest of the Mississippi River all the way to Minnesota. There were also several long-standing treaties between the United States and some of the Native American tribes who dwelled in those areas. These agreements delineated the areas open for settlement by the Americans and those reserved for the Native Americans. According to the *Land Ordinance of 1785,* settlers from the various states were allocated lands on which they could build farms. The settlers purchased the land from the federal government at a discount, which was a good source of revenue stream for America.

The culture of the Native Americans, however, was very different from that of the Americans. Tribes were accustomed to establishing hunting grounds as they saw fit and followed the herds wherever they grazed. Therefore, the tribes tended to spread their hunting activities on to areas that overlapped the farms of Americans. It was a question of survival because herds tend to relocate frequently in search of water and grazing land. As a result, the tribes often attacked Americans who had fenced in the land. In addition, the tribes had signed treaties with the Americans with great reluctance after living many years without having to heed property rights or conform to American standards. To make matters worse, many of the Americans who settled in the Northwest broke treaties with the tribes and encroached on their lands too. Even the Indian agents hired by the government turned a blind eye to the abuses. There was also racial prejudice on the part of both Americans and tribesmen, because there was such a wide disparity in lifestyle.

To protect themselves from the settlers, some of the Native Americans formed the *Western Confederation* with the support of Great Britain which regularly supplied them with weapons to fight off the Americans.

This confederation fluctuated in terms of its membership due to the status and availability of the tribes. Among many others, the tribes consisted of:

Shawnee

Lenape, also called the Delaware Nation

Seneca

Cherokee

Chippewa and Ottawa tribes

Miami (This should not to be confused with Miami, Florida. They were the tribes in Indiana and Michigan.)

The Americans had an alliance with the Chickasaw and Choctaw tribes, who were bitter enemies with the tribes in the *Western Confederation.*

Battle of Heller's Corner

In 1785, George Washington launched a force of 1,400 men in Indiana under the leadership of Colonel John Hardin. His scouting party was led by Major James Fontaine and Captain John

Armstrong. Most of the tribes in this battle were from the Miami people. Little Turtle was their chief, and he is said to have been one of the cleverest of the tribal warriors. At Heller's Corner, he spotted the American forces and sent out a decoy, a lone tribesman, to lure them into believing he was returning to his village from a hunt. Hardin sent out a company of troops led by Major Fontaine, and they raced after the warrior only to find themselves in a deep swamp!

Hardin's remaining troops were then suddenly surrounded by many warriors and were heavily outnumbered. 129 militiamen were slaughtered.

Realizing that the situation was more alarming than he initially thought, Washington sent out a more vigorous force in 1791 under Major General Arthur St. Clair. It was difficult to recruit experienced men from the states to serve in the Northwest Territory, so many of the new soldiers weren't sufficiently trained and most lacked the kind of skills necessary to deal with the kind of tactics Native Americans employed. The tribes again were led by Little Turtle. In addition, he was joined by the chieftain, Blue Jacket, who led the combined forces of the Shawnees and the Lenapes.

Before even going into battle, many of St. Clair's new recruits deserted. These men had simply entered the militia seeking a brief adventure and grossly underestimated the hardships of serving in the military. St. Clair was also ill himself and that fact alone made him a mediocre model for his soldiers. Many of the deserters were picked off by the tribesmen who were following them.

Battle of the Wabash

In 1791, St. Clair then moved toward the Wabash River in Indiana. He had his militia set up a camp and instructed them to bring their weapons with them to their meals. However, they failed to do so and left their rifles stacked up near their tents on their first night there. Little Turtle and his warriors descended upon them *en masse* while they ate. Most of the terrified new recruits ran off. The more experienced soldiers, however, retrieved their muskets and fired off a couple of volleys. The native warriors then retreated into the woods and hid there. The warriors were outside the visual range of the soldiers, so the soldiers let up their guard. Suddenly, without warning, thousands of warriors surrounded one of St. Clair's battalions and killed as many as they could. St. Clair was forced to retreat with his remaining men, but was pursued by the warriors who nearly wiped all of them out.

Washington sought out Anthony Wayne, whom he knew from his sterling reputation during his service in the American Revolution. He was nicknamed "Mad Anthony Wayne" because he was a ferocious and fearless soldier of amazing agility and hit the enemy with overwhelming force. Anthony accepted the position of general. He then thoroughly trained American troops in forest warfare tactics, and they marched into the Ohio Valley to engage the tribes who were slaughtering the settlers there.

Battle of the Fallen Timbers

This confrontation took place around Toledo, Ohio in 1794. Wayne went into the region with his Chickasaw and Choctaw warriors. For their battlefield, the tribal warrior, Blue Jacket and some other tribes from the *Western Confederation* chose an area strewn with fallen trees as it would slow down the advance of Wayne's troops. Despite those obstacles, Wayne staged a bayonet charge, and his other troops surrounded the tribes on three sides. The warriors then fled to the Maumee region in Ohio where there was a British fort. Much to their surprise, the Native Americans were refused entry because Great Britain was reconsidering its relationship with the United States. Consequently, the warriors were then forced to disperse.

The Treaty of Greenville 1795

This treaty was made between the major tribal confederations and the Americans. It firmly established areas that would be open for

American settlements on areas West of the Mississippi in the state of Ohio and Southward through Indiana. The Ohio territory was the region most involved in the Northwest Indian War. Among the American signatories was General Anthony Wayne and Meriwether Lewis, an officer during the Whiskey Rebellion. The tribes were represented by Chief Blue Jacket and Little Turtle among others from the *Western Confederation.* Lewis later became part of the two-man team of Lewis and Clark who extensively explored the Northwest.

The Native Americans didn't utilize currency, so they received useful goods valued at $20,000 in exchange for ceding specified regions in the Northwest. In addition, they agreed not to use those lands for hunting and not to intrude on the lands belonging to settlers.

Chapter 10 – Washington Reelected

Even though George Washington longed to return to Mount Vernon, not just one, but both of the recently formed political parties nominated him to serve as president again. The Federalists nominated John Adams to serve another term as vice-president. The Democratic-Republicans nominated George Clinton, the governor of New York, as vice-president. Washington was then elected to serve another term and John Adams won a second term in his capacity as vice-president. Washington's second term ran from 1792-1797. His cabinet included:

1. Secretary of War – Henry Knox

2. Secretary of the Treasury – Alexander Hamilton; replaced by Oliver Wolcott, Jr. in 1795

3. Attorney General – Edmund Randolph (until 1794), William Bradford (until 1796), and Charles Lee (until the end of the term)

4. Secretary of State – Thomas Jefferson (until 1793), Edmund Randolph (until 1794), and Thomas Pickering (until the end of the term)

Washington realized that there were still some unresolved issues pending since his last term:

- Foreign affairs related to the French Revolution in particular

- The continued presence of British forts within the boundaries of the United States

- Unresolved issues left in abeyance since the signing of the *Treaty of Paris*

- The internal dissension in the government between Hamilton and Jefferson

The United States and the French Revolution

In 1789, the storming of the Bastille took place, initiating the French Revolution, which started as a civil war against an absolutist monarchy. The cry for liberty and freedom by the French was, in great part, influenced by the success of the American Revolution. Like America, they wanted social change. The French Revolution engendered positive American support because it was a struggle much like its own. But France wanted American support in more tangible ways by providing troops, money, and supplies. Because this occurred at a time when America was still desperately trying to pay back its war debt, Washington was vehemently opposed to providing American support. Washington was a practical man who kept meticulous records of his own expenses and understood the necessity of financial survival. A person or a country can be ruined by debt.

Thomas Jefferson and Alexander Hamilton supported France idealistically, but neither man wanted to provide American financial or military support. This was one of the few times that Jefferson and Hamilton agreed with each other.

The French Revolution expanded when the French attacked the British-owned Duchy of Holland in 1793. Great Britain, who had made its peace with America, was its greatest trading partner. By virtue of that relationship, they craved American support. France, on the other hand, had supported America in the Revolutionary War, so the French felt that America should ally with them. Therefore, the American government was wedged between the support of Great Britain and France.

After the expansion of the French Revolution, George Washington still felt that this was not the time to take a position in the dispute and issued the *Neutrality Proclamation of 1793*. It stated that America was not taking a position in the war between Britain and France, and the president threatened to take legal action against any American who violated that neutrality.

Neutrality Proclamation of 1793 and National Uproar

Washington's cabinet and Congress were opposed to becoming involved, because another war would not only increase American debt, but America might see nothing but war in its infancy as a new nation.

Many of the Americans supported France and some of the more idealistic among them wanted the U.S. to get involved. When Washington forbade Americans to privately take part in the French revolutionary war efforts, there was a louder outcry. In an anonymous letter to the president, one citizen said, "The cause of France is the cause of man, and neutrality is desertion." John Adams, his vice-president, wrote about the excitation of the people, stating,

> "Ten thousand people in the streets of Philadelphia, day after day, threatened to drag Washington out of his house, and effect a revolution in the government, or compel it to declare in favor of the French Revolution against England."

To quell American unrest and support his own agenda of strengthening the powers of the executive branch, Hamilton turned the issue into a partisan one. Under the pen name, "Pacificus," Hamilton wrote an essay bolstering support of Washington in the *Federalist*. He gave the essay a bias that supported the Federalist agenda when he said that all Americans should recognize that Washington, as President, knew what was good for the country and more respect should be given to the central government. Jefferson was furious about this partisan ploy. Although Jefferson agreed with the *Neutrality Proclamation,* he favored France. In response to Hamilton's article, Jefferson recruited James Madison to write a retort under the pen name "Helivicus." Again, the hostility between Jefferson and Hamilton resurfaced, much to Washington's annoyance.

Citizen Gênet – The First Political Refugee

Edmund-Charles Gênet was a French ambassador during the French Revolution when the Girondin political faction was in control. Gênet was an ebullient man and became very popular with Americans. He was sent to the United States to garner support for its war against Great Britain. Instead of presenting himself to Washington in Philadelphia, as was the accepted protocol for foreign representatives, Gênet sailed to North Carolina, commissioned some of the old British vessels seized during the Revolution and converted them into French privateering ships to raid English ships. Although he was aware of America's stance on neutrality, Gênet defied it and began recruiting Americans to staff those vessels. Not only that, but the clever man funded Democratic-Republican societies in the states.

The American administration demanded he stop the recruiting effort and return the ships he commissioned. Gênet privately threatened the administration, saying he would ignore the president and appeal directly to the American people. Hamilton leaked this out to the press. The American people were highly incensed that a foreigner would defy their well-beloved president and ceased their support of Gênet. At that time, France also beheaded their king, which served to change people's minds about supporting them anyway.

Next, Washington contacted France and requested that Gênet be recalled. When Gênet's vessel arrived in a French port, military officers searched his luggage, trying to confirm a wild rumor that he was transporting the missing French heir to the throne, a 10-year-old boy, back to France. After this, Gênet discovered that a new political faction had taken over. Since Gênet had been given his position as an ambassador under the Girondist faction, he would be dismissed and most likely arrested by political opponents. Fearing arrest and perhaps even the guillotine, he turned around and desperately returned to America. Observing the proper protocol this time, Gênet docked in Philadelphia and begged Washington for political asylum. In his generosity and magnanimity, the president welcomed him. Edmund Gênet became America's first political refugee.

Thomas Jefferson Resigns

In 1793, Jefferson still tried to draw Washington into his continuing differences with Hamilton by bringing up not only idealistic, but personal objections about Hamilton, even to the point of misquoting him. Washington's keen mind pierced through Jefferson's hidden agenda which he felt was the fact that Jefferson may have wanted Washington to dismiss Hamilton from the cabinet. The president wouldn't take the bait. Jefferson became frustrated, felt alienated, and quit his post. Washington was disappointed because Jefferson was not only popular with the people but he was insightful and talented in other ways. Edmund Randolph replaced him in 1794.

Fugitive Slave Act 1793

Washington tried to be discreet and secretive about his attitudes toward slavery, especially in Philadelphia where he had his headquarters as president. Pennsylvania had a gradual emancipation policy to which they scrupulously adhered. In addition, the majority of Pennsylvanians were Quakers who were also abolitionists. Washington's feelings about slavery evolved significantly over time, as he was conflicted about his belief in the equality for all, including slaves. It offended his innate sense of morality more and more strongly as time went on.

The *Fugitive Slave Act of 1793* implemented a clause in the US Constitution giving slave-owners the right to capture runaway slaves and bring them back to their houses or estates. Because it was written into the Constitution, Washington felt he had to sign it. That was eventually eliminated by the Thirteenth Amendment in 1865.

The Warring Brown Brothers: The Slave Trade Act of 1794

John Brown was an ambitious Rhode Island merchant. Aside from molasses, rum, and cocoa, he traded slaves, as his father did before him. His brother, Moses Brown, became a Quaker, and like his religious brethren, he owned no slaves as he believed in the principles of freedom for all. He was diametrically opposed to his brother's involvement in the slave trade. Moses started a well-publicized campaign to eliminate slavery altogether. Even though his efforts weren't always successful, he persisted through legal means to mastermind the passage of anti-slavery legislation in Rhode Island. His publicity efforts provided the major impetus for opposition to the slave trade in the Northern United States, and he contributed to the passage of the *Slave Trade Act of 1794* by Congress, forbidding the overseas shipment and sale of slaves to America. Predictably, that act backfired on Moses' own brother, John, who was the very first person convicted under the *Slave Trade Act*.

Washington wholly supported the elimination of the slave trade because it would be a gradual way to pursue elimination of the institution altogether. Washington said, "...it is among my first wishes to see some plan adopted by the legislature by which slavery in this country may be abolished by a slow, sure and imperceptible degree."

The John Jay Treaty 1795

Even though the British were expected to honor the *Treaty of Paris* after the Revolution, they maintained forts in New York, Vermont, Michigan, and Ohio. The John Jay Treaty specified the British forts within US territory and demanded that those forts be abandoned. Among them was a fort in the Maumee River region of Ohio, Fort Miami, where the tribes who were engaged in the Northwest Indian War attempted to seek refuge.

The British who had been providing the Native American tribes with rifles, guns, and ammunition agreed to discontinue that practice. In exchange, America agreed to permit the tribes to trade with the British in the Canadian territory without interference, with a clearer territorial boundary being set up between America and Canada.

In addition, the Americans agreed to grant Great Britain a "most-favored nation" status when trading with the United States and allowed Americans to trade with the British West Indies as well.

National Controversy

There were other key points introduced in the treaty which Great Britain refused to honor:

1. Discontinuation of the impressment of American seamen

2. Compensation for merchant ships seized during the American Revolution

3. Monetary compensation for kidnapped slaves belonging to Americans

This treaty was negotiated in secret at the behest of George Washington. He knew it would be very controversial so he didn't want interference during the negotiation stage. Once the treaty was signed and publicized, many people protested. Effigies of John Jay were burned in a number of states. A slogan was created and appeared in shop windows and houses of many towns. It said: "Damn John Jay! Damn everyone who won't damn John Jay! Damn everyone that won't put lights in his window and sit up all night damning John Jay!"

James Madison was its most vocal opponent and attempted, although futilely, to deprive funding to enforce this law. Washington and Alexander Hamilton were fervent supporters of the treaty. In a very close vote, the treaty was approved by Congress along with the funding for it.

Although Washington promoted and supported the John Jay Treaty, he also knew there were weaknesses in it. However, he was an immensely practical man and realized that this treaty was better than none at all.

Relations with Spain – Pinckney's Treaty of 1795

The American administration wanted to shore up its relations with Spain, because the Spanish had entered the war that raged in Europe. Spain was also concerned because it feared that England and the United States would form an alliance and the US would become a springboard to attack Spanish settlements in current-day Florida. In an attempt to prevent such an occurrence, Spain sent their ambassador, Manuel de Godoy, to make an initial contact with the president.

Washington jumped on this opportunity because he wanted duty-free access to the Mississippi River and the Port of New Orleans for the country. In 1793, Spain owned what is currently the state of Florida, the Port of New Orleans, and a Southern section of land that is now the state of Mississippi. That region severely restricted American shipping to New Orleans. Washington sent Thomas

Pinckney from South Carolina to Spain with the task of negotiating the matter. As a result of this treaty, a definitive border was established in the United States, and Spain agreed to permit America free access to the Mississippi. In exchange, the United States stated its intentions of friendship and peace with Spain, and would agree to drop the agreements made between former colonial officials for Spanish protection from the Yazoo tribes who claimed some of the land in southern Mississippi. This treaty established an open door to America for expansion into the West.

Foreign alliances, particularly permanent ones, bothered Washington. When Pinckney went to negotiate the treaty with Spain, the Spanish wanted America to sign an alliance with them. Washington specifically told Pinckney not to agree to an alliance, but to give Spain what they asked for anyway. He didn't want to be bound by other obligations to foreign countries in the future. This was an important feature that Washington emphasized in his farewell address.

Farewell Address

Washington asked Hamilton and Madison to present him with a draft for his final address to the people of the country. He declined to run again because he was tired, having been worn out by the wars he had fought and directed. He felt old before his time.

Two main threads of thought arose in Washington's farewell address: 1) that of avoiding foreign entanglements and alliances, and 2) the pitfalls of engaging too heavily in political party factions.

In terms of foreign relations, Washington stressed that commercial interests would be to America's benefit, but should be removed from the political stage. He said,

> "The great rule of conduct for us in regard to foreign nations is in extending our commercial relations, to have with them as little political connection as possible.... A passionate attachment of one nation for another produces a

variety of evils. Sympathy for the favorite nation, facilitating the illusion of an imaginary common interest in cases where no real common interest exists, and infusing into one the enmity over the other, betrays the former into a participation in the quarrels and wars of the latter without adequate inducement or justification."

Ever since 1792, when James Madison and Thomas Jefferson founded the Democratic-Republican Party, George Washington felt that political parties were not only divisive, but could betray national interests. He had painful memories of the arguments between Alexander Hamilton and Thomas Jefferson. So, when he gave his farewell address, he made a point of warning the American people about the problems created by political parties. He said,

"The alternate domination of one faction over another, sharpened by the spirit of revenge, natural to party dissension, which in different ages and countries has perpetrated the most horrid enormities, is itself a frightful despotism...The disorders and miseries which result gradually incline the minds of men to seek security and repose in the absolute power of an individual; and sooner or later the chief of some prevailing faction, more able or more fortunate than his competitors, turns this disposition to the purposes of his own elevation, on the ruins of public liberty."

Chapter 11 – Peace at Last

Home at Mount Vernon

At Mount Vernon, Washington could be more relaxed. He dressed in plain clothes, but was always very neat. It was his habit to rise very early—two hours before daybreak in the winter and at sunrise in the summer. He took a horse from the stables and visited some of his lands in the morning before breakfast. Despite the fact that he was in his mid-sixties, he was a graceful and sure rider. On one occasion, when Washington was entertaining his good friend, General Harry "Light-Horse" Lee, he inquired about buying two horses from him. To that request, Harry just laughed and politely refused to sell any to Washington. When asked why not, Lee replied that Washington would want them at a tremendous discount.

For breakfast, he usually had johnnycakes, honey, and tea before continuing with his rounds. His adopted son, George Custis, used to tell the occasional stranger who stopped by asking to see the president, "You will meet, sir, an old gentleman riding alone, in plain drab clothes, a broad-brimmed white hat, a hickory switch in his hand, and carrying an umbrella with a long staff – that person, sir, is George Washington!"

During the evenings, many people would come by to visit. Most of them were strangers, curious about what Washington looked like in person, and express appreciation for his services to the country. They were usually invited to dine with him and Martha.

He often mused with his guests about his own death, commenting that he wanted to hear ahead of time what others will say about him after his death. That way, he said, he might have a little while to correct whatever negatives might be brought up.

After dinner, he lit the candle at his writing desk and tried to answer all the letters he received, of which there were many. He and the Marquis de Lafayette, in particular, kept up a vigorous correspondence. Lafayette considered Washington a father figure to him and even named one of his children after the president.

Plantation Problems

When George Washington returned to Mount Vernon, he was faced with a problem related to the profitability of his plantations. His lands had suffered from years of neglect. In addition, his one-crop system of primarily raising tobacco was quickly becoming less and less cost-effective. The drawbacks he faced had to do with the soil depletion caused by tobacco, the fluctuating prices of the tobacco market, and the cost of using slaves to harvest the crop. Tobacco was very labor-intensive, and he had to give it up on all but a section of his land. Fearful that he might become destitute in his old age, Washington studied the new agricultural methods and hired experienced farmers to guide him.

In 1792, Arthur Young of England published several volumes called *The Annals of Agriculture and Other Useful Arts*. After reading some articles Young wrote, Washington wrote to Young with questions. As result, Young sent him his publication. Washington was very grateful for it, and wrote back to Young with the comment, "Agriculture has never been among the most favorite amusements of my life, though I never possessed much skill in art, and many years of total inattention to it…but shall return to it with hope and confidence." Young responded to Washington indicating that his skills as a good general would put him into a good stead for being successful with his new attempts in farming.

Washington immediately set out putting the new agriculture into practice. He ordered some Rotherham plows from Yorkshire and a threshing machine. He also invested in farm equipment such as ox carts, mortising axes, wheat and corn drills, shovels, and rakes with iron teeth. He also purchased a machine to gather clover seeds.

During his retirement, Washington experimented with all types of vegetables as the soil had a very high clay content. He had raised alfalfa for years, but eventually turned to chicory. Besides being used for salads, the Southerners, even to this day, use chicory as a flavor additive for coffee. When Washington kept livestock, it was used for animal feed.

By the time he retired, Washington couldn't be called a "planter" anymore, but a farmer.

George Washington and the Slavery Issue

In the 1700s, slaves were an integral part of the economy in agrarian states, particularly the South. Like many of the enlightened philosophical thinkers of the time who believed in liberty and equality for all, Washington was burdened with the obvious contradiction between human freedom and the ownership of an enslaved population in his presidential residences, his farms, and plantations. In 1799, he had 317 slaves. He first inherited slaves at the age of eleven.

With regard to the matter, Washington said he wanted

> "…to liberate a certain species of property which I possess very repugnantly to my own feelings, but which imperious necessity compels, and until I can substitute some other

expedient by which expenses not in my power to avoid (how well disposed I may be to do it) can be defrayed."

The "imperious necessity" of which he spoke appears to be a rationalization he created to explain why he kept slaves. Washington may have been afraid that he would outlive his wealth, and that he and his family would be destitute without the economic crutch slavery provided.

George Washington was a detail-minded and demanding administrator. The necessity of making changes to his agricultural methods in order to keep the land arable forced him to insist that his slaves learn new ways of doing things. Management of the farms was more strictly enforced, and Washington increased the burdens of his slaves. Washington also kept close track of profits and losses. His papers and records reveal meticulous calculations in terms of cost efficiency. His expectations of the quality of work from his slaves was quite high.

Despite his prejudices, it was said by visitors to Mount Vernon that he treated his slaves far more humanely than did other Virginians. Washington himself had criticized some of the other slave-owners who "...are not always as kind, and as attentive to their slaves as they ought to be."

Perhaps through a feeling of guilt or his personal warmth as a person, he kept his elderly and ill slaves, insisting that they continue to be supported by his estates for the rest of their lives. In addition, he opposed splitting up the families of slaves. When he was made Commander-in-Chief, a slave in Boston by the name of Phyllis Wheatley wrote a poem to him in which she said:

"Proceed, great chief, with virtue on thy side,

Thy every action let the goddess guide;

A crown, a crown, a mansion,

And a throne that shine with gold unfading,

WASHINGTON, be thine."

Washington wrote a letter of gratitude to her saying that he was undeserving of her tribute and that she was a strikingly talented poet. He also invited her to come and visit him, but it is unknown as to whether or not she did.

Washington's slaves were illiterate, so he wanted them to get a basic education and learn trades other than farming. He had his neighbors and friends, who were able and willing, to teach them some basic understanding of reading, writing, and arithmetic. He also hired people to teach them how to be carpenters, wheelwrights, millers, weavers, seamstresses, and midwives.

Changing Attitudes Toward Slavery

Prior to the Revolution, slavery was an acceptable practice. However, the principles of liberty and freedom for all were imprinted on his mind. He had lived through the consequences of tyranny and limits on freedom placed by the absolutist monarch in England. His views on slavery quickly evolved after that experience. In addition, he also discovered that many agrarian areas in the North didn't use slaves and yet were economically feasible, so he knew it could be done, but didn't know how.

Because the *Slave Trade Act of 1794* proposed a gradual change, Washington supported it. While it wasn't total abolition, it forbade the importation of slaves from overseas. In 1780, Pennsylvania had passed a law that the sons and daughters of slaves would become free at the age of 28. The states of Rhode Island, New Jersey, and Connecticut followed suit. These efforts had positive results as he observed farms in the North that weren't supported by the use of slaves prosper.

During the Revolution, Washington had also seen black soldiers fighting for the American cause. They were freed men, but had been inspired by the same ideals of all Americans. Although Congress discouraged the practice, it wasn't forbidden. So, during the Revolution, Washington proposed a technique of reorganizing some forces in the Rhode Island militias that mixed freed blacks with new white recruits. This was perhaps the first attempt at racial integration. It worked to a limited degree.

As he aged, Washington's economic need for slave labor decreased. He admitted that he had more slaves than was needed to support his farms. However, he had a dilemma. Washington loathed selling them because he no longer wanted to support the continuation of the institution of slavery. He said,

> "I have more working Negroes…than can be employed to any advantage in the farming system. To sell the overplus I cannot, because I am principled against this kind of traffic in the human species…What then is to be done? Something must, or I shall be ruined."

Washington was also afraid he would be impoverished if he freed all his slaves. If he freed the overage, he was afraid they would not be able to survive on their own. Likewise, he feared that some would abandon their families and create emotional hardship on those who chose to remain. In addition, they might be abused by the unscrupulous.

In his retirement, Washington tried to launch an experiment calling for some lots on his lands to be rented out to experienced Scottish and English farm managers. Washington intended to have some of his slaves become tenants on those farms and be freed. However, when Washington tried to find farm managers to take on the project, none were interested.

Chapter 12 – The Last Days of a Noble Man

Washington Called Back to Service

In 1798, Washington received a request from John Adams, the president at the time, to again return to the service of his country. Until that time, America had assumed neutrality in the European wars. However, in that year, France declared war on Great Britain and wanted American support. Because the United States maintained neutrality, France harassed American ships and forcibly impressed their sailors. To ameliorate that, John Adams sent secret ambassadors called "X," "Y," and "Z" to France. However, President Adams felt he needed to prepare for war just in case the situation couldn't be contained.

Washington hurried to Philadelphia to a meeting between himself, Alexander Hamilton, and Pinckney, both of whom were now major-generals. Although Adams had asked Washington to assume the position of commander-in-chief, Washington requested that he not serve in the field unless war actually broke out. Seeing that Washington had become feebler, Hamilton and Pinckney agreed but asked that he act as a consultant. Washington indicated that an initial force of 10,000 men should be assembled and trained. He also pointed out the fact that French military tactics would be much different from that of the British, and that they would attack rapidly and suddenly and move directly into the interior of the country. He advised Hamilton as to how best to recruit the men and suggested that America expand its very modest navy. When they noticed that Washington was getting rather exhausted as the days went on, Hamilton and Pinckney thanked him on behalf of President Adams, and he returned home.

Illness and Death

On December 12, 1799, Washington left to make his usual rounds at Mount Vernon. Although he left at 10 AM, he didn't return until mid-afternoon. It was a rough winter that year, and snow was falling that day. A frigid wind was blowing, but Washington felt that his heavy coat was enough. He had a brief repast, and then insisted on continuing to inspect his lands, as there were some trees he wanted cut down.

When he returned in the evening, he didn't change his clothes, which was very unlike him. The following day, the snowfall continued and became heavier. Washington indicated he would stay at home because his throat was very sore and he was probably coming down with a cold. His voice became very hoarse and he was becoming weaker, and he asked that someone read to him about the debates that took place at the Virginia Assembly about the election of a senator and state governor. In particular, he wanted to know what the representative, James Madison, said about the new nominee for president, James Monroe.

Washington seldom took medicine—a factor that may have helped him develop a rigorous immune system. However, he wasn't invulnerable to disease. His wife was extremely concerned when he could barely speak and had labored breathing. She sent out for the family doctor, and she had her husband take a drink of molasses, butter, and vinegar in the meantime, but he wasn't able to drink a drop. One of their servants was trained in the process of bleeding. This was a practice common in the 18th century, and it was believed that bodily toxins could be eliminated that way.

When the doctors arrived, he did another bleeding, and then had Martha call for two more doctors. All three doctors executed another bleeding, but it had no positive effect. They put a poultice on Washington's neck and helped him gargle with vinegar and tea, then prepared a steam inhalation of vinegar and water. They offered Washington something to drink, but he was still unable to swallow. Finally, though, he was able to swallow, due to the inhalations, but only a little bit. It did not help him very much, though, and he knew he was approaching death.

Washington was able to speak, but his voice was hesitant and still hoarse. He called for his personal secretary, Tobias Lear. Washington frankly said he wouldn't survive much longer, and asked Tobias to arrange his military accounts, settle his books and see to the accounting that still needed to be done.

The following day, he asked to be dressed and sat up in a chair for a while, but he had to lie down again. Martha, Tobias, and a few of his servants came in to join him. When his doctors came in, they raised him up in the bed just a little. Then, with great strain, Washington said, "I feel myself going, I thank you for your attention; but I pray you to take no more trouble about me, let me go off quietly, I cannot last long." After that, his family and his dear friends gathered around. His last words were "'Tis well." He then died peacefully. The date was December 14, 1799.

Cause of Death

George Washington died from what today's doctors call epiglottitis, a failure in the epiglottis, which is the "flap" that opens and closes over the windpipe while swallowing. It isn't a common disorder. Epiglottitis is often caused by a severe streptococcus infection that can be triggered by pneumonia. In addition, the excessive bleedings that doctors performed in the 18th century were also seen as an aggravating factor.

Slaves Freed by Virtue of His Will

In 1782, Virginia passed the "Manumission" bill permitting its residents to free their slaves in their wills or by choice. In fact, thousands of slaves were freed shortly after the passage of that law. George Washington decided to free all his slaves after he died. He wrote he did that "…as an act of atonement for a lifetime of concurrence in human exploitation." However, he couldn't free those slaves that were the legal property of his wife. Martha's former husband had slaves he bequeathed to her and George didn't have the legal right to free them, so they remained as her property. Several years after George died, though, Martha freed her own slaves. Many of them, however, elected to stay because they felt they were happy to be with her at the estate.

For at least thirty years after George Washington's death, some of his freed slaves returned periodically and volunteered to maintain the property around his tomb at Mount Vernon.

Conclusion

George Washington was an aristocrat but discovered within himself transformative qualities that converted him into a man with no airs or pretenses. He was ambitious but discovered that his ambitions were contagious. Leadership seemed to come naturally to him, so he was left with no other route but to inspire and lead. Loyalty is the reward of good leadership. And as he looked out at his ragtag regiments during the American Revolution, he felt the insatiable need to respond with his own loyalty to them.

Washington towered over other men, not only by virtue of his height, but by virtue of the strength he radiated. He was one of the rare commanders who was able to gallop in the front of a battalion which was falling back and motivate them forward despite enemy fire. Because of his fearlessness and courage, many battles were won that would have otherwise been lost.

Sharing the glow of freedom – that energetic force that coursed through the veins and arteries of his soldiers – Washington spent the winters at Valley Forge alongside them. George Washington never planned on being a president, but he knew he could do it and do it well. Power was something that needed to be shared in a democratic society, and he permitted Congress to sometimes choose unwisely and learn from their mistakes. He had to fight to get the John Jay Treaty passed in 1795, knowing it would reap disquiet. However, Washington was an intelligent man who knew that it was better to get the British to agree to some of its precepts, rather than reject the whole treaty.

Although he would have wanted to serve longer, he knew his body wouldn't permit him to. Slowly, he knew he was fading into the twilight of history and died happy commenting about the future of America: "'Tis well."

Part 3: John Adams

A Captivating Guide to an American Founding Father Who Served as the Second President of the United States of America

Introduction

John Adams once wrote, "People and nations are forged in the fires of adversity." That was very much Adams' experience. Although he was often maligned, he didn't deserve it. Having been born in the English colony of Massachusetts in 1735, he not only witnessed a new nation emerging from the shell of infancy, but he also participated in its growing pains. Adams was a man who was frequently asked to assume roles in which he had little experience, like that of a diplomat to France and England. In a sense, he was a part of the vanguard that the government had thrown into the fray.

But why would the government choose him to represent their interests? Perhaps the main reason was that John Adams was a lawyer and understood the legal significance of treaties and agreements. He was also a simple and objective man who knew how to get to the heart of an issue in quick order. However, the French and British were confused by his direct approach. They preferred charm decorated with solicitousness and obsequiousness, and Adams often had to tread water. Even his wife was criticized because her gowns weren't up to the standards of the nobility she encountered there. The one quality he had that aided him well during these times was the fact that he was tough and not easily discouraged. He threw all his energy into a task in order to serve his country.

John Adams was a deep thinker unless his ire was aroused. Generally, he tried to resolve the issues that most annoyed him. Unlike a lot of the other hot-headed Patriots during his time, Adams was well aware of his shortcomings. When asked to write the Declaration of Independence, he said, "I am obnoxious, suspected and unpopular." No doubt the members of the Continental Congress chuckled at that. Adams kept no secrets when it came to the way he felt, especially when it came to British officials. Even British General William Howe was made aware of this when Adams leaped up and led his delegation out of the room when he realized that Howe tried to resolve the Revolutionary War without the authority to draw up a treaty.

Historians have cast aspersions on Adams for conducting the secret XYZ Affair because it was ineffective. However, he was cheered in the streets of Philadelphia after telling the country that he turned down France's bid for peace because America was expected to offer generous bribes to French Foreign Minister Talleyrand in exchange for no interference in American shipping. Because he wouldn't pay the bribes, French privateers attacked the American ships. As a result, America feared engaging France in a war. Adams, however, was instrumental in limiting that war, known as the Quasi-War, to naval engagements.

Despite Adams' successes, the opposing party—the Democratic-Republicans—predicted that John Adams would be a one-term president. That he was, but it was due to a number of unfavorable factors—most of which were unavoidable. First of all, he had to raise money for a national navy and a military force. This created unpopular taxation, but those fleets and forces became crucial in the years that followed. Adams also witnessed some of the most vicious political battles between the Federalists and the Democratic-Republicans during his presidency. However, Adams was tough and weathered through that crisis.

Despite some of the controversial policies that John Adams enacted, he was a president that guided the young country of the

United States to its feet. It is to his credit that he was able to maintain neutrality while Europe waged yet another war. With the country still in its nascent stages, the country would have floundered under such a heavy debt and perhaps would have never become what it is today.

Chapter 1 – John Adams: Political Activist

In 1735, John Adams was born in Braintree (currently Quincy), Massachusetts, in a small saltbox house, a style that was typical of the colonial era and characterized by its sloping roof. Ever since he was born, John Adams' father, John Sr., planned on his son becoming a Congregational minister like he was. Although young John was raised in a family that was dedicated to pursuing and upholding the beliefs of the church, he himself had no inclination to join the ministry. When he was a young student, he often played truant while attending Latin school, and his intense dislike of the headmaster there also discouraged him from taking any interest in becoming a minister. Adams felt that some preachers "pretended sanctity" and sounded like "absolute dunces" when they addressed their congregations. However, he did appreciate the values imparted through religion, and his later writings reflected his deep sense of spirituality.

Besides being a minister, John's father was also a farmer. The family leased their land in the beginning, but later, Deacon Adams bought a nine-acre lot which he later expanded into a 35-acre estate. The Adams' family had an active orchard, as the family was quite fond of apple cider, and grew vegetables—mostly staples like corn and potatoes. The family also owned some barnyard animals who would graze on the slopes of their land. Braintree was truly a beautiful area to settle down and raise a family in. It was situated in a river basin and was very fertile. There were meadows, woods, and streams, and the people themselves were very friendly as well. The people of Braintree leased land from each other, and in times of drought, the entire community shared their food with each other. About the family farm and its environs, young John Adams wrote, "I take great pleasure in viewing and examining the magnificent prospects that lie before us in this town."

But Adams wasn't content to live there forever, and in 1751, he entered Harvard University. Like many young men in his position, he wasn't sure what career path to take. These were tumultuous times for the thirteen colonies who were under the dominion of Great Britain. By the time John Adams graduated from Harvard, most of his peers had entered the military to make a living. John didn't choose to follow suit as he wanted to make his mark on history. He felt that he could make more of an impact as a lawyer than a soldier. To earn money for his tuition in law school, Adams taught school in Worcester and then studied law under John Putnam, a respected attorney in the community. In 1758, he was admitted to the bar. Although he was offered a job as a registrar of deeds, he turned it down and returned home, hoping to find a more exciting opportunity. Back in Braintree, Adams opened a small practice to help clients resolve local legal disputes.

While living once again in his hometown, John met a woman named Abigail Smith, who intrigued him. She was straightforward in her speech and never hesitated in carrying on debates with Adams about politics and social issues. His father was fond of Abigail, but his mother was hesitant since Abigail was the daughter of a humble farmer. After noting that he continued to court her, his mother accepted her, and he married Abigail in 1764. They lived on the farm he inherited from his father, who had died in 1761. John had once fancied that he might become a gentleman farmer, but the unrest in Boston, and indeed in all of the colonies, became a paramount concern.

John Adams and the Stamp Act

Times were changing in the thirteen colonies. The Seven Years' War (1756-1763) was mostly fought in Europe, but a portion of the war spilled over into North America. That segment was called the French and Indian War. Great Britain had instigated it as they wanted to expel the French from the North American mainland to increase their colonial holdings. After the war ended in 1763 with a British victory, Britain needed to find a way to pay off the debt incurred from the Seven Years' War, and they looked at the colonies as a way to both pay back their debts and reap a profit.

John Adams and his neighbors began to voice their extreme discontent with the monarchy and Parliament in England, who high-handedly rejected any objections the Massachusetts Bay Colony made in regard to the tax burden. The whole colony festered with unrest. To keep abreast of the events that affected Massachusetts, John often attended many of the town meetings in Boston, which was located nearby. At one such meeting, he met James Otis, a prominent leader of the city, who vigorously talked to the residents about the injustice of the newly-passed American Revenue Act, also known as the Sugar Act, of 1764, which actually lowered the tax on sugar. However, the colonists resented taxes that the English themselves didn't have to pay and viewed them as an infringement on their rights. At that meeting, Otis shot up and with great fury shouted, "Taxation without representation is tyranny!" Having been heavily influenced by the dynamism of Otis, John considered using his own knowledge of the law in the political arena.

To raise revenue for Great Britain, the British Parliament passed the Stamp Act of 1765. This act required that colonists pay for a special stamp that was placed on many papers carrying written material. When John Adams heard of this, he became incensed. Lawyers often need to use voluminous amounts of paper for their legal documents, and this directly affected his practice. In response to this crushing tax, Adams penned a series of articles under the pseudonyms, "Humphrey Ploughjogger," and "Mr. U." In the fall of the year 1765, he had them published in the *Boston Gazette*. It was an effort to make the reaction of an ordinary colonist to the Stamp Act known to the British authorities. In the letters, he warned their governor that colonists would resist these acts by refusing to buy the English products they regularly sold to the colonies.

> I do say, I won't buy one shilling's worth of anything that comes from old England, till the stamp act is repealed, nor I won't let any of my sons and daughters; I'd rather the Spittlefield weavers should pull down all the houses in old England, and knock the brains out of all the wicked great men there, than this country should lose their liberty. Our forefathers came over here for liberty of conscience, and we have been nothing better than servants to them all along this 100 years.

One of the more scholarly pieces he wrote was entitled *A Dissertation on the Canon and Feudal Law*, and it was published in the *London Chronicle*. Adams felt that an intellectual appeal to Great Britain might coax them into examining the colonial grievances more objectively. He used references from history and pointed out how the mindless application of feudal ideas create slaves and leave societies in ruins. John Adams' cousin, Samuel Adams, on the other hand, was belligerent about the unjust taxation and suppression. He favored violent protests as opposed to peaceful resistance. Samuel often met with his countrymen in the low light of dusk under a tall old elm tree in Boston—later dubbed the "Liberty Tree"—and suggested in engaging in more violent protests against the British officials stationed in Massachusetts. Samuel Adams' group called themselves the Sons of Liberty, and it was decided from the onset that they would operate in secret. Their singular goal was to undermine the high-handed rule of the colonial governors and the red-coated regiments that patrolled the cities and countryside. While they started out simply burning an effigy of Andrew Oliver, a local tax collector, mob violence broke out in various quarters of Boston. The Sons of Liberty were also instrumental in the destruction of the home of the English-appointed lieutenant governor of the colony, Thomas Hutchinson. John Adams eschewed these acts of vandalism and continued to urge the people of Massachusetts to engage in passive resistance. He rejected violence as the most appropriate means to deliver a message, and that remained a goal throughout his entire life. Although John did eventually join the Sons of Liberty, it was with the purpose of keeping abreast of events in Massachusetts, as he still preferred the use of reasoning and the law as a means to right a wrong. Others, like James Otis and Boston selectman John Hancock, recommended this as well.

The Commonwealth of Pennsylvania and some of the other colonies hired the statesman Benjamin Franklin to represent them directly in England and present a case for a reduction in taxes. Due to Franklin's efforts, the mounting pressure, and rise in violent protests in the colonies, the Stamp Act of 1765 was repealed in 1766.

Townshend Acts

During the years of 1765 through 1770, England's Cabinet was undergoing a troublesome turnover. William Pitt the Elder was one of the most capable parliamentarians in England. He had the uncanny ability to assess a need and propose a practical solution. After Pitt campaigned with the prior Prime Minister Lord Rockingham for the repeal of the Stamp Act, King George III burdened him with the duty of selecting new Cabinet members. Unfortunately, though, Pitt became ill. This created problems because he now couldn't monitor the performance of the new Cabinet members he selected.

Charles Townshend was one of the men Pitt appointed, and he accepted the role of Chancellor of the Exchequer. Townshend was an energetic man, and he was eager to please the king because he was politically ambitious. Therefore, he was determined to obtain revenue from the colonists but only managed to compound the problem. Between 1767 and 1768, he convinced Parliament to approve a number of revenue-raising mandates:

- *The New York Restraining Act of 1767*

This act obligated the colonists to house and support British soldiers as they had been doing since the French and Indian War. Because so many of these soldiers were quartered in New York, this act was specifically written for them.

- *The Revenue Act of 1767*

Townshend was a clever man, and he determined what products could not be manufactured in the colonies and would need to be purchased from Great Britain, which included items such as glass, painters' pigments, tea, and paper. A tax was placed on each of those items.

- *The Indemnity Act of 1767*

The colonies often bought tea smuggled into the country by the Dutch because it was less expensive than the British tea. To help the floundering British East India Company, the British permitted the company to sell directly to the colonies. The colonists still had to pay a tax, but it was less than they had been paying, and the British hoped that this would spread some goodwill. However, this act infuriated the colonies because it helped create an English monopoly on tea.

- *The Commissioners of Customs Act of 1767*

Customs on products shipped to the thirteen colonies were administered by British officials in England. Great Britain then established customs houses in the colonies. Most of them were housed in Boston, and the purpose of this act was to make sure that the laws were enforced better and that smuggling decreased.

- *The Vice-Admiralty Court Act of 1768*

This was an effort to curtail the smuggling of goods from other countries. Although penalties had regularly been levied for smuggling, the cases had been tried in colonial courts. This act required that smuggling cases be heard by a court appointed by the Royal Navy.

John Adams: Clever Counsel

In 1768, a case came up before the Vice-Admiralty Court in Massachusetts related to the newly passed Townshend Acts. John Adams demonstrated his peerless abilities as a defense lawyer in this case, which was brought against John Hancock, a well-known shipper in Boston. The case was a prime example of the misapplication of two of the Townshend Acts—the Customs Act and the Vice-Admiralty Act.

Because of the smuggling that occurred in the port of Boston, the British officials were on high alert. An English warship, the HMS *Romney*, was sent to Boston to stand by in order to eliminate the incidents of smuggling.

When Hancock's ship was docked, the British Board of Commissioners attempted to board it to inspect the cargo. However, they lacked the proper paperwork, so Hancock refused to permit the inspectors aboard. When they returned the next day with the appropriate warrants, he had his men unload the vessel, which included 25 kegs of wine. Hancock then paid the taxes on the alcohol to Thomas Kirk, the customs official. Once that was accomplished, Hancock went home. However, the British agents tallied at the dock and began to think that his shipment of wine had been very small. They suspected that more wine had been offloaded into smaller vessels before the *Liberty* docked. The commissioners weren't required to inspect the smaller ships as they could easily dock and unload cargo. They would have let the matter go, but Thomas Kirk then changed his story. He told the British agents that Captain Marshall of the *Liberty* locked him in the hold and threatened his life if he reported anything amiss. To make matters worse, Kirk went on to say that he heard the sounds of seamen unloading cargo while he was being confined. This revised statement was then reported to Comptroller Benjamin Hallowell who instructed Joseph Harrison, the Customs Collector, to seize the vessel. Harrison alerted the HMS *Romney* and asked them to assist. A few seamen at the dock suggested that Harrison notify John Hancock before taking action, but Harrison ignored their advice. Therefore, the HMS *Romney* attempted to seize the *Liberty*, and a fight broke out. Eventually, the sailors calmed themselves down and disembarked from Hancock's sloop. Then the *Liberty* was seized. A crowd had noted this commotion from the shore, which swelled to about 3,000 people. They tore through the port district searching for Hallowell and Harrison but couldn't find them. So, instead, the angry colonists broke all the windows in Hallowell's house and hauled Harrison's pleasure craft ashore. They dragged it to the Liberty Tree where they watched it burn. Riots erupted all over the city. This frightened not only Hallowell and Harrison but the entire Board of Commissioners who sought refuge aboard the HMS *Romney*.

According to the court records, Hancock was charged with failure to pay the duties on the wine reportedly unloaded from his ship. Hancock denied it and retained John Adams as the counsel for his defense. Court officials arrived from Great Britain for the trial, but the case was poorly handled by the British authorities.

It also didn't help the British authorities that Adams' legal mind was like a vise, and he seized upon the errors and inconsistencies in the conduct of the British court officials. First of all, they hadn't appointed judges within the deadline specified, so Adams tried to have a mistrial declared because of that. Adams' next targets were the witnesses called by the prosecution. Because of his two disparate affidavits, Kirk's testimony needed to be corroborated. Therefore, witnesses were needed. However, the customs official who was serving with Thomas Kirk admitted he was asleep during the incident and was unable to testify. To make matters worse for the Crown, their star witness, Joseph Maysel, was a man who had a history of perjury, so he was rejected as a credible witness, and his testimony was never heard. Captain Marshall was the captain of the schooner at the time so he could have been called as a witness; however, he died before the trial took place.

John Adams also didn't argue on the basis of whether there was or wasn't wine smuggled from the *Liberty* when it was at sea. He argued on the technical grounds that 1) the Vice-Admiralty Court hadn't chosen its judges in time for the trial and missed the proscribed deadline, 2) the death of Captain Marshall, 3) the testimony of Thomas Kirk couldn't be corroborated, and 4) Joseph Maysel couldn't be cross-examined having been discredited as a witness. Due to the embarrassment caused by the inept officials and the riots this case triggered, the newly formed Vice-Admiralty Court decided to drop all the charges!

Chapter 2 – From Counsel to Patriot

Tensions in the colonies continued to be high, especially due to the presence of increasing numbers of British soldiers in or near the port of Boston. Mobs of colonists flocked around the city. On one occasion, a crowd gathered around a store owned by a known Loyalist. They shouted and threw rocks, breaking a window in his house. A customs officer who lived nearby responded by firing shots. Tragically, he accidentally killed Christopher Seider, an eleven-year-old. Emotions were already at a fever pitch, and this only managed to outrage the colonists more. British soldiers were on high alert.

Defense Attorney for the British Soldiers: The Boston Massacre

Fistfights between colonists and soldiers were commonplace all over Boston after the *Liberty* affair. On March 5, 1770, a riotous crowd gathered in front of a customs house, and British soldiers under the command of Captain Thomas Preston rushed to the scene. A colonist threw an object, knocking one of the soldiers down. Shots rang out upon the crowded street. Preston hollered out an order to cease fire, which they did, but it was too late. Sixteen colonists lay bleeding upon the cobblestones; five of them died due to their injuries. More soldiers raced to the scene. In an effort to quell the rioting public, Governor Thomas Hutchinson announced from the safety of town hall that Preston and his soldiers would be put on trial. The crowd then quieted down.

The Governor's Council scheduled the case for the end of October of that year and decided to hear the case at Castle William rather than Boston in an attempt to eliminate bias in the jury selection. In addition, there were no Bostonians on that jury.

There was some difficulty in naming an attorney for the defense, but as an honorable attorney, John Adams accepted the role of defense counsel. He believed that all people had the right to legal counsel regardless of their guilt, innocence, or public sentiment. In his defense, Adams carefully described the nature of the violence on the part of the colonists because they hit the soldiers' rifles with sticks and threw snowballs at them constantly. He indicated that it was a provocation on their end. In his closing statement, Adams said that a verdict should only be based on the facts of the case and not on the public sentiment toward Great Britain. He then quoted Algernon Sidney, an English parliamentarian, who said that the law "…is inexorable to the cries and lamentations of the prisoners…and deaf as an adder to the clamors of the populace." Two of the British soldiers were convicted, but the rest of the defendants, including Captain Preston, were acquitted. Today, Castle William is called Fort Independence.

After his experience defending the soldiers from the Boston Massacre, Adams felt that issues could still be resolved between the thirteen colonies and Great Britain, although it would take great effort. Adams' opinion changed considerably in the next two years, however, due to new, more repressive laws that applied to the thirteen colonies. These laws didn't apply to British citizens living in England, and since the citizens in the colonies viewed themselves as British citizens, they felt they were entitled to the same rights. Adams felt that the opinions that Great Britain had of the colonies had "undergone as many changes as the moon."

Transformation into Revolutionary

In 1772, the great statesman, Benjamin Franklin, was sent copies of thirteen letters sent from the governor of Massachusetts, Thomas Hutchinson, and the lieutenant governor, Andrew Oliver, to the British Parliament. These letters suggested that there should be a curtailment of the rights the Massachusetts colonists were originally entitled to as English subjects. Although Franklin didn't want the letters made public, John Adams felt that they should be. He said that Hutchinson had professed to be a defender of liberty, but his real sentiments were revealed in these letters. Adams had some of the content published in the *Boston Gazette*.

There were other changes afoot that affected the accountability of the governor and his top officials. The governors of Massachusetts had been paid for their services by the colonial legislature since the founding of the colony. The British government started paying the salaries of the colonial governors and judicial representatives in the colonies. This would shift the accountability of the provincial judges and representatives from the colonists to the Crown. During that crucial year, Governor Hutchinson gave a speech to the people of Massachusetts in which he insisted that the powers of the British Parliament over the colonies were absolute. The people were furious. In response, John Adams, Samuel Adams, and a lawyer and minister named Joseph Hawley III created a resolution that stated independence was a much better alternative than tyranny.

After the changes were made to the justice system as a result of the Vice-Admiralty Act of 1768, Hutchinson started applying its provisions by moving some of the trials from Massachusetts to England. This enraged the colonists. They couldn't afford to pay for colonial lawyers to travel to Britain and lodge there, and they also felt that the juries there would be biased.

The Boston Tea Party

Because the colonists had no representatives in the British Parliament, they viewed the Townshend Acts and the later Tea Act of 1773 as discriminatory and illegal. To protest their lack of representation in Britain, the citizens of Boston targeted the tea shipments, as it was the most popular drink in the colonies. In the winter of 1773, tea shipments arrived in Boston, but the people rejected it. Hutchinson responded by forbidding the ships to return to England with the tea, so they remained moored there in the harbor. John Adams wrote in his diary that accepting the tea would be tantamount to "giving up American posterity to ignominy, desolation and oppression and to poverty and servitude."

On December 16, 1773, the Sons of Liberty, some of whom were disguised as Native Americans, forcibly boarded the ships and dumped the tea overboard—over 92,000 pounds of it! This deliberative action was called the Boston Tea Party. John Adams said, "This destruction of the tea is so bold, so daring, so firm, intrepid and inflexible, and it must have important consequences, so lasting that I can't help but consider it an Epoch in History."

The British were vengeful. They felt that these colonists needed to be disciplined like naughty children, and their next move aimed to do just that.

The Coercive Acts

In 1774, Great Britain passed a series of punitive measures called the Coercive Acts. The passage of these laws wasn't as much of a legislative scolding as the Crown had hoped for. It was more of a provocation.

The Coercive Acts were called the Intolerable Acts by the colonists and consisted of the following:

> 1. *The Boston Port Act* – This closed the port of Boston until the destroyed tea had been paid for.

2. *The Massachusetts Government Act* – Town meetings in Boston were to be restricted, and the Governor's Council was no longer to be elected by the colonists; it was manned by people appointed by the governor, who served directly under the government of Great Britain.

3. *The Administration of Justice Act* – This allowed for British soldiers and sailors charged for offenses under the Massachusetts legislation to receive a trial in Great Britain if the royal governor deemed that a fair trial in Massachusetts was not possible.

4. *The Quartering Act* – This applied to all colonists and allowed for the quartering of British soldiers in buildings owned by the colonists, which were to be made available upon demand

5. *The Quebec Act* – This act, although not related to the other acts when it was passed in the British Parliament, was still seen as one of the Intolerable Acts by the colonists. This enlarged the boundaries of the Province of Quebec and granted reforms that were very favorable to the Catholics living in the region.

The First Continental Congress

In the fall of 1774, the colonists decided to meet in secret in Philadelphia after the passing of the Intolerable Acts, and Adams was one of the individuals chosen to attend as a delegate for Massachusetts. Peyton Randolph, a wealthy planter from Virginia, was elected as the president of the Congress. Adams was very active in 1774 and met with all of the influential leaders in the colony at every meal, the tavern at night, and at the regularly scheduled meetings in Carpenter's Hall. The first issue discussed was the implication of the Intolerable Acts. He listened very carefully to what people said and recorded the comments he felt were crucial in framing a colonial reaction. Some of the delegates from Massachusetts were Samuel Adams; Thomas Cushing, a vociferous and popular lawyer and merchant; and Robert Treat Paine, a conservative who felt that reconciliation with Britain was still possible. Members of the First Continental Congress split along two lines: the conservatives and the rebels. For 22 grueling days, they argued. Adams spent a great deal of time trying to develop a compromise. Although some of the delegates felt it was futile, the Continental Congress decided to send a letter of grievances to King George.

One of the grievances on the list had to do with Massachusetts. In 1774, Thomas Gage replaced Hutchinson as governor. However, Gage was also the British general in charge of the colonies. The grievance stated: "The Commander-in-chief of all your Majesty's Forces in North America, had, in a time of peace, been appointed Governor of a colony." To the colonists, there seemed to be a conflict caused by serving in both capacities.

Among the other grievances were objections to the fact that the colonists had no representation in the British Parliament, the alteration of the justice system which had affected the impartiality of the judges, the many duties and taxes that were levied on the colonists, and the quartering of British troops on private property belonging to the colonists. As a lawyer, John Adams was particularly perturbed by the alterations in the justice department. Adams objected to the fact that the colonist's right to a trial by a jury of his own peers was now changed because of the Vice-Admiralty Court Act. A colonist could now be coerced into going to a court where Royal Navy officials would preside and no colonial peers would be allowed to participate in the jury.

The letter was overly polite and regularly punctuated with compliments for the fairness of the king. In parts, it begged for relief but confirmed loyalty to England by stating to the king, "Your royal authority over us and our connection with Great Britain we shall always carefully and zealously endeavor to support and maintain." One of the most conservative members of the First Continental Congress was Joseph Galloway, a lawyer from Pennsylvania. He was very critical of the letter of grievances. Galloway was against any revolutionary violence and was a self-admitted Loyalist. He did, however, prefer that legislature be established in the colonies similar to the House of Commons in England. To promote his opinion, Galloway presented a meticulously worded proposal to be sent to Great Britain. It was totally rejected. Disgusted by what he considered traitorous discussions, he stormed out before the meeting was adjourned. The man then impulsively joined General Howe's British regiment! Despite the fact that many colonists felt their rights were being infringed upon, there were still quite a few who remained loyal to the Crown, which often only furthered the tensions felt in the colonies.

In the middle of their discussions one day in September, the session was interrupted by the sudden arrival of Paul Revere. Rushing into the meeting room, Revere presented the Suffolk Resolves. They were composed by Dr. Joseph Warren, president of the provincial council of Massachusetts. The Suffolk Resolves proposed that the council continue to meet despite the fact that the governor had prohibited such meetings. In addition, the Suffolk Resolves asserted that Massachusetts should state its non-allegiance with the governor and end all trade with Great Britain. The Continental Congress endorsed these resolves. The delegates agreed that their respective colonies should participate in the embargo and encourage self-reliance so the colonies could manufacture what they need rather than depend upon shipments of British-made products.

As part of the agenda, it was recommended that the colonies set up their own militias and collect weapons and military equipment. Many, if not most, realized that war was inevitable and imminent.

Earlier in the sessions, Adams and the Continental Congress had received an inaccurate report delivered by a special messenger on September 6 that reported soldiers had fired on people in Boston. Patrick Henry was quick to respond, "The distinctions between

Virginians, Pennsylvanians, New Yorkers and New Englanders are no more. I am not a Virginian, but an American." In actuality, the alleged incident was exaggerated because there was no shooting. As a precaution against any hostile actions, Governor Gage and his men started checking out some of the magazines and armories in the area. They were observed by some of the colonists, and news of this search, later dubbed the Powder Alarm, raced around the colonies along with its inaccuracies. After hearing the report, the Sons of Liberty quickly formed a militia and marched toward Charlestown. When General Gage discovered that, he kept a cautious watch on Massachusetts. After the initial session of the Continental Congress was adjourned, Adams published a series of letters in the *Boston Gazette* under the pseudonym "Novangelus." In essence, these letters alerted colonists to not let the British remove their rights as citizens lest they become like the vassal states of Europe and incur hardships as a result.

After the Powder Alarm occurred, Massachusetts set up an alarm system by which local residents and colonial leaders would be notified if there was unusual activity on the part of the British soldiers in the colony, specifically if they left Boston where they were stationed. This system was extremely useful as it served as a way to alert the local militias to arm themselves and defend the colonists against any aggressive actions. Members of the group whose job it was to initiate the alarm were called Minutemen, and they were among the first to fight in the upcoming war.

Chapter 3 – The Second Continental Congress

The Conciliatory Resolution

In February of 1775, several influential members of King George's Cabinet attempted to avoid the pending war with the colonies with what was entitled the Conciliatory Resolution which would grant some of the colonists' demands. The original proposal was penned by William Pitt the Elder, who had been ill but briefly returned to his post as prime minister. He had a reputation for being more liberal in dealing with the colonies and proposed that more freedoms should be given to the colonies so they could rule themselves. Also, Pitt felt that some of the provisions of the Coercive Acts should be repealed. There were reportedly fierce arguments that followed the presentation of Pitt's proposal, so only a weakened version was passed and sent to the individual colonies. It indicated that the colonies who were willing to pay for the common defense and administer justice against those who resisted British authority in the colonies would be excused from paying some taxes but not those that would interfere with control of commerce.

The Battles of Lexington and Concord

As a result of the work of the First Continental Congress, the colonists began building up storehouses of arms. Many of these were on the private properties of the colonists since they knew the British were aware of the location of armories and weapons depots in the colonies. Boats came ashore at the Charles River toward Charlestown near the road to Lexington and Concord. The Minutemen that spotted them sent out an alert about Gage's activities, and at nightfall on April 18, 1775, one of the church officials hung two lanterns in the steeple of the Old North Church. The prearranged signal was that one lantern meant the British were arriving via a land route (which would have taken longer) and two lanterns meant they were coming by sea. Those two lanterns informed the colonists that the British were coming inland from the Charles River. Three Patriots, Paul Revere, William Dawes, and Samuel Prescott, rode through the local towns, spreading the word. Shortly after that, the colonial militia met with John Adams and John Hancock briefly at Lexington Common, which was south of the Charles River. Gage organized a unit of 700 British soldiers and gave them orders to search the colony of Massachusetts for weapons. The men concluded that Gage and the British redcoats were going to head for Concord where there was a weapons depot. All the weapons in it had already been hidden, but the British didn't know that. Since the British force was so large, the colonial militia dogged them. Several hundred townspeople also arrived. Major John Pitcairn, leading the British out of Lexington, saw the militia near a bridge and commanded them to disarm. The militia, under Colonel John Parker, didn't comply. A shot was fired; it is still unknown to this day which side shot first. The British then let loose a volley of shots. Eight members of the militia were killed, and ten men were wounded.

From there, the redcoats marched on to Concord in search of weapons. The colonial militia confronted them there also. Gunfire erupted, and 73 British soldiers were killed. The colonists lost 49 men, including one of their commanders, Isaac Davis. John Adams recorded in his diary, "The battle of Lexington, on the 19th of April, changed the instruments of warfare from the pen to the sword."

Adams rode to a local militia encampment at Cambridge (formerly Charlestown) and remarked that there was "great confusion and much distress." He also noted there wasn't enough artillery and provisions there. Following that visit, Adams rode the route where the battles had taken place, asking questions of the inhabitants. After those conversations, he was convinced that the colonies had reached the point of no return. The war had begun.

As he was preparing for his journey to Philadelphia for the Second Continental Congress, Adams realized that a revolutionary fever had infected everyone he met. By the time he reached Philadelphia, crowds of people had gathered around Adams and those he had traveled with on the way there.

On the Way to Independence

The Second Continental Congress assembled in 1775 and ran until 1781. The same delegates that collected in Philadelphia were the same as those at the First Continental Congress, along with some new delegates which included Thomas Jefferson, the young statesman from Virginia, as well as James Wilson, an accomplished lawyer, and Benjamin Franklin, a prolific writer and inventor, from Pennsylvania. Lyman Hall represented Georgia, the only colony without a delegate at the First Continental Congress. At the time, that colony was having a problem with a Native American rebellion and needed the support of British troops, so they had refrained from attending. John Hancock was another delegate sent from Massachusetts. Adams knew Hancock from when he had defended him on the charge regarding his shipping business. Peyton Randolph, an established attorney, was elected the president of the Congress again, but the very popular Hancock replaced him later on when Randolph was called back to Virginia by the governor.

The first item on the agenda was what came to be called the Olive Branch Petition. It was proposed and written by John Dickinson, the author of the *Letters from a Farmer in Pennsylvania* which were written in protest to the Townshend Acts. Unlike many of the other delegates, Dickinson felt that there was a clear distinction between Parliament and the king. Therefore, he felt that another petition should be sent directly to the king so he could redress the grievances of the colonies, which might result in reconciliation with Great Britain. A few others in the Congress supported the petition as well.

John Adams, however, rejected the Olive Branch Petition, and other delegates agreed with him. A debate followed. Adams stepped out of that assembly briefly, but Dickinson followed him into the yard and argued with him vehemently, saying "If you don't concur with us in our pacific system, I and a number of us will break off from you in New England, and we will carry on the opposition by ourselves in our own way." John Adams was angry and retorted, "I am not to be threatened into an express adoption or approbation of measures which my judgment reprobates." Adams and Dickinson never spoke to one another privately again during the meeting. Despite the protests against it, a sufficient number of delegates voted that the Olive Branch Petition be sent to the king, and so, it was.

The next item on the agenda had to do with making a declaratory statement related to the rights of the colonies to provide arms for their quickly forming militias. Although that task had already begun after the First Continental Congress, Benjamin Franklin felt that a workable procedure needed to be specified in writing. John Dickinson wrote the final draft, working upon the earlier draft written by Thomas Jefferson, called the Declaration of the Causes and Necessity of Taking Up Arms which was adopted in July of 1775.

The Conciliatory Resolution proposed by Britain had finally reached the Continental Congress and was discussed at length.

John Rutledge, a lawyer from Charleston, South Carolina, asked the crucial question, "Do we aim at independence? Or do we only ask for restoration of rights and putting us on our old footing as subjects of the crown?" The Congress split into two factions over the matter. Even those who felt that a war might be necessary imagined that just the Battles of Lexington and Concord would be sufficient to convince Great Britain to put the colonies back on the same footing they were before the heavy taxation was imposed. In addition, there were London merchants who petitioned England to reconcile, so that trade could be normalized. Some of the merchants in Philadelphia and New York were in favor of reconciliation.

The opposition, however, felt that the resolution was "too little, too late," and they made an issue out of the fact that the colonies weren't even permitted to raise their own revenues to provide for themselves in terms of defense and justice. Throughout the summer of 1775, those in favor of reconciliation weakened. Realizing that they weren't even going to be funded for curtailing raids from Native Americans and had little by way of supplies for border protection, the colonists drew up regulations to guide the state militias plans for a rudimentary navy and took over foreign policy.

John Adams then stood up in the assembly, stressing that this was an issue that required patience. He said, "We must suffer people to take their own way" although path they take may not be the "speediest and surest." The Congress took fourteen months to discuss the Conciliatory Resolution, but also remembered the words of King George III who said that the hostilities in the colonies formed a "wicked and desperate conspiracy." Suggestions arose in Congress about the creation of an army. James Wilson of Pennsylvania objected. However, despite that Congress rejected his opinion about making yet another overture of peace. In the heat of the moment, Samuel Adams leaped up and called those who supported reconciliation the "tools of a tyrant."

John Adams then boldly proposed that the Congress appoint a general. Adams felt that there was one member of the Congress well suited for that role, and that man was George Washington. A large militia unit was already in Charlestown, Adams added, and an army could start with them. The assembly concurred, and Washington became the commander-in-chief of the Continental Army. Washington was ready for the challenge, so he immediately left the Congress in order to recruit troops.

In the summer of 1775, Richard Penn, the lieutenant governor of Pennsylvania, and Arthur Lee brought a copy of the Olive Branch Petition to Lord Dartmouth, the British representative in the colonies and asked for a response. Dartmouth forwarded it to England and reported back a month later, "We were told that as his Majesty did not receive it on the throne, no answer will be given." However, this is not what happened. The British already knew its contents because they intercepted a packet of letters aboard a ship. One of the items in the packet was a private letter from John Adams to a friend that showed he wasn't in favor of the petition. The British were aware that John Adams was an influential leader among the colonists, and the British realized that there wasn't a consensus among the people. The Olive Branch Petition also reached England around the time of the Battle of Bunker Hill, so it became a moot point anyway.

The Battle of Bunker Hill

While the Second Continental Congress was in session, colonial militiamen heard a rumor that the British planned on fortifying the hills around Boston. To prevent British infiltration into the colony, Colonel William Prescott sent in his men to occupy those positions under cover of darkness. On the morning of June 17, 1775, the British, under the command of General William Howe, attacked them. Even though the colonists had the advantage of higher ground, they lost the battle because their ammunition ran out. Despite their victory, the British incurred a lot of casualties.

Following that, King George III issued the Proclamation of Rebellion. It stated that portions of the colonies were in "open and avowed rebellion" against Great Britain. Even though the American supporters in England told their monarch that the actions of the British were driving the colonies toward declaring independence, he persisted in getting the proclamation passed.

Two months later, Great Britain passed the Prohibitory Act, which essentially closed all of the ports of the colonies to foreign trade. When that act was passed, the Continental Congress sent the Connecticut merchant, Silas Deane, on a secret mission to France to secure weapons and assistance in furthering their cause. Deane secured heavy weapons along with the help of the famous Major General the Marquis de Lafayette. Deane was also instrumental in smuggling badly needed goods to the colonies during the closure of Boston Harbor. Some of those supplies arrived in North Carolina and were shipped north, and more were brought to the Continental troops with Lafayette's assistance.

The Lee Resolution

In 1776, Richard Henry Lee made a motion, recommending that a resolution be passed declaring independence of the colonies. That body would, he said, "best conduce to the happiness and safety of their constituents in particular, and America in general." John Adams seconded that motion. This resolution was carefully reworded and called the Lee Resolution. The proposal was approved in May of that year, and the stage was set for the writing of the Declaration of Independence. Three committees were appointed to develop the wording of the resolution, and Adams himself served on two of the three committees.

The final resolution, completed in July of 1776, stated:

> Resolved, that these United Colonies are, and right ought to be, free and independent States, that they are absolved from all allegiance to the British Crown, and that all political

connection between them and the State of Great Britain is, and ought to be, totally dissolved.

That it is expedient forthwith to take the most effectual measures for forming foreign Alliances.

That a plan of confederation be prepared and transmitted to the respective Colonies for their consideration and approbation.

The Declaration of Independence

One of the committees that arose from the Lee Resolution was known as the Committee of Five. They were tasked with the job of drafting a statement that declared the colonies' independence to the world. The Committee consisted of John Adams, Thomas Jefferson, Benjamin Franklin, Roger Sherman of Connecticut, and Robert Livingston from New York.

After outlining the general principles of freedom, many of which were inspired by Thomas Paine, an English statesman, and discussing its content, Jefferson suggested that John Adams write the initial draft of the Declaration of Independence to present to the Second Continental Congress to vote upon. He declined Jefferson's recommendation, saying:

> Reason first: You are a Virginian and a Virginian ought to appear at the head of this business. Reason second: I am obnoxious, suspected and unpopular. You are very much otherwise. Reason third: You can write ten times better than I can.

Virginia was generally recognized as the wealthiest of the thirteen colonies so having their approval was of the utmost importance. John Adams was also a forceful man who recognized his own limitations, one of them being a tendency to be abrasive at times. Thomas Jefferson was noted as a prolific writer and had received many accolades for the quality of his writing. Therefore, the

Committee approved of Thomas Jefferson to write the first draft of the declaration.

As per his reputation for speed, Thomas Jefferson produced the Declaration of Independence in 17 days. Other members of Congress made some changes, and it was then sent out to all the colonies for ratification.

While the Declaration of Independence was circulating throughout the colonies, more British warships were arriving in the port of New York. George Washington scrambled to set up fortifications on the western end of Long Island in the area currently known as Brooklyn, but Manhattan Island itself was poorly defended. The colonial troops were fresh and inexperienced because Washington didn't have sufficient resources to train them. Not only that, but some of the new recruits were insubordinate, and some quit when Washington initiated a program of discipline. The Continental Congress recognized this and appointed Adams as the administrator of the Board of War and Ordinance. Adams realized that soldiers should be paid for their services and that they needed an incentive to fight in addition to patriotism. Therefore, as his first act, Adams had the Continental Congress pass resolutions providing salaries and a grant of land for the men if they remained in military service. In addition, he had regulations passed regarding discipline and set up a special committee to arrange for provisions and supplies.

On July 4, 1776, the Declaration of Independence was passed. But because the War for Independence was happening faster than military preparations were progressing, New York fell to the British. General William Howe, who replaced Thomas Gage as the head of the British army in the colonies, attempted to put the war to an end and called upon the colonies to send representatives to Staten Island for a conference. John Adams, Benjamin Franklin, and Benjamin Rush, a physician from Philadelphia, met with him. Howe tried to assuage the group by saying that he viewed them as legitimate British subjects. To that, Adams replied, "Your

Lordship may consider me in what light you please, except for that of a British subject." After fruitless discussions with Howe, the delegation realized that General Howe had no authority to formulate a treaty anyway, and they promptly left.

The Articles of Confederation

In 1776, at one of the sessions of the Continental Congress, the colonists realized that they were acting in the capacity of a government that was separate from that of British America. The Continental Congress appointed John Dickinson to head a committee whose purpose was to draw up a united plan for a government that had representation from each of the colonies. The Congress then contacted the colonies and informed them to set up local governments of their own and write their own constitutions. After that happened, the Congress proposed that the colonies call themselves "states." This conversion of the term from "colony" to "state" had to be ratified by each colony, and it wasn't until 1790 that the entire process was actually completed.

Expenses related to the funding of a united government was also an issue. The Continental Congress finally decided that the financial obligations of each state would be determined upon the relative physical size of each state.

The tools and procedures for functioning as a representative government also needed to be clarified. The Congress drew up a series of thirteen articles, called the Articles of Confederation, to which each state would adhere. Amendments could be added to those articles via a voting procedure which required that at least two-thirds of the states approve them. The Articles of Confederation, after much debate, was passed in 1781.

This finalized structure was commendable, but some glaring factors were overlooked. Although there was a voting procedure in place, there was no consistent system enacted to levy and collect taxes, regulate trade, and conduct commerce, no set policy for conducting foreign affairs, no standard monetary policy, no national army or navy, and no judicial system for enforcing laws. In addition, no one particular person or persons were in charge of the new country, and there was no staff to support them.

The weaknesses of the Articles of Confederation became a stumbling block for John Adams in the years to come when he was called upon to function as a diplomat.

Chapter 4 – John Adams: Diplomat & Constitutionalist

As the administrator of the Board of War and Ordinance, Adams knew that the states weren't likely to win the Revolutionary War without the assistance of other nations. He presented this dilemma to the delegates of the Continental Congress, and they agreed. To attract the support of France in the war effort, Adams presented the idea that a favorable trade agreement might arouse their interest. At that point, though, the war wasn't going well, so France would have been unlikely to respond to a direct request for military assistance.

It was a known fact that Benjamin Franklin was popular in France due to the intense interest of the French in many of his innovative inventions. They also enjoyed him personally. Therefore, the Congress sent him there as a goodwill ambassador with the hopes that he might be able to convince France to offer military assistance. Having heard about the colonists' desire for independence from Silas Deane who consulted with him the year before, Lafayette was enthusiastic about helping out and went to America unofficially in 1777. When he was introduced to George

Washington, they related to each other so well that they became lifelong friends. Due to Franklin's endeavors, a very skilled Prussian lieutenant, Baron von Steuben, who was in France on business, also expressed an interest, so he traveled to America to help as well. One of von Steuben's greatest strengths was his ability to train new recruits. He did that at Valley Forge, Pennsylvania, where the Continental Army was encamped for the winter. The colonial soldiers loved him as he was very humorous and witty. In later years, John Adams' son, Charles, lived with von Steuben for a time. It was rumored that they were homosexuals.

John Adams: Commissioner to France

Back in the states, the Continental Congress was growing impatient. Franklin was already over in France, but there was no commitment yet on their part. So, in November of 1777, they appointed John Adams as a commissioner to France to obtain an agreement. Arthur Lee, who had written some intense essays against the Townshend Acts, was also sent there as an aide in the negotiations. The journey across the Atlantic was hazardous, and they arrived later than they expected. Shortly after they had arrived, Adams and Lee conferred with Franklin to develop a treaty. Adams himself wrote the original draft. The French foreign minister, the Comte de Vergennes, signed the Treaty of Alliance and Treaty of Amity and Commerce but only after hearing about the Continental victory at the Battle of Saratoga in 1777. After that battle, France finally felt that the colonists' resolve was strong and that they might have the ability to win against France's perennial enemy, England.

Adams and Lee then met with Franklin to make some changes to the treaty to have them approved. The three commissioners had many differences among themselves, though. Adams felt that Franklin came across as too loyal to the French and seemed to be too old for the job. Lee, on the other hand, disliked Franklin intently and refused to cooperate, so he was sent to Spain to attempt to get their help. Adams, however, endeavored to create a working relationship with Franklin. Adams was concerned that France had yet to take any action to aid the states and contacted de Vergennes in that regard. However, Adams was unaware that de Vergennes was also focusing on the newly declared war between Britain and France over control of the West Indies when he suggested that France send over a naval fleet. De Vergennes was incensed about what he considered to be Adams' impertinence. He also disliked Adams because he spoke French very poorly. During the course of their negotiations, Adams admitted to de Vergennes that the value of their dollar had dropped. De Vergennes insisted that Adams write to the Continental Congress to get them to restore the dollar to its original value when trading with France under the treaty. That would, of course, cause a delay in the negotiations, but it was more of a tactic by de Vergennes to get rid of Adams for a while.

Adams still voiced his frustrations at the lack of progress on France's behalf though. The treaty with France had been made two years prior, and while France had dispatched Jean-Baptiste Donatien de Vimeur, better known as simply the Comte de Rochambeau, to assist George Washington in 1780, France had yet to do anything of significance. While Adams furiously wrote letters about this, de Vergennes wrote his own to the Continental Congress and informed them that he would only work with Franklin, and he later informed Adams of the same. Adams' diplomatic mission was the result of mishandled efforts on the part of an immature nation not yet familiar with dealing with foreign powers and who was also not careful enough to keep all channels of communication open.

Ambassador to the Dutch Republic

In 1780, John Adams went to the Dutch Republic. He didn't initially go in an official capacity, but he was later assigned the role of ambassador to the States-General, the administrative body of Holland. Adams knew that America desperately needed a loan, not only to help finance the war but to pay off their war debt. He sent numerous letters to the Dutch government, but there was no response, and many of the banks that Adams approached were reluctant to meet with him. One of the reasons for this was the fact that Holland hadn't yet recognized the right of America to achieve independence from Great Britain. The Dutch also depended heavily upon England for trade and wanted to remain neutral in the American War of Independence. Interestingly, the Dutch proposal of neutrality angered the British and drove them to declare war on Holland at the end of 1780. During the following year of 1781, the British Lieutenant General Charles Cornwallis surrendered to George Washington at Yorktown, Virginia, and the American War of Independence was over.

In April of 1782, Adams finally received a response from the Dutch government and met with Prince William V of Orange. Holland finally recognized American independence in exchange for a Treaty of Amity and Commerce between America and their own country. In October of 1782, Adams made a proposal to that effect, and Dutch officials signed it after making a few changes. Adams then proudly stated in a letter to Robert Livingston,

> Upon the whole, I think the Treaty is conformable to the principles of perfect reciprocity, and contains nothing that can possibly be hurtful to America, or offensive to our allies, or to any other nation, except Great Britain, to whom it is indeed, without a speedy peace, a mortal blow.

Once the Dutch treaty was signed, Adams met with Joan van der Capellen, a Dutch nobleman who was a champion for the American cause. He had met der Capellen earlier, but the financier wasn't willing to commit any funds without his government's acknowledgment of American independence. To further aid John Adams, der Capellen introduced him to some bankers and advocated a loan for America. Due to van der Capellen's intercession and the new treaty, two very prominent bankers came forward to help America's cause—Nicolaas van Staphorst and

Wilhelm Willink. When Adams returned to America, he had a guaranteed loan of two million dollars.

The Yorktown Campaign: End of the American Revolution

Before Adams made progress with the Dutch though, the war had already come to an end. In 1781, the American Revolution involved the land forces commanded by George Washington, the Comte de Rochambeau, and the Marquis de Lafayette. These troops marched the entire length of the United States from Pennsylvania and Delaware all the way to Virginia. Naval forces paralleled them at sea in the Atlantic and were led by French fleets under François Joseph Paul, the Comte de Grasse, and Jacques-Melchior Saint-Laurent, known as the Comte de Barras, of the French Navy. The American land forces and the French naval forces combined were massive. The British land forces were heavily outnumbered, and they only had a small number of warships—about 63—and those were reportedly small.

Lieutenant General Charles Cornwallis had been the general in charge of the British forces in the south. In 1780, he was defeated at the Battle of Kings Mountain in South Carolina and again failed at the Battle of Cowpens, also in South Carolina, in 1781. He was promised reinforcements by General Henry Clinton, who was in Philadelphia. However, those reinforcements were delayed and didn't leave the harbor until a month later. In the meantime, Cornwallis sent out a message to Clinton, saying, "If you cannot relieve me very soon, you must prepare to hear the worst." The Continental Army and the French Navy soon after began a siege on the city of Yorktown, Virginia, on September 28. Although Cornwallis attempted to escape via the nearby waterways at Gloucester, he was unsuccessful. On October 19, 1781, he surrendered. He then sent General Clinton a letter stating:

> Sir, I have the mortification to inform your Excellency that I have been forced to give up the posts of York and Gloucester, and to surrender the troops under my

command, by capitulation on the 19th instant, as prisoners of war to the combined forces of America and France.

Negotiator: Treaty of Paris

In 1782, Adams was appointed as one of the American Peace Commissioners to help formulate the terms of the Treaty of Paris, which officially ended the American War of Independence. Benjamin Franklin, Thomas Jefferson (although he did not go to Europe like the other commissioners), Henry Laurens, and John Jay were tasked with working with Adams to negotiate with British, French, and Dutch officials.

John Adams had his 16-year-old son, John Quincy Adams, the future president of the United States, and his 13-year-old son, Charles, accompany him to France. John Quincy acted as his secretary, and Charles attended school in both France and the Netherlands. Both of his sons learned a number of languages while there.

While in Europe, Adams worked alongside a number of men to finalize the Treaty of Paris, and each brought along their own distinct advantages. Benjamin Franklin, the publisher and printer, had extensive experience in dealing with the British as well as the French. The British knew he was a clever inventor and scientist, and he had also been an agent for American commercial interests in the past. The officials of Great Britain treated him well because he was a very powerful representative of America. Henry Laurens was a merchant and a rice planter from South Carolina. He had experience working in the Netherlands and also had a good business relationship with Richard Oswald, one of the British officials assigned to help negotiate the treaty on behalf of England.

John Jay, a former president of the Continental Congress and a lawyer, was also sent because his sharp mind and sense of objectivity would help iron out any disagreements among the parties who would be discussing the terms.

Representing England was Richard Oswald and David Hartley. Oswald was a trader and had a good relationship with Ben Franklin, who once said of him that he was a man with an "air of great simplicity and honesty." Hartley was a respected member of Parliament, and he had positive relationships with Benjamin Franklin and Lord Rockingham, the prior prime minister of Great Britain. The British prime minister during these negotiations was Lord Shelburne, a man whose history showed that he was understanding of the rights of Americans.

The French, led by the French Foreign Minister Vergennes, proved to be difficult to deal with over issues related to fishing rights in Newfoundland, Tobago Island, and Gibraltar. In fact, these disagreements stalled the formulation of the treaty. Most of the arguments stemmed from the fact that France, in their competition with England, wanted more restrictive measures than was deemed necessary. Therefore, John Adams and John Jay overruled Franklin's pro-French stance and decided to negotiate with Great Britain directly. Jay, Laurens, and Adams preferred that all parties make separate pacts with France regarding commercial interests. Franklin was an agreeable and humble man, so he gave them the leeway they requested.

There were ten points cited in the treaty with Great Britain:

> 1. Britain would acknowledge the independence of British America to be a free and sovereign country called the United States of America.
>
> 2. The boundaries of America would include the thirteen states and all the land over to the Mississippi River.
>
> 3. The United States would be granted fishing rights off Newfoundland and in the Gulf of Saint Lawrence.
>
> 4. Debts would be paid to the creditors on either side.

5. Americans would make restitution on confiscated lands belonging to British subjects that were seized during the war.

6. In the future, America would refrain from confiscating any land belonging to a British subject.

7. Prisoners of war would be released, except for British slaves who were still in America.

8. America and Great Britain would each have access to the Mississippi River.

9. Territories captured after this treaty would be returned without compensation.

10. Ratification would occur within six months.

The Treaty of Paris was signed on September 3, 1783, officially ending the war. It was a part of the set of agreements between the United States, Great Britain, France, Spain, and the Dutch Republic known as the Peace of Paris.

France also signed what was called the Treaties of Versailles of 1783. It granted France fishing rights in the west coast of Newfoundland and the Gulf of Saint Lawrence. The other points in this mutual treaty related to the possession of various islands in the Atlantic Ocean and near Europe and India.

The Dutch Republic participated in the peace process as well with their own treaty. They had a good relationship with France and worked with them so that they could regain the possession of their territories in the East Indies and the small country of Cape Apollonia in Africa that had been annexed by Great Britain. There was also a guarantee that there would be no British interference with oceanic traffic.

Spain gave up control of Florida to the British in exchange for Cuba. In addition, they received possession of French territories west of the Mississippi along with the Port of New Orleans.

Ambassador to England

Now that America was an independent country, it was vital to appoint ambassadors to represent their interests in foreign counties. In 1785, John Adams was appointed as the first American ambassador to Great Britain. His wife, Abigail, accompanied him there, and his son, John Quincy Adams, who was serving an American diplomat in Russia, came over to join his father as well. John Adams' rather challenging task was to warm up the relations with England following the revolution in order to reestablish trade between the two countries. Although Adams was successful in his relationship with King George III, the king had some reservations due to Adams' rocky relationship with France.

Adams had difficulties with some of the officials and courtiers in England. Before the war, Adams was a good friend of Jonathan Sewall while he was serving as the British attorney general of Massachusetts. During John Adams' ambassadorship, Sewall served as an attorney for King George. However, Sewall had a falling out with Adams due to their differences over the war and Adams' lack of social graces. Sewall said of Adams that "His abilities are undoubtedly equal to the mechanical parts of his business as ambassador, but this is not enough...he has none of those essential arts or ornaments which constitute a courtier." Sewall also added that he felt Adams was "quite out of his element." He had difficulty in blending pleasure with business, as the English were wont to do. Adams tended to ruminate and worry about the fulfillment of his duties as ambassador, and one of those concerns revolved around the payment of war debts.

According to Article 4 of the Treaty of Paris, Americans were expected to pay their debts back to English creditors. However, not all of these debts were repaid. In retaliation, some British soldiers still remained on American territory at forts that they had constructed prior to and during the revolution. Although Adams made a concerted effort to resolve those issues, there was no response from Congress, and he felt unsuccessful and frustrated.

One of the reasons for the failure to collect monies to pay debts stemmed from a weakness in the Articles of Confederation. The Articles failed to provide for the enforcement of its precepts, causing John to reach a stalemate in that regard.

Shay's Rebellion

After the War of Independence, Adams' state of Massachusetts was inflicted with a cash shortage because foreign and state merchants began demanding that payments be made in hard currency. Prior to this, the merchants were satisfied with payment made in goods.

In 1786, a rebellion broke out highlighting four unresolved issues: failure to pay the salaries of Revolutionary War veterans, the high taxes the state of Massachusetts levied, the lack of value in the Continental dollar, and the confiscation of farm property from those who were unable to pay with hard currency. Hence, the courts were bombarded with petitions and complaints from mostly the merchants and war veterans. When the militia was called out, violent protests in the streets and towns continued. James Warren, who headed up the militia, wrote to Adams saying that "We are now in a state of anarchy and confusion bordering on civil war." Adams was extremely concerned and anxious about the situation; he was afraid that the United States might collapse while it was still in its nascent stages. He even suggested that these rebels should be executed. About a year later, the insurrection was stopped, and its leaders fled to other states. There was some loss of life during this rebellion, but Shay's Rebellion brought about a strong motive to correct the situation on a national level.

Constitutional Convention

Therefore, the Philadelphia Convention, better known now as the Constitutional Convention, was called into session in September of 1787. George Washington was unanimously elected as president of the convention. The assembly then decided to write a new constitution for the country because the Articles of Confederation had proven to be ineffective. John Adams didn't attend this convention as he was still serving in England, and neither did Thomas Jefferson, who was in France in a similar capacity.

The Articles of Confederation had deleteriously affected John Adams' performance, and some of the Founding Fathers discussed the problems flowing from these Articles and determined that the weaknesses were:

1. The national government had no power to impose taxes as it only relied upon the willingness of states to contribute if a need was presented. If the states failed to remit payments, there was no way to compel them to do so. Therefore, the country was underfunded and unable to pay its war debt.

2. The government had no power to impose duties or tariffs on foreign imports or to regulate interstate commerce as well as international commerce. As a result, American ports were flooded with goods, and the growth of American manufacturing was stunted by the competition.

3. There was no standardized currency, and the Continental dollar used during the war was worthless.

4. While various states may have had militias, there was no army or navy to protect the entire country, no system for recruiting people to join the armed forces, and no means to pay them.

5. There was no tool created to enforce the legislation that was included in the Articles of Confederation passed by the Continental Congress.

6. Although the Treaty of Paris allowed free access to the Mississippi River, there was no means to prevent a country from breaching that agreement.

7. Very often, the passage of new laws was often deadlocked when the Congress failed to produce a 2/3 majority on a vote.

8. The national government wasn't empowered to make treaties.

9. The voting system, which was based upon the size of a state, created a lopsided majority in favor of the Southern states. Therefore, the Northern states had no say in the measures that were passed.

While the issues of the Articles of Confederation were being nailed down and the United States Constitution was being created, Adams was becoming increasingly frustrated with his lack of progress. John Jay was the secretary for foreign affairs at the time. Because Adams was having enormous difficulties with his post in Britain, he asked Jay to be relieved. Jay politely assented, so Adams and Abigail returned to Massachusetts.

"Old Peacefield"

The purchase of a delightful farm and home called Peacefield while Adams was still in England served to take the sting out of a disappointing stint as the British ambassador. Of it, he said, "Improving my garden has more charms for my fancy than residing at the Court of Saint James." The farmhouse had been built in 1731, so it needed work, of course, but it had the makings of a lovely garden. There was an orchard on the property which was overgrown but still thriving. Abigail was excited and brought two cuttings with her from England—a white and a red rose bush. The roses represented the 16th-century insignias of the House of York (the white rose) and the House of Lancaster (the red rose). She also planted lilacs at the entryway. Those lilac bushes are actually still there today, now tended by the National Park Service.

Chapter 5 – John Adams: Vice President and Then President under the New Constitution

The Philadelphia Convention was attended by 55 of the 75 state delegates. They determined that they had to develop an effective organization that would resolve the weaknesses in the Articles of Confederation and that would establish a national government to lead all the states. After voting on plans submitted by several states, they decided upon establishing three branches of government: the executive, legislative, and judiciary branches, branches which are still used today in the United States.

The executive branch is made of a president, vice president, the Cabinet, and various departments and agencies. The president is the head of state and the government, the commander-in-chief, and the chief diplomat with the duty to name an attorney general and a postmaster general. The president can sign treaties and pass or veto legislation proposed by the legislative branch. The vice president is the presiding officer of the Senate (a part of the legislative branch) and takes the place of the president if he cannot fulfill the duties of his office, for example, due to death, illness, resignation, or removal. In 1789, the executive branch had two departments at the time: Foreign Affairs (later renamed State Department), to handle commerce, treaties, and international relations, and the Treasury Department to levy, collect, and distribute taxes according to the formulas laid out by Congress.

The legislative branch consists of a Senate and a House of Representatives, collectively known together as Congress. Prior to the establishment of the Constitution, the number of state representatives was determined based on the size of the state. However, that created bias. To resolve that, the Convention decided to have two senators per state, and the number of representatives in the House for a state depended upon the population of it. The function of the legislative branch is to pass laws.

The judicial branch was also created, separating the states into judicial districts. A US Supreme Court was also set up under Article III of the Constitution. The framework for the lower courts was created by the first Congress in the Judiciary Act of 1789 after the first president was elected. In the beginning, the president appointed the justices to the Supreme Court. Later on, those justices were subject to the approval of the Senate. The Supreme Court justices were also initially assigned to particular districts and traveled there to hear cases, much like circuit courts. In time, that was changed, and the Supreme Court now sits in Washington, DC. Their function, still to this day, is to enforce the laws of the land.

The first US Constitution was created in 1787. It had seven articles, eleven amendments, and the Bill of Rights, which contained ten items. One of the original 11 amendments wasn't ratified—one that would have required each district to not exceed a population of 50,000. More amendments were passed in later years, and today, there are 27 amendments in all.

James Madison and Alexander Hamilton contributed a great deal of the writing to the US Constitution. Nine states ratified the document on June 21, 1788, the required minimum needed to pass; however, the Constitution didn't go into effect until March 4, 1789. The Constitution was eventually ratified by all the states, although this didn't happen until 1790.

When John Adams served as ambassador to Great Britain, he could have particularly benefited from the improved Constitution, especially Article I which would have given him the money to pay off foreign debt (from the Treasury), the power to take action against those who had failed to pay their debt (through the judicial department), and the ability to intercede with issues related to international commerce (through the state department).

Presidential Campaign

According to the US Constitution at that time, the president of America was elected by the majority of votes from the electors of each state. Whoever came in second in the count was appointed as vice president. For the 1789 election—the first one in the new nation of America—it was expected that George Washington would be elected. John Adams was also very popular and was a serious contender for the presidency as well. After the ballots were counted, Adams received 34 electoral votes and Washington got 69. Although he wasn't surprised that Washington won, Adams was upset that Washington received twice as many votes as himself. However, unbeknownst to him, Alexander Hamilton had written letters to some of the electors disparaging Adams. In one of them, he said:

> He is a man of an imagination sublimated and eccentric; propitious neither to the regular display of sound judgement, nor to steady perseverance in a systematic plan of conduct; and I began to perceive what has been since too manifest, that to this defect are added the unfortunate foibles of a vanity without bounds, and a jealousy capable of discoloring every object.

In addition to other criticisms, Hamilton contended that a person in high office should seek the advice of his advisors and others well respected in the areas of political philosophy. He also suggested that John Adams would be too arrogant to seek advice from capable and reliable sources.

John Adams – Vice President

Having come in second, John Adams became the vice president. As vice president, he presided over the Senate. The very first debate Congress had was a curious one—what title should be given to the president and vice president, and how should they be addressed? Adams had a reputation for being rather aristocratic and suggested that the government of the United States wouldn't command respect around the world unless its chief executive had a "superior title." Adams especially liked the suggestion made by Representative George Tucker of South Carolina: "His Highness the President, Protector of the Liberties of the United States." Thomas Jefferson felt that particular title was "superlatively ridiculous." Adams' preference for extraordinary titles made him the subject of laughter and ridicule, and some people even jokingly called Adams "His Rotundity," a reference to his rather ample waistline. It was decided that the president would simply be called "Mr. President."

Adams also felt that he, as vice president, should live in an impressive home. So, he and his wife moved into the Richmond Hill mansion in New York, which was the first national capital under the Constitution.

Later on, during the second session of the US Congress, the Residence Act was passed, establishing the location of a national capital. Washington, DC, situated inside the borders of Maryland and Virginia, was envisioned as the central location of the original states. Those two states donated land for the creation of the capital, and funding was approved to erect majestic buildings for the use of federal officials and their staffs.

Despite the progress the nation was making in establishing itself, John Adams was unhappy with his role as vice president, serving two terms under George Washington. However, it might be said that he contributed to his own displeasure. Hamilton's comment that Adams wasn't one to seek advice might have been well founded as Adams seemed to feel that the president should seek his advice instead of the reverse. He also felt the vice presidency role was an "inactive" one. In his personal papers, he sarcastically wrote: "My country in its wisdom contrived for me the most insignificant office that ever the invention of man or his imagination contrived or his imagination conceived." He also cynically remarked that "Franklin electrified (George Washington) with his rod – and henceforth these two conducted all the policy, negotiations, legislatures and war." However, it is worthy to note that Adams rarely attended Cabinet meetings, thus limiting himself.

Election of 1796: President John Adams

John Adams associated himself with the Federalist Party, which was also called the Pro-Administration Party. The Federalists espoused the concept of a strong central government and were basically conservative and pro-business. During Washington's term, the First Bank of the United States was established to provide for the stabilization of the fiscal policy and empower the government to pay debts and charge excise taxes and tariffs. Most of the Federalists lived in the northern states where manufacturing and business were prime occupations. In terms of trade, they preferred to deal with Great Britain, and the John Jay Treaty, negotiated in 1794, named Great Britain as their most favored trading partner.

The Democratic-Republican Party, created by Thomas Jefferson and James Madison, stood for the principle that states' rights were more important and that a highly centralized national government would be deleterious for the common man. In terms of trade, the Democratic-Republicans favored France over Britain. And as for the national bank, they were dead set against that, imagining that greedy Northerners would take undue advantage of farmers from rural America in the southern states.

Adams ran for the presidency in 1796 as a Federalist against Thomas Pinckney, also a Federalist. The Democratic-Republicans ran Thomas Jefferson and Aaron Burr. Jefferson was extremely popular and favored as the top contender. However, the Democratic-Republican predilection for France made voters hesitate to vote for him as France was in the throes of the French Revolution, a violent grassroots movement that rocked the country and shook the entirety of Europe.

John Adams had strong opinions against the newly established French Republic because he felt that it was a form of unicameral legislation—that is, controlled by one political body without input from the opposition—and that there would be nothing "to restrain them from making tyrannical laws." In 1790 and 1791, he had anonymously published the *Discourses on Davila* in the *Gazette of the United States*, a Federalist publication. Davila was a 17th-century writer who wrote about the French wars of religion of that era. Adams' essay was originally meant as a translation, but he transformed it into a political commentary supporting a government with bicameral representation with checks and balances. Having both parties represented in the executive branch wasn't quite what Adams had in mind, however, but it did happen in Adams' 1796 election. Adams won 71 electoral votes, and Jefferson won 68, making him the vice president. It was an incredibly close election. To date, this was the only election in the history of the United States where the two top offices were held by individuals from different political parties.

In establishing his Cabinet, Adams selected those who had served during Washington's administration. Historians indicate that Adams wasn't particularly close to any of them but wanted continuity. Jefferson himself was surprised because he knew about the personal attitudes the men in the Cabinet had toward Adams.

Most of them were in agreement with the policies of Alexander Hamilton, another Federalist, and sometimes even rejected Adams' input on issues. Jefferson was quoted as having once said, "The Hamiltonians by whom he (Adams) is surrounded are only a little less hostile to him than to me."

The XYZ Affair

In 1793, England and France were at war. France, at that time, was in the hands of the Jacobin party and the National Assembly, establishments that arose during the French Revolution. Because of America's close trade relations with England, Adams wanted to maintain neutrality and avoid being drawn into a war. As he was concerned about how to prevent that, Adams approached Congress in 1797, indicating that American defenses should be strengthened in case of a threat. The Democratic-Republicans reacted negatively to this because they heavily supported the French Republic and didn't want to offend them. However, the Federalists agreed with Adams' precautions and wariness. Once Adams became aware of the possible reaction of France, he wanted to smooth over relations with them, so he sent three peace commissioners over there— Elbridge Gerry, Charles Pinckney, and John Marshall. This maneuver was labeled as a "peace commission," and the details weren't released to the public.

Gerry was a member of the Federalist Party and an exporter from Massachusetts who had familiarity with trade. He was considered a moderate by the Federalists. Charles Pinckney came from a Southern background and was more sensitive to the needs of those who were less fortunate. John Marshall was a staunch conservative and Federalist who believed in a strong central government and preferred Britain over France. In terms of America's public position, he preferred to express neutrality in foreign affairs.

In order to affect a positive outcome for the envoys, Vice President Jefferson met with the French representative in America, Joseph Letombe. He urged Letombe to convince France to spend a long time with the negotiations, saying, "Listen to them and then drag out the negotiations at length and mollify them by the urbanity of the proceedings." Jefferson felt that John Adams would only be a one-term president and thought that France would fare better under a new president, preferably himself. Adams did have a negative view of France, due in part to the treatment he received from them while he was an ambassador. Unfortunately, he made that attitude obvious in a rather bellicose speech to Congress just prior to the departure of his peace delegation.

Upon their arrival in France, the three peace envoys met with Charles Maurice de Talleyrand, the French foreign minister. However, Talleyrand harbored ill feelings toward John Adams, having heard his speech to the US Congress. As a result, Talleyrand met with the American delegation very briefly. He then referred them to three agents who had the code names X, Y, and Z. The French emissaries indicated that they would refrain from hostilities if the US would grant the Republic of France a 12-million-dollar loan, if President Adams apologized for his offensive remarks about France in his speech, and if they made another payment to the avaricious Talleyrand personally.

Adams was incensed and considered that an insult. He publicly announced that the mission was a failure without elucidating any specifics, as he didn't want to create even more friction between the two countries. Then he reiterated his need to strengthen the country's defenses. Because neither Congress nor the public knew why the peace effort had failed, rumors flew about. The Democratic-Republicans, in particular, felt that Adams was hiding positive information related to France because of his prejudice. Congress then required Adams to release the details about the XYZ Affair. When he did so, the Democratic-Republicans were embarrassed, and the American public was shocked. Adams popularity soared to new heights among the public for taking this honest and courageous standpoint. The country's attitudes understandably began to turn against France, and the Federalists sent out anti-French propaganda. Congress was alarmed by the

French reaction to the peace mission, and laws were passed that strengthened the United States Army and Navy. Of course, Congress had to raise taxes as well to support that.

John Adams was extremely leery of being responsible for permitting another war to occur so soon after the War of Independence, so he and the Federalist-dominated Congress passed a series of four laws, known as the Alien and Sedition Acts, to prevent the French from having undue influence in America.

The Alien and Sedition Acts

These acts were passed by a narrow margin in 1798 and severely restricted immigration by requiring that a foreigner wait fourteen years before applying for citizenship. In addition, the president was permitted to accuse anyone as being a threat to the security of the United States and had the right to deport him. Any publication that was critical of the US government was also forbidden. Because Adams and many members of his Cabinet were Federalists, those laws also protected them from criticism. The Democratic-Republicans had been weakened after the XYZ Affair, but they felt that the Alien and Sedition Acts were unreasonably harsh. They argued strongly that these laws were unconstitutional because they directly restricted the freedom of speech. Many outrageous arrests were made because of those laws, and notable people from both political parties were imprisoned on scurrilous charges.

For example, Roger Griswold and Matthew Lyon, both of Connecticut, were expelled from the House of Representatives and arrested for sedition. It seems that Griswold, a Federalist, had read some anti-Federalist articles penned by his fellow congressman, Matthew Lyon. At one session in the House, Griswold chased after Lyon with a hickory stick. After catching up to Lyon, Griswold struck him a number of times on his shoulders and head. Lyon then spit tobacco at Griswold in retaliation. Although it's true that they could have been arrested for assault, they were arrested by virtue of the Alien and Sedition Acts. Furthermore, when a man by the name of Anthony Haswell tried to pay the fine for the release of Matthew Lyon, he, too, was arrested!

Likewise, a journalist, Thomas Cooper, went to prison for writing critical articles about Adams. In issuing their verdict, the court said that Cooper was "a person of wicked and turbulent disposition." James Callender was subjected to the same fate when he penned an anti-Federalist pamphlet, *The Prospect Before Us*. Benjamin Franklin Bache, the publisher of the *Philadelphia Aurora*, a newspaper that supported Jeffersonian thoughts, was also arrested for his articles that attacked John Adams. He called him the "old, querulous, bald, blind, crippled, Toothless Adams." Abigail Adams often spoke to her husband about the politics of the day, and she flew into a frenzy when she read words that attacked her husband. She called Bache of the *Aurora* newspaper insolent and abusive and called the man a "lying wretch." Bache was the grandson of Benjamin Franklin, and because of his relationship to the famous scientist, his detractors referred to him as "Lightning Rod Junior."

22 other people were charged under these acts. Usually, these charges represented a devious form of negative politicking rather than true sedition or treason.

Chapter 6 – To Fight or Not to Fight: The Quasi-War

The Quasi-War has been called such because it wasn't a declared war. Due to hostilities with France that had affected America after the XYZ Affair failed in its peace mission, French vessels started attacking American merchant vessels. They were intent upon inspecting the ships for weapons and equipment bound for England and other countries who opposed France during their revolutionary war period (1789-1799). In 1798, just two years into the Adams' administration, Congress approved of hiring privateers to patrol the shore and rescinded all treaties with France. John Adams also proposed that America replenish their navy.

Naval Engagements

James McHenry of Maryland, the secretary of war, authorized 25 American warships to be built. The fear of a war with France was heightened when a French vessel, *La Croyable*, came precariously close to the state of New Jersey. It wasn't a commercial vessel; it was commandeered by privateers. Once that happened, the *La Croyable* was seized off the shores of Egg Harbor, New Jersey, and impounded. *La Croyable* had also been responsible for capturing a British merchant vessel earlier along with one owned by a Philadelphia company.

On the high seas, the USS *Constellation* engaged the French ship *La Vengeance* in the vicinity of the West Indies as it headed toward America's southern shore. The French ship was actually heading back to France with passengers, but the signal flags hoisted by the two ships weren't understood, and the USS *Constellation* gave chase. Captain Thomas Truxton of the *Constellation* demanded surrender, but the French refused. Both ships opened fire. In the half-light of the reflection from gunfire, the USS *Constellation* lost its rigging, and *La Vengeance* limped its way to Curacao where the French captain was forced to beach her.

More than a dozen US merchant vessels were attacked by the French during 1798. Only one American ship was seized, the *Retaliation*, which was outgunned by two French warships. The captain, William Bainbridge, was detained at the French island of Guadeloupe in the West Indies. Governor Victor Hugues of that island wanted to preserve trade and be guaranteed neutrality, so he attempted to bargain with Bainbridge. However, Bainbridge knew that the American seamen who had been captured by the French before this had been mistreated, and he used this incident to draw attention to that. Instead of cooperating with the French authorities on the island, he protested, knowing it would reach the national media. In addition, he indicated to the French that he wasn't authorized to grant neutrality. Since the French governor was sincere, he released the American sailors that the island held, including Bainbridge. Hugues then sent a communique to President Adams. That letter, though, was accompanied with the threat that should their neutrality proposal be denied, any American sailors found off their shores would be executed.

To continue in their efforts to protect American shipping interest in other areas of the Caribbean, the USS *Merrimack* was launched by the noteworthy shipbuilders of Newburyport, Massachusetts, for service in 1799. She was tasked with escorting American merchant ships, and as one of its first actions, the *Merrimack* captured *L'Magicienne*, the former *Retaliation*, outside of the Caribbean. In naval warfare, it was fairly common to seize enemy ships and refit them for use by one's own navy. Following that, the USS *Merrimack* took the French ships *Bonaparte 7, Ganges,* the *Phoenix, Ceres,* the *Brilliant*, and the schooners *John* and *Godfrey*, the latter of which was the property of the British navy.

Armed Forces and Political Strife

Without approaching George Washington, Adams appointed him the head of the ground forces in this Quasi-War. Washington was then 67 years old and retired. He graciously accepted, but he didn't feel physically capable of adequately serving in the role of commander-in-chief at that age. He accepted Adams' appointment for the sake of the country but added the caveat that he must be free to choose his own leaders or he wouldn't take the post. The former president was given permission to do so, and he chose Alexander Hamilton, a man that Adams distrusted, to do the actual work involved in organizing and managing the army. John Adams had initially wanted two Democratic-Republicans to fill the associate positions in order to maintain a balance in political factions, but the vociferous Federalists in Congress objected to that. Adams reluctantly relented because his dear wife Abigail was ill, and Adams wasn't prepared for a political battle on top of the stress he was already dealing with.

Besides Alexander Hamilton, Washington selected Charles Pinckney, James McHenry, and Henry Knox to be his top advisors. McHenry declined the position, but the other two men were anxious to fill the roles. Washington, who had suffered from a perennial lack of supplies during the War of Independence, stressed that Alexander Hamilton should be sure that his soldiers had sufficient supplies. As it so happened, there was no ground war phase of the Quasi-War, but it helped to establish the precedent that Congress needed to appoint someone to make arrangements for military equipment, uniforms, and supplies. That would require more taxation, and Adams' administration imposed the Direct House Tax of 1798, which was essentially a property tax. It might come as no surprise that Adams became very unpopular because of it.

John Fries Rebellion

The Direct House Tax of 1798 was levied upon individuals' buildings based upon the number of windows and their land. In the 18th century, glass was expensive because it had to be imported, and people whose homes had more windows were usually wealthier. Tax assessors were sent to the states, but they encountered a great deal of resistance from the people living just outside Philadelphia. When the assessors arrived, the inhabitants ridiculed them and forced them off their property. John Fries, an auctioneer in Pennsylvania, had a general impression about the reactions of the people of his own state because of his occupation and helped to instigate an uprising. Fries held town meetings, prompting the farmers of the area to hold rallies and protest. Having been incensed by the new taxes, the farmers harassed the assessors, and the people of the state itself called upon their local militias to arm themselves and drive the assessors away.

In January of 1799, the US Marshal was sent by the federal government to Pennsylvania, armed with arrest warrants. He located twelve men who were responsible for tax resistance and arrested them. He then had them transported to a temporary jail in Bethlehem, Pennsylvania. The next day, 400 armed men, led by John Fries, arrived at the jail. To quell the crowd, the marshal released a few men as a sign of good faith and started negotiating with Fries.

In response to this action though, President Adams issued orders to the Pennsylvania state militia to march over there and stop the insurrection. When they arrived, they promptly arrested John Fries and 31 others. Those men were jailed in Philadelphia and charged with treason—an offense that might result in execution. According to the law, an attempt to resist the enforcement of a federal law was the same as waging war against the United States. Most of them were released after a short period, except for John Fries and two others who were charged with treason.

Their trial was held in April of 1799, and Fries and the other two men were convicted of treason and sentenced to hang. However, a mistrial was declared when one of the jurors admitted that he had decided ahead of time that they should be hanged.

In 1800, another trial was held. The judge, Richard Peters, and Supreme Court Justice Samuel Chase presided at the trial. At this trial, Fries and the others were once again found guilty of treason and were sentenced to be hanged. However, John Adams pardoned them. Alexander Hamilton was confused by the pardon and responded angrily by saying that it was the "most inexplicable part of Mr. Adams' conduct." When it was published, that statement created a rift in the Federalist Party because it gave rise to arguments amongst the party members themselves.

End of the Quasi-War

By the spring of 1799, the French had let up on their intensive attacks on American ships due to the French losses that occurred overseas during their engagement in the revolutionary wars. In addition, the political landscape had shifted in France, and their focus turned toward internal events. In November of 1799, Napoleon Bonaparte—a former naval commander—staged a coup d'état and took over France. Consequently, the naval battles with America were of little interest, and France announced they wanted to make peace with America.

In his role as the head of France, Napoleon Bonaparte made a lot of reforms and wanted to end the Quasi-War with America. Alexander Hamilton was a presumptuous man, and when he heard about Bonaparte's overtures for peace, he rushed over unannounced to see Adams. Hamilton wanted to convince him to forego a treaty and simply create an alliance with Britain to restore the influence of the Bourbons, who were the ancestors of King Louis XVI, the king the French had violently executed during their revolution. Adams was amused by that, and in his papers, he said, "I heard him with perfect good humor, though never in my life did I hear a man talk more like a fool."

On September 30, 1800, his envoys—Oliver Ellsworth, William Davie, and their leader, William Vans Murray—signed the Treaty of Mortefontaine on behalf of the United States, putting an end to the Quasi-War. The old Treaty of Alliance and Amity between the United States and France in 1778 had already been rescinded at the start of the Quasi-War, but it was now permanently terminated.

Political Rancor

Alexander Hamilton continued to fuel the tensions within the Federalist Party because of his overwhelming need to control its direction. He had many followers but managed to make a number of political enemies. James McHenry, the secretary of war, was one of them.

Further differences arose among the Federalists because of an argument between Adams and McHenry where Adams impulsively fired McHenry. Adams also took that opportunity to ask Timothy Pickering, the secretary of state, to resign. Pickering, it was later discovered, was opposed to making peace with France, and he was in office during the negotiations over the Treaty of Mortefontaine. Pickering adamantly refused to leave, so Adams dismissed him outright and replaced him with John Marshall, the man he wanted to take McHenry's place. The position of secretary of war went to Samuel Dexter instead. The Federalists were, indeed, becoming fractured over policy differences.

Judicial Appointments

In 1798, John Adams appointed Bushrod Washington as an associate justice of the Supreme Court. Adams originally asked John Marshall to serve, but Marshall was running against a Democratic-Republican, John Clopton, in Congress as one of the representatives for Virginia. Marshall won the majority of votes in that race even though he was a member of the Federalist Party—a party that usually wasn't popular in the Southern states.

Bushrod was a friend of Marshall's and was, therefore, Adams' second choice. This was a recess appointment: that is, an appointment made while Congress wasn't in session. Normally, Congress must approve of judicial appointments, but the Constitution states that the president has that power if Congress is in recess. After Congress reconvenes, they are then expected to vote for the continuance or discontinuance of the appointment. Recess appointments became a stumbling block for many US presidents as time went on.

Alfred Moore served on the Supreme Court from 1800 to 1804. He replaced Justice James Iredell, from Washington's administration, who had retired. Most historians indicate that Moore's service was unremarkable, but he was also a sickly man who served for only five years.

In 1800, Adams approached John Jay to serve as the chief justice after the resignation of Oliver Ellsworth, who had become extremely ill. However, John Jay, who had been the first chief justice of the Supreme Court, turned down Adams' appointment. John Jay had become disgusted with party politics during the year of 1800, and he was particularly incensed when Hamilton tried to manipulate the electoral laws. Jay was a "purist," meaning he believed that the political process should be honorable and that both appointments and elections should be decided by the people without undue influence.

After Jay declined the appointment, Adams sought out his secretary of state, John Marshall, to assume the position. Marshall served out his role as secretary of state and then assumed the position of chief justice after Adams left office. Marshall was perhaps one of the most learned men in the justice department and authored many books. As chief justice, he altered the way the Supreme Court did business. Up until 1800, the Supreme Court was very much like a traveling circuit court. However, as cases became more complex and involved constitutional matters, Marshall saw to it that the Supreme Court operated independently.

Chapter 7 – 1800: The Politics of Dissension

The Capitol of the United States

In 1790, Congress had approved of the building of the United States Capitol. By 1800, many of the buildings had been erected, and John Adams was the first president to reside in the President's Mansion which resided on a small hill in the center of the city. This mansion was later renamed by the more recognizable name of the White House. Nearby stood Congress Hall, which later became the United States Capitol building. Pierre (or Peter, as he went by that name in the United States) Charles L'Enfant designed the city itself, while Dr. William Thornton and Stephen Hallett were the architects of the United States Capitol. James Hoban, an architect from Ireland, was chosen to design the President's Mansion. The architects were awarded the positions in a competition held during George Washington's presidency.

John Adams visited some of the nearly completed buildings in 1800 as he readied himself for the upcoming presidential campaign. He and Abigail moved into the President's Mansion in the late fall of that year just as the campaign was heating up.

Political Warriors

The campaign for the election of 1800 was one of the most contentious of 19th-century America. The rivalry of the two political parties—the Federalist and Democratic-Republican Parties—was malicious and negative. Throughout the campaign, wild rumors flourished, much to the titillation of American readers, and many believed them.

Thomas Jefferson and Aaron Burr of the Democratic-Republican Party ran against Adams. Jefferson was convinced that the Federalist Party betrayed the cause of liberty by granting too much power to the national government. He was a champion of states' rights and felt that a strong central government would be oppressive. Aaron Burr was very popular in New York politics, and that helped him win room on the ticket. He and Jefferson were an unlikely pair, though, as Burr was heavily involved in banking. Jefferson himself had a negative opinion of banks and associated them with the wealthy aristocracy.

John Adams was one of the Federalist candidates along with Charles C. Pickney of South Carolina. Charles Cotesworth Pinckney was known to the people as one of the agents sent by Adams to negotiate the failed XYZ Affair. After his return from France, he became disillusioned with the French in general but came across as a political moderate. Because he was a Southerner and had military experience (unlike Adams), the party felt that he might be successful as a candidate.

As soon the political battle formations were drawn up, the rumor mill started grinding. Because of Adams' aristocratic mannerisms, one rumor stated that Adams was plotting to have his son, John Quincy Adams, marry a daughter of King George III. The Federalists, on the other hand, cast Jefferson as a pro-French radical, saying that he would carry on a Reign of Terror, much like Robespierre did under the French Republic. The smear campaign that was conducted is uncomfortably similar to the campaigns of today in which each side attempts to hurl accusations at the other regardless of their validity.

What's more, the debt from the Quasi-War was tremendous because America had taken out a lot of loans to build their navy. As a result of the Direct House Tax of 1789, many Americans fell into economic hardships. Although Democratic-Republicans had encouraged the Quasi-War, that was quickly forgotten when they stirred the public's emotions with incessant propaganda against the reelection of John Adams. His political enemy and fellow Federalist, Alexander Hamilton, wasted no time in disparaging Adams. During the course of Adams' campaign, he wrote an inflammatory letter to some electors. Although decorated in elaborate and heavily tailored terms, he inserted comments like:

> Mr. Adams has committed some serious errors of administration; that in addition to these, he has certain fixed points of character which tend naturally to the detriment of any cause of which he is the chief; that he has furnished deadly weapons to its enemies by unfounded accusations, and has weakened the force of its friends.

Some Federalists urged Hamilton not to send the letter, but he ignored their advice. Hamilton followed that letter up with a pamphlet denouncing Adams' decisions to discharge Pickering and McHenry. In addition, Hamilton suggested that the electors should vote for Charles Pinckney, the other Federalist running against Adams.

Adams wasn't the only one that Hamilton harbored ill will toward. He also disliked Aaron Burr, just as Burr did him. Now that he was Jefferson's running mate, it inflamed their antipathy toward each other. Burr reportedly saw to it that Hamilton's otherwise private letter to the electors was made public; Hamilton had originally planned on just a public release of his follow-up pamphlet against John Adams. Their rivalry contributed to divisions within the Federalist Party.

In 1800, William Duane, who had taken over the *Philadelphia Aurora* after Bache, published a letter written to Tench Coxe that said there were still men influenced by Great Britain in the US government. The letter was private, but somehow, it was revealed. Adams was not just embarrassed; he was furious. The whole intent of the letter had been taken out of context and written in such a way as to imply that Adams himself had some degree of loyalty to Great Britain. Word spread that Duane was also being sought by authorities who wanted to charge him under the Alien and Sedition Acts. As a result, Jefferson interceded, indicating Duane had to be let out until he could find an attorney. After that, Duane went into hiding until the end of Adams' administration.

It was hard for the public to relate to Adams, even without slanderous words being printed against his character. Abigail and John liked to travel in style, even though Adams wasn't really considered all that wealthy. He and Abigail enjoyed the pomp and circumstance, and that led to a lot of criticism related to their being aristocrats and monarchists. In 1799, when they were traveling in their entourage through New Jersey, ceremonial cannons were fired as a salute. Hearing that, Luther Baldwin, the driver of a garbage scow in Newark, New Jersey, rushed out from a local tavern, shouting, "There goes the president and they are firing at his arse!" He then followed that up with the comment, "I do not care if they fire thro' his arse!" As expected, he was arrested then convicted and imprisoned on the charge that he spoke "seditious words tending to defame the president and the government of the United States."

Election Results and Ramifications

This election was different than the elections before as the voting regulations had changed. Five states now allowed qualified voters to vote for the federal electors. That number had been seven in the 1796 election. The other states adopted a "winner-take-all" system, also called plurality-at-large voting. At-large voting means that a representative is elected to vote for a district, town, or state; this was banned in 1842, as it was determined to be biased and could lead to gerrymandering, a system in which districts are split in such a way as to favor certain candidates.

It is possible this new system didn't aid John Adams and Charles Pinckney, who both lost the election. Charles Pinckney received the least number of votes of all the candidates (64); however, Adams only gained one more vote than Pinckney. Thomas Jefferson and Aaron Burr were tied at a vote of 73-73. In that case, the Constitution stipulated that the winner must be selected by the House of Representatives. Each state represented in the House had one vote, and a supermajority determined the outcome. The final vote came to 10-4 in favor of Jefferson.

After this vicious and slanderous campaign, the Federalist Party started to disintegrate. Analysts say the split was due to the antipathy of Hamilton and Adams. In addition, political thinkers indicate that the platform of the Federalist Party eventually evolved into that of today's Republican Party, and the Democratic-Republicans, who actually referred to themselves as the Republican Party back then (the name Democratic-Republicans is used to differentiate themselves from the current Republicans), became the current-day Democrats.

Shortly after taking office, Thomas Jefferson released everyone who had been imprisoned under the Alien and Sedition Acts and gave them an official apology. In 1800, the Alien and Sedition Acts expired, although a segment called the Alien Enemies Act remains in effect to this day. This act allows for an alien to be deported if he or she is determined to be dangerous to the nation's security during a war.

Chapter 8 – John Adams: His Thoughts and Retirement

Back to Old Peacefield

John Adams was a farmer at heart, so he wasn't crushed by having lost his bid for another term as president. John Adams' son, Charles, who had accompanied him on his ambassadorship in Paris, achieved a bad reputation while attending Harvard University because he became an alcoholic who was often involved in drunken antics on campus. Following his graduation, he passed the bar and apprenticed briefly under Alexander Hamilton. After that, Charles borrowed a lot of money from his father, presumably to open up a law practice. However, he squandered the money and abandoned his wife, Sarah, and his two daughters, Susanna and Abigail. In 1798, John felt that Charles was a "madman possessed of the devil" and disowned him. Charles died of cirrhosis of the liver in 1800. When John and Abigail retired to Peacefield, they welcomed Charles' wife and their daughters to live with them.

John Quincy Adams lived nearby with his wife and children. He visited his parents quite frequently and often stayed with them for weeks on end. It was convenient for John Quincy because he had entered politics in Massachusetts.

Attitude on Slavery

In 1801, two fervent abolitionists—George Churchman and Jacob Lindley—sent John Adams a letter, enclosing a copy of Warner Mifflin's late 18th-century pamphlet against slavery. As a Quaker, Mifflin didn't condone slavery and spent most of his life campaigning against the practice. As part of his campaign against slavery, Mifflin sent out pamphlets and letters to the influential politicians of the day.

George Churchman was a Pennsylvanian Quaker who opened Quaker schools and promoted the education of women as well as men. Jacob Lindley, also from Pennsylvania, was a Presbyterian minister who served as a missionary in Africa and later became the first president of Ohio University.

John Adams responded to the letter by saying:

> Although I have never sought popularity by any animated speeches or inflammatory publications against the slavery of Blacks, my opinion against it has always been known and my practice has been so conformable to my sentiment that I have always employed freemen both as domestics and laborers, and never in my life did I own a slave.

Because John Adams wasn't extremely vocal about his stance against slavery, Mifflin and Churchman were unaware of it. Adams, knowing that slavery was a divisive issue, tended to avoid bringing it up.

In 1822, he wrote to Thomas Pickering, expressing his disappointment that the Constitution of the United States did not abolish slavery. It had appeared in an earlier draft of the Constitution, but it was ultimately rejected in the final version.

John Adams believed in a gradual transition in order to free the country from the evils of slavery. Because of the economic dependency of the South upon slavery, he felt that sudden emancipation would be not only a divisive issue but also a traumatic one as well.

The Rise of His Son

John Adams' son, John Quincy Adams, followed in his father's footsteps by becoming a lawyer and then entering the field of politics. After having lost the 1800 election, John Adams was gratified to learn that his own son had been elected as a senator of Massachusetts. Like his father, he was also a Federalist, but he became disenchanted with that party and became a Democratic-Republican later in life. He also befriended James Madison, who appointed him as an ambassador to Russia. In addition, he also served as an ambassador to England as his father did. By 1817, John Quincy Adams became secretary of state under President James Monroe, and in 1825, he even became president, a year before his father died.

Adams on Monarchy

Adams was often criticized for favoring a monarchical form of government, but he rejected the opinions of those who said he felt positively about monarchies. In a letter to Thomas Jefferson, he said he never promoted such a thing and challenged anyone who could find evidence to the contrary. However, a critical reading of his documents appears to show ambiguity with regard to the "aristocracy." For example, in 1779, when formulating the state constitution for Massachusetts, he said, "We have so many men of wealth, of ambitious spirits, or intrigue, of luxury and corruption, that incessant factions will disturb our peace without it." Adams was referring to the powers of the three branches of government, but he felt that there should be one individual bestowed with power over all three branches. Without that person, Adams felt that the government would "be run down like a hare before the hunters." As for the Governor's Council, Adams preferred that the members of such a council had the right to approve or reject appointments related to civil, judicial, and military positions.

Despite his respect for a more "elite" composition of that council, he manifested some fears about the control of a republican form of government by aristocracies, especially new ones. Adams intensely disliked some of the emotional corruption of politicians but said that "There are as many and as dangerous aristocratical demagogues as there are democratical."

He seems to have ended up with a contradictory concept about the structure of a government. On the one hand, he had an antipathy toward the oligarchy of the rich classes who would deprive the people of their rights but also suggested that the upper echelon of society be curbed by a strong executive. Curiously, the result could be just the same; only the doer would change.

Adams did feel, however, that monarchies historically outlived democracies. He is quoted as saying, "Remember, democracy never lasts long. It soon wastes, exhausts and murders itself. There never was a democracy yet that does not commit suicide."

Literary Endeavor: *In Defense of Constitutions*

Adams wrote a 3-volume series while abroad called *In Defense of Constitutions* in 1787. In it, Adams delineates the various forms of governments, even including those in ancient times. It contains a survey and discussion of various types of governmental republics from history and went on to espouse political philosophies from the past, like those of Anne Robert Turgot and Richard Price, who were both accomplished statesmen and writers. One of the reasons John Adams explored the structure of governments is that, unlike today, there were no contemporary democracies or democratic republics upon which to model a new government that would work for America. The United States wasn't set up as a pure democracy anyway, and the founders recognized that. The Founders intended it to be a democratic republic. Adams said that if all men were able to follow natural law, a government would be unnecessary. However, people are subject to their passions, and such unbridled freedom would invite abuse without the law.

James Madison, who helped to write the Constitution, based his writing upon the recommendations of the delegates of the Constitutional Convention; he personally defined democracy as a "pure democracy," meaning "a society consisting of a small number of citizens to assemble and administer the government in person." To Madison, a republic yielded "a government in which the scheme of representation takes place." That is, the people elected representatives who, in turn, administered the government. It is noteworthy that Madison never applied the term "democracy" to the government of America. He preferred to use the term "republic."

There was some confusion as to the definition of "republic" anyway. To Adams, the term "republic" meant:

> Could be no other than a government in which the property of the people predominated and governed; and it had more relation to property than liberty. It signified a government in which the property of the public, or people, and of every one of them, was secured and protected by law.

Adams emphasized the law to be the external factor that guided the actions of all, including the people elected to office. He felt that civil law was absolutely necessary as a mechanism to restrain men from falling upon their natural weaknesses, regardless of their posts or positions within the structure. However, Adams modified the concept that men must be subject to the law to mean that there should be sufficient flexibility so that they are not slaves to its literal interpretation. In addition, he stressed the fact that any law needs to be a "good law" and that it protects both the majority and the minority. He said that "laws are neither made by angels, nor by horses" and that there needs to be a system of checks and balances in place.

Historians have criticized *In Defense of Constitutions* as being too voluminous and mostly paraphrased or quoted from other sources. Only the last few essays or "letters," as they were called, appear to have sprung from Adams' own thoughts. Although Adams was complimented on some of the scholarly material in the beginning, political writers called the huge series "incoherent" and "disorganized." Adams did have a tendency to start on a project, heavily invest his mind into it, but then either leave it unfinished or unedited, which is what may have happened with this work. He also never finished his own autobiography.

Adams Reconciles with Jefferson

Thomas Jefferson and John Adams had been on a friendly basis during the initial years of America. They had worked together on the content of the Declaration of Independence and had even communicated with each other when Jefferson was the American ambassador to France in 1785 and Adams was the country's ambassador to England. However, the two political parties of the nation—the Federalists and the Democratic-Republicans—became more widely disparate, and Adams and Jefferson had grown apart. Jefferson's on-going support of France, even during their revolutionary war period, was another bone of contention between them. The tumultuous election of 1800 played a very strong role in driving these two idealistic and committed patriots apart even further.

At one point, Abigail wrote a letter of sympathy to Thomas Jefferson on the death of his daughter, Polly. In his response, though, Jefferson threw out a barb toward Adams about his "unkind appointment" of federal judges toward the end of his presidency but said he "forgave" him for it. Judges appointed just as a president was leaving office were called "midnight judges," and at the time, they weren't subject to congressional approval. Abigail, still stinging from the slander spread during Jefferson's campaign, retorted with annoyance over that.

Benjamin Rush, a physician and signer of the Declaration of Independence, wanted to reunite the two and wrote a number of letters to both of them. John Adams was the first to break the ice. In 1812, he wrote to Jefferson, saying, "Madame joins and sends her kind regards to your daughter and your grandchildren as well as to yourself." Jefferson speedily replied. After that, Adams wrote to Jefferson, "You and I ought not to die before we have explained ourselves to each other." That they did, and they more calmly discussed the political implications of America, including those issues upon which they differed. The pair exchanged about 158 letters after their reconciliation.

John Adams developed heart disease but lived for many years after the diagnosis. He died of congestive heart failure at the age of 91. It is curious to note that both John Adams and Thomas Jefferson died on Independence Day, July 4, of 1826. Adams' last words were "Jefferson still lives," but he was wrong by about five hours.

Conclusion

John Adams lived through one of the most difficult times in early America. His presidential predecessor, George Washington, had fame thrust upon him because of his contribution in winning the American War of Independence. When Adams came into office, America was heavily conflicted politically and financially. War became a distinct possibility while America was still undergoing growing pains. Adams successfully kept the nation from becoming involved in another war, but he is rarely given credit for that.

Prior to his tenure as president, Adams was placed in the position of ambassador more than once but became frustrated due to the failure of the Continental Congress to set up a workable system of laws to back him up. Although he was sometimes described as being "abrasive," the uncomfortable situations with which he had to deal with would try the patience of any reasonable man. Adams was a lawyer who had a sharp mind and could destroy opponents by pointing out the contradictions in their own arguments. Honesty was perhaps the strongest of all his traits. During the XYZ Affair, he adamantly refused to accept bribes, even though they may have resolved the differences between France and the United States.

Because Adams raised taxes during his presidency, he became extremely unpopular during his administration. However, he had seen unhappy results when a young nation is insufficiently financed and forced to depend upon other countries, which could lead to undesirable entanglements. America gained a navy and an army as a result of those taxes and now had the means to maintain its integrity and independence, as well as gain the respect of other nations.

He was a firm believer in the balance of power within the government. Long before it was written into the Constitution, Adams promoted the separation of the government into three branches—the executive, legislative, and judicial. That separation of powers proved to be one of John Adams' greatest insights, as it was written into the final US Constitution, which was ratified in 1788. During the preliminary discussions on the Constitution, the issue of the abolition of slavery had arisen, but feelings on the issue were mixed, so it wasn't included. With regard to John Adams, he was one of the few Founding Fathers who never owned a slave. Instead of succumbing to the economic advantage of having free labor on his farm, he insisted on hiring only freemen to assist him.

John Adams had the honor of having a son, John Quincy Adams, who also became president of the United States, serving from 1825-1829. Only he and George H.W. Bush (1989-1993) had sons who also became a president.

Part 4: Thomas Jefferson

A Captivating Guide to an American Founding Father Who Was the Principal Author of the Declaration of Independence and the Third President of the United States

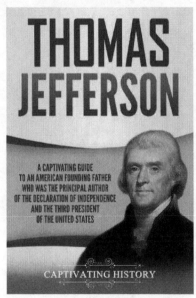

Introduction

Although one can speak of Thomas Jefferson in a tediously factual way, he was an enigma. Historically, he is noted for writing the Declaration of Independence, which was a daring and courageous statement of the rights of Americans and, indeed, of all people. Hidden beneath the many cloaks of legalistic terminologies that he was fond of using, all the strengths and vulnerabilities of Jefferson as a man were there too. Like many people of today, he had a difficult childhood. He also liked to party while in college and loved to play the fiddle. The names of his friends and colleagues are featured in all the history books of yesteryear and today—Patrick Henry, John Adams, George Washington, Lewis and Clark, Benjamin Harrison, and Lafayette. Thomas Jefferson also knew the scoundrels of the day like Benedict Arnold and Aaron Burr. He was not only a lawyer, a statesman, and a founding father of the USA, but a political and moral philosopher. He even rewrote the Bible.

Above all, however, he was human. As such, Thomas Jefferson was susceptible to weaknesses as well. Jefferson had frequent migraines, something for which he was often teased by his dear friend, James Madison, who became the fourth President of America. When he got married, he took a month off from work to spend time with his new bride. Although he seldom showed it in the State House or the Capitol, he was emotional. He wrote love poems for his wife, and was inundated with righteous anger when his people cried out against the oppression at the hands of a grandiose and greedy British king. Jefferson's sword was his humble quill pen, but it was just as powerful as a thundering cannon.

With reference to slavery and the civil rights of Native Americans, he held contradictory opinions and even argued with George Washington about the issues. Among his friends were some Native Americans and he is alleged to have had a child or more by a black woman, Sally Heming.

Thomas Jefferson craved neither fame nor fortune, but fame he received...the fortune, he did not. Although he was believed to have had an extravagant lifestyle, he mismanaged his finances. Aside from his lack of financial prowess, he became a pillar of history and symbol of independence.

Chapter 1 – Young Jefferson Leaps into Adulthood

Jefferson's Terrible Teens

Most who read about Thomas Jefferson may think that he is just a typical wealthy colonial politician in early America who lived a charmed life. Not so! Scholars who have studied his memoirs eventually noticed that he never spoke about his mother. When he wrote about his life as a teenager, he reflected:

> *When I recollect that at fourteen years of age the whole care and direction of myself was thrown on myself entirely, without a relative or friend qualified to advise or guide me, and recollect the various sorts of bad company with which I associated from time to time... I am astonished that I didn't become as worthless to society as they were.*

In the year 1757, when Jefferson was fourteen, his father died. Thomas didn't know his father that well because he was away frequently. When his father died, Peter Jefferson left his entire estate to his wife, Jane. According to the laws of Virginia, where the Jefferson's resided, that left her in full control of the money. Thomas had to wait until he was 21 years old before he could inherit it. There were ten children in the family, so she scuttled Thomas off to a boarding school. On weekends, his mother insisted that he return home to their plantation, Shadwell, to help her out.

Implications seem to highlight the view that his mother was rather domineering. When he wrote to his uncle about her death, Thomas presented the information in a glib matter-of-fact manner: "My mother died about eight o'clock this morning in the 57th year of her age." He was also noted for having a rather dim view of women who express themselves, preferring that they be quiet and of reserved demeanor. He also felt that they should never discuss politics. One's opinions about women are often based upon their relationship with the mother figure, so it might be conjectured that his future opinions about other women would be colored by that.

Jefferson was sometimes afflicted with migraine headaches and even dysentery, which attacked him sporadically throughout his life. Researchers have indicated that this was very likely a psychologically-related symptom of repressed anger. He had recurrent headaches whenever issues regarding his mother arose too.

Education

While under the guardianship of Rev. Maury, Jefferson built up a distrust of Anglicans. Maury, disparaged the Native Americans, or Indians, as they were called in those days. He said they were "temptations to evil." Yet, Thomas had a Cherokee hero in his childhood by the name of Ontasset with whom he used to visit. Ontasset even took a voyage to England to plead the case of Indian needs with the king. Jefferson greatly resented Reverend Maury's attitude and this served to create within Thomas a distrust of the clergy. Later in life, Jefferson even wrote a "revisionist-style" Bible that eliminated all references to the miracles and resurrection of Christ in which most avowed Christians believe (see Chapter 8).

Under Maury's supervision, however, Jefferson learned the classics and five languages. In 1759, he was accepted by the College of William and Mary in the historic town of Williamsburg, Virginia.

Jefferson Partied!

During his first year at college, Jefferson did what any red-blooded college student would do—he partied!

After he wasted nearly the whole year in frivolity, he checked on his financial situation and deeply regretted his policy of "spend, spend, spend." Not only had he been neglecting his studies, but he was consuming a lot of the money his mother had allotted for him to attend college. Besides the money reaped from the plantation under the auspices of his mother, his sisters were going to depend upon him for additional support when he graduated.

Jefferson Fiddled!

Jefferson met Patrick Henry, the famous American patriot and orator, at Williamsburg. Henry could play the fiddle by ear and taught Jefferson. When Thomas visited acquaintances while at Shadwell, he livened up their parties with his fiddle. He was also invited to his instructors' homes to entertain at their dinner parties.

After his dissipated first year, Thomas applied himself rigorously. Humbly, he admitted that learning cannot be reached by some "royal road;" it must be earned. After he directed his focus on his studies, he became well-rounded educationally and was an exceptional student because he loved to read. Among his studies are those familiar to all college students—history, science, ethics, the languages and the classics. Like so many other deep thinkers before and after him, Jefferson eventually turned to that of philosophy, which laid the foundations for his life after college.

The Pivotal Year: 1765

In those days, the thirteen colonies in America were English territories. When Jefferson heard about the obnoxious passage of the Stamp Act upon America, he attended a session of the House of Burgesses, a legislative governing body in Virginia. There, Jefferson witnessed his good friend, Patrick Henry, stand up and say with a voice of thunder, "Caesar had his Brutus, Charles the First his Cromwell, and George the Third might profit from their example...If this be treason, make the most of it!" Jefferson understood the crucial significance of Henry's statement with regard to the Stamp Act and the attitude of the British royalty toward America. In one of his letters, he wrote, "As long as we were young and weak, the English whom we had left behind, made us carry all their wealth to their country to enrich them...They at length began to say we should do whatever they ordered us." Jefferson was then determined to apply his legal knowledge toward securing freedom for all Americans.

Personal Life

In 1765, Thomas Jefferson's favorite sister, Jane, died. She was only 25 years old. Jane was Thomas' intellectual equal, and he thoroughly enjoyed his discussions with her. He was thrown into a period of deep grief.

His sister, Martha, married shortly afterward, but he still had to help provide for his mother and other siblings: Lucy, Randolph, Peter, Elizabeth, Mary, and Anna. Elizabeth was mentally handicapped and often needed attention. Jefferson and his siblings always tried to watch out for her.

Monticello

Across from the family home at Shadwell, Jefferson began construction on his new home which he called Monticello, meaning the "mountain." Tourists who visit this plantation residence note the fact that it is located on a steep hill near the foothills of the Piedmont mountain chain. Local flooding was frequent in that area of Virginia, so that's why he sought higher ground. At the time it was first built, Monticello was a simple, small house of brick. He employed his creative skills in expanding the estate. In 1770, Jefferson moved into the South Pavilion of the residence while it was being built. Jefferson designed the new house in the 18th-century neo-classic style. It resembled a European villa.

In 1772, he married Martha Wayles Skelton, a widow. Isaac Granger, a servant, said of her, "Mrs. Jefferson was small...Polly low like her mother and longways a pretty lady." Jefferson related later in his extensive journals about "years in uncheckered happiness" with her. In fact, even after he had secured a seat in the House of Burgesses in Virginia in 1769, he missed nearly a month in attendance. Where was he? Home with his dear Martha! Jefferson was described by contemporaries as a man who craved privacy in his personal life.

Jefferson named his first daughter after his deceased sister, Jane. In the year 1776, the girl died. She was merely 18 months old.

Jefferson's Contradictions About Slavery

Jefferson is known to have owned a large number of slaves. However, a study of his attitudes toward slavery creates a mosaic. In the American South, the economy depended upon this abhorrent practice of keeping slaves. However, in examining the dynamics of Jefferson's thought, a change was taking place. In 1768, he took on sixty-eight cases related to emancipation. In one of his cases, *Howell v Netherland*, he said: "...Under the law of nature, all men are born free, and every one comes into the world with a right to his own person, which includes the liberty of moving and using it at his own will." In those days, that was nearly tantamount to heresy. It is interesting to note that Jefferson also used the phrase "all men are born free" when he penned the Declaration of Independence eight years later.

Jefferson believed that every slave had the right to petition for emancipation. His contemporaries in Virginia began seeing him as a revolutionary with beliefs that broke the traditional lifestyles of the landowners in Virginia. In a short period of time, after he himself became the master of the plantation, he provided for the emancipation of the children of his slaves. Although he kept trying to abolish transatlantic slave trading, it wasn't halted until 1807.

He did, however, feel that emancipation of all slaves should be a gradual process. The Southern planters were heavily dependent upon it, especially for growing tobacco, a labor-intensive ordeal. Jefferson felt that sudden emancipation would create a split between the North and the South. His prediction was correct, because slavery was one of the pivotal issues that triggered the Civil War in America.

Jefferson's gradual emancipation plan was:

1. An abolition of the slave trade

2. Reduction of violent physical penalties for the misbehavior of slaves

3. Improvement of the living conditions for slaves and their families

4. Establishment of a date at which time those who were born into slavery would be declared free

5. All freed slaves should be deported from the United States

The last item, in particular, gives one pause. He was rather aristocratic in his beliefs and felt that the two races would never be able to function in the same society. Similarly, he thought that most former slaves wouldn't be able to function independently. In that sense, he was prejudiced.

The 4% Solution

So, why did Jefferson continue to own slaves? He had a burdensome debt due to the money he owed for the payment of his education (about $24,000 dollars or £17,000) and the administration of his plantation.

In the October 2012 issue of the Smithsonian magazine, Henry Wiencek said that in 1792, "Jefferson said clearly for the first time…that he was making a four percent profit every year on the birth of black children." Archeologists have also excavated part of a neighboring tract on the Monticello estate around the area once known as "Mulberry Row." This was the section on which some of his slaves raised their families. What they found were some rather shabby dwellings. Jefferson also had a number of buildings used as naileries in which his slaves worked. The archeologists located them and noted kilns, coal, charcoal, metal rods, and slag used for the manufacturing process. It was a growing business for Jefferson, because there was a lot of construction during the Colonial Era and nails were needed.

When his father-in-law, Jack Wayles died, he willed his slaves to Jefferson who willingly accepted them. Jefferson already had a number of them himself including the Hubbard and Fossett family. Wayles's estate included the Hemings family. In 2017, archeologists working at Monticello found what might be the dwelling belonging to young Sally Heming and possibly her family. This was discovered below the basement at Monticello, no doubt because Sally was a household slave for Jefferson's daughter, Martha. Results of their excavation aren't yet published.

Did Thomas Jefferson Have Sexual Relations with Sally Heming?

In 1802, the Federalists who were dissatisfied by the election results stirred up a controversy against Jefferson. In one of the newspapers, a journalist by the name of James Callender reported that Jefferson had "...kept, as his concubine, one of his own slaves." The slave to which he subtly referred was Sally Heming. Rumors flourished. During the latter years of the 19th century, two of the descendants of Sally Heming, Madison and Eston Heming, claimed that Thomas Jefferson was their father. The debate was also bolstered by the fact that descendants of Jefferson along that line were mulattos.

A 1998 investigation of DNA evidence reported in *Nature* magazine stated that Thomas Jefferson fathered Sally Heming's last child. However, when the investigation was repeated by the Thomas Jefferson Heritage Foundation, the geneticists questioned that conclusion. All they had to go by was the appearance of a unique gene that resides on the male chromosome (the Y-chromosome). Their findings indicated that the ancestor of Eston Heming could have been Field Jefferson, Thomas' paternal uncle. Thomas Jefferson may also have carried that genetic marker, but there is no definitive proof to that effect because Jefferson had no surviving male sons. Therefore, a comparative analysis couldn't be made.

Most scholars accept the view that Jefferson did father one or more children by Sally Heming.

Chapter 2 – "Two if by sea!" – Jefferson: Evolution into a Revolutionary

Assertion of American Rights and Freedom

In the year 1774 and at the age of 31, Jefferson was just an ordinary member of the House of Burgesses in his native Virginia. That house was just the lower house of the legislative assembly, but Jefferson still boldly stood up and presented *A Summary View of the Rights of British America*.

Despite his short amount of experience as a legislator, he courageously enclosed that treatise in a letter addressed to King George III, the reigning monarch of Great Britain. It was written in a style that was respectfully courteous but had the deliberate punch of accusations couched within it. In describing the domination of England and its sovereign, he utilized words such as "unwarrantable encroachments," "usurpations," "series of oppressions," "spirit of tyranny," "treasonous," and the like. His legal arguments revolved around the right of the people in America to enjoy the same rights and benefits as the people of England. He argued for free trade and the removal of all taxes and fees that wouldn't be required of any other British citizen. He further presented the case that England should permit Americans to pass their own laws for their own colonies and that England should honor those decrees.

Well-worded statement was also included into the record at the House of Burgesses in Virginia. It was so popular that it was reprinted numerous times. After noticing that his *Summary View of the Rights of British America* had been circulated even among the British public, Jefferson was besieged by a series of his recurring migraine headaches. He was unaccustomed to such notoriety, so he was anxious.

There was already unrest and rebellions against British oppression. Back in 1765, the infamous Stamp Act had been passed. However, the colonists harassed the British tax collectors to the point that they resigned out of frustration. Since the Stamp Act required the purchase of paper from England, the Americans boycotted paper shipments or made private deals with the British merchants to smuggle it in. As a result, the Stamp Act was repealed just a year after its passage!

In England, two of the prime ministers—the elder Thomas Pitt and Lord Chatham—pronounced two-sided remarks related to American independence that basically belittled the colonies. In the denigrating words of Lord Chatham: "I love the Americans because they love liberty...but they are the children; they must obey and we prescribe."

The First Continental Congress

Back in 1773 at the behest of the English prime minister, William Pitt, a tea tax was levied on the Colonies. As result, the incensed colonists raided a tea shipment and hurled barrels of tea leaves into Boston Harbor. Many of the rebels were disguised as Native Americans. The British followed up in 1774 with a blockade of the port. Under the influence of Jefferson, Virginia issued objections to the closing of Boston Harbor by England. Britain then followed up their siege with subsequent repressive legislation called the "Coercive Acts." The Americans disparaged the Coercive Acts and called them the "Intolerable Acts."

After the passage of the Coercive Acts, John Adams, governor of Massachusetts, leaped into action. He formed a new legislative body within the colonies to assert the rights of the Americans. Essentially, it amounted to a new colonial-based government, which was called the Continental Congress. This body acted as a brewing ground for the call of independence from England.
Rumors of War

In the dim-lit taverns in the evening, candles burned well into the night, as the people of the towns and villages gathered. The anger toward Great Britain was fomenting. There were some who could foresee the kind of devastation that an all-out war might bring. They were afraid of the mighty power that the British regiments displayed as they marched around the mansions of the royal-appointed governors. Most of the people in the colonies were native Englishmen and the mere suggestion of turning traitor to the authority of the Crown offended their sense of righteousness and propriety. On the other hand, many of these people were so adversely affected by the oppressive taxation that their farms and businesses were cash-strapped. The women gossiped over their backyard fences complaining about the difficulties they faced when attempting to buy goods at the market. The paper used for books their children used at the schools was heavily taxed and textbooks were becoming ragged because they weren't readily replaced. Farm families worked hard to be able to pay for the taxes levied on paper by England and barely had enough money left to allocate produce from their vegetable gardens for their own consumption.

Political divisions began to form among the Americans. Some of the settlers from different towns and areas were already becoming classified as "Tories," meaning that they supported King George. Today, there is a historical hotel, the Black Bass Hotel in

Lumberville, Pennsylvania, that – unlike other historical hotels built during Colonial America – proudly boasts, "George Washington did *not* sleep here!"

The Americans anticipated a military response on the part of Great Britain. In 1775, private militias formed in Pennsylvania and many of the Northeastern States. The Americans stealthily hid their weapons in the farmhouses and villages around the countryside rather than the designated arsenals. These were clever men who knew the terrain well and could fight in the dense woods or leap up from behind rocks and fences, having learned their guerilla-style skills from hunting.

In Massachusetts, the British governor, Thomas Gage, predictably had his soldiers search the countryside for the stashes of weapons. The only significant item they found was one cannon! While the British military looked for ammunition and artillery, a colonial group called the "Sons of Liberty" hid themselves and watched their progress. Then they sent word out to the Americans in the area.

"One if by land; two if by sea!"

The colonists knew that the bulk of the British forces was occupying Boston Harbor. However, they also knew that those who were at Boston would be joining up with another British contingent, but didn't know from where they were going to arrive. On land or by sea? So, a patriot by the name of Paul Revere and his companion, William Dawes, devised a system to alert the people. Men were dispatched to the tower of the Old North Church in Boston Harbor to hang out lanterns in order to send the message far and wide. If one light was held out, that meant the British were coming by land or if two lights were shown, the British were coming by sea. On a dark night in April 1775, two lights shone bright over the black waters of the harbor. A British naval fleet landed its military regiments at Dorchester Heights just South of Boston Harbor. It was therefore clear that they were going to cross the Charles River! All the people near the port of Charlestown awoke, formed their militias, and marched toward Lexington to surprise the British.

The Battles of Lexington and Concord

The British army was highly regulated and obstinately adhered to their traditional formations. They were surprised by this ragtag group dressed in leather wearing coonskins caps. Suddenly the colonists emerged from behind trees and stones. A rifle went off. It was the "shot heard round the world"— a phrase from the first stanza of Ralph Waldo Emerson's *Concord Hymn*. The American Revolution had begun! With the Americans in pursuit, the British found themselves scuttling back and forth between the towns of Lexington and Concord trying to unite all their different forces, some of who were still rummaging through the farmhouses and municipal buildings hunting for the hidden weapons that were no longer there.

Jefferson was a lieutenant under the prior Royal Governor, Baron de Botetourt. After the Revolutionary War began, George Washington appointed Jefferson as a colonel of the militia for his county of Albemarle, Virginia. In 1776, he was also elected to Virginia's House of Delegates.

The Battle of Brooklyn, also called the Battle of Long Island

In March of 1776, the colonial militias engaged with the British troops in a series of skirmishes. At that time, the English regarded their military response as the repression of a civil war instigated by subjects of the Crown. They underestimated the significance of the colonial rebellion.

In August, the British turned their attention to New York Harbor. The British navy landed on the shores of Staten Island at what is now known as the "Narrows." The Narrows is a very small waterway between Staten Island and Brooklyn at the Western end of Long Island. Today the Verrazano-Narrows Bridge spans that passage. Washington and his troops were entrenched at Brooklyn waiting for the British onslaught. A vicious battle broke out. While engaging the Americans there, General Howe arrived from the south and attacked the Americans from the rear. Washington and his army then retreated northwest to the island of Manhattan. This military action was a distinctive British victory. Although the colonists lost, it didn't deter them from pursuing their dream of freedom.

Chapter 3 – Jefferson and the Declaration of Independence

Out of Philadelphia came many political pamphlets and writings. Thomas Paine, a recent immigrant from England was also a political philosopher committed to humanism. He decried the attitudes related to monarchy and recognized the integrity of the individual. Paine emphasized his belief that people had the right to choose for themselves as to which form of government was best for their own societies. In January of 1776, he anonymously published a large pamphlet called *Common Sense*. In it, he outlined the kinds of organizational frameworks that could support human rights. He followed that up with his *Common Sense* newsletters. His work challenged the hereditary rights of the royalty to run Great Britain. His style was deliberately simple enough that one needn't be skilled in the study of ancient philosophies to understand it. The response in Philadelphia was overwhelming.

Jefferson read the document at Monticello. The principles presented in *Common Sense* matched those of Jefferson and influenced him to develop those concepts further. When trying to determine the true author of *Common Sense*, many at the time felt that Jefferson wrote it. Paine's style was much more direct, however. Paine wasn't from the upper class and disliked tip-toeing through the legalistic language that Jefferson used as a man steeped in law. The two men actually communicated with each other on political matters later on.

The Virginia Constitution

George Mason, a short, stocky man, was a member of the landed gentry of Virginia. He had heard about the eloquence of Thomas Jefferson and began a friendly correspondence with him. In some of his letters, he and Jefferson complained about the state of their tobacco crops for two years straight, as the weather had been too inclement for successful growth. Like Jefferson, Mason also lost his father at a young age.

Mason busied himself by rallying the patriots in Virginia and serving in the Virginia House of Delegates along with Jefferson. Mason and Jefferson frequently spoke about arsenals of weapons, supplies, and tentative plans for the battles they knew were coming. George Mason and Jefferson even sent a missive to George Washington, requesting that he be the Commander-in-Chief—an appointment which Washington readily accepted.

The delegates from Virginia tasked themselves with developing the Virginia Constitution. Mason knew his own weaknesses, one of which was the fact that he peppered his documents with sarcastic and brutally frank remarks. The other legislators toned down that language in the Virginia Constitution, but most of the elements written by Mason still remained. In its final form, the initial paragraphs, called the "Bill of Rights" of Virginia, accused King George III of Great Britain of "...detestable and insupportable tyranny." At the end of the lengthy document, after specifying all of the offenses committed against the colony, the entire body agreed to write, "By...several acts of misrule, the government of this country (America), as formerly exercised under the crown of Great Britain, is TOTALLY DISSOLVED."

The Virginia Constitution influenced Thomas Jefferson when he wrote the Declaration of Independence (see later).

Jefferson: Delegate to the Second Continental Congress

Thomas Jefferson had envisioned a career spent in the courtrooms, defending citizens in legal matters. However, that wasn't his destiny. He had been elected as a Delegate to the Second Continental Congress representing his dear state of Virginia in 1775. Jefferson had what his admired philosopher, John Locke, called a "tabula rasa," or "clean slate" because this was the first time he served as a delegate. There, in Philadelphia, he worked with George Mason, George Wyeth and James Madison, a new statesman who later became an American president. Then, of course, there was Patrick Henry whom he knew from college. In addition, he had the assistance and advice of the portly Mr. Benjamin Harrison and the reserved Mr. Edmund Pendleton, both conservatives. Jefferson came across as calm and intellectual but was considered somewhat of a "radical" in the opinion of the conservatives who attended.

The Second Continental Congress – The Declaration of Independence

The year was now 1776. In a room in Philadelphia, a Committee of Five men bent over a candlelit table discussing issues of liberty. Due to the patriotic and eloquent presentation of *A Summary View of the Rights of British Americans*, Jefferson was invited to attend by the leader of this committee, John Adams, governor of Massachusetts. Along with Jefferson, Adams contacted Benjamin Franklin of Pennsylvania, Roger Sherman of Connecticut, and Robert Livingston from New York. They pulled out a copy of the "Halifax Resolves," also known as the Lee Resolution. It was a ratified resolution passed by the colony of North Carolina earlier in the year that boldly resolved the thirteen colonies needed to declare their independence from Great Britain. They also pulled out a copy of the Virginia Constitution. These resolutions were the clarion call for all Americans to take concerted action. Thomas Jefferson was now in attendance, and George Mason recruited him to write the first draft of the Declaration of Independence.

Jefferson particularly admired Mason's initial words in the Virginia Constitution, "That all men are by nature equally free and independent, and have certain inherent rights…" A slight alteration of those words was included in the Declaration of Independence. Those concepts were common principles upon which humans formulate their beliefs.

Many of the statements within the Declaration of Independence were derived from the Virginia Constitution. George Mason managed to get in some of his very pointed wording, meant to absolutely clarify the position the colonies were pursuing in no uncertain terms. For example: "He (George III) is at this time transporting large Armies of foreign mercenaries to compleat [sic] the works of death, desolation, and tyranny, already begun with circumstances of Cruelty and Perfidy scarcely paralleled in the most barbarous ages, and totally unworthy of a Head of a civilized nation" was included.

After some revisions, the Committee of Five presented the Declaration of Independence to the Second Continental Congress. Each state was represented with fifty-six state delegates. Contrary to popular opinion, not all the states voted for independence. A few abstained but reversed themselves. In the long run, only New York continued to abstain. The Declaration was ratified based on a 12 to 1 decision.

According to the historian, Merrill Peterson, "The Declaration of Independence endowed the American Revolution with high moral purpose united to a theory of free government."

American Reaction to the Declaration of Independence

About 60% of the Americans were in favor of the sentiments expressed in the Declaration of Independence. However, there were some who felt very strongly that they should remain loyal to

Great Britain. As natives of England, they were reluctant to alter their long-held beliefs, and felt that it might be possible to work out a compromise with Great Britain. In addition, these loyalists may have been afraid of King George's reaction. Many of them had heard about and even seen the British forces in action in Europe.

British Reaction to the Declaration of Independence

The reaction in Great Britain was mixed. Some of the members of the British House of Lords felt that the royal policies toward the colonies had driven them to revolt. The Duke of Manchester compared the American relationship to the Crown with that of the Roman Empire under dictatorship. Many of the elites in England, though, thought that these uprisings would be short-lived. That was a mistake.

The learned writers of Great Britain wrote a number of articles in their newspapers that took the words in the Declaration out of context. In a picayune fashion, they minced the words and criticized the phraseology, ignoring the import of the whole document. In other writings, they appear to have deliberately misconstrued its meaning to the point that it looked ridiculous. At other times, they implied that the Americans were ignorant and mocked them. For example, when commenting about the Declaration's wording "All men are endowed by their Creator with the unalienable right of life...," one writer quipped, "How far they may be endowed with this unalienable right I do not yet say, but...their gentry assume to themselves an unalienable right of talking nonsense!"

King George's Reaction to the Declaration of Independence

Fortified by his victory at Brooklyn, King George said of the leaders who wrote the Declaration of Independence, "For daring and desperate is the spirit of those leaders, whose object has always been domination and power, that they have now openly renounced all allegiance to the crown, and all political connection with this country." Nevertheless, General Howe, who commanded British troops at Brooklyn, was reluctant to believe in the depth of the American commitment. This sentiment was typical of many of the English. The colonists, after all, were their fellow Englishmen and women. Much of the British population, including the elites, felt there was still a chance of reconciliation.

King George, however, was an arrogant and proud monarch. Despite the fact that England was in severe financial straits, he was a man who was easily insulted and inclined to maintain the overinflated image he had of himself regardless of the cost.

Chapter 4 – Jefferson: The "War" Governor of Virginia

In 1779, Thomas Jefferson was elected Governor of Virginia. This occurred during the heaviest engagements between the British and the Americans during the Revolution. When Jefferson first alighted the steps of his gubernatorial offices at Williamsburg, the British Army was in the process of leaving New York Harbor, after which they started moving southward by both land and sea. The "Redcoats," as they were sometimes called, had been exploring possibilities in Georgia as well as North and South Carolina.

General Gates of the Continental Army in North Carolina requested that Jefferson send men and troops to help thwart the British. Unfortunately, Jefferson couldn't find enough well-trained men to repel the British. He said to the general, "We find it very difficult to procure men." Jefferson attempted to rally some troops from the countryside and dispatched them to the Carolinas. These new volunteers were willing to go, but there was an insufficient number of them and they had little or no background in military service. In order to respond to these calls from the State Militia and the Continental Army, Jefferson was also forced to issue draft lotteries in order to recruit men for military service, but their only experience was in hunting animals. The general severely criticized him for this.

Although Jefferson wasn't a great military leader, he made a good governor, especially with his background in law and philosophy. In 1780, he was re-elected governor.

Jefferson's Bill for Establishing Religious Freedom – 1777

During his youth, Jefferson's headmaster, Rev. Maury, had always irritated him with his obstinacy and insistence that everyone should adhere to the principles of the Anglican Church. The Anglican Church was the Church of England, and Jefferson, who had friends among Native Americans had made the freedom of religion a priority among his causes even when he was young. The Virginia Statute for Religious Freedom was among the 126 bills he helped write. Thomas Jefferson did believe in God, but also believed very strongly that no one should be coerced into believing in any religion against his will. This statute met up with some opposition as to the way in which it was phrased, so it was revised on a number of occasions before its final passage. In his personal letters, there is a copy of it. In part, it reads, "…all men shall be free to profess, and by argument maintain, their opinions in matters of religion…". Jefferson felt so strongly about it that he left instructions that he wanted that bill mentioned in his epitaph. This bill was the precursor to the First Amendment of the US Constitution in later years.

The Raid on Richmond – 1781

Jefferson's state failed to take the precaution that the Northerners did by hiding their arms and ammunition. Virginia's armaments were still in the arsenals. Details about the War in the Northeast hadn't reached the Southern States so the loyalists in the area were astonished when the British raided their stores of ammunition. Some of them even publicized a formal complaint to the British-appointed governor in the *Virginia Gazette*:

"We humbly beg leave to represent to your Excellency that the inhabitants of this city were this morning exceedingly alarmed by a report that a large quantity of gunpowder was, in the preceding night while they were sleeping in their beds, removed from the public magazine in this city and conveyed on board one of his Majesty's armed vessels lying at a Ferry on James River."

As governor of Virginia, Jefferson moved the state capital to Richmond because it had a foundry nearby for the manufacture of ammunition and would be well-supplied. The British Army was moving toward Virginia at that time. The contingents it contained were commanded by Sir Henry Clinton and General Benedict Arnold. Benedict Arnold had originally been on the American side, but became disillusioned. He felt that America wouldn't win the war, so he turned traitor.

Thomas Jefferson had to step away from his gubernatorial duties when he heard that the British were sailing up the James River toward Richmond. Jefferson's Virginia militia knew of the pending arrival of the British forces but was delayed in confronting them, so that left Richmond without an effective defensive force. Therefore, when Arnold and his men disembarked, they were met by only a small volley of musket fire. The American Revolution had arrived at Jefferson's doorstep!

Hastily Jefferson ordered a full-scale evacuation of the city. He, his staff, and others in his offices fled. Arnold's troops then marched triumphantly into Richmond. From Richmond, Arnold boldly sent off a letter to Jefferson demanding that he surrender any weapons that were in the hands of the militia, threatening to lay the city to waste. Jefferson was furious. After he received a curt response from Jefferson, Arnold ordered his men to burn what they could in Richmond. They not only burned down the governmental buildings, but homes. Then they besieged the plantations and plundered jewelry and paintings. The Virginia Militia finally arrived under the command of General Matthews and gave chase, but many of his men were ill. Nevertheless. they struggled northward but Arnold set up a new fortification at Portsmouth, Virginia to deter them.

Jefferson himself wrote to General Washington about the state of the war efforts in Virginia. He said:

> *"A number of privateers and small vessels which are constantly ravaging the shores of our Rivers prevent us from receiving any aid from the counties lying on navigable waters…we are too far removed from the others scenes of war to say whether the main force of the enemy be within this state."*

In the same year, the General Assembly of Virginia investigated an inquiry into the humiliating defense during the raid at Richmond and Thomas Jefferson's possible culpability in the affair. As result of their sessions, Jefferson was exonerated of any wrong-doing, but he decided he wasn't going to run for re-election.

Siege at Yorktown, Virginia - 1781

The famous American-born statesman, Benjamin Franklin, was dispatched to forge an alliance with other European countries in order to secure military help. One of the most effective partners in the newly forged alliance was France. As result of Franklin's appeal, France immediately sent a large fleet of naval vessels to the American shore.

Upon hearing of the bloody attacks in Virginia and other areas in the South, General George Washington hastily marched the Continental Army South from New Jersey. Simultaneously, the French General de Rochambeau and Admiral DeGrasse moved into the bay at Yorktown, quickly followed by Comte de Barras. Heavy artillery pounded the British on the banks and they fled westward. Just west of them were Washington's land forces.

After unloading his land troops, de Barras' men gave chase to the fleeing British who were under the command of General

Cornwallis. As Cornwallis and his men moved westward, they were suddenly confronted by Washington's huge force. They were totally wedged in and surrendered.

It took a long time to negotiate a treaty, because European countries were also involved. The Continental Congress then appointed Thomas Jefferson, along with Benjamin Franklin, John Jay and Henry Laurens as negotiators. The Treaty of Paris was signed and America was now independent. The year was 1783.

Death of His Wife and Children

Two years prior to the signing of the Treaty of Paris, Jefferson lost three of his youngest children to the whooping cough. In 1782, his wife, Martha, was also ailing and close to death. In reference to her pending death, Jefferson is recorded to have written in his private journal, "...every time I kiss thy hand to bid adieu, every absence which follows it, are preludes to that eternal separation which we are shortly to face."

Chapter 5 – The Many Roles of Thomas Jefferson 1785-1800

Thomas Jefferson – Minister to France 1785-1789

Benjamin Franklin, whom Jefferson knew from his service at the Second Continental Congress, had been sent to France as an ambassador in order to secure military aid and financial support for the American Revolution. In 1784, Jefferson was appointed to succeed Franklin and went to Paris. While in France, he met frequently with the Marquis de Lafayette who came to America and fought alongside George Washington.

Jefferson had a lot in common with Lafayette. They both shared the same views on liberty. Lafayette asked for Jefferson's input regarding a document he was drafting to present to King Louis XVI regarding individual rights. Jefferson was impressed with it because it asserted to the king that all have equal rights and deserve a fair system of taxation. The final draft was presented to the king in 1789. During the same year, the French Revolution broke out. Jefferson was there on the day of the Storming of the Bastille, July 14, 1789.

Following that, Jefferson left for home, but was called back by George Washington himself to serve as secretary of state.

Thomas Jefferson – Secretary of State 1790-1793

His colleague and friend, George Washington, appointed Jefferson secretary of state in 1790. In that office, it was his role to follow the prescriptions of the administration that had appointed him. Washington was the president at this time, and he wanted to maintain a position of neutrality in the French Revolution.

The "Adam and Eve" Letter

Jefferson was, at heart, partial to French interests. He was in favor of the sentiments of the French with reference to their struggles to rid themselves of the domineering power of its monarchy. Washington wanted America to take a neutral position, but Jefferson held a contradictory opinion. He was in favor of the ongoing French Revolution and made his thoughts known publicly. In 1793, he wrote a letter to William Short, the American Charge d'Affaires to France. In that letter, Jefferson expressed his support of the French revolutionaries. He said, "Were there but an Adam and Eve left in every country, and left free, it would be better than it now is." Jefferson, in the same letter, went so far as to say that he considered "France as the sheet anchor of this country (the US) ..." The United States had only just been founded, so neutrality was the wiser choice at that time. In addition, the US had a large war debt and was hardly in a position to risk any kind of partiality that might lead to involvement in yet another expensive armed conflict. Jefferson's letter arrived just prior to the execution of the French monarch, King Louis XVI. George Washington was extremely displeased with Thomas Jefferson for failing to follow his recommendation of declaring American neutrality. The untimely arrival of Jefferson's "Adam and Eve" letter just prior to King Louis' execution was also an embarrassment for Washington.

Jefferson and the Michaux Affair

Again, in violation of Washington's policy of non-interference, Jefferson himself secretly made contact with Andre Michaux, a French political agent, who was attempting to undermine Britain's and Spain's interest in the territories that stretched from Louisiana to Canada, just east of the Mississippi River. Jefferson expressed his support for Michaux and offered his assistance. Although he may have been free to do so personally, it was against US policy for a secretary of state to do such a thing, as it would be viewed as the policy of the American president.

Jefferson vs. Hamilton Banking

Throughout his life, Jefferson had taken out substantial loans. Many of those were to pay for his education, as well as his general living expenses while he was working his way toward becoming a statesman and legislator. While Washington was president, Alexander Hamilton, as Secretary of the Treasury, proposed that the federal government set up a national bank. Jefferson was dead-set against that and argued the issue incessantly with Hamilton. He pointed out that Congress' "enumerated powers" did not encompass the establishment of a bank. Hamilton retorted that the wording meant Congress was free to take up whatever issues they pleased. Jefferson countered by restating the words in the Constitution that said Congress should only consider issues that are "necessary and proper." Establishment of a national bank wasn't "necessary" in Jefferson's opinion and wasn't among Congress' "enumerated powers." While this is an important distinction, it is a question of not only definition and semantics, but the rights of the federal government to establish a national bank. Jefferson preferred that the American States alone have the right to approve of banks within their borders. Jefferson's underlying objections had to do with a fear that a federal bank would create a monopoly and only the wealthy elite financiers would profit from it. He feared that a federal bank, for example, wouldn't make allowances for farmers when their crops failed. A state bank, however, would be aware of local conditions.

Jefferson also foresaw a class conflict that a national bank might create. He felt it would foster a new class of financiers whom Jefferson considered as "non-producers." They would simply get wealthy by handling paper currency rather than through the exertion of manual labor. He also feared that politicians and companies would set up secret alliances with the government and corruption would run rampant. The establishment of a national bank centralized governmental power placing it into the hands of a few. In addition, Bank officers running a national bank wouldn't necessarily be aware of the needs of everyone across the country. His fears were also founded on examples of the agrarian-based economy in the South. Jefferson once warned, "We are to be ruined by paper!"

Despite Thomas Jefferson's vigorous efforts, Hamilton's version was accepted and the first bank was established in 1791. It issued paper currency backed up by the gold standard. The bank also handled the payments of foreign debt, including those incurred from the war.

The John Jay Treaty

John Jay was an American statesman who had assisted in the drafting of the Treaty of Paris. From 1789-1795, he was the first Chief Justice of the United States.

After the Treaty of Paris was signed, there were still some unresolved issues remaining between England and the US after the Revolution. Among those were:

- The British occupation of forts on US territories around the Great Lakes region and in upstate New York

- The Americans wanted compensation for the vessels that were seized by the British during the war

- The need for a definitive border between America and Canada

- Payment of pre-war debts incurred by the British

Because John Jay was knowledgeable about the Treaty of Paris, he proposed a treaty to resolve the above issues. For years, these issues were debated. Border issues were those that were more easily solved, but subsequent entanglements about trade with England (who controlled Canada and some of the West Indies) caused some dissent.

Washington wanted Jefferson's support for the John Jay Treaty because it would settle some of the open issues after the war, and regain a "most favored nation" status for the US in conducting trade with England. With regard to some of remaining matters like the northern US border, compensation for debts incurred before the Revolution and the seizure of American vessels were to be decided through arbitration.

Washington wanted Jefferson to follow his lead in supporting the John Jay Treaty, because it stabilized relations with Great Britain after the war was over. Although Jefferson also wanted to stabilize relations with England, he still felt that America would be giving up too much because of the John Jay Treaty. Instead, he wanted a settlement that compensated America for losses incurred due to the war. The American public felt as Jefferson did and abhorred the John Jay Treaty. Nevertheless, Congress passed it but only by a narrow margin.

After the passage of that treaty, Washington's adversaries shouted insults at the president. Jefferson did nothing to curtail such hate speech. George Washington also had to deal with the long and tedious legal debates Jefferson had with those who disagreed with him. So, in 1793, Washington asked Jefferson to leave his post of secretary of state. In 2017, the political analyst, Stephen Knott, wrote an article for the magazine, *National Interest,* calling Jefferson "America's worst Secretary of State!" After all, Jefferson didn't represent the Washington administration very effectively. Instead, Thomas Jefferson had virtually transformed his role as secretary of state into a proverbial "soap box" for persuading Americans to follow his own lead. The animosity between George Washington and Jefferson became stronger after that. When Washington died in 1799, Jefferson didn't even attend the funeral!

Political Parties Form 1791-1793

During George Washington's administration – the very first one in America – foundations for partisan divisions were established. Washington himself was opposed to political parties, as he didn't want this new nation split over political differences so early in its history.

Despite Washington's objections, partisan politics caused the formation of two parties – the Federalist Party and the Democratic-Republicans. The Federalists supported a strong central government and the Democratic-Republicans supported a decentralized structure that granted more rights to the states.

Among the founders for the Federalist Party were Alexander Hamilton, John Jay and John Adams. Thomas Jefferson and James Madison were credited as the Founders of the Democratic-Republicans.

Thomas Jefferson – Vice-President 1797-1800

1796 was the first year in which political parties played a significant role in presidential elections. Unlike today, the vice-president could be a member of the opposing party. The winners of an election were based upon a straight count. The one with the highest number of ballots would be the president, and the person with the second highest number would be the vice-president. That system made it possible for individuals from two different parties to be elected.

The outspoken second president of the US, John Adams, was a Federalist who believed in a strong central government. Jefferson knew Adams from his tenure in the Continental Congress in Philadelphia. He had admired him, but after hammering out the Virginia Constitution with his own contemporaries, Jefferson began to realize that much of his own background as a member of the landed gentry had colored his views. While looking around at the members of the upper classes in Virginia, he began to notice that new Americans like Adams may indeed be recreating the aristocracy Jefferson received nearly the same number of votes as Adams did – Adams received 71 electoral votes and Jefferson received 68. Thus, Jefferson considered running for President in the future.

Virginia and Kentucky Resolutions

In 1798, President John Adams and the Congress passed a series of bills known as the Alien and Sedition Acts. It provided the US government with the power to deport any immigrant whom they considered a threat to the country. Jefferson was very opposed to that, as it might prompt a rejection of immigrants on the basis of nationality, political inclinations, or even on the basis of personal prejudices. Therefore, if one was a Democratic-Republican, he or she could be deported or imprisoned on the grounds of being seditious simply because they held different political views. At that time, a fully-functioning court system under an independent Department of Justice didn't exist. That meant that decisions were wholly placed upon executives of the federal government. And, in 1798, that was the Federalist Party.

Thomas Jefferson often had long political discussions with the noted statesman, James Madison, whom he had met at the Second Continental Congress. They agreed in their political views and became fast friends when Madison moved to Virginia.

After convening with political figures in the state of Virginia and its neighboring state, Kentucky, Madison and Jefferson noted that both states strongly opposed the Alien and Sedition Acts. To record the opinions of both states, Madison and Jefferson composed the Virginia and Kentucky Resolutions. Jefferson and

Madison did this anonymously. Both states passed the Virginia and Kentucky Resolutions in 1798 which served as a legislative protest to Adams' Alien and Sedition Acts.

Chapter 6 – Thomas Jefferson, The Third President of the US

The year of 1800 marked the beginning of one of the most contentious elections in American history. Two of the most vital issues that loomed large in the minds of American voters were the Alien and Sedition Acts and taxation. Many were opposed to the policies of John Adams who was running as an incumbent especially with regard to those two factors. Jefferson, as a Democratic-Republican, was opposed to the Alien and Sedition Acts and in favor of lower taxes.

A Fistfight Explodes into a National Event!

Even minor events aroused the sensitivities among Americans with regard to immigration. One Sunday, an Irish immigrant, John Connor, arrived at his church to see a crudely posted notice on the entryway: "Natives of Ireland, who worship at this Church are requested to remain in the yard after divine service, until they have affixed their signatures to a memorial for the repeal of the Alien Bill." After the pastor had the notice removed, a member of the congregation disagreed with the pastor's reaction and shouted to him, "You impertinent scoundrel!" One of the parishioners, Dr.

James Reynolds, pulled out a pistol. Another church member, James Gallagher, struck Reynolds, dislodged his grip on the gun, and then kicked him where he fell. A massive fistfight broke out and spread to the churchyard. Needless to say, the perpetrators were hauled into court.

The group of four Irishmen were charged on the basis of the Alien and Sedition Acts. The prosecutor labeled them "treasonous" and therefore "dangerous" to the government of the United States and called for their deportation.

Although the Irishmen were all acquitted, this triggered a war of words between the two political parties. Like today, the media in the eighteenth century was just as noisy. Following that occurrence, the *Philadelphia Aurora*, which was the mouth organ for the Democratic-Republicans, and the *Federalist Gazette* prolonged the argument over those laws.

In addition, national divisions and outright skirmishes over the imposition of the Alien and Sedition Acts infuriated a lot of people. Men who were using the media to express their political agenda had been imprisoned and/or fined. These weren't violent men in the eyes of the public and the ideals of freedom were seen as sufficient reason to refrain from turning opposing political opinion into an act of treason.

The issue of immigration and the possibility of politically biased application of such laws to favor the party in power at the time, the Federalists, highlighted one of the other deleterious effects of the Alien and Sedition Acts.

Taxation

Early in his administration, John Adams had raised federal taxes significantly. One of the factors that caused this was the money Adams spent building new battleships to combat French raids on American shipping lanes. Those raids were a spillover from the French Revolution. France was trying to draw America into their war. Adams tried to settle it by secretly communicating with

French agents. This was called the "XYZ Affair." Adams' attempt ended in failure. As result, it led to a two-year undeclared war with France called the "Quasi-War." That war was fought entirely at sea. The Democratic-Republicans wanted a cessation of the French raids on American ships, but preferred that the matter be handled diplomatically. The Federalists, on the other hand, favored an expansion of hostilities. That would have been even more costly. Too much American money had already been spent at war, and – besides – it wasn't until the end of Adams' administration that the issue was settled and hostilities were halted.

Outcome of the Election

There was also deep dissent within the Federalist Party leading to disunity, so Adams lost his bid for the presidency and so did Charles Pinckney – both Federalists. In the year 1800, Thomas Jefferson and Aaron Burr – both Democratic-Republicans – received 73 electoral votes each. In the case of a tie, the election was to be decided by the House of Representatives. The House appointed Jefferson president and Burr became the Vice-President.

The Louisiana Purchase 1803

Jefferson had been criticized for his support for France because of the raids on American shipping before John Adams' debacle over the issue was resolved. Thereafter, relations between France and the United States were still somewhat delicate. Shortly after his election in 1800, Jefferson received word that the Spanish had ceded a massive area just west of the Mississippi to France. The results of that were:

- France could now cut off access to Westward expansion

- It threatened the freedom of the port of New Orleans shipping along the Mississippi and restricted access to the Gulf of Mexico

Napoleon Bonaparte of France himself was in dire need of funds because he was contemplating war with England. He was much more interested in European expansion than in the administration of such a huge swath of American land. So, Napoleon offered to sell it to the United States.

The Louisiana territory was about 800,000 square miles, or 2,000,000 square kilometers. Arkansas and Missouri, in particular, were anxious for America to acquire this territory. Despite the fact that Jefferson's acute legal mind questioned whether or not it would be legal for the federal government alone to purchase this land, Jefferson was wise enough to realize that this was a golden opportunity. In 1803, he purchased it for the United States.

Jefferson & the Impeachment Trial of Samuel Chase – 1804

The judiciary branch had been set up by the revised US Constitution of 1789. The intention was to separate this branch from the executive and legislative branches. When Jefferson became president, most of the court justices were Federalists, including Samuel Chase. Chase's legal decisions tended to be in favor of Federalists, while he was much more vindictive toward defendants who were Democratic-Republicans. In one case, Chase even tried to sentence John Fries of Pennsylvania to death for Freis' opposition to the federal excise taxes imposed under President John Adams. Because he spoke up against a president, Fries was charged with sedition. (The sentence was later set aside.)

After the election of Thomas Jefferson, Justice Chase became involved in controversy yet again when he vociferously objected to changes in Maryland's law that he perceived as being too liberal by following the Democratic-Republican agenda. He said in front of a grand jury in Baltimore that such changes would cause the "…Constitution [to] sink into mobocracy, the worst of all possible governments." People were astounded when they heard about it.

That incendiary statement was highly inflammatory rhetoric focused against the Democratic-Republicans and Jefferson was furious. So, he and other Democratic-Republicans in the House of Representatives impeached Chase on the basis of judicial misconduct. Chase argued back that the court could only convict him under the constitutional definition of high crimes and misdemeanors, and that his diatribe couldn't be classified as such. When the case moved up to the Senate for a vote, they acquitted him.

Thus, a higher standard was placed upon the courts with regard to the serious action of impeachment. In Chase's case, they ruled that no justice could be removed on the basis of his political beliefs. As a precaution, however, they recommended that justices refrain from making statements either in or outside the courtroom that are highly charged politically. This case marked a precedent that is still used today.

The Barbary Pirates

Even though the French privateering had effectively been halted, America still wasn't free from pirates. The Barbary Pirates were the most common ones. They were mostly composed of Berbers from Algiers and Tripoli. After the Revolutionary War, the colonies had lost the protection of the British warships, so fierce fleets of swift vessels manned by these pirates ferociously raided American merchant vessels. America wanted to accelerate trade with Europe and needed to have unimpeded access to the Mediterranean Sea. The US reluctantly paid tribute to the pirates in order to cease these arbitrary attacks. This practice amounted to legalized extortion. After America had financed the Louisiana Purchase, it didn't need to go into deeper debt so Jefferson decided not to pay the Barbary Pirates anymore. Fortunately, John Adams had increased the strength of the American Navy so Jefferson was able to use those ships to wage an all-out war against the Berber ruffians.

Initially, the early battles against the petty Tripoli tyrant went badly. American sailors were captured and taken into slavery. Jefferson was humiliated. Then he reached out to the Europeans who were likewise subject to the Barbary savagery. Finally, after years of battles in the Tripoli and Algerian harbors, he was assisted by the Greeks and Arabs. Peace was finally reached in 1804. On the shores of the North African city of Tripoli, an American flag was raised. It was the first time in history that the American flag flew over foreign soil. There is a phrase in the Marine hymn of today commemorating that event. Jefferson didn't have to pay tribute any longer, but still had to free his captive sailors. Rather than enter into lengthy and contentious legal arguments, he paid ransoms to secure their release.

The Shoshone Native American Girl & the Lewis and Clark Expedition

After the Louisiana Purchase, Thomas Jefferson wanted to find a route that would provide access to the Pacific. Jefferson, a prolific reader, had read about the expeditions of Captain Cook in search of the infamous Northwest Passage. Although those explorations were forged through the frozen seas of Northern Canada, Jefferson had hoped for something that would help America develop trade. In addition, he wanted the Louisiana territories explored, as well as areas that lay west of there. He then had Congress finance an exploration. The Spanish had possession of the American Southwest at that time, but the far northwest was free to explore.

Jefferson knew of a hardy explorer from his own county in Virginia (Albemarle) and commissioned him to explore that vast territory. His name was Captain Meriwether Lewis. Jefferson invited him up to Monticello to study in his library which contained books on natural history, geology, and the sciences. Jefferson had compiled his own study of the languages of the indigenous people in America and gave it to Lewis to help him communicate with the tribes. After spending some time at Monticello, Lewis recruited Lieutenant John Clark and a group of military volunteers to assist. They called themselves the *Corps of Discovery.*

Lewis and Clark moved up the Missouri River with their men and built Fort Mandan in the Dakota territory. Along the journey, which was made mostly by canoe, they met many indigenous peoples from various tribes. After traversing the land of the Sioux, they came across a 16-year-old Native American girl by the name of Sacajawea. She was of the Shoshone tribe, but had been kidnapped by another tribe and put into slavery. A French fur trapper, Toussaint Charbonneau, had married the girl thus freeing her. Lewis and Clark hired Charbonneau and took his wife, Sacajawea, with them. Sacajawea was a knowledgeable and skilled woman of many talents. She spoke a number of Native dialects and assisted in translation. During the year-long trip, she had an infant son and gave birth to yet another son. If it wasn't for Sacajawea's courage, Lewis and Clark could have lost their diaries during a freak storm that broke out on a raging river.

After Clark died, Lewis, Sacajawea and the other men returned, bringing with them notes and the specimens that Jefferson had requested. When the expedition was concluded, Charbonneau and Sacajawea returned to North Dakota with their children. Lewis sent them money to help support their children.

Jefferson's Puzzling Stance on Native Americans

Thomas Jefferson believed in freedom for all men, including Native Americans. After learning about the various tribes from his own childhood experiences and what he gleaned from the diaries from the Lewis and Clark expedition, he felt that the best course of action for dealing with the Native tribes was either assimilation or forced removal of the Native tribes further west. That was a harsh stance, but he felt that the American culture and that of the Native Americans were significantly different and justified relocation.

In addition, he knew that these people were true naturalists. They had a deep and respectful understanding of the earth and how to cultivate it. After all, they were the ones who introduced the colonists to the growing of maize (corn). Therefore, he felt that Native American resettlements in the West would be successful.

Jefferson's "Civilization Program"

Jefferson knew that the culture of the Native Americans was vastly different from that of the English and subsequent European immigrants. It was Jefferson's wish that the Native Americans learn the agricultural techniques of the Americans and settle on farms rather than hunt freely on the open range. Most of all, Jefferson wanted to avoid the bloodshed that resulted from conflicts with American farmers and townspeople.

He did want the Native Americans to live on their lands in peace but didn't want them to migrate or engage in their nomadic traditions.

In 1803, Jefferson sent a confidential letter to Congress making two suggestions to bring about the cessation of the bloody fights between the Native Americans and the whites:

> First: to encourage them to abandon hunting, to apply themselves to the raising of stock, agriculture and domestic manufacture, and thereby prove to themselves that less land and labor will be needed to survive and flourish.

> Secondly: to multiply trading houses among them, and place within their reach those things which will contribute more to their domestic comfort, than the possession of extensive, but uncultivated wilds. This program, of course, could be considered one-sided and deprived the Native Americans of their rights.

Chapter 7 – Jefferson Re-Elected in 1804

Although the election of 1800 was a trying one for America in its infancy, the election of 1804 was a landslide in favor of Thomas Jefferson. He received all of the electoral ballots except for Delaware and Connecticut. He handily won because of his role in the Louisiana Purchase that allowed American citizens who wanted to settle in the Ohio Valley or the newly formed states lying just east of the Mississippi River to have all the protections the American government could offer. George Clinton also ran in the election and became Vice-President. Clinton had a remarkable military career and that made him popular with the American people.

Conspiracy against Jefferson: Aaron Burr

Although Jefferson had political disagreements with Hamilton as a Federalist, he was somewhat distrustful of Burr. In the 1800 Election, Jefferson discovered that Burr had engaged in underhanded schemes.

In 1805, Burr conspired to gain control of territories in Texas. Spain had ownership of that land but agreed to lease it to Burr, whose objective was to gain control of some land in the West. Only an Eastern portion of Texas was included in the Louisiana Purchase of 1803. Burr desired ownership of Western Texas, which was part of what was called "Spanish Texas." His plan was to set up a new country on his own! Joseph Daviess, the district attorney for Kentucky, got word about Burr's plans and notified Jefferson. The president dismissed his letter as a political ploy. However, Daviess was persistent and brought charges of treason against Burr.

The governor of Louisiana, James Wilkinson, was contacted by Burr who wanted him to join the conspiracy. Instead of partaking in the treacherous plot, he contacted Jefferson as well and confirmed Daviess' accusations. Then Thomas Jefferson sat up and took notice. Thomas Jefferson's cabinet examined the evidence and Burr was arrested in 1806.

The judge at the trial was John Marshall. In his decision, Marshall indicated that Burr hadn't committed an overt act of war against America because that land wasn't part of America at that time. In addition, Burr was caught before he could execute his diabolical conspiracy. Therefore, a treasonous act hadn't actually occurred. Burr was acquitted.

Despite the verdict, Burr's political career was obliterated by this episode. He then fled to England and later to France.

The Chesapeake Affair - 1807

During the years 1803-1815, the Napoleonic Wars between England and France were raging in Europe. America had declared neutrality in that war, as they were still recovering from the Revolution.

In order to win a victory over France, Britain needed more fighting seamen so they patrolled off the shores of America in search of British sailors who deserted. Some of them were deserting and enlisted in the American Navy. Britain dispatched a number of warships to stop these American ships to seize any English sailors that might be on board.

In 1807, England dispatched a British warship, the HMS Leopard, to the port at Norfolk, Virginia. A US Frigate, the USS Chesapeake, under the command of Commodore James Barron, was preparing for a voyage to the Mediterranean. Suddenly, the HMS Leopard approached Barron and demanded to search the ship for deserters. Barron refused. After that, the HMS Leopard fired at the USS Chesapeake broadside. As result, several Americans were killed and others were injured including Barron. As result of the attack, the Chesapeake was severely damaged and unable to counterattack. Barron was left with no choice but surrender. The British then boarded the ship and arrested four sailors, only one of whom was actually British.

Jefferson had the naval confrontation in Chesapeake Bay investigated, along with other stop-and-search incidents offshore. It was discovered that as many as 4,028 Americans had been seized by the British in addition to 1,000 ships. Also, French vessels were also conducting stop-and-seize activities, but the number of these events were fewer. The secretary of state, James Madison, reported this to Congress and filed an official complaint with Great Britain and France.

There was an uproar in America over the Chesapeake incident in particular. It touched all the sensitivities of the Americans, as it only served as a cruel reminder of the Revolution. It certainly looked like England –and to some extent France – were trying to suck America into a war. Jefferson realized that something drastic had to be done, but desperately wanted to avoid armed conflict.

The Embargo Act of 1807

Jefferson drew up a law and proposed it to Congress. It contained two facets: 1) Cease American trade at foreign ports, and 2) place extra restrictions on shipments from Great Britain.

Congress hastily passed it.

The Embargo Act was ill-advised because Southern farmers were adversely affected. New England had also been shipping material and manufactured goods to Europe as well. Merchants in America felt that they would rather risk losing some ships than be bankrupted by allowing their ships to sit idle in the ports. Trade was essential and Jefferson had acted impulsively, as did the members of Congress. Just days prior to Jefferson's exit from office, the act was repealed in 1808.

The Non-Intercourse Act - 1809

The Embargo Act was replaced by the Non-Intercourse Act in 1809. This was a compromise. The Non-Intercourse Act only forbade trade with France and England, while other European ports were open to American shipping. The law wasn't practical because it was unenforceable. Due to this interference in naval trade, America was drawn into the War of 1812. This is what Jefferson had feared. His term expired that year, but he didn't want to run again. A 19th-century historian, James Schouler, paraphrased a sentence from Jefferson's personal writings which says it best: "He wanted to retire from the public stage and pass the rest of his days in domestic ease and tranquility, banishing every desire of hearing what went on in the world."

Livingston v. Jefferson: The Batture Case

Thomas Jefferson returned to Monticello in 1810, but was immediately thrown into the spotlight again when a man by the name of Edward Livingston claimed to own a plot of land, called a "batture," along the Mississippi. Jefferson had the title to that land, and when he discovered the intrusion he had Mr. Livingston removed. Livingston sued. Jefferson was astonished and upset, since he was not only an attorney but a former president being sued by a civilian. Jefferson felt that this case was embarrassing and insulting. Jefferson then hired three attorneys—George Hay, William Wirt, and Walter Tasewell—to participate in his defense.

Albert Gallatin, a lawyer and a Democratic-Republican who served as Secretary of the Treasury under Jefferson, assisted in the defense as well. In 1810, Jefferson conducted legal research on the issue and sent it to Gallatin from Monticello. In an 1810 letter to him, Jefferson said: "I know that even a federal jury could not find a verdict against me on this head, but I go fully into the question of title because our characters are concerned in it, and because it involves a most important right of the nation."

Jefferson prevailed in the long run, but the case was decided outside of court, which he found disappointing. He preferred to have a definitive record of the case in order to establish a precedent.

Chapter 8 – Intellectual, Writer, Farmer

Jefferson's Letter Writing

Even though Jefferson had said that he wanted to leave public life and concern himself with life on his plantation, he couldn't help but express himself on various political topics. He also used a lot of his time to send courteous messages and express gratitude to dignitaries whom he met while in public office. Thomas Jefferson always admitted that he wasn't a great orator like his friend Patrick Henry, but was a prolific writer even though he was very wordy. He enjoyed writing, and realized from his past experience that his efforts helped the people of this nation.

Many of his correspondences were with the Marquis de Lafayette, whom he met in France at the very beginning of the French Revolution. During that time, he and Lafayette discussed that Revolution at length. Lafayette was horrified by the bloodshed caused by the conflict, and desperately tried to help his people work out a more diplomatic solution. Unfortunately, he was unsuccessful. Instead, the French people followed the lead of the fiery Napoleon Bonaparte whose hidden agenda was imperial conquest. Jefferson, in one of his letters, praised Lafayette for his peace-making attempts saying, "I found you were right...but unfortunately, some of the most honest and enlightened of our patriotic (French) friends, are closet politicians merely, and do not weigh the hazards of a transition from one form of government to another."

Founder, University of Virginia 1819

Although the College of William and Mary was Thomas Jefferson's *alma mater,* he became rather disillusioned about it after the American Revolution. His problems were related to the College's strong religious ties to the Anglican Church. Jefferson disliked any kind of religious involvement. The College of William and Mary, named after William III and Mary II, king and queen of England in the 17th century, existed at a time when England was required to adhere to the tenets of the Church of England, which is the Anglican church. In 1777, Jefferson passed the Freedom of Religion Act and was a staunch believer in religious freedom for all. His *alma mater,* however, required all their students to study the Catechism approved by the Anglican Church. Of course, Jefferson was very much against that. The college also didn't have a strong science department, and ever since the Revolutionary War, enrollment was dropping.

In 1817, Jefferson sent a flurry of letters to other former graduates and influential men with the suggestion that a new centrally-located university be built in Virginia. Toward that interest, they met to discuss it. One of the former graduates of the College of William and Mary, James Monroe, owned some property near Charlottesville and donated it for the proposed college.

Jefferson had a wide variety of interests and skills. One of them was architecture. In fact, prior to the American Revolution, he had been asked by the British-appointed governor, Lord Dunsmore, to design another building for the College of William and Mary. In 1772, he sketched out a draft for such a building. Lord Dunsmore responded that he liked the design and an adaptation of Jefferson's design was used there. Due to his success with that project and with the design of Monticello, Jefferson applied his architectural skills toward designing the new college he envisioned in Virginia. He pictured the college as a village, consisting of a number of buildings targeted for specific purposes. In fact, Jefferson designed a number of campus buildings there that exist to this day.

In 1819, Jefferson and his other sponsors proposed the institution to the General Assembly of Virginia and it was approved. It was called Central College, but the name was later changed to the University of Virginia. The University credits Jefferson with being its chief architect.

Initial Curriculum

As per Jefferson's wishes, students weren't required to take religious courses. They were, however, free to enroll in the divinity school. Among the primary majors the university offered were:

- Medicine
- Mathematics
- Law
- Chemistry
- Ancient and modern languages
- Moral philosophy
- Natural history

In November of 1824, he hosted an event for four hundred guests including the Marquis de Lafayette to see the new college. After recruiting professors from both England and the United States, it opened on March 7, 1825, with Thomas Jefferson as its first rector. He was succeeded by his friend, James Madison.

Monticello Vineyards and Vegetable Gardens

Thomas Jefferson loved horticulture. His plantation was like a laboratory and he experimented with a wide variety of crops. In his *Garden Book*, Jefferson took copious notes about the successes and failures in his gardens.

Jefferson's vegetable gardens served a practical purpose, as its produce was used by the staff and all the residents of Monticello for consumption.

Jefferson continually dabbled in growing grape vines at Monticello cultivated from the European species called *Vitis vinifera*. He especially remembered it from his experiences as the Ambassador to France. The *Vitis vinifera* yields a tasty and delicate wine. However, that particular variety didn't grow well in the difficult moist climactic conditions in Jefferson's orchard at his estate because he grew it near a native species called *Vitis labrusca*, the fox grape. The *Vitis labrusca* variety carries the *phylloxera* louse, which isn't harmful to plants with exception of Jefferson's grape, the *vinifera*. In the 19th Century, no one realized that because it was native to Europe and hadn't yet been cultivated in America. He also reportedly grew *Vitis rotundia*, a grape that is native to the South. Of course, that was successful and Jefferson stored it in the wine kegs at Monticello.

Jefferson was primarily a vegetarian. He said, "I have lived temperately, eating little animal food, and that as a condiment for the vegetables which constitute my principal diet." Among the vegetables he planted were:

- Eggplant
- Tomato
- Sesame
- Okra

- English pea
- Asparagus
- Artichokes
- Kale

After the Lewis and Clark expedition, Lewis brought back some plant roots from their journey. Among those was Salsify, which is a little-known root vegetable called "oyster root." Jefferson discovered that it could be used as a tasty thickener for soups and stew, so he grew that as well. He dearly loved salads and asked his kitchen staff to add it to them.

Fruit Orchard

It is amazing to note that Jefferson experimented with 150 varieties of fruit. He grew a wide variety of apples, especially those suitable for making cider. He also had peach trees by the hundreds, along with apricots and cherries. Gooseberries and strawberries were grown in his "fruitery," as he called it. Jefferson also grew fig trees propagated from roots he had shipped in from France.

Flower Gardens

Jefferson loved flowers and had roots for perennials sent to him. Most of the flower beds were along winding paths to allow room for the orchards. He had his daughters and granddaughters care for them.

Wheat and Clover

His staple crop was wheat. At Monticello, there were about 5,000 acres. After the harvest, Jefferson planted clover which restores the nitrogen in the soil. It is also a useful ground cover that discourages the growth of weeds.

He didn't just have Monticello; Jefferson also had smaller farms which he called Lego and Thufton. He had inherited 300 acres at Thufton as part of his patrimony and grew vegetables for his family and staff there. In 1783, he bought the 819-acre Lego farm.

Jefferson used a portion of that for pleasure, because it had a beautiful brook and was picturesque. The rest he used for growing vegetables.

Some of Jefferson's Inventions

Three notable inventions are attributed to Jefferson:

- The Moldboard Plough
- The Wheel Cipher
- The Macaroni machine

The Moldboard Plough

To prevent erosion, he redesigned the curvature on the blades of his plows to cut deeper into the soil. Unlike the one invented by Charles Newbold in 1797, Jefferson's had a double edge on it and his plow was lighter. His earlier designs were wooden and followed his mathematical formula. Later on, he had it cast in iron. Improved versions of his moldboard plow are still sold today.

The Wheel Cipher

When Jefferson was in France as an ambassador, he became involved in the solicitation of aid to finance the Revolutionary War. He also requested ships and military forces. When he noticed that his correspondence had been opened and read before delivery, he invented a wheel cipher to convert written material into code. He sent some wheel ciphers to his correspondents as well, and all their correspondence was encrypted.

The Macaroni Machine

When he was a minister to France, he developed a macaroni machine and delighted Lafayette and his other French guests with his pasta creations. It consisted of an iron box into which a wheat paste was placed. The paste was then pressed into the unit and forced out through holes at the end. The wheat paste was made from durum wheat which could be grown at Monticello.

The Jefferson Bible – 1819

Jefferson had a long-term project he had pondered over with regard to religion. He toyed with the idea of writing his own instructions for leading a good life. His initial premise was to write a book with a review of the moral philosophy promoted by Jesus Christ. In 1798, he wrote it, and simply called the book *The Philosophy of Jesus.* When Jefferson was reviewing some of his written material, he discovered he'd lost the book. From his discussions about the book in his early private papers, scholars believe it contained just the words of Jesus Christ alone, without the added narrations from the evangelists.

Because Jefferson wanted to replace it somehow, he wrote another book about Jesus Christ. That one he titled: *The Life and Morals of Jesus of Nazareth.* Toward that effort, Jefferson painstakingly took a Bible and fastidiously cut out the printed sentences from his favorite sections of that Bible. Then he delicately glued them on to fresh paper. Biblical researchers investigated the volume and noted that he eliminated any references to a declaration of Christ's deity and stories about the miracles attributed to him including the Resurrection.

With reference to his own beliefs, Jefferson called himself a Christian, but with the caveat that he believed in the doctrines preached by Christ as opposed to his divinity.

Thomas Jefferson believed in the freedom of religion and had the Virginian government pass a statute that protected that right (see Chapter 4). He was also always critical of the accouterments of ceremonial garb such as ornately woven vestments and detested such displays as "instruments of riches and power."

Chapter 9 – Thomas Jefferson's Declining Years

Collar the Dogs!

As discussed earlier, Thomas Jefferson used to spend a lot of time writing letters. People knew that and contacted him about legal and other matters. His correspondents were thrilled to receive replies from someone so notable. Occasionally, he would make attempts at humor—usually dressed up in his legalistic wording. Opportunities for that arose whenever someone sent him a letter addressing an issue that evoked an emotional reaction on his part. In 1811, he received a letter by Peter Minor to ask that he be instrumental in supporting some regulations regarding pet dogs. Minor felt that they were nuisances who sometimes destroyed property.

It just so happened that Jefferson wasn't particularly fond of dogs either. He did have sheepdogs at Monticello, but made an exception in that case, as they served a useful function.

In response to the letter, Jefferson said:

> *I participate in all your hostility to dogs, and would readily join in any plan for exterminating the whole. But as a total*

extirpation cannot be hoped for, let it be partial. I like well your outlines of a law for this purpose: but should we not add a provision for making the owner of a dog liable for all the mischief done by him and requiring that every dog shall wear a collar with the name of the person inscribed who shall be security for his honest demeanor?

Curiously, Jefferson's private letters were simply signed, "Th. Jefferson."

The Tearful Visit of the Marquis de Lafayette

In 1824, Lafayette contacted James Monroe, the current president, about visiting the US. The nation honored him because Lafayette was instrumental in helping the country during the American Revolution. He toured twenty-four states. During that time, he greeted the President, veterans of the Revolution, dignitaries, statesmen, writers and other American citizens all along the way. Lafayette made it a point to visit Fayetteville, North Carolina, a city named after him. After that stop, he went to visit his dear friend, Thomas Jefferson. Jefferson and Lafayette kept up a healthy correspondence through the years, but they hadn't seen each other in person since 1789.

On the day of Lafayette's arrival at Monticello, an excited assembly waited on the front terrace. Lafayette was preceded by a train of carriages and a large contingent of military cavalrymen in dress uniforms. Then a bugle sounded, and the guest of the nation pulled up in a fine carriage. Jefferson's grandson, Jefferson Randolph, described their heartwarming meeting: "As they approached each other, their uncertain gait quickened itself into a shuffling run, and they exclaimed 'Ah, Jefferson! Ah, Lafayette!' Then they burst into tears as they fell into each other's arms."

Toward the end of the dinner Jefferson served, James Madison and his wife arrived, and the excitement of greetings started all over again. The next day, Jefferson and Lafayette visited the University of Virginia and celebrated at a banquet. Jefferson's voice had now grown weak with age so he had to have someone else read the speech he wrote.

Jefferson's family and many of his friends visited Lafayette and Jefferson at Monticello for the next eleven days. The two close friends spent many hours in front of a blazing fireplace reminiscing.

Jane Smith, a dear friend of the family, described the emotional tenor of those days well: "The sun shone every day – the Indian summer became every day softer: we walked on the roads that circled the mountain. And in the evenings, we strolled on the terrace."

Second National Bank – 1816

Henry Clay was a statesman and a Congressional representative. He was instrumental in setting up the Second National Bank. Despite his objections to central banking, Jefferson knew there was little he could do about it except suggest some modifications and encourage the Bank supporters to add protective measures. Clay, also a Democratic-Republican, was pleased with Jefferson's suggestions. One of Jefferson's recommendations called for tariffs on imported goods, and Clay added that to the revised charter. More fiscal refinements were added. Those alterations protected the bank to some extent, but unfortunately not the people.

Panic of 1819

During the year of 1819, there was an economic panic. Banks had been freely giving out loans for agricultural products and real estate, resulting in inflation. The corruption Jefferson alluded to years earlier occurred. Embezzlement was rampant. The situation was aggravated when there was a downturn in the economy after a number of disastrous harvests. Many state banks collapsed and the Second National Bank was nearly insolvent.

The Second National Bank then mercilessly called in loans, and many people defaulted. That included a friend of Jefferson's by the name of Wilson Cary Nicholas. Unfortunately, Jefferson had co-signed two loans for him amounting to $10,000 each. When Nicholas died, the value of Nicholas' estates had also plunged in value. Sale of that land wouldn't be sufficient to cover the balance of the loan plus interest. As co-signer, Jefferson was the responsible party.

The Verge of Bankruptcy

Although Jefferson had accumulated an enormous debt himself, the debt that he incurred after the death of Wilson Nicholas was a heavy burden. The year was now 1826, and Jefferson was 83 years old. Nevertheless, he was an honorable man and desperately tried to pay off his debts. When he first retired, Jefferson thought that the money he saved from his salaries as minister to France, secretary of state, vice-president, and president would serve to help to cover some of his living expenses. In addition, he thought the profits from his farms would supplement that. Unfortunately, those profits were practically negligible. Prior to his retirement, Jefferson had been so heavily focused on his legal and political career that he didn't devote enough energy into budgeting his expenses carefully. Jefferson became alarmed and distressed when he discovered his miscalculations.

On a personal level, Jefferson also wanted to bequeath Monticello to his single surviving daughter, Martha Jefferson Randolph, but that was going to be difficult, given what he owed on his loans. As a solution, Jefferson felt that he might be able to pay off his debts by selling off parcels of land at Monticello and his farms, and still be left with a portion of Monticello he could bequeath to Martha.

When people were deeply in debt during those days, it was a common practice among landowners in the South to hold land lotteries in order to satisfy debt. In February of 1826, he petitioned the legislature to permit such a sale. Despite some objections, his plan for the lottery sales was approved. Americans were horrified to hear about Jefferson's misfortune. They not only bought parcels of land from him, but donated money to this man who had accomplished so much for them. However, the value of land was very low at the time, and the entire figure after the sales and donations only came to around $16,500. That covered only 17% of Jefferson's remaining debt.

Jefferson was tired, sick and sadly knew that the debt would be passed on to his heirs.

Jefferson's Illness and Death

Since the spring of the year 1826, Jefferson was bedridden. He had suffered from rheumatism as he aged, but now had severe intestinal and urinary disorders. His family and friends rushed to his bedside during his final hours.

Thomas Jefferson took his last breath on July 4, 1826 — exactly 50 years since the Declaration of Independence was ratified. That wasn't coincidental. It was providential, because the people of America have been living in freedom ever since.

Conclusion

Thomas Jefferson was a virtual superhero in the landscape of freedom and liberty. The dream of freedom he envisioned was bought at a great price, because this man spent all his waking moments toiling with his quill pen to make that freedom real. Independence for his nation started when Jefferson declared it so. Just 1,458 words in the Declaration of Independence made all the difference. It was a majestic work written by a man without a crown.

When the American people yearning to be free came to Jefferson in hopes he would lead them to experience that liberty in their houses of state, he became a governor. When the Americans wanted to bring their message overseas, he became their ambassador. When they wanted him to head up their nation, he became their president. Whatever the American people asked of him in the name of independence and liberty, he complied. Thomas Jefferson wasn't consumed with the glories of leadership; he came to serve the American people to the best of his ability. That was his passion.

Part 5: John Jay

A Captivating Guide to an American Statesman, Patriot, Diplomat, Governor of New York, the First Chief Justice, and One of the Founding Fathers of the United States of America

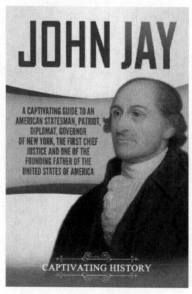

Introduction

John Jay was a master statesman and strategic diplomat who associated with all the great men of his day in the mid-18th century. However, his contemporaries said that he was modest and humble. They indicated that they could be at a party or gathering and guests had to coax him into discussing his role during the American Revolution or as the first Supreme Court justice of the new nation.

John Jay was tall and thin, not noted for his physical strength, but for his courage. One time, in the midst of a riot over body snatchers, he walked out into the middle of it! It was a foolhardy gesture, as he was injured, but that injury helped quiet down the embarrassed crowd around him. When he was burned in effigy over the Jay Treaty he negotiated, he was unperturbed and even joked about it.

Perhaps he had a darker sense of humor due to the fact he grew up in the midst of heartaches and tragedy. One of his siblings, Nancy, was blinded after her bout with smallpox, and his brother, Peter, was partially blind. John's other brother, Augustus, had a severe learning disability as well as emotional difficulties. His sister, Eva, was often overcome with fits of hysteria. John and his wife had to care for them when his father became older.

Although he was wealthy at a young age, John Jay wasn't infected with greed, as were some of the powerful men in colonial

America. As governor of the newly-founded New York State, he could have confiscated estates and public lands but refrained from doing so. In any case, the various disabilities and physical maladies that afflicted his siblings reduced his income significantly. John was a true family man and always sought news of his family when away from home, which was often. During the Revolution, in particular, he had to make constant arrangements and go to any expenses in order to keep his family safe.

Perhaps his greatest contribution during his political life was his dedication to the duty to serve his country. When he became the first chief justice of America, he established the groundwork for fairness and neutrality in decision-making. Many of the principles he established in the 19th century are practiced today by this high court. His foresight was extremely acute, and leaders of America sought out his opinions even during his retirement. He was a role model for patience and fairness, and he manifested these qualities in his roles as a jurist, the governor of New York, and the ambassador to Spain, France, and England. None of his positions were easy ones. Every issue he confronted in his political life was a negotiation, and he was expected to referee various opposing factions. Almost magically he developed practical results that were "win-win solutions."

John Jay is a Founding Father who is often overlooked, and few people realize the extent and impact of his contributions to the new nation. He might not have been a part of the Constitutional Convention, but he passionately argued for a more powerful, yet balanced, centralized form of government which eventually led to the passing of the U.S. Constitution. John Jay's work provided for the expression of liberty and justice in a viable society, and he designed a functional and dynamic process that still works today.

Chapter 1 – From Tyranny to Freedom

The "Divine Right to Rule?"

In 17th-century France, King Louis XIV—also called the "Sun King"—clouded the European sun with his own glory. Like all absolute monarchs, Louis really believed that God himself bestowed upon him the power and right to rule his country just by virtue of heredity. What a glorious world he experienced, as the whole country revolved upon his whims and wishes!

Like a god, King Louis XIV of France expected glory and even adoration. Autocracy was also easier if everyone was of the same religion. In France, during King Louis XIV's reign, the Catholic religion was the state-mandated religion. That way, pulpits could be platforms for his agenda. Because his promulgations were announced by the clergy, they gave people the impression that his rulings were doctrine. In 1685, King Louis tore down the church John Jay's great-grandfather attended. Why? Because Augustus Jay and his family weren't Catholic; they were Huguenots. Huguenots are Protestants following the traditions of John Calvin, a Protestant reformer. Prior to the ascension of King Louis, the French were free to practice other religions by virtue of the Edict of Nantes of 1598, but King Louis XIV revoked that in 1685.

When that occurred, armed cavalry soldiers called "dragoons" went from town to town trying to force the Huguenots to convert to Catholicism at the point of a gun. The Huguenots, including

John Jay's great-grandfather, were harassed, denied positions in civil service, and discriminated against. Their churches were torn down or repurposed. Initially, the Huguenots were allowed to emigrate, but many were highly educated, and France didn't want to lose a skilled labor force. Consequently, emigration was forbidden —or else. Persecutions followed when people refused to conform.

Religious Refugees

As a result, Augustus Jay clandestinely arranged to leave with his wife and family and flee to the British colonies. In 1690, with the help of friends, he procured passage to South Carolina. Finding the climate far too humid and mosquito-ridden there, the Jays traveled to Philadelphia. At that time, Philadelphia wasn't much more than a carriage stop spotted with farms. Augustus Jay was a merchant, accustomed to setting up shop in city districts, but Philadelphia in the late 17th century was far too underdeveloped to support a profitable commercial enterprise, so the Jays left there and moved to New York. This area had originally been settled by Peter Stuyvesant and the French Huguenots who built their Dutch Reformed churches there and set up a nascent mercantile culture. What's more, most of the settlers spoke French like the Jays. The colony had originally been called "New Netherland," and current-day Manhattan was called "New Amsterdam" when Augustus arrived. It thrived under the directorship of Peter Stuyvesant before it was ceded to the British after the Anglo-Dutch War in 1665. The British, however, permitted the continuation of the Dutch-found enterprises. Today, many areas in New York are named after Peter Stuyvesant.

Augustus Jay set up a thriving business in the harbor city of New York, selling wheat, timber, iron ore, and other products. As New York was in its infancy stage, there was a need for all of those items for consumption and construction. His business was extremely successful. He married Anna Marie Bayard in 1697. They had four daughters and one son. Their son, Peter Jay, John

Jay's father, followed him into the business. His venture was so successful that he was wealthy by the time he was just 24 years old! In 1728, he married Mary Van Cortlandt in the Dutch Reformed Church. Van Cortlandt Park in Westchester County, New York is actually named after her family.

Heartaches and Victories of the Jay Family in the Early Years

Although the Jays were wealthy merchants, they had their share of family heartaches. Peter and Mary's firstborn was a girl, Eve, or "Eva" as she was sometimes called. Eva wasn't very healthy as a child and had a fragile ego. She tended to have fits of hysteria at times and needed a lot of emotional support. Peter's eldest son, Augustus, who was named after Peter's father, had a learning disability. Peter and Mary tutored him carefully, and he managed to master some academic skills. Of course, there were no schools in those days that catered to children with learning problems. Two of Peter's other children, Peter Jr. and Anna Marika (also known as "Nancy"), contracted smallpox at a young age, and the disease left Nancy blind and Peter Jr. with partial sight. Peter Jr. managed a business later in life but needed the support of his father and siblings after John Jay's father passed away. Some of Peter and Mary's children didn't survive for very long. They had a boy, Jacobus, who died as an infant. Another son, Frederick, died of smallpox when he was just a child.

In 1732, though, Mary gave birth to James. He was a precocious and bright child with no physical disabilities. Peter and Mary were delighted about that, but New York was besieged by another smallpox epidemic the same year, so Peter and Mary desperately wanted to protect their uninfected children from the horrors of smallpox. Fortunately, they were in a comfortable economic situation, so they moved away from the city. Peter found a beautiful lot in Rye, New York with a house, orchards, outbuildings, sheds, and the like. There, Peter planned on starting a plantation where he could retire and become a gentleman farmer.

In the year 1747, they had another child, Frederick, who bore the same name as their deceased son.

Despite all of their hardships, the children harmonized well. Mary spent a lot of time caring for her two disabled children and giving emotional support to Eva as needed. The Jays had as many as nine slaves to assist in the raising of their children and to work on the plantation. Both Mary and Peter were delighted with young James and John as they grew older. About John, Peter once said, "Johnny is of grave disposition, and takes to learning exceedingly well." His brother, James, was a very studious lad as well. The young boys were the bright lights of the family.

John was, by nature, intellectually curious. This was the Age of the Enlightenment in America. The Enlightenment era in America promoted the use of individual reasoning to create new systems of understanding. As the thirteen colonies that composed British America, this land was wide open to ideas that differed from those in traditional Europe.

James Jay and Ben Franklin

James was very intelligent and had an intense interest in both medicine and science. In 1750, his father sent him to Bristol, England where he lived with his great-uncle's family and was educated there. After primary studies, he studied medicine at the University of Edinburgh in Scotland and obtained an M.D. in 1760. Upon his return, James opened up a private practice. In addition, he raised funds for King's College (now Columbia University). For that effort, he was knighted by King George III, thus becoming Sir James Jay. In the mid-18th century, he met Benjamin Franklin, the famous inventor and statesman. Franklin wanted to open a college in Philadelphia, and James volunteered to secure funding for it. He was immensely successful and secured a number of endowments for the college. It had been chartered under the name of University of Philadelphia and later became an Ivy League college.

Like Ben Franklin, James was an inventor as well. He invented invisible ink which was used to disguise messages in personal correspondence. This was particularly helpful when letters were censored by colonial authorities in British America. Experimentally, James sent letters to his brother, John, who was very excited about the discovery. Occasionally, the two left the letters unsealed just to tempt the British authorities into censuring them. Because the actual content of the letters appeared elsewhere on the paper than the superficially chatty portion, they discovered that this ink could be successfully employed. It was also a source of secret amusement for James and John. The two of them felt that this ink could be used to convey messages about the British authorities in the colonies and utilized to alert the people about possible threats from the more oppressive British authorities. John and James had a very close relationship at that time although the intensity of their relationship later changed.

John Jay: The Incident at the College Dorm

Like James, John was precocious and intelligent. As a child, he attended grammar school under Rev. Stoop and the vigilant tutelage of his mother. The young man excelled in academics, as he could handle Latin and French, the language of his forefathers. He had an organized mind, so mathematics and the study of law appealed to him. He was also well aware of the tribulations his great-grandparents suffered and the negative effects of restrictive laws when religious edicts were passed in Europe. In New York, the Charter of Liberties established by the national assembly gave free rights to the settlers in terms of religion. They also had the right to elect their own mayor and a colonial assembly. The power of the colony was limited by the royal governor of the colony, and the atmosphere they sometimes created for the colonists wasn't always amicable.

In 1760, he enrolled at King's College. He was fastidious in his studies and attentive to detail. That quality is very beneficial in analyzing the law, as every phrase and qualification has meaning.

John Jay's astute mind was suitable for the legal profession, and he was often at the top of his class.

Even though he was scrupulously studious, John was just as normal as other college lads. Just before his graduation, Jay and his close buddy, Robert Livingston Jr., and some companions got involved in horseplay in their dorm. Their energy exploded one evening, and the rambunctious group started throwing furniture. They threw chairs around and then heaved the sturdy study table clear across the room. Suddenly, the president of the college itself, Myles Cooper, happened to walk into the room, nearly stumbling on the broken table. He was furious! Red-faced John was the closest one to the table but vehemently denied responsibility for the vandalism. When prodded, he adamantly refused to snitch on anyone. The administration didn't give up, though, and John had to appear before the college board. When asked about the identity of the perpetrator, Jay said that no college bylaw required him to tell. It was a convincing argument that showed his propensity to be an excellent lawyer, and this weighed in their decision of whether he should be refused the right to graduate. Because of his laudable college grades, the college authorities decided to let the matter slide, and John graduated with his class.

General Thomas Gage, who served on the British Governor's Council in New York and later in the American Revolution, attended John Jay's graduation ceremony at St. George's Chapel. Not too many members of John's family attended his graduation though. John's father had to look after Eva because she was very ill, as was Mary Jay. Mary had rheumatism and was besieged by a serious bout of the illness. John's older brother, James, was then living in England studying to be a physician, so he was also unable to be there. His brother Augustus most likely did attend, but there is no record as to who else was there except Frederick.

Law Clerk

In 1764, through the assiduous help of his father, John was able to start reading law under the illustrious colonial lawyer, Benjamin Kissam, who was also his father's attorney. Peter and Mary had originally planned on John becoming a minister, but John preferred to apply himself to the nuances of the law. His personality was well suited for that as he was acutely aware of the details and circumstances surrounding actions. His father wasn't really surprised by his choice but knew how difficult the career would be. He wanted John to become a good lawyer as opposed to one who is merely mediocre. So, he cautioned his ambitious son to persevere in the practice of the law, saying, "I hope you'll closely attend to it with a firm resolution and that no difficulties in prosecuting that study shall discourage you from applying very close to it, and if possible, from taking a delight in it."

Kissam was an extremely busy lawyer and had other men running his office in New York. Jay admired him because he was a pious man and most agreeable, and Jay trusted him implicitly. Kissam respected Jay's abilities; he once told John, "Your whirl of imagination bespeaks the grandeur of the intellectual source from whence the current flows." The first phase of becoming a licensed lawyer was to act as a law clerk and process paperwork, file motions, and the like. It was tedious work, as the clerks sometimes were only required to simply copy material into the official records. Unlike other law clerks, Kissam's law clerks were enveloped with a lot of cases in the summer of 1764. The colonial courts dealt with the precepts of English common law and were left fairly free to manage their own agenda. As a student of the law, Jay was expected to keep abreast of the most notable cases of the day. One of the most controversial decisions was that of *Forsey v. Cunningham*, and it whetted his appetite to eventually open up his own practice.

Forsey v. Cunningham

John Jay's former college colleague and good friend, Robert Livingston Jr., was the son of the famous court justice in colonial New York. Robert Livingston Sr. was one of the associate justices who heard the famous case of *Forsey v. Cunningham* in 1764. As part of his clerical duties for Kissam, John attended the proceedings in the case. It was an important case as it addressed the fundamental legal rights of the colonists who were also considered to be English people, which should entitle them to the same rights as those who lived in Great Britain.

In 1764, Associate Justice Livingston, William Smith, and David Jones heard the case in the New York court, presided by Chief Justice Horsmanden. The issue was triggered when a violent altercation broke out between two businessmen—Thomas Forsey and Waddell Cunningham—over a business deal. John found this particularly interesting because his father was also a merchant.

While carving out their business agreement, tempers flared. The episode turned violent, and Cunningham seriously injured Forsey with a sword. Forsey, who only had a horsewhip to protect himself, was critically injured. After a lengthy recovery, Forsey charged Cunningham with criminal assault, and he was found guilty. Forsey then followed up with a civil suit because his injuries were so severe. He demanded a trial by jury, and the jury ruled in Forsey's favor, awarding him damages. Cunningham wasn't satisfied and appealed, claiming the verdict should be set aside. According to English law, the only way a verdict in a jury trial could be reexamined was if a writ of procedural error could be obtained. Cunningham had none, and the justices refused to hear him.

Still determined to win the appeal, Cunningham approached English Lieutenant-Governor Cadwallader Colden of New York, who issued a stay of judgment until the case could be reheard.

Colden was appointed by the Crown and was the royal representative. The stay of judgment Colden issued infuriated the colonists because their legal rights were being limited on the whims of the colonial authorities in collaboration with the English king. This was a blatant challenge to the colonists' right to trial by jury. The New Yorkers felt that Cunningham was a manipulative and devious bully who used Lieutenant-Governor Colden to support his viewpoint. As a result, there were demonstrations in New York, and Colden was burned in effigy.

Chief Justice Horsmanden reheard the case and upheld the original verdict. Horsmanden and the other justices indicated that no royal prerogative could overturn a legally-rendered verdict in a jury trial. John Jay said, "We claim all the rights secured to the subject by the English constitution, and particularly that inestimable right to trial by jury." The final verdict in this case bounced back and forth for years. It wasn't resolved until after the war for independence when the colonists were no longer bound by English common law and the exercise of the royal privilege.

That case influenced John Jay to publish a book called *Commonplace Book* which not only outlined the ordinary procedures to observe in court cases but contained extraordinary material that wasn't likely to arise in everyday matters. Procedures like the one employed to decide the *Forsey v. Cunningham* case were discussed in his book.

Chapter 2 – Yearning to Be Free

As evidenced in the *Forsey v. Cunningham* case, colonists were victims of absolutist rule from King George III. Great Britain in the late 18th century may have been a constitutional monarchy, but there was a wide gap between the law and its rightful application. Other injustices occurred as well. In 1765, England was saddled with war debt and inflicted the colonists with a crushing tax by the passage of the Stamp Act. It didn't refer to stamps, per se, but a tax on an embossed symbol placed on paper used by colonists. In order to create any kind of legal document, it was mandated that lawyers use this English paper. Benjamin Kissam refused to pay it in protest, as did many of the other lawyers in New York. The people did too, and they reused old paper or made their own paper from stripped saplings or clothing. Lieutenant-Governor Colden, who interfered in the *Forsey v. Cunningham* case, was again hung and burned in effigy outside Fort George in lower Manhattan, not far from Kissam's office. Mobs of youths, farmers, sailors, and merchants flooded the streets to rebel against the passage of this infamous Stamp Act. Kissam had to send John and his staff home and close up his office for over a week as a result. After nightfall of the first day of the riot, a faction of the rioters raced to the home of an English major, Thomas James, broke into his house, damaged the furniture, broke mirrors, stole the silver, slit the wall paintings, and sliced up the chair upholstery. As a vengeful epilogue, the rioters smeared butter and lard all over what remained.

Benjamin Franklin, the noted statesman, was sent to England to protest the Stamp Act and other unfair trade taxes levied by the English government. Two years later, in 1767, Franklin successfully had the Stamp Act repealed.

Recognizing the failure of the Stamp Act, Charles Townshend, the Exchequer of England, identified items that the colonists couldn't easily manufacture on their own, like paint and glass, and taxed those instead. About those taxes, Jay wrote to the English authorities:

> Before we had recovered from the distresses which ever attend war, an attempt was made to drain this country of all its money, by the oppressive Stamp Act. Paint, glass and other commodities which would not permit us to purchase of other nations, were taxed; nay although no wine is made in any country subject to the British state, you prohibited our procuring it of foreigners without paying a tax, imposed by your parliament, on all we imported...These exactions are lavishly squandered on court favorites and ministerial dependents.

In no uncertain terms, Jay was referring to the extravagant lifestyle of King George III and his family and favored friends in the court. In his mind, Jay felt that there was no justification for levying such taxes, as the English didn't have such taxes in the British Isles. It was purely for the colonists in British America.

The colonies had already been paying taxes regularly to the British to finance the debt incurred as a result of the Seven Years' War, which was mostly fought in Europe. What is called the French and Indian War was a phase in that war, and that part was fought in the colonies. The colonies themselves had actually paid 40% of the costs involved as a result of that war and lost a lot of men in those battles. Thus, the Stamp Act and the Townshend Acts were superfluous taxes perceived as unjust. John Jay, along with other colonial lawyers, objected to it, not on the basis that is was a tax but upon the constitutional right of England to impose it because the colonies had no say in the legislation from England that affected them. In the Massachusetts General Assembly, the patriot, James Otis Jr., leaped up at a meeting and shouted, "Taxation without representation is tyranny." That became a slogan of the colonists' position, and they resisted the imposition of the Townshend Taxes by establishing a boycott on English goods.

John Jay's Debating Society

While at Kissam's, John was active in one of the debating clubs traditionally held between those studying law and those who had recently passed the bar. Jay was a lover of peace, and the Society debated about the riots in the city. They introduced a topic on the issue about the "the blessings of order and tranquility and the pernicious consequence of faction and riot." The debating society was not only an intellectual study group but a social occasion. John Jay's group in New York argued issues related to natural law, ethics, law enforcement, and political theory. One of the issues they discussed was whether it was better to have a hereditary monarch or an elected one. John Jay was very outspoken on that topic, saying that a nation's representative should be selected based on merit rather than heredity. In addition, he stated that a representative must also be held responsible for his decisions.

Britain Oversteps English Law

In 1766, Benjamin Kissam brought John Jay with him when he defended a colonist, William Prendergast, against a charge of high treason for his participation in a local rent riot. British regiments had been brought in, and the riot became violent, resulting in one death. The Crown became involved and rounded up a number of witnesses supporting the Crown who claimed that this insurrection was a high crime of treason against the British authorities. According to English law, private grievances weren't supposed to merit a charge of "high treason," so this was highly irregular. However, the presiding judge, Justice Daniel Horsmanden, served at the king's pleasure, so he felt compelled to charge Prendergast with high treason. Despite Kissam's efforts to point out this violated British law, members of the panel were biased in favor of the Crown. Prendergast was convicted of high treason and sentenced to be hanged, castrated, disemboweled, and beheaded! After Prendergast's wife, Mehitable, traveled all the way to the governor's house and begged him for mercy, he was pardoned.

However, Governor Moore was well aware of the volatility in the colonies at the time and was also cognizant of the highly questionable foundation upon which that verdict was decided. Wisely, he convinced the king to officially pardon Prendergast.

In 1768, John Jay was admitted to the bar, and his appointment was approved by the colonial governor. John was only 23 years old when he was awarded his license to practice law. Robert Livingston Jr. also passed the bar. He and John Jay then decided to open up their own practice in New York.

John Jay and Robert Livingston, Counselors-At-Law

This wasn't the best time to start up a law practice. Because the Townshend Acts levied taxes on goods that couldn't be manufactured in the colonies, it sent the economy of colonial America into a depression. That left less money in the hands of people who might want to employ the services of a lawyer. Therefore, the partnership of Jay-Livingston didn't generate many clients. When John's brother, Augustus, retired from promoting the Jay family interests, John replaced him. The bulk of Jay's cases at the Jay-Livingston law firm were from John Jay's family, but there weren't many cases from this collection. Kissam also referred a few other cases to him, saying, "I wish you good success with my consignments, and hope they'll come to a good market. If they don't, I am sure it will not be the factor's fault; and if my clients' wares are bad, let them bear the loss."

In 1769, John Jay was appointed as secretary to the commissioners appointed by the king to settle the boundary between New York and New Jersey. John's appointment to the commission was recommended by his former mentor, Benjamin Kissam. John Jay's partner, Robert Livingston Jr., didn't have much work at all, so he spent many of his hours visiting his family home at Clermont in the Hudson Valley, north of the city, and hoped for better times. Then, in 1770, Livingston became the Chancellor of New York and in charge of New York's foreign affairs. His aptitude in legal affairs became known due to the fame of Kissam who spread the word, so he was consulted by the County Court of Common Pleas. His skills were tapped to help out with the legalities of determining the New York-New Jersey border. Because Livingston and Jay's careers had now veered into different directions, the partnership was dissolved.

John Jay's Public Law Practice

Because of his stellar performance regarding the New York-New Jersey border, John Jay rose rapidly up the ranks and in 1770 served at the County Court of Common Pleas in Westchester County. Not only that, but he had as many as eighteen cases in the Supreme Court of Judicature of New York City. The sudden onslaught of unexpected business took its toll on John physically, however. He developed fluid buildup in his body, causing swelling in his muscles. In addition, Jay fought back a long-lasting fever. With the introduction of some remedies accompanied by more exercise, he was eventually able to overcome that difficulty. In 1773, Jay then had 136 pending cases in the supreme court and 118 in the Court of Common Pleas. Most of his caseload consisted of civil litigation, debt collection, and insolvency issues, but some were of a minor criminal nature such as battery and assault.

John Jay became famous for his fearless defense of those who suffered from meddling with the royal authorities. In 1773, he defended Nathaniel Underhill in an election controversy over his position of mayor. In that case, *King v. Underhill*, the attorney for the Crown objected to Underhill's election. Again, the Crown was attempting to override the rights of the citizens to elect their own mayor and attempted to unseat Underhill through legal means. Through legal machinations, John Jay obtained two continuances until the Crown attorneys lost interest in the case. That was the technique he saw employed in the *Forsey v. Cunningham* case. Jay had learned the importance of persistence in legal matters when it seemed clear defendants were being discriminated against. As a result of Jay's perseverance and delay tactics, Nathaniel Underhill successfully remained in office for the remainder of his term.

Bloomer v. Hinchman

He also tried some cases in the High Court of the Chancery, which superseded the Common Court of Pleas. Matters that were within its purview had a direct bearing on the interpretation of English law. In 1770, one case, that of *Bloomer v. Hinchman*, was between a clergyman and a representative of the congregation. The Crown had the right—but not the obligation—to appoint rectors to religious offices but wasn't responsible for paying them. The English governor exercised his right to appoint the rector of the church and replaced a Presbyterian minister with Joshua Bloomer, an Anglican. Bloomer took over the parish and served for a number of months. Unhappy with this meddling from the English authorities, Robert Hinchman, the congregation's vestryman, refused to pay Bloomer his salary. Bloomer sued for the amount of the salary due to him. Bloomer's lawyers were John Jay and the more senior lawyer, John Tabor Kempe. Kempe, his co-lawyer, chose to ignore all of Jay's motions and was totally uncooperative. This incensed Jay, and he publicly confronted him in a fearless manner. Jay felt that his own reputation was besmirched by this public defiance and demanded that Kempe explain his actions. Kempe refused to respond for reasons unknown. Observers of this case noted that Jay was virtually unafraid of risking the enmity of Kempe who was an influential man in the court system. As might have been predicted, the congregation wanted the religious freedom they had been accustomed to, and Hinchman won the case. Jay appealed that verdict, and it was referred to the Privy Council in England. The case was never ruled upon due to the outbreak of the Revolutionary War though. What impressed the commentators, however, wasn't the delay in the appeal, but Jay's boldfaced courage to confront Kempe.

Most of the cases John tried were in the common court, but some of the cases which he had were heard in the chancery court. Chancery courts handle matters related to wills, land estates, and other issues not covered by the common courts. Legal fees for cases heard in the chancery court paid considerably more money, and Jay's practice was becoming quite lucrative.

Chapter 3 – Freedom Is Expensive

Through his friend and former law partner, Robert Livingston Jr., John met the love of his life—Sarah Van Brugh Livingston, who was Robert's second cousin. She was the spunky daughter of William Livingston, a fiery patriot who later became governor of New Jersey. It was said of Sarah that the "rosy fingers of pleasure paint her cheeks with double crimson." Etchings of Sarah portray a very attractive woman with long flowing curls and rosy cheeks. They were married in 1774. The *New York Gazette* which carried their wedding announcement said she resembled all of Jane Austen's heroines.

John and Sarah had to cut their honeymoon short, however, because Boston Harbor was becoming littered with British vessels. Massachusetts was alarmed, as were all the colonies. This happened as a result of the Coercive Acts passed in 1774, locally called the "Intolerable Acts" by the colonists. These five acts stated:

o The Boston Port Act – This closed the harbor until reparations could be made for the dumped tea.

o The Massachusetts Governing Act – This required that the colonial governor and other officials were appointed directly by the Crown.

o The Administration of Justice Act – This allowed any British soldier charged with the murder of a colonist to have his case heard in another colony or in England.

o The Quartering Act – This permitted the governor to house British soldiers in unoccupied buildings on the property of any citizen, although with compensation.

o The Quebec Act – This extended the borders of Quebec into the Ohio Valley

John and Sarah had to rush home because John was one of the New York delegates to the colonial assembly, and he had to attend a meeting of the assembly. Jay rapidly secured a coach and rushed off to Carpenter's Hall in Philadelphia where the conference was being held. He and Thomas Jefferson were the youngest members of that meeting. As a result of this gathering, it was proposed that the colonies would hold regular meetings in the interest of protecting their rights. John Jay then dispatched a letter for the citizens of Boston on behalf of New York, saying, "We sincerely condole with you in your un-exampled distress, and to request your speedy opinion of the proposed congress, that if it should meet with your approbation, we may exert our utmost endeavors to carry it into execution." They became known as the Continental Congress, and future Continental Congresses continued to take place without the permission of the royal authorities.

Battles of Lexington and Concord

Events were happening at a staccato pace in Massachusetts when the British warships were anchored in Boston Harbor. The local patriots, Samuel Prescott and Paul Revere from the secretive Sons of Liberty patriot group, formed a notification system to alert the colony if the British sent troops into the colony. The signal appeared in the lanterns of the Old North Church in the harbor.

One lantern meant that the British would infiltrate via land; two lanterns meant they would come in by sea. Around midnight of April 19, 1775, two lanterns blazed from the church tower, and word spread.

Once the British regiments disembarked from their ships on the St. Charles River, their military mission was to seek out and confiscate all stored weapons belonging to the colonial militias. Without concern for personal property or respect for the colonists, British troops marched upon the towns of Lexington and Concord, rummaging through arsenals, then barns, storage sheds, and even tavern basements searching for arms and artillery. Little was found as it had been already hidden elsewhere by the clever colonists. The colonial militiamen hid behind stone walls and bushes and followed the British soldiers as they moved through the two villages and countryside. In Lexington, a huge regiment of British troops spotted the colonists hidden behind bushes and stone walls, and they panicked. Suddenly, a shot rang out. A volley of shots followed that. In the end, eight militiamen were killed, and one British soldier lay dead.

To this day, no one knows if a British soldier or colonial militiaman fired the first shot, but it was "the shot heard round the world," according to the poet Ralph Waldo Emerson.

The Olive Branch Petition

In May of 1775, delegates of the Continental Congressional meetings reconvened in the Philadelphia State House. John Jay was on the committee which drafted a petition to send directly to King George III himself. As an alternative to war, this committee sought to set up an understanding between the colonies and Great Britain. The Olive Branch Petition was an appeal to England to become more flexible in its policies toward the British colonies. Jay and his fellow committee members included the most prominent personages in colonial America. Among them were Benjamin Franklin and John Dickinson. John Jay and John Dickinson were the primary authors of the document. Dickinson, as well as John Jay, is considered to be among the Founding Fathers of the United States. Twelve of the thirteen colonies signed this petition. Only Georgia didn't, as they were hoping for British military support in a skirmish with some native tribes who were attacking their farms there.

John Jay and the other colonial representatives also felt that the Battles of Lexington and Concord would give impetus to the fact that the colonists were firm in their resolve. However, John Adams, a radical patriot from Massachusetts, stood up at that meeting and indicated that he didn't feel that the Olive Branch Petition would be successful or even worth pursuing. John Jay found Adams to be rather abrasive in his approach, as Jay tended to be much gentler. Although Jay initially had ill feelings about Adams, seeing him as too hot-headed and impulsive, he did patch up their differences later in his life. Regardless, John Adams was correct because it was reported that the irate king didn't even read the petition!

The Second Continental Congress 1775

The Continental Congress again assembled in Philadelphia in May of 1775. The initial aim of this colonial assemblage wasn't independence but a defensive technique for the preservation of their rights under the English constitution in case British troops came ashore in any of the other colonies after the Battles of Lexington and Concord. In order to defend their rights, the colonists knew they had to arm themselves and create a military force. Their immediate military goal was to destroy any British fortifications that were already being built within the colonies.

Most of the New York population were either businessmen, lawyers, or entrepreneurs. There were no well-known New York colonists with a lot of military experience, however, who could head a colonial militia. John Jay, the New York delegate, knew of a lawyer from New Hampshire who had some recent military experience. His name was John Sullivan, the son of an Irish settler. He was a major in the New Hampshire militia and successfully conducted raids on the British fortification Fort William and Mary at New Castle in the colony. New York readily assented to his appointment. Later on, he became a very successful general who coordinated with George Washington in some of his most momentous actions.

The Second Continental Congress didn't want to overlook anything in view of the fact that a possible armed conflict was imminent. It appointed John Jay to write to the British citizens of Canada because the colonies didn't want the Canadian settlers to rise up against them. In his address to the Canadians, especially the French Canadians, Jay stated:

> We, for our parts, are determined to live free, or not at all…As our concern for your welfare entitles us to your friendship, we presume you will not, by doing us an injury, reduce us to the disagreeable necessity of treating you as enemies.

John Jay's letter was also an attempt by the Continental Congress to enlist the support of the Canadians against the British, who dominated them as well. As a result of Jay's efforts and that of his relative, James Livingston, some of the Canadians formed the 1st Canadian Regiment.

The Clandestine Arms Shipments

Records show that in 1775 Comte de Vergennes, the foreign minister of France, covertly arranged to help the colonists with their conflict against Great Britain. As stated earlier, the main shipping port of Boston was blockaded by the British, but the French knew ways to circumvent the British ships. De Vergennes was clever and even employed neutral Dutchmen to secretly act as intermediaries and get military supplies to the colonies on a network of merchant ships. An American merchant, Silas Deane, was directly instrumental in the arms shipments.

Chapter 4 – New York in Crisis

The Olive Branch Petition to which Jay contributed was unsuccessful, so all of the delegates to the Second Continental Congress recognized that war would be necessary in order to achieve independence from Great Britain. However, this Congress in and of itself didn't feel they should declare war without the approbation of the colonies. In 1776, the Congress selected a committee of five men consisting of John Adams of Massachusetts, Robert Livingston of New York, Benjamin Franklin of Pennsylvania, Thomas Jefferson of Virginia, and Roger Sherman of Connecticut to choose someone to draft a definitive statement declaring independence in order to send it to all the colonies for approval. Initially, the committee chose John Adams to write it, but he declined, giving a number of reasons for that. Among his reasons was one that cited one of his self-admitted personality flaws that might mitigate against making the most ideal presentation: "I am obnoxious, suspected, and unpopular." Then Adams looked at Thomas Jefferson and commented, "...you can write ten times better than I can." Jefferson then agreed to do it.

John Jay wanted to contribute something to this document, and as he was becoming more sensitive about the issue of slavery, and in view of the fact that such a declaration was to advocate liberty and freedom for all, Jay wanted to have something inserted into the document that would call for the gradual emancipation of slaves in America. He wasn't successful with that, however, and didn't get the opportunity to fight for it, as there was a serious situation brewing in New York.

In May of 1776, John Jay was suddenly summoned by his own colony to return to New York because of a local problem. The citizens of New York indicated that the political situation in New York was critical due to the antipathy of the loyalist supporters and hostilities between them. To demonstrate their anger, the colonists had toppled a statue of King George III mounted on a horse, which stood in a park at the southern tip of Manhattan.

In order to maintain order, John Jay established a convention to be held in Albany, New York, to elect leaders for a provisional government of the colony so there would be local leaders who could get support for the cause of independence. Jay then directed the election of new participants to form a provisional government of New York. That government would be independent from the British-appointed governor. The next main task of this convention was the formulation of a constitution for New York.

Simultaneously, Thomas Jefferson wrote the Declaration of Independence in Philadelphia, which declared the colonies as independent states no longer under the rule of the British monarchy, and members of the Second Continental Congress signed it. Jay wasn't one of the signatories because he was in Albany at the time because of his duties in New York. However, Philip Livingston, Francis Lewis, Lewis Morris, and William Floyd from New York did sign the Declaration. William Livingston was the uncle of John Jay's former law partner, Robert, who also attended the Second Continental Congress. Each of the delegates was tasked with taking copies of the Declaration of Independence to the thirteen colonies for ratification.

Roving Government in New York

In June of 1776, word came to John Jay and the nascent provisional government that General Howe of England had just sailed into the port of New York with a fleet of warships. The New York Convention quickly moved to White Plains from Albany, which was closer to New York City. The colonists were then ordered to remove the lead frames from their windows, brass door knockers, church bells, and any other metal items that could be melted down for artillery for the newly-forming troops. New York had been unprepared for such a sudden armed threat, and the patriots hectically collected what weapons they could use for their defense, as well as erecting redoubts for an inland invasion. Meanwhile, at his meeting hall in White Plains, John Jay was given a copy of the Declaration of Independence which was sent for ratification. Because so many members of the New York Convention were back at home preparing to defend New York, the convention lacked a sufficient number of members to legally sign the ratification documents on behalf of the colony, so New York was forced to abstain. John Jay knew his constituents supported the Declaration of Independence for the most part. John Jay, on behalf of New York, wrote an official letter of support to the Continental Congress saying, in part:

> Resolved unanimously, that the reasons assigned by the Continental Congress for declaring these united colonies free in independent states are cogent and conclusive, and that while we lament the cruel necessity which has rendered this measure unavoidable, we approve the same, and will, at the risk of our lives and fortunes, join with the other colonies in supporting it.

John Jay was authorized by the New York Convention to obtain metals and materials needed to fight a war. After that order, Jay left and rushed up to Connecticut. There he procured carriages, horse teams, and sloops, and made an agreement with a foundry in Salisbury, Connecticut to manufacture cannons. Within a very short time, Jay had twenty cannons and cannonballs sent to West Point where the colony had a major fortification.

Traitors Imprisoned!

After the Declaration of Independence was signed, the Continental Congress created the Committee for Detecting and Defeating Conspiracies of which Jay was a member. He and his committee were in charge of uncovering British conspiracies. Upon the establishment of this committee, the provisional New York government passed a resolution called the Bill of Attainder, declaring that those colonists who lent active support to the British were guilty of high treason. John Jay himself was vehemently opposed to that, though. In his own upbringing, he heard fearsome stories about the persecution of his father, his family, and friends due to their beliefs. Over Jay's objections, the committee created a passport system to identify those who were patriots and arrest the others who supported the British. The "Tories," or those who sided with England in the opening battles of the American Revolution, grew in size and strength as the people discovered the proximity of the British troops to New York. The anti-American spy network that exacerbated this divisiveness had to be stopped. Jails and even churches were used as makeshift prisons for the Tory supporters. The colonists of New York became very polarized as time went on.

John Jay continued his opposition to the imprisonment of Loyalist-leaning people in New York. It was his opinion that it encroached on a person's individual rights by virtue of their political opinions, and he appealed for less vigorous prosecutions.

Battle of Long Island; Conquest of Staten Island

George Washington, one of the delegates to the Continental Congress, had been confirmed as commander-in-chief of the Continental forces. When he got word about General Howe at New York, he raced out of the Continental Congress meeting with a preestablished force of 3,000 troops. That force increased exponentially to about 19,000 men within a short period of time. Washington set up a fort in the Bowery, at the tip of Manhattan Island, and a battery of cannons. The New Yorkers who lived on Long Island had built a number of fortifications on the higher ground of current-day Brooklyn Heights. Brooklyn Heights and western Long Island was a strategic point between the Atlantic Ocean and the East River and thus vulnerable.

Unfortunately, these fortifications had been hastily constructed, and there were some passes in the Heights that gave the enemy access to Manhattan. In 1776, the British invaded Brooklyn under cover of darkness. Washington fired off his cannons from Manhattan in response and also sent a segment of his forces to Governors Island between the East River and the tip of Manhattan, but they were forced to move out from there to defend Brooklyn.

Washington then crossed the East River and put up a stern defense on the island. The British, however, staged more attacks that were successful and kept moving west. In the process of attempting to locate passes through Brooklyn Heights, the British threatened the families living there, and some were forced to lead the enemy through the accessible passes. Washington was short of troops and consulted with his generals. They realized that the Continental force was at a distinct disadvantage in Brooklyn and advised him to pull his troops off Long Island and retreat to Manhattan.

There were initially 45 British vessels in New York Harbor. Within a short period, 130 more ships arrived and anchored off Staten Island between New York and New Jersey. Staten Island wasn't well defended, and the panicked American population switched to the British side in the interest of their own safety and survival. More British troops poured in along with 400 more ships accompanied by their mercenary soldiers—a force of 8,000 Hessians who were mercenary troops from Germany. As the British troops invaded, Washington pummeled them with cannon fire from Manhattan and rapidly constructed forts along the East

River. Because he still hadn't attracted many more colonists to the Continental Army, he was outnumbered two to one.

The Great Fire of Manhattan of 1776

Lacking sufficient men and resources to beat back the British army, Washington consulted with his advisors as to his next move. Some of them suggested that he set fire to lower Manhattan to prevent the British regiments from finding refuge there. This idea was scuttled, so Washington and his troops moved farther north. However, a fire did actually break out. Historians suggest that the fire was set by patriots. Seeing the fire, the British were furious because they were depending upon quartering their troops in the houses of the colonists in New York. To exact revenge, the English arrested up to 200 patriots there. They also hanged the spy, Nathan Hale, one of the most memorable martyrs in the name of the Revolution. Before the noose was drawn around his neck, Hale uttered these famous words: "I regret that I have but one life to give for my country."

Howe Attempts to Secure Colonial Surrender

By the end of December in 1776, the British general, William Howe, now in New York City, attempted to persuade the colonists to surrender and offered everyone "pardon." Howe then tried to contact General Washington three times. It wasn't until his third attempt that Washington responded saying, "Those who have committed no fault need no pardon."

Because of this offer of "pardon," more of the colonists were weakening their resolve and turned traitor. After that occurred, John Jay wrote one of the most forceful and emotionally charged appeals of his career:

> They tell you, if you submit, you shall have PROTECTION – that their king breathes nothing but peace – that he will revise (not repeal) all his cruel acts and instructions, and will receive you into favor. But what are the terms on which you are promised peace? Have you heard of any

except absolute, unconditional obedience and servile submission? Why should you be slaves now, having been freemen ever since the country was settled?

Jay then reminded everyone about the oppressive taxes the Parliament charged at their will and pleasure. He also pointed out that these British who offer "peace" arrived armed with weapons to spill the blood of Americans. He then vigorously continued, indicating that these soldiers who offer peace, will "...order your country to be desolated, your brethren to starve and languish, and die in prison."

The British troops made their way up the Hudson River which lies to the west of Manhattan. The colonists had troops stationed at Fort Washington in upper New York in what is the Bronx today. On November 16, 1776, the Continental troops engaged the British regiments. General Howe, General Hugh Percy, and their Hessian ally, Wilhelm von Knyphausen, forced the colonial fort commander to surrender.

General Washington then chased General Howe and confronted him at White Plains. By now, Washington had recruited more colonists, and new recruits continually joined up. Unfortunately, there was precious little time to train the new men, and the colonists lost the Battle at White Plains.

White Plains lies very close to Rye, New York, where John Jay's parents and some of his siblings lived. The children who still lived at home included Nancy who was blind, Peter who was only partially-sighted, and Frederick. They were all in critical danger of being overrun by the British. Jay asked to be allowed to temporarily leave his position at the New York Convention and see to their safety.

Jay's Family Relocates

John made arrangements to move his family to Fishkill which was the site of a colonial military prison holding British prisoners with a nearby hospital. There were many colonial troops at an adjoining encampment there so Jay felt they would be safer there. Jay then headquartered the New York government to Poughkeepsie nearby. Jay returned to New York and steadily had shipments of gunpowder and arms brought into the harbor. He also made arrangements to pick up secret shipments of arms from France which were arriving in North Carolina. These were the weapons smuggled into the country per agreement with the secret emissary of Comte de Vergennes whom Jay had met during the First Continental Congress.

John Jay temporarily moved into his father-in-law's house with his wife. This Georgian style mansion is called Liberty Hall and later became the residence of New Jersey governors. In 1776, John's son, Peter, was born there. Sally's family was from the important family of the Livingstons, and Jay knew she had a support network there, but he wanted to be assured of her good health and well-being. So, when he was away, Jay also wrote to her during the tumultuous year of 1776 asking about her safety.

Chapter 5 – John Jay in the Midst of the American Revolution

Washington and his ragged forces were forced by the overwhelming number of British forces in New York to retreat to Morristown, New Jersey where they encamped for the winter of 1776. The state of the American Revolutionary War was precarious.

The New York Constitution of 1777

John Jay was the primary writer of the constitution of New York, and he was assisted by Robert Morris, a noted financier of the war, and Robert Livingston Jr., Jay's good friend and brother-in-law. He and the other convention members of New York spent much of the time between 1776 and 1777 moving their meeting locales because most of New York City and current-day Westchester County was occupied by the British. Jay and the convention members had started out in Albany in upstate New York. Because of the war situation in New York, the convention moved to Harlem, Kingsbridge, Philips's Manor, Fishkill, White Plains, Poughkeepsie, and finally to Kingston, farther upstate.

The final constitution presented some initial statements about the motives behind why the colonists felt that declaring a final separation from England was absolutely necessary. The subsequent sections had to do with the structure of the New York government. Three divisions were established: executive, legislative, and judicial. It called for the election of a governor representing the executive branch, and the elections of 24 senators and 70 assemblymen representing the legislative branch. It also laid out a basic structure for the judicial branch with specific mention of the right to trial by jury—a right that was severely compromised by the British. John Jay was appointed the first chief justice of New York. Jay wanted an article added to the New York constitution against the continued practice of slavery. However, he was unable to stay for the approval of the final constitution because of the terminal illness of his mother. Jay assigned Gouverneur Morris to present that proposal prohibiting the continuation of slavery. Unfortunately, it was defeated.

Death of John Jay's Mother

His dear mother only survived a few days after John Jay's arrival at Fishkill, and she was buried on the property in a private cemetery. Then John dallied for a while to comfort his aging father in his grief.

While at Fishkill, John Jay was visited by Washington, who had left his winter encampment in New Jersey. The commander-in-chief wanted to brainstorm with Jay about possible military moves. Washington asked Jay if he felt that the colonists should become more involved in Canada which the British had won on an earlier engagement, the Battle of Quebec in 1775. Jay indicated that they should not pursue that front, and Washington deferred to his opinion.

General George Washington was now being assisted by the Marquis de Lafayette who brought privately hired French troops along with weapons and some ships. Lafayette was a well-experienced military commander who could lead military divisions. Washington's Continental forces had been growing exponentially, so this was an opportune time to score some victories against the English. He had General Benedict Arnold (who later became a traitor) and the very capable and experienced Commander Horatio Gates, who commanded a magnificent cavalry regiment of sharpshooters, join the Continental forces. Captain Morgan of Virginia also assisted and led his famous light infantry, and Henry Dearborn had a well-trained ground infantry force. A mercenary engineer from Poland masterminded the building of a formidable fortress called Fort Bemis, right on the Hudson River at New York, and it was to be used for the Continentals. New York was finally building up its defensive network.

Battle of Saratoga: Turning Point

General John Burgoyne of the British army had easily seized Fort Ticonderoga which was on the border of New York and Canada. That victory made him overconfident, and he slowly marched his troops southward toward Washington. That granted Washington plenty of time to regroup and ready his forces.

In September of 1777, Burgoyne attacked. General Arnold rushed out to confront him but was dismayed by General Horatio Gates who held back, hesitating. Arnold rushed forward anyway, supported by Morgan's cavalry and Captain Henry Dearborn's infantry. The Continental Army won the battle. It was a tremendous victory and manifested the seriousness and the strength of the colonists to prevail in the Revolution.

Treaty of Amity and Commerce

Ben Franklin, the first ambassador to France, had been over there in order to secure a commitment from France to ally with the colonies in their struggle for independence. The French sympathized with the colonists but didn't make a firm commitment until after the Battle of Saratoga ended in a monumental victory for the Americans. The Marquis de Lafayette, who was already participating in the American Revolution, was also in France to help Franklin with his mission. In 1778, King Louis XVI approved a Treaty of Amity and Commerce which was shepherded through Parliament due to the efforts of Franklin and Lafayette, as time was of the essence. Other provisions granted both France and America the right to a safe harbor in either country for both warships and commercial vessels with supplies.

As a result of this treaty, America received 80,000 troops, fleets of French warships, and a many rifles, cannons, and military equipment for the American Revolution. Official shipments started in 1778. General de Rochambeau and General de Barras then arrived on American shores along with their own seamen and more supplies.

John Jay's Brothers

John Jay was the kind of brother who saw his role as the protector of the family. Through this chaotic time, he was extremely concerned about his family and his elderly father because the enemy was infiltrating towns and cities in New York. Frederick—also known as Fady—was the youngest of the Jay clan. Fady was a merchant like his father. His business, unfortunately, was interrupted during the Revolution, so he lived with the family at Fishkill and served in the New York Militia and the New York Assembly. When the British intruded into the vicinity of the Jay dwelling at Fishkill, John quickly sent a letter to Frederick, tasking him with providing for the safety of the family. In his letter, John said, "…either you or James [his other brother] will undertake to attend constantly to our good old father and his unfortunate family. Otherwise, I shall at all events return for that purpose." Fady explored Kent, Connecticut as a possible city in which to relocate the family and made other contacts there, but they never came to fruition. Fady contacted John and assured him that he had made arrangements to move the family to Poughkeepsie, which was safe at that time. John felt relieved and proceeded with the business of organizing the new government.

John's other brother, James, was a physician who studied medicine in Scotland. He returned to the colonies and opened up a successful practice. However, he had a convoluted history. In 1762, he had gone to England to raise funds to support King's College that had initially been chartered by King George II. King George III appreciated his endeavors and knighted him, and James then became "Sir James Jay." However, his method for fundraising was later called into question and triggered a bevy of lawsuits. They weren't totally resolved for many years. John Jay and his family were embarrassed by James' financial manipulations.

When the American Revolution erupted, James was a fervent but vindictive type of patriot. He was a member of the New York Assembly and actively promoted the passage of the Bill of Attainder, which punished loyalists in the colonies for their support of England. John had been irate about that, as he believed that people shouldn't be prosecuted for their political beliefs.

John Jay: Move to Philadelphia

In 1777, John Jay was called upon to serve as president of the next session of the Continental Congress. The majority of the members of the Congress preferred Jay because the opposing candidate, Henry Laurens, still favored reconciliation with Great Britain. Jay knew it was much too late for that, as England showed no flexibility.

After winning the election, John Jay resigned as chief justice of New York and moved to Philadelphia. Jay served from 1778 to 1779, and he worked hard with the Continental Congress to try to resolve the differences and disputes between New York and the states in order to present a unified front. There were also commercial concerns regarding trading policies as well. He worked with the other New York delegates to develop thirteen resolutions that represented these agreements between New York and the states. That document was sent to George Clinton, the current governor of New York.

The Spy

When John Jay was in New York in 1778, it came to his attention that the English were continually trying to locate loyalists within the colony and recruit them to join the British regiments. Jay alerted the Continental Congress and was placed on a secret committee to eliminate that practice. Toward that effort, Jay found a poor man who had a reputation for heroism and hired him as a spy. The man, whose name reportedly was Harvey Birch, spied on the British and even got arrested by local authorities who were concerned about his eavesdropping and association with the British. One time, he was sentenced to the gallows under the barbarous Bill of Attainder, but members of Jay's underground committee bribed the jailer to free him. When Jay was appointed as minister to Spain, he had the Continental Congress clandestinely appropriate the money to pay Birch, but Birch refused it, saying he did this for his country. Although many of the facts surrounding Birch's activities were kept secret, James Fennimore Cooper wrote a novel in 1821 called *The Spy*. As the setting for the novel, Cooper used the Jay family's property at Rye as the background setting.

Minister to Spain

In 1779, Spain had expressed an interest in helping America during the American Revolution. To iron out an agreement to that effect, John Jay was sent to Spain. He was able to get some loans from the government to help finance the Revolutionary War. However, Spain was extremely wary about the Revolution in general, fearing it might lose control of East Florida if the war was to spread to that area. They did, however, aid in expelling the British from some Southern forts and from West Florida. Toward that effort, Spain was instrumental at the Battle of Pensacola, fought primarily at sea. In the process of the Revolutionary War, Spain annexed the Bahamas in the Caribbean Sea. Jay couldn't get Spain's definitive recognition of American independence though, but he did secure a loan from them for $170,000 which was a goodly sum in those days.

John Jay frequently took his wife with him on his trips to European countries. Sarah was with him in Spain and was with child. In 1780, she gave birth to Susan. However, there were difficulties immediately following the birth, and Susan died in Madrid. Just two years later, in 1782, Sarah gave birth to another daughter, Maria, in Spain.

Washington's Devious Strategy

In 1781, Comte de Rochambeau and George Washington discussed strategies. There were 3,000 Continental and 4,000 French soldiers in Rhode Island, so Washington felt that they should plan a major action in New York. However, Rochambeau suggested that they move farther south because there was a French fleet under Comte Francois de Grasse in the West Indies that could sail north and join them. De Grasse had 3,000 more men supported by marines along with artillery and military equipment. Washington and Rochambeau then decided upon an attack in Virginia which had a deep-water port. However, Washington kept the operation secret and even sent out missives that said New York was to be the major target. It appeared that way to Lieutenant General Henry Clinton when he observed the movements of the troops from Rhode Island. This made it necessary in Clinton's mind to continue to man the fortifications around New York Harbor. Washington and Rochambeau then started their arduous march south by land.

The British under Lieutenant General Charles Cornwallis were in the Carolinas with Hessian mercenaries, but his movements were being followed carefully by the Marquis de Lafayette who had been sent down south. Lieutenant General Henry Clinton, the commander-in-chief of all the British forces, ordered Cornwallis to move northward to secure a harbor. First, he told Cornwallis to do it at Portsmouth and later told him to secure the harbor at Yorktown, Virginia. Cornwallis moved toward Yorktown but then spotted de Grasse's large French fleet out at sea heading toward the Chesapeake Bay. When he reached there, he encountered a

British fleet. There, the two naval forces engaged in the Battle of Chesapeake Bay. De Grasse handily won the naval battle, thus reducing the number of fighting men so the Franco-American troops wouldn't have to confront them later on. Washington and Rochambeau, who were just arriving, set up their defensive positions at a distance from Yorktown. De Grasse then moved toward Yorktown and arranged his ships in such a way that Cornwallis couldn't escape into the open ocean.

After Rochambeau and Washington had arrived and settled in, they set up redoubts surrounding Yorktown itself. De Grasse had his artillery and equipment debarked earlier for that use, and two Virginia militias also set up fortifications closer to the coast. The Americans were fortified in the south by Lafayette and Baron von Steuben, Washington was in the west, and the north and northwest were defended by Rochambeau's men who had encampments and redoubts. Both the Americans and the French had heavy artillery units on the open ground between the coast going inland.

Cornwallis and his forces were wedged in on the coast except at the southeast where they had two redoubts built. All in all, the British were heavily outnumbered. They had at their disposal 9,000 troops while the Franco-Americans had more than 16,000! Seeing the discrepancy in numbers, Cornwallis sent a message to Clinton for reinforcements.

The French artillery was too plenteous, though. Huge guns, mortar rounds, and howitzers fired upon the British defenses on land. In addition, American cannons and French guns pounded at the British frigate, the HMS *Guadeloupe*, and the British scuttled it to avoid its capture. The Continental soldiers moved east toward the shore and fired all night as Washington didn't want them to have enough time to make repairs. Although the English ground troops fired a countless number of volleys inland, these troops were heavily outnumbered by the combined American and French forces. Some of the British guns went silent, and many of the soldiers deserted when they got pushed back toward the shoreline.

The French then destroyed the HMS *Charon*, their large warship. The *Charon* roared into flames, and other smaller English ships likewise caught fire. Cornwallis was forced to send out another dispatch to Clinton about the promised reinforcements as he didn't think he could hold out too much longer.

During the night, the French ground forces sneaked up to one of the redoubts while the Continental soldiers moved toward the other one. They did this in total silence in order to have the advantage of surprise. Once discovered, the British defenders fired on the Continentals and the French heavily. The British defenses were ineffective though, and both redoubts were taken. This left the city of Yorktown exposed, allowing the Franco-American forces to move in and fire ceaselessly.

Cornwallis tried to move away from the Continental forces by stealing or renting smaller ships in order to cross the York River and head toward Gloucester Point. This retreat was thwarted by a sudden storm, however. Forced to face Washington and Rochambeau with their massive numbers, Cornwallis sent out a soldier waving a white handkerchief and surrendered. This marked the end of the American Revolution.

Chapter 6 – Treaty of Paris and Repercussions

The American Revolution ended with Cornwallis' surrender in 1781, but the Treaty of Paris wasn't officially signed until 1783. Reasons for that were myriad, but the focal point for the delay centered around the differences in the personality traits of the participants in the negotiations. The participants included:

America:

1. Benjamin Franklin

2. John Jay

3. John Adams

4. Henry Laurens

England:

1. Richard Oswald

2. David Hartley

3. Charles James Fox

4. The Earl of Shelburne

Delicacy Demanded

England had gone through changes in its government during these negotiations. Thus, Oswald and Hartley helped formulate the initial articles, and Fox and Shelburne contributed to them. King George III also made his views known from the sidelines, and the ministers had to take his viewpoints into consideration.

While John Jay was attempting to design a workable structure for a treaty, his egotistical brother, James, meddled in the process and tried to grab attention. He wanted to be credited for resolving the differences between the various parties. So, he got himself arrested by the British who were still occupying the colonies. He was then taken to England and released. While there, James tried to meet with the parties involved. James also went to France and Holland to ascertain their positions. John was extremely incensed by James' machinations. James Jay had no authorization to negotiate a treaty, and it was no wonder the negotiations were taking so long! Gossip raced around America about James Jay, and he again embarrassed John. The New York Assembly even withdrew James' membership for his insolence. In 1782, John Jay complained to a close friend about James, saying, "After making so much bustle in and for America, he [James] has, as is surmised, improperly made his peace with Britain, I shall endeavor to forget that my father has such a son." John rarely ever spoke with James after that.

There were at least two versions of the final treaty. Prior to the arrival of John Jay, John Adams, and Henry Laurens, Benjamin Franklin had forged a deal with Comte de Vergennes, the French Minister of Foreign Affairs. The American governmental body, called the "Confederation Congress," was opposed to France's involvement. This put John Jay and the others in a precarious position. The personalities of the three Americans were also vastly different, and Jay felt he had to keep the interrelationships as compatible as possible. Yet Jay was a man with his own personal opinions as well, as he mistrusted France. Benjamin Franklin disliked John Adams, and the feeling was mutual. Jay respected Franklin but also knew Franklin wasn't a lawyer. As a lawyer, Jay managed its legal aspects as those would impact relations with Great Britain for years to come. Jay was proper and careful in his communications but sometimes found that Adams came across abrasively. Henry Laurens was somewhat of a reluctant participant, but the Confederation Congress finally persuaded him to join with the others. However, Laurens had been charged with treason by England because he was a patriot and had been imprisoned in the Tower of London until 1781, so neither he nor the English negotiators related well to each other. Therefore, the footing upon which this treaty was formed was on shaky ground.

Hurdles

The French version of this treaty had been premature and was derived from Franklin's opinion that America had to adhere to the commercial aspects of the Treaty of Amity and Commerce of 1778. Yet England was the primary country involved in the American Revolution, not France. Some of the French negotiators wanted to give France exclusive rights to the use of the Mississippi River and Canada. If that was agreed to, America would have lost a great deal, particularly with regards to the Mississippi and the possible expansion of America into the lands west of the Mississippi. Because of the crucial aid of France during the Revolution, Franklin felt that was a debt owed to them. However, by so doing he seemed to be willing to sacrifice America's rights to the Mississippi and just "give" Canada to France.

The next major issue involved the fishing rights off the coast of Newfoundland. John Jay met with Richard Oswald of Great Britain, and England regarded these fishing rights as crucial to its economy. Likewise, America wanted to benefit from fishing in the North Atlantic. So, America, England, and France wanted those rights. In addition, France wanted to maintain control over Tobago and Senegal. The Treaty of Paris was accompanied by the Treaty of Versailles which granted France control of Tobago and Senegal, as well as fishing rights off Newfoundland.

John Jay and John Adams objected to the restrictions on the Mississippi and French control of fishing rights off Canada, as it eliminated England from the basic negotiations and might open up a new possible war between France and England. In addition, the two of them felt that there was some trickery on France's part that went unrecognized by Franklin. Jay and Franklin argued about that point in particular, each trying to convince the other. Franklin then realized that Jay may have been correct in his suspicions that France had an ulterior motive and agreed to discontinue his nearly exclusive dealings with the Comte de Vergennes. Franklin still felt, however, that his own opinion was correct but deferred to John Jay. As a result, Jay and Franklin maintained a lifelong friendship after that.

Consequentially, the Confederation Congress insisted that Franklin apologize to Comte de Vergennes about eliminating him from the final negotiations. He did so because Jay, Adams, Franklin, and the representatives from England were willing to allow France to retain Tobago and Senegal. That was one of de Vergennes' primary interests. Fortunately, de Vergennes was gracious about being dropped from the final negotiations, but it took some effort.

Spain

Spain's main contribution to the American Revolution was financial. The country was also intensely interested in regaining West Florida about which there were disputes with Great Britain. John Jay concurred with that opinion, as he sensed that Spain would be more cooperative in giving America free and unadulterated access to the Mississippi River. Henry Laurens entered into the negotiations later than the others and was instrumental in dealing with Spain to develop the final agreements in the Treaty of Paris.

Treaty of Paris 1783

The key points of the treaty:

1. Recognition of American independence from Great Britain

2. Establishment of American boundaries to include the former British American colonies westward to the Mississippi River, northward to the southern border of Canada, and southward down to Florida. England would have possession of Canada. Spain would be entitled to Florida and the lands west of the Mississippi.

3. Great Britain would cede West Florida to Spain. France would cede Canada to Great Britain. Spain would surrender the Bahamas to the British.

4. Great Britain would evacuate from any territories it occupied during the Revolution and dismantle their forts.

5. America would be granted fishing rights off the coast of Newfoundland.

6. Property confiscated by America that belonged to the British would be returned, and restitution would be paid if applicable. Slaves that were taken during the course of the war would be returned to their prewar owners.

7. America would have rights to the Mississippi River.

8. War debts would be repaid.

Return to New York

Upon his arrival in New York, Jay received a welcome letter from the mayor and city council. The people of New York congratulated him on the successful Treaty of Paris, saying, "You have executed the important trusts committed to you with wisdom, firmness and integrity, and have acquired universal applause." The mayor presented him with a gold box signifying his accomplishments abroad. Bells from the old church chimed, and a cannon thundered his victorious homecoming.

During his absence, John Jay's elderly father had died at Fishkill. New York was still in the process of British evacuation, which delayed the family's return to their estate at Rye. Jay's father, Peter, bequeathed the majority of the family lands at Rye to his son, Peter Augustus, and a portion of it to John. John's allotment was seventy acres, and he named that area "The Locusts." During the Revolution, a lot of damage was done to the buildings there until Peter was able to rebuild it and the family moved back. Due to his obligations, John could only spend some of the summers at Rye. He put a family friend, Captain Samuel Lyons, in charge of his sector of the estate until it, too, could be developed.

The home was warm with all the people from his family: Peter, of course, and his wife Mary Duycinick; her niece, "Effy"; Jay's brother, Augustus; Eva, his older sister with her son, Peter Jay Munro; his blind sister, Nancy and Frederick, who cared for their elderly father at Fishkill during his declining years.

John Jay's lovely wife, Sarah "Sally" Livingston Jay, was also delighted to be home. Sally was in fragile health, but this large family was there to help her when Jay had to leave on business.

Secretary of Foreign Affairs

This office was successively named the "Secretary of War," the "Secretary of Foreign Affairs," and the "Secretary of State," which it is still known as today. John Jay served in that role from 1784 to 1789. This was a nascent position which unfortunately gave rise to abuse, particularly with reference to the collection of debt. Terms for the repayment of loans accrued due to the war debt. Various parties often faced impediments placed by the debtors, and clarification was needed related to debt collection according to the Treaty of Paris. Some debtors fabricated reasons why they couldn't be responsible for the entire amounts due and that caused dissension. The other overwhelming factor was the availability of money and the policies of those who controlled it. These issues, however, weren't settled until 1802.

Foreign Affairs Under the Articles of Confederation

The original Continental Congresses now morphed into the Confederation Congress under the Articles of the Confederation. During the American Revolution, the Articles of Confederation represented what could be considered the first U.S. Constitution. In its new form, the Confederation Congress was weak as it lacked the power of a true national government. Americans had struggled for so long against the absolute power of Great Britain that they moved in the opposite direction of the kind of government the British held. By virtue of these Articles, most of the power was in the hands of the states. Those states frequently fought with each other, creating wide disparities between their policies. Three key issues were immediately impacted: the enforcement of provisions from the Treaty of Paris, payment of war debt, and the funding of a national military force. In essence, the national government was powerless.

The British were required under the Treaty of Paris to dismantle the forts they still had in the states. However, the national government had no tool to use for enforcing that. The Confederation Congress also had no treasury and had to appeal to the states to "contribute" money to pay off the war debts. Yet Jay was saddled with the job of creating a system of stable American currency, as each state had its own paper currency and credit agreements in order to establish terms for debt collection. Not only that, but Jay held the position of being the negotiator for the repayment of war debts between America, England, France, and Spain.

In 1785, Thomas Jefferson was a peace commissioner for some of the European countries and was sent to Paris in the interest of debt collection. John Jay and Jefferson exchanged a flurry of letters in that regard. According to Jay, "our treasury and credit are in a sad situation." The indebtedness was exacerbated by money paid to the

Barbary pirates operating in the Mediterranean Sea. These pirates raided ships from nations with whom they had no right of passage agreements. Those nations which had the right of passage usually paid an annual tribute—much like one paid to an extortionist. Before the Revolution, America didn't have to concern itself with that because that task was in the hands of Great Britain. After the war, America was on its own, and its merchant vessels were subject to seizure by the pirates. In fact, an American brigantine had been seized. Jefferson wrote to John Jay in that regard, indicating that an American navy needed to be built. He said, "Our trade to Portugal, Spain and the Mediterranean is annihilated unless we do something about it."

Without a federal military force, there were also difficulties Jay faced when the borders of the United States were threatened with invasions. Tribal encroachments often led to conflicts between the settlers and the tribes. The Native American and Canadian tribes had nations that spread across a number of borders and sometimes conducted raids in the Ohio Valley. After the Treaty of Paris, it was vital to maintain border security from English-dominated Canada and Spanish Florida. Some of the states objected to contributing to defense because each state had its own militia. The coordination of the militias of more than one state to participate in a united defensive action became a logistical nightmare.

While state funds could be obtained to finance counterattacks against intruders, it was first necessary to obtain approval from every state in America. That could be done, of course, but it took an incredibly long period of time to get approvals.

John Jay then spoke to Alexander Hamilton and James Madison who were serving in the Confederation Congress. Like Jay, both of these representatives felt that the Articles of Confederation were too weak to form the backbone for the new nation. In 1788, Jay published the Address to the People of the State of New York on this subject:

The Congress under the Articles of Confederation may make war, but are not empowered to raise men or money to carry it on—they may make peace, but without power to see the terms of it observed—they may form alliances, but without ability to comply with the stipulations on their part—they may enter into treaties of commerce, but without power to enforce them at home or abroad.

Chapter 7 – Constitution and Court

The governmental structure of America under the Articles of Confederation directly affected John Jay in his crucial role as secretary of foreign affairs. It diluted his effectiveness in dealing with foreign countries, shaking their confidence. Foreign governments needed to see that the United States spoke with one voice, operated as one union, and that all states would observe treaties made with foreign nations.

Federalist Papers

To promote a change to the Articles of Confederation, John Jay, Alexander Hamilton, and James Madison wrote the *Federalist Papers*, which played a significant role in the articles formed in the U.S. Constitution, and had them published in all the states. They felt that the weaknesses of the Articles of Confederation represented a reaction against the former domineering control of England over policy and practice. Therefore, these Articles tended to put too much power into the hands of the states, thereby weakening the central government nearly to the point of paralysis. The three published their papers under the pseudonym "Publius," which is derived from the Latin word, *"publicus,"* meaning the "people." In "Federalist No. 2", Jay opined that the transformation of states into individual and distinct confederacies would "put the continuance of the Union in the utmost jeopardy."

In his Federalist Nos. 3, 4, and 5, he stated that the country could protect itself from the intrusion of foreign forces and influence if it spoke in a unified voice. He said that "a good national government affords vastly more security against dangers [than] that sort that can be derived from any other quarter." He went on to give the example that there had been several skirmishes with the Native Americans provoked by the leniency or neglect of certain individual states and that it resulted in unnecessary bloodshed. In "Federalist No. 5," in particular, he argued that too much state control over foreign affairs might trigger competition between states in terms of power and cause each state to become distrustful of one another. If that happened, for example, a foreign government might favor the interests of the Northern states over the Southern states and cause a division within the United States, or they might send foreign fleets to one state to influence the behavior of another. This resulted in the formulation of Article I, Section 8 of the Constitution, known as the "Dormant Commerce Clause." It stated that Congress (but not the president) has the right to regulate commerce with foreign nations. Of course, the president could make recommendations, which he so did in numerous instances. In "Federalist No. 6," John Jay presented a possible scenario for harming commercial interests in order to satisfy an exclusive interest or passion on the part of a powerful person in one state. That issue was addressed by Article I, Section 10, which forbids states from entering into their own private agreements with a foreign power.

"Federalist No. 64" is particularly significant. In this essay, John Jay indicated that the president should be entitled to make treaties with the consent of 2/3 of the members of the Senate. That touched off a debate among Alexander Hamilton, John Jay, and James Madison. In a clause in that essay, it says that the president "…by and with the advice and consent of the Senate, is empowered to make treaties, provided two thirds of the senators present concur." Jay intended by the use of that language that the president himself would have the final power with regards to a treaty and was not obliged to take the advice of the Senate. He felt that only the president understood the issues at stake, while states did not have sufficient knowledge about a foreign government to make the final decision.

According to Article VI of the U.S. Constitution—otherwise known as the "supremacy clause"—the central government alone has the exclusive right to make treaties. States have no rights to negotiate treaties with foreign countries.

John Jay and the Body Snatchers

In 1788, New York experienced what they called the "Doctor's Riot." It wasn't conducted by doctors but was the result of citizens reacting to the clandestine practice of grave robbing. Dissection of the human body was forbidden by law. There were still some of the vestiges of superstition within the minds of men, so the means of obtaining corpses for study was relegated to an underground practice. The notion of having one's body disinterred and dissected struck fear in people. Curiously, even Shakespeare had these words in his epitaph:

> Good friend, for Jesus' sake forebeare
>
> To Digg the dust enclosed heare;
>
> Bleste be the man that spares these stones,
>
> And curst be he that moves my bones.

Doctors and medical students needed to study the anatomy of corpses for educational purposes, though. So, in the heart of night, grungy men crept around graveyards and disinterred bodies to sell to these anatomy classes. According to urban legends that flourished at the time, it was said that arms and legs of bodies were found on the grounds outside these clinics. New Yorkers were finding open graves and even discarded body parts in various dark alleys and the dirty streets in lower-class neighborhoods.

In the beginning, the burial grounds of African Americans were desecrated. The American society had a prejudicial attitude toward African Americans at that time and didn't react much when these graves were robbed. However, when the practice spread to white people, the New Yorkers were incensed and horrified. On one occasion, it was rumored that the nude body of a partially dissected woman was discovered. She was a person from the middle class according to the tale.

Another case was that of a young boy who reportedly was struck with a severed leg when he was peering into a basement anatomy class. It was said that the boy recently lost his mother and was severely traumatized by this incident. He ran home and reported it to his father who checked the grave and found it empty. The man then organized a band of people to go on the prowl trying to capture the possible body-snatchers. Mobs formed near the New York Hospital where they broke into the laboratory and were appalled by what they saw there. There were bodies boiling in kettles and organs displayed on walls. Their equipment was consequently destroyed, and the citizens gathered up the dissected parts of the corpses and carted them out for reburial.

John Jay and Alexander Hamilton—both New Yorkers—rushed into the streets and tried to calm the unruly mob. As he was speaking to a crowd, Jay was struck by a rock on his head and had to be hospitalized. As a result of his head injury, John Jay was only able to contribute five essays to the *Federalist Papers*.

It wasn't until the 19th century that reformed laws were put into place. These new laws allowed dissection for medical purposes, but there were strict guidelines regulating that practice.

The U.S. Constitution 1787-1790

Members of the Continental Congress debated about the Articles of Confederation, and it was decided that the Articles of

Confederation was too weak. Rather than modify them, the members of the assembly determined that all of them should be rejected, and a new set of precepts should be adopted that could be used for the nation. To set a different tone, members called their sessions the "Constitutional Convention."

Several state delegates presented plans that could form the basis of a national constitution, and heavy debates commenced having to do with them. James Madison was assigned the all-consuming job of collecting the notes from all the states' delegates and putting the material into a summary document. He was later persuaded by the delegates to write the Bill of Rights, which was an addendum to the draft of the Constitution. The United States Constitution was ratified in 1788, with all the states having ratified it by 1790.

The Anti-Federalist Papers

The entire issue of states' rights vs. federal rights was in contention because of the weight of the power of those two entities. Papers were written under the pseudonyms "Brutus" and presented reasons for the rejection of the U.S. Constitution. Although the Constitution had been passed in 1790, these *Anti-Federalist Papers* were published through the years 1787 to 1788. In criticizing John Jay's Federalist essays, "Brutus" said that this Constitution would eventually annihilate the powers of the individual states. History has indicated that the writer of this section of the *Anti-Federalist Papers* was John DeWitt, a delegate from Duchess County in New York. Others have attributed the "Brutus" essays to Robert Yates, a statesman from New York who was a justice on New York's supreme court.

According to Jonathan Marshall in *The Journal of Libertarian Studies* of Amherst University, "Historians by and large have assumed that the Anti-Federalists were consumed with purely domestic, parochial concerns...except perhaps on the issue of commercial regulation." In 1791, the Tenth Amendment was added to the Bill of Rights and formed part of the U.S. Constitution. It was written basically to attempt to satisfy the objections of the Anti-Federalists who opposed a strong central government.

Chapter 8 – John Jay, Chief Justice and Gubernatorial Candidate

After the U.S. Constitution was passed, there was a reorganization in the federal government. In 1789, George Washington renamed the position of secretary of foreign affairs to "Secretary of State," as it included not only dealings with foreign countries but negotiations between the states and those foreign countries. Washington then asked John Jay to assume this newly defined position, but Jay turned it down. Jay's passion was that of a trial lawyer and felt that he would be more productive in a legal role.

The fledgling U.S. Constitution established the Supreme Court when the Judiciary Act of 1789 was passed. Washington offered John Jay the position of chief justice, and he readily accepted. Washington responded, "In nominating you for the important station which you now fill, I not only acted in conformity with my best judgement, but I trust I did a grateful thing to the good citizens of these United States." The initial judges that Washington selected were:

1. William Cushing

2. James Wilson

3. John Rutledge

4. James Iredell

5. John Blair

William Cushing of Massachusetts was the chief justice of that state. His most notable state case had to do with a slave named Quock Walker who sued for freedom based on the language of the new Massachusetts Constitution. Cushing charged his jury to consider that "a different idea has taken place with the people of America, more favorable to the rights of mankind." After the jury considered the arguments, the court decided that slavery was inconsistent with the state constitution. Another jury in the state also ruled for the freedom of another, slave Elizabeth Freeman, who coincidentally was aptly named. Cushing was a welcome addition to the Supreme Court.

James Wilson was a professor of law at the College of Philadelphia which later became the University of Pennsylvania. While he was well trained in the legal profession, he also believed in practicality in developing his legal decisions. He also felt that even those without legal training should have some background in understanding the law. His lectures were reprinted in the academic community, and the law department of the University of Pennsylvania presents his viewpoints in their studies. Wilson, with his practical-minded approach, helped balance out the views of the others who were more addicted to the letter of the law.

John Rutledge of South Carolina owned slaves and supported the institution of slavery. He was wealthy and absorbed in what he considered was his higher social status. He resented anyone who disparaged him and had a hot temper. Some people in his state called him "Dictator John Rutledge." One time, the owner of a tavern in his state reportedly insulted him, and he stormed into the House of Representatives in South Carolina requesting that the man be banished from the state. Predictably, they refused.

Although he served on the Supreme Court, he resigned before participating in any rulings because he was appointed to the Court of Common Pleas and Sessions in South Carolina. Washington had only selected him because he wanted all segments of American society to be represented.

James Iredell from North Carolina was the youngest of the Supreme Court justices. He was a fervent and impassioned patriot and wrote a number of essays supporting freedom. Iredell heavily lobbied for the passage of the U.S. Constitution but only after it was appended with the Bill of Rights. Iredell wasn't a rich man and even on occasion was debt-ridden, but he managed to emerge from that situation successfully and become a very wealthy man. Washington wanted both the wealthy and the less wealthy adequately represented.

John Blair of Virginia heralded from Williamsburg and attended the College of William and Mary there. He was a military man who served in the French and Indian War but later studied law. His law practice initially was small when he was elected to the House of Burgesses, the English version of a state House of Representatives before American independence. He rejected the stridency of Patrick Henry, considering him to be too extreme in his oratories. When the United States was formulating its Constitution, Blair was instrumental in writing Virginia's plan called the Declaration of the Rights of Virginia. After he was appointed to the Virginia Court of Common Pleas, he ruled in the important case of the *Commonwealth of Virginia v. Caton et al.* that stated a court had the right to rule a legislative act as unconstitutional. This mirrored the later monumental decision given in the well-publicized case *Marbury v. Madison*. His background made him a good selection for the highest court in the land.

Structure and Functioning of the Early Supreme Court

The Supreme Court worked as circuit courts under the Judiciary Act of 1789. These justices traveled to different locales to hear cases and to make themselves known to the citizens. John Jay's territory included New York and New England. He was very popular, especially in Boston. Harvard College even awarded him an honorary degree of Doctor of Law. Invitations from noted people poured in whenever he held court in their state. He rode by horseback throughout New England and once said that he spent more time in the saddle than on the bench!

For those who were called "Anti-Federalists," the founding of the Supreme Court posed a threat. They were afraid that it could become a tool for national tyranny. Federalists, on the other hand, saw the need for a strong central government, as they were concerned about preserving unity among the states. Initially, it was composed of circuit courts and district courts. The Supreme Court itself heard cases in which constitutionality was questioned or the sovereignty of a state was brought into question. Other cases involving serious crimes and civil cases entailing at least $500 or more were heard by the circuit courts that formed the Supreme Court. Smaller district courts had jurisdiction over civil cases involving $100. These circuit courts were presided by two chief justices and a district court judge. An attorney general and U.S. Marshals were appointed to coordinate matters. At that time, five associate justices were appointed to assist Jay. Every party to a case was given the right to representation and were permitted to represent themselves if they wished or hire someone else (usually a lawyer) to represent them. The attorney general had the responsibility to represent the entire state.

The Neutrality Crisis

One issue of critical importance presented itself in the early days of the Supreme Court. In 1789, French mobs stormed the Bastille prison, touching off the French Revolution, which was essentially a rejection of the monarchy and fluctuating reorganization of the power structure. There were riots all over Paris, and the politics in the country was in chaos. In 1793, King Louis XVI was executed. Europe reacted with alarm, as Britain and many of the central European countries were also monarchies and feared the spread of radical ideas in their own territories. France, then being run by the National Assembly—the French people's representative body— invaded Dutch lands and interfered with British commerce. British allies in Europe aided them in fighting the French. By 1793, not only England but the Netherlands, Austria, Prussia, Spain, Sardinia, and Portugal were at war with France. Washington feared that America would be drawn into a war that would not only cost lives and money but also hamper the growth and development of America as a new nation. President Washington wanted to declare neutrality, but there was an impediment. Back in 1778, the U.S. and France signed the Treaty of Alliance, guaranteeing that America would provide military aid to France in case of a war against England.

Washington's proposal of neutrality set off a firestorm of controversy within America. Alexander Hamilton, the secretary of the treasury and the well-known conservative statesman, was in favor of neutrality. The secretary of state, Thomas Jefferson, was personally pro-France but realized that neutrality would be safer. However, he suggested that perhaps America shouldn't make an official declaration of it, even suggesting that countries "bid" for America's neutrality. In April of 1793, Washington issued a proclamation which required America to pursue "friendly and impartial relations toward belligerent powers." It also threatened prosecution against any American offering or providing military aid to those powers.

Proclamation of Neutrality and the Genêt Affair

During the early stages of the French Revolution, everyone carried the title "Citizen." In April of 1793, a Frenchman by the name of Citizen Genêt was appointed to be the French minister to the United States. A violation of the Neutrality Proclamation arose regarding Citizen Genêt. France wanted Genêt to recruit American seamen and purchase a few old British warships that had been confiscated during the war and send them back to France.

Proper protocol called for Genêt to first pay his respects to President Washington, but he deliberately ignored that in view of the Neutrality Proclamation. He landed in South Carolina, knowing he would be well received. And he was correct in his assessment, as there were parties in his honor. The Americans were extremely grateful for French aid, and the French were honored and celebrated in this country. He continued with his plan to purchase old British vessels or having privateers confiscate them. He then further planned on recruiting American seamen to commandeer his ships and began hiring infantrymen for a militia to engage the Spanish in Florida. Next, Genêt set out for Philadelphia, garnering more recruits along the way. Among the first British vessels the pirates took was the *Little Sarah*, a brigantine. Before much time had passed, ports along the Eastern seaboard were full of confiscated ships, and the American public cheered the effort while condemning the British. Then Genêt had those ships outfitted for the Anglo-French War. The *Little Sarah* was docked at Philadelphia, and its refurbishing was complete. When Genêt had the new ship ready to leave port, Governor Mifflin of Pennsylvania sent out his militia in order to halt the voyage. Washington was home at Mount Vernon because of the death of his estates' overseer and wasn't aware this was happening at the time, and Thomas Jefferson was away in the country. Therefore, Mifflin sent out the secretary of state of Pennsylvania, Alexander Dallas, to speak with Genêt. Dallas met up with Genêt on the dock. Shouting ensued, and he refused to abide by the order to stay. Mifflin also sent a message to Jefferson who rushed over and met Genet at his room in a local tavern. Genêt warned Jefferson that the *Little Sarah* was full of American patriots who were going to fight for France and that they had best refrain from taking any action. Seeing that a skirmish might break out, Jefferson had Governor Mifflin dismiss the militia. Then, futilely, he tried to persuade Genêt to wait for Washington's return. Then Genêt unleashed a tirade berating America for breaking its treaty with France and criticized the Constitution as well. Finally, Jefferson calmed down Genêt, but the persistent Frenchman threatened to go directly to the American people to ask them to approach Congress and have them recommend that the Neutrality Proclamation be dropped.

In the meantime, Genêt had left port. In an effort to head off Genêt's departure to sea, the secretary of war, Henry Knox, and Jefferson discussed putting cannons on Mud Island in the Delaware River, as Genêt had been headed that way. Jefferson disagreed saying that bloody consequences could occur. By the time their discussions were over, the *Little Sarah* was docked at Chester, Pennsylvania. With Washington out of town, Governor Mifflin along with Knox and Jefferson were hesitant to take any definitive action. They were also concerned about what should be done about the Americans Genêt claimed to have on board. Jefferson then thought that he might suggest to the president approach John Jay about that. While those discussions continued on, the Little Sarah sailed down the Delaware River to Gloucester Point, Virginia moved into open waters.

Jefferson sent a packet of letters about the Genêt Affair to Mount Vernon for the president to read upon his return. Washington was very perturbed about the affair but became furious when he discovered that Jefferson had quickly retreated back to his country hideaway. Washington sent him a stern notification that he return so the crisis could be resolved.

Pacificus-Helvidius Debates

An uproar among many U.S. citizens resulted when Genêt's publication hit the newspapers. There was also a strong partisan reaction to the Genêt Affair as it related to the Neutrality Proclamation. Alexander Hamilton and James Madison debated about the constitutional rights of the executive branch and the legislative branch to make rulings regarding foreign affairs.

That disagreement set off what was called the "Pacificus-Helvidius Debates." Hamilton, under the pseudonym "Pacificus," wrote that the president was well within his rights to issue this executive order. "Helvidius" was the name James Madison chose to present the opposing point of view and wrote that the Neutrality Proclamation created a new construct not written in the US Constitution.

Faced with this dissension from the American public and other influential statesmen who demanded that Congress repeal the Neutrality Proclamation, Washington sought the opinion of the Supreme Court.

Supreme Court Ruling

John Jay and the justices declined to offer their advice to George Washington regarding the Genêt incident. This was unusual at the time, and the issue still arises today having to do with the solicitation of a legal opinion versus a legally-rendered verdict based on law and interpretation of the U.S. Constitution. The justices said that they wouldn't present their opinions unless it was as a result of a verdict rendered in litigation. This was called the "Rule against Advisory Opinions." In addition, the court carefully explained that their role didn't include giving advice to the executive branch of government. They said:

> ...these considerations afford strong arguments against the propriety of our extra-judiciously deciding the (president's) questions...especially as the power given by the Constitution to the president of calling on the heads of departments for opinions, seems to have been purposely as well as expressly limited to *executive* departments.

Washington was disappointed that the court wouldn't rule on this but now faced a dilemma. He discussed it with Congress, and together, they decided that the president should contact France asking to recall Genêt. Astonishingly, France complied with that request without objection, and Genêt left the U.S. However, when

Genêt approached a port in France, his luggage and documents were laboriously searched by the military. Much to his horror, he then discovered that a new political faction, the Montagnards, had taken control of the National Assembly. Because he had been sent by a rival political faction, the Jacobins, Genêt was deathly afraid he might be sent to the guillotine. Panic-stricken, he had his vessel turn back and hurried to Philadelphia to see George Washington. Humbly, he begged Washington to grant him political asylum. Washington graciously welcomed Genêt to the United States, and Genêt moved to New York and became involved in politics.

Jay, as chief justice, had remained neutral in the Genêt matter but later on did write an article for newspapers delineating the factual details about it. He indicated that Genêt defied President Washington who told him not to promote his cause directly to the American people because it violated the Neutrality Proclamation. Genêt charged Jay with libel, after which Jay told the newspapers to reprint Genêt's public letter that stated he was going to deliberately disobey the president. Once he knew the truth would be exposed, Genêt didn't pursue the lawsuit. Libel cannot be successfully prosecuted unless the material presented is untrue.

Justice John Jay and the National Bank

When he was first appointed chief justice, John Jay was approached by Alexander Hamilton, a fellow Federalist, who was trying to establish a national bank. In order to garner additional support for his proposal, he contacted John Jay in 1791 in his capacity on the Supreme Court. Hamilton wanted to add the support of that Court to his promotion of the national bank. On the grounds of neutrality, Jay wouldn't comply. He later wrote to Hamilton advising him that private property would not be secure in a national bank. He said "…while Congress thought themselves authorized to take such liberties, private property could not be secure in a national bank." Jay was a firm believer in the sanctity of private property, having come from a family whose property was stripped from them in monarchical France.

Hayburn's Case

Jay was instrumental in confining his Supreme Court to strictly judicial matters. The justices registered their objections to an Act of Congress that decided that the Court should hear cases relating to the Invalid Pensions Act. Congress had voted that an invalid from the war was required to submit his application to the Court if it was appealed. Jay and the others felt that this was an unjustifiable use of the Court. *Hayburn's Case* was an example of this, and the justices claimed the federal law supporting that unconstitutional. As a result, the Invalid Pensions Act was repealed.

Alexander Chisholm v. Georgia

In 1793, John Jay presided over his associate justices to hear the well-known case of *Alexander Chisholm v. Georgia*. It involved the jurisdiction of the Supreme Court, which was important in view of the ongoing friction between states' rights and federal rights. In this case, a South Carolina citizen named Robert Farquhar sued the state of Georgia for monies owed from a Revolutionary War debt. Georgia indicated it wasn't required to appear because a sovereign state was immune to prosecution by a private citizen in the Supreme Court unless they consent to it. Four of the six Supreme Court justices, including John Jay, ruled in favor of the defendant because Article 3 of the Constitution permitted suits against states by private citizens.

This case gave rise to the passage of the 11th Amendment. That amendment took the position that Justice Iredell had written. It says that a state cannot be sued by an individual of another state in federal court without the state's consent. The only exception that can occur is if the U.S. Congress denies the state immunity in the particular case under consideration.

Ware v. Hylton

After the American Revolution, the Treaty of Paris required that American debtors be paid for debts owed to them from British creditors including those incurred before the Revolution. However, the state of Virginia had passed a law which forgave these debts. Arguing for the American debtors was John Marshall, who later became a chief justice; Patrick Henry, the famous patriot; Alexander Campbell; and James Innis. Although they were split in their opinion, the majority of justices voted for the nullification of this Virginia statute and declared that the British creditors could legally collect the debts.

Calder v. Bull

The Supreme Court rendered a monumental verdict on this case which is still practiced today. It passed a verdict that declared:

> 1. Congress is forbidden to pass *"ex post facto laws."* When a person performs an act that isn't criminal at that time, he or she cannot be convicted if such an act is later designated as criminal.

> 2. The Supreme Court cannot declare that laws passed according to its own state constitutions are in violation of a state's law. That prerogative resides within the state itself.

> 3. No one can be forced to do anything that a law doesn't require.

John Jay Runs for Governor

Jay had long been associated with the Federalists who believed in a strong national government, but the Anti-Federalists were starting to unite into a political party themselves. They called themselves "Democratic-Republicans." Many Federalists were businessmen, entrepreneurs, or manufacturers. The Democratic-Republicans were mostly farmers, small craftsmen, and traders.

They had this long-sustaining fear that tyranny in some form would infiltrate the country because of the wealth and influence of the Federalists who were mostly in the north. In upstate and western New York, many were engaged in the agrarian culture. They felt that the growing wealth of the state and indeed the country was due to unrestricted financial speculation. Prior to 1795, the secretary of the treasury, Alexander Hamilton, established the first national bank. He set it up as a means to finance the war debt initially. The Anti-Federalists felt that loans extended by this bank were a means of enslaving the people. They feared that the wealth seemed to be concentrated in the hands of bankers and businessmen, leaving them to the mercy of greedy financiers. The Democratic-Republicans criticized the structure of such loans, saying that it opened the door to corruption and usury.

In 1792, John Jay ran for governor of New York against the incumbent, George Clinton. The Federalists presented their position as being one of change and progress. They pointed out the fact that a rotation of leaders was desirable and presented themselves as civil reformers. That election was not unlike those of today, as rumors about the new candidate proliferated the media. One of the stories circulated indicated that John Jay had secretly colluded in the sale of a huge tract of land in New York extending all the way up to the Canadian border, and the potential owner planned on making it part of the British territory. It wasn't true. Another rumor attributed this fabricated quote to him: "There ought to be in America but two sorts of people, the one very rich and the other very poor." The farmers in New York during the 1790s depended upon slavery, and Jay was noted for his stance on the freedom of slaves, although he favored a gradual dissolution of the practice.

Critics of the John Jay gubernatorial campaign indicated that Jay's supporters didn't produce any compelling agenda other than the fact that the state needed a change and that George Clinton had been in office for too long. In order to help boost his chances, he chose Stephen Van Rensselaer as his running mate. Rensselaer was a landowner with very liberal views on the treatment of his tenants, even giving them perpetual leases at low rates. However, Jay didn't or couldn't convey the fact that a strong central government would ensure unity, not dictatorship, so it was a tight race.

The tallies from the polls from three counties were mishandled as they hadn't been delivered to people authorized to collect the ballots. Because of this technicality, the canvass committee, the committee in charge of determining whether or not ballots are properly processed, rejected the validity of those ballots. Therefore, Jay lost the election. Of the valid votes cast, he actually won 49% of the votes while Clinton won 50%. Had the votes been handled correctly, John Jay would have won according to analysts.

Chapter 9 – The Jay Treaty and John Jay as Governor

The Treaty of Paris signed in 1783 had a number of weaknesses that were left unresolved. Some of those issues had to do with:

1. The British withdrawal from forts on American territory

Although the Treaty of Paris required that the British withdraw from their forts on American territory, no firm date was established. Thus, in 1794, English regiments still occupied and defended those forts, most of which were near the Canadian border.

2. Native American Rights

The Treaty of Paris was very nonspecific about Native American territories in northern Maine, Massachusetts, and the Pacific Northwest, including the rights of tribes living in Canada.

3. The impressment of American seamen by the British and the seizure of American vessels

4. The failure of the British to return confiscated property to the Americans, specifically slaves

5. Impediments placed by the Americans having to do with the collection of debts due to private parties in England

6. Trading Rights

There had been a restriction of American exports to Great Britain and other countries in Europe since the war between Britain and France broke out. England was only given a "favorable" status in trade as a result of the Treaty of Paris.

In view of the fact that the war between England and France caused difficulties since English ports were sometimes closed to American shipping, George Washington sent John Jay to England to solve the issue. His son, Peter, had just graduated from King's College, and John took him along to act as a secretary. They met with William Pitt the Younger, the prime minister.

The Jay Treaty of 1795

As a result of the Jay Treaty, only three issues were resolved:

A. The British withdrew from eight of its forts along the Northern frontier.

B. The Native Americans near the border and over the Canadian border were given the liberty of entering each other's territory in the United States. To aid that effort, firm borders were drawn up between the contiguous United States and Canada. That was of particular concern to Great Britain at the time.

C. England gave America the status of "most favored nation," in trading privileges. America then reciprocated.

Consequent Backlash

The Americans were angry that John Jay couldn't resolve the other issues. Americans were still being impressed into service on English warships, and merchant vessels were being confiscated by pirates (aka "privateers"). The Southerners were upset that their purloined slaves hadn't been returned to them from England. Some of the English were abolitionists, but Britain did recruit slaves for their wars in the British West Indies—a contradiction between their purported ideals and actual practice.

The followers of the newly burgeoning Democratic-Republicans were incensed that America failed to establish commerce with France which had given it so much support during the Revolution. This eventually evolved into the creation of the party platform for Democratic-Republicanism under Thomas Jefferson and James Madison.

As a consequence of the proposed Jay Treaty, there were protests in the streets of Philadelphia, New York, and even Boston. People scrawled graffiti on buildings saying, "Damn John Jay! Damn John Jay! Damn everyone who won't damn John Jay! Damn everyone who won't put lights in his windows and sit up all night damning John Jay!" People burned his image in effigy in the city streets. John Jay even quipped that he could travel the streets from Philadelphia to Boston solely by the light from his effigies!

Washington was kindlier toward Jay. In his wisdom, he knew such matters would take time, but little by little they would be resolved. The American public, on the other hand, was impatient. It became a political party matter when the Democratic-Republican part of the state of South Carolina had the audacity to pass a resolution calling for a trial of John Jay on charges of treason and even lamented the fact that America didn't employ the use of the guillotine!

Many people even became angry with George Washington over the Jay Treaty, feeling that their liberties were in jeopardy because of the preferred status granted to England in terms of trade. Some members of the Democratic-Republican party even called for his impeachment.

French Reaction

The Democratic-Republicans sympathized with France in terms of trading rights and lobbied for the House of Representatives not to sign the treaty. Much to the surprise of everyone, thirteen members of the Democratic-Republican party joined the Federalists in voting for the treaty.

There were serious repercussions regarding the fact that Great Britain was given a "most favored nation" status by virtue of the Jay Treaty which led to a serious incident in French relations during John Adams' administration. This was dubbed the "XYZ Affair" to maintain secrecy during the negotiations.

By the year 1795, over 300 American merchant ships were confiscated by France because they didn't provide legal proof that they weren't carrying arms or armaments for England. The waters off coastal American were strewn with both British and French ships. There were naval engagements in the Western Atlantic between France and American ships because of the French privateers.

New York Gubernatorial Election 1795

Jay won the gubernatorial election against Robert Yates. It was a close race, but the Democratic-Republicans had yet to become the more prominent political party in New York which was still a mostly Federalist state.

Jay then resigned as chief justice of the Supreme Court and became a foresighted governor. Painfully, he remembered the burning of his dear city in 1776, and New York was virtually defenseless as a result. He also knew of the English and French ships offshore, either of whom could invade the state again. Therefore, he saw his first obligation as one to create a suitable defensive force. In 1789, there had been money set aside for the building of a navy with a budget of $950,000. That was a considerable sum in those days. Benjamin Stoddard, a capable manager and businessman, had helped raise the funds for building the first American Navy. Jay's predecessor, George Clinton, had laid some groundwork for the construction of effective fortifications in New York, and Jay began working on perfecting the project. Henry Knox, the secretary of state at the time, had hired Charles Vincent, a French military engineer. Vincent was succeeded by Joseph Francois Mangin as the engineer. Jay discussed the situation with him, and Mangin proceeded to work on establishing protections on the many waterways around New York City. The former governor had originally feared an invasion from England, but the Jay Treaty reduced that threat, so New Yorkers began to grow complacent. Jay, on the other hand, warned his state legislature and the people that France was now the new threat and New York was still vulnerable. He said, "Imbecility invites insult and aggression and experience of ages proves that they are the most secure against war who are best prepared to meet it."

Mangin first focused his attention upon the territorial waters around Staten Island, Long Island, and Manhattan. During the American Revolution, Staten Island had been annexed by the British, and the British also entered Manhattan by crossing over Long Island at Brooklyn. At Jay's behest, Mangin proposed the use of Governor's Island, Bedloe Island, and Oyster Island for naval fortifications. Much later on, Bedloe Island became Liberty Island where the Statue of Liberty stands. Instead of Oyster Island, nearby Ellis Island became the famous site that housed immigrants to the American shores. Governor's Island was used for harbor defenses for the British during the Revolution but was used for administrative offices and the Coast Guard station at this time. Today it's a national park.

Uphill Battle for Funding

In 1796, Jay sent an envoy, his wife's cousin, Edward Livingston, to the national government but was shocked when the House of Representatives refused to provide funding. In 1797, Congress allocated $365,000 for coastal defenses. Jay then sent Ebenezer Stevens, a Revolutionary War veteran, on a mission to have them earmark some funds for the defense of New York. Squabbles over land ownership and administrative arguments totally clouded the issue, and again, New York was unsuccessful. The support of New

Yorkers was also fading until a fire broke out near Wall Street. That aroused interest in the funding campaign.

John Adams was elected president in 1797. As one of his initial acts, he conducted secret negotiations with France to avert war. This was called the XYZ Affair as the French agents didn't want to be identified. Adams sent a national peace delegation to France in 1797-1798. Subsequent reports indicated that the peace commissioners were met with a very cold reception, and the effort was unsuccessful. That also alarmed the New York populace.

Realizing that they weren't going to get federal funding, John Jay and the leading New Yorkers, Alexander Hamilton, Ebenezer Stevens, Matthew Clarkson, and Aaron Burr formed a committee to try to encourage New Yorkers to fund the project themselves. Jay called for a session of the New York Congress in Albany in 1798. Finally, they were able to secure some limited funding— $150,000. That was targeted to be spent on completing the partially constructed defensive installations on the islands in the inner harbor.

Fort Jay

During the American Revolution, George Washington had built an earthen work fortification, but it lay in ruins. In view of the fact that the French might attack and in view of the overall fact that a new country needed defenses in every state, John Jay campaigned incessantly for funds. In his letter dated January 19, 1797, Jay said, "I am strongly impressed with the importance of our being always in a state of defense." He obtained some state funding and was able to initiate construction of a more permanent fort on Governor's Island. Unfortunately, the yellow fever epidemic broke out, and construction proceeded very slowly. Later on, he was able to persuade the U.S. Congress to designate some money for further construction. The entire project wasn't finished until 1806, but Congress placed Fort Jay under the direction of the Army Corps of Engineers.

The Quasi-War of 1798

The defensive war fought during John Adams' administration was called a "Quasi-War" because it was undeclared. It came about because of unresolved issues related to the Jay Treaty and the confiscation of American ships and impressment of their sailors by France. John Jay had made all those initial military plans because he had been wary there would be a war between France and the United States. In 1798, it looked like a war might start when a French privateer boldly confiscated a merchant vessel right inside New York Harbor. President Adams became particularly alarmed and forcefully designated funds to create the inauguration of an American Navy. Hamilton, who had been serving as an inspector general of the military, was made the potential commander-in-chief of the American army in the event that full-scale war broke out.

Political infighting reached a deafening pitch, and Federalist John Adams appointed George Washington instead. However, he did that without asking Washington! Washington agreed, indicating he would not actively participate but serve more as a consultant. In addition, Washington insisted he select his own subordinates. Those subordinates—Charles Pickney, James McHenry, Henry Knox, and Alexander Hamilton—were Federalists.

This war was fought entirely at sea. The rather modest U.S. Navy damaged the French frigate *La Vengeance* off the shores of New Jersey. The American warship, *Enterprise*, captured two more French privateering ships as well as *Le Berceau* near Boston. More action took place in the West Indies where several French privateers were hiding and disrupting U.S. commerce in the South Atlantic. Many American ships escorted U.S. merchant ships into Boston and the Southern ports. One of the most famous Navy ships was the USC *Merrimack*, a 24-gun warship. Another was the USS *Constitution*, also called "Old Ironsides," which was later refitted and today is used as a historical attraction. The *Merrimack* and the USS *Constitution,* the *L'Magicienne, Bonaparte, Phoenix, Niger, Amelia*, and the *Brilliant*.

John Jay: Federalist

In 1800, John Adams lost his bid for president. The Federalist Party was much maligned in the state of New York because advocates of the Democratic-Republican Party sponsored by Thomas Jefferson formed their own local societies and associated the Federalists with a return to the domineering structure of the old monarchy of England. The Democratic-Republicans tended to look upon the Federalists, who believed in a strong central government, as a threat to the rights of the states and individuals. Their preferences centered around the working man and especially favored farmers. Democratic-Republicans felt that the states were sovereign entities and resented regulation by the central government. Democratic-Republicans associated the Federalists with the wealthy manufacturers in the Northern states, preying upon those in the Southern states who generally had lower incomes.

On the other hand, John Jay looked at the issue differently. He felt that different economic and business interests might cause a split in the United States. He wrote an on-going series of essays for the Federalist newsletter, along with Alexander Hamilton, expressing his concern. In "Federalist No. 5" under the pseudonym "Publius," he wrote:

> Different commercial concerns must create different interests, and of course different degrees of political attachment to and connection with different foreign nations. Hence it might and probably would happen that the foreign nation with whom the SOUTHERN confederacy might be at war would be the one with whom the NORTHERN confederacy would be the most desirous of preserving peace and friendship. An alliance so contrary to their immediate interest would not therefore be easy to

form, nor, if formed, would it be observed and fulfilled with perfect good faith.

The Democratic-Republicans were firm believers in the strict, if not the literal, interpretation of the U.S. Constitution. They felt that this Constitution satisfactorily curtailed the powers of the central government and prevented it from encroaching on states' rights. They pointed out the fact that any right not granted the federal government by the Constitution was under the control of each of the states.

In 1795, Alexander Hamilton proposed the First Bank which was presented as a national entity. Jefferson and James Madison insisted that such a proposal was unconstitutional, saying that the Constitution didn't have any provision for banking and it favored the Northern interests. In addition, Jefferson argued that it violated state laws related to property. Hamilton was much more interested in generating financial devices to pay off war debts by establishing credit. Interest on loans then could be used to help pay off some of that debt. When the First Bank failed due to overspeculation by investors, the Democratic-Republicans pointed to that indicating that their argument was proven. Hamilton put in a temporary measure to prevent wild speculation and managed to save it in its last hours. The Second National Bank was surprisingly approved in 1816 by the president at that time, James Madison, and was designed to prevent abuses.

In terms of foreign affairs, John Jay, then the secretary of foreign affairs, considered the central government needed to be more effective and more powerful to protect America's interests abroad. To combat the Democratic-Republican attitude that the Federalists favored the Northerners, Jay stated that it was Congress that shouldered the responsibility of representing the interests of all states and all political factions. He reminded his readers that state representatives "have joined with the people in thinking that the prosperity of America depends upon its Union."

John Jay didn't make party membership a priority in selecting his appointees to serve under him when he was governor. Once, he was presented with a potential nominee for public office by someone who indicated that the person's affiliation with the Federalist Party should qualify him to be a nominee. To that, Jay replied, "That, sir, is not the question; is he fit for the office?" His son, Judge William Jay, said that his father read the opinions of all sides on an issue before making a decision. William commented that John Jay "...at times took papers of opposite politics, that he might obtain more full information of passing events."

George Washington, when he wrote his Farewell Address in 1796, revealed his own concerns about the consequences of divisions caused by political parties. Washington personally shared that concern with John Jay, saying that some parts of the United States—while they meant well—were averse to the government because they feel their liberties were endangered. He further said to Jay, "The trouble and perplexities which they occasion, added to the weight of years which have passed upon me, have worn away my mind more than my body."

Chapter 10 – John Jay During His Initial Retirement

John Jay retired in 1801 because he was psychologically and physically drained. He went to his property in Bedford, New York—now called Katonah—where he had a small farm. There was a handful of cattle there which he sold and replaced with a flock of sheep and raised a few horses, as he always liked riding. The property had a lot of trees planted by Jay himself. Sarah was staying with the Livingstons in New Jersey and planned on joining John when she recovered. She wrote to her daughter, now at Bedford, saying that she experienced excessive heat in her back with fever, chronic coughing spells, and heart palpitations. Medical treatment was primitive in those days, and it is difficult today to conclude what the true nature of her illness was. The doctors were giving her "increased doses of opium and decoction of small quantities of bark." "Bark" was the colloquial name for quinine, as it comes from the cinchona tree and was imported from South America via the West Indies. Quinine was often used to reduce fevers in those days but was ineffective for that. It did, however, tend to increase the heartbeat as a side effect and may have actually caused, rather than cured, her palpitations. She was delighted with their farm though and saw it as a place where she could relax and spend her declining years together with her husband in the solace and comfort of the country. However, not long after Sarah arrived, she was stricken with more episodes of her rheumatism and then developed influenza. In 1802, just a month after joining John, Sarah died in her sleep. He was devastated by the loss and never fully recovered emotionally. Their daughter, Ann, took over the household and the raising of her younger siblings. Her older brother, William, then moved in along with his wife and six children. The house had been expanded to accommodate them. Shortly, the whole house was alive and singing with the voices of children.

Water Rights Issue

While enjoying his life as a gentleman farmer, John Jay was occasionally contacted by civic leaders and private people about legal and state matters. In 1810, a company in the city of Mamaroneck wanted to increase its water supply and applied to the legislature for permission to flood part of Jay's property. Jay was always particularly sensitive on the issue of private property and lodged an official objection to the legislature about it. In his presentation, he admitted that the state had a right to take property for its own needs but cannot compel a private citizen to grant such use to another citizen, even if they did own a company.

United States on the Verge of War

One of the unresolved issues after John Jay developed his Jay Treaty of 1795 was the interference of American trading and the impressment of sailors. Both George Washington and John Jay were aware that the Jay Treaty might give rise to further difficulties but, in the interest of peace at that time, postponed dealing with the issue. In 1807, that led to an isolated incident that occurred at sea off the coast of Virginia. It involved the British ship, HMS *Leopard*, and the American frigate, *Chesapeake*. The British attempted to seize its naval deserters from the *Chesapeake*. Commander James Barron of the *Chesapeake* put up little resistance when his ship was attacked by the *Leopard*, and he surrendered his vessel to the British. After he was allowed to return to port, Barron was relieved of command. Thomas Jefferson was president of the U.S. at the time and tried to reassert American rights to freedom of the sea as a neutral party. England responded belligerently and announced they would not only seek out British deserters but impress American sailors along the shipping lanes. Thomas Jefferson retaliated by passing the Embargo Act of 1807, closing U.S. ports to foreign trade.

The Little Belt Affair

Despite the embargo, British ships sailed along the American coast. In 1811, a British ship, the HMS *Guerriere* stopped an American ship, the USS *Spitfire*, off the coast of North Carolina and seized an American sailor from the ship. Another incident occurred shortly thereafter involving the *Little Belt*, which was a small sloop-of-war named after *"Lillebaelt,"* the Danish name for a Danish ship taken by the British in another war. When patrolling, Captain Rodgers of the huge American warship, the *President*, mistook the *Little Belt* for the *Guerriere* because of poor lighting. Rodgers then pursued the sloop. The *Little Belt* attempted to avoid an altercation, but the captain of the sloop failed to identify himself or give the identity of the ship, and Rodgers continued the chase. A shot rang out, and both ships fired upon each other. The *President* carried 56 guns, while the *Little Belt* only carried 22. The sloop lost all its guns, and eleven English seamen died. That sloop wasn't involved in the impressment of American sailors and was much smaller than the American warship, so the British were furious. These hostilities triggered the onset of the War of 1812. `

The War of 1812

England and Napoleonic France were at war at that time, and the British were suffering from the lack of fighting men. So, they continued to interfere with American shipping in order to forcibly impress American sailors. Thomas Jefferson and his presidential successor, James Madison, both blamed the Federalists and the Jay Treaty for laying the groundwork for this abuse. Neither Jefferson nor Madison wanted to go to war over this, but Congress grew louder, calling for another war. Finally yielding to popular opinion, President Madison declared war on Great Britain in 1812. Most of the Federalist contemporaries of John Jay felt that the declaration of war was foolhardy. John Jay published his response saying, "In my opinion, the declaration of war was neither necessary nor expedient." The older Federalists then founded what they called the "Peace Party."

In the meantime, the British maintained their forts in the American Northwest, the Great Lakes, and the land just west of the Mississippi River, although they were supposed to abandon them per the Treaty of Paris. In order to weaken America, England supplied Native American tribes with weapons to attack American settlers. This is exactly what John Jay predicted when he wrote to Thomas Jefferson about it. In 1785, he had said, "...we have to apprehend an Indian war, and to suspect that Britain instigates it." Before the onset of the War of 1812, England fostered the intent to recruit Native Americans to become their allies in that war and curtail American expansion westward. It worked. Hundreds of tribes united, Tecumseh's Confederacy being the most formidable. America was able to attract the support of the Native American nations in the Southeast and the Seneca of the Six Nations Tribe in New York.

Invasions of Canada

James Madison mistakenly thought that the conquest of Canada would come easily. However, immigrants who had settled in Upper Canada may have been more pro-American, but they weren't interested in supporting the war. General Zebulon Pike was killed in action in Upper Canada, and control of that area stayed under the control of the British. General Prevost, commanding the English troops, had financial difficulties keeping his Canadian troops supplied. Lower Canada was more heavily populated, but its citizens were loyal to Great Britain for the most part. General Isaac Chauncey was able to maintain American control of Lake Ontario. General Hull, commanding the American forces in the Detroit and Michigan area, had inexperienced soldiers under his command. He was forced to surrender to the British Commander Henry Proctor and Tecumseh, who assisted him.

Commander Oliver Perry fared much better at Lake Erie, however, and American troops prevailed. The Americans now had control of Lake Erie and the territories lying just south of it. The northern border in that area conformed very closely to the Canadian border drawn up by John Jay.

Indiana Territory

General Henry Harrison was then commanding the American troops and persuaded many of the Native American tribes to withdraw from the war in exchange for property rights. The Native American tribes that were participating in the War of 1812 were then depleted.

Tecumseh's Defeat

Tecumseh tried to unite more tribes to expand his tribal forces and relocated his warriors to Upper Canada. General Henry Harrison then moved northward and pursued him. The British general, Henry Proctor, in Canada joined up with Tecumseh in the Ontario province. At what was called the Battle of the Thames, Tecumseh was killed. His tribal confederacy was totally disbanded, and Proctor with his British units made a hasty retreat.

Burning of Washington

In 1814, Napoleon was defeated, and the European front in the war between England and France wound down. That left many more British troops able to engage the American army. President Madison had as his commanders two very inept generals, William Winder and Tobias Stansbury, who were in charge of defending the Chesapeake Bay and its bordering states of Maryland and Washington, D.C. The British used their expanded forces to invade Washington and set it afire, including the White House. James

Madison, his family, government officials, and Madison's Cabinet barely escaped.

The Battle of Baltimore

After the British successfully invaded Washington, the Americans put a great deal more effort into strategic planning. The British left Washington and moved northward toward Baltimore. They planned an attack by land and sea. General Smith leading the American forces sent General John Sticker out to engage the British. That was intended as a delaying tactic so that Smith could bolster up defenses in the city of Baltimore. Although the Americans deliberately retreated after those defenses were ready, the British commander, Robert Ross, was killed and had to be quickly replaced. When the British moved farther north and inland, they were blasted with cannon fire. When orders went out, the British on land removed themselves to the ships in the harbor. Their intent was to attack Fort McHenry which was on a peninsula in the harbor. British Commodore Alexander Cochrane then prepared his warships to assault Fort McHenry. General Smith had strategized that action, readying many cannons and George Armistead's powerful artillery force to beat back the British assault. The British were forced to retreat until their ships were out of range but continued with bombings and mortar fire. The battle continued for over a day, but the British were ineffective due to the fact that Fort McHenry had been carefully reinforced. When morning came, the Americans raised a huge American flag over the fort. The British retreated by sea and headed toward New Orleans.

In the harbor just outside the action, an amateur poet and a professional lawyer named Francis Scott Key was aboard a ship overlooking the battle. He was there to negotiate the release of an American doctor being held by the British. While he waited to engage in his negotiations, he watched the battle and wrote the future national anthem, the *Star-Spangled Banner*, which was originally called "Defense of Fort McHenry."

Maritime Issue Still Unresolved

One of the major reasons the Americans wanted to go to war in 1812 was to resolve one of the issues left in abeyance since the Jay Treaty of 1795—the impressment of American sailors in order to serve in the European wars, particularly the Napoleonic War. The Treaty of Ghent ended the War of 1812, and the British returned all the property they had taken in the Pacific Northwest as well as confiscated slaves to their owners in the U.S., but with the provision that both sides would work toward ending the slave trade. Territory in Canada that had been conquered by Americans was also returned. Historians such as Pierre Berton said the war "was fought for no good reason." John Jay and a number of the other Federalists predicted that, and Jay himself said that the War of 1812 "was ill-advised."

John Jay on the Rights of Native Americans

Thomas Jefferson was an influential member of Congress; he was the principal formulator of the Land Ordinance of 1784. The Land Ordinance had dealt with the slavery issue, forbidding slavery in unsettled lands west of the Mississippi, among other issues. John Jay was concerned about the Northwest Territory and the slavery issue but also wanted to draw Jefferson's attention to the plight of Native Americans when Congress dealt with unsettled lands. He said to Jefferson that "Indian affairs have been ill managed." Then Jay spoke more forcibly, saying that Native Americans had been murdered and America unjustly confiscates their tribal lands. He also pointed out the fact that educational opportunities were denied to them. John Jay was very instrumental in the passage of the Northwest Ordinance of 1789 which replaced the Land Ordinance of 1784. Article III of the Northwest Ordinance specifically took up this issue by stipulating that the tribal lands Native Americans inhabited shall not be taken from them. Additionally, that article encouraged the establishment of educational programs for the Native Americans.

Chapter 11 – John Jay: The Final Years

Despite the fact that John Jay was becoming less physically active, his mind absolutely raced through all the concerns he knew would become important in America's future. There were so many factors that should define the United States as a land of liberty, unencumbered by those factors that could cause dissension between the states and between America and foreign countries.

John Jay and the Slavery Issue

A number of the Founding Fathers, including John Jay, held dichotomous viewpoints on slavery. Like his evolution from a man who presented England with the Olive Branch Petition to an American patriot, his views on slavery changed. He did own slaves himself but favored gradual emancipation. In a letter to Egbert Benson, a lawyer and another Founding Father, Jay wrote, "I purchase slaves and manumit them at proper ages and when their faithful services shall have afforded a reasonable retribution." By 1782, his slaves were elderly, and he felt that it was his obligation and that of his family to support them. He said to his brother, Frederick, "As to old servants, who have expanded their strength and youth for the family, they ought and must be taken good care of, while we have the means to do so."

In 1783, while the Jays were in Paris negotiating the Treaty of Paris, they had an elderly slave with them, Abbe. Abbe ran away from them but was imprisoned. John asked Sarah to secure her release because she was ill. Abbe was extremely reluctant but eventually consented and returned to America with them. After that, the Jays took care of her. Unfortunately, she was mortally ill and died. Another one of his slaves, Peter, who belonged to Jay's brother, Fady, defected and joined the British forces in Canada. Fady later freed some of his own slaves, but a few chose to stay on as paid workers.

By the year 1798, John had six slaves and decided to leave them to his son William with the provision that he free them totally. In 1785, he, Alexander Hamilton, and a few other prominent men founded the Manumission Society in New York whose intent was the gradual emancipation of slaves. In the same year, the Manumission Society lobbied for the passage of an act forbidding the sale of slaves in the state, and it was successfully passed into legislation. This society also promoted boycotts of businesses that were involved in the slave trade whether in the state or outside of it. Newspapers were also targeted if they advertised the sale of slaves.

John Jay and the Missouri Compromise of 1820

In 1819, the United States was in the process of admitting new states to the union as either "slave states" or "free states." The proposed "slave states" were considering techniques used to tax their citizens. The Missouri Compromise indicated that each slave was to be considered ¾ of a person for tax purposes. John Jay received a pamphlet on the matter while in his retirement and published his opinion. He forcefully wrote,

> The obvious dictates both of morality and policy teach us what our free nation cannot encourage the extension of slavery, nor the multiplication of slaves, without doing violence to their principles and without depressing their power and prosperity.

The Kidnapping Club

Richard Riker was one of the members of the Manumission Society. He served as the district attorney for some of the counties shortly after John Jay left his office as governor. He signed the inaugural papers of the Manumission Society but betrayed the principles it stood for. In his position, he had the identities and locations of freed slaves, and he hired men to kidnap and sell them to the South. He and his conspirators, Daniel Nash and Tobias Boudinot, established an underground route to take the former slaves, particularly children, to the Southern states for sale at auctions. He and his cohorts did this by snatching the former slave before he or she received their certificate of emancipation. Hence, the African American had no proof to show that they were, indeed, free. It is not a coincidence that an island Riker inherited from his ancestor, Abraham Rycken, is now called "Riker's Island" and houses a prison. African American abolitionists of the 19th century attributed that to Riker's deplorable activities which violated the law regarding slave trading.

Act for the Gradual Abolition of Slavery

John Jay had long regretted the fact that the New York Constitution didn't carry an article regarding the gradual abolition of slavery as he had wanted in 1782. In the year 1799, under Jay's urging, the state of New York passed a bill declaring that the children born of African American parents would automatically be free. New York was one of the last Northern states to pass such a bill. It met with difficulty in the state congress, though, because the initial draft of the bill attempted to delineate the rights of freed African Americans. Many different versions were floated, but none reached the quota needed for passage. When the bill was rewritten that didn't define these rights, it was passed. Unfortunately, that seemed more like lip service than a practical piece of legislation as there was no way the state could enforce its adherence. What's more, the final bill required that all freed children serve apprenticeships until the age of 28 for the males and 25 for females. The reluctance to abolish slavery was still evident in 1817 when New York passed a corollary to the bill stating that those born before 1799 would be free but only after ten years had passed. That way, slave owners would have slaves during their productive years. However, when they got older and less able to support themselves independently, they would be freed.

This compromise was made to suit individual needs but especially for the farmers in upstate New York, who were descended from the old Dutch who settled in the state prior to its annexation by the British.

Like his father, William Jay was opposed to slavery and campaigned against it vigorously. William served as a judge in the Court of Common Pleas during his father's retirement years. However, his anti-slavery views brought about his dismissal from his position as a jurist.

African Free School

In 1794, John Jay realized that African Americans people had the right to be educated just as White people are and solicited donations to establish a school for African Americans. He once wrote, "I consider education to be the soul of the republic...I wish to see all unjust and all unnecessary discriminations everywhere abolished, and that the time may soon come when all our inhabitants of every color and denomination shall be free and equal partakers of our political liberty." The first school, located in Manhattan, started out with 40 students. As the student population grew, he helped create more schools in larger buildings within the city. Initially, it had exclusively White teachers but later on hired African Americans as teaching assistants and finally employed African American teachers. By the time they closed in 1827, they had educated over 1,000 students.

John Jay and Religion

Regarding the American Revolution, John Jay saw it as an example of the interposition of Heaven and compared the victory that resulted from that to the "emancipation of the Jews from Egyptian servitude." After the ratification of the U.S. Constitution, he counseled people about the fact that liberty shouldn't be misconstrued to mean that licentious behaviors should be excused. He saw America as a free country, but that didn't mean that its society was free to do as it pleased. After his retirement, he related a conversation he had with an atheist:

> I was at a large party, of which…several…spoke freely and contemptuously of religion…An atheist very abruptly remarked that there was no God, and he hoped the time would come when there would be no religion in the world. I very concisely remarked that if there was no God there could be no moral obligations, and I did not see how society could subsist without them.

He perceived his position as the chief justice as being charged with passing judgments that were in keeping with the moral law. He felt that the practice of the law was not to be seen as a vehicle for carrying out personal vendettas, and he maintained high standards for himself when he was the governor of the state. During his term of service, Hamilton once asked him to gerrymander the state in order to manipulate electoral results in favor of the Federalists. Jay firmly refused to do so, seeing such an action as an unjust use of his power.

Despite his strict view on morality, Jay wasn't an overly religious man. As a child, he attended the Dutch Reformed Church but felt that people needn't exclusively follow the creed of any particular religion. In his retirement years, he attended the National Protestant Episcopal Church. His church attendance was irregular, especially as he aged, and his son William said, "He was always a scrupulous, but not superstitious observer of the Sabbath."

However, some analysts indicate that Jay's views on religion seem confusing. He was a devout Protestant and had a strong preference for Christianity but not that practiced by the Roman Catholic Church at the time. His objections appear to focus upon the Roman

Catholic tendency to involve itself in setting political policies. When he was a member of the Constitutional Convention, Jay questioned the propriety of starting new sessions with a prayer. He wasn't concerned with the separation of church and state, through the act of praying itself, but as to whether or not a particular prayer would offend another denomination because of its wording.

John Jay did, however, firmly want Christianity to be the foundation for moral guidance. He said it was impossible to "…maintain both order and freedom, both cohesiveness and liberty apart from the moral precepts of the Christian religion."

American Bible Society

He felt that everyone had the freedom to worship in his or her own manner. John Jay relied upon the Bible for guidance and as a moral code of conduct. He once said, "In forming and settling my belief relative to the doctrines of Christianity, I adopted no articles from creeds but such only as, on careful examination, I found to be confirmed by the Bible." In 1816, the American Bible Society was founded, and John Jay served as its vice president. Jay's son, William, was also one of its founders.

In 1821, Jay was elected president of the American Bible Society. Their first headquarters were in New York.

The American Bible Society's main objective was and still is the publication of and distribution of free Bibles. Beginning in the 19th century, the Society also offered classes and lectures related to issues of the day that it felt related to the practice of morality in society. The Bible was also translated into different languages in order to reach a wider reading audience. That even included the Lenape language of the Delaware Nation, a Native American tribe. In time, it produced Christian literature but saw to it that their contexts showed no denominational leanings. In keeping with its precepts, the American Bible Society forbade any comments or notes within the texts that might show a preference of one particular denomination.

When John Jay was nearing death, he is recorded to have been asked if he had any words for his children. To that, he replied, "They have the Book."

Illness and Death of John Jay

John Jay in his later years had been undergoing painful and severe rheumatic attacks. His relatives also indicated that he had been diagnosed with some disease of the liver as well. John Jay himself said that his most serious illness was the "incurable" one of old age! In 1814, a political colleague of his, Rufus King, invited him to attend a celebration after the overthrow of Napoleon Bonaparte. He wrote back and declined, citing his poor health. Gouverneur Morris asked Jay to come to the city and stand as a godfather for his son, but Jay also politely declined that request, saying that he could no longer travel. His partner in the 1783 Treaty of Paris and second president of the United States, John Adams, renewed their relationship in old age, and they commiserated about the ailments that accompanied it. Jay replied that he hadn't had a day that he felt well for twelve years, writing, "It rarely happens that the maladies and infirmities which generally accompany old age will yield to medical skill; but happily for us, patience and resignation are excellent palliatives."

In 1827, his condition turned critical, and the doctors concurred that his illnesses couldn't be treated effectively. His son, William, who was handling his personal papers and affairs felt that his father would want to be informed of the hopelessness of any cures for his condition. William then approached his father and told him the bad news. He indicated in his biography that his father took the news without any emotional reaction. In fact, William wrote that his father later demonstrated "cheerfulness and animation."

Medical knowledge was limited in those days, but it's conjectured that he died of a stroke. Later historians indicate it was "palsy," which is a partial paralysis and a symptom of a stroke. He died on May 17, 1829, at the age of 84 and was buried in Bedford, but his remains were transferred to Rye, New York, where his body rests alongside his wife in a private cemetery.

Conclusion

John Jay might be considered the most overlooked of the Founding Fathers. Even though he was the first chief justice of the Supreme Court, Jay was a humble man for his entire life and never sought fame or glory. He may have even lost his first attempt to run for governor of New York simply because he was so reluctant to brag about his own qualities and refused to disparage other candidates. That quality of fairness made him the most ideal man to serve as a justice. Although he was an admitted Federalist, he always made efforts to carefully review all the issues that the opposition brought up.

John may have come from a wealthy household and became wealthy himself, but he weathered many personal hardships within his family from physical afflictions and tragedies. His own father was a religious refugee, so he understood the tragic effects of persecution. His political life was peppered by criticisms from a number of Americans who—all too frequently—demanded that his diplomatic efforts yield perfect results. John Jay merited the admiration of George Washington, Ben Franklin, Alexander Hamilton, and John Adams. During the course of his life, John Jay never asked for a political office but considered it his duty to fulfill whatever position the country wanted and needed him to serve.

He was one of the prime negotiators of the Treaty of Paris, which marked the end of the American Revolution. His work on the Jay Treaty met with tremendous criticism, but Jay did manage to reestablish trade with England, define the borders of Canada and the contiguous United States, and secure just rights for the Native American tribes. He had the foresight to understand that the Jay Treaty was only a stepping stone for future negotiations. As a minister to Spain, he not only obtained financing for the Revolutionary War efforts but laid the foundations for amicable relations between the two countries. John Jay also pulled his state of New York from the devastation rendered by the fires set at the beginning of the Revolution to a fully-functioning state with a viable constitution.

The Founding Fathers and historians today agree on the fact that John Jay was crucial in the shaping of the U.S. Constitution. He looked toward creating a country that would be prominent in influencing world affairs in the future. John Adams, the second president of the United States, might have put it best, saying that John Jay was "of more importance than the rest of us."

Part 6: James Madison

A Captivating Guide to an American Founding Father Who Served as the Fourth President of the United States of America

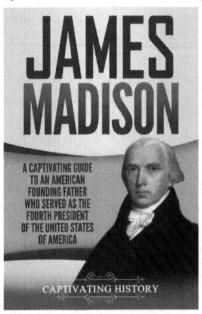

Introduction

James Madison earned the title "Father of the Constitution." How did this man who was diminutive of stature with a weak constitution produce such an energetic document? Through more than 200 years, it stands like a silent sentinel to protect the freedom and independence of the American people.

It was a time when the Americans were weary from the tumult of the Revolution, but Madison's job had barely begun. He realized that it was up to him now to help fashion the future of a country that would outlive him.

Although characterized as introverted and pensive, Madison had a ferocious absorption to persevere until he could effectively shepherd the Constitution through all the logistical stages necessary to make it real.

They said he was "humorless," but James Madison and his dear wife, Dolley, built an ice cream parlor in the White House. Dolley's favorite flavor – Oyster! Oh, my…He was a wordsmith and a punster. His sense of humor was dry and subtle, and he once used an amazing pun to justify an expense. It will send any reader into a fit of laughter as it did Thomas Jefferson.

On the night before Washington D.C. was burned by the British in 1814, the redcoats had the audacity to eat Madison's supper and drink his homemade cider. On occasion, he felt like he was surrounded by assassins due to the gross incompetence of some of the people he had mistakenly recruited to serve on his cabinet. The oversight of one of them resulted in the burning of Washington which destroyed all but one of the governmental buildings.

James Madison was the only person who could win a debate against the infamous Patrick Henry, the most charismatic and fiery orator of his age. Madison wasn't theatrical, but his logical arguments grabbed hold of the truth like a vise.

He was plagued by physical weakness most of his life and even embarrassed himself when it showed. Madison came to be known for his brain not his brawn. So, how did James Madison live until the age of 84? Force of will – an unbroken power that propelled him to work every day of his life for those whom he would never meet, the Americans who live today in unity and freedom.

Chapter 1 – Jemmy

Early Life and Education

James Madison, born in 1751, was the eldest son of a Virginia tobacco planter, James Madison, Sr. As a youngster growing up at home in Port Conway, Virginia, James Madison was affectionately called "Jemmy." Jemmy had eleven brothers and sisters. Two of his siblings died in infancy, one was stillborn, and two more died very young. James wasn't a healthy child, and his parents worried about him. He also had occasional attacks that he himself likened to epilepsy. However, that didn't stop him from playing with his brothers and a few of the children of his father's 108 slaves. James' father was one of the wealthiest landowners in the colony of Virginia, and his plantation was called "Mount Pleasant."

In 1760, when he was ten, the Madisons moved to Montpelier, a larger piece of property in the foothills of the Blue Ridge Mountains in Virginia. There his father created a plantation. It provided extra room for buildings devoted to maintaining farm equipment, a blacksmithing shop, and stables.

James wasn't an athletic boy. To compensate, he directed most of his energy toward intellectual pursuits and thoroughly enjoyed reading. By the age of eleven, he'd read all the books in his father's library. He was then sent to the Donald Robertson School, where he studied under Robertson for about three years. Of course, they didn't call him "Jemmy" at this very strict school, but he was known as "Mr. Jamie."

All well-to-do boys learned the classics, and he was a gifted student. James really admired Robertson, the headmaster. In describing Donald Robertson, Madison once said, "All I have been in life I owe largely to that man." That was a fitting tribute for a teacher who was especially interested in him.

When he completed his primary education at the Robertson school in 1767, James was sixteen—still too young to enroll in college. To prepare him for more advanced studies, his father hired a tutor by the name of Rev. Thomas Martin, the rector of Brick Church. He moved into the family residence and also taught James' brothers, two of his younger sisters, and even some of the neighborhood children.

College Enrollment

Most Virginians attended the College of William and Mary in Williamsburg, VA. It was one of the most notable colleges in the colonies and was attended by children of the landed gentry.

However, there were several mitigating circumstances that dissuaded the Madisons from advising James to attend there. First of all, Williamsburg was located in the Tidewater region of Virginia. The belief at that time was that this was an unfavorable climate for James who wasn't that healthy, and he would have been particularly susceptible to illness during what they called the "sickly season"—July through October. Williamsburg could be oppressively hot and humid during the summer and early fall, a stark contrast to the mountain air that James grew up with. Secondly, his tutor hailed from New Jersey College (later called Princeton University) and seldom lost an opportunity to promote his alma mater. Also, his parents decided that James shouldn't attend the College of William and Mary since it was known as a "party school," to use today's term. According to the Anglican preacher in Williamsburg, Rev. William Yates, some of their professors "...played all night at cards in public houses in the City, and often were seen drunken in the street."

The Arduous Journey to the College of New Jersey at Princeton

James compensated for his lack of physical strength through sheer determination and strength of will. Stubbornly, he made the 300-mile journey to Princeton by horseback with a couple of friends and a slave. There were ferry crossings at the Potomac near the estates of George Mason and George Washington. The crossings were rather treacherous in those days because these ferries were nothing more than glorified rafts, and the riders had to hold their horses steady as the rafts crossed. The first ferry he took navigated the Susquehanna River. After disembarking, he and his companions moved through Wilmington, Delaware, which was a quaint village in the late 18th century. From there, they went north along the coast. Madison was amazed by the crops that were grown there, as they were different from those grown in Virginia. There were sheep farms and fields covered with clover and flax in the area.

After crossing the Schuylkill River by ferry, they visited Philadelphia. It had a sizeable population of 25,000 even then. Neither James nor his companions had ever seen a city that size. Stately mansions and government buildings lined Market Street. There were carefully laid paths through Philadelphia lit by the lanterns on lampposts—something James hadn't seen back home. From there, they took the ferry from Philadelphia into Trenton and then on to Princeton. The oldest building on the college property was Nassau Hall, which is still there today.

James had lived a sheltered life up to that point, and this trip was a wondrous new experience. There has never been any mention of mishaps on the route in the histories, so it is assumed Madison made the trip unscathed. By horseback, it most likely took about ten days, but he was a skillful horseman. Upon his arrival, James excitedly wrote to Rev. Martin saying,

"I am perfectly pleased with my present situation; and the prospect before me of three years of confinement, however terrible it may sound, has nothing in it, but what will be greatly alleviated by the advantages I hope to derive from it."

James Madison: Prankster and Protester!

Even though James was rather short and didn't have the physical prowess of his college mates, he wasn't considered odd and actually had numerous friends. The boys at the college liked to play practical jokes and James was no exception. The most common of these pranks involved greasing the feathers from chickens and throwing the oily feathers on the sidewalks. While they hid, they laughed as other students slipped on the feathers. Other pranks were the ringing of the chapel bells in the middle of the night, lighting firecrackers, and peering through telescopes at girls on the campus!

The college professors always educated their students about current political events and their relationship to political philosophy. The college president, John Witherspoon, often said, "Just by reason of being what they are, people have certain God-given rights. These rights cannot be given by kings and taken away by kings." James considered that statement awe-inspiring. It emphasized the innate rights every human has within – ones that should be defended.

One of the most momentous political events that occurred while he was at college was the passage of the Stamp Act. This was passed by King George III of England upon his subjects in the American colonies in order to finance his war debt from the French and Indian War (1754-1763) fought between Britain and the British colonies. Once the tax had been paid, a stamp was impressed upon the paper which the colonists had imported from England. It was looked upon as a punitive tax by the colonists. In order to deliver a message to King George, the colonists initiated a boycott of British-made paper and other imports.

Madison and his fellow students decided to make their voices heard as well regarding this abominable tax. Ever alert to the world around them, Madison and his fellow students discovered that English merchants were trying to disrupt the boycott. Often these merchants sent messages ahead via horseback or human carriers to Philadelphia, so Madison and the others served on rotating watches until they could intercept a message from one of these messengers by a little "old-fashioned" subterfuge. Taking the letter with them, they descended upon the campus dressed in homemade clothes rather than the fine broadcloth imported from England. After gleefully lighting a bonfire, they ceremoniously hurled the letter upon it and cheered.

College and Subsequent Illness

The students were heavily regulated in New Jersey College. They had to rise at 5:00 AM and attend a prayer service an hour later. After an hour for breakfast and study hall, they attended classes. Lunch was served at noon and classes reconvened at 3:00, continuing until 5:00 PM when they had their evening prayers. After that, they were required to study. There were mentors who paraded the dormitories at 9:00 curfew to be sure the students were either studying in their rooms or asleep.

James excelled in his studies and graduated in 30 months. However, he was too ill to attend his own graduation and was unable to make the journey home right away. So, he continued to reside at Princeton where he studied theology and Hebrew with Witherspoon. In 1772, Madison was well enough to travel back home.

Although he was anxious to go home and tutor his brothers and sisters, James felt weak and ill upon his arrival. His father and mother became alarmed and sent him to a spa for a while to regain his health, but that was a futile effort. The drastic change from the excitement of college to the bucolic life on the plantation depressed him even after he left the spa. His emotional state exacerbated his physical condition. Seeking support or perhaps sympathy, he wrote to a college friend saying, "I am too dull and infirm now to look out for any extraordinary things in this world for I think my sensations for many months past have intimated to me not to expect a long or healthy life."

What cured Madison was his interest in political philosophy and the current events that were erupting in his country. The hostility between America and England grew daily. As darkness fell and shadows lengthened, he could hear his father hollering about it to his mother, Nelly, in the great room. Vividly remembering the passion that he felt as a protestor in Princeton, his spirit quickened and vigor rushed through his small frame. He decided that his life's work would be in politics.

Chapter 2 – Spirit of the Revolution

The Revolutionary War Breaks out 1775

The calls to go to war with the oppressive policies of Great Britain over the thirteen colonies in America were loud and shrill. In the taverns, the markets and the parlors, the people were furious about England's discriminatory taxation and denigrating policies. The colonies were helping the British pay their own debts, and had yet had no voice in their Parliament. The hostility was at fever pitch.

While Madison and his colleagues in Virginia were planning to declare their own independence from Great Britain, a musket shot was fired from behind a bush on a farm in Massachusetts. The famous American poet, Ralph Waldo Emerson, called that the "shot heard 'round the world." To this day, no one knows who fired the first shot, but one of the most momentous wars ever fought had just begun. Stiff red-coated soldiers from a duty-bound British regiment traipsed back and forth between the towns of Lexington and Concord, exchanging fire with colonial settlers dressed in hand-hewn clothing with coonskin caps on their heads.

Later, even more English disembarked at the great harbor of Boston from their numerous vessels. Everyone in Virginia realized that time was of the essence. The colonies were still voting on the foundational documents to declare independence, realizing that any statements they adopted would become the framework for generations to come.

Drummed out of the Military 1775!

It was traditional for the sons of the gentry to enlist in the state militias. James' father was a commissioned colonel in the Virginia militia. When the American Revolution broke out in 1775, he was fifty-three and served on the Orange County Committee of Public Safety as chairman. The Committee of Public Safety was an organization that actually created a kind of "shadow government," in anticipation that the British governors would be expelled or otherwise rendered ineffective.

Like his father, James was commissioned as a colonel in the militia. When the first day arrived for him to report for duty, he fainted! Determined to fulfill his duties, however, James recovered and subjected himself to training. His emotional states sometimes triggered physical symptoms. It was said he became an excellent marksman. However, in time, his fellow soldiers realized that he lacked the rigor to withstand warfare but was an excellent thinker. Even they felt as he did that his career lay in politics, not the military. He was a man of brains, not brawn.

Madison was drummed out of active military service in a manner of speaking but garnered plenty of support for his first stint into the political arena from his former fellow militiamen and others who knew him. In 1775, he was elected to represent Orange County at the Fifth Virginia Convention. The Virginia Conventions were patriot legislatures held secretly at various locations outside of the knowledge of the English-dominated House of Burgesses to discuss the issues related to independence from Great Britain.

Fifth Virginia Convention 1775-1776

Virginia was the most populous of the colonies and keenly felt its responsibility to contribute to the national discourse by declaring itself independent from Great Britain and formulating its constitution.

As two of the representatives from Virginia, Madison and his uncle, William Moore, made the long trip to Williamsburg to meet with the other county delegates. Edmund Pendleton, a former member of the Virginia House of Burgesses, served as the president of the Virginia convention. That body was a legislative group of elected landowners from each colony.

James Madison, 25-years-old, and Thomas Jefferson, 33-years-old, were among the group's youngest members. Basic political viewpoints were discussed at the Virginia Convention, especially those of the empiricist John Locke and other Enlightenment philosophers. The delegates wanted to base their constitution on sound political philosophy to give them focus and direction.

Patrick Henry was the representative from Hanover County in Virginia. He is best known for the quote, "Give me liberty or give me death!" Henry was a fiery and persuasive orator. On May 15, 1775, Virginia voted in favor of independence, saying that their delegates are to "be instructed to propose to the respectable body to declare the United Colonies free and independent states."

As result of the Convention, the Commonwealth of Virginia then published a document entitled the Declaration of the Rights of Virginia and proposed that a constitution for the Commonwealth of Virginia be drawn up.

Declaration of the Rights of Virginia

George Mason, one of the most experienced members and the representative of Fairfax County, was a bold speaker who was very forward and outspoken. His words were extremely powerful and he wrote most of this document. In it, he stated:

"Whereas George the third, King of Great Britain and Ireland, and elector of Hanover, heretofore entrusted with the exercise of the kingly office in this government, has endeavored to prevent the same into a detestable and insupportable tyranny, by putting his negative on laws the most wholesome and necessary for the public good...and by which several acts of (British) misrule, the government of this country, as formerly exercised under the crown of Great Britain, is TOTALLY DISSOLVED."

The Virginia Convention signed this document on June 12, 1776 and appointed Richard Henry Lee as their delegate to the national assembly, the Second Continental Congress.

The Declaration of the Rights of Virginia became the foundation for composing the final bill of rights to be added to the draft of the first U.S. Constitution. Segments of it were also used to formulate some of the statements contained in the Declaration of Independence penned by Thomas Jefferson in 1775.

Madison and the Constitution of Virginia 1776

James Madison and George Mason are credited with composing the state constitution. Their contributions resulted in the formulation of 16 sections, reflecting political philosophies regarding the rights of every person and the means by which they can protect those rights. To those sections, Mason's *Declaration of the Rights of Virginia* were added with some modifications. One of the modifications Madison felt strongly about was freedom of religion. He had admired Daniel Robertson, his headmaster when he was a boy and John Witherspoon, President of the College of New Jersey. Robertson was an Anglican, but Witherspoon was a Presbyterian. Virginia at the time had mandated Anglicanism as its accepted religion.

Back in the year 1773, Madison had heard that Virginia had imprisoned Baptist preachers, and was outraged by that. By way of making a fair comparison with other colonies, he wrote to William Bradford, a well-known statesman in Pennsylvania, asking for a copy of the Pennsylvania colonial charter. He knew that most Pennsylvanians were Quakers and wanted to see if they had a mandated religion. As he suspected, the Pennsylvania charter honored religious freedom. Madison then vowed that he would have the notion of religious freedom included in the Virginia Constitution and it was ratified to include that. In Section 16, it states:

"That religion, or the duty which we owe to our Creator, and the manner of discharging it, can be directed only by reason and conviction, not by force or violence; and therefore all men are equally entitled to the free exercise of religion."

A number of years later, Madison made a rather prophetic statement about freedom of religion when he said, "...religion and Government will both exist in greater purity the less they are mixed together." Today, the separation of church and state is a policy upon which the United States stands.

The Declaration of Independence 1776

Madison's colleague, Thomas Jefferson, was considered an eloquent and incisive writer. He was recruited by five of the most persuasive attendees at the Second Continental Congress (1775-1781) to write the *Declaration of Independence*. Among the reference documents Jefferson used to compose his draft were the *Declaration of Rights of Virginia* and the Virginia Constitution which was written by James Madison and George Mason. On July 4, 1776, the final form of the *Declaration of Independence* was signed by the delegates at the Second Continental Congress.

During the Second Continental Congress, the issue of getting some foreign support was brought up. Benjamin Franklin, the senior statesman from Philadelphia, was selected and he went to France in 1776 to negotiate the French as allies. France was chosen because they were perennial enemies of England, especially after having fought the Seven Years' War against them less than 10 years prior to this.

The freedom of the states, while laudable, made very little allowance for the pressing need to direct the country forward. As yet a division of the government into three branches hadn't yet been delineated and no real way to enforce a means to pay its war debt. Most likely that shortcoming was due to the fact that the Americans had lived so long under the domination of a strong central power, the king of Great Britain. Therefore, they were extremely sensitive about reproducing a monarchical structure like the one they were abandoning, so a great deal of thought had to go into establishing a central governmental authority. They then formulated the *Articles of Confederation* which gave the central government some very limited authority. These articles delineated the powers and functions of a central government and had sections devoted to defining states' rights, judicial powers, the post office, matters related to wars, a method to collect state funds to support the war effort, terms for members of Congress, and voting procedures.

In 1777, The Second Continental Congress passed the *Articles of Confederation,* and sent them to the thirteen states for ratification. That process took 3½ years.

Battles of Saratoga 1777

While the Second Continental Congress was still in session, the British under General Burgoyne engaged the Continental Army at two battles near Saratoga, NY. The English had moved south from Canada and were attempting to separate the colonies in New England from those in the South. Burgoyne anticipated reinforcements, but they didn't arrive in time. The Continental troops, however, were growing as most New England militias joined in. After huge losses of men and equipment, the British surrendered. This was a significant victory for the Continental Army.

France noted this victory and felt that the colonies had the stamina and willingness to see the Revolution through until its end. Therefore, they contacted Benjamin Franklin and agreed to ally with them in their war of independence. In addition, Spain was likewise impressed and also agreed to offer their support.

The delegates at the Second Continental Congress were very encouraged by this.

Madison Loses 1777 House Election

In the meantime, James Madison ran for election to the Virginia House of Delegates. However, he was still relatively naïve and unaccustomed to the process of political campaigning. In order to win over voters, political candidates customarily provided free drinks for them. It is much the same as it is today. Madison was a purist in terms of proper conduct, so he disliked those influential techniques. He said that he objected to "the corrupting influence of spirituous liquors." That was a hard lesson because history reported that Madison was rather upset about losing the election. Nevertheless, he had the spirit and vigor of a patriot and knew that he had something valuable to contribute to the constitutional process.

Governor's Council Instead

The Governor's Council in Virginia was now taking on the functions of the Council of Public Safety on which Madison's father once served. An opening occurred on the Council and the illustrious Patrick Henry nominated him. Madison was immediately awarded a seat on the Governor's Council. The vivacious Patrick Henry was one of the most prominent members of that council and was aware of Madison's unfortunate loss in the Virginia House of Delegates. He didn't want the extraordinary talents of this young man to lie fallow during such a crucial time, however. Many of the Virginians were well aware of Madison's spirit and talents, and he won by an impressive majority.

Filled with gratitude for what may have otherwise have been a year of sequestered political silence, Madison excitedly rushed to Williamsburg to take his seat. The year was 1777.

Chapter 3 – The Governor's Council – The Second Continental Congress and its Aftermath

Governor's Council 1777-1780

There was a shortage of housing in Williamsburg when the council was in session, but fortunately James' older cousin, Rev. James Madison, had a spatial home there and offered him lodgings there. The Rev. Madison was the new president of the College of William and Mary. While there, James made the acquaintance of a number of learned men from the graduates and faculty of the College of William and Mary. They were impressed with Madison's skills and engaged him in experimental astronomical projects and philosophical discussions.

It was the nitty-gritty job of the Governor's Council to plan for the newly-forming divisions of the Continental Army. George Washington had sent out a request that all the colonies contribute to the war effort saying that his army might "starve, dissolve or disperse" if it didn't receive shipments of food. First, the council had to fill the mundane function of seeing that food was sent expeditiously. Meat was sent along with shipments of salt to cure the meat. Uniforms and supplies needed to be purchased and also shipped to the troops. Madison and the other members hurried an expedition into the Mississippi Valley arranged to secure more provisions for a detachment from the Continental Army Washington sent to confront the traitor, General Benedict Arnold and his troops who were moving toward Virginia.

As soon as his term of service in the Governor's Council was over, James Madison was elected as Virginia's representative in the Second Continental Congress and started serving there in 1780. This Congress had been meeting in a number of sessions between 1774 to 1781.

Madison at the Second Continental Congress

In 1780, James Madison was anxious to get to Philadelphia to join with the other members at the session that was being held there. Of those who didn't yet know him, Madison was not only one of the youngest members there, but possibly the shortest too! He stood only 5' 4". Next to Jefferson, who was physically impressive at 6' 2" and the difference was stunning. However, what he lacked in stature was compensated by his vision and force of will. It wasn't long before other members were spellbound as he spoke in clear concise terms that summarized his key points in just several statements.

The turnover was high during the session that Madison attended. This was mostly due to circumstances at the delegates' farms and businesses and the events occurring during the American Revolution. In Madison's state of Virginia, farmers were suffering because many of their workers were participating in the Revolution, or attempting to build up defenses in the area when they received word that British troops were on their shores.

The Second Continental Congress disbanded when all the states had ratified the Articles of Confederation in 1781. The new government was then called the "Confederation Congress."

Battle at Yorktown 1781

Washington was encamped at Morristown, NJ during the winter, which was frigid. However, after he heard that the English General, Charles Cornwallis, had placed Charleston, South Carolina under siege Washington marched his troops southward to meet up with them.

The British Surrender 1783

There was a major convergence of British vessels and land troops squeezing down upon Yorktown as spring approached. Once the British disembarked their vessels, they headed inland to join their infantry units. The French forces, who were assisting the Americans, followed them. General Cornwallis and his British troops were confronted on their flanks from the French soldiers. Then Washington moved toward Cornwallis' army from the west and the British were hemmed in from both sides. Left with no other choice, Cornwallis surrendered. When Prime Minister North of England got word, he said, "Oh my God, it's over!"

In 1783, the Treaty of Paris was signed. Benjamin Franklin, John Adams and John Jay represented the thirteen colonies. It had three main terms:

1. The American Revolution was officially ended.

2. Great Britain acknowledged that independence of the colonies.

3. The boundaries of the colonies were established.

1783: A "Dear John" Letter to James Madison Arrives!

During this time, Madison met a lovely girl by the name of Catherine Floyd at one of her family's social functions. Her father was a prominent political figure in Long Island, New York with strong ties to the state of Connecticut.

When Madison first spotted Catherine Floyd at a dance, it was a case of "love at first sight." He called her "Kitty." Although he didn't have much money, Madison scraped enough together to have miniature portraits of each of them painted and encased them in a pendant to hang from a chain around their necks. James even sent her an oval pendant of his braided hair. He was very much in love with her. They dated for three years.

Madison's predictable mistake was the fact that he was so utterly committed to his work that he postponed personal pleasures in order to create a long-lasting foundation for the people of the America-yet-to. While Madison was engaging in his political duties, Kitty's father planned a nice family vacation for the Floyds in Connecticut in 1783. While there, Kitty met a medical student from Connecticut and broke off her affair with Madison. All that he received was a glib letter. Madison was heart-broken. In fact, when he was older, he blotted out her name on every letter he had written to a friend or colleague which mentioned her name. To this day, historians say that he never really got over the affair. When Madison succumbed to an emotion, it was deep and sustaining.

Financial Problems in the New Nation

After his attendance at the Second Continental Congress, Madison and the other delegates at that Continental Congress noted that there were problems created by deficiencies in the *Articles of Confederation* that the states ratified in 1781. Primarily, those Articles stated the new government, the Confederation Congress, had to depend upon the states to pay for war debt, but had no real power to enforce that. Due to adverse economic conditions, many of the states didn't remit the funds. Therefore, the country was virtually bankrupt. Consequently, the new nation was unable to pay its soldiers or pay back the war debt owed to France and Spain who had supported it. What's more, states were competing with each other over interstate commerce.

Due to the poor economic conditions, banks from which people had taken out loans were starting to foreclose on some of those who couldn't pay. Farmers' properties were being confiscated and they had no means by which they could move their crops. In 1786, there was growing unrest especially in Massachusetts. Daniel Shays, a Revolutionary War soldier who hadn't been paid, organized a rebellion later called "Shay's Rebellion." Thousands of rebels attacked large numbers of courthouses and other government buildings.

In 1787 when the rebels attacked the arsenal at Springfield, the military responded. They deliberately shot over the heads of the rebels, but some were killed in the skirmish that followed. Eventually, soldiers managed to disburse the rebel leagues. Shay himself fled to Vermont.

During the same year, John Hancock, the famous signatory of the *Declaration of Independence* was elected governor. One of his first actions was to pardon the rebels.

As result of Shay's Rebellion and the financial crisis created by the weaknesses of the *Articles of the Confederation,* members of the former Continental Congress called for a session in Philadelphia to revise the *Articles of Confederation.* It was called the "Philadelphia Convention" and was later called the "Constitutional Convention." This meeting was scheduled to begin in 1787.

In preparation for this convention, Madison studied the structures of other governments as well as the *Articles of Confederation*, and published the results of his study, called the "Vices of the Political of the United States." He also circulated it among the members who were expected to attend.

Madison's "Vices of the Political System of the United States" 1787

Madison's main difficulty with the *Articles of Confederation* revolved around the counterbalance of states' rights and the rights of the national governing body. Some of the items he cited as weaknesses were:

1. Lack of required compliance by the states to requisitions in the *Articles of Confederation*

2. Allowance for the violation of federal law by the states

3. Tacit permission for states to trespass on the rights of other states

4. Lack of unity that affects the common interest

5. Lack of a provision for the ratification of the *Articles of Confederation* by the <u>people themselves,</u> as opposed to just the legislative assemblies

6. Lack of some protection from partisan groups to promote candidates to seek office through merely ambition and personal interests of their supporters

7. Inability of the national government to enforce its precepts or support an army

All of those factors severely weakened the executive function of the national government. Madison also felt that the executive function should be separated from the legislative functions.

Madison at the Philadelphia Convention 1787

It was difficult to convene enough state delegates to attend this session after the Second Continental Congress was concluded in 1781, so Madison discussed that issue with other noted members. To drum up support, he suggested that George Washington be requested to come out of retirement and attend. The tactic worked and other states decided to send representatives.

George Washington was elected chairman of the Philadelphia Convention. Attendees changed as some retired their seats and others took their place. Benjamin Franklin was perhaps the oldest member. Gouverneur[i] Morris from New York, who was held in high regard as a veteran statesman, was likewise there. Other members included Alexander Hamilton of New York, William Paterson of New Jersey, Daniel Carroll of Maryland, Edmund Randolph and James Madison from Virginia. Towns, cities, and colleges in those states bear the names of these famous statesmen today.

The members of the Convention decided from the onset that their goal wouldn't necessarily consist of making modifications to the *Articles of Confederation.* They felt that it might be vital to rewrite the document and call it the U.S. Constitution. It was also agreed at the Convention to keep the proceedings secret until the sessions were completed.

Chapter 4 – James Madison: Father of the Constitution

The Constitutional Convention 1787

After the delegates agreed that they would open themselves up to changing the entire content of the *Articles of Confederation,* this meeting was called the "Constitutional Convention" and its outcome was to be called the U.S. Constitution. Elements of the *Articles of Confederation* that were still seen as valuable would be retained. The delegates also felt the session would be open to the entire assembly, but granted themselves the opportunity of separating into committees as needed. In addition, the membership agreed to meet for as many sessions as absolutely necessary, but also agreed to keep in mind the fact that an excess amount of time would have deleterious effects upon the country.

In addition, the delegates elected George Washington the president of the Convention.

James Madison's Role

James Madison was called the "Father of the Constitution" because he organized the various meetings and appealed to the elected delegates for continued participation in the process of producing the final text. He wanted an unambiguous document that would apply to all Americans then and in the future. He was the *ipso facto* leader of the Constitutional Convention and spearheaded all the logistics to create a cohesive force. About him, William Pierce, a captain during the American Revolution and representative from South Carolina, said "… every person seems to acknowledge his (Madison's) greatness. In the management of every great question he evidently took the lead in the Convention…he always came forward as the best-informed man of any point in the debate."

The "Springboard"

To kick off the initial debates, two plans were presented from the floor. James Madison wrote the first one considered – the Virginia Plan. William Paterson who was active in formulating the state constitution of New Jersey and N.J.'s first Attorney General, wrote the N.J. Plan.

The Virginia Plan

1. Three branches of government—executive, legislative, and judicial—with term limits set for members of each. The executive would be appointed by the legislative assembly.

2. A bicameral Congress would serve as the legislative body, and the numbers of these legislators would be determined by the state populations. One segment of the bicameral congress would be directly elected by the people, and the other segment composed of state legislators would have the right to nominate and/or veto a member.

3. A law that was in contradiction to a federal law would be negated as illegal.

4. Legislation could be vetoed by the "Council of Revision," consisting of the national executive and one or more Supreme Court Justices.

5. A process of appeal was to be established by which members of the legislative branch could apply to have a Council of Resolution decision reconsidered.

The New Jersey Plan

1. Three branches of government—executive, legislative and judicial—with the chief executive to be elected by the legislative branch and who would be elected yearly without being allowed to run for re-election.

2. The members of the judicial branch, called the "Supreme Tribunal," were to be appointed by the federal executive.

3. A unicameral Congress with 2-7 representatives per state, depending on population.

4. A federal executive could compel non-compliant states to obey a federal law.

5. A citizen could be prosecuted under the laws of the state in which a crime is committed.

6. The legislative body, called the "Congress," had the power to charge tariffs for international trade.

7. Congress could collect taxes from the citizens and states. State taxes were based on population and 3/5 of the slaves residing therein (called the "Three-Fifths Compromise").

8. Naturalization policies would be established.

Discussion and Objections

Once William Paterson of New Jersey examined the Virginia Plan, he uttered, "Shall I submit the welfare of New Jersey, with five votes, in a council where Virginia has sixteen? Neither I nor my state will ever submit to such tyranny." Many of the other states had that as a major objection to the Virginia Plan. Arguments arose. Another difficulty that was cited was the fact that states would grow in size as the years went on. All members wanted their final document to be something that everyone could depend upon generation after generation.

Roger Sherman of Connecticut was the second eldest member of the Congress and was known for his terse tone. However, his words were pointed and cut into the heart of the matters under discussion. He made as many as 160 motions during the debate. James Madison made as many as 177 motions.

Oliver Ellsworth of Connecticut was a firm believer in strong states' rights. Later in life, he became the third Chief Justice of the country. Ellsworth, like his colleague, Sherman, also disliked the disproportionate representation of the larger states for the final document. These two men worked together to present a structure to Congress that would meet the needs of all the states. James Madison's objections consistently circled back to one issue: that of states' rights vs. federal rights. Throughout the debates, most of the representatives were making states' rights stronger than those of the federal government. Madison did manage to persuade some of the representatives to alter their thinking and word the Constitution in such a way that more power was granted to a central government.

The Connecticut Compromise

By way of compromise, Sherman and Ellsworth proposed that there be two bodies in the legislative branch, one of which would depend upon a state's population and the other that would be composed of two representatives. That became today's House of Representatives and the Senate. Article Five of the today's U.S. Constitution reads: "...no state, without its consent, shall be deprived of its equal suffrage in the Senate."

James Madison was virtuous in terms of developing a final Constitution that would be more than just an amiable confederation of states. He wanted a fair and balanced Constitution with checks and balances. In his letter to George Washington, he said, "I have sought for middle ground, which may at once support a due supremacy of the national authority, and not exclude the local authorities wherever they can be subordinately useful." The balance between federal rights and states' rights is a delicate one.

He suggested that "ratifying conventions" be established with separately elected representatives to analyze the final proposed Constitution. To resolve item #6, he proposed that the U.S. president be elected separately from the Congress and be elected by the people of the country through a system of electoral ballots. Up until that point, the president of the Continental Congress was elected by the people who attended the convention.

Madison discussed these issues with Alexander Hamilton, a delegate from New York. John Adams jumped into that discussion because he reread the *Articles of Confederation* and foresaw the possibility that the new country might become no more than an assemblage of self-serving states. Another flaw the delegates saw was the fact that the more populous states had more power than smaller ones. To resolve that, the delegates decided that the legislative branch should contain congress members – the House of Representatives – based on population, but each state would have two representatives to serve on a Senate regardless of population. Hamilton and Adams had a lot of influence among the members and together the three men convinced the members that another session should be held in order to iron out these disparities.

As the people of America were reorganizing their lives and recovering after the Revolutionary War, each of the states had their own agenda. Above all, James Madison knew that any country couldn't stand on its own if it was divided. He remembered the lyrics of the "Liberty Song" sung during the Revolution. The lyrics were composed in 1768 by John Dickinson, president of Delaware who was also in attendance at the Constitutional Convention.

The Federalist Papers 1787-1788

Three of the founding fathers of the United States—James Madison, Alexander Hamilton, and John Jay—published a series of essays called *The Federalist Papers* in order to boost support and interest in the ratification process. So as not to influence any of the readers, they published these essays under a pseudonym, "Publius." Thomas Jefferson, who was one of the most respected of the statesmen, called *The Federalist Papers* "the best commentary of the principles of government which was ever written."

Madison wrote 29 of the essays, the most famous of which is "Federalist No. 10." He was concerned that political factions would become so strong that one faction might overwhelm the legislative process. He wanted the United States to have a clear balance of powers. He stressed the demarcation between a democracy and a republic. In a pure democracy, all the citizens of a country have one vote to pass or veto a law. In a republic, elected representatives of the individual states have the responsibility to take the time to study a proposal and determine the suitability of a proposal as applied to the circumstances of the state they represent. For example, a rural state might be more affected by an agrarian law than one in the North. He said:

> *"...it may well happen that the public voice, pronounced by the representatives of the people, will be more consonant to the public good than if pronounced by the people themselves, convened for that purpose...it is this circumstance principally which renders factious combinations less to be dreaded."*

Madison wrote 29 of the 85 *Federalist Papers*. Hamilton wrote 51. John Jay was seriously injured in New York in 1788 and therefore was only able to write 5 of the 85 *Federalist Papers*.

The Final Draft

James Madison fervently took notes during all the sessions, wrote the first draft and presented it to the assembly. Although some minor modifications were made, it was passed by the assembly.

Ratification Process

A two-thirds majority was needed in order for the Constitution to become the law of the land. By June of 1788, enough of the states had ratified the Constitution, and that is considered to be the date the U.S. Constitution was passed. However, some of the states only signed on the condition that there would be amendments added to the document and others didn't ratify it in its unamended form.

These additions form what is now known as the Bill of Rights. Madison wrote twelve, ten of which passed. A brief synopsis:

1. This amendment had four parts: the freedom of religion and separation of church and state, freedom of speech and the press, freedom to assemble peaceably, and the right to approach the government for a redress of grievances.

2. The right of the people to bear arms.

3. Soldiers cannot be quartered in a house without the express permission of its owner.

4. The right of the people to be free from unlawful searches and seizures.

5. This amendment had five parts: the right to trial by jury, except in the case of military courts for military personnel; no one can be tried twice for the same crime; no one can be compelled to be a witness against oneself[ii]; freedom against confiscation of property without fair and just compensation[iii]; and no one can be deprived of life or liberty without due process of law.

6. This amendment has two parts: in criminal prosecutions, a defendant has the right to a speedy trial; and every defendant shall have right to have legal representation.[iv]

7. The right to a trial by jury applies to controversies in which $20 or more is at stake.

8. This amendment had two parts: excessive bail shall not be levied on any defendant, nor shall cruel or unusual punishments be inflicted.

9. Rights not specified in the Constitution cannot be used to deny other rights of the people.[v]

10. Powers not delegated in the Constitution, or prohibited by a state, are reserved to those respective states or to the people.[vi]

By May 29, 1790, all thirteen of the states ratified the Constitution including the Bill of Rights. The votes:

Connecticut – 128 for; 40 against

Delaware - 30 for; 0 against

Georgia – 26 for; 0 against

Maryland – 63 for; 11 against

Massachusetts – 187 for; 168 against

New Hampshire – 57 for; 47 against

New Jersey – 38 for; 0 against

New York – 30 for; 27 against

North Carolina – 194 for; 77 against

Pennsylvania – 46 for; 23 against

Rhode Island – 34 for; 32 against

South Carolina – 149 for; 73 against

Virginia – 89 for; 79 against

Chapter 5 – Congress or Not: That Is the Question

After the ratification of the U.S. Constitution, Madison ran for the Senate representing the state of Virginia. However, the eloquent, but nevertheless boisterous statesman, Patrick Henry from Madison's own county of Orange blocked him with his own hand-picked nominees, James Monroe and Henry Lee. Patrick Henry intensely disliked Madison's emphasis on increasing the strength of the federal government. In a book review for the *Harvard Law Review*, Klarman, a legal historian, stated, "If Madison is a hero of Ratification, then Patrick Henry is the villain."

Patrick Henry: A Political Enemy

Henry Lee wrote to Madison in November of 1788 telling him of Patrick Henry's opinion of him: "Mr. Henry on the floor exclaimed against your political character and pronounced you unworthy of the confidence of the people in the station of Senator. That your election would terminate in producing rivulets of blood throughout the land." Henry was a feverish debater at the meetings of the Confederation Congress, but Madison counterposed Henry's emotive appeals with solid rational arguments in favor of passing the Constitution in its final form. That was enough to convince Edmund Randolph, another Virginia representative, to change his mind. This may have further angered Henry. Henry preferred the school of thought that gave the states more control, as he felt that a strong central government would result in increasing the power of Northern financiers and bankers at the expense of the Southern farmers and plantation owners.

Madison actually suspected that Patrick Henry's hidden agenda was to separate the North from the South. Madison then decided to run for the House of Representatives, because he had more support to run for this office. Hearing about this, Patrick Henry attempted to preclude Madison from running for that office, too, by attempting to pass a one-year residency requirement. Because Madison was living in New York to serve in the Confederation Congress, he wasn't a legal resident of Virginia at the time he applied to run for House of Representatives. Patrick Henry also nominated the very persuasive James Monroe in hopes that Monroe would beat Madison in the race. His attempts were futile. James Madison was elected to the U.S. House of Representatives.

James Madison: Ghostwriter

George Washington ran in the very first presidential election held in 1789. He had communicated with James Madison during the Confederation Congress and the meetings regarding the U.S. Constitution. Washington admired Madison's literary style and his caution in the wording of official documents. Knowing that he was about to be elected president (there were no other candidates), he knew he had to make his first inaugural address memorable and wanted the input of Col. Humphreys. Washington had Humphreys as his aid-de-camp during the Revolution and felt he had a great deal of integrity and loyalty to the country. Humphrey's response was 73 pages long! Hoping to get a more condensed version, Washington sent Humphrey's manuscript to James Madison for a suggested revision. He also asked that Madison's response be confidential and sent through a third party, Fontaine Maury, who was the postmaster at Fredericksburg in Virginia. In the interest of non-disclosure, Madison wrote back with his draft and assured the president that he would retain no copy of the document. To date, there is no copy of Madison's original notes for this among his writings. James Madison was a man who kept his promises.

Madison in the House of Representatives

The first order of business for the U.S. Congress was the presidency. In 1789, the Senate and House met in a joint session and counted the ballots from the electoral college for the presidential election that was held in 1788 under the new Constitution. The results indicated that George Washington was the first president and John Adams the first vice president. The results, of course, weren't surprising.

Major Legislation

The Tariff Act of 1789 – This required that taxes be collected to pay the interest on the Revolutionary War debt and tariffs be collected on imports, including those on domestically-produced alcohol. Madison tried to mediate on this bill as concessions to Southern growers but failed to get enough support.

Establishment of the First Bank of the United States in 1789 – Following Alexander Hamilton's framework, this passed over the opposition of James Madison and Thomas Jefferson.

The Assumption Bill (1790) – This was based on the Financial Report on Public Credit and delineated the national debt and assumed the funding of all state debt.

James Madison had objected to the Assumption Act of 1790 and wanted lower rates to be paid by the states, especially the South. However, the Congress really wanted this passed, so they made a deal with Madison. In exchange for his positive vote, they promised to move the U.S. capital to the Virginia-Maryland border, which was later to become Washington D.C. This was discussed by Hamilton and Madison over dinner! This was the very first compromise in the United States between sitting members of Congress—one of many to come in the history of the country.

The Residence Act of 1790 – As per the compromise between Hamilton and Madison, members of the U.S. Congress had the cornerstone laid for the District of Columbia In 1792. James Madison in his "Federalist Paper No. 43" had written that the nation's capital should be located in a territory independent from any other state.

Appropriation of Funding for the John Jay Treaty – In 1794, George Washington asked the Supreme Court Justice, John Jay, to negotiate a treaty between the United States and Great Britain in order to force them to cease seizing ships and impressing American sailors among other things. The House didn't have the right to approve of treaties (the Senate does). The Senate signed off on the treaty by a vote of 20 to 10. The House approved the funding in a very close vote of 51 to 48. That was only the beginning of much turmoil to follow.

George Washington wanted the John Jay Treaty to go into effect in order to establish a "most-favored nation" status for Britain as a trade partner because most American imports came from England. There were four basic goals in the treaty: 1) Stop the kidnapping of American sailors to help Britain in their war with Napoleon, 2) England must abandon their forts near the Great Lakes, 3) England must compensate America for the ships they seized, and 4) England must compensate American slave owners for the slaves they stole.

Because Jay failed to secure all the points in his treaty with Great Britain, specifically those relating to the abduction of sailors (Item #1) and the stolen slaves (Item #4), many Americans – the Southerners in particular – were outraged. By failing to get Britain's consent regarding compensation to the slave owners, it affected the profits of Southern plantations. Both the Northerners and the Southerners felt that Jay's failure to get Britain to stop impressing American sailors implied that the practice was acceptable. The John Jay Treaty, as it turned out, infuriated many Americans and John Jay was burned in effigy over it!

18th Century Graffiti: "Damn John Jay!"

In Boston—the city which the British entered at the start of the American Revolution—emotions were still brittle toward the English who had slaughtered so many of their men. Someone actually scribbled on a fence,

"Damn John Jay! Damn everyone who won't damn John Jay! Damn everyone that won't put lights in his windows and sit up all night damning John Jay!"

Madison was very vocal in his opposition to this treaty that the Senate passed nearly in secret. Washington brashly told Madison, "The nature of foreign negotiations requires caution, and their success must often depend on secrecy." He then schooled Madison by adding, "The power of making treaties lies in the President, with the advice and consent of the Senate."

Consequently, Madison's only tool would be for the House to deny funding for the treaty implementation and enforcement. In 1796, the House of Representatives finally appropriated funds for the treaty. James Madison didn't give up, however. He then drafted legislation asserting that the House had a right to review treaties. Due to the appeals of Fisher Ames, the congressional representative from Massachusetts, Madison's motion failed. That was most unfortunate because the Jay Treaty came back to haunt Madison during his later presidency.

The Rise of Partisan Politics

Two political parties emerged as distinct entities after the passage of the John Jay Treaty, the Federalists and the Democratic-Republicans. Curiously, those two parties resembled the political parties in England, the Tories and the Whigs.

The Federalist Party 1791

Those who tended to favor a strong central government rather than the supremacy of states' rights were called Federalists. Although Washington preferred that more power be put into the hands of the federal government, he abhorred political parties. However, after much persuasion, he stopped objecting to the term "Federalist" being employed with reference to himself.

The other notable feature that characterized the Federalists was the fact that many of their policies favored Northern commercial interests. When Washington's vice-president, John Adams, ran for the presidential election in 1798, he announced himself as a Federalist.

James Madison's nemesis, Alexander Hamilton, is considered the founder of the Federalist Party.

The Democratic-Republican Party 1792

Although Madison first supported the Federalist Party, as can be seen in his work prior to his congressional terms, he altered his affiliation. Initially, he had followed the lead of Alexander Hamilton who believed in a strong central government, but became more disillusioned with that point of view after Hamilton was so influential in establishing a national bank in 1789, the Assumption Bill, the Tariff Act of 1789, and the John Jay Treaty of 1794.

Madison's objections to the national bank had to do with the fact that he felt it was unconstitutional because it wasn't an article in the Constitution. Madison's fears were prophetic because many were forced into bankruptcy when there was a financial crisis in the 1790s. The national bank, mostly run by Northerners, demanded that the Southern planters make good on their loans, without any extensions granted in consideration of the fact that the Southerners were the largest borrowers. Madison also felt that the Assumption Act of 1790, having to do with the war debt, and the

Tariff Act of 1789 favored the Northerners rather than the farmers in the South which was primarily agrarian. As it so happened, the Tariff Act also led to the Whiskey Rebellion in 1794 because domestically-produced alcohol carried a tariff if it was sold to other states. The Southern states manufactured whiskey from their grain. Actually, the farmers in Pennsylvania were also affected and there was a lot of violent outbursts as a result of it, including the tarring and feathering of tax collectors!

Madison objected to the John Jay Treaty on the basis that it gave preference to Great Britain as a trading partner. Madison preferred that this status be given to France as did Thomas Jefferson. After all, France aided America during the Revolutionary War.

James Madison and Thomas Jefferson were the founders of the Democratic-Republican Party. They supported states' rights but modified that with the extenuating circumstance that there must be a central government that reserves some powers over the states.

Partisan Politics Becomes Strident

Due to Madison's harshly-worded objections to the John Jay Treaty, Washington and he rarely ever communicated after that. Hamilton and Madison also had disputes over since the establishment of the national bank. Hamilton even brought his Federalist views to a personal level when he warned that these political factions would become "potent engines, by which cunning, ambitious, and unprincipled men will be enabled to subvert the power of the people and to usurp for themselves the reins of government." When he said, "cunning, ambitious, and unprincipled men," he was referring to Madison especially.

To combat this notion, Madison and Jefferson recruited Philip Freneau, Madison's college friend, to write the *National Gazette* in 1791. The solitary purpose of this newsletter was to attack the Federalists and extol the opinions of Democratic-Republicans. Freneau was bold enough to send Washington not just one, but *three* copies of the *National Gazette* daily! Washington referred to Philip Freneau as a "rascal."

The Federalists, on the other hand, had a political organ called the *Gazette of the United States*. The partisan politics in American today dates back to the 18th century, as do the liberal and conservative newspapers.

Chapter 6 – Delicate Dolley – Manipulative Hamilton – Wild Lyon

Dolley! Dolley!

In the year 1794, James Madison met the lovely Dolley Payne Todd in Philadelphia. (The U.S. House of Representatives was located in Philadelphia during 1790-1800.) Dolley and her mother ran a boarding house for congressional members in that city. Dolley also attended many of the social events along with the politicians and their wives. Madison instantly liked her, as Dolley was an attractive twenty-six-year-old woman with beautiful brown eyes. She was also a Southerner like Madison. One day, Madison asked Aaron Burr—who would become Thomas Jefferson's vice-president—to introduce them.

They dated for just a few months and married each other in 1794. In order to marry, Dolley had to sever her membership in the Society of Friends (the Quakers). She was very much in love with James and therefore did so. Dolley was a very friendly socialite with poise and grace. "James Madison was forty-three at the time but was infatuated with her.

Dolley's niece, Mary Cutts, commented about their relationship:

"Mr. Madison dearly loved and was proud of his wife, the ornament of his house – she was his solace and comfort, he could not bear her to leave his presence, and she gratified him by being absent only when duty required. No matter how agreeably employed she was, her first thought and instinct seemed to tell her when she was wanted."

Dolley was a widow, having lost her husband and son to the yellow fever. Her other son, Todd, did survive, however. Between 1794 and 1797, Todd, James Madison, and Dolley lived together in their Philadelphia house. The interior of that house is much the same now as then. Today, it is privately owned but is registered as an official historical site and is open for tours.

The Election of 1796

In 1796, Washington retired and a new election was held.

Four principal people ran in the 1796 election. The results:

1. John Adams – Washington's former vice-president – Federalist — 71 votes

2. Thomas Jefferson – Democratic-Republican — 68 votes

3. Thomas Pinckney – Federalist — 59 votes

4. Aaron Burr – Democratic-Republican — 30 votes

Hamilton's Trick Backfires

Alexander Hamilton was a Federalist like Adams. However, he had some arguments with Adams and preferred Thomas Pinckney as president. So, he influenced the presidential electors to withhold their votes for Adams and asked them to vote for Pinckney instead. Pinckney was from a Southern state, so Hamilton was convinced that some of the Democratic-Republicans from the South would vote for Pinckney, who was also a Federalist. His scheme leaked out though, and many of the electors from the North—mostly those from New England—decided not to vote for Pinckney at all.

Thomas Jefferson, on the other hand, was famous for his contribution, the Declaration of Independence, and was an eloquent speaker. The electors in the Southern states almost unanimously voted for him.

Thus, this is the first time in American history that the president and Vice President came from different political parties. Today, the president and vice-president run on the same ticket.

Madison and Jefferson Object to Adams' Alien and Sedition Acts

James Madison kept up frequent correspondence with his colleague, Thomas Jefferson. Their focus was to balance out some of the policies of John Adams and his Federalist Party. In 1798, Adams signed the Alien and Sedition Acts into law.

The Alien and Sedition Acts gave new powers to the President to deport foreigners and make it more difficult for new immigrants to achieve voting status. Harrison Gray Otis, a Federalist and supporter of the Alien and Sedition Acts, said that it was not in America's interest to "invite hordes of Wild Irishmen, not the turbulent and disorderly of all the world, to come here with a basic view to distract our tranquility."

A "Wild Irishman" Goes to Jail!

Matthew Lyon was an immigrant from Ireland who later became a manufacturer. He also helped to establish the state of Vermont. Lyon had an uncanny knack for instigating violence. He even ended up in a brawl on the floor of the House of Representatives when Representative John Griswold of Connecticut and other Federalists mocked him! It spawned many political cartoons of the day. According to eyewitnesses, Griswold hit Lyon with his cane, and Lyon picked up a pair of tongs to defend himself. Such exhibits no longer occur on the House floor because of the House rules today.

Lyon, however, was what one would call a "loose cannon." He later accused John Adams from the floor of the House of displaying "an unbounded thirst for ridiculous pomp." Adams responded by throwing Lyon in jail for violating the Alien and Sedition Acts. The Democratic-Republicans were incensed by this.

Federalist-inspired newsletters, on the other hand, announced support of the Alien and Sedition Acts. Democratic-Republican newspapers wrote articles criticizing it. To make matters worse, several publishers of the Democratic-Republican papers were charged under the Sedition Act.

Such was the nature of the emotional reactions that these acts caused.

Historians indicate that about 25 arrests were initiated by the enforcement of that law. The Democratic-Republican Party was the party most adversely affected by it because the non-English immigrants tended to join the Democratic-Republicans. Jefferson and Madison saw this act as a ploy to discredit the Democratic-Republican Party. And, in effect, it was. James Madison then made a point of emphasizing the fact that those acts violated the spirit of the law by working with Jefferson to create the Virginia and Kentucky Resolutions.

The Virginia and Kentucky Resolutions 1798

James Madison and Thomas Jefferson reacted vehemently to the Alien and Sedition Acts and they agreed that these acts were unconstitutional. Under anonymity, they drew up the Virginia and Kentucky Resolutions and presented them to these respective state legislatures. Madison was the anonymous writer of the Virginia Resolution. In it, he said:

> *"That this state (Virginia) having by its Convention, which ratified the federal Constitution, expressly declared, that among other essential rights, 'the Liberty of Conscience and of the Press cannot be cancelled, abridged, restrained, or modified by any authority of the United States."*

Those resolutions brought the issue of states' rights vs. federal rights into the foreground. They also addressed the issue of the constitutionality of a piece of legislation. James Madison is famously remembered for pointing out the constitutionality factor. In 1798, there was no other recourse for appealing an act of Congress.

Chapter 7 – Secretary of State and Fourth President

In 1801, Thomas Jefferson was elected the Third President of the United States and appointed James Madison as his Secretary of State. Of all the issues he had to deal with, the case of Marbury v. Madison was the most famous and is studied by every first-year law student in America.

Marbury v. Madison 1803

James Madison's first task as secretary of state for Jefferson was this landmark decision, heard by Chief Justice John Marshall in the Supreme Court. In 1803, William Marbury petitioned the Supreme Court to honor his nomination as a justice of the peace in Washington County, Washington D.C. Marbury's appointment was confirmed during the last days of John Adams' presidency. Because it was among the many last-minute appointments, Marbury's confirmation papers didn't reach Adams' desk before he left office. Therefore, Adams never signed the document. Marbury was among many "midnight judges" that the Federalist Adams had tried to appoint before Jefferson took office.

When William Marbury's confirmation papers were forwarded to James Madison, the current secretary of state, Jefferson instructed Madison not to deliver nor honor it. Madison obeyed Jefferson.

Marbury then brought the case to the Supreme Court. When his case reached the Court, the Court demanded that James Madison hand over the document. Following the instructions of the president, Madison refused.

This case presented a dilemma in which the Chief Justices had to rule on. Their verdict revolved around three points. First of all, the Supreme Court already had the right to judicial review, that is, to determine the constitutionality of an action taken by the executive or legislative branch of government. Secondly, the power of the Supreme Court had limits. The Constitution clearly delineates that the nomination of Justices is at the discretion of the president. That meant that Thomas Jefferson had the personal discretion to approve of Marbury's appointment or not as he had with any other nominee. In addition, the powers of the Supreme Court are limited by the Constitution. It cannot force a sitting president or a secretary of state, for that matter, to take an action regarding a political appointment. They would be, in essence, assuming the privilege of the executive branch. Thirdly, this case also lay outside of the jurisdiction of the Supreme Court. Again, as per Article III of the Constitution, the Supreme Court has "original jurisdiction" only in cases "affecting ambassadors, public ministers, consuls, and those in which the state is a party." The Marbury case should have been heard by an appellate court (a lower court). Therefore, the Supreme Court had no jurisdiction in the case.

The Marbury v. Madison case was based upon the Judiciary Act of 1789. The Judiciary Act delineated the scope and limitations of the Supreme Court. Part of that act (Section 13) was judged to be unconstitutional because the Supreme Court was not permitted by the Constitution to order that Marbury be appointed to his post.

The Louisiana Purchase 1803

Although Madison lacked experience in foreign affairs, Jefferson implicitly trusted him. This was a delicate time in Europe as nearly all the countries were at war since Napoleon in France conquered or controlled many nations there. John Adams adamantly maintained neutrality, and Jefferson likewise wanted the United States to stay out of the conflict. However, Jefferson and Madison followed the events carefully because that European war could spread to America.

Over 800,000 square miles of territory that lay west of the Mississippi River was the property of France. That meant that Napoleon could create a satellite empire bordering the U.S. This was fertile farmland, and the wealthy port of New Orleans in southern Louisiana gave ready access to the Atlantic Ocean. Fortunately, Napoleon was in needs of funds to finance his war and was considering the sale of the land. Word reached the U.S., and Jefferson snapped up this opportunity to expand the United States. Consequently, he told Madison to open negotiations with Napoleon in order to secure the Louisiana territory. Madison, in turn, recruited James Monroe, a former senator from Virginia, and Robert Livingston, the U.S. minister to France, to meet with French representatives. James Monroe had experience with France when he was the foreign minister under George Washington. The delegation was successful. Monroe and Livingston signed the Louisiana Purchase, which nearly doubled the size of America. After this notable agreement, Livingston is recorded to have said, "We have lived long but this is the noblest work of our whole lives...The United States takes rank this day among the first powers of the world."

A Most Curious Expense

In 1805, President Jefferson and James Madison wanted to hammer out an agreement with the Tunisian envoy, Sidi Soliman Mellimelli, in order to halt the raids of the Barbary pirates against U.S, merchant vessels in the Mediterranean. Mellimelli was a Muslim. As it so happened, Dolley Madison had meticulously prepared a dinner for the diplomatic party for them in the White House at 3:30 PM. However, after she discovered that it was scheduled during the sacred month of Ramadan, when Muslims fast during the day, she graciously changed the dinner to after sunset, as per their belief.

As part of his entourage, Mellimelli brought several concubines for his own personal pleasure at night. Madison justified this requisition from his funding source as "appropriations for foreign intercourse." He and Jefferson laughed long and hard at that pun.

As result of his diplomacy, Mellimelli put an end to his piracy. There were, however, some other attacks from pirates from some other smaller countries in North Africa, but they were minor, and taken care of handily.

The Contentious Embargo Act of 1807

It was Madison's job to uphold American neutrality in the Napoleonic War which was raging in Europe. In the meantime, American merchants were conducting trade with both France and Great Britain, both of which were engaged in the war on opposite sides. Despite all attempts, it seemed as if both of these countries were going to bait the U.S. into joining the war when their warships intruded on the shipping lanes in the Atlantic. Britain, running short of fighting forces, raided American harbors, impressed American sailors, and seized U.S. vessels. France followed suit. In 1807, as many as four thousand U.S. sailors had been kidnapped along with one thousand ships. France seized over five hundred U.S. ships, including their cargoes and sailors as well.

France vehemently reacted to prevent Britain, as its enemy, to profit from the acquisition of these resources, so they closed off trade with any and all foreign countries who were neutral. Great Britain reacted by the doing the same. In order to punish England and France and prevent the possible loss of lives and property, Jefferson conferred with James Madison and together they agreed to establish the Embargo Act which prohibited foreign trade. Jefferson had thought that the Americans would be patriotic and cooperate with this and hoped that this economic blow would result in a change in England and France's policy. The consequences of the Embargo Act were disastrous. The Americans were severely affected by the economic hardships that came of it.

Smuggling was rampant. Naval skirmishes broke out in the Lake Champlain area due to British intrusions from Canada. Jefferson even sent in the Navy to quell those, but without any long-lasting resolution.

In 1808, Jefferson's presidential term was nearly over. Shortly before he left office, Congress repealed the Embargo Act and replaced it with the Non-Intercourse Act of 1809, forbidding trade to only France and England. Like its predecessor, the Non-Intercourse Act was ineffective because it was unenforceable.

Jefferson was anxious to leave the White House and recommended James Madison as his successor. Despite America's strenuous objections to the Embargo Act and the Non-Intercourse Act, James Madison was elected to the presidency.

President James Madison 1808–1817

One of the first things James Madison and Dolley did when they moved into the White House was to set up a section in the basement to make ice cream. Reportedly, her favorite flavor was something that would offend the American tongue today—oyster! She wasn't the first to serve ice cream though. Thomas Jefferson and John Adams did too. Dolley was the perfect hostess for the president. She dressed herself tastefully and decorated the White House elegantly, as would be expected by the dignitaries of the times. Dolley also had the envious ability to remember names.

Jefferson passed to Madison the unfortunate legacy of the disaster wreaked by the violation of American rights on the high seas. Americans were suffering from food shortages and had an oversupply of unsold manufactured goods originally slated to be shipped to France and Britain. That led to widespread unemployment in America. Desperately, Congress was trying to resolve this dilemma without going to war.

Macon's Bill Number 2

Macon's Bill Number 1 was voted down in 1809 by the House of Representative because it forbade trade from England and France. In terms of trade, nearly 80% of American imports came from England.

The House agreed to consider an amended version in 1810.

The U.S. Congress passed this bill, but James Madison forcefully objected to it because it was fraught with potential difficulties. Macon's Bill Number 2 lifted embargoes against England or France if one of them would honor American's neutrality. As a bargaining chip, the bill agreed that the United States would cease trade with the opposing country, be it France or England.

Napoleon was a clever politician and leaped at this opportunity. He immediately agreed that France would honor American neutrality. America, per the agreement, ceased all trade with Great Britain. Madison had launched opposition to the Macon Bill because he sensed that Napoleon would ignore its precepts. Madison was correct. Additionally, as Madison feared, the British were infuriated with this bill because it implied, in effect, that America was allying itself with French interests.

Hostilities escalated between Great Britain and the United States. The American people were incensed by England's failure to respect American shipping rights. What's more, the British continued to impress sailors from American vessels. As a matter of fact, many of those sailors were actually British, but the desperate merchants chose to ignore that in order to obtain the goods they needed. Napoleon benefited from the fact he was luring America into the war as well. That would deplete British efforts to engage him. Everything that the American government attempted seemed to be totally ineffective in restoring stability to the economy and good relations with both France and Great Britain. Americans revisited the emotions of the past, those that they felt just prior to the Revolutionary War. Wars and rumors of war circulated in all the parlors and taverns of America, and hostilities resurrected as the Revolutionary War veterans hollered patriotic slogans well into the night.

The "War Hawks" Descend!

James Madison understood the truth behind the bravado, that is, the cost of war to lives and property. He had seen first-hand the deterioration of Southern plantations after the war when traveling home from his stint at New Jersey College (Princeton University). He had weathered through the difficulties experienced in the Virginia Militia. Above all, he understood that the logistics of fighting a war were challenging to a young country. Toward that effort, he made an assessment of assets including ships, munitions, and the training of a fighting force—all of which would cost money and result in war debt.

Henry Clay was the newly-elected hot-headed but persuasive senator from Kentucky. Like so many Americans, he recommended declaring war on Great Britain. Likewise, John Calhoun the South Carolinian representative in the U.S. House spearheaded the call for a "Second War of Independence."

The hidden agenda for the call for war was the fact that Canada was perceived as being vulnerable. The English dominated Canada but lacked the ability to conduct defensive or offensive actions on land. It was an opportunity for annexation.

At this point, Madison knew that it was impossible to prevent Great Britain from attacking U.S. interests and re-establishing trade with them. In June of 1812, he asked Congress to declare war and they did so.

"Mr. Madison's War"

The War of 1812 became known by the dubious term of "Mr. Madison's War" by its detractors despite the fact that he had no control over the John Jay Treaty, the Embargo Act, or the Non-Intercourse Act. In addition, he made his objections known about Macon's Bill Number 2.

Among the causes for America's entry into the War of 1812 were:

1. The flawed John Jay Treaty

2. The Embargo Act

3. The Non-Intercourse Act

4. Macon's Bill Number 2

Attitudes toward the war split along party lines and the North and South. Most Federalists came from New England. They were the manufacturers and the merchants who were much more interested in restoring trade with Great Britain to its pre-war level than they were to fight. As result of Northern opposition to the war, states in New England refused to commit their militias to the war effort and sat out the entire war. The Southerners were more responsive. Most of them were Democratic-Republicans who felt their honor was assailed by the wholesale impressment of sailors and the naval battles that had been fought off their Southern coasts.

The Siege of Fort Mackinac under Bumbling Leadership 1812

Fort Mackinac housed a large trading post near the border of Canada. The Native Americans and Canadian traders used it to trade furs and goods. Lieutenant Porter Hanks commanded the American division at Fort Mackinac on an island between Lake Michigan and Lake Huron. He didn't know about the status of the potential war. Madison's Secretary of War William Eustis hadn't sent any messages to him, although the war had already started. Hanks knew there was a pending war, so he sent messengers out and quietly waited for the response.

In the meantime, the British commander, Charles Roberts, was just south of the fort. Roberts dispatched some spies, who discovered the Americans at the fort were uninformed. Roberts seized this opportunity by rolling a huge cannon into the woods and fired it at the fort. Hanks was caught by surprise. Totally unprepared for battle, he immediately raised a flag of truce and surrendered without a fight.

Madison was furious and issued orders to place Hanks under court-martial. Madison also dismissed his war secretary, William Eustis, once he discovered his gross incompetence and replaced him with John Armstrong who had Revolutionary War experience.

Battle of the Thames 1813

The British had been recruiting Native American warriors and Ontario tribes to help them fight the war, promising them land in the Northwestern United States for their effort. Because of the British victory at Fort Mackinac, the tribal confederations started to join up. The Shawnee chieftain, Tecumseh, had been conducting a campaign to unite as many tribes as possible in a confederation. At Thames River, off of Lake Huron, he gathered a modest force of 1,000 native tribes, with the British contributing about 700 soldiers. The Americans, on the other hand, had been gaining immense strength and had the support of some of the Native American tribes. At Thames, there were 2,000 American soldiers under William Harrison armed and ready, and they anticipated more reinforcements.

The British, under Henry Proctor, attempted a frontal assault, but failed to create any fortifications. He was forced to surrender because he couldn't defend the area. Tecumseh and his legions didn't surrender, however. So, General Harrison dispatched a unit under Colonel Johnson to take them on. Although the tribes fought bravely,

Tecumseh was killed near a swamp there. Once the other tribes heard of his demise, they retreated. This was a notable American victory.

Napoleon surrendered in 1814 and was exiled. That freed up a great deal of British forces to fight America. In addition, their naval forces were patrolling offshore, raiding trading vessels at every opportunity.

In August, the British had numerous warships, war sloops, and many transport vessels in the Chesapeake Bay under the commands of Admiral Alexander Cochrane and Rear Admiral George Cockburn. General Richard Ross arrived from the south and disembarked his transport ships. He then attacked and defeated American regulars at Bladensburg, Maryland. Bladensburg lies just northeast of Washington D.C.

Cochrane and Cockburn moved up the tributaries of the Chesapeake, including the Potomac River. After meeting up with Ross and his ground forces, they decided upon a combined naval and ground invasion. Ships attacked Fort Washington and Alexandria. General Ross now had a choice of attacking Baltimore or Washington.

When Madison heard the news of the proximity of the British regiments, he became alarmed. However, John Armstrong, the secretary of war, informed him that there wasn't any danger. General William Winder guarded the route to Baltimore, but moved Eastward in case the Americans moved in from the coastal areas. To replace his forces, he dispatched Brigadier General Tobias Stansbury who protected the intersecting routes to Washington, Baltimore, and Georgetown.

Unfortunately, Stansbury made a major tactical error and moved his troops further east in order to protect his flank. Seeing that Washington was now wide open for an invasion, British Commander Ross rapidly marched toward the capital.

Burning of Washington D.C. August, 1814

One evening, as dinner was being served at the White House to Madison and his guests, one of Madison's freed slaves galloped up to the White House waving his hat rapidly. Loudly, he called out to them, "Clear out! Clear out! General Armstrong has ordered a retreat!"

In the confusion, James and Dolley got separated. On Dolley's part it was deliberate, because she and the servants rushed about trying to save some of the national treasures and some silver.

Among those was a very famous painting of George Washington by Gilbert Stuart in 1796 during his last year in office. Although it is widely believed that Dolley herself rescued this portrait, that isn't true. Jean-Pierre Sioussat, the doorkeeper, and Magaw, the gardener, are the two who saved the painting. Dolley then went to Georgetown to stay with a friend overnight.

Ross, accompanied by British Admiral George Cockburn and his forces, marched up Maryland Avenue and entered the White House. Seeing Madison's grand dinner there, they ate it themselves and drank the wine. Then they looted the building and set it aflame. The conflagration was intense, so much so that even metal melted. The British then burned 3,000 books in the Library of Congress. All except one of the government buildings were destroyed.

Before they could reconnoiter, a vicious tornado assailed the entire city. Two British cannons were ripped from the ground, and roofs blew off buildings sending debris all over. The English then fled.

Madison and his staff had relocated to Brookeville, Maryland. Madison took a strongbox with him which contained the entire treasury of the United States. He and Dolley joined up again the following day.

Secretary of War Resigns in Disgrace

Madison felt like he was surrounded by assassins. He had fired his secretary of war, William Eustis, for failing to prepare the American troops at the Great Lakes. Now his new secretary of war, John Armstrong, failed to adequately prepare for the British attack on the nation's capital. The toughest man he knew was James Monroe and he recruited him for the position of Secretary of War. James Monroe later became a U.S. president.

Battle of Baltimore 1814

After seeing Washington D.C. reduced to crumbling stone and smoldering ruins, Madison knew that this destructive war must end. Secretary of War James Monroe came through for him. He immediately rallied eleven thousand American soldiers to overwhelm the British who moved northeast toward Baltimore.

The pounding from nineteen British warships went on for three full days and raged on three fronts, Fort McHenry, North Point, and Hampstead Hill, all of which were located on a small peninsula in a choke point of the Chesapeake Bay. British regulars disembarked and went ashore where they were confronted by men from the Virginia and Pennsylvania militias. This time, the British vessels were equipped with rockets and mortar rounds. It was a loud battle. The sky filled with bursting bombs and red starbursts from the explosives. Cannons pommeled Hampstead Hill, and the infantry fired countless rounds of rifle fire and engaged in hand-to-hand combat.

The Americans had fortified the city of Baltimore and its fort, Fort McHenry, as well. The British commander,

Robert Ross was killed by an American sharpshooter at North Point. At Hampstead Hill, the Americans pounded the British regiments with one hundred cannons, backed up by long-range artillery fire from Fort McHenry.

At the star-shaped fort, the battle mercilessly raged on for twenty-seven hours. American defenders were joined by the Maryland militia. They fired thousands of rounds from their cannons and rifles. During the battle, the Americans boldly replaced the tattered American flag over the fort with a huge new one.

Determined to halt this war, Madison and Monroe had dispatched a truce ship offshore as soon as this brutal battle was over. Aboard that ship was a poet by the name of Francis Scott Key. He was aboard to negotiate the release of a Dr. William Beanes whom the British had taken as a prisoner of war. Leaning up against the side of the ship, he watched the bombardment and saw the massive American flag waving in the air over the fort. Then he penned the lyrics for the "Star-Spangled Banner" which became the national anthem of the United States.

After the Battle of Baltimore, the British retreated, but some naval fleets headed toward New Orleans. They were stubborn and felt that they might be able to annex this vital port for England. Inspired by the astounding victory in Baltimore, the Americans, under General Andrew Jackson, roundly defeated the British. Three hundred British were killed and over twelve hundred wounded or captured. It was the end.

The Treaty of Ghent 1815 – All Is as It Was

There were no significant territorial changes due to the War of 1812. The Canadian author, Pierre Berton, once wrote, "It was as if no war had been fought, or to put it more bluntly, as if the war that was fought was fought for no good reason." In that sense, he was wrong, because this war proved to the British that America would fight for its independence right down to the last man standing. The spoils of "Mr. Madison's War" were national pride and freedom.

Chapter 8 – Partial Retirement and Death

James Madison was far too mentally active to ever fully retire. Whatever he lacked in physical stamina was compensated for by his intelligence. His entire life wasn't devoted to his own health, but the health of the young United States.

In 1817, James Madison returned to his beloved plantation home at Montpelier, Virginia. Dolley was a hostess extraordinaire, so he entertained his political friends, neighbors, and family under her watch.

Financially, Madison didn't do well. Although it seems paradoxical, his profits plummeted due to the peace he himself had engendered after the War of 1812. In order to help in the payment for the overhead, he applied for loans, but was turned down as a poor credit risk. Madison was then forced to sell parcels of land and took out mortgages on the remaining land.

The "Brutus Affair"

James Madison would most likely have preferred to worry about finances than a set of notes from the Constitutional Convention of 1787 that reached print in the year 1821. It attacked Madison where it hurt the most—the formulation of the U.S. Constitution. This publication was originally written by Robert Yates under the pseudonym Brutus. That was certainly a fitting moniker for the document.

Yates participated in the Constitutional Convention for only one month. Nevertheless, he apparently had taken notes as he listened to Madison's lines of reasoning on the various points elucidated for the proposed Constitution. In one of the papers, Yates reported that Madison said the Senate would serve as a check "on the democracy" and that Madison alluded to the "instabilities of the other branches (of government)." When Madison was working on the U.S. Constitution, he believed in a strong central government, but not one that would stifle the rights of the states. However, Yates' document appeared to make Madison's views look like a wholesale sabotage of states' rights.

In some of his personal letters, Madison complained that Yates' notes at the Convention were "egregious," "erroneous," and "mutilated." He was very offended by the publication and concerned about the purity of his legacy. Madison wanted the American public to read his own notes at the Convention, not someone else's interpretation.

The printing of this 1821 manuscript was actually executed by John Lansing, Jr., as Yates had died in 1801. Lansing and Yates both vigorously opposed the adoption of the U.S. Constitution.

It should be remembered in this context that James Madison spearheaded the ratification of the U.S. Constitution, but he did not compose the entire document. It was submitted to all the delegates at the Constitutional Convention for their approval and/or modifications. The final document represented the voice of all the members who attended.

Role in the University of Virginia

This university was the brainchild of Thomas Jefferson, America's third president. James Madison, Jefferson, James Monroe, Chief Justice John Marshall, and others were instrumental in planning for the college. James Madison was its second rector. Madison and

Jefferson collaborated in the selection of books to be included in the university library. This university was to be Jefferson last public act for America and he knew it.

He and James Madison were close friends for years and cherished that friendship. In Thomas Jefferson's last letter to Madison, he wrote,

> "The friendship which has subsisted between us, now half a century, and that harmony of our political principles and pursuits, have been sources for constant happiness to me through that long period...You have been a pillar of support through life. Take care of me when dead, and be assured that I shall leave you my last affections."

Madison replied to him writing,

> "You cannot look back to the long period of our private friendship and political harmony with more affectionate recollections than I do...Wishing and hoping that you may yet live to increase the debt which our country owes you, and to witness the increasing gratitude which alone can pay it, I offer you the fullest return of affectionate assurances."

One of the concerns both Jefferson and Madison shared was the fact that both of them owned slaves. Both were acutely aware of the contradiction between their beliefs in the freedom of all people and the denial of those very same rights to their slaves. In his later years, it bothered Madison a great deal.

Madison and the Slavery Issue

In 1783, letter James Madison had written to his father saying that he would have to sell one of his slaves:

> "I do not expect to get near the worth of him; but cannot think of punishing him by transportation merely for coveting that liberty for which we have paid the price of so

much blood, and proclaimed so often to be the right &
worthy pursuit of every human being."

Many Southerners, and even some Northerners, were trapped in an economic system that denied them a reasonable income without free labor. Earlier in his life, Madison tended to ignore the issue, but now the issue deeply depressed him even to the point of obsession at times.

When younger, Madison had been subjected to a lot of noisy criticism due to slavery. One of his complainants, Benjamin Franklin, once made an analogy between slave owners and Muslims enslaving Christians. That appeared in Franklin's journals late in his life. Many other Northerners were even ruder, and there was a lot of potential here for embarrassing Madison during his retirement.

In 1819, Madison received a letter from Robert Walsh, a British citizen, inquiring about the reasons why the abolition of the slave trade wasn't included in the Constitution. Madison clarified Walsh's assumption that it wasn't included. He pointed out that it had been, but many of the delegates had scruples about putting the word "slaves" into the document. He also indicated to his correspondent that the phrase the framers of the Constitution used was "the migration and importation of persons." He added that the delegates at the Constitutional Convention of 1787 wanted to prohibit the slave trade between states as well. However, many of the states, Madison said, were reluctant to have that go into effect immediately. So, a compromise was agreed, stating that any such prohibition would go into effect between the years 1800 and 1808. The Prohibition was passed in 1808.

Madison also alluded to the fact that the slavery issue was problematic because of states' rights as they applied to new states asking for admission into the United States.

Madison's Opinion on the Missouri Compromise of 1820

New states that applied to join the United States were required to declare whether they would be "slave states" or "free states." Missouri applied as a slave state and Maine applied as a free state. Heated debates arose in Congress regarding whether Congress had the right to rule on slavery or not. A compromise, called the Missouri Compromise, was passed. Its provisions indicated that Missouri would be admitted as a slave state and Maine as a free state. What's more, it attempted to set a geographic line separating states that would be permitted to become slave states. This questionable solution was for the purpose of balancing the number of free states with the slave states.

Madison was extremely critical of the arguments in Congress about its authority to regulate slavery between states. It didn't, according to Madison.

After Madison's death, the Missouri Compromise was declared unconstitutional in a Supreme Court case, known as the Dred Scott decision, in 1857.

The "Back to Africa" Colonization Plan 1816 and 1820–1821

James Madison had futilely hoped that the prohibition of the foreign importation of slaves and the spread of already owned slaves into the new states in the West would create a diffusion when people took their slaves with them.

Madison noted that black slaves who had been freed or arrived at the shores of the United States as free men were discriminated against. To prevent that, the American Colonization Society founded a colony in Africa where they felt these people could live under the benefits of liberty and freedom. It was called Liberia. In 1821, thousands of free black men moved there. It's interesting to note here that the British did a similar thing by establishing the African state of Sierra Leone as early as 1780.

In 1833, James Madison became the president of the American Colonization Society. He also became one of the most rigorous supporters of the establishment of Liberia. In a letter to Robert Evans of Philadelphia, Madison said that the prejudices of both races were "unalterable."

Madison even calculated the costs of such a resettlement plan. However, it would cost five times the cost of the War of 1812. A round of loud criticism resounded especially on the part of the Northern Federalists, so the plan was reworked.

In Defense of the Constitution

In 1832, at the age of 81, James Madison had to fly into public political action once again. For years after he led the creation of the U.S. Constitution, many people confronted him with questions regarding it. Madison passionately objected to being misconstrued or misunderstood. Furthermore, he despised it when citizens deliberately mischaracterized his intentions in order to bolster support for their own agendas.

In South Carolina during the presidency of Andrew Jackson, a tariff was passed that had a damaging effect upon the South in particular. Southerners called that the "Tariff of Abominations." So, the citizens of that state tried to declare these tariffs null and void in a matter related to the business of South Carolina. That led to a subsequent debate on the right to nullify a federal law.

The Nullification Crisis 1832-1833

South Carolina invoked the doctrines they claimed were established by Thomas Jefferson and James Madison and stated that those doctrines gave it the right to nullify laws passed by Congress. James Madison himself indicated that wasn't his intention, nor did the Constitution allow for a state to nullify a federal law. Other states joined in the debate saying that their positions were supported by statements made in the Kentucky Resolutions as well as the Virginia Resolutions. Jefferson wrote the Kentucky Resolutions and Madison wrote the Virginia Resolutions.

In his final letter to Jefferson, Madison wrote that he would defend his legacy, so he lashed out against any insinuations that Jefferson, or he himself for that matter, supported nullification. When talking about Jefferson's stance, Madison said, "It is remarkable how closely the nullifiers...shut their eyes and lips, whenever his (Jefferson's) authority is ever so clearly and emphatically against them."

Madison forcefully defended himself in that regard also. He promoted the notion of "interposition," which gave the states the right to *question* the constitutionality of a law. That, of course, didn't mean a state alone could nullify a federal law. In his essay, Christian Fritz of the Heritage Foundation said, "Madison emphatically rejected the attempt by a single state to nullify national laws."

Unfortunately, the result of the nullification crisis led to a serious ramification. If a state cannot nullify a law, it leaves the door open to secession from the Union.

In 1832, the president at the time, Andrew Jackson, issued the "Proclamation to the People of South Carolina," reasserting the supremacy of federal law. Because of continued debate on the issue in South Carolina, Jackson then passed the "Force Bill" in 1833, indicating that its actions amounted to treason and he threatened the use of military force if necessary.

Madison the Farmer

During his retirement years at Montpelier, James Madison worked as a farmer would. He utilized different fertilizing methods and alternated his crops from tobacco to wheat. This was important, as Madison observed the prices of his main crops at the market. He even was elected as the president of the local Agricultural Society.

He advised his fellow growers never to exhaust a field and to use methods of crop rotation, even leaving some of their fields vacant for a season.

Madison was one of the earliest proponents of environmentalism. He often asked the question in his presentations to the Agricultural Society as to what the best ratio of plants to animals (including humans) was that would achieve a natural balance in nature.

His recommendations included those of proper irrigation and the use of oxen rather than horses for plowing. Madison opposed the sale of animal hides, like those of cows, indicating that it amounted to exploitation of the animals and didn't even earn them enough money to pay for animal feed.

Financial Crisis Due to Madison's Stepson

During their life together, James and Dolley had a lot of trouble with Todd Payne Madison. Todd was James' stepson and James permitted Dolley to be the disciplinarian when he was young. Dolley wasn't very good with that at all. Ralph Ketcham, one of Madison's biographers, was very kind in his assessment of the boy's comportment when he said that Todd never felt "at ease" at Montpelier because it wasn't his boyhood home. Nevertheless, that doesn't explain his behavior. He drank excessively and sometimes traveled about shooting his gun just for fun. At one time, he invested in a "sure-fire" scheme to obtain a storehouse of gold. Of course, the plan failed.

To help Todd develop a sense of responsibility, Madison gave him an administrative role at the plantation. That effort failed because he often left his post in order play cards and get drunk at the various pubs in the area.

After that, Todd moved between New York, Washington D.C., and Philadelphia. He continued to gamble a great deal. Dolley tried to pay some of Todd's loans and James paid others about which she had no knowledge. In 1824, Todd nearly went to prison because of a fraudulent check charge. Fortunately, one of Madison's friends,

Richard Bache, made good on the check. Nevertheless, Todd continued to take out loans he had no hope of repaying unless he won at the gambling tables.

Consequently, he ended up in prison. James was only able to bail him out when he had a crop of tobacco that sold at a higher price— the first one in years. These expenses severely cut into Madison's finances reserved for his retirement. All in all, Madison spent about $40,000 between the years of 1813 to 1836 on Todd's gambling debts.

His Darling Niece and Dear Friends

Madison and Dolley's grandniece, Mary Cutts, used to call James Madison "Uncle Madison." In her memoirs, she said that James was "a dear lover of fun and children." James and Dolley never had any children between them, so Madison appreciated his nieces and nephews and loved to watch them play.

Death of James Madison

In 1832, he knew the end was close when he wrote, "My bones have lost a sad portion of the flesh which clothed and protected them, and the digestive and nutritive organs which alone can replace it are too slothful in their functions."

One morning, when Madison's niece, Nelly Willis, served him breakfast, he couldn't swallow. She didn't understand why he couldn't and asked him what was wrong. Madison replied, "Nothing more than a change of mind, my dear." Then his head fell back and he stopped breathing as quietly as a candle loses its flame. The date was June 28, 1836.

One of his slaves, Paul Jennings, truly admired and loved James Madison. In fact, he took care of him when he was ill and was there when he died. Of him, Jennings wrote,

> *"Mr. Madison, I think, was one of the best men that ever lived. I never knew him to be in a passion...For six months before his death, he was unable to walk, and spent most of*

his time reclined on a couch; but his mind was bright, and with his numerous visitors he talked with, had as much animation and strength of voice as I ever heard him in his best days."

Conclusion

James Madison was a wordsmith and used his remarkable abilities to place solid rationale upon the heated debates related to the issue of independence from Great Britain in formulating the U. S. Constitution, its amendments. He penned the state Constitution of Virginia along with George Mason. As Secretary of State under Thomas Jefferson, he manifested extreme loyalty giving rise to the notable Marbury v. Madison decision that denied the states the right to arbitrarily declare an item in the Constitution unconstitutional. That case set a precedent in the Supreme Court.

Without Madison's intervention, the United States would just be an amiable confederation of states. James Madison had the highly commendable ability to relate to legislators with sincere respect and was flexible enough to compromise.

James Madison has gone done in history as the "Father of the Constitution." He could have been its grandfather and defender as well. He was the man who shepherded it through Congress during a time of recovery from the Revolutionary War. That was a role that America imposed upon him and one he played well into his 80's. Perhaps it could be said that no one but James Madison could have performed that feat which has benefitted all Americans today.

Part 7: Alexander Hamilton

A Captivating Guide to an American Founding Father Who Wrote the Majority of The Federalist Papers

Introduction

Alexander Hamilton, unlike many of the other Founding Fathers of the United States, was born outside of wedlock and was an orphan at the age of thirteen after his mother died. He and his brother grew up in the West Indies on the islands of Nevis and Saint Croix, which are now part of the Virgin Islands. They spoke French on Nevis, which is where he was born. Alexander's mother, Rachel, ran away from her legal husband, James Lavien, because he terrorized her. She later met John Hamilton and lived with him in a common-law relationship. They had two boys—Alexander and James. When his business went bad, John abandoned Rachel and the two boys who were just in their pre-teens. She ran a small shop supplying sailors for their trips abroad, and she managed with the money she had.

In February 1768, his mother died of yellow fever, after which her legal husband returned and confiscated everything they owned, which the law allowed at the time. There they were, two adolescents thrown into the world, depending on the charity of friends and neighbors. That perhaps is one of the reasons why Alexander Hamilton was fiscally sensitive and always anxious about funding and finance, not only for himself but for the new nation of the United States, where he emigrated when he was in his late teens. It is no wonder then that he became the first Secretary of the Treasury of the United States and that he even saved banks from financial collapse.

His home island of Nevis was a rough place to live. Gruff sailors covered with brine frequented the port that he lived by where frightened African slaves were sold in the market square. Life there was based on survival, and Alexander Hamilton's first occupation in his new country of the United States was as a military officer. He was brash and fearless. It was he that stood along with General George Washington during the surrender of General Charles Cornwallis at Yorktown, Virginia.

Hamilton had a brilliant mind. Although the law was his calling, he was blessed with charisma that could persuade even the stoniest of hearts. As a prolific writer, he never shied from presenting his legal (and personal) opinions regarding the political issues of the day.

Temperamentally, he was a warm and cordial companion but could effectively rebut anyone who disagreed with him, and—for some reason—he was always surprised when he lost. Hamilton, unfortunately or fortunately, was brutally honest and told everyone what he thought. People like that can attract many friends but just as many enemies. Politically, he was a Federalist in support of a strong national government but would occasionally support a rival candidate if he felt that the rival candidate would do a better job for the country. He gave up any presidential ambitions he had for himself due to a highly publicized illicit affair, but he continued as an expert campaigner and powerbroker for others. His resiliency was truly astounding.

Alexander Hamilton and Aaron Burr, a banker and an entrepreneur, were political rivals for nearly fifteen years. After running for president along with Jefferson and being relegated to becoming just vice president, Burr attempted to run as the governor of New York. Hamilton then vociferously opposed him. When Burr lost that election, he blamed Hamilton and challenged him to the most historical duel of the 19th century. As a result,

Hamilton died, and a country mourned him. However, his legacy lives on.

Chapter 1 – From Nevis to Boston

Nevis was once a tropical island with luscious plants spotted with brightly colored flowers dripping nectar onto the rich soil, but that was gone after it was settled. Instead, it became a place of devastation. In the 1750s, Nevis was under the possession of the King of Norway and Denmark. The indigenous people were the dark-skinned Nevisians ruled over by Chief Tegremond until Denmark took possession of the island. The Europeans there were French Huguenots who had escaped France when they were being persecuted because of their religion. Dr. John Fawcett, Hamilton's grandfather, was a French Huguenot—a Protestant reformer who rejected the domination of Catholicism in 17th-century France. About him, Hamilton wrote, "My grandfather by my mother's side of the name of Fawcett was a French Huguenot who emigrated to the West Indies in consequence of the revocation of the Edict of Nantes and settled in the island of Nevis...he practiced as a physician." The family records are poor, as the name "Fawcett" is also spelled as "Faucett," "Fawcette," and even "Fosset" on some documents. On this tropical island, John Fawcett met Mary Uppington, an Anglican, and married her. Besides practicing medicine, John was a gentleman farmer and lived from circa 1680 to 1745.

After Dr. John Fawcett died, he left quite a bit of money to his sons and daughters, including Rachel, Hamilton's mother. In 1745, Rachel and her mother Mary moved to the nearby island of Saint Croix (currently one of the U.S. Virgin Islands). While there, Rachel was approached by a man named Johann Michael Lavien. He was very dazzled by Rachel's lovely clothes and thought she was independently wealthy, so he fancied that he could buy a sugar plantation and become a respected landowner. Rachel already owned sixteen slaves from the indigenous population, which Lavien imagined he could use for his potential plantation. Anxious to have her daughter marry into wealth, her mother, Mary, persuaded Rachel to marry Lavien. She followed her mother's advice, and they had a son, Peter, in 1746, but the marriage was a rocky one. Lavien was an avaricious and cruel man. Unable to tolerate his abuse any longer, Rachel complained bitterly and ran away in 1750. After locating her, Rachel's vengeful husband imprisoned her at Fort Christiansted in Saint Croix, which was a practice under Danish law for a disobedient wife. After her stint in confinement, Rachel was still so frightened of her husband that she abandoned him and their young child and fled to the island of Nevis just west of there.

Rachel never returned home and escaped to the British West Indies—a chain of islands just northwest of there. There, she met James A. Hamilton, a Scottish merchant and entrepreneur. They fell in love with each other, and he took her to the island of St. Kitts and later back to Nevis.

However, there was a problem. Rachel was still legally married to Johann Michael Lavien, so the Scottish Presbyterians wouldn't recognize a marriage between Hamilton and Rachel Fawcett Lavien. Thus, they cohabited. In 1753, they gave birth to a son, James Jr., and on January 11th, 1755 (or 1757), they gave birth to Alexander. Once Rachel's husband, Johann Michael Lavien, heard about this in 1759, he divorced Rachel on the grounds of desertion. James Hamilton called Lavien a "fortune hunter, bedizened with gold." Rachel and her common-law husband did well together until James Hamilton experienced a severe downturn in his business and disappeared.

Years later, Alexander wrote to his brother, James Jr., asking, "But what has become of our dear father? It is an age since I have heard from him though I have written...I entreat you, if you can, to relieve my doubts, and let me know how or where he is, if alive, if dead, how and where he died." His brother didn't have any definitive information, but family records later revealed that Alexander's father wrote to him from the island of Bequia in the Grenadines in 1786. That group of islands lies southeast of Nevis, very close to the shore of South America. According to the records, the young men found out that their father sold his lot of land and moved 100 miles northward, settling on the island of St. Vincent. He never made any effort to contact his two boys again.

Rachel's Unfortunate Legacy

Rachel was now left to care for her two sons by herself. She rented out a shop in Christiansted from which she sold clothing, plantation equipment, and supplies for the sailors and planters. She and her two boys, when they were old enough, worked hard, and they were able to buy some furniture and silverware for their modest dwelling. Because of the religious laws, children from illegitimate marriages were forbidden from receiving an education in the Anglican church schools. Thus, Rachel enlisted private tutors and paid for that by teaching classes at a local Jewish school.

Although this island would normally appear to be a virtual paradise for vacationers, it wasn't. This was a relatively poor area full of people who were struggling for survival. Many of the Nevisians were slaves, and they worked the plantations for a handful of wealthy planters who separated themselves from the populace. Luckily, the slaves and the freed Nevisians were often given Sundays off and sold some of their handmade wares in the street markets. Freed slaves had larger stalls there and ran their businesses in the heart of the busy port city.

The cargo that traversed this port sometimes carried disease, particularly yellow fever. That disease was quite common in the 18th century as it could be easily carried from African monkeys and mosquitoes. In the year 1768, both Alexander and his mother contracted it. The illness bypassed James Jr. for reasons unknown. Both Alexander and his mother underwent primitive 18th-century treatments—bloodletting, enemas, and the use of a risky herbal product, valerian, which adversely affects the liver. Alexander survived the yellow fever, but the primitive treatments his mother was subjected to were ineffective, and she died on February 19th before the sun had even risen. Now, Alexander and James Jr. were orphans. As soon as Rachel's estranged husband, Johann Michael Lavien, received word of her demise, the avaricious man went to probate court and claimed the rights to his wife's money and goods, showing no interest in the two boys. Because Rachel had deserted him, the court awarded everything to Lavien. The two dazed boys were at the mercy of their friends and what relatives they had. Their nearest relative was a cousin, Peter Lytton of Saint Croix, and he donated the black drape for Rachel's coffin. Lytton then had a parish clerk conduct a brief funeral. As she wasn't permitted burial in a church cemetery, he had her buried on his property on the outskirts of Christiansted. The court then made James Jr. and Alexander wards of Peter Lytton and his wife, Ann, Rachel's sister. Lytton, like so many of the planters in the region, ran into setbacks on his plantation and went into heavy debt. The court records reported that Lytton became totally despondent and either "stabbed or shot himself to death" in July of 1769. Lacking foresight, what goods and cash Peter still had was bequeathed to his mistress, Ledja, and their mulatto son. Unfortunately for Hamilton and his brother, Peter Lytton's brother, James, died shortly thereafter, so the boys were at the mercy of poor Ledja who couldn't support them. Because Peter was bankrupt at the time of his demise, he also left nothing in his will to his wife or the boys, either. History has no record of what happened to Ledja and her son, but James Jr. and Alexander Hamilton were now wards of the state.

Clerkship

After Peter's death, a local carpenter, Thomas McNobeny, took in James as an apprentice, and a Scottish merchant, Thomas Stevens, oversaw Alexander's upbringing. Only the landowners and larger import-export offices brought in a decent income that could help in the support of the boys. Everyone else on the island was either engaged in menial work in the fields or labored in the counting houses of clerks and money changers.

Auctions were held under the tents in the sandy streets of Christiansted. There were many import-export businesses in the busy port, including that of Beekman and Cruger, who later became Kortright and Cruger. Nicholas Cruger saw some promise in Alexander and created an apprenticeship for him. Alexander came across as precocious and intelligent and was excited about being able to work. Cruger then apprenticed Alexander to his establishment to work alongside his own son on Saint Croix. Kortright and Cruger was an import-export firm which conducted business between New England and New York, as well as to the French West Indies. Alexander was a little under thirteen years old at the time, and his role was that of a clerk. Unfortunately, he hated the work, although he performed it well. While there, Alexander admitted to his older foster brother, Edward Stevens, "I condemn the groveling condition of a clerk, or the like, to which my fortune condemns me, and would willingly risk my life though not my character, to exalt my station."

In time, however, Cruger noted that Hamilton was capable of much more than just bookkeeping, and he permitted him to do more work. Young men during the 18th century were often entrusted with a great deal of responsibility during their years as apprentices. Fortunately, Alexander was left in charge of his employer's office when Edward Stevens was away, which gave him broader experience. He was able to handle the bills of lading, the inspection of cargo, and even advised the ship's captains.

Alexander was very pleased with this added responsibility and often wandered about the port, which was packed with clipper ships and sloops carrying rum, sugar, grain, flour, and even timber. Besides the traditional trade that kept this port extremely active, the docks were also replete with smugglers. That secretive collection of swarthy-looking men not only smuggled in contraband but engaged in slave trading under the authority of the import-export company Hamilton worked for. Occasionally, notices appeared in the *Royal Danish Gazette*: "Just imported from the windward coast of Africa and to be sold on Monday next by Mssrs. Kortright & Cruger at said Cruger's yard, three hundred prime slaves." Alexander looked upon these unfortunate black men dragged up from the cargo hold of their ships and put on display to sell to the highest bidder. Most were naked, drenched in sweat, and terrified. Having been confined to close quarters below deck, they were blinded by the bright light of the tropical sun and bent over, squinting. Alexander immediately felt sympathy and treated them decently but realized he was helpless in terms of resolving their dilemma.

Hamilton and the other young men in the region were required to enlist in the local militia. There were a number of revolts and rebellions in the area, as the islands attracted a motley group of foreigners. In addition to that, there were slave rebellions, and Hamilton had to fight with the other members of the militia in order to quell them. He wasn't unsympathetic to their struggles, but he was given no choice when he was ordered to attack them during a revolt. After seeing the cruelties imposed upon these slaves, Hamilton thought of his own impoverished beginnings and was deathly afraid he, too, might meet their fate. Their lowly position in life instilled in him a fear of never being able to elevate himself above his own station and becoming as needy as the slaves. Hamilton had to survive on his wits and his desperate need to make a living in a harsh environment.

Hamilton's only escape was his fervent intellect and imagination. He read and consumed the printed word like a glutton. Books took him to other places where life might be more palatable. He even penned a few short poems, which were accepted for publication in the *Royal Danish Gazette*. For one of his submissions, he decided to write a piece about a hurricane that ravaged the island. Saint Croix was subject to a great many vicious hurricanes, but the hurricane of 1772 was particularly horrifying. Below follows a portion of that essay:

> Good God! What horror and destruction—it's impossible for me to describe—or you to form any idea of it. It seemed as if a total dissolution of nature was taking place. The roaring of the sea and wind—fiery meteors flying about in the air—the prodigious glare of almost perpetual lightning—the crash of the falling houses—and the ear-piercing shrieks of the distressed, were sufficient to strike astonishment into angels.

Then he showed it to the pastor of a Scottish Presbyterian church he occasionally attended, Reverend Hugh Knox. Knox was astounded by the sophistication of Hamilton's writing style and said that he would submit it to the *Royal Danish Gazette* for Alexander and enclosed a letter written by Hamilton that said:

> I am afraid, Sir, you will think this description more the effort of imagination than a true picture of realities. But I can affirm with the greatest truth, that there is not a single circumstance touched upon, which I have not absolutely been an eyewitness to.

Knox was well aware that the Church wasn't supposed to educate illegitimate children, but he considered that policy unfair and took a special interest in Alexander. So, he tutored him in the sciences and humanities. Knox had a large library, and Alexander took full advantage of it. When he wasn't working, Hamilton read some of the works of Alexander Pope, a poet of that day, and Plutarch, the Greek-Roman chronicler. Reverend Knox then started a fund to send Alexander to the United States. Many people in the community, including Hamilton's firm of Kortright and Cruger, financed him to go to the colonies in British America for a proper education. They knew this boy was special and that his talents should be employed toward more productive ends.

Boston

The "West Indian boy," as he was known, arrived in the port of Boston in October of 1772 and was met by Hugh Mulligan, a customer of the Cruger firm where Hamilton had worked. Through Hugh, Hamilton met Hugh's brother, Hercules Mulligan, when he moved to New York and Hercules offered him lodging there. Hercules then arranged for Alexander to take some college preparatory courses at Elizabethtown Academy in New Jersey in 1773. There, Hamilton met the illustrious William Livingston, who shared the same religious faith with him, that of Presbyterianism. Livingston was a wealthy man and was in the process of building an estate there, now called Liberty Hall. Hamilton was then boarding at Elizabethtown Academy and often visited Livingston, as did many of the other young men from the academy. In the winter, Hamilton even lived with the Livingstons. Following his term at Elizabethtown, Hamilton applied to the College of New Jersey (later Princeton University) on the condition that he would be put on the fast-track as he wanted to complete his education as soon as possible. They turned him down because of that condition, but he had simultaneously applied to King's College (currently Columbia University) in New York and was accepted in 1773 as a special student.

During the early 1770s, there were rumors and whispers about rebellion against the British control of the colonies. There were political unrest and protests due to the increase of taxes levied upon them. In the taverns and on the college campuses, colonists began to split into camps—those who supported British domination were known as the Loyalists and those who fostered rebellion were known as the Patriots. Hamilton had come from a background of repression in Nevis and Saint Croix, and here was a country that promised more freedom and opportunity. Alexander—while attending the King's College—formed a debating club. He was incensed by the offenses against the rights of the colonists and was tired of being simply a victim of his circumstances.

In late 1772, the British East India Company, which imported tea to America, was in financial straits. Tea was the most popular beverage in America, and the British levied a tea tax upon the colonists to make up for the shortfall. The colonists had already been incensed at the fact that they had no representation in the British Parliament, and they now realized that they had no control at all over the export taxes they remitted to Great Britain. When the Patriots dumped barrels of tea overboard into the Boston Harbor in December 1773 at the event later called the "Boston Tea Party," Hamilton cheered and presented an energetic appeal to his debating club members, saying that such protests "will prove the salvation of North America and her liberties," otherwise "fraud, power, and the most odious oppression will rise triumphant over social happiness and freedom." When Hamilton heard the contrary opinions of the president of King's College, Myles Cooper, he was astonished because he had always respected Cooper's viewpoints. Cooper wished for the country to continue to be subservient to Great Britain. At one time, Cooper was even heard to have called the people of Boston a "crooked and perverse generation," adding that their colonial charter should be rescinded. That puzzled Hamilton, who had always considered himself to be a good judge of character.

Following the Boston Tea Party, the colonies elected delegates to meet in Philadelphia and discuss how to deal with Britain's oppressive actions. This assembly became known as the

Continental Congress, and William Livingston himself was elected as a representative.

Hamilton's college president, Myles Cooper, was among a group of Loyalists who were very active in their opposition to that congress. One member of Cooper's inner circle was another Anglican minister, Samuel Seabury, who published a retort about the impropriety of holding such meetings in a long pamphlet called *Free Thoughts on the Proceedings of the Continental Congress held at Philadelphia, Sept. 5, 1774; Wherein their errors are exhibited, their reasonings confuted.* Seabury signed the lengthy thesis "A. W. Farmer," and it was published in the *New York Gazetteer.* In this, Seabury states:

> Will you choose such committees? Will you submit to them should they be chosen by the weak, foolish, turbulent part of the country people? Do as you please, but by HIM that made me, I will not. No, if I must be enslaved, let it be by a KING at least and not by a parcel of upstart lawless Committeemen.

In 1775, while he was still attending college, Hamilton, who was never averse to controversy, anonymously wrote *A Full Vindication of the Measures of the Congress from the calumnies of their enemies in answer to A Letter under the signature of A. W. Farmer.* In it, he moved to a discussion of the rights of man to make his own choices, questioning very directly:

> What then is the subject of our controversy with the mother country—It is this: whether we shall preserve that security to our lives and properties which the law of nature and the genius of the British constitution and our colonial charters afford us, or whether we shall resign them into the hands of the British House of Commons, which is no more privileged to dispose of them than the Grand Mogul?

Chapter 2 – From Pen to Sword

It took only four days for Hamilton and his classmates in New York to hear the news that the port of Boston was closed to all but British warships. Then Hamilton and his colleagues from college got word about a clash between the British regiments and the patriotic militia from Boston, the Minutemen. General Thomas Gage, the British Governor of Massachusetts Bay Colony, had infiltrated the interior of the colony in search of hidden caches of weapons. The Minutemen, aided by patriotic locals, followed the British regiments through Concord, and a deadly conflict broke out in Lexington on April 19th, 1775. What Hamilton and his classmates heard was that the losses of the British numbered 73 and 49 Patriots lay dead near a bridge crossing.

Anger erupted amongst the colonists, and on April 24th, thousands of students and New Yorkers protested at city hall. In May, a group who knew that Hamilton's college president, Myles Cooper, had Loyalist leanings rushed into his campus residence. An alumnus by the name of Nicholas Ogden woke Cooper, and the frightened man in his nightcap peered out the window. Even though he had political differences with Myles Cooper, Hamilton and his friend, Robert Troup, didn't feel that he deserved to be injured. So, he and Troup held off the mob on the stairway.

Hamilton hollered to the crowd that violence against this defenseless man would only hurt their cause. His words weren't entirely effective, but it allowed Cooper enough time to escape and rush toward the Hudson River. After wandering around all night in his nightclothes, Cooper came upon a British warship, boarded it, and headed back to England!

Many colonists still discussed the possibility of reconciliation with Great Britain. Hamilton picked up his pen again and sent out some bold letters against reconciliation that were published in the *New York Gazetteer*. That newspaper was a Loyalist-leaning paper, but it often printed letters from the Patriots, as it had done in the "A. W. Farmer" letters. The Rivington Press, which published the *Gazetteer*, was destroyed by an angry mob, and the presses were damaged beyond repair. Afterward, a sign was placed outside the shop which read, "The printing of the *New York Gazetteer* will be discontinued until America shall be blessed with the restoration of good government." Hamilton had been upset by the pending attack on Myles Cooper, and now he felt the same about the livelihood of James Rivington, the printer. He wrote to John Jay, a well-known statesman who had married William Livingston's daughter. Jay was from New York and was also a delegate to the First Continental Congress. Hamilton said to Jay that although he felt the newspaper was detestable, he was concerned about the lawless nature of the colonists' retaliation.

Hamilton spoke to some of the other students at King's College, and they decided to join a newly forming militia. The militia drilled behind St. Paul's Chapel, which was nearby. The militia called itself the "Corsicans," later renamed the "Hearts of Oak." Every morning, Hamilton drilled with the other college volunteers under Edward Fleming, who used to be a captain in a British regiment.

Some of the Governors' Councils in the colonies had also been suspended by the British, so there was a need for a colonial-based assembly to recall the Continental Congress into its second session in May 1775. They called again upon delegates from each of the colonies to meet in Philadelphia to plan a course of action. The members of the assembly had no authority to govern but took it upon themselves to form a provisional government. They then circulated a resolution among the colonies advising that each should declare independence from Great Britain. After some discussion among the colonies, it was agreed to. Richard Lee of Virginia then proposed that the colonies as a unit declare themselves independent from Great Britain. So, the Articles of Confederation were drawn up, the group recognized the need to form foreign alliances for military aid, and a paper currency was issued called the Continental Dollar. Plans were then made to create a formal declaration of independence, and Thomas Jefferson, the prolific young writer from Virginia, was chosen to write it. At that meeting, George Washington, who had military experience while working under British commanders, was chosen as the Commander-in-Chief of the Continental Army. Word went out, and colonial recruits came from all parts of the colonies. Some even trained themselves, forming smaller units and looked for opportunities to join up with the main forces.

New York had established a local Provincial Congress and formed an artillery company to defend the colony. There, Hamilton met a friend of his, William Livingston. Hamilton not only had the experience from his college militia drills, but he had studied up on military tactics and told Livingston about it. Then he was introduced to Colonel Alexander McDougall, a Scotsman, who was pleased to hear about Hamilton's knowledge and even recommended that Hamilton be the captain of an artillery company. His college roommate, Robert Troup, also spoke with John Jay on Hamilton's behalf. Alexander Hamilton was then appointed the Captain of Artillery for the Provincial Government of New York. Hamilton then dropped out of school, but the school was suspended shortly thereafter at any rate because of the unrest in the colonies.

As a captain, Hamilton became popular with the men when he negotiated their pay, which was to be the same as the forces recruited for the regular Continental Army George Washington was forming.

On June 28th, 1776, George Washington discovered a traitor among his Continental Army, a man named Thomas Hickey. Hickey had organized a plot to murder Continental officers and revealed the location of colonists' magazines to the British, after which they were blown up. To make an example of him, Washington had him convicted of treason, and he was hanged at the Bowery in the southern area of Manhattan Island. Today, little is known of that event.

In July, Admiral Samuel Graves had now assumed command of a large number of British man-of-war ships, and they were sitting just below Manhattan at Sandy Hook, New Jersey, ready to stage an amphibious attack on Manhattan Island. In the meantime, Washington had gathered as many as 20,000 Continental troops. The newly formed army lacked sufficient ammunition, so Washington issued orders to remove any leaden window frames in order to melt them down to make bullets. To the northeast, the British commander, General William Howe, had his brother, Admiral Richard Howe, sail up through the Narrows in their warships. The Narrows is a deep waterway between Staten Island and Long Island paralleling the East River alongside Manhattan. Colonel McDougall made contact with General Washington and was told to station Captain Hamilton and his troops at the Battery, located at the southern tip of Manhattan. From their vantage point, they could observe the whole action.

On July 12th, Captain Hamilton was confronted with a 44-gun battleship, the *Phoenix*, and a 28-gun frigate, the *Rose*, with its guns firing. Hamilton's artillery unit fired incessantly upon the ships, and then Hamilton had his men light the cannons. To the horror of his soldiers, the cannons malfunctioned, blowing up six of his own men and wounding others. Due to the lack of experience of many of his men, more mishaps occurred. Hamilton was emotionally crushed by this circumstance and rapidly learned that war was a dirty and brutal business and hardly a reliable one.

Washington's ragtag troops were scattered in fortifications built up on Brooklyn Heights at the southern end of Long Island. However, thousands of British and the mercenary Hessian troops penetrated those defenses, threatening the lives of the people living there. The British had at least twice as many enemy forces than the Continental Army had at that time.

In August, Hamilton, under the Continental Artillery Captain John Lamb, ordered the seizure of 24 cannons from the Battery. They stole up the shore and started dragging the cannons away, but a Loyalist had given the British advance warning. The British then opened fire on Hamilton and his men from a barge they had just offshore. Hamilton and his unit returned fire but kept tugging on the cannons. Hercules Mulligan, whom Hamilton had roomed with in New York, was also in his regiment, and the two fought side by side during this action. As a result of their efforts, Hamilton and Mulligan were able to take 21 of the 24 cannons, which they dragged uptown to city hall.

Stealthily, Washington and his troops in Brooklyn Heights were forced to make a nighttime retreat. The British then pillaged their farms and devastated the countryside of Brooklyn, which Washington had to abandon because there was nothing he could do to stop them.

Washington and his troops then marched to White Plains, New York. The Americans dug in around the base of Chatterton Hill and planted themselves in various positions up the hill. Hamilton mounted the hill and placed his 2-gun battery at the top. The British then moved in from Brooklyn Heights, swarming the area, and began climbing the hill. Every time the British made any progress, they were beaten back by the Americans toward the nearby town of Sleepy Hollow. In the course of their halting progress, the head of one of the Hessians was blown off, and that gave rise to "The Legend of Sleepy Hollow," which is about a headless horseman who haunts the region.

Later in the battle, Colonel Johann Rall joined up with the British forces with thousands of more men. Ferociously, they split up Hamilton's militia, who were forced to cross the Bronx River and rejoin Washington's main division in the hills.

Following that, Lieutenant-General Hugh Percy also arrived, thus reinforcing the British, and they planned on surrounding Washington. However, a driving rain fell, and they were forced to delay their plans. That was fortunate for Washington and his men, who would have been hopelessly outnumbered and defeated but were now offered the opportunity to retreat.

Surreptitiously, Hamilton and his men kept calm during the orderly retreat, crossing the Hudson River and moving into New Jersey. As they moved southward, Washington reorganized his men and posted young Hamilton high on the riverbanks with rifles drawn to pick off the British who were likely to pursue them downstate. Hamilton directed volleys against columns of British regiments marching on the lower ground. They were headed toward the Raritan River on the way to the capital city of Trenton, New Jersey.

Washington had Hamilton hold up the rear of his forces, and they moved west across New Jersey, marching southward from New Brunswick and crossing the Delaware River and encamping alongside it. They were then directly west of the Hessians, who were stationed at a garrison nearby. The enemy was celebrating at the home of a Loyalist in Trenton the day after Christmas. Captain Hamilton and his associate, Captain Forrest, took their artillery company and covered King's Street and Queen's Street which led into the city. Then Washington and his men began their attack. Hamilton and Forrest—along with Edward Hand's Pennsylvanian units—fired upon the garrison, and Lieutenant Andreas Weiderhold hollered out "Der Feind!" ("The Enemy!"), summoning his soldiers who came rushing out. Hamilton and the other Continental troops met heavy action on lower King's Street and Queen's Street. They killed and captured hundreds of them. During the street fighting, the commander of the second unit of the Hessian divisions, Johann Rall, was fatally wounded. This battle, known as the Battle of Trenton, was a tremendous victory for the Patriots. The Continental forces then moved back to the Pennsylvania side of the river to plan their next strategy. Washington and his officers felt that an attack on Lieutenant-General Charles Cornwallis and Lieutenant-Colonel Charles Mawhood at Princeton would be feasible.

In January of 1777, Washington's troops awoke in the middle of the night then secretly sailed back across the Delaware River. From there, his forces moved northeast along the trail called the Post Road toward Princeton and spotted the British. Washington shouted to his men, "It's a fox chase, my boys!" Hamilton's 5th regiment, along with the Virginia Continentals, pounded the British under Lieutenant-Colonel Mawhood. The British fell in such large numbers that Mawhood ordered a retreat. Most of the British soldiers followed Mawhood outside of Princeton, but a smaller unit rushed down the street and hid in Nassau Hall, the city administration building. Hamilton grabbed his cannons, collected his men outside the structure, and pommeled the building. Some of Hamilton's men then stormed the door and broke it down. A white flag waved from one of the windows, and 194 of the British soldiers surrendered. It was yet another triumph for the Continental Army. After the battle, a senior officer remarked about Hamilton, "I noticed a youth, a mere stripling, small, slender with a cocked hat pulled down over his eyes, apparently lost in thought, with his hand resting on a cannon, and every now and then patting it, as if it was a favorite horse or pet plaything."

Washington encamped at various places in New Jersey, moving about frequently to avoid detection. In the spring of 1777, Washington was moving southward along the eastern border of Pennsylvania. Hamilton and his artillery force were then ordered to take possession of a flour warehouse so the British couldn't seize it. As he was riding, Hamilton's horse was shot out from under him, and he had to swim across the Schuylkill River to rejoin Washington.

Washington later sent young Hamilton to secure reinforcements to protect some of the areas around Philadelphia. Hamilton approached General Horatio Gates with the request. After Gates selected a brigade, Hamilton noted that the very small body of men Gates gave him had all the earmarks of being new recruits, so he demanded more troops with experience as well. Gates was astonished at Hamilton's brashness, but he also realized that this young man wasn't easily fooled and responded with what Hamilton knew was needed.

Hamilton as an Aide de Camp

Washington was impressed with Hamilton's performance in Brooklyn, Trenton, and Princeton. Desirous of having this brave and brash young man continue to serve with him, Washington promoted Hamilton to the rank of lieutenant-colonel. John Laurens from South Carolina as well as Aaron Burr from New Jersey were also aides-de-camp. All of them were not only skilled militarily but had clerical knowledge and could write well. Hamilton and the others served under Washington for four years and worked with intelligence operations, negotiations, diplomacy, and served as his emissaries as well. Hamilton served as Washington's aide-de-camp from 1777 to 1781.

In the year 1777, the French military colonel Marquis de Lafayette arrived with forces to help in the effort, even though France wasn't officially an ally yet. Washington knew that Hamilton spoke French fluently because his mother was a French Huguenot, so he had the Marquis speak with Hamilton on his behalf. In time, Hamilton befriended Lafayette, and the French Marquis even spent time with Hamilton and his family several years later.

During the Revolutionary War, they marched alongside each other throughout New Jersey. At the Battle of Monmouth on June 28th, 1778, they parted company temporarily when Burr and Laurens had their horses shot out from under them. Laurens recovered, but Burr had been more severely injured, so it took him more time.

The Battle of Monmouth took place near the Monmouth Courthouse in New Jersey. When the Continental Army was near the courthouse, Washington's officers suggested various actions they might engage in against the British troops, under Sir Henry Clinton, who were in the area. General Charles Lee felt that it might be better to subject the British to running skirmishes, which would use far fewer men. Washington then sent out Hamilton to assess the situation. Hamilton reported back that the British army was quite formidable there and would require a huge number of Continental forces along with supportive forces to back them up in order to achieve victory, saying to Washington, "To attack in this situation without being supported by the whole army at a distance, would be folly in the extreme." Instead, Hamilton suggested an attack on the British rearguard. Lee, on the other hand, was convinced that the British were practically invincible, and it would be far better just to harass them and kill the stragglers. Washington thought about it and then ordered Lee to attack with 5,000 men with a backup force under the Marquis de Lafayette, who was about a mile away. During the course of the Battle of Monmouth, Hamilton noted that the British were reinforcing their flank, so he sent word to the Marquis de Lafayette to join up with him. Rather than stay in the fight while waiting for Lafayette's reinforcements, though, Lee and his group retreated. Washington was furious and took off looking for Lee. Finding him, Washington insisted Lee make a stand. After the Battle of Monmouth, the British proclaimed a victory, but so did the Americans. The results of this battle were inconclusive, leading to no clear advantage on either side.

Hamilton was so dissatisfied by the conduct of Lee that he felt that Lee was either "a driveler in the business of soldiership or something worse." When Lee heard that, he wrote a letter to Washington and demanded a court-martial against Hamilton. Henry Laurens, his fellow officer and friend, testified along with Hamilton that Lee participated in a disgraceful retreat that was neither necessary nor ordered. As a result of the court-martial, Lee was reprimanded and convicted on three counts: 1) disobedience to orders, 2) misbehavior in making an unnecessary, disorderly, and shameful retreat, and 3) disrespect to the commander-in-chief. He was found guilty on all three counts, and he was suspended from the army for a year.

After the war, Lee went to Philadelphia and published his "Vindication," "damning George Washington…and congress." He also struck hard against Hamilton and Laurens, calling them Washington's "hatchet men."

Hamilton and Laurens became very close friends. In a letter to Laurens in 1779, Hamilton said to him, "I have written you five times since I left Philadelphia and I should have written you more had you made proper return. But like a jealous lover when I thought you slighted my caresses, my affection was alarmed and vanity piqued." Some speculate the two might have been involved in a homosexual relationship, although there isn't enough evidence for this to be proven.

In the position as Washington's aide-de-camp, Hamilton was in the midst of all the jealousies and politicking of the men who frequented Washington's offices. During that time, Hamilton also kept a close watch on the naïve Continental Congress and was critical of those who were individualistic and favored states' rights over that of a strong national government. Hamilton always expressed himself freely and made his opinions known among his contemporaries. Sometimes that got him into trouble, especially when people exaggerated his words or put a negative spin on what he said. In a coffee shop in Philadelphia, someone spread the rumor that Hamilton said, "It was high time for the people to rise, join George Washington, and turn congress out of doors." Of course, he had said no such thing, but there were many who were envious of Washington's fondness for Hamilton. Many politicians considered Hamilton to be no more than an ignorant military officer who "needed to be put in his place."

When these stories circulated, Hamilton suspected that the sources were from the supporters and friends of General Charles Lee, who was humiliated after the court-martial. Meticulously, Hamilton traced the story to Francis Dana, a member of the Continental Congress. Dana, however, claimed he heard it from Reverend William Gordon, who regularly sent Washington advice about the war. He loved scandals and gossip, and he frequently spread falsities. Once he even accused another aide-de-camp, Joseph Reed, of promoting the support of Charles Lee as a replacement for George Washington as the commander-in-chief.

Gordon repeated the rumor that Hamilton had denigrated Congress at the Philadelphia coffee shop, and then in 1778, he boldly wrote to Washington that "You have some treacherous person about you that betrays you and our officers to the enemy." Hamilton knew Gordon was referring to him.

Gordon had secretly hoped that perhaps Washington would hire him to be a spy to ferret out subversives in the troops. Washington was impatient and annoyed with this, calling it "tittle-tattle" that would only delay their business of war. However, the politicians in those days were incurable gossip-mongers, and Washington's words did little to stop the spread of rumors.

Marriage

While Hamilton functioned as Washington's aide-de-camp, he was stationed near Morristown, New Jersey, during their winter encampment there in 1780. Eliza Schuyler, a New York socialite, had been staying with her aunt nearby during this time. Hamilton had met her briefly at the Schuyler Mansion in Albany when he had been meeting with some dignitaries on Washington's behalf. Hamilton wanted to marry into wealth. In fact, he even asked for a marital reference from his friend, John Laurens. He said to John, "She must be young, handsome (I lay most stress upon a good shape) sensible (a little learning will do), well-bred. On politics, I am indifferent as to what side she shall be on, I have arguments that will easily convert her to mine." Those charismatic qualities of his served Hamilton well throughout his life and did much to determine his motivations and political drive.

Eliza was wealthy, as her father, Philip, was a rich slave trader. Hamilton had nothing by the way of money or land but pursued her nevertheless. Hamilton had met her several times at the Schuyler mansion. Although Hamilton's efforts were fruitless, he kept up a correspondence with Eliza. Hamilton was bright and charming, and Eliza's father was impressed with him, despite the fact that Hamilton wasn't from a wealthy family. Therefore, he didn't mind the disparity in their social statuses.

While Hamilton was stationed with Washington at Morristown, New Jersey, Eliza was staying with her aunt nearby, and Hamilton enjoyed her company whenever he had the opportunity. Eliza became intrigued with Alexander, and by April, she and Hamilton were engaged.

Hamilton, as an aide-de-camp, resumed his duties at Morristown. Then it came to pass that Major John André was captured in a plot with Benedict Arnold to capture West Point and was charged with treason. Eliza told Hamilton that she had a crush on him as a young girl, and she asked Hamilton to intercede on his behalf. In order to impress Elizabeth, Hamilton interceded and asked for mercy for André after he was captured.

They took a very brief honeymoon, after which Eliza joined Hamilton in New Windsor, near Trenton. During their downtime, Eliza and Hamilton worked together on some of his political writings, including financial advice for Robert Morris, a Patriot and merchant who oversaw some of the procurement of supplies for the war.

Alexander and Eliza had eight children. Their first son, Philip, was born in 1782, and in 1783, they moved to Wall Street, which was in a wealthy area of New York City. Hamilton had his eye on status. A year later, they gave birth to a daughter, Angelica, a sensitive child who stayed with the Schuylers in Albany during the war. They had six other children after that, including John Church Hamilton, who wrote his father's biography.

Hamilton at the Siege of Yorktown

As his work became more clerical, Hamilton yearned to be given a field command. He then asked Washington if he could step down from his role as aide-de-camp and serve actively in February 1781. Although the president hesitated at first, he finally relented in March and assigned Hamilton to a light infantry unit under Lafayette which was bearing down on Yorktown, Virginia, in September of 1781. The British commander, Lieutenant-General Charles Cornwallis, was there, but the harbor was blocked in by the French fleets of Admiral de Grasse to protect the Continental forces inland. Cornwallis was low on supplies because he couldn't gain access to the shore and was desperate for help. He had been promised reinforcements from General Henry Clinton from up north, but they hadn't arrived yet.

Hamilton was in charge of deconstructing Redoubt No. 10, built by the British outside Yorktown. In order to do that, Hamilton's artillery needed to get within firing range of the British regulars. Feverishly, he had his Continental and French soldiers quietly sneak up the earthen domes of the redoubt and then rip apart the hastily constructed wooden fences and tear out the spikes meant to slow their advance. Upon reaching the top of the dome, Hamilton and his men stormed down on the British troops, shooting round after round from their muskets. Many of the surrounding redoubts were being simultaneously attacked. This action caught the trenched-in British by surprise, but the fight continued on for three more grueling days. On October 17th, a huge white flag was waved from Cornwallis' division, and it was over. A little over 155 British soldiers lay dead on the uneven field saturated with blood, littered with twisted metal and torn-up uniforms. 28 Americans and 60 French were killed. The British band played "The World Turned Upside Down" as the two opposing sides met to declare the end of the hostilities on October 19th:

> A ragged band they called the Diggers
>
> Came to show the people's will
>
> They defied the landlords; they defied the law;
>
> There were the dispossessed
>
> Reclaiming what was theirs.

Alexander Hamilton and John Laurens were two of the junior officers who stood behind Washington at the official surrender ending the American Revolution.

Chapter 3 – Onset of Hamilton's Political Career

Now that the Revolutionary War was over, Hamilton resigned his military commission and studied law. He passed the bar in 1782—an amazing accomplishment in such a brief period of time. Hamilton was brilliant and took to the study of law rapidly. He voraciously studied one of the standard reference books in the field at the time, Sir William Blackstone's *Commentaries on the English Common Law*. He immediately attracted wealthy clients in his home state of New York, like maritime insurance companies and wealthy merchants. In 1779, New York passed "An Act for the Forfeiture and Sale of the Estates of Persons who have adhered to the Enemies of this State, and for declaring the Sovereignty of the People within the same," or, for short, the "Confiscation Law." By that law, whoever was convicted of loyalty to the British Crown forfeited their real and personal property, and the state was then permitted to seize and sell it. After the war, Hamilton realized that the country needed the former Loyalists, so he disagreed with this law and felt that they shouldn't be abandoned or exiled. Hamilton looked upon the former Loyalists as fodder for building a new nation whose central government had strength and was in support of the Federalist agenda, those who favored a strong central government. He looked upon these people as being able to help ensure the country didn't become just a weak confederation of states—each with their own agendas—which would most likely detract from the union. If an ex-Loyalist experienced success in this new nation, where his property rights were respected, he might indeed help them mature into a fully united America.

Another act passed in New York around this time was the Trespass Act of 1783. It allowed Patriots whose property had been seized or damaged by Loyalists or the British to collect damages. Hamilton defended clients accused of breaking those laws, regardless of whether they were Patriots or former Loyalists.

Of the cases Hamilton defended, three of them were landmark cases—*Lloyd v. Lewis* (1784), *Rutgers v. Waddington* (1784), and *Post v. Leonard* (1786). In the *Lloyd v. Lewis* case, Scudder Lewis was required to work John Lloyd's land for the British who had confiscated it during the war. Hamilton helped clarify the fact that a man—regardless of whether he was a Patriot or Loyalist—should not be convicted of aiding the enemy by virtue of the confiscation law because the land didn't belong to him and he worked it under duress. In the *Rutgers v. Waddington* case, the owner of a tavern, Eleanor Rutgers, was forced to flee her tavern when it was confiscated by the British. The tavern was then run by Mr. Joshua Waddington, who rented it from the British occupiers. In 1784, Rutgers sued Waddington for the rent. Hamilton defended Waddington and won the case by proving that the Treaty of Paris, signed on September 3rd, 1783, stipulated that the British were due the payments as a war debt. Furthermore, it trumped the Trespass Act in that case because it was a state law and in contradiction with the Treaty of Paris.

In the case between Anthony Post and James Leonard, Hamilton utilized the tool of judicial review, which calls for a reanalysis of the case by certified judges. In that case, Leonard had acquired the property after a judgment of forfeiture and proved it couldn't be confiscated after the fact.

Hamilton wrote two essays in *The Federalist Papers* regarding the confiscation law. In them, he said that in the case of a conflict, "the Constitution ought to be preferred to the statute."

The procedure of judicial review was later employed in the famous *Madison v. Marbury* case heard before the Supreme Court. When there is a constitutional collision between two mandates—one passed by a state and another by the U.S. Constitution—it is the constitutional law which prevails. Although there may be many cases meeting that criteria, even today, each of those cases needs to reach the level of the higher courts, perhaps even the Supreme Court, before a precedent can be established.

Aaron Burr and the Confiscation Acts

Aaron Burr disagreed with Hamilton's opinion. He felt that the properties that had been confiscated from the Loyalists during the Revolution should be redistributed among the Patriots and sold at a cut-rate price if the grantee wished. Along with other people, Burr seized property belonging to Loyalists. He was the grantee of 2 pieces of property at Trinity Church in southern Manhattan, 300 lots on Houston Street, and 3 shares of the Bank of New York. According to the new stipulation on the Confiscation Acts, Burr had to see to it that those lots were returned to the previous owners.

Congress of the Confederation

While Hamilton was practicing in New York, he was appointed as the New York representative for the newly forming Congress of the Confederation, or the Confederation Congress, to create federal laws for the new nation.

Briefly, there were thirteen articles:

> 1. The union shall be called the "United States of America."
>
> 2. Each state had its own powers in addition to those listed in the articles.

3. The union is a "league of friendship."

4. People may travel freely among the states, and criminals must be returned to their own states to face trials.

5. Each state had between two to seven members, and there is one vote per state.

6. The central government handles foreign relations, trade agreements, and declarations of war.

7. States may assign military ranks below that of general.

8. Money is to be raised by each state to support the central government.

9. Congress passes laws and handles foreign affairs like peace, war, and treaties.

10. A committee called the Committee of States acts for the central government when it's not in session.

11. Canada may join the union, if desired.

12. The union will pay war debts.

13. The Articles of Confederation will be perpetual unless altered by the states and Congress.

The Articles of Confederation were ratified on March 1st, 1781.

There were serious flaws with these articles. First of all, they emphasized the separation of the states, putting little weight upon the united aspect of the states and denying the central government the power it needed to enact measures passed by Congress. Although money came up in terms of paying war debts and supporting the central government, no method of collection nor enforcement was specified. It almost sounded as if such monies were to be donations. Hamilton, in 1780, indicted that the failure of the central government to regulate commerce resulted in a different procedure for buying and selling manufactured goods in each state. There was no court system established, save the fact that a criminal had to be returned to his or her own state. And each state had only one vote regardless of the size or population of the state.

Hamilton was unhappy with the weaknesses he saw in the articles, as he felt they didn't have sufficient power to run an entire nation. Early into the process, Hamilton disagreed with the proposed ideas, saying that "the confederation itself is defective and requires to be altered; it is neither fit for war, nor peace." While he understood that the states were oversensitive to having virtually no power of their own, he was also critical of the fact that a federal government that could do nothing but ask or recommend that the states provide sufficient resources to support an army and navy, pay for staff of learned men to analyze proposed legislation, or have any powers of enforcement would get nowhere. In 1780, he wrote a number of letters to James Duane, whom he knew through the Livingston family. Duane was a prominent lawyer, a member of Congress, and later became a senator in New York. Hamilton wrote to him saying,

> 1. The fundamental defect is a want of power in Congress...It may however be said that it has originated from three causes – an excess of the spirit of liberty which has made particular states show a jealousy of all power not in their own hands;

> 2. A diffidence in Congress of their own powers, by which they have been timid and indecisive in their resolutions, constantly making concessions to the states; and

> 3. A want of sufficient means at their disposal to answer public exigencies and fulfill their engagements with the army.

One of the cited flaws manifested itself almost immediately. Article 12 indicated that the union shall pay its war debt, but that didn't happen as planned.

The Newburgh Conspiracy

In March 1783, the army was encamped at Newburgh, New York. Many of the soldiers had yet to be paid and didn't receive the pension they'd been promised. Robert Morris, a wealthy financier who had been funding many of the military efforts, was now forced to take out loans, but he could no longer do so and still stay solvent. A delegation of influential officers, including Hamilton's friend General Alexander McDougall, and Robert Morris met with Congress regarding the matter.

Congress was divided on the issue, even though the treasury was empty. It was suggested that an "impost tax" be charged, but not all the states were willing to participate. General McDougall then sent out a letter under the pseudonym "Brutus," warning of a possible mutiny forming.

Washington got word of this crisis, and Hamilton advised him to intervene by manifesting his support of the military but to do it in a gentle way so that Congress would be coaxed to respond. Washington understood the impact of personally appearing before a crowd, so he rushed up to Newburgh to address the war veterans. The men were shocked by his unexpected visit. Washington addressed them courteously and asked them not to "sully the glory" they had attained and expressed full confidence in Congress. He then fumbled for his spectacles to read a letter and apologized to the men, saying, "Gentlemen, you must pardon me. I have grown old in the service of my country and now find that I am growing blind." This subtle chide won the day, and the crowd disbursed in shame. Everyone knew Washington never asked to be paid for his service.

Despite this protest, Congress failed to pass a tax twice—in 1783 and in 1785—to pay for this war debt.

Shays' Rebellion

In 1786, Massachusetts tried to resolve the issue of local war debt by levying a tax in the state. That tax was quite high—even higher than the taxes paid to Great Britain before the war. The farmers, mostly in western Massachusetts, had received some money from the state to compensate for expenses incurred during the war. However, it was insufficient. These farmers had taken out loans from the banks to plant new crops and hadn't yet found a profit on their harvest, so they couldn't make all their payments. Their Continental Dollars were now worthless because its value had diminished since the end of the war. They didn't have silver or gold to use as a form of currency either. Then the authorities in Boston started to arrest the deadbeats and begin foreclosure procedures. At first, the farmers attempted to resolve these issues in court, but the judges were denied entry by the angry mobs. An ex-soldier by the name of Daniel Shays rose up among them and took 600 armed men to shut down the main courthouse in Springfield. General William Shepard, head of the state militia, arrived and negotiated with Shays. Events quieted for a while after the Massachusetts legislature offered leniency in terms of loan repayments. They passed another bill setting stiff penalties for the rebels in custody and freed the sheriffs from responsibility if any insurgents were killed. That infuriated the public, and Governor James Bowdoin hired 4,400 troops under General Benjamin Lincoln.

The year was now 1787, and the rebellion had only escalated. The mob attempted to raid the Springfield arsenal but was met by General Shepard. Shepard's men fired above their heads at first but then shot some of the rebels. A section of the militia also assaulted a farmer along with his family in Groton.

Yet another rebel, Luke Day, and his men arrived to help out, and they were joined by Eli Parsons and 600 more men from the mountains. General Benjamin Lincoln then chased them northward, and the group finally disbursed by the end of August.

When John Hancock was elected governor, he pardoned the rebels. Hamilton and even Madison agreed that the national government needed to be stronger but that it also needed to establish fairer taxes; to them, the rebellion was the logical outcome of fiscal mismanagement. Although he rarely attended the sessions of Congress, Hancock attended the sessions related to the writing of the state constitution. This constitution was written by John Adams, and Hancock wholeheartedly approved of it. It was passed in 1780.

Trade Debt Crisis: Tariff Wars

Those states that had ports found it necessary to impose duties and tariffs on vessels that docked there for the purpose of conducting trade. That included not only foreign ships but those from other states. Bias entered into the system when some ports set up protectionist trade barriers between certain states which they perceived as being in direct competition with products manufactured from their own respective states. For example, the port of New York imposed clearance fees for ships also trading with New Jersey.

In 1786, at the behest of James Madison, a young statesman from Virginia, a meeting of representatives from the affected states met. The meeting was originally called the "Meeting of Commissions to Remedy Defects of the Federal Government," and it was later called the Annapolis Convention, named for the city in which it took place.

Only twelve delegates from five states showed up, one of whom was Alexander Hamilton. At that convention, it was determined that more decisive action must take place in order to resolve the problems, which now were of national importance. It was decided, therefore, that a serious rewrite of the Articles of Confederation was needed.

The Battle for State Recognition: Vermont vs. New York

The Confederation Congress was now meeting in order to rewrite the Articles of Confederation, and the people who considered themselves citizens of the "Vermont Republic" wanted representation at the convention. That area was originally designated as either a part of the state of New Hampshire or of New York in a disputed area called the New Hampshire Grants. But that was back in the year 1764, prior to the Revolution. There was a group of protesters in that territory who objected to those classifications called the "Green Mountain Boys," who were led by a dynamic man called Ethan Allen. After the war, the people who lived there didn't want to be a part of either New York or New Hampshire. They wanted to instead form a separate state called Vermont. During 1777, "Vermont" applied for statehood but was repeatedly denied, even though they had their own state government in place. New York insisted that Vermont was a part of New York, but Vermont vehemently objected. Then New York Governor George Clinton took the extraordinary measure of asking Congress to declare war on "Vermont." Congress was aghast at this and rendered no decision on the matter.

Alexander Hamilton, as a well-respected New Yorker, realized that it was up to him to step in and restore the peace so that the convention could go about its job of formulating a new constitution. Toward that end, Hamilton contacted their representative lawyer, Nathaniel Chipman, and they both agreed that Vermont merited the status of a separate state. However, such a change would be time-consuming, as New York was reluctant to give up some of its landholdings there.

Kentucky was also having similar difficulties, as the neighboring state of Virginia was trying to claim it as part of their state. Kentucky argued that they were recognized as "Kentucky" under the prior Articles of Confederation but had been dropped as a recognized state for this new Confederation Congress.

In 1788, Hamilton wrote that these matters should be the first order of business under the new constitution: "One of the first subjects of deliberations with the new congress will be the independence of Kentucky for which the southern states will be anxious. The northern will be glad to find a counterpoise in Vermont."

The entire matter was finally settled when New York gave up its claim on Vermont and resolved their fiscal encumbrances. Vermont and New York eventually ironed out their difficulties, but Vermont wasn't recognized as a state until 1791, after the Constitutional Convention. In 1792, Kentucky was granted statehood.

Constitutional Convention

In 1787, representatives of the states were elected to attend the Constitutional Convention that was to be held in Philadelphia between 1787 and 1789. George Washington was the undisputed president of the convention, and Alexander Hamilton was the delegate from New York. Hamilton had a preference for a strong central government, not unlike that of Great Britain. Therefore, he made a speech early in the convention supporting what was later called a "President-for-Life." He made this proposal as he wanted the U.S. president to establish policies without having to be concerned about his own reelection. As a safeguard, he suggested that a president could be dismissed for what he termed "bad behavior." He said, "The supreme Executive authority of the United States to be vested in a Governor to be elected to serve during good behavior—the election to be made by Electors chosen by the people in the Election Districts."

Hamilton also recommended that some privileges be added to the executive branch: 1) veto power; 2) responsibility to direct a war effort, but the Senate alone would have the power to declare war; 3) the power to make treaties approved by the Senate; 4) the appointment of officials for departments of war, foreign affairs, and finance, and 5) the ability to pardon crimes except that of treason.

Hamilton's vision was to have a legislative division consisting of a Senate and a house assembly. Senators would be elected for life, while house members would be elected periodically.

For the judicial department, Hamilton supported a life-term for the justices, provided they demonstrated what he called again "good behavior."

The members of the Constitutional Convention were surprised at Hamilton's proposal that a president should serve for life, and they called Hamilton's proposal the "British plan." One of the other delegates, James Madison, felt that Hamilton was a sympathizer of a monarchical structure of government.

Members of the convention deviated from Hamilton's British plan in terms of the role of the chief executive. However, they agreed with him in terms of a tripartite division; that is, that the government should be divided into three branches—the executive, the legislative, and the judicial. They also differed with his view that senators should be appointed for life.

It was further determined that an executive branch should handle the implementation of laws passed by Congress, the power to veto a law—unless two-thirds of Congress approves it—sign treaties with other nations, and the power to grant pardons to those convicted of federal crimes. It was to be supported by four heads of cabinets: 1) Secretary of the Treasury; 2) Secretary of State; 3) Secretary of War; and 4) Attorney General.

The legislative branch, or Congress, would be bicameral, that is divided into two: the House of Representatives and the Senate. Laws would be proposed, discussed, and debated by the House and then by the Senate. If the piece of legislation had sufficient support, it was to be passed along to the Senate for debate and voted upon.

Congress was to have the right to tax the citizens. In addition, Congress would establish an annual budget for the country and have the power to declare war. The Senate, not the House of

Representatives, however, was to have the ability to ratify treaties with other countries.

The judicial department would interpret the application of laws to particular situations. Juries would be appointed by the courts unless the defendant waived that right. The juries would then decide the guilt or innocence of the defendant, and the judge would pass sentence. If a jury trial was waived, the judge was to decide the case instead.

Although Hamilton had some reservations regarding the document in its final form, he far preferred this to the weaker Articles of Confederation and urged the people of New York to sign for ratification. The Constitution was then circulated among all the states for ratification, and it was ratified on June 21st, 1788.

Most of the people were expecting a modification of the Articles of Confederation, but this was a new and very different document from what the people expected.

The Federalist Papers

In order to shore up support from the states for the passage of the new Constitution, Alexander Hamilton, John Jay, and James Madison wrote 85 essays known as *The Federalist Papers*. Hamilton wrote under the pseudonym "Publius," a name he had used before. They were published in the largest newspapers in the region, including the *Independent Journal* and *The Daily Adviser*, in October 1787, and they were constantly reprinted in newspapers throughout the colonies for the rest of the year. In January 1788, they were published in book form, and it was titled *The Federalist: A Collection of Essays, Written in Favour of the New Constitution, as Agreed upon by the Federal Convention, September 17, 1787.*

After Hamilton died, a list came out, saying that Hamilton had written two-thirds of the essays alone. However, scholars now believe that some of those essays were indeed written by James Madison. This doesn't mean that Hamilton's contributions were lessened in any way. Hamilton wrote an astounding 51 articles, while James Madison wrote 29 and John Jay wrote only 5.

Some of the most influential essays that Hamilton wrote include Federalist No. 70, where Hamilton states that the country needs one chief executive, and Federalist No. 78, where he lays the groundwork for the idea of judicial review by the federal courts. In Federalist No. 6, Hamilton warns against competition among the states and says that men "have in too many instances abused the confidence they possessed; and assuming the pretext of some public motive, have not scrupled to sacrifice the national tranquility to personal advantage or personal gratification." In Federalist No. 34, Hamilton spells out the kinds of questions citizens should consider concerning taxes. "Suppose then the convention had been inclined to proceed upon the principle of repartition of the objects of revenue, between the Union and its members in PROPORTION to their comparative necessities; what particular fund could have been selected for the use of the States, that would not either have been too much or too little for their present, too much for their future wants?"

There were incessant arguments among the people about the general structure of this new government. People split into two groups: the Federalists and the Anti-Federalists. The Federalists were those who envisioned a strong central government, while the Anti-Federalists felt that a strong central government would squelch the rights of individual states. Violent written rebuttals full of hyperboles raced back and forth in the press. Each side painted nightmare scenarios of what would happen if the other side was to prevail.

When the governor of New York, George Clinton, read the Constitution, he called it "a monster with open mouth and monstrous teeth ready to devour all before it" and scribbled off his own pieces under the pseudonym "Cato." He had firm objections against a stronger central government. Patrick Henry of the former Massachusetts Minutemen characterized it as "the tyranny of

Philadelphia," and he even drew a comparison between the document and the "tyranny of George III." Hamilton, in particular, was hit with personal criticisms by those who knew he had used the pen name "Publius." These comments alluded to the fact that he was illegitimate and foreign-born. Knowing from whence the barbs were flung (Governor Clinton and his supporters), Hamilton handled it more objectively. It isn't known whether or not Clinton's supporters realized this was Hamilton's contribution, but he addressed the wider issues of international relations, and—in defense of the Constitution—he reminded his readers to note the series of checks and balances in this type of republication government not found in other political systems.

The First Election

New York City was considered the first capital of the United States. George Washington was elected as the first president of the country, as was expected, and John Adams was the vice president. For his Attorney General, he chose Edmund Randolph, who had served during the Constitutional Convention; for his Secretary of War, he chose Henry Knox, whose performance during the French and Indian War was excellent; for his Secretary of State, he chose Thomas Jefferson, who was excellent at foreign relations; and for his Secretary of the Treasury, he chose Alexander Hamilton, whose financial skills were known to him from his service as his aide-de-camp.

Washington wanted his Cabinet to be a group of people who had different ideas about governance. He liked the interchange of various ideas, hoping that one member might present the same issue from a different viewpoint.

Washington was an adept judge of personality and realized that there would be distinct differences between his fellow Virginian, Jefferson and the New Yorker Hamilton. Hamilton felt very strongly about the priority of national rights over states' rights in particular instances. However, Washington hoped that these two intellectuals might find some common ground between their two viewpoints that would satisfy most of the states. Washington also had the ability to understand their different political philosophies and lead them toward a compromise. Unfortunately, both were incredibly stubborn, and that never happened. They both became bitter political rivals over the sovereignty of states' rights and national rights, and neither one seemed to be able to compromise.

The Foreign War Debt Crisis

Not only were the Revolutionary War veterans owed money, but the foreign governments from whom America borrowed money were demanding payments. America's ambassador to England, John Adams, was placed in a very difficult position when he served there. Because the Articles of Confederation didn't allow a national government to enforce procedures for the collection of war debts, his only resource was to approach Congress and "ask" that they contribute funds. In addition, England had failed to remove some of its forts from northern New York through the terms of the Treaty of Paris. Adams had little power to have his own militia dismantle the forts. The heads of the British garrisons indicated that they would do so once the Americans had released the British property seized during the war.

Adams, as an ambassador, had also secured loans from wealthy Dutch bankers, but the federal government, again, had no financial machinery in place to satisfy these loans either. Likewise, the French government took enormous risks of both money and men to help America become independent.

Chapter 4 – Economy and the First National Bank

Hamilton and the Debt Crisis

One of America's first orders of business had to do with the procedures for paying its debt through its newly established Department of the Treasury under Alexander Hamilton. He called for the input of James Madison and Thomas Jefferson to tackle that issue. The country owed about 54 million dollars, and the states owed about 25 million. Hamilton expressed that concern very explicitly in his first report on public credit. He said:

> That exigencies are expected to occur in the affairs of nations in which there will be a necessity for borrowing. The loans in times of public danger especially from foreign war, are found an indispensable resource, even to the wealthiest of them. And that, in a country such as this, is possessed of little active wealth, or in other words, little moneyed capital, the necessity for that resource in such emergencies be proportionally urgent.

After the U.S. Constitution came into effect on March 4th, 1789, the new government had the authority to raise revenues through taxation. Through the Treasury Department, Hamilton had the freedom to charge a lower interest rate on land. Starting in 1790, he made regular payments to the French government. However, the total expenses incurred by the U.S. government exceeded the amount of money in the U.S. Treasury, so Hamilton sought out private loans through Dutch bankers. That helped to some extent, but money was still owed to the French. James Swan, an American banker, stepped in to assist and visited France to negotiate a settlement. He bought up the American loans, then turned around and sold those loans to others in exchange for a higher interest rate on the repayments. Americans and even the British, although unknowingly, bought shares in these securities. He did well with those, and the debts were finally being repaid.

The First Report on Public Credit

In January of 1790, Hamilton presented a three-part provision for paying back their debt using government bonds:

> 1. The foreign debt must be paid in full per the treaties.

> 2. The principal amount of the loan would be paid. Interest rates of four percent would be paid on short-term bonds; six percent interest would be paid for long-term bonds.

> 3. State debts would be assumed by the federal government, and interest wouldn't be due until 1792.

During the course of the war, federal certificates had been sold at a percentage of their stated value in order to raise capital rapidly. James Madison, whom Hamilton thought would support the provision, vehemently objected. Because the principal was to be paid in full plus interest, this would provide a windfall profit for those—mostly the wealthy Northerners—who had the resources to invest in the certificates. That would discriminate against those of lesser means who weren't able to purchase these certificates, like farmers, Madison said.

Hamilton felt that it was vital to pay state debts at their full price because some of the states had already been paid while others hadn't. The plans to repay the loans still owed to the federal government by some states were designed in such a way that the tax burdens would be evenly spread over the states for the next three years. The difficulty with this was the fact that it would be a logistical nightmare tracking down those individuals within the states that should be paid more. Hamilton admitted that there would be some inequalities, but he felt that those who received more money would reinvest it in the country. This is what is known today as the "trickle-down" theory.

 The debate continued in Congress for months. In addition, the press issued bitter criticisms toward Hamilton, calling his plan the "bastard of eastern speculators." After a great deal of time had passed and it was ascertained that there weren't enough sufficient votes in Congress to get a bill passed, Jefferson asked that Madison and Hamilton sit down to a dinner meeting to hash it out. As most of the opposition resided in Virginia, Madison and Jefferson felt they could muster the sufficient votes needed to pass a bill if Hamilton would agree to move the country's capital near the Potomac River, which was around the halfway mark between the North and the South. Hamilton agreed, indicating that this transition from Philadelphia, which was the current U.S. capital, needed to be gradual in order to assuage the concerns of the public in and around Philadelphia.

The now-famous "dinner deal" was the last time that Alexander Hamilton, Thomas Jefferson, and James Madison would work together and emerge in a "win-win" situation.

The Second Report on Public Credit and the National Bank

In December of 1790, Hamilton indicated that, in order to handle these transactions, a national bank should be established. Madison and Jefferson, among others, objected to the establishment of the bank on the grounds that is was unconstitutional, and Washington was hesitant about it as well. Hamilton, however, argued that the government should not refuse to do for a nation what they could do for a person. There were private banks and corporations in the states run by individuals and boards of directors. In addition, this bank would not be an agency of the government, and Hamilton indicated that a government was, by its nature, sovereign.

Southerners like Madison and Jefferson simply didn't trust banks. First of all, such a bank would have special privileges that private banks didn't have, and it would diminish the importance of state banks who kept the smaller investors in mind. Secondly, this bank would be more of a profit-making vehicle for the wealthy who had more to invest, and they were more likely to invest their money in manufacturing than farming. Thirdly, this bank would be run by the wealthier investors who would cater to the needs of their friends more than the common good, and there was nothing in the Constitution giving the federal government the right to establish a bank in the first place.

Usually, banking and finance were handled by the Northerners, and the trust level between the North and the South was shaky. In order to include the contribution from the South, Hamilton stressed that fact that the United States, up until this point, had been too dependent upon imports from Britain and Europe in general. To balance that off, he encouraged the agricultural market to produce more crops and ship some overseas. In addition, they levied tariffs on imports from Great Britain and other countries. To stimulate new businesses, Hamilton also subsidized some new industries. Washington was convinced by Hamilton's arguments and signed the Funding Act of 1791. The bank was also chartered in that year and was set to expire in 1811. The First Bank of the United States was built in Philadelphia.

Initial Steps Toward Capitalization

To start the bank off on a good footing, custom houses were set up for the collection of tariffs owed by foreign shippers under the Customs Bureau, which had been established in 1789. During the Revolutionary War, smuggling was common. Therefore, shipping routes and smuggler networks were already in place, so they simply fired up once again. In order to prevent the non-payment of tariffs, the country used the Revenue Cutter Service, which had been active during the war. As part of the Funding Act of 1790, those ships were armed, and arrangements were made to build more. It was their function to guard the eastern shore of the United States, enforce the tariffs, curtail piracy, and later on prevent the slave trade from reaching the country's shores when it was prohibited in early 1808. In addition, they could transport government officials and even carry the mail. Ben Franklin had already been the Postmaster General in 1753, and he was made responsible for creating and regulating mail delivery, utilizing the Revenue Cutters. In 1792, the Post Office Department was created. Postal inspections were systematized, and their function was to prevent the smuggling of contraband and other abuses. The Revenue Cutter Service later evolved into today's U.S. Coast Guard.

In 1784, 1785, and 1787, Northwest Ordinances were passed, granting ownership of unsettled lands west of the Mississippi River in order to expand the area of the United States. Those territories were wide and open ranges. However, they eventually wanted to apply for statehood in order to have all the rights and protections provided by the federal government. Part of the process for achieving statehood was to have the government sell plots of land. That resulted in monetary resources for the federal treasury, although it wasn't enough to pay off the country's foreign debt.

Hamilton's goal, like that of all Americans, was to be self-sufficient enough to buy and sell among the states, as well as to promote a healthy export business. Unlike Jefferson and Madison, George Washington didn't feel that the country was destined to be primarily an agricultural society. In 1789, Washington chided Congress, saying that free people should "promote such manufactories as tend to render them independent of others for essential." Congress asked Hamilton to prepare a report on the state of manufacturing in the country in order to make plans to establish a more independent economy.

The U.S. Mint

The First Bank of the United States had issued U.S. paper currency, but people were using the Spanish peso in addition. Hamilton felt that the United States should also have its own coinage. Therefore, in 1792, the Coinage Act was passed. It was the first building to be built under the Constitution, and its first coins were the ten-dollar gold Silver Eagle coin and the silver dollar. Coinage for less than that was created in denominations from a half-penny to fifty cents.

The Beginning of Industry

Hamilton wanted America to develop its own industries and manufacture truly American products, not only to pay off the war debts but to support the American people who lived within the country. In fact, the population was steadily increasing, and the administration needed to see to it that their economic needs were met.

In 1790, Alexander Hamilton appointed Tench Coxe, an economist and merchandizer, as the Assistant Secretary of the Treasury. Coxe had served as a delegate at the Continental Congress from 1788 to 1789. During the course of his mercantile experiences in England, Coxe indicated that the textile industry in England was superior to that in America. Interested in the industrial improvements that England possessed, they hired a man, Andrew Mitchell, to check out textile-making devices that were used over there. Mitchell made sketches of the machinery he was able to observe and passed them along to America.

While there, Mitchell discovered a British weaver named George Parkinson, who worked with an invention created by Richard Arkwright of Lancashire. He had created a device called a "spinning frame," which—when combined with horsepower, hydropower, and, later, a steam engine—could convert cotton to something called "cotton lap," a precursor in the yarn-making process. After improvements to his unit, Arkwright received a patent for another one of the units used in the process, a card-making machine. It was capable of producing long skeins of yarn suitable for weaving and crocheting. With a combination of those machines, Arkwright opened up cotton mills in Great Britain. In March of 1791, the U.S. government awarded a patent to Parkinson for his design for a flax mill, even though the affair had a tint of industrial espionage. There were, though, differences between Arkwright's designs and Parkinson's.

After that, Tench Coxe established the "Society for Establishing Useful Manufactures or S.E.U.M." The society envisioned creating automatic processes for the manufacture of other goods, such as women's shoes, stockings, hats, carpets, and the like. William Duer along with three other financiers of the society, Alexander Macomb, John Dewhurst, and Royal Flint, were also major investors in the First National Bank.

Hamilton helped Coxe write the prospectus for the society to help distribute to potential investors. An initial stock offering was made, and it was an enormous revenue-raising measure to help the burgeoning company. The capitalization of the company would come in part from the purchase of government bonds. They selected a site near the Passaic Falls in New Jersey, which could be used to supply the hydropower needed to operate the machinery. Hamilton then showed it to Governor William Paterson, who was very excited about the profit this would bring into his state. In his honor, the city for the site of the plant was called Paterson. From that point on, Paterson grew as an industrial city.

Report on Manufactures

In 1791, Hamilton indicated that America was, in effect, isolated from the rest of the world in terms of commerce. Manufacturing needed to be set up like that of the Passaic Falls project. In fact, once other manufacturers and merchants heard about the industrial plan, they wanted to emigrate to the United States. To them, it was a land of opportunity and new untapped markets.

Hamilton figured that the addition of moderate tariffs for imported goods could raise revenue without threatening the growth of home industries. A portion of those tariffs, he reasoned, could be used to provide subsidies for start-up companies. Given a sufficient profit from tariffs, that money could be targeted to build roads and canals.

There was, as might be predicted, a great deal of opposition to this report. Most of the country had, up until 1790, been agrarian-based. James Madison, in particular, objected to the preference given to those involved in manufacturing unless it was handled properly. He feared that corruption and favoritism would enter the system because politicians might be unduly influenced. The farming community had no subsidies, and many felt that put them at a distinct disadvantage. Today, however, that situation is reversed because farming is subsidized, mostly due to the cost of land in the agrarian sector and unpredictable weather.

Eventually, Congress adopted most of Hamilton's policies in this report because of the protective nature of tariffs. However, it remained a bone of contention between the North and the South up until the Civil War (1861 to 1865.)

Dawn of the Political Parties

The delegates of the Constitutional Convention differed significantly on one issue—that concerning the amount of power granted to the executive branch and the power granted to Congress. The Articles of Confederation had been scrapped due to the fact that nearly all of the power rested in the hands of the states, leaving the executives with virtually little. The president, therefore, couldn't make treaties, charge tariffs, or the like. Once the Constitution was ratified, the central administration held more power, but it was balanced off with checks and balances due to things like congressional vetoes.

The two parties at the time were the Federalists, who sought to have a strong government and weaker state governments, and the

Anti-Federalists, who_preferred that more power be held by the states than the central government. In time, with the rise of Thomas Jefferson, a wider party platform was developed. He and James Madison formed what was called the Republican Party, although historians refer to it as the Democratic-Republican Party or the Jeffersonian Republican Party to differentiate it from the Republican Party today. It opposed the centralizing feature of the strong national government that the Federalists believed in, and they believed that the states should have more power and a greater say in the functions of the federal government. This party began around the year 1792.

The Democratic-Republican Party could be viewed as a counterreaction to the policies of Alexander Hamilton. Men like Thomas Jefferson saw in Hamilton an imitation of the British style of government, and they feared that a system such as that could lead the nation back to a despotic tyranny that was so typical of Europe. Not to be overlooked is the fact that an agrarian economy and a manufacturing economy differed in many ways. Both Jefferson and Madison came from an agrarian background and had experienced the manipulations of financial networks that could deleteriously harm the everyday man who was limited by economic conditions, environment, climatic conditions, and other forces of nature over which he had little control. It wasn't until later that factors entered in to limit the power of the manufacturing sector, like global competition, prices on world markets, foreign wars, and international political conditions.

Today, the best corollary for the evolution of the United States political parties might be said in this way: The Federalists of today are now Republicans, and the Democratic-Republicans are today's Democrats.

Chapter 5 – The Time the Troubles Start

The Early Banks

The first bank established in the United States was the Bank of North America in 1781. The Continental Congress chartered it, and the first shareholders were Ben Franklin, Thomas Jefferson, and Alexander Hamilton. It offered the high interest rate of fourteen percent on its dividends. Boston opened the Massachusetts Bank in 1784. New York petitioned for another bank to service its many customers and opened the Bank of New York in 1784. It wasn't entirely capitalized, so it wasn't chartered at that time. The first shareholders were William Seton, Alexander McDougall, Alexander Hamilton, and Aaron Burr.

The Banking Prejudice and Aaron Burr

Hamilton wrote the charter for the Bank of New York in 1791. The Bank of New York, a private bank, was generally quite successful but was discriminatory. What it failed to do was loan money to those who were followers of Thomas Jefferson and the Democratic-Republicans. All the banks were run by the Federalists until Aaron Burr came along. Burr was a Revolutionary War veteran who later became a lawyer and then a senator in 1791 after having defeated Philip Schuyler, Hamilton's father-in-law. Burr was a Democratic-Republican and a big player in the political power complex in New York, especially after gaining the support of George Clinton. It is curious to note that Burr lived just a block away from Alexander Hamilton.

Burr was determined to forge his way into banking so that the Democratic-Republicans could have a foothold in it. In an insightful but rather devious proposal, Burr indicated that a source of fresh water was needed for the city of New York and worked with Alexander Hamilton, William Seton, and three other Federalists in a bipartisan effort to accomplish that through what was called the Manhattan Water Company. The bill was passed into law by the New York Congress.

However, the Manhattan Water Company was just a puppet company and pumped very little water. When its charter was written, Burr managed to cleverly sneak in a clause "to employ surplus capital in any moneyed transactions or operations not inconsistent with the and constitution of this state or of the United States." That allowed the water company itself to not only take deposits but make loans. Those loans were open to the Democratic-Republicans and represented a major change in the banking industry. Now, the Federalists no longer had a monopoly on loans. Eventually, the Manhattan Water Company merged with Chase National Bank to form the Chase Manhattan Bank, which was one of the earliest institutions that formed the current J.P. Morgan Chase company.

The Bank Panic of 1792

The price of the securities in the First National Bank rose quickly, as investors were interested in the purchase of the government-backed bonds. However, in the spring of 1792, the price of the securities suddenly started to fall. Investors panicked, and as they did so, more investors pulled out. When the prices of the securities were falling, Hamilton wrote to William Duer of the Society for the Establishing of Useful Manufactures, saying, "I trust they (the funds) are not diverted. The public interest and my reputation are deeply concerned in this matter." As a matter of fact, Duer had taken thousands of dollars from the society's funds, so all of that money was now missing. John Dewhurst, another investor, had taken 50,000 dollars for a loan to purchase textile equipment, but he absconded with the money. That problem dovetailed into one of their own creation. The two men had concocted a scheme to take out loans from elsewhere and get a minor monopoly on selling securities. When the prices of the securities fell, Duer couldn't make his payments; neither could Malcomb, and—of course—Dewhurst was among the missing. Both Duer and Malcomb were imprisoned. Dewhurst went bankrupt and fled to England where he continued with his manipulative speculating.

Hamilton used some of his own money and got a loan from William Seton of the Bank of New York to help resolve the crisis within the S.E.U.M. Because of that, the S.E.U.M. was able to offer some of its programs in Paterson.

As for the national bank crisis, it was exacerbated by a parallel crisis in the Bank of New York. Hamilton again approached his friend, William Seton, asking that he purchase more of the public debt. However, because of all those requests, the Bank of New York was overextended. New speculators also thought they had a new source of revenue in this bank, but the bank had to curtail back, as they had little left in reserve. While it didn't fail to make the periodic payments to the securities investors, the Bank of New York couldn't renew its 30-day loans, so investors had to go elsewhere. They were then forced to sell their securities, but the prices fell drastically.

In March of 1792, the National Bank resorted to what was called the "Sinking Fund Commission," which was composed of Vice President John Adams, Attorney General Edmund Randolph, Secretary of State Thomas Jefferson, and Chief Justice John Jay. Hamilton proposed that the national securities be put on the open markets. They needed a majority vote, but John Jay was away. They voted on the measure anyway, but the vote was half for and half against. After much discussion, however, Randolph was persuaded to change sides, and the measure was passed. Hamilton also guaranteed that the government would buy up to 500,000 dollars of securities in case the National Bank was stymied by too much collateral.

In a series of contracts with William Seton of the Bank of New York, they offered him bank loans collateralized by national debt securities at a higher interest rate—seven percent. In addition, they guaranteed to have 150,000 dollars available in open-market loans. The crisis was successfully averted, and the financial conditions reverted back to normal.

The Whiskey Rebellion

There was no income tax in 1790. However, to help make up the shortfall in paying war debt, Hamilton proposed to the Congress that a tax be charged on domestically produced spirits and whiskey. Because it was considered a luxury rather than a necessity, he felt it would have little reaction. He was wrong. Farmers in western Pennsylvania, in particular, rose up in a rebellion which lasted until 1794. Nearly all of the farmers had whiskey stills, as the alcohol could be made from the byproducts of the grain they harvested. It could also be made from corn, wheat, and barley—all of which the farmers grew in abundance. After hearing the practical complaints, Hamilton reduced the amount charged. However, he gave the larger distilleries more of an advantage, as it took more money to operate them safely and produce a high-quality product. Every still had to be registered, which was a hardship on the smaller manufacturers. Inspectors and tax collectors arrived at these establishments, infuriating the distillers. It reminded them of the times when the British inspectors canvassed their towns in search of customs and duties.

Resistance and harassment of these excise tax collectors were rampant. Some of the men's homes were broken into and ransacked. Collectors were tarred, feathered, and marched in the streets. Writs (which are like warrants) were written liberally against those who refused to pay the excise tax. William Findley, who was one of the congressional officials from Pennsylvania, had the law made to be more practical by requiring that the smaller offenders be heard in local courts rather than traveling miles and miles to Philadelphia. He objected to many of Hamilton's more stringent measures, which he felt would do harm to the smaller farmers. Many historians indicate that Hamilton's heavy-handed approached triggered some of the violence that followed.

The rest of the government writs were given to the parties concerned without incident, but it didn't stop there. In July 1794, Federal Marshal David Lenox, who was joined by General John Neville, made his rounds around western Pennsylvania until they were shot at by the men who were holed up at Miller's farm. The next day, at least thirty men surrounded Neville's home, and they demanded the surrender of the federal marshal, who they believed to be inside; he actually went home following the events the previous day. Neville responded to their demands by firing a shot that killed one of the men outside. They opened fire but were unable to dislodge Neville. So, they came back the next day, this time with nearly 600 men. Ten U.S. Army soldiers also arrived to aid Neville in the fight. Following negotiations that went nowhere, the women and the children were released unharmed before both sides began shooting. Some died in the crossfire, including Major James McFarlane, a veteran of the Revolutionary War who sided with the rebels. McFarlane was given the funeral of a hero, but that only served to arouse the hatreds manifested between the two opposing forces.

Rumors then proliferated that crops, too, would be taxed. Farmers in those areas started to feel that this would result in a repeat of the excessive taxation levied by Great Britain during the Revolutionary War. An uprising occurred in Hagerstown, Maryland, over this issue. The people rushed to their armories and took weapons and ammunition to prepare for an imagined incursion from the national government, forcing as many able-bodied men to join them as possible. Washington reviewed his troops at Fort Cumberland, Maryland, and put "Light-Horse Harry" Lee in charge. They met with little resistance, and the crowds disbursed.

George Washington himself donned his military uniform and led an army of nearly 12,000 men to western Pennsylvania. The formidable size of his force was sufficient enough to disperse the rebels.

Washington's Watermelon Army

After the uprising at Miller's farm, Washington explored western Pennsylvania further. He marched at the head of what was called a "Watermelon Army." The Watermelon Army may have had the appearance and the abilities of an army, but its function belied its appearance. Washington took the opportunity to march through these rural areas in Pennsylvania, Maryland, and Virginia to admire the appearance of the various villages and towns and praise the progress they had made since the devastation of the Revolutionary War battles fought on their land. These people weren't rebels, he noted; they were hard-working, patriotic Americans working together to build a society. From time to time, he stopped and met with the community spokesmen, asking them about their grievances and their hopes and plans for the future. Washington took his time talking to them, and he stayed in many of their farmhouses.

This trip had two results: 1) It showed the population that the national government had the power and strength to quell insurrections, and 2) the national government had the ability to listen to and respond to the needs of the common people who lived in the states.

Outcome

Many of the rebels involved in the insurrection disappeared westward into the mountains. Only two were captured—Philip Wiggle and John Mitchell, one of whom had assaulted a tax collector and the other whom burned down a house. Although they were sentenced to death by hanging, Washington pardoned them. He was desperately trying to keep the country united. The tax on domestic whiskey was later rescinded under the following presidential administration—that of Thomas Jefferson—in 1801.

Crisis of Another Sort

Hamilton was a feverish worker, but he could be jovial and charming at the social events he attended. Often, he and his wife, Eliza, were entertained by Martha and George Washington. Hamilton liked arriving late at parties, relishing the attention he received when he did so. Most people found him very pleasant and agreeable. When he spoke, everyone tended to stop speaking so as to catch his every word. The ladies were especially fascinated by his charm and grace.

His graciousness and generosity got him into trouble in 1791. As he often traversed the walkways of the city of Philadelphia, he came across many admirers. Hamilton was a good-looking man with a calm demeanor, so people felt comfortable approaching him. One day, a demure woman by the name of Maria Reynolds walked up to him and asked that he visit her in her boarding house where she might discuss an urgent matter with him privately. Foolishly, he met her there. Maria then asked him for some help because her husband had abandoned her. Did he perhaps have some money he could spare so she could take care of herself? He agreed, excused himself, and later returned with some money for her. Maria cried about the vulgarity of her husband, James. Then she added that she still truly loved her husband but that her distress over the abuse was overwhelming. Hamilton felt pity for her, and perhaps that only added to his attraction to her. The two of them began having intimate relations with each other, and his affair with her only escalated over the weeks. They frequently met during the summer and fall to continue in the wild and torrid relationship.

In truth, Maria had a local reputation for engaging in prostitution, although Hamilton didn't know that. The neighbors said that Maria's husband was well aware of Maria's promiscuity and of

Hamilton's relationship with her. James Reynolds knew full well that Hamilton stood to lose a lot should the affair be made public, so he seized the opportunity and insisted on 1,000 dollars in December to keep the matter private. Hamilton paid the money and ended his relationship with Maria. However, Reynolds wrote Hamilton in January 1792 to invite him to visit his wife again. Maria, who might have been manipulated into the scheme by her husband, began to write and seduce Hamilton whenever she knew her husband would be away, and it was too much for Hamilton to resist. After these visits, Hamilton would send thirty or forty dollars. The last payment he sent was in June 1792, which might have been the end of the affair.

In November 1792, Reynolds was imprisoned for counterfeiting and speculating on veterans' back pay, and he wrote to Hamilton for assistance. However, Hamilton refused to help, and not even Maria's letters would sway him otherwise this time. James Reynolds' accomplice, Jacob Clingman, who had also been imprisoned, informed some of Hamilton's rivals that Reynolds had information they could use against their political opponent. James Monroe, a Virginia statesman, Frederick Muhlenberg, the speaker of the House of Representatives, and Abraham Venable, a representative from Virginia, visited Reynolds in jail, who only hinted at Hamilton's misconduct before disappearing after his release from jail. However, the three men believed that Hamilton was involved in the crime Reynolds and Clingman were charged with, not that he was involved in an affair. They even visited Maria, who confirmed their suspicions that Hamilton was involved in speculation, giving them some of his notes that he sent.

Instead of immediately making the matter public, Monroe and the others decided to confront Hamilton directly. Hamilton then revealed the actual truth to them and gave them the letters from the Reynolds'. The three men were satisfied with Hamilton's explanation and decided to keep the matter private. However, Monroe did retain copies of the Reynolds' letters and sent them to

Thomas Jefferson, Hamilton's perennial nemesis. Jefferson held on to those letters until later on.

The harm that could have been caused by that episode loomed large in Hamilton's mind, and he spent years ruminating about it. In 1797, a muckraker by the name of James Callender obtained the notes from Monroe's committee about the Reynolds-Hamilton affair and wrote a series of pamphlets about it. Callender published them, adding his own embellishments to the story.

The Possible Duel: Hamilton vs. Monroe

After Hamilton left his post in the Department of the Treasury, the publicity about the Reynolds affair had deleteriously affected his public life. Hamilton suspected that the information about his affair had been released by James Monroe and met with him along with two witnesses, Hamilton's brother-in-law John Church and his friend, David Gelston, to discuss it. When confronted, James Monroe denied any knowledge about the release of the information regarding the committee investigation. The witnesses reported that Monroe leaped up and hollered at Hamilton, shouting, "Do you say I represented you falsely? You are a scoundrel!"

To that, Hamilton replied, "I will meet you like a gentleman."

"I am ready. Get your pistols," Monroe shouted.

The two witnesses, Church and Gelston, then stood between the two men until their sanity returned.

Monroe himself was highly agitated about Hamilton because he had been suddenly recalled from France by George Washington in 1796 where he had been an ambassador. George Washington had given him no reason for it either. Monroe felt that he was dismissed from his ambassadorship to France because of Hamilton's influence. That wasn't true at all, though. Monroe was recalled because Washington heard a rumor from Senator Gouverneur Morris that Monroe was stirring up anti-American sentiment in France. It also wasn't true that Monroe was stoking anti-American sentiment or that he had released information about the Reynolds-Hamilton affair to a muckraker. Monroe's secretary, James Beckley, had. Beckley was a clerk who had worked with Munroe and the other investigators, and he had made his own copies and handed them off to James Callender.

Despite being upset with Hamilton, Munroe promised him that he would get to the bottom of what happened and send him a full explanation of it. However, Hamilton was not appeased with the explanation he received a week later. He zeroed in on Munroe not refuting Clingman's charges of him misusing government money, a crime that was more serious to him than adultery. He demanded that Munroe refute them, which he declined to do. Things escalated again, and Munroe eventually told Hamilton that they could settle things in a way "which I am ever ready to meet." This could be seen as a veiled challenge of a duel.

Hamilton took it as such, and he accepted, saying that his second would visit to finalize the details. Monroe chose Burr to be his second, and it was Burr, oddly enough, the man that later killed Hamilton in a duel, that resolved the tensions between the two men. Burr delivered a letter to Hamilton from Munroe which stated that Munroe had misunderstood Hamilton's previous letter and denied issuing the challenge. However, perhaps so he didn't appear to be a coward, he told Hamilton that if he wished to fight that he should arrange it with Burr. Burr managed to convince the two to avoid it, saying they were being childish.

By mid-August, the two had settled down. However, Hamilton still felt that his reputation was still tarnished, so he decided to go public with the story. On August 25th, he printed the *Observations on Certain Documents*, later known as the Reynolds Pamphlet, where he admitted the entire affair but denied all charges of corruption.

Since Hamilton included his correspondence with Monroe in the pamphlet, Monroe wondered if things really were settled between the two. It is unknown how the drama between these two Founding

Fathers settled itself as the two were still discussing the possibility of a duel in early 1798. Perhaps Hamilton was more interested in getting a new foothold in politics when relations between the United States and France heated up, causing him to forget about the petty squabble between himself and Monroe.

Chapter 6 – Empowerment of Political Parties

There are always groups and social centers within communities and countries that rise from a common root, like veterans' organizations, patriotic endeavors, hereditary groups, fundraising societies, and the like. Politics is no exception. Sometimes social clubs morph into political organizations. As these groups evolve, they often change focus or direction, depending upon the needs of the community.

The Society of the Cincinnati

The Society of the Cincinnati was a patriotic organization established, and it was composed of officers of the Continental Army and French soldiers who had participated in the American Revolution. It was originally formed during the Continental Army's encampment at Newburgh, New York, in 1783. Within ten years, members of the society were composed of many of the Founding Fathers like George Washington, General Henry Knox, and General von Steuben. The society held social events at which many of them conversed about political topics. Although George Washington himself declared no political party, most of the members of this society were Federalists. Originally, the society was based on a hereditary membership, but that requirement was later abolished. Alexander Hamilton succeeded George Washington as the society's president in 1784.

Most of the members were also wealthy, and many were landowners or involved in areas of advanced finances. Eventually, the society established state societies, where they often discussed matters involving the constitution and governance of their state. A large number of the members were from the northeastern states, and they exercised control of banks and industries. Prejudices arose as the state societies tended to favor their own members.

As the years progressed, this organization became more political.

The Tammany Society, Aka Tammany Hall

The Tammany Society used Native American terms to symbolize themselves as true or "pure" Americans. Early on, they declared themselves as a political entity. Although it had members from both political parties, the inclusion of the powerful George Clinton brought in representation from the Democratic-Republicans. By 1798, it became a political club of highly placed Democratic-Republicans. Its purpose was to create party unity on various issues and to support certain candidates for elections while opposing others. The Clinton family was one of the most powerful families in New York and controlled the Tammany Society for years. Hamilton spent a lot of energy enlisting the support of the ex-Loyalists and moderate former Whigs to wrest political control from the over-powerful Clinton faction. To this day, many cities, towns, and even streets in the tristate area bear the name of "Clinton." The society used the tactic of attracting the most recent immigrant population, making promises to them if their favorite candidates were elected. In time, the Tammany Society became very corrupt, exchanging political favors for money and/or lucrative positions in the local governments.

The Tammany Society primarily operated in New York. In the late 18th century, the Tammany Society met in an upper room of city hall that was often called "Tammany Hall." Although they moved their conference room to a Nassau Street tavern, the name stuck. Tammany Hall adopted the aim of countering the Federalist Party and their political candidates. Another ambitious politician, Aaron Burr, a Democratic-Republican, used the power of the Tammany Society to help him rise up in political circles. In 1789, Clinton was the governor of New York, and he appointed Aaron Burr as the state attorney general. Two years later, in 1791, Clinton was instrumental in getting Burr elected as a New York senator. Philip Schuyler, Alexander's father-in-law, served as a U.S. senator for the state of New York from 1789 to 1791, but due to the rising influence of Tammany Hall, he lost that election to Aaron Burr. Hamilton was furious and personally held that against Burr. In 1796, John Adams' wife, Abigail, who was quite astute about politics, told her husband that the Democratic-Republicans might have been considering Burr to run against Adams for the presidency.

Hamilton wasted no courtesies when he spoke about Burr. "He is for or against nothing, but as it suits his interest or ambition. He is determined as I conceive, to make his way to be the head of the popular party and in a word, to become like an "Embryo-Caesar" in the United States."

Jefferson vs. Hamilton

Hamilton was a strong and smart man. Despite the fact that he said he preferred the quiet life, he thrived on controversy and spent a great deal of his life involved in it. To Hamilton, engaging in the war between the political parties was like a game of tug-of-war. Jefferson also felt that way. In 1798, he said, "In every free and deliberating society, there must, from the nature of man, be opposite parties, violent dissension and discord; and one of these, for the most part, must prevail over the other for a longer or shorter time." According to Jefferson, the Federalists held the belief that "the executive branch of our government needs the most support." As for Jefferson's view of his own party, he said, "The republicans

[Democratic-Republicans] compose the only form of government which is not eternally at open or secret war with the rights of mankind." Jefferson often defined his party not in terms of what it stood for but for what it didn't support.

When a national bank was proposed, Jefferson and Hamilton argued incessantly. Jefferson was vigorously opposed to banks under the auspices of a national government. Jefferson was a Southerner, and Southerners were often hurt by private bankers from the North, who would seize their farms if they defaulted on their loans. Hamilton, on the other hand, was more concerned about the status of America in the eyes of foreign countries, so he wanted to be sure that America gained the reputation for paying its loans and resolving its debt.

Since the Revolution, Great Britain had no ambassador in the United States. Hamilton felt it would be prudent to invite a British ambassador to the country and reopen communications between Britain and America for the economic advantage both would receive. Prior to the Revolution, there was a brisk trade between Britain and America that had slackened after the war. Because there was a common link between the two countries culturally, it would have been advantageous to exchange ambassadors. Hamilton's unofficial envoy to Great Britain, George Beckwith, agreed, saying, "We think in English and have a similarity of prejudices and of predilections." James Madison and Thomas Jefferson felt differently, however, and considered Britain to be corrupt and greedy. They preferred France as a major trading partner instead. Hamilton, on the other hand, harbored a deep antipathy for France and considered them "dangerous" because of the somewhat chaotic events going on in the country at the time. Although he had befriended Lafayette, Hamilton felt that close relations with France would be disastrous as it might trigger a trade war.

Madison favored tariffs levied against Great Britain based on tonnage, which would have made the fees higher. Both Madison and Jefferson cited the fact that Great Britain had yet to relinquish their forts on American soil, which was an agreement in the Treaty of Paris. In truth, however, America hadn't yet paid its war debt nor returned all the property belonging to British citizens in America, which is one reason the British held onto the forts.

Jefferson was the secretary of state at that time and should have been drawn more fully into this discussion about trade. However, he wasn't. Hamilton had already met with the unofficial British envoy, George Beckwith, in 1791 and later on covertly met with the official British ambassador, George Hammond, and groundwork was laid for trade relations. Hamilton had overstepped his bounds by manipulating foreign policy, which was the duty of Jefferson as the secretary of state, but Hamilton was concerned about too much involvement with France. As it turned out, that was a fortuitous occurrence because France was on the verge of bankruptcy in the late 1700s. The expenditures of the Wars of the Coalition and their financial aid to the United States during the American Revolutionary War had nearly exhausted the French treasury. In addition, the extravagant spending of the royal monarch, King Louis XVI, and his wife, Marie Antoinette, had cut further holes into the French economy.

Due to the economic trauma, the French people rebelled, deposing their king in 1792 and setting up a new government run by a mixed group of French militants that eventually evolved into the Legislative Assembly, which was headed up by a political faction called the Girondins and then later the Jacobins. Those who fell out of favor were executed on that frightening apparatus known as the guillotine during the Reign of Terror. King Louis XVI himself was even guillotined, along with his wife about nine months later. After that, France declared war on the British monarchy and was cheered on by Thomas Jefferson and other Democratic-Republicans. That support was short-lived. When that war spread to other monarchies in Europe, the situation became precarious for the United States.

George Washington wanted to declare neutrality, but the Treaty of Alliance and Amity signed after the Revolution required that America ally itself with France. Washington met with his Cabinet. Hamilton reasoned that the treaty should not be adhered to if it was dangerous to other nations with whom America had relations. Secretary of War Henry Knox agreed. Thomas Jefferson and Edmund Randolph, however, supported the alliance with France. Jefferson and Hamilton engaged in a shouting match, and the argument continued until Washington put a stop to it. Washington then cast the determining vote and passed the Proclamation of Neutrality on April 22nd, 1793.

During that same year, a Frenchman by the name of Edmond Genêt had been seeking support for France during the Revolution and was already in the United States. He broke protocol and undermined Washington's Proclamation of Neutrality by failing to greet President Washington upon his arrival and purchasing some confiscated British ships for France. In addition, he recruited Americans to serve as privateers on those ships. Genêt had landed in South Carolina, and the South, in particular, favored France due to Jefferson's influence. He was even met with a parade!

Although Jefferson was pro-French, he was angry with Genêt over his political *faux pas*. So was Hamilton, and that was one of the few issues on which Jefferson and Hamilton agreed.

Genêt continued with his recruiting efforts and showed no sign of relenting. Washington then dispatched a letter to France demanding that Genêt be recalled. Genêt demanded that America make its periodic payments to pay back the war debt. Both Jefferson and Hamilton indicated that the payment should be delayed, although they disagreed as to how. Hamilton wanted to write a stern letter, but Jefferson wanted one that was more cordial. An argument, once again, ensued between the two of them. And again, Washington had to step in and decided to send the more polite version.

Totally exasperated by his dealings with Alexander Hamilton, Thomas Jefferson attempted to resign from his position as secretary of state. Washington persuaded him to hold off until the fall-out from the Genêt affair had passed. Jefferson ended up resigning on December 31st, 1793.

As for Genêt, he sailed for France. However, upon his arrival, he sadly discovered that his political supporters, the Girondins, were no longer in control. He feared for his safety, so, he turned around and sailed back for the United States. This time, he abided by the protocols, landing in Philadelphia, and he begged Washington to let him remain in the country. Washington granted his request. Genêt settled down and married the daughter of Governor George Clinton of New York. After that, Genêt faded into history.

The Jay Treaty of 1794

In 1793, when France and England were at war, George Washington consulted the members of his Cabinet, including Alexander Hamilton, concerning his wish to maintain neutrality. The United States was just in the process of establishing its own policies regarding internal taxation, the nature of the country's credit, and the status of the manufacturing sector. At that time, the country was in no position to fund a war, having fought a long and bloody war for independence on their own soil. Washington then sent Justice John Jay over to Great Britain to draw up a treaty of peace. This treaty placed Britain on a "most favored nation" status, which would give them preferential treatment for trade purposes and maintain neutrality simultaneously. Hamilton, it is said, penned most of the treaty for John Jay to carry over there, if it could be passed by Congress. Most of the members of Congress at that time were Federalists and roundly supported it. However, many of the Democratic-Republicans in Congress felt that some similar allowances should be given to France. Because the Federalists had the majority in Congress, though, it passed with the required two-thirds majority.

Unfortunately, it wasn't the most ideal of all treaties, giving rise to arguments in Congress and among the people. Not all points in the treaty were addressed, including those that required that the British close up their forts still on American soil. In addition, the impressment of American sailors still continued, compensation for merchant vessels confiscated during the war hadn't been made, and there was no compensation for kidnapped slaves.

Hamilton and Slavery

Hamilton had his own stance on the issue of slavery. He had seen the sufferings of the slaves on his home island of Saint Croix. He saw their squalor. At the firm of Kortright and Cruger, slaves were occasionally auctioned off, although that wasn't their major function. Hamilton was in charge of keeping order with the slaves but disliked that immensely. In 1777, he wrote critiques against the planters at Saint Croix using biblical language, saying, "O ye who revel in affluence see the afflictions of humanity and bestow your superfluity to ease them. Say not, we have suffered also, and thence withhold your compassion. What are your sufferings compared to those? Ye have still more than enough left. Act wisely. Succour the miserable and lay up a treasure in heaven."

In his writings, he often compared the condition of slavery to the manner in which Great Britain treated the American colonists. Through his church, he befriended Elias Boudinot, a Cherokee abolitionist, and that association led him to consider joining the Manumission Society after the Revolutionary War. Although Hamilton abhorred slavery, he placed his personal ambition ahead of taking any forceful actions to abolish the practice.

In 1779, Henry Laurens and Alexander Hamilton recommended to George Washington that he recruit African slaves to help in the war effort, telling him that they would make excellent soldiers. Hamilton also sent a letter to John Jay in that regard, saying, "The dictates of humanity and true policy equally interest me in favor of this unfortunate class of men." The army sent Hamilton and Laurens to South Carolina to recruit troops made from the slaves living there. Once there, they proposed to the legislature that they should raise these battalions, which the owners of the slaves would be given contributions. At the war's end, those who survived would be free men. Many of the Founding Fathers felt that blacks were inferior, but Hamilton, who had lived among them in the West Indies, never felt that way. After the war, Hamilton joined the Manumission Society in 1785, which supported freedom for the slaves. He served as its president briefly. Some of the other members were John Jay, Gouverneur Morris, and Rufus King. As president of the Manumission Society, Hamilton loudly protested about how citizens were circumventing state laws against slave sales by exporting slaves from other states. Oddly enough, however, the Manumission Society's administrators themselves owned slaves, and Hamilton attempted to remedy that but without success. Many of the leaders of the new nation felt that emancipation of slavery should be a gradual process, and Hamilton grudgingly signed bills in the new Constitution that supported that. He set his priority instead upon supporting bills that would strengthen the cohesiveness of the union.

Eliza's family owned slaves, and his mother-in-law willed her slaves to her. Neither she nor Alexander took possession of them, though. There was some evidence that Eliza sold them, however. During Hamilton's life, there was never any evidence that he himself owned any slaves.

Alexander Hamilton Resigns

Hamilton had become increasingly frustrated with his role as secretary of the treasury as the opposition to his policies increased. He also tended to stir up very strong feelings among Congress and other influential men in the community. Hamilton personally had a heavy-handed way of dealing with issues and was headstrong—a personality trait that worked to his disadvantage. At home, his wife had a miscarriage during the time when the Whiskey Rebellion was in progress, and he couldn't help comfort her when she needed him most. This sad event caused him to focus more on affairs at home. In addition, he was only receiving about 3,000 dollars for his services as the secretary of the treasury, and he knew he could make much more as a lawyer. That would help his family and help him feel better about himself. So, in the year 1795, he tendered his resignation to George Washington. Hamilton, however, fully intended to participate in politics but more as someone who operated behind the scenes.

A Possible Duel Between Alexander Hamilton and James Nicholson

James Nicholson, a retired naval officer with the Continental Army, became a Democratic-Republican during the rise of Thomas Jefferson. Nicholson also belonged to the Democratic Society of New York. In the year 1795, he was involved in a political debate over the Jay Treaty of 1794. Hamilton had apparently sent a proposed resolution to one of the committee meetings of the Democratic Society, "declaring it unnecessary to give an opinion on the treaty." The committee summarily rejected it, after which Hamilton later got into an argument with Josiah Hoffman, a Federalist lawyer, and James Nicholson, a member of the Democratic-Republicans. Not only that, but Nicholson accused Hamilton, via a friend of Hamilton's, of investing some of the U.S. Treasury funds into a British bank. The friend asked Nicholson for proof of this, and Nicholson indicated he could produce it if Hamilton attempted to run for public office. Hamilton then sent a letter to Nicholson demanding proof. Nicholson reiterated that there was proof and warned Hamilton that there might be consequences should this come to the public eye.

Letters flew back and forth between them, sometimes two per day. In one of the letters, Hamilton challenged Nicholson to meet him face-to-face at Paulus Hook. Paulus, today a section of Liberty State Park, is in Jersey City, and that area was often used for duels in the 18th century. As it turned out, DeWitt Clinton, among others, met with Nicholson with a draft of an apology letter for him to sign. The draft said, in part, "The subscribers (Clinton et. al.)

having been made acquainted with the correspondence between Mr. Hamilton and Mr. Nicholson relative to a controversy that took place between them on Saturday before last, do hereby certify the same has been settled in a satisfactory and honorable way to both parties."

Washington's Retirement

In 1796, Washington longed to take refuge again in the private life sector, and he decided not to seek the office of the presidency for another term. Although he didn't publicly deliver it, Washington published it in the *American Daily Advertiser* after Alexander Hamilton helped to rewrite it. The initial draft of the address was written by James Madison when Washington first considered retirement. During 1796, the Genêt affair had had a profound effect on George Washington and was reflected in that address. Although it wasn't the only example, Genêt's attempt to prevail upon the liberty promulgated by America toward the end of the 18th century was extremely presumptuous and highlighted Washington's caution about foreign entanglements, which was one of the major themes of his speech. The second major theme had to do with political factions. He was emotionally exhausted by acting as a referee between Thomas Jefferson and Alexander Hamilton. Like Jefferson, Hamilton was very partisan, and—as a matter of fact—Washington had to modify Hamilton's draft of his farewell address quite a bit in order to remove some of its harsh wording.

Washington stressed the word "unity" in the address to give impetus to the commonly held core beliefs of all Americans, regardless of their political party. He spoke of each region of the country and stressed the contributions of each to the whole union. He warned the American people to be wary of influential and persuasive power brokers. He said that powerful political factions "are likely in the course of time and things, to become potent engines by which cunning, ambitious and unprincipled men will be enabled to subvert the power of the people." He did, however, make an exception to that opinion by indicating that the parties can serve as a check on the powers of the government.

Chapter 7 – The Bitterly Fought Elections

The Contested Election of 1796

In the year 1796, John Adams, the vice president under George Washington, and Thomas Pinckney—both Federalists—ran against Thomas Jefferson and Aaron Burr, the two Democratic-Republicans. As soon as the campaign was under way, an essay appeared in the *Gazette of the United States*, a Federalist newspaper. It was signed by "Phocion." It warned its readers that Thomas Jefferson was having an affair with his slave, Sally Hemings, and added that Jefferson planned on freeing all the slaves. That latter notion alone struck fear in the hearts of the Southerners, who had developed an economic dependency on slavery to support their plantations. Of course, the idea that a white man would have intercourse with an African American slave offended the sensibilities of the prejudiced. The essay also went on to accuse Jefferson of having run away from the British soldiers during battle while the courageous Alexander Hamilton stayed his ground and fought with the Patriots. Alexander Hamilton was, in fact, the person who wrote under the pseudonym "Phocion."

During the campaign, Hamilton wrote to the federal electors privately, advising them to vote for Thomas Pinckney, hoping that it would convince them to elect Pinckney rather than John Adams. Because Pinckney was from the South, he assumed that some of the Southerners would be more likely to vote for Pinckney than Adams. Hamilton's scheme was revealed to some electors before the voting took place, however. So, instead of the Northern Federalists following along with Hamilton's recommendation, they voted for Adams but withheld their second ballots from Pinckney, as each elector was given two votes. Instead, they simply left their second vote blank. There were other electors who didn't know about the scheme ahead of time, so it was estimated that Adams might have lost five votes in New Jersey and two in Connecticut.

As a result of the election, John Adams obtained 71 electoral votes, and Thomas Jefferson received 68. That wasn't the result that Hamilton expected. In addition, for the first time in U.S. history, the president and the vice president were from two different parties (back then, whoever had the highest number of votes became president while the person with the second-highest number became vice president).

The Quasi-War

John Adams was president from 1797 to 1801. During his administration, there was an undeclared war between France and America called the "Quasi-War." The Quasi-War was fought from 1798 to 1800, and it was a naval battle stemming from the forceful impressment of American sailors and the destruction of their ships. Fears of yet another war permeated the population. The administration was also obsessed with concerns that French operatives would infiltrate the country, causing Adams and the Federalist-controlled Congress to pass the Alien and Sedition Acts. Adams, in particular, knew that another war could ruin the country, and he didn't want to leave that to be his legacy. Fear of infiltration by France within the country led to a great deal of mistrust and paranoia on the part of the administration, leading them to curtail the free press. Hamilton was of the opinion that some of the editorials in the press were written by anti-American aliens. As a result of the enforcement of the Alien and Sedition Acts, innocent people who were just journalists and commentators were imprisoned as a result. The increased anxiety prevailing in the country also resurrected fears about Great Britain gaining renewed strength, which had first occurred during the vice presidency of John Adams under the Washington administration when the very unpopular Jay Treaty of 1794 was in effect. Even at this late date, there was still British influence in the unsettled lands of the Pacific Northwest.

Alexander Hamilton: Major-General

Adams also called upon George Washington, who was now retired, and asked him to organize preparations with some major officers in case there was ground combat. Although he was quite feeble at the time, Washington always answered the call of his country. Toward this effort, he traveled to Philadelphia. Washington stipulated that he choose the individual with whom he would work. Major Alexander Hamilton was then promoted to Major-General and was chosen to head up the operation. Recalling the difficulty he had getting supplies and equipment during the Revolution, Washington stressed to Hamilton that he needed to focus on that crucial aspect. Washington further gave him complete authorization to conduct operations if a ground war broke out, indicating that he himself wouldn't be physically up to the task. He then tasked Hamilton with the recruitment efforts and arrangements for the procurement of supplies.

In order to provide funding if such a war broke out, Hamilton contacted Oliver Wolcott Jr., the current secretary of the treasury, Senator Theodore Sedgwick from Massachusetts, and William Loughton Smith of the House Ways and Means Committee. The House Ways and Means Committee is a tax-writing group selected from members of the House of Representatives who decide how to go about collecting taxes. Unfortunately, Smith was asked to leave as Hamilton felt he was too slow to act and instead took on the responsibility himself. Instead of being taxed on their land, people were taxed on the number of windows they had in their houses. While this may seem strange today, glass was a valuable commodity in the early 19th century. Those who had more windows were generally wealthier. There was also another tax passed that was similar to the old Stamp Act. German farmers in southeastern Pennsylvania demonstrated against these taxes. Once the threat of war had passed, those taxes were rescinded.

The Explosive Election of 1800

This election was one of the most contentious and fiery elections in American history. Thomas Jefferson and Aaron Burr ran on the side of the Democratic-Republicans against John Adams and Charles Cotesworth Pinckney, both Federalists. Burr influenced Tammany Hall to collect donations from its membership for the campaign of Jefferson and himself and persuade electoral delegates to vote for their ticket. He also played into the Federalists' hands by becoming lukewarm about France in case some of the assemblymen were of that mind. He then saw to it that his supporters were merchants, mechanics, and workmen who would typically be attracted to Federalist candidates. Burr felt that befriending the influential people and building loyalties, especially among the assemblymen of New York, could sway an election. Jefferson's campaign workers also made many attempts to get him elected. They spoke to their influential friends and family about Jefferson's positive characteristics. Jefferson tended to do his campaigning "behind the scenes" by writing letters to those he knew. Burr, on the other hand, campaigned actively for himself. He visited Connecticut and Rhode Island, giving speeches. He said that what the country needed now was someone who could forge regional alliances between the Northern manufacturing states and the South, a person who could get Democratic-Republican support even in the Northern states. Of course, Burr was from New York, so he filled that qualification.

Since each elector had two votes, Burr stressed to the Democratic-Republicans that they should be sure to cast one vote for himself and one for Jefferson. Occasionally, electors would just vote for one man and withhold their second vote. That, he indicated, might result in Jefferson becoming president and John Adams vice president.

For the Democratic-Republicans, the key to getting the New York vote was Aaron Burr. Jefferson, however, was uncomfortable with Burr's style of campaigning. He and many others saw Burr as being selfishly ambitious. He never came across at election time as a "team player." Burr was a shrewd and calculating politician, and Jefferson felt that he really didn't hold on very tightly to Democratic-Republican values. Burr was a New Yorker who never turned a hoe in his life, so Jefferson found it hard to believe that Burr believed in the rights of the Southern farmers.

As for Hamilton, a Federalist, he had disparaged John Adams and Charles Pinckney in prior publications, but, of course, he didn't want Jefferson or Burr to win. In his published letters, Hamilton attempted to soften his formerly negative aspersions against John Adams and recommended that the Federalists vote for John Adams or Pinckney—whichever they preferred. Jefferson and Burr, meanwhile, crisscrossed New York trying to round up support.

In an effort to weaken Hamilton's role within the Federalist Party, Burr was able to secure copies of confidential letters sent to members of Congress and published sections of them in the Democratic-Republican newspapers. However, it did more than diminish support for the Federalists. It helped fracture the party. The noted statesman Rufus King said, "I have little or no doubt the letters [written by Hamilton and published by Burr] will lay the foundation of a serious opposition to General Hamilton amongst the Federalists, and that his usefulness hereafter will be greatly lessened."

It was. As a result of the 1800 election, Jefferson won 73 electoral votes, and Aaron Burr won 73. Adams won 65, and Pinckney won 64.

In the case of a tie, the responsibility passes onto the House of Representatives. In 1800, that meant the responsibility passed along to John Marshall, who was the secretary of state and who had to monitor a new election between Jefferson and Burr.

A minimum of at least nine votes from the sixteen states was needed to break the tie. Burr received votes from six of the eight states controlled by the Federalists. Seven of the states controlled by the Democratic-Republicans voted for Jefferson. Hamilton rigorously embarked on a frenzied letter-writing campaign, reminding people that he considered Burr more "dangerous" than Thomas Jefferson. Hamilton even wrote to Secretary of State John Marshall in that regard. During his frenetic attempts to prevent Aaron Burr from becoming president after this tie vote of 1800, Hamilton called Burr a "profligate, corrupt, bankrupt, and an unprincipled man" who was looking to cheat Jefferson out of the presidency. Throughout the campaign and even prior to that, Burr had heard accusations that he was an adulterer, that he forced women into prostitution, that he accepted bribes, and that he stole from the escrow funds of his legal clients. Other anonymous brief notices showed up in print that further disparaged Burr. Hamilton also wrote letters to some of the most influential Federalists he knew, including, Oliver Wolcott, Theodore Sedgwick, Gouverneur Morris, Harrison Gray Otis, John Rutledge, John Marshall, and James Bayard. As revealed in his letter to Samuel Bayard, Hamilton wrote a number of grievous negatives about Burr, going so far as to imply that Burr could become an "unruly tyrant" who would limit the liberty and freedom of the people. Bayard convinced nine Federalists not to vote for Burr, and they instead passed in blank ballots. Tie votes kept reoccurring, and the House had to hold the voting again on a number of occasions. Finally, Hamilton was able to influence the electoral voters, and as a result,

Thomas Jefferson became president with Aaron Burr as the vice president.

Aftermath

The election of 1800 stimulated a lot of animosity among Americans. Adams also wrote to Abigail that his journey home would be burdened. Upon his arrival, it is said that he rushed into his farming work to distract himself. The *Philadelphia Aurora* insulted him in their columns, saying that Adams "needed to be cast like polluted water out the back door, and who should immediately leave for Quincy that Mrs. Adams may wash her befuddled brains clear."

During that same year, John Adams' son, Charles, died of alcoholism. Jefferson had received that notice accidentally and forwarded the missive to Adams, kindly expressing his sincerest condolences. It was a gentle letter full of empathy and understanding.

Now thrown into forced retirement, Adams was not only depressed, but he was also angry, and he kept ruminating about the turmoil and tribulations of this election. Abigail Adams said, "Party hatred, by its deadly poison, blinds the eyes and puts venom into the heart." As a consequence of the nastiness and insults that Jefferson engaged in during electioneering, Adams broke off his relationship with him. It wasn't until thirteen years later that they reconciled.

The Fatal Duel of Hamilton's Son, Philip

One night, in 1801, Alexander Hamilton's eldest son, nineteen-year-old Philip Hamilton, and his friend, Stephen Price, came across George Eacker and a friend attending a comedy in New York entitled *The West Indian*. Eacker was an accomplished lawyer in the city who was rising the social ladder in New York society. He had been chosen to give a speech for the Fourth of July Independence Day celebration four months earlier, which was sponsored by the Tammany Society. According to most listeners,

Eacker's speech was "good," but some of the members of the Democratic-Republican society felt that there were insinuations made in the oration against the Federalist agenda. Philip and Richard were angry about the remarks made during it, and they intruded into Eacker's box seat and began taunting him about some of the supposedly offensive remarks. Then Eacker turned to Price and Philip Hamilton and quipped angrily, "It is too abominable to be publicly insulted by a set of rascals!" The term "rascal" in those days was a hot-button term that implied a challenge to a duel. To that retort, Price and Philip became even more enraged. Philip then shouted, "Who do you call damn'd rascals?"

The generally accepted procedure for a duel is to appoint "seconds," who are trusted friends to act as witnesses. It is their function to try to elicit an apology by the one who has apparently offended the honor of the other. Although movies have portrayed it, duels are never preceded by a blow or slap on the face. If the apology fails to be procured, duelists may announce in advance that they will use dummy bullets or shoot in the air, but no one says they will aim toward a less lethal area of the body. The seconds load the pistols but don't cock them, and then the pistols are presented to the duelists. Each duelist stands ten yards apart. If neither falls on the first shot, the shooting continues for two or three shots until someone falls. There are only three possible outcomes when a duel takes place: 1) One party is injured and bloodied. If that is sufficient retribution for the winner, the duel is ended. If the party isn't satisfied, the duel continues. 2) If a duelist isn't able to proceed because of a serious wound, the duel is considered over. 3) If either party is fatally killed, the duel is over.

John Church of the Schuyler family attempted to negotiate peace among the three but was unsuccessful. Two duels were scheduled—one between Stephen Prince and George Eacker and the other between Eacker (if he survived) and Philip Hamilton. Price and Eacker faced each other on November 22nd, 1801. Both shot, but both parties missed each other. The parties agreed that they were satisfied. Whenever that happened, it was the traditional practice to abandon the attempt. Alexander Hamilton, according to the *New York Evening Post*, wasn't aware of the planned duel at the time. However, historians have said that he probably did know about it, indicating that the lack of publicity was most likely an effort to protect Alexander from rumors that he was involved. Dueling, although frowned upon, isn't technically illegal in all of the states today, but if a duel did take place, people could still be convicted on charges like manslaughter. However, back then, many of the prominent politicians were against it, such as Ben Franklin, John Adams, and Thomas Jefferson. Some men who had military experience tended to practice it to settle issues and felt it was a respectable way to defend their honor and integrity.

The second duel—between Hamilton and Eacker—was scheduled for the next day later, November 23rd, 1801. It was to take place again in Weehawken, New Jersey, on a sandbar near the current Jersey City. In fact, this would be the same place where his father would later be mortally wounded in his own duel. Philip took his father's advice and didn't fire first. However, neither did Eacker. They stared at one another for a few moments before lifting their pistols. Eacker fired first, according to witnesses, hitting Philip above his right hip. The bullet went through his body, though, and actually lodged itself in his left arm. Philip fired in response, but it is possible that it was an involuntary spasm as the bullet did nothing to Eacker. Falling to the ground, Philip's face turned white as his wounds started bleeding profusely.

The young man was lowered into a rowboat and taken across the Hudson River to the home of Hamilton's sister-in-law, Angelica Church. Alexander contacted the family physician, David Hosack, and both of them raced to the scene. Philip lay on the bed all night in total delirium with his eyes darting back and forth. According to Henry Dawson, a witness to the event, Alexander fainted from grief when he arrived. Eliza, who was also there, was three months pregnant with Alexander's youngest son at the time. Friends arrived shortly. Finally, after fourteen hours spent in agony, Philip confessed his faith in Christ and died. Alexander, it was said, was so distraught that he could barely stand during the funeral service and needed his friends to hold him up. Eliza herself was inconsolable. Alexander's youngest son was named "Philip" or "Young Philip" after his deceased brother.

Alexander sunk into a deep depression for many months following the death of his son. His close friends said it took him months to reply to the many sympathy letters he received after the event. He had been very close to Philip and raised him to follow his own beliefs. Philip, it was said, was very much like his father, so it's no surprise that he reacted so vehemently to Eacker's comments.

After Philip's death, his sister, Angelica who was only seventeen years old, had a mental breakdown. The psychiatrist, also a relative, said, "Upon receipt of the news of her brother's death in the Eacker duel, she suffered so great a shock that her mind became permanently impaired, and although taken care of by her devoted mother for a long time, there was no amelioration in her condition."

Chapter 8 – Bottom of the Curve

While Alexander Hamilton wasn't a strong supporter of Jefferson, he did recognize that Jefferson had integrity and was devoted to his principles. After the Federalist Party started to weaken, Senator Gouverneur Morris of New York was cognizant of Hamilton's position after the 1800 election. He wrote in 1801 and said that Hamilton appeared to be in "the awkward situation of a man who continues sober after the company are drunk." About Burr, Morris said, "Thus you see that Mr. Burr is resolved to preserve himself in a situation to adhere to his former friends, engagements, and projects; and to use the Federalists as the tool of his aggrandizement."

Hostility continued to brew between the Federalists and the Democratic-Republicans. Each party had their respective reasons for doing so, but the political crisis only continued to grow. Everyone was looking for a scapegoat. The Democratic-Republicans, in particular, were worried about what the Federalists might do. Rumors of violence permeated the taverns and parlors.

George Washington didn't declare a political party affiliation, although many of his viewpoints and decisions were similar to the Federalist agenda. In fact, many people referred to him as a Federalist. His successor, Adams, was a declared Federalist. After the election, all eyes looked toward Jefferson as a Democratic-Republican to ascertain the differences in how the parties ran the country. The Democratic-Republicans were more interested in a protectionist position, which would generally remove America from the world stage and focus upon agrarianism and development within the country itself. Predictably, Thomas Jefferson decreased government expenditures, thus lowering excise taxes, giving relief to the companies and farmers involved in the manufacture and distribution of whiskey and the sale of other goods among the states. Progress had finally been made toward the repayment of war debts, due to the efforts of Hamilton. In addition, the reduction in government spending would leave even more money available for private enterprise. During the initial phase of his presidency, Jefferson reduced the size of the United States Navy as well as other related expenses. That alone reduced the national debt from 83 to 57 million dollars. Now American shipping could be of a commercial rather than a military nature.

Under Jefferson, Albert Gallatin was appointed the secretary of the treasury. With Jefferson's approval, Gallatin followed through with much of the same policies established by Alexander Hamilton, who had preceded him.

The War of the Barbary Pirates

That relief was incredibly short-lived, though. Jefferson, as foreign minister under Washington, had negotiated with the Barbary pirates, the largest piracy operation in the southern Mediterranean. A treaty was made with the Barbary state of Morocco in 1784. Although it did involve paying tributes to the pirates, it seemed to preserve the peace with the exception of Algiers and the Tripoli pirates. In 1801, just after Jefferson took office, the Dey of Algiers demanded a tribute of one million dollars every year. Also, in 1801, the Pasha of Tripoli demanded 225,000 dollars, but Jefferson refused to spend more. For the protection of American shipping, Jefferson asked Congress to allocate money to send over one schooner and then six frigates to protect the merchant vessels. His new secretary of state, James Madison, wrote to the Pasha of Tripoli, indicating to him that it was the president's intention to send this initial squadron over to negotiate peace, but that failed when the Pasha of Tripoli declared war on the United States. Jefferson approached Congress with a request for the funds to finance this mission and obtained it under the "Act for the protection of commerce and seamen of the United States against the Tripolitan Cruisers." Hamilton disagreed with Jefferson's solution, arguing that a formal declaration of war needed to be passed by Congress. Jefferson ignored that and asked his newly appointed secretary of war, Henry Dearborn, to intercede. Dearborn argued with the president, but there was no time for prolonged debate, so Jefferson himself sent Commander Edward Preble to go to Sicily to obtain the support of King Ferdinand of Spain and secure the use of gunboats and two warships. Because of this, Jefferson had been forced to break his promise to reduce the size of the navy.

Jefferson's newly appointed secretary of the navy, Robert Smith, sent more ships under Commander Preble, including the *Chesapeake*, *Argus*, *Constellation*, *Constitution*, *Enterprise*, and *Philadelphia*. The American ships set up a blockade of the Barbary ports and raided the pirates' ships. In 1803, during the naval maneuvers in the Mediterranean, Captain Bainbridge, his ship the *Philadelphia*, and his men were kidnapped and taken prisoner. In retaliation, Lieutenant Decatur stole aboard a Tripoli ship and captured it. Ground forces were disembarked and marched across North Africa all the way to the Tripolitan city of Derna, where the Barbary soldiers were defeated.

The Great Louisiana Purchase of 1803

The Seven Years' War between England and France and its allies, which lasted between 1756 and 1763, was mostly a European conflict which spilled over into the British Colonies before the American Revolution. One of the phases of it was known as the French and Indian War, which was waged between the British

Americans and the French, both with their Native American allies. The goal was to control this vast amount of land amounting to about 828,000 square miles west of the Mississippi River. After the Seven Years' War was over, the secretive treaty, the Treaty of Fontainebleau in 1762, ceded the territory to Spain. After American independence, the United States obtained the rights to use the Mississippi River for navigation and shipment of goods to and from the Port of New Orleans, which was still owned by Spain. Until 1798, the Americans were permitted to store goods there until they were shipped overseas or somewhere more local.

In 1800, Spain, in need of funds, was in the process of transferring the Louisiana territory and New Orleans back to France. Jefferson had long coveted this land as he could expand the United States westward and create more states there. So, he sent Robert Livingston, his U.S. minister to France, to open up negotiations in 1801. The Port of New Orleans, in particular, was essential for American trade.

Napoleon Bonaparte now had control of France, and he sent in a military force to protect it. The Southerners were also afraid that Napoleon would free all of the slaves in Louisiana, which might cause slave revolts in the Southern states. The opposite happened. Napoleon wanted the wealth in the islands of the Caribbean more. In 1802, General Charles Leclerc was sent to Saint-Dominique and reestablished slavery. British and Spanish forces became involved in a conflict over Saint- Dominique and its nearby islands. Concerned that hostilities would break out between the French and the settlers already there, Jefferson declared neutrality. The people on Saint-Dominique managed to secure a victory, declaring independence under the new name of Haiti in 1804.

Jefferson quietly worked with a French noble by the name of Pierre Samuel du Pont de Nemours. Du Pont was living in the United States at the time, but he was able to contact Napoleon directly, and Jefferson wanted to know what Napoleon's intentions were in regards to the Territory of Louisiana. Without informing

Livingston, his foreign minister to France, Jefferson sent James Monroe over there in 1803. Napoleon attempted to regain control of the all-important island of Saint-Dominque but was met with extreme resistance. Already, Napoleon had lost a little over 24,000 to 25,000 men out of the original 31,000 sent there during the aforementioned expedition to Saint-Dominque alone, and he was growing weary of trying to conduct a war on two fronts—one on the European continent and another one across the Atlantic Ocean. Also, because Napoleon couldn't control Saint-Dominque, no sugar shipments would be forthcoming, which was their prime commodity there. Since he wouldn't have sufficient revenues from the colonies, he didn't see much of a point of holding onto Louisiana. Plus, Spain had yet to finish the transfer of the territory to him, so Napoleon might have been spurred on by spite, selling something to the United States that wasn't even his quite yet.

In 1803, just a few days before James Monroe's arrival, the treasury minister of France, François Barbé-Marbois approached Robert Livingston and offered to sell not just New Orleans but all of the Louisiana Territory to Jefferson. Jefferson was astonished that Napoleon was willing to sell that much land and raised his initial offer from ten million dollars for New Orleans to fifteen million dollars for the Louisiana territory. That would be equivalent to about 600 billion dollars today, and acquiring the territory doubled the size of the United States.

Hamilton approved of this purchase wholeheartedly and even complimented Jefferson for agreeing to this sale. Several months before the treaty was ratified, Hamilton wrote, "This, it will be allowed, is an important acquisition not indeed as a territory, but as being essential to the peace of prosperity of our western country, and as opening a free and valuable market to our commercial states." The treaty was ratified on May 2nd, 1803.

Political Partisanship: Trial of Samuel Chase

Aaron Burr, Jefferson's vice president, was bypassed in terms of having an intimate role in the Jefferson Cabinet, besides presiding over the 1803 impeachment trial of Justice Samuel Chase, whom Jefferson perceived as his political enemy. Chase heavily supported the Federalists but made the error of carrying on a political soliloquy from the bench against the Democratic-Republicans. He said to the grand jury that the country was "headed down the road to mobocracy, the worst of all governments," and he implicated that the Democratic-Republicans would extinguish all liberty and freedom. Jefferson wrote to Representative Joseph Nicholson, indicating that Chase should be charged with seditious behavior. The three charges had to do with comments stemming from Chase's conduct during the treason trial of John Fries during the Whiskey Rebellion and the trial of James Callender on libel charges, as well as the vicious comments he made about the Democratic-Republicans, mentioned above, to a grand jury in Baltimore. In his earlier Federalist letters under the name of "Publius," Hamilton had been very critical of Samuel Chase, even though he was a Federalist. Hamilton felt that he was corrupt and used his position to aggrandize his own reputation.

Although political partisanship was rampant during the campaign for the 1800 election for president, it was not intended to be practiced by a Supreme Court Justice. However, in 1804, this was not as strictly practiced as it is today. Samuel Chase was opposed to the repeal of the Judiciary Act of 1801, an act which restricted the members of the Supreme Court in such a way that they could be chosen according to the party that was in office. Chase, it was alleged, showed seditious behavior when he lambasted the Democratic-Republicans from the bench. If he was convicted, that would mean that he had committed a "high crime and misdemeanor." In order for that to happen, two-thirds of the jury had to choose to convict him.

As a Democratic-Republican, Burr wasn't sympathetic with Chase, but he strictly observed court etiquette in the execution of his role of presiding over the trial. Although Chase was old and frail, Senator William Plumer of New Hampshire observed that Burr insisted that Chase find his own seat, as was customary, and not be provided with the table he had requested. Plumer said, "Although rightfully concerned about maintaining an atmosphere of judicial decorum, Burr had lost much of his 'easy grace' and consummate tact that made him an effective presiding officer." Curiously, attendees in the courtroom were also snacking on cake and apples, but Burr said he didn't notice that when it was brought up.

As was his practice, Burr was impartial when passing judgment. He indicated that the criteria for impeachment wasn't met, and Samuel Chase was freed.

The Election of 1804

Jefferson began to suspect that Burr was only aligned with the Democratic-Republicans because he felt that he would gain political ground by doing so. Jefferson was also astonished that Burr didn't graciously step down in favor of Jefferson during the 1800 election.

Due to the results of the 1800 elections, the Twelfth Amendment to the U.S. Constitution was passed in June 1804, just in time for the new presidential election. Under this amendment, one would cast a vote for the president and another vote for the vice president—in other words, the person who won the second most votes would no longer be automictically vice president. Jefferson, of course, was going to run again as president, but he did not choose Burr to be his running mate; instead, he chose George Clinton

Running for the Federalists was Charles Cotesworth Pinckney, a Southerner who ran previously in the 1800 election. He was chosen because he was a planter who contributed during the administration of John Adams and the Quasi-War. Rufus King, a well-respected lawyer who served Jefferson despite the fact that he was a Federalist, ran as his running mate.

Due to the strong economic status of the county, the Louisiana Purchase, and Jefferson's own popularity, he easily won the presidency, attaining 162 electoral votes to Pinckney's 14 votes.

The 1804 New York Gubernatorial Race

Jefferson's suspicions about Burr were correct. Instead of being a loyal Democratic-Republican, Burr also campaigned among the Federalists against Morgan Lewis in the 1804 New York gubernatorial election. Lewis came from a respectable military background, as did Burr, and was an assemblyman in New York in 1789 and 1792. George Clinton was New York's previous governor and was very popular. However, now that he would be Jefferson's running mate in the presidential election, he was no longer a political threat. The seat was wide open.

Even though Burr was a Democratic-Republican, he had supporters among the Federalists, especially a splinter group called the Essex Junto, which was made up of powerful politicians from the New England states. Several years prior to this, they had offered Hamilton a position in a clandestine plot to separate New England from the union. Hamilton refused to participate, but word had it that Burr indicated he might be interested in this. Hamilton told the Federalists that the result of voting for Burr might be a "dismemberment of the Union." According to Hamilton, Burr could then become chief of the "Northern portion" and might be a "despotic chief." Hamilton also said Burr was a man of "irregular and insatiable ambition." Hamilton then added that his political rival, John Lansing, would be a better governor because he could keep New York united.

In February of 1804, Hamilton gave a speech to that effect to his fellow Federalists in Albany. Hamilton always was a charismatic and respected individual. Just a few months before the gubernatorial election was held, Lansing decided not to run and was replaced by Morgan Lewis. Burr ran as an independent, but he had the support of many at Tammany Hall as well as the radical Federalists. Lewis, on the other hand, wasn't associated with

Tammany Hall, but he had the backing of the former Democratic-Republican governor, Clinton.

A little over 58 percent of the "Clintonian" Democratic-Republicans voted for Lewis, and he won the election. Burr received almost 42 percent of the vote.

The Duel Between Alexander Hamilton and Aaron Burr

In early 1804, at a dinner party at Judge John Tayler's home, both Tayler and Hamilton dreaded the possibility that Aaron Burr might be elected governor of New York. James Kent, another illustrious Federalist who was at the table, expressed the same fear. Dr. Charles Cooper, another guest, then characterized Burr as a "dangerous man and one who ought not to be trusted with the reins of government." Cooper wrote that in a letter which ended up being printed in the *New York Evening Post* in July of that year. It wasn't uncommon for letters to be intercepted and deliberately misdirected to the press.

When that letter hit the light, Cooper was peppered with questions. On one occasion, Cooper was quoted to have said, "I could detail to you a still more despicable opinion which General Hamilton has expressed of Mr. Burr." Cooper's letter was reprinted in the *Albany Register* on April 24th, 1804, and when Burr read it, he lost his temper and shot off a letter to Alexander Hamilton.

Hamilton responded that the language of Dr. Cooper "plainly implies that he considered this opinion of you, which he attributes to me, as a 'despicable' one; but he affirms that I have expressed some other still 'more despicable' without however mentioning to whom, when or where." Then Hamilton said that between gentlemen, the distinction between the words "despicable" and "more despicable" weren't worthy of discussion.

Hamilton didn't respond to Burr's reply right away, so Burr wrote more letters. Other letters then went back and forth between the two. Burr's communications were full of free-floating anger and evidence of the increasing paranoia of a man who was now obsessing over a word.

In these letters, the term "honor" was often mentioned. That was a cue used to signify a duel. Even though the practice had been forbidden by state laws in both New Jersey and New York, it wasn't well enforced in the former state. One of the most common places for duels was Weehawken, New Jersey, in the heights near the Palisades, the same place where Philip Hamilton had his duel three years before. This wasn't a heavily trafficked area, and a duel was scheduled there for July 11th, 1804. Both groups rowed across the Hudson River separately, and Burr's group arrived first. William Peter Van Ness, a federal judge, stood for Aaron Burr and Nathaniel Pendleton, a New York judge, stood for Alexander Hamilton. Hamilton's group arrived about a half hour later, whose boat also included a physician, Dr. David Hosack.

It was common for the two combatants to deliberately miss their first shot, shooting at the ground to demonstrate their courage in participating in a duel at all. After this shot, the duel could then come to an end. Although they could fire again, few did, and usually, both left and called the matter closed. Because the people who stood in as seconds had their backs turned, they couldn't see exactly what happened. In the early morning hours of July 11th, 1804, two shots cracked out, breaking the deadly silence. Van Ness and Pendleton swung around and saw Hamilton lying in a heap upon the dusty ground, bleeding profusely from his abdomen.

Hosack later related that Hamilton regained consciousness only briefly after he applied smelling salts. He told Doctor Hosack, "I did not intend to fire at him." Then he told the doctor he had lost all feeling in his lower limbs and said no more. He was carried by boat to the Greenwich Village home of William Bayard Jr., a New York banker, and died there the following morning after receiving communion from Bishop Benjamin Moore. All his seven living children and his loving wife Eliza were there at his bedside when he breathed his last.

There are a few versions told about the duel, and it was said that Hamilton aimed above Burr's head, prompting Burr to think that Hamilton was shooting at him; others said that he fired into the ground, which was the more traditional way. The newspapers reported that a ball was later found to have gone through the limb of a cedar tree about thirteen feet above Burr's head, but some claim that Hamilton's pistol went off accidentally when he fell.

The country went into a frenzy over the duel. There was disagreement over who shot who first and whether or not the duel would have been resolved with an apology by Hamilton. For the most part, people considered Burr to be a murderer. Hamilton was popular, and many hung on to his every word when he published his opinions about American issues. The newspapers which leaned toward the Democratic-Republican faction, however, had difficulty defending Burr, so instead, they targeted the Federalist press for its campaign assailing the reputation of Burr. During those years, this duel indicated that party politics was not only vicious but also violent.

There is one rock at the duel site called the "Death Rock," upon which it is said Hamilton's head was propped up after the duel. Alexander Hamilton is buried at the Trinity Churchyard in lower Manhattan.

The Destiny of Aaron Burr

Both Hamilton and Burr were at the bottom of the curve in their political careers at the time of Hamilton's death, but Burr had new and exciting plans for the future. Aaron Burr hadn't forgotten the appeal from the radical Federalists in 1800 who proposed a secession of the New England states from the union. It wasn't the first time this kind of notion crossed his mind. In 1795 and again in 1796, he had proposed that America invade some of the Spanish lands in Texas. He knew the Spanish didn't have the disciplined military that the British had. After seeing that Jefferson was able to gain acres of land from France at the Louisiana Purchase, he visited some areas there in 1805. While exploring the region, he met Harman Biennerhasset, a lawyer, who owned a lot of land in the Ohio River valley. He also met with a former Continental Army officer, James Wilkinson, and hired him along with Biennerhasset to help conquer the Spanish-owned territory of south Texas and part of Mexico. Burr wanted to cede from the union and set up his own private empire in that fertile area. Burr didn't have access to a lot of funding, so he contacted an Englishman by the name of Anthony Merry, with whom he discussed ideas about attracting the interest of the British in American territory west of the Mississippi. Although he tried, Merry wasn't very influential in Britain and couldn't attract their interest. Following that, Burr and his companions went about recruiting men for a force.

Burr's conspiracy came to the attention of President Thomas Jefferson, and in 1807, Burr was put on trial for treason. The prosecution asserted that Burr's plan for land acquisition included some land that was a part of the Louisiana Purchase of 1803. However, it was discovered during the trial that the document upon which they based the evidence was an uncorroborated letter from one of Burr's alleged conspirators, John Wilkinson, so the court threw out this solitary piece of evidence, and Burr was acquitted.

After the case, Burr fled for Europe, living there from 1808 to 1812. Upon his return to New York, he reopened his law practice in order to pay some of his past debts, which were substantial. He lived in relative obscurity, using the pseudonym "Edwards," his mother's maiden name, when he could. He married again in 1833, but the marriage only lasted a few short months. In 1834, Burr died of a massive stroke.

The Hamilton Progeny Lived On

Although Hamilton's daughter, Angelica, had suffered a mental breakdown after the death of Hamilton's eldest son, her younger brother, Alexander Jr., attended Columbia College and then began the study of law as his father had done. He was also a military man like his father and later resumed the practice of law, becoming a federal attorney, a legislator, and later on a realtor. Likewise, Hamilton's fourth child, James, had a similar career in the military and law. He married Mary Morris, the daughter of Robert Morris, a financier of the Revolution whom his parents knew well. Curiously, James differed with his father's views on banking and opposed national banks to service the government and was a heavy supporter of Thomas Jefferson. It's interesting to note that he named his main residence the "Nevis House" after his father's birthplace.

On the morning before Alexander Hamilton's fateful duel, he called for his twelve-year-old son, John Church Hamilton. Related in his later years, John Hamilton said that on that day, he drew John close and "taking my hands in his palms, all four hands extended, he told me to repeat the Lord's Prayer." In 1834, John Church Hamilton wrote a biography of his father's life.

Alexander's son, William, was only six years old at the time of the duel. When he became an adult, he moved to Illinois and was involved in the legislature for a while. Later on, he became a lead miner of all things. Little Eliza, who was four when her father died, cared for her mother until her death in 1854. "Young Phil," who was the youngest, was said to have "manifested much of his father's sweetness and happy disposition, and was always notably considerate of the feelings of others, and was punctilious to a fault in is obligations."

Conclusion

In August 2015, the musical *Hamilton* opened on Broadway. One of the most notable quotes from that performance was "How does a bastard, orphan, son of a whore and a Scotsman, dropped in the middle of a forgotten spot in the Caribbean by providence, impoverished, in squalor grow up to be a hero and a scholar?" One might simply respond that America was a land of liberty that supported the rights of the individual, regardless of their social standing. That is true, to an extent, but it takes more than rugged individualism to become universally recognized as a Founding Father of the United States. It takes extraordinary courage to rise above one's social station in life and reach for what seems to surpass one's own abilities.

Hamilton was a soldier with unmitigated valor during the American Revolution because he felt his beliefs and those of his countrymen were worth dying for. Hamilton's credo was like the U.S. Constitution itself, which was wrapped up in his astute mind—the mind of a man convinced in the ideals of the new American nation. He was, however, a stubborn man who argued with his learned contemporaries like John Adams, the second president of the country, and the third president, Thomas Jefferson. Unlike many of the other Founding Fathers, Hamilton was never wealthy, but that never stopped him from expressing his views when he wrote essays for *The Federalist Papers*. For a man who wasn't wealthy, he understood finances and managed to pull America out of debt after the war and resolve a banking crisis.

As he looked upon the possibility of death, Hamilton knew he would never be president because of his affair with Maria Reynolds. So, he planned to go where destiny would lead—to a life of being a campaigner extraordinaire and what is today called a "power broker." Just that, and nothing more. Hamilton's words spoken hundreds of years ago to thousands of patriotic Americans will never fade from the language of liberty, freedom, and, above all, truth. Hamilton once said, "I thought it my duty to exhibit things as they are, not as they ought to be." And that is the way it was on that fateful day of July 11th, 1804.

Part 8: James Monroe

A Captivating Guide to the Founding Father Who Served as the Fifth President of the United States

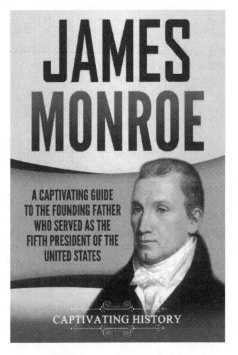

Introduction

From plantation owner to diplomat to U.S. President, James Monroe was known for his tenacity in pursuing what he thought was right, while also being honored for his fair policies, such as the Monroe Doctrine and policies to develop the country's infrastructure. These traits were recognized in 1816, when the West African country of Liberia, changed its name to Monrovia, in honor of James Monroe. It serves as the only international capital named after a U.S. President, and only one of two capitals in the world named after a U.S. President—the other being Washington, D.C.

James Monroe shares another badge of honor with George Washington in that the two were both unchallenged candidates for the presidency. Washington ran unopposed for his second presidential term in 1792 and Monroe held the same honor in 1820.

In losing both parents during his teenage years, Monroe was forced to drop out of school to help with his younger siblings. Despite this, he later attended college and went to law school. That he was counted on for his diplomatic skills demonstrates his sense of fairness, and paved the way for his presidency.

The United States, in its infancy during his lifetime, gained its foothold in history thanks to people like James Monroe and the peers of his day: George Washington, Patrick Henry, Thomas Jefferson, John Quincy Adams and James Madison.

James Monroe is probably best known for the Monroe Doctrine, a policy challenging European colonization and interference, but he was also an integral part of many other policies such as the Missouri Compromise.

Regardless of where his focus was required, Monroe met challenges head-on, whether it was working to improve the infrastructure of the country during his presidency, or working to end unjust practices such as the British impressment of U.S. sailors.

A family man, a diplomat, a soldier, a lawyer, a farmer and a president... no matter what capacity he was called on to serve, James Monroe did so with confidence and tireless perseverance.

Chapter 1 – His Early Years

James Monroe was born on April 28, 1758, during the fervor to colonize North America. His birthplace, in Westmoreland County, **Virginia**, was a partially wooded area of the colony.

Long before his birth, his family moved to Virginia to live in the 'virtual paradise,' as described in one 1649 pamphlet that circulated in London. Monroe's paternal grandfather emigrated from Scotland and began working a large piece of land in the area, while his maternal grandfather emigrated to Virginia from Wales.

By the time Monroe was born to Spence Monroe and Elizabeth Jones, the family owned 600 acres of land that Spence was farming. By many standards, the Monroe family would be considered upper-class, due to the fact that Spence owned land and slaves. Monroe also had four siblings: Elizabeth, Spence, Andrew and Joseph.

His mother taught Monroe and his siblings—Elizabeth, Spence, Andrew and Joseph—during their early years and when Monroe was 11, he was allowed to enroll in Campbelltown Academy, a school run by Reverend Archibald Campbell. Monroe was known as a bright pupil, excelling in Latin and mathematics.

Even then, he was drawn to friends who would later be politically inclined, including classmate John Marshall, who became the fourth Chief Justice of the United States, serving in that position from 1801 to 1835.

Despite his love of learning and his close friendships, Monroe was only involved with the school for parts of the year, since he was often needed at home to work on the farm. When he was 16, he left the school permanently, being thrust into adulthood following his mother's death, soon followed by his father's death.

Monroe inherited his family's farm and at least one slave, but he was still too young to manage such responsibilities.

His sister, Elizabeth, had already married, and Joseph Jones, their mother's brother, took in the three Monroe boys. Childless himself, Joseph not only acted like a surrogate parent, but also had a major influence on the direction that Monroe's life took. A member of the House of Burgesses himself, Joseph introduced James to influential Virginians, including George Washington, Patrick Henry and Thomas Jefferson.

Joseph also enrolled Monroe in the College of William and Mary in 1774. Perhaps ironically, the college would later grasp on to a bit of his history by purchasing the plantation he owned in later life.

If he had expected a peaceful college tenure, Monroe would have been wrong. By 1774, unrest had seized the hearts of the colonists. Britain enacted a series of restrictive laws after the Boston Tea Party. The "Intolerable Acts" as they became known, took away the self-governance of Massachusetts colonists, but incited fury throughout the 13 colonies.

Monroe himself became involved in the opposition to Lord John Murray, the 4th Earl of Dunmore, who was serving as the governor of Virginia at the time. Perhaps in anticipation of an uprising, Lord Dunmore ordered the removal of military supplies from the Hanover militia.

The act backfired, and Lord Dunmore took his family and fled the Governor's Palace, which was then raided by Monroe and other college classmates. They seized swords and an estimated 200 muskets for the militia.

Two years later, in 1776, Monroe dropped out of college and joined the Continental Army in the 3rd Virginia Regiment. Although he hadn't finished college, his intelligence and aptitude earned him the rank of lieutenant, serving under Captain George Washington.

He would later study law, but would never return to the college classroom. However, at 18 years old, Monroe was well on his way to making his mark on American history.

Chapter 2 – The Revolutionary War

As a lieutenant, Monroe had several months of training before his regiment was called north where they participated in two battles, known as the New York and New Jersey Campaign.

In the fight for control over New York City and New Jersey, Washington's troops were pushed back over the Potomac River by the British, under the command of General Sir William Howe.

Although morale was low and the winter was brutal on the soldiers, the Continental army regrouped and went on the attack again, this time on a Hessian encampment. Although they were stealthy, Monroe and Washington's cousin, William Washington, caught the attention of a local farmer and doctor John Riker. Learning that they were American soldiers on their way to a surprise attack, Dr. Riker joined them, assuming that he might be of some use.

The attack was successful but James was shot in the shoulder. An artery was severed and he was bleeding profusely. Fortunately, the doctor that they encountered on their way to the attack was on hand and stopped the bleeding, essentially saving Monroe's life.

The battle was deemed a victory for the patriots, and an estimated 900 Hessians were killed. However, there were many casualties on the American side as well, which were depicted in the famous painting *The Capture of the Hessians at Trenton, December 26, 1776*, by John Trumbull. In the painting, Monroe is captured as being attended to by Dr. Riker.

He was also depicted in another famous painting called *Washington Crossing the Delaware* by Emanuel Gottlieb Leutze. In it, Monroe is credited as the man who was holding the flag. However, some historians insist that Monroe crossed the Delaware well beyond Washington's famed crossing.

For his efforts, Monroe was promoted to the rank of captain and sent home to recover from his injuries. Under his new role, he also began to recruit soldiers for his own company, but was unsuccessful.

To that end, he asked to be returned to the front and started working with General William Alexander, also known as Lord Stirling. During this time, he also befriended the Marquis de Lafayette, a young Frenchman who volunteered his efforts against the British in retaliation for the killing of his father in the Seven Years War.

Lafayette induced Monroe to view war as the resistance to political tyranny, which no doubt influenced Monroe's actions in the political arena. The two remained close, and their friendship would prove fortuitous later during the French Revolution.

Monroe returned to battle and fought in the Philadelphia Campaign, an effort to capture the city, which was, at the time, where the Second Continental Congress was located. On the British side, the British General William Howe succeeded in the campaign, although his slow progress was heavily criticized for not coming to the aid of John Burgoyne's troops in a campaign that essentially forced the French to join the war.

During that campaign, Monroe met up with his old school chum, John Marshall, and the two hunkered down to wait out the brutal winter in the same quarters at the Valley Forge encampment.

In the summer of 1778, Monroe participated in the Battle of Monmouth. Perhaps ironically after surviving the brutal winter, the New Jersey battle ushered in soaring temperatures and killed many soldiers on both sides.

Constantly facing financial challenges, Monroe decided to resign his commission later that year. He wasn't out of action for long, though, because in December 1778, the British captured Savannah and his home state took steps to raise four regiments.

Bolstered with letters of recommendation from former commanders Washington and Stirling, as well as a letter from Alexander Hamilton, James returned to Virginia to try to get his own command. Although he was made lieutenant-colonel of one of the regiments, he faced the same struggle as he did after his injury at Trenton: he couldn't recruit enough men to join his regiment.

Once again, his challenges turned into an opportunity. His uncle suggested that he change career directions and start studying law, which would later bolster his political ambitions. Monroe moved to Williamsburg and by 1780, was studying law under Thomas Jefferson, who was then the governor of Virginia.

Monroe never entirely relished the idea of practicing law, but he was very interested in politics, and was convinced that establishing a law practice was the most practical way to advance his political career.

While studying with Jefferson, Monroe accompanied him to Richmond, where the state capital was now established, largely because it would be easier to defend from the British, who were starting to concentrate their focus on the southern colonies.

The governor named Monroe a colonel in the army and he was expected, once again, to recruit men. For the third time, he was unsuccessful. Monroe returned home, and wasn't present when the British raided Richmond in 1781.

Then, the war turned a corner. It was at the Siege of Yorktown where Lafayette held Cornwallis' troops with his own army of 5,000 American soldiers, with an additional 1,500 French troops. With Washington's forces 200 miles away, Lafayette was ordered to prevent the British forces from escaping. They did so until Washington could arrive in early September, surrounding the British army.

To Monroe's frustration, he also missed the Siege of Yorktown, which proved to be the final battle of the Revolutionary War.

By this point, though, Monroe's tenure with the war was over and he moved on to a new phase in his life.

Chapter 3 – Early Political Career and Family Life

James Monroe passed the Virginia bar exam and began practicing law in Fredericksburg, an effort partially funded by the sale of the plantation he had inherited.

At the same time, he won his first political appointment and in 1782, was elected to the Virginia House of Delegates, the successor to the House of Burgesses, of which his uncle was a member.

He first served on the state's Executive Council and the following year, was elected to the Congress of the Confederation, the governing party of the United States, where he served until his tenure concluded three years later.

While serving in Congress, he became interested in the country's expansion west and was part of the governing body that wrote the legislation for the Northwest Ordinance, the first organized area of the United States.

In 1776, he married Elizabeth Kortright, the daughter of Lawrence and Hannah Kortright. The family was wealthy, although they had taken a hit financially because Lawrence was considered by many to have loyalist sympathies.

Her father's political views hardly affected James when he met the beautiful Elizabeth at a local theatre. When they married, Elizabeth was 17, nine years younger than James.

The two were married in her father's home in a ceremony presided over by Reverend Benjamin Moore, the second Episcopal bishop of New York. Interestingly, while his participation with the Monroe marriage was noteworthy, Reverend Moore is best remembered for giving communion to Alexander Hamilton on his deathbed, after Hamilton was mortally wounded in a duel with Aaron Burr, then the Vice President of the United States.

James and Elizabeth honeymooned on Long Island and then returned to New York City where they lived with her father until Congress adjourned that year.

It was perhaps a bittersweet time for Elizabeth's father, Lawrence, who never remarried after losing his wife, Hannah in childbirth. Elizabeth had four older siblings. No doubt the house felt empty when James resigned from Congress with the intent to return to his legal career in Virginia.

Lawrence was in New York with Elizabeth gave birth to their first child, Eliza Kortright Monroe, in December 1776. James Spence Monroe was born two years later, but died when he was 16 months old. Historians did not record the cause of death, but it is known that he was sick for several days before he succumbed to his illness.

"An unhappy event has occurr'd which has overwhelmed us with grief," James Monroe wrote to his friend, James Madison in 1800. "At ten last night our beloved babe departed this life after several days sickness... I cannot give you an idea of the effect this event has produc'd on my family, or of my own affliction... This has roused me beyond what I thought was possible... [sic]"

Despite the devastation, time continued on. James and Elizabeth had another daughter in 1804, whom they named Marie Hester Monroe. Although they could not have known it at the time, Marie would later be the first presidential child to be married in the White House.

After moving back to Virginia, Monroe became a state attorney, and then chose to serve another term in the Virginia House of Delegates.

In 1788, Monroe was selected as a delegate to the Virginia Ratifying Convention, a group of 168 members who met to determine if they would ratify or vote against the proposed United States Constitution. After deliberating from June 2 through June 27, the Virginia convention narrowly voted to ratify the convention, making it the tenth state to ratify the Constitution.

Monroe was one of the 79 members to cast his vote against ratification, largely because he supported the addition of a bill of rights, which was not included at that time. Monroe, like others, feared that a central government could cast a shadow over the rights of individual states.

James and the other anti-federalists (although they called themselves "federalists for amendments") weren't ready to give up the fight and planned to put in power a Congress that would amend the newly-adopted Constitution. Under the urging of Patrick Henry who vehemently opposed ratification, James ran against James Madison for a seat in the First United States Congress.

Although they were political opponents, the two maintained their friendship and often traveled together. When the vote was held, Monroe was elected by more than 300 votes.

Monroe decided that it was time for another change.

After the defeat, Monroe returned to his law practice and also took up farming in Charlottesville, but not for long. In 1790, Senator William Grayson died. Only one of two elected senators who voted against ratifying the Constitution, perhaps it was only natural for Monroe to be elected to finish out Grayson's term.

After the term was completed, Monroe went on to win the reelection in 1791, a position he held until he was asked to bring his diplomatic talents overseas.

Chapter 4 – Ambassador to France

War was once again on the horizon, but not on the young United States' shores. In the late 1790s, the French Revolutionary Wars loomed, and conflicts with both Britain and France were impacting trade with the United States.

In response to these foreign concerns, Washington, who was serving as president, appointed two new ambassadors in 1794. Federalist John Jay was named the ambassador to the United Kingdom and James Monroe was sent to France as the United States ambassador in that country.

Not one to be separated from his family for extended periods, Monroe gathered his family and traveled to France. Prior to their departure, Elizabeth gave herself a crash course in French culture to make sure that she did not offend society. She need not have worried—between her diligent studies and her American charm; she was given the nickname "La Belle Américaine."

Elizabeth's love for the French was evidenced in later years as she adopted many European customs when serving as First Lady. For example, each guest who dined with them had their own servant, as was the norm in French aristocracy, and the family frequently conversed in French.

It was a precarious time in France, to be sure, but Monroe was confident enough in his diplomatic skills to not only keep his family safe, but to also assist others who had become victims of the French Revolution.

Thomas Paine was instrumental in influencing people in the colonies to revolt against the British with his popular pamphlet, *Common Sense*. His nature to incite rebellion followed him to Britain after the American Revolution and then to France, where he was elected to the French National Convention, supposedly without being able to speak French.

Paine's fervent writings got him in hot water once more, this time in France. In 1791, he released *Rights of Man,* highlighting his perspective on the French Revolution. As he continued to condemn the revolutionaries who were executing hundreds via the guillotine, the government that once supported him turned against him.

In December 1793, Paine was arrested and imprisoned in Luxembourg Prison, a move that caught the attention of Ambassador Monroe.

Upon Monroe's arrival in France, one of his first tasks was addressing the French National Convention, giving a speech on the benefits of republicanism. He received a standing ovation for his efforts and used this and other successes to secure Paine's release from prison.

Not one to sit still herself, Elizabeth Monroe took it upon herself to visit Adrienne de Lafayette, the wife of Monroe's good friend from the American Revolution.

Madame Lafayette was also imprisoned in 1792, following a movement to control all nobles. At first, she was placed under house arrest, but after the 1794 Reign of Terror, she was transferred to La Force Prison. She was comparatively fortunate: her grandmother, mother and sister were all executed. However, diplomacy prevailed in her situation and after several months at La

Force Prison, the Monroes were instrumental in her quiet release from prison.

The Lafayette family had already been granted American citizenship and upon her release, she and her family were given American passports.

While Monroe's time as ambassador saw many successes, including trade protection, it was a short-lived tenure. His counterpart in Britain helped orchestrate the Jay Treaty between the U.S. and Britain. The ambassador to France was outraged because he was not fully informed of the treaty's nature, which damaged U.S. relations with France.

However, the Jay Treaty was quite beneficial for the United States, due to the many concessions the British made, including an agreement to leave the Northwest Territory. It also facilitated U.S. trade in the British East Indies and not only improved trade between Britain but also led it to agree to compensation for its acts against American shipping.

In return, the U.S. agreed that it would not fund privateers in ports hostile to British interests. The treaty also ordered those Americans who owed money to British merchants before the war to pay up.

Overall, the treaty was considered an important step to prevent future animosity between the two countries; however, those benefits did not console either Monroe or France. Washington called on James to convince the French that the treaty was benign, but the country was not convinced.

Frustrated, Washington demanded that Monroe return to the U.S., convinced that the ambassador was failing to "safeguard the interests of his country."

In return, Monroe harbored a concern that Washington's sensibility may have been compromised by his age.

Chapter 5 – James Monroe: Slave Owner

He and his family made the return voyage in November 1796, but being on home soil did not alleviate Monroe's frustration. He started to pen his experiences as ambassador, which turned into a 400-page defense. In it, he highlighted his concerns that the treaty, while strengthening ties with Britain, would undermine relations with   France.

The family was also struggling financially. Although he received a stipend of $9,000 for living and working in France, they soon found that this wasn't enough to sustain them, between the higher cost of living and their social obligations. After all, the reason they were in the country was to maintain or even improve relations with the European country, so they could hardly cut corners and eliminate social engagements.

Just for the cost of passage home and to ship their belongings, Monroe was forced to take out a mortgage on his new home in Virginia.

For a while after his return, James concentrated his efforts on practicing law and farming. Prior to leaving for France, he purchased a 3,500-acre plantation in Albemarle abutting Jefferson's plantation. Although he had aspirations to build a mansion on the land, he ended up building a much more modest six-room house after his return to the U.S. It was supposed to be a temporary structure, but because he was on the move so much, his family ended up living in it for two decades.

The Ash Lawn-Highland is now simply known as Highland. While he often owned an estimated 30 to 40 slaves at any time, a common practice with large landowners in the south during that era, by 1810, he owned 49 slaves living at Highland. (At the time, his neighbor, Jefferson, owned 147 slaves.)

Because he was so often away from Highland due to his political duties, the plantation was frequently controlled by overseers and slaves were often swapped back and forth between Highland and another piece of property that Monroe owned.

In July 1826, *The Central Gazette* featured an advertisement for the capture and reward of two of Monroe's slaves. Known only as George and Phebe, the two escaped and were assumed to be making their way toward Loudon or heading toward a free state. "If taken in the county," the ad read, "I will give a reward of Ten Dollars: or Fifteen Dollars if taken out of the county and secured in any jail so that I get them again."

The two were never found.

Interestingly, Monroe's perspective on slavery was divided. While he depended on slaves and in his lifetime owned as many as 250 slaves, he never freed any of them. However, in a letter to John Mason in 1829, Monroe called slavery "one of the evils still remaining, incident to our Colonial system."

During Monroe's first year as president, the Society for the Colonization of Free People of Color of America—more commonly known as the American Colonization Society (ACS)—was created upon the premise of relocating freed slaves or free-born blacks to Africa. The colony was located on the Pepper Coast of West Africa.

Some felt that this was a veiled attempt at upholding slavery, but the organizers, which were mostly Quakers, felt that this provided the relocated colonists a better opportunity for freedom in Africa.

In just over the first two decades, 4,571 emigrants were sent across the ocean. Unfortunately, disease ran rampant and of those, there were less than 2,000 survivors by 1843. However, the colony did thrive and reached economic stability. In 1847, the area known by then as Liberia, declared its independence.

Because of his support of the ACS, the capital of Christopolis was renamed Monrovia and the name remains.

Many years later, Monroe was forced to sell Highlands in 1828. All of his slaves were also sold and sent further south, although it is unknown if the man who purchased them, Colonial Joseph White, honored Monroe's stipulation to keep the slave families together.

Chapter 6 – The Governorship & Return to France

In 1799, Monroe was elected to serve as the governor of Virginia. While the governor had fewer duties at this time, he was able to persuade the state to make some infrastructure improvements, such as making changes to transportation. He also urged the legislature to improve the educational system.

One of his primary duties was overseeing the militia when it was activated, but recalling the struggles the fledgling militia had in the beginning of the Revolutionary War, Monroe called for better training for the soldiers.

A year into office, he did call out the militia in response to what is now known as Gabriel's Rebellion, an effort by the slaves on a nearby plantation to rise against the slave owners. The rebellion was squashed and the slave Gabriel was hanged, along with 27 other slave conspirators.

In his letter to Jefferson on September 15, 1800, Monroe seemed to question the punishment. "We have had much trouble with the negroes here," he wrote. "The plan of an insurrection has been clearly proved, & appears to have been of considerable extent. Ten have been condemned & executed, and there are at least twenty perhaps forty more to be tried, of whose guilt no doubt is entertained. It is unquestionably the most serious and formidable conspiracy we have ever known of the kind: tho' indeed to call it so is to give no idea of the thing itself. While it was possible to keep it secret, wh[ich] it was till we saw the extent of it, we did so. But when it became indispensably necessary to resort to strong measures with a view to protect the town [Richmond], the publick arms, the Treasury and the Jail, wh[ich] were all threatened, the opposit course was in part tak[en]. We then made a display of our force and measures of defence with a view to intimidate those people. Where to arrest the hand of the Executioner, is a question of great importance. It is hardly to be presumed, a rebel who avows it was his intention to assassinate his master... if pardoned will ever become a useful servant and we have no power to transport him abroad—Nor is it less difficult to say whether mercy or severity is the better policy in this case, tho' where there is cause for doubt it is best to incline to the former council. I shall be happy to have y[our] opinion on these points [*sic*]."

In his response five days later, Jefferson mulled over Monroe's concerns. "Where to stay the hand of the executioner is an important question," he said. "Those who have escaped from the immediate danger, must have feelings which would dispose them to extend the executions. Even here, where every thing has been perfectly tranquil, but where a familiarity with slavery, and a possibility of danger from that quarter prepare the general mind for some severities, there is a strong sentiment that there has been hanging enough. The other states & the world at large will for ever condemn us if we indulge a principle of revenge, or go one step beyond absolute necessity. They cannot lose sight of the rights of the two parties, & the object of the unsuccessful one. Our situation is indeed a difficult one: for I doubt whether these people can ever be permitted to go at large among us with safety. To reprieve them and keep them in prison till the meeting of the legislature will encourage efforts for their release. Is there no fort & garrison of the state or of the Union, where they could be confined, & where the presence of the garrison would preclude all ideas of attempting a rescue. Surely the legislature would pass a law for their exportation, the proper measure on this & all similar occasions? I hazard these thoughts for your own consideration only, as I should be unwilling to be quoted in the case; you will doubtless hear the sentiments of other persons & places, and will hence be enabled to form a better judgment on the whole than any of us singly & in a solitary situation."

Regardless of Monroe's concerns, the country felt it needed to do something to avoid further insurrections after Gabriel's Rebellion and even more restrictions were placed on blacks, whether slave or free. For example, they were forbidden to gather in groups, they could not be educated and they were forbidden from outside work.

Whether it was a disturbance with slaves or others, Monroe tried to balance what was fair and right. As Jefferson said, "Monroe was so honest that if you turned his soul inside out, there would not be a spot on it. [*sic*]"

While Gabriel's Rebellion was one of the notable points of Monroe's tenure as governor, he also made several other changes in this role. For example, he furthered an effort to create the state's first penitentiary, providing an alternative for even harsher punishments.

He also worked to enhance communication with the legislature by giving the first State of the Commonwealth address, once again setting a precedent for others to follow

A year into his governorship in 1780, Monroe threw his efforts into helping Thomas Jefferson win his bid for the presidency. Not only did he use his position to influence the state's presidential electors but he also toyed with the idea of using the militia to force a favorable outcome for Jefferson. The militia was not called out in the end, but it exemplifies how passionate Monroe could be when he took up a cause.

For his efforts, when Jefferson was elected president, he named Monroe as his Secretary of State.

Monroe's term wrapped up as governor and Jefferson reached out to him once again. This time, he asked Monroe to make "a temporary sacrifice to prevent the greatest of all evils in the present prosperous tide of our affairs." Jefferson sent James back to France to assist with the negotiations with France for the purchase of New Orleans. In 1800, France was given the Louisiana territory from Spain as part of the Treaty of San Ildefonso.

Since the city was so close to the mouth of the Mississippi River, the United States was determined to purchase New Orleans. And it was good timing, too. Napoleon Bonaparte would have loved to keep hold of it, but the country was still reeling from the high costs of war.

After much negotiation overseas, James was integral in the Louisiana Purchase, obtaining not just New Orleans but the entire territory of Louisiana—all 530 million acres of it— for the bargain price of $15 million.

Even though the U.S. government had initially authorized 50 million francs, just over $9 million at the time, the purchase was considered a huge win for America. Not only was New Orleans secured, but now the country had bragging rights to so much additional land, it was difficult at best to comprehend the parcel of land it just acquired—one that nearly doubled the size of the United States.

One of Monroe's main objectives during the four years he was a diplomat in Britain was to try to extend the Jay Treaty, the very treaty that he had so opposed when it was created.

By this time, the terms of the treaty had expired but by 1806, Monroe had effectively negotiated a new treaty with Britain. He was surprised to find that, after all that work, Jefferson refused to move it further for ratification. Although he was essentially told that he could do better in his negotiations, particularly since there was no clause to address U.S. seaman impressment, Monroe vehemently claimed that this was the best they could do with Britain.

It was a frustrating time for Monroe. Not only was he aggravated by Jefferson's rejection of his hard work in securing the best terms he could, but the news that his friend and neighbor was refusing to support the work he did to negotiate the new treaty was almost too much.

This also happened in addition to several challenging months when he traveled to Spain to try to convince the country that the Louisiana Purchase indeed included the western section of the Florida territory as well—a premise the Spaniards refused to consider.

So, when Monroe's tenure as the British ambassador was up, he returned home, prickling with frustration.

However, as luck would perhaps have it, 1808 was another presidential election year and Monroe was temporarily buoyed by the Old Republicans (also referred to as Quids) to run against his friend, James Madison, for the Democratic-Republican nomination.

Some say that Monroe's campaign was in a halfhearted retaliation for what he felt was Madison's lack of support for his failed treaty attempt. Other historians champion Monroe for stating their similarities, with the exception to foreign policy issues.

Regardless, Madison won his party's nomination and became the fourth president of the United States. Monroe, ever moving forward, was elected to the Virginia House of Delegates in 1810 and then served as Governor of Virginia for most of 1811 when he was once again called on by a president – this time, Madison sought his help.

If one assumed that there was any animosity between the two, it was quickly squelched when, three years into his tenure as president, Madison appointed Monroe as his Secretary of State.

This diplomatic role required Monroe to focus once again on foreign relations, primarily with Britain and France. At this point, the French and British were at war with each other once again, which necessitated a delicate balance in relations with both countries as an objective third party.

Chapter 7 – The War of 1812

Tensions between America and Britain continued to escalate, largely due to the animosity between Britain and France.

At the time, Britain had the largest navy in the world and was actively blockading several French ports. The navy was also tasked with maintaining a military presence around their other colonies in the British Empire.

To meet the demands, Britain increased their fleet to 170 ships, but with limited manpower, Britain attacked American ships and forced their sailors aboard. This impressment had been a growing concern, and was now escalating toward a dangerous tipping point.

At the same time, Britain was trying to prevent America from trading with France, while France was doing the same. America, with a much smaller fleet, tried to stay neutral and not side with either country.

However, neither France nor Britain viewed the United States as a neutral country and both targeted America's trade practices. The primary offender, though, in the newer country's eyes, was Britain for its tendency toward impressment, which was responsible for capturing between 5,000 and 9,000 American sailors in less than a decade.

One of the most notorious examples of British impressment was with what is known as the Chesapeake Affair. Taking place off of the coast of Norfolk, the British warship HMS Leopard clashed with the USS Chesapeake, an American frigate. The Leopard pursued and attacked the Chesapeake.

Leopold commander Salusbury Humphreys ordered the removal of four crew from the Chesapeake after her commander, James Barron, surrendered after firing one shot. The men were tried for desertion and one was hanged. The others were sentenced to 500 lashings, but their sentences were later commuted.

Monroe intervened once more and negotiated the release of the captives. However, the British impressment actions continued, which heightened tensions between the two countries.

On top of that, the Americans suspected that Britain was behind riling up the Native Americans in the country and providing the supplies for carrying out raids against the colonists. If the British could be instrumental in allying with the Native Americans and pushing back the Americans, a neutral Native American state could be created to serve as a barrier between the U.S and Britain's interests in Canada.

Some people were clamoring for war once more. "War Hawks" Henry Clay and John C. Calhoun started making the case, along with new Congressmen.

For the most part, the Congressman from the South and the West were in support of the war, but those from New England, who depended on trade with Britain—or lack thereof by this point—opposed the warmongering.

Perhaps if the treaty that Jefferson had rejected had instead been passed, the relationship with Britain wouldn't have deteriorated to this point. However, there was no looking back for Monroe, and he instead focused his efforts as Secretary of State on how to best protect American's interests.

On June 18, 1812, with Monroe's support, President Madison officially signed a declaration of war against Britain, kicking off the War of 1812.

There were several battles over the next few years, but America still had comparatively fewer troops than Britain. To their benefit, though, British focus was split between the pesky Americans and fighting the war against Napoleon. During the first few years of the war, Monroe was instrumental in fortifying the military presence in Florida.

Beyond these efforts, Monroe was focusing his own efforts where needed and was serving in any way that he could to support his country. With his military history, he tried to give advice to the Secretary of War, John Armstrong, an attempt that Armstrong wholeheartedly rejected.

With the effective defeat of French troops in 1814, the British were immediately able to redouble their efforts and send more troops to America to fight. Still, Armstrong minimized the British capabilities, which would prove to be a bad military decision. While he was effectively turning his back on the British threat, Monroe often joined local troops who were patrolling the coast for signs of a growing threat.

Monroe wanted to return to battle, but Jefferson gently rebuked the efforts. Finally, when British troops were closing around the Americans in the Chesapeake Bay, he tasked himself with changing the troop deployment at Bladensburg. Brigadier General Tobias Stansbury had formed three lines of men, but Monroe repositioned them, inadvertently spreading them too far apart.

The British broke through the lines and then moved on to Washington, D.C. On August 24, 1814, the British burned several governmental buildings. In retaliation for the Americans attacking

York in Ontario, they then turned their attention to the White House.

Fortunately, Madison and his wife were not in residence. The president, having ridden to meet with troops the previous day, told his wife to be on alert. If she saw signs of an attack, he instructed her to gather important papers and flee.

She managed to make it out in time, but not before securing a large portrait of George Washington. One can only imagine their collective relief when they finally met up with each other at a predetermined meeting place!

Their concerns were not unfounded and the British troops first ransacked the White House and then set it on fire, destroying the structure and further bruising the spirit of the American people.

While some members of Congress wanted the White House moved to a different location within Washington, or a different city altogether, Madison moved quickly to have reconstruction commence before a decision to move the location could be finalized.

Madison called in the original architect, James Hoban, to rebuild the executive mansion according to the original plans, but urged a quicker timeline in the rebuilding. In fact, while the first White House was built in 10 years, the replacement was constructed in three years' time.

Deeply disappointed in Secretary of War Armstrong's refusal to heed warnings about troops marching on Washington, Madison removed him from his position. Armstrong was quick to note that Monroe's actions may have led to the British breaking through their lines, but Madison was insistent in his removal.

Following on the heels of Armstrong's dismissal, Monroe was named the new Secretary of War. For the first time, one person held both the Secretary of State and the Secretary of War positions.

The tide of the war turned a year after his appointment as the Secretary of War. September 11, 1814, saw the Battle of Plattsburg Bay on Lake Champlain. This turning point ushered in a new peace treaty between American and British advisories. The Treaty of Ghent was signed on Christmas Eve of that year, signaling the end of the war.

Unfortunately, news traveled quite slowly at that time and it took nearly two months after the treaty was signed in Belgium to reach parts of the United States. By then, the Battle of New Orleans had already been executed and deemed a victory by the Americans.

Although the odds were stacked against the Americans in this battle, determined leadership by Major General Andrew Jackson and a successful conglomeration of U.S. soldiers, Choctaw tribesmen, free blacks and city aristocrats saw tremendous success for the defending party.

There were an estimated 100 American casualties to Britain's 2,000 wounded and killed. Jackson, nicknamed "Old Hickory" for his unwavering toughness, was escalated to high esteem and Monroe would later lavish praise on the war hero by saying, "History records no example of so glorious a victory obtained with so little bloodshed on the part of the victorious."

A month after news of the tremendous victory in the Battle of New Orleans reached the east coast, the news of the Treaty of Ghent finally crossed the ocean as well.

The treaty did not address two of the most pressing issues that brought the war—British impressment and recognizing the neutrality of U.S. vessels—the treaty did make room for expansion into the Great Lakes region, and was considered a diplomatic victory.

Chapter 8 – The Fifth President

James Monroe's wartime leadership bolstered confidence in his ability to succeed Madison as president in the 1816 elections. This time, the odds were much more in his favor.

While America could not claim victory over the War of 1812, the government and military did demonstrate to the American people that once again, it could push off its oppressors. The fact that the political party Monroe and Madison belonged to, the Democratic-Republican party, was in support of the war gave them the necessary credibility to launch another successful presidential bid.

The Federalist party, on the other hand, loudly opposed the war, which partly led to the party's later collapse. As it was, the Democratic-Republican party had already made concessions toward Federalist practices and policies, including tariffs to protect national interest as well as creating a national bank. This heightened Monroe's political party even more in the eyes of their supporters.

His opponents in the caucus were New York Governor Daniel D. Tompkins and William H. Crawford, Secretary of the Treasury.

Crawford later deferred to Monroe, hoping to promote himself as a possible successor, and Monroe beat Tompkins to secure his name on the ballot, with Tompkins in position as his Vice President.

Monroe's political opponent was Rufus King, the man he replaced as ambassador to Great Britain in 1803, but there were not many people who backed the Federalist party or its nominee at that point.

When the votes were counted, James Monroe secured 183 of the 217 electoral votes, beating out King by a landslide. In fact, Monroe won all states except for Connecticut, Delaware and Massachusetts.

When he was inaugurated on March 4, 1817, the warm, sunny day matched the optimistic climate. At noon, the temperature was about 50 degrees, marking a beautiful day for the inaugural speech to be held outdoors.

Originally, the inauguration was slated to be held inside in the Capitol, in the House chamber. However, a heated debate ensued between the House of Representatives and the Senate about which chairs would be used for the event—the Senate wanted their gold-painted chairs to be used for the event.

In retrospect, it was beneficial that the oath of office took place outside because it allowed a large crowd estimated between 5,000 and 8,000 to bear witness.

Consequently, they decided to chance the winter weather and hold the inauguration on a temporary stage in front of the building, which was serving as the temporary Capital after the British invasion.

His speech started out humbly, showing his gratitude for the honor of serving the American people as their President. "I should be destitute of feeling if I was not deeply affected by the strong proof which my fellow-citizens have given me of their confidence in calling me to the high office whose functions I am about to assume," he said.

Standing in front of the Old Brick Capitol, which was serving as the temporary capitol after the British invasion, his speech enthusiastically moved to an upbeat tone. "During a period fraught with difficulties and marked by very extraordinary events the United States have flourished beyond example," he said. "Their citizens individually have been happy and the nation prosperous."

Interestingly, Monroe used the words "happy" or "happiness" nine times in his speech. It was not because he lacked a thesaurus, but he truly felt the positivity as surely as one feels the sun on his face.

And why not? The country had just thrown off an enemy country once more, and the country had ample room to grow.

"Fortunate as we are in our political institutions, we have not been less so in other circumstances on which our prosperity and happiness essentially depend," he said. "Situated within the temperate zone, and extending through many degrees of latitude along the Atlantic, the United States enjoy all the varieties of climate, and every production incident to that portion of the globe. Penetrating internally to the Great Lakes and beyond the sources of the great rivers which communicate through our whole interior, no country was ever happier with respect to its domain. Blessed, too, with a fertile soil, our produce has always been very abundant, leaving, even in years the least favorable, a surplus for the wants of our fellow-men in other countries."

Within the speech were words of warning, though; warning of what the country could become. "It is only when the people become ignorant and corrupt, when they degenerate into a populace, that they are incapable of exercising the sovereignty. Usurpation is then an easy attainment, and an usurper soon found. The people themselves become the willing instruments of their own debasement and ruin. Let us, then, look to the great cause, and endeavor to preserve it in full force. Let us by all wise and constitutional measures promote intelligence among the people as the best means of preserving our liberties."

Also, he suggested that the peace they had at the time may be temporary. "Dangers from abroad are not less deserving of attention. Experiencing the fortune of other nations, the United States may be again involved in war, and it may in that event be the object of the adverse party to overset our Government, to break our Union, and demolish us as a nation. Our distance from Europe and the just, moderate, and pacific policy of our Government may form some security against these dangers, but they ought to be anticipated and guarded against."

Monroe, with his wartime experience, was already anticipating what might happen. "To secure us against these dangers our coast and inland frontiers should be fortified, our Army and Navy, regulated upon just principles as to the force of each, be kept in perfect order, and our militia be placed on the best practicable footing."

While he went on to discuss fortifications and other suggestions, he also emphasized the importance of building and maintaining the country's infrastructure. "Other interests of high importance will claim attention, among which the improvement of our country by roads and canals, proceeding always with a constitutional sanction, holds a distinguished place. ... Nature has done so much for us by intersecting the country with so many great rivers, bays, and lakes, approaching from distant points so near to each other, that the inducement to complete the work seems to be peculiarly strong."

At the end of his speech, his tone turned humble once more. "In the Administrations of the illustrious men who have preceded me in this high station, with some of whom I have been connected by the closest ties from early life, examples are presented which will always be found highly instructive and useful to their successors." But his focus was not only his past experience; to be successful as president, he needed the support of other officials.

"Relying on the aid to be derived from the other departments of the Government," Monroe concluded, "I enter on the trust to which I have been called by the suffrages of my fellow-citizens with my fervent prayers to the Almighty that He will be graciously pleased to continue to us that protection which He has already so conspicuously displayed in our favor."

With the troubles of the country now being laid on his shoulders, Monroe also felt the tug of family commitments, particularly with his wife, Elizabeth. It is likely that her health was starting to fade at this point. While no official records are pinpointing her particular ailment, many people theorize that she had epilepsy.

Interestingly, while Monroe's wife was once held precious by the French when he served as the ambassador, the new role as First Lady proved a more difficult transition. Following in the footsteps of the vivacious former First Lady, Dolley Madison, Elizabeth was considered more aloof and standoffish. It is ironic that she was considered one of the most beautiful women in her generation and at 48 years old when Monroe took the office, her youthful appearance likely made her failing health more improbable in society's eyes and rumors started to circulate that she may be suffering from mental illness.

At the same time, Elizabeth also adopted the more European custom of stepping away from social obligations, bringing many of the social policies Dolley had enacted to a screeching halt.

Even though the inaugural reception was held at the Monroe's home on I Street, she was not present at his swearing-in, and was absent during the reception at their home.

On the holiday when patriotism reigned high, July 4, Elizabeth chose to spend the time in Virginia instead of being on hand for the annual Independence Day festivities. Because of this, many of Washington's society chose to boycott Administration receptions.

She neglected to make social calls, and many of Washington's society felt slighted, to the point that it became a topic of discussion at a cabinet meeting in December 1817.

While Elizabeth had withdrawn from the social spotlight, she did throw her efforts into decorating the White House. It had been built in three years, but it still lacked the furnishings worthy of a presidential family. Some say that Elizabeth tapped into her experiences in Europe to furnish the house; others claim Monroe made the choices himself and then deferred to Elizabeth. However, most agree that the Monroes tapped into their own finances to help with the furnishings, further pushing the family into the great crevasse of debt that the president would spend years trying to escape.

Chapter 9 – First Presidential Tour

Monroe's optimistic presence during his inauguration was extended through the early months of his tenure as President as he took the show on the road, so to speak, to meet with the people who elected him and to help build national trust.

After leaving Washington, D.C., on May 31, 1817, his first stop was in the Baltimore area, where one of his goals was to inspect Fort McHenry. The *Baltimore Patriot* captured the respect of the troops. "Although it was rather the wish of the President to perform his present tour without receiving any public demonstration of respect, the heads of the war and navy departments have, very properly, conceived it incompatible with all usage, and derogatory to the high office he holds, to wave the accustomary military and naval honors on his visit to the different posts and stations."

Upon leaving Baltimore, he elected to travel by steamboat, a rather hazardous decision, as the boats did not have high safety ratings at the time. In one estimate of the boats' dangers, there were explosions in one out of every five that took to the water between the years of 1811 to 1851.

Next, he traveled to Frenchtown, Maryland, and then Newcastle, Delaware. Here he and his traveling companions took a barge to Fort Mifflin.

Monroe spent a few days in early July in Philadelphia, visiting a number of different buildings and inspecting a Revolutionary War battleground, before taking a horse and traveling through New Jersey.

A June 12, 1817, newspaper article from the New Brunswick, New Jersey, *Fredonian* had nothing but glowing reports of Monroe's character. "All considerations of party were merged in the general wish to honor the man of the people—the dignified, yet affable— the illustrious, yet unassuming President," the article read. "No one can become acquainted with President Monroe, without being enamored of his simplicity; warmed by his engaging deportment; and charmed by his unaffected conversation."

In mid-June, Monroe spent more than a week in the New York City area, inspecting military structures, visiting hospitals and even a prison in the area.

Once again, the President took to the steamboat, this time on the *Connecticut*. He spent several days in the New London and Hartford, Connecticut, area. Even his clothing of choice received comments and compliments as it was a subtle throwback to his participation in the Revolutionary War.

"The Dress of the President has been deservedly noticed in other papers for its neatness and republican simplicity," wrote the *Connecticut Herald* in its June 9, 1817, issue. "He wore a plain blue coat, a buff under dress, and a hat and cockade of the revolutionary fashion. It comported with his rank, was adapted to the occasion, and well calculated to excite in the minds of the people, the remembrance of the day which 'tried men's souls.'"

Sadly, the tour wasn't without its issues. According to a July 8 edition of the Salem *Gazette*, one presidential salute in Pawtucket, of which there were many during Monroe's tour, badly injured a man in a cannon discharge. As a result of the accident, Smith Slocum had to have his arms amputated above the elbows because they were so badly damaged.

It was on his next major stop where the famous nickname for Monroe's early presidential administration was coined. "The Era of Good Feelings" has often been credited as being named here. He timed his visit for so that he could be in Boston during the July 4 celebrations.

Based on the extensive newspaper articles and extensive diary entries, his stay in the Boston area was hardly a relaxing one. Not only did he visit the naval yard and toured ships and military arsenals, he also took in several gardens and made appearances at no less than 16 separate households—all in five days.

One of those stops in the Boston area was in Quincy, where Monroe paid a call to John Adams at his mansion.

Monroe's tour even took him as far north as what is now known as Maine, although the area was still a part of the state of Massachusetts at that point. He traveled as far north as Portland, Maine, receiving tremendous cheering and participating in animated conversations.

One can only imagine how touched he was when he entered Scarborough, Maine, passing under an archway of greenery and roses, which read, "UNITED WE STAND." When he arrived at the archway, Monroe left his carriage and walked under the greens.

According to a written recollection from Isaac Adams, chairman of the committee to welcome the president, "A living Eagle, a native of our own forests and the symbol of our martial prowess, perched on the summit of the twentieth arch, and under the canopy of stars, by which it was surmounted, apparently watching, with intense curiosity and surprise, the concourse of people passing under him, heightened in the bosom of every beholder, the interest of this lovely spectacle."

"It was a delightful sight to behold this haughty monarch of the feathered tribe, the pride of the forest, encircled by the blaze of the stars that he loves, stifling, for a moment, his untamed spirit of liberty; and gratefully spreading his pinions, as the chief of the nation passed, which had chosen him the whole range of animated nature, as the emblem of its glory and strength."

On July 17, President Monroe left the Maine territory and reentered New Hampshire, where local dignitaries escorted him through Dover, Rochester and Milton.

In Concord, committee chairman Thomas W. Thompson spoke of the optimism for more cohesiveness with the citizens of the United States. "Upon this auspicious occasion, party feelings are forever buried—and buried, we would hope, forever. A new era, we trust, is commencing."

The President passed into Vermont on July 23. Not only was he treated with the same respect, and returned it with a humble conversation, but he also spoke of the lush greenery the state was known for. One account while Monroe was on the banks of the Connecticut River, noted that, "The President, although born in the fertile regions of the South, could not suppress his admiration at the flourishing and productive state of the country upon this river."

In response, Monroe said in his speech, "I have approached the state of Vermont with peculiar sensibility. On a former visit, immediately after the war, I left a wilderness, and I now find it blooming with luxuriant promise of wealth and happiness, to a numerous population."

While in the area, he spoke with students of the Windsor Female Academy, telling them, "I take a deep interest as a parent and citizen, in the success of female education, and have been delighted, wherever I have been, to witness the attention paid to it."

After leaving Windsor, the entourage passed through Woodstock and Montpelier, before coming to Burlington, on the shores of Lake Champlain. Although the lake is smaller in comparison to the Great Lakes, Monroe understood the significance of the fortifications with the lake and passionately recalled its importance as a turning point in the War of 1812.

"The eventful action on your lake and its invaded shores," he said, "can never be contemplated without the deepest emotion. It bound the union by stronger ties, if possible, than ever."

Monroe moved on to speak of the exposure of the frontier areas and pledged to support them. "You may feel assured that the government will not withhold any practicable measures, for the security of your town; nor have I ever doubted that preparation for defense in time of peace, would ever prove the best economy for war."

On the western shores of Lake Champlain, he was met by citizens of Plattsburgh, New York, who focused on the vulnerability of living where they did. In turn, Monroe assured them that after the war's conclusion, the United States took steps to convince that British that "we had every reason to look for a permanent peace."

When Monroe arrived at Sackett's Harbor, one of the first areas the British tried to invade in the War of 1812, he met with several veterans of the Revolutionary War. In their address to the President, the men said collectively, "It is with pleasure that we, a few of the survivors of the revolution, residing in this part of the country, welcome the arrival of the chief magistrate of the union. It is with increased satisfaction we recognize in him one of the number engaged with us in the arduous struggle of establishing the independence of the country."

"We have lived, sir, to see the fruits of our toils and struggles amply realized in the happiness and prosperity of our country, and Sir, we have the fullest confidence, that under your administration, they will be handed down to our posterity unimpaired."

He traveled west even further, stopping over at Niagara Falls and meeting with the citizens of Buffalo, and then Detroit. Both areas had fallen victim to the British propensity for fires, but were slowly rebuilding.

In Detroit, he acknowledged their remote part of the territory, and urged the citizens to be ready for any further acts of aggression. "Aware of your exposed situation, every circumstance material to your defense in the possible, but I hope, remote contingency of future wars, has a just claim to, and will receive my attention. For any information which you maybe able to give me, on a subject of such high importance, I shall be very thankful.

"Your establishment was of necessity, in its origin, colonial; but on a new principle," he continued. "A parental hand cherishes you in your infancy."

It was time to turn the corner and start for home.

After his stop in Detroit, Monroe proceeded through Ohio, a state which only 50 years before was fully wild and barely touched by settlers. Philemon Beecher, chairman of the committee in Lancaster, Ohio, commented on their state's interest in following Monroe's tour to date. While they welcomed him wholeheartedly, they appeared somewhat embarrassed in their modest environs.

"If in your reception here," Beecher said, "we cannot, from the infant state of this part of the Union, exhibit the highest refinements of the most polished society, we flatter ourselves that the offerings of the West are accompanied with the warm and honest feeling of our honour thus voluntarily done us; and with the affection for him, who in this season of examination, has not overlooked us."

After Monroe departed from Lancaster, he traveled through Delaware and Columbus, Ohio. He received a reception in Chillicothe, Ohio, that was similar to the reception in Lancaster, but there was an additional layer of pride in Chillicothe Mayor Levin Belt's address to Monroe.

"The progress of the arts and sciences has not reached, in our state, the height of which they possess in some of our sister states," Belt said, "but our love of country and devotedness to her welfare is not surpassed by any."

Monroe later met with citizens of Zanesville and Putnam, Ohio, where he once again was greeted with a lengthy speech, to which Monroe responded with an equally verbose speech. He impressed upon them the fact that, while he was happy to meet the citizens of the country he now governed, they should not forget that he is a fellow citizen as well.

On September 5, Monroe toured Jefferson College in Canonsburg, Pennsylvania, where an address to Monroe expounded on the qualities of the institution. "We have ever viewed sound morality and intelligence as the great supports of free government, and the principal guarantee of our rights and privileges, both civil and religious."

In response to this speech, Monroe upheld the qualities of virtue and religion and complimented the college for its efforts to educate students with these things in mind.

In part of his speech, Monroe said, "Educated in these principles, we can, with confidence, repose our free government and the interests of our beloved country in their care, assured that they will preserve, protect, and cherish them, with equal honor and advantage."

Later that day, Monroe arrived in Pittsburgh. The next morning, he met with Pittsburgh's representatives and gave a recap of his experiences thus far on his tour. "I have seen, with great interest, in this Tour, the most satisfactory proofs of the rapid growth of this portion of our union; of the industry of its inhabitants; and in their progress of agriculture, manufactures, and the useful arts."

There, at the junction of the Monongahela and Allegheny rivers, Monroe took pride in mentioning his success in securing New

Orleans, nearly 2,000 miles away, allowing for secure passage without the threat of foreign barriers.

After leaving Pittsburgh, the pace of the tour picked up as Monroe headed back to Washington, D.C. Within a week of fast travel and hard riding, the group reached Fredericktown, Maryland, and proceeded to the capital city.

The people of Washington, D.C. greeted him with enthusiastic joy upon his arrival on September 17. The vacuum created when he went on his tour three months before was finally filled once more.

Benjamin Orr, Mayor of Washington, D.C., represented the sentiment of many in the nation's capital when he spoke to Monroe the next morning. "Mr. President," he said, "In the tour which you have just finished, we have sympathized with you in your fatigues, and exulted with you in the extraordinary demonstrations of the nation's love, which, though sometimes oppressive, are always grateful."

Monroe's pleasure as he recalled his tour was evident in his response. "I shall always look back to the important incidents of my late Tour with particular satisfaction. I flatter myself that I have derived from it information which will be very useful in the discharge of duties in the high trust confided to me; and in other respects, it has afforded me the greatest gratification."

"In all that portion of our country, through which I have passed, I have seen, with delight, proofs of the most conclusive, of the devotion of our fellow citizens to the principles of our free republican government, and to our happy union. The spontaneous and independent manner of which these sentiments were declared, by the great body of the people, with other marked circumstances attending them, satisfied me that they came from the heart."

It was time to return his focus to matters of running the country, such as appointing his cabinet. Secretary of War John Calhoun was from South Carolina and Benjamin Crowningshield hailed from Massachusetts. Crowningshield was appointed as the Secretary of the Navy. The two were part of a geographically balanced cabinet, along with the recently appointed Richard Rush of Pennsylvania and Massachusetts resident John Quincy Adams.

The following year, he would take to the road again to tour other parts of the United States.

Chapter 10 – Second Presidential Tour

Monroe's first tour to the north afforded him the time and ability to meet with citizens, inspect military installations and devise a plan to defend the frontier and areas exposed to the Atlantic Ocean. Conversely, his second tour was much shorter, and took him to the Chesapeake Bay area.

The tour kicked off after Congress adjourned its 1817-1818 session. On this tour was his Secretary of War and Secretary of the Navy. Near the end of May 1818, Monroe and his group departed from Washington, D.C. One of their first stops was Annapolis, where Monroe lived in 1793 and peace negotiations commenced after the Revolutionary War.

Annapolis Mayor John Randall recalled the atmosphere of Maryland's capital city at the time that Monroe resided there. "The rigor of the season at that time was unfavorable to a view of the situation of the place and its surrounding waters, the prospect of which is now expanding and embellished by the military establishments erected by the United States, which of course will come into your observation."

In turn, Monroe's speech also recalled those events. "In recurring to the period of 1783, when Congress was held their session here, you bring to view, incidence of the highest degree important. It was then, and here, after a long and arduous struggle, which secured our independence, that the Treaty of Peace was ratified. It was then, and here, but the lustrous commander of our revolutionary armies, after performing Services, of which a grateful country can never forget, nor time obliterate, restored his commission to the authority with whom he had received it. To me these events... were particularly imposing an impressive. It was then, in very early life, that I commenced my career in the National Council, and which I have since so long continued. To me again, so many of those who were present at those great events, some of home, were parties to them, affords me the greatest gratification."

After leaving Annapolis, Monroe spent quite a bit of time touring the Chesapeake Bay area, which, at the time was the largest bay in the country. Monroe examined all facets of the bay, strategizing the best way to defend it, should war again come to America's shores.

On June 7, 1818, Monroe arrived in Norfolk, Virginia, where he was greeted by dignitaries. Mayor John Holt spoke: "The personal attention, sir, which you have thought proper to bestow on measures adopted by the general government, for the defense of our Inland Frontier, and Seacoast, and the establishment of naval arsenals, confidently assures us, our country will reap the full benefit of these measures from your extended observation, practical knowledge, and judicious discrimination."

Monroe assured the people of Norfolk in his return address that they would be well defended. "No object is more interesting to the United States than the adoption of a judicious system of defense, and the establishment and construction of such fortifications as may be found necessary for the security of our Maritime and Inland Frontier. Such a system, well-executed, may prevent wars, and it cannot fail, should war become inevitable, to mitigate their calamities."

After spending some more time in Virginia, Monroe returned to Washington, D.C., on June 17, 1818.

Several months later, when addressing Congress once more, Monroe concluded respectfully to God. "When we view the greater blessings with which our country has been favored, those which we now enjoy, and the means by which we possess of handing them down unimpaired, to our latest posterity, our attention is irresistibly drawn to the source from whence they flow. Let us, then, unite and offering our most grateful acknowledgments for these blessings to the Divine Author of all good."

First Lady Elizabeth Monroe maintained her departure from society, often relying on her eldest, Eliza, who was by then married to prominent attorney George Hay. Eliza had been educated in French schools, including one headed by Madame Campan, who served as Marie Antoinette's lady in waiting.

While Eliza upheld Elizabeth's nod toward social exclusivity, the Monroe daughter did cultivate many politically strong relationships, such as Hortense de Beauharnais, and Caroline Bonaparte, who respectively became Queen of Holland and Queen of Naples.

And while she was often seen as standoffish, Louisa Catherine Adams, wife to James Quincy Adams, appeared a staunch supporter of Elizabeth, speaking of her in effusive, complimentary terms. "The Drawing room was full tho' not crowded and we had altogether a very pleasant evening. Mrs. Monroe as usual looked beautiful," Louisa wrote in her diary.

And, in a letter to John Adams after an encounter with Elizabeth, Louisa wrote, "She was dressed in white and gold made in the highest style of fashion and moved not like a Queen (for that is an unpardonable word in this country) but like a goddess."

Chapter 11 – The Era of Good Feelings Challenged

With his two lengthy tours behind him, Monroe settled into the challenges that would later define his presidency.

In 1817, determined to improve relations with Britain once again, Monroe was determined to oversee demilitarization in the Great Lakes area. On April 16, 1818, the Senate ratified the Rush–Bagot Treaty between the United States and Britain, limiting both countries to one military vessel and one cannon on Lake Ontario and Lake Champlain. These countries were also permitted two military vessels on the remaining Great Lakes.

In what was considered the largest demilitarized zone, the treaty resulted in 5,527 miles of the east-west boundary.

"I have the satisfaction to inform you that an arrangement which had been commenced by my predecessor with the British Government for the reduction of the naval force by Great Britain and the United States on the Lakes has been concluded," Monroe said triumphantly. "By this arrangement useless expense on both sides and, what is of still greater importance, the danger of collision between armed vessels in those inland waters, which was great, is prevented."

The Florida territory, under Spanish rule, was starting to become a problem for the United States. Not only was Spain proving to be an absentee parent, but skirmishes with the Native Americans in the area were requiring the attention of the United States military once more.

General Andrew Jackson was called on to march into Florida with 4,000 troops. Seizing the fort in St. Augustine, he discovered illegal slave trading, and troublesome gun sales to the Native Americans there.

Additionally, it was common practice for slaves who escaped their masters to hide out in Florida, gaining sanctuary from Seminole and Creek tribes.

Congress was worried that this might be perceived as a threat to Spain, and some demanded that Adams be removed from his position, but Monroe defended the move in Florida. "Spain had lost her authority over it," he said. "And, falling into the hands of adventurers connected with the savages, it was made the means of unceasing annoyance and our Union in many of its most essential interests."

Secretary of State John Quincy Adams was called in to tenderly negotiate the purchase of Florida. He stressed that Florida was "a derelict open to the occupancy of every enemy, civilized or savage, of the United States, and serving no other earthly purpose than as a post of annoyance to them."

The Adams-Onis Treaty was signed on February 22, 1819, by Adams and Luis de Onís, Spanish minister, and two years later, the eastern part of Florida was turned over to the United States. "By this cession, then, Spain ceded a territory in reality of no value to her," Monroe concluded.

There was no money exchanged in the sale, but it did agree to pay legal claims of Americans against Spain for as much as $5 million. In fact, there were 1,859 claims from more than 720 incidents, which were handled by Daniel Webster and William Wirt, as well as other attorneys.

In addition, the United States gave up any claim to the Texas territory, for the time being.

Tensions with Spain were put to rest with the treaty but the problems were far from over for Monroe.

In 1819, the first major depression struck since the constitution was ratified. Known as the Panic of 1819, the economy began to collapse as the global economy adjusted itself after the Napoleonic Wars.

Additionally, westward expansion and real estate speculation demanded increased credit extended by the Second Bank of the United States. The resulting effects were widespread. People were thrown into debtors' prisons, land was devalued and dropped from an estimated $70 an acre to $2 per acre, unemployment rose and countless banks were bankrupt.

People turned against Monroe for not doing enough to prevent the depression. Although Monroe was convinced that this was a normal part of any economy, he did press Secretary of Treasury William Crawford to relax mortgage payments on land purchased from the United States itself.

The depression ended officially in 1823, but there were other problems Monroe was facing.

In February 1820, the Missouri territory sought to join the Union as a state and a bill was put together and submitted to the House of Representatives. It was then that Congressman James Tallmadge, Jr. offered the Tallmadge Amendment.

The amendment, if passed, would prohibit more slaves from being introduced into Missouri. It also stated that all future children of slave parents would be freed when they turned 25 years old.

Three days later, the bill passed in the House of Representatives, but those amendments were then rejected in the Senate and in December 1819, Alabama was allowed into the union as a slave state. At this point, the number of free states and slave states were equal.

In January 26, 1820, the House of Representatives passed a similar bill introduced by New York's John W. Taylor, which allowed Missouri into the Union as a slave state, at the same time that a bill was introduced to admit Maine as a free state. At that point, in February, the Senate decided to put the two ideas together and passed a bill allowing Maine in while also allowing Missouri to enter into the union as a slave state.

Monroe was deeply affected by the impact of the compromise. In his personal notes found, he wrote in February, "The idea was that if the whole arrangement, to this effect, could be secured, that it would be better to adopt it, than break the union. Neither did Mr. Barbour, nor any other person alluded to, favor this, but to save the union, believing it to be in imminent danger."

Others were acutely aware of Monroe's concerns, and the next month, John Henry Eaton wrote to Jackson on behalf of the president. "The agitation was indeed great I assure you," Eaton wrote. "Dissolution of the Union had become quite a familiar subject. By the compromise however restricting slavery north of 36½ degrees we ended this unpleasant question. Of this the Southern people are complaining, but they ought not, for it has preserved peace, dissipated angry feelings, and dispelled appearances which seemed dark and horrible and threatening to the interest and harmony of the nation. The constitution has not been surrendered by this peace offering, for it only applies while a territory when it is admitted congress have the power and right to legislate, and not when they shall become States."

On March 6, the President signed the compromise, but the discussion was far from over. In fact, the debate continued throughout the nation.

In April, Jefferson wrote to John Homes. "I had for a long time ceased to read newspapers or pay any attention to public affairs, confident they were in good hands, and content to be a passenger in our bark to the shore from which I am not distant. but this momentous question, like a fire bell in the night, awakened and filled me with terror. I considered it at once as the knell of the Union. it is hushed indeed for the moment, but this is a reprieve only, not a final sentence."

"I perceive you have strong foreboding as to our future policy," Calhoun later wrote to Andrew Jackson in June 1820. "The discussion on the Missouri question has undoubtedly contributed to weaken in some degree the attachment of our southern and western people to the Union; but the agitators of that question have, in my opinion, not only completely failed; but have destroyed to a great extent their capacity for future mischief. Should Missouri be admitted at the next session, as I think she will without difficulty, the evil effects of the discussion must gradually subside."

Not all was dismal in the era though. Monroe's first term saw the wedding of his second daughter. Maria Hester Monroe became the first presidential child to be married in the White House. In March 9, 1820, Maria married Samuel L. Gouverneur, her first cousin and a White House staffer.

Although held at the White House, the wedding was very private. Only 42 close friends and family were invited to attend. Perhaps because of the backlash, the couple planned to attend several balls.

Nine days after Maria and Samuel were married, they attended their first ball at Stephen Decatur's house. During the ball, Decatur was challenged to a duel, which he accepted. Within that week, he was killed in the duel. Society fell into mourning and the upcoming festivities were canceled.

Chapter 12 – Reelection and Building the Country

James Monroe's first term was coming to a close and he was urged to seek another term. By this time, the Federalist party had completely collapsed, so there was so challenger and Monroe was the second president in United States history to run unopposed.

The electoral vote was not unanimous, however. William Plumer from Epping, New Hampshire, cast his vote for John Quincy Adams. Some of his opponents thought that he did this just to ensure that George Washington was the only president unanimously elected. The contention is a practical one—Plumer had so much respect for the first president that he named one of his six children George Washington Plumer.

However, Plumer emphatically stated that he submitted his vote in the Electoral College because he felt the president to be incompetent. When submitting his vote for Vice President, Plumer also voted against Monroe's running mate, Daniel D. Thompkins; instead, he cast his vote for Richard Rush.

Even John Adams, the man who had been part of founding the Federalist party, came out of retirement to cast his vote for Monroe.

Unlike his first inauguration, it was cold and snowy on Monday, March 5, a day after the inauguration was initially scheduled. This marked the first time the country was temporarily without a president since Washington took office, and after Monroe's first term expired at noon on March 4, Senate President Pro Tem John Gaillard took up the duty of President for a day.

Gaillard's duties were hardly taxing and the inauguration took place the next day in a snowbound capital after snow began on that Saturday.

At an estimated 28 degrees, as noted by John Quincy Adams, Monroe's second oath of office was made inside the House Chambers. However, the ceremony was a festive one and they were regaled by the Marine Corps Band in their first appearance in an official event, playing "Yankee Doodle Dandy" at the conclusion.

While his Vice President, Daniel Tompkins, was on hand during his first inauguration, he was in New York at the time of the 1821 inauguration and chose not to travel to Washington to be sworn in for the second time.

At first, the president was hesitant about making a speech, since it was actually not required by the Constitution. However, his advisors strongly suggested that he should make a speech. Rising to the occasion, he constructed a speech that was more than 4,400 words long and lasted for more than an hour.

There were concerns that the floor might buckle under the weight of the waterlogged spectators, but others were more concerned with staying awake through the entire speech.

Once again, Monroe started out with a humble tone. "I shall not attempt to describe the grateful emotions which the new and very distinguished proof of the confidence of my fellow-citizens, evinced by my reelection to this high trust, has excited in my bosom," he began in his speech.

Monroe also spoke about the economic struggles they were still encountering. "Our commerce had been in a great measure driven from the sea, our Atlantic and inland frontiers were invaded in almost every part; the waste of life along our coast and on some parts of our inland frontiers, to the defense of which our gallant and patriotic citizens were called, was immense, in addition to which not less than $120,000,000 were added at its end to the public debt."

However, he explained, it was imperative that the country remain a neutral global presence. "At the period adverted to the powers of Europe, after having been engaged in long and destructive wars with each other, had concluded a peace, which happily still exists. Our peace with the power with whom we had been engaged had also been concluded," he said. "Respecting the attitude which it may be proper for the United States to maintain hereafter between the parties, I have no hesitation in stating it as my opinion that the neutrality heretofore observed should still be adhered to," he stated, as impractical as it sounded. "Europe is again unsettled and the prospect of war increasing. Should the flame light up in any quarter, how far it may extend it is impossible to foresee. It is our peculiar felicity to be altogether unconnected with the causes which produce this menacing aspect elsewhere."

Domestically, though, neutrality may not have been possible. Monroe highlighted some of the struggles with the Native Americans. "The care of the Indian tribes within our limits has long been an essential part of our system, but, unfortunately, it has not been executed in a manner to accomplish all the objects intended by it. We have treated them as independent nations, without their having any substantial pretensions to that rank. The distinction has flattered their pride, retarded their improvement, and in many instances paved the way to their destruction." And while he seemed empathetic, he did not turn away from pushing the United States boundary ever west. "The progress of our settlements westward, supported as they are by a dense population, has constantly driven them back, with almost the total sacrifice of the lands which they have been compelled to abandon. They have claims on the magnanimity and, I may add, on the justice of this nation which we must all feel. We should become their real benefactors; we should perform the office of their Great Father, the endearing title which they emphatically give to the Chief Magistrate of our Union."

This time, Elizabeth was present at the swearing in.

Without the necessary time to transition into the executive mansion he already occupied, it was time to move on with his presidential duties.

With the addition of Missouri and Maine, the United States continued to grow and with that, the need for a better infrastructure was evident.

"When we consider the vast extent of territory within the United States," he said, "the great amount and value of its productions, the connection of its parts, and other circumstances on which their prosperity and happiness depend, we can not fail to entertain a high sense of the advantage to be derived from the facility which may be afforded in the intercourse between them by means of good roads and canals. Never did a country of such vast extent offer equal inducements to improvements of this kind, nor ever were consequences of such magnitude involved in them."

Monroe was concerned that the Constitution did not give the government the authority to construct or maintain a national transportation system and asked Congress to amend the Constitution.

However, Congress refused to make any amendments, deciding instead that it gave the government too much power.

In 1822, though, Congress passed a bill to make improvements on the Cumberland Road, also known as the National Road. The roadway ran from Wheeling, Virginia, to Cumberland, Maryland.

Monroe vetoed the bill on May 4. "It is with deep regret," he said in his veto message, "approving as I do the policy, that I am compelled to object to its passage and to return the bill to the House of Representatives, in which it originated, under a conviction that Congress do not possess the power under the Constitution to pass such a law."

"A power to establish turnpikes with gates and tolls, and to enforce the collection of tolls by penalties, implies a power to adopt and execute a complete system of internal improvement," he explained. "I am of opinion that Congress do not possess this power; that the States individually can not grant it, for although they may assent to the appropriation of money within their limits for such purposes, they can grant no power of jurisdiction or sovereignty by special compacts with the United States. This power can be granted only by an amendment to the Constitution and in the mode prescribed by it."

However, the issue was not dead and the President turned to the Supreme Court justices and others to discuss his concerns.

Two years after he vetoed the bill, Monroe signed a bill to fund surveys and estimates for the road. One year later, in 1825, he signed a bill to extend the road all the way to Zanesville, Ohio. On July 4 of that year, the ground was broken for the road in Ohio.

Now that national obligations were addressed, Monroe tackled foreign concerns. During this time, Latin American territories were attempting to remove themselves from Spain's grasp. With his own revolutionary experience, Monroe could certainly sympathize with his southern counterparts but he maintained the attempt at neutrality that he upheld and refused to side with either party.

However, when Argentina, Columbia, Chile, Peru and Mexico all won their independence from Spain, Monroe felt he could make an official move. In March 1822, Monroe instructed his Secretary of State to write instructions for the officials he would be sending to these countries as their ministers.

Despite his initial hesitancy, this move made the United States the first to officially recognize these countries, and set the stage for the rest of the world to follow.

Within the instructions Adams dictated, the United States declared that they would support Republican efforts, while also working toward treaties of commerce on the basis of what was known as the 'most favored nation.'

In the meantime, Spain and Britain were bristling for a fight. Britain wholeheartedly cheered Spain's looting these colonies, and the trade restrictions they might bring on.

Adding to the international tensions was Russia. Although Monroe said in his second inaugural speech that, "I have great satisfaction in stating that our relations with France, Russia, and other powers continue on the most friendly basis," Tsar Alexander was eyeballing expansion along the Pacific coast. After Russia defeated Napoleonic France, the tsar deemed himself the head of the Holy Alliance, a group of monarchs from Russia, Prussia and Austria who were dedicated to staunch liberalism and secular views.

In 1823, Tsar Alexander pronounced that the area north of the 51st parallel would be held for Russian interests only. In response, John Quincy Adams, once the first ambassador to Russia, refused to honor the claim as Secretary of State.

With the major world powers still in a state of flux, Adams and Monroe determined it was time to take a stand for American soil once and for all.

While the verbiage was encapsulated in his address to Congress on December 2, 1823, the message rang loud and clear to nations planning to capitalize on North American lands.

"At the proposal of the Russian Imperial Government, made through the minister of the Emperor residing here, a full power and instructions have been transmitted to the minister of the United States at St. Petersburg to arrange by amicable negotiation the respective rights and interests of the two nations on the northwest coast of this continent," Monroe said as he transitioned into what is now known as the Monroe Doctrine.

"A similar proposal has been made by His Imperial Majesty to the Government of Great Britain, which has likewise been acceded to. The Government of the United States has been desirous by this friendly proceeding of manifesting the great value which they have invariably attached to the friendship of the Emperor and their solicitude to cultivate the best understanding with his Government. In the discussions to which this interest has given rise and in the arrangements by which they may terminate the occasion has been judged proper for asserting, as a principle in which the rights and interests of the United States are involved, that the American continents, by the free and independent condition which they have assumed and maintain, are *henceforth not to be considered as subjects for future colonization by any European powers.*"

"It was stated at the commencement of the last session that a great effort was then making in Spain and Portugal to improve the condition of the people of those countries, and that it appeared to be conducted with extraordinary moderation. It need scarcely be remarked that the results have been so far very different from what was then anticipated. Of events in that quarter of the globe, with which we have so much intercourse and from which we derive our origin, we have always been anxious and interested spectators."

Once again, Monroe selected a word he often chose in his speeches: happy. "The citizens of the United States cherish sentiments the most friendly in favor of the liberty and happiness of their fellow-men on that side of the Atlantic."

The President spoke of the country's desire to remain neutral and would only take up arms to defend her lands. "In the wars of the

European powers in matters relating to themselves we have never taken any part, nor does it comport with our policy to do so. It is only when our rights are invaded or seriously menaced that we resent injuries or make preparation for our defense."

And in turn for steadfast neutrality, Monroe said, the United States expected the same consideration on their soil. If this did not happen, there would be ramifications. "We owe it, therefore, to candor and to the amicable relations existing between the United States and those powers to declare that we should consider any attempt on their part to extend their system to any portion of this hemisphere as dangerous to our peace and safety. With the existing colonies or dependencies of any European power we have not interfered and shall not interfere. But with the Governments who have declared their independence and maintain it, and whose independence we have, on great consideration and on just principles, acknowledged, we could not view any interposition for the purpose of oppressing them, or controlling in any other manner their destiny, by any European power in any other light than as the manifestation of an unfriendly disposition toward the United States."

Monroe noted that Spain and Portugal remained unsettled and continued by saying, "Our policy in regard to Europe, which was adopted at an early stage of the wars which have so long agitated that quarter of the globe, nevertheless remains the same, which is, not to interfere in the internal concerns of any of its powers; to consider the government de facto as the legitimate government for us; to cultivate friendly relations with it, and to preserve those relations by a frank, firm, and manly policy, meeting in all instances the just claims of every power, submitting to injuries from none."

In other words, the President concluded that no country should get involved with matters of other countries. "It is still the true policy of the United States to leave the parties to themselves, in hope that other powers will pursue the same course."

The frank statement, which wasn't coined as the Monroe Doctrine until 1850, clearly drew a line in the sand. And while the young, feisty country may not have been able to ward off a full-on attack from another military powerhouse, by this time, the United States and Britain were once again on amicable terms. With Britain staunchly supporting the declaration, the United States could be confident in naval support from Britain should the need arise.

This has been considered the first significant policy issued by the United States in her defense and in support of the Western Hemisphere. To date, it has been referred to on a handful of occasions.

Of course, relations with Britain continued to wax and wane. In 1842, President John Tyler applied the Monroe Doctrine to warn their sometimes-allies off from Hawaii, as the United States began the process of taking the territory into her fold.

During the Mexican-American War, President James Polk enacted the Monroe Doctrine to annex what is now the state of Texas. After that, President Theodore Roosevelt utilized the policy to underscore the United States' presence in the Philippines as well as the Caribbean and Central America.

Perhaps the most widely known application of the Monroe Doctrine in recent history was in 1962, when President John F. Kennedy led the country in mitigating the Cuban Missile Crisis. No stranger to the doctrine, Kennedy also referred to it the previous year during the Bay of Pigs invasion. While the military action was short-lived, the United States was destined to tussle with Cuba's government the following year.

On October 16, 1962, Kennedy convened his Executive Committee after the country became aware of several nuclear missiles in Cuba. After much military discussion and maneuvering, the president addressed the country on October 22.

"This Government, as promised, has maintained the closest surveillance of the Soviet military buildup on the island of Cuba,"

Kennedy began in his speech. "Within the past week, unmistakable evidence has established the fact that a series of offensive missile sites is now in preparation on that imprisoned island. The purpose of these bases can be none other than to provide a nuclear strike capability against the Western Hemisphere."

A few days later, on October 29, the president was asked directly about the Monroe Doctrine in a news conference. He responded, "The Monroe Doctrine means what it has meant since President Monroe and John Quincy Adams enunciated it, and that is that we would oppose a foreign power extending its power to the Western Hemisphere. And that's why we oppose what is being--what's happening in Cuba today. That's why we have cut off our trade. That's why we worked in the OAS and in other ways to isolate the Communist menace in Cuba. That's why we'll continue to give a good deal of our effort and attention to it."

Known as a cornerstone of American policy, the Monroe Doctrine has proven to be a powerful tool in protecting the country from foreign threats.

A year after the Monroe Doctrine was released, Monroe invited his good friend Marquis de Lafayette to return to America. It was time, he thought, to instill the "spirit of 1776'" to the younger generation of Americans.

In a letter to Lafayette dated February 24, 1824, Monroe said, "I wrote you a letter about 15 days since, by Mr. Brown, in which I expressed the wish to send to any port in France should you point out, a frigate to convey you hither, in case you should be able to visit the United States. Since then, Congress has passed a resolution on the subject, and which sincere attachment of the whole nation to use expressed, whose ardent desire is once more to see you amongst them. At which you may yield to this invitation is left entirely at your option, but believe me, whatever may be your decision, it will be sufficient that you should have the goodness to inform me of it, and immediate orders will be given for a government vessel receipt for to any port you will indicate, and convey to you then the adopted country of your early youth, just always preserved the most grateful recollection of your important Services. I send to you herewith the resolution of Congress, and add thereto the assurance of my high consideration and of my sentiments of affection."

Despite Louis XVIII's disapproval of the trip, Lafayette departed French shores on July 13, 1824, and the Revolutionary War hero did indeed return to America with a full hero's welcome in New York City.

After several days in New York, Lafayette traveled to Boston where he was warmly greeted. "Greetings! Friend of our fathers!" boomed Edward Everett, the politician who gave the "Other Gettysburg Address" before Lincoln's famous speech. "May you be welcome on our shores! Happy are our eyes to look upon your venerable features! Enjoy a triumph, which is reserved for neither conquerors nor monarchs, the assurance that here in all America there is not a heart which does not beat with joy and gratitude at the sound of your name."

In September of his great tour, Lafayette journeyed to the many of the same cities as Monroe did through his first presidential tour: New Haven, Connecticut; Providence, Rhode Island; Portsmouth, New Hampshire, Saco, Maine.

He then headed south, stopping in Washington, D.C., and then went on to Mount Vernon where he visited Washington's tomb. An emotional Lafayette, at Washington's final resting place, said, "The feelings, which on this awful moment oppress my heart don't leave me the power of utterance. I can only thank you, my dear Custis for your precious gift and pray a silent homage to the tomb of the greatest and best of men, my paternal friend."

Among his 13-month trip, Lafayette traveled through Louisiana, Mississippi, Georgia, South Carolina, North Carolina, Tennessee and Kentucky. During his trip to Louisville on the steamboat

Mechanic, the ship sinks. While everyone reached shore safely, Lafayette lost both possessions and money.

He is also the guest of honor at the White House in early December. Even Elizabeth Monroe makes a rare public appearance at a reception in his honor.

By the time Lafayette boards the American warship, the *Brandywine*, to return home, John Quincy Adams is the next president.

Chapter 13 – Post Presidency

Following in the footsteps of his presidential predecessors, James Monroe decided not to run for a third term as president.

His eighth annual message as the President would be his final one. While steadfastly providing updates on the health of the country, his final words were bittersweet. "I can not conclude this communication, the last of the kind which I shall have to make, without recollecting with great sensibility and heartfelt gratitude the many instances of the public confidence and the generous support which I have received from my fellow citizens in the various trusts with which I have been honored. Having commenced my service in early youth, and continued it since with few and short intervals, I have witnessed the great difficulties to which our union has been surmounted. From the present prosperous and happy state I derive a gratification which I can not express. That these blessings may be preserved and perpetuated will be the object of my fervent and unceasing prayers to the Supreme Ruler of the Universe."

Monroe's presidency ended on March 4, 1825, when John Quincy Adams was sworn in as the sixth president of the United States.

In another presidential first, Monroe became the first presidential escort the President-Elect to the swearing-in ceremony. While the two rode in separate carriages, the strength of the party's unity and their own friendship could not be denied.

And, in another example of presidential camaraderie, the Monroes were permitted to remain in the White House for an additional three weeks, as Elizabeth had fallen ill and was too sick to leave the White House.

When she had recovered, the Monroes traveled to their home in Oak Hill, located in Loudoun County, Virginia.

After the presidential world, life settled into a quiet routine. Elizabeth focused her efforts on her family and the Monroe daughters often came to visit.

Supporting Jefferson's focus on the University of Virginia, James Monroe regularly attended Board of Visitors meetings and served as the rector for a time. He was also appointed to the Virginia Constitutional Convention and in 1829, he was asked to serve as the presiding officer.

However, his health was failing and he was forced to withdraw from his final civic duty.

Monroe also turned to writing, spending a considerable time penning a book that compared the current political clime to other nations, both ancient and modern. It may be the premise of this book that was inspired by Monroe's words: "If we look to the history of other nations, ancient or modern, we find no example of a growth so rapid, so gigantic, of a people so prosperous and happy."

However, as much as he wanted to write this book, it proved too much, so he chose another subject and began writing his autobiography. That would never come to fruition either.

Soon, tragedy struck. In 1826, Elizabeth became ill once more. Whether it was a weakness from her malady or an epileptic seizure, no one knows for sure. Sadly, she fell into an open fire and was severely burned.

In even more tenuous health circumstances, Monroe's beloved wife lived for three more years, often in considerable pain from her burns. On September 23, 1830, Elizabeth passed away at the family home in Oak Hills. She was 62 years old.

Despondent, Monroe was said to have sat by the fire after her death and systematically fed page upon page of his private letters to and from Elizabeth into the fire. It is one of the reasons much less is known about the personal life of this President than most others of his status.

Elizabeth was interred at Oak Hills, a place Monroe himself left not long after. With his financial woes ever dogging him, he moved in with his daughter, Maria. Even then, the former President knew he would not live much longer.

His friend, John Quincy Adams visited him for the final time in 1831. The two men discussed the current affairs in Europe, but Adams opted to cut the visit short, afraid he was tiring Monroe.

About 3:30 p.m. on July 4, 1831, James Monroe, war hero, diplomat and fifth president died in New York City in his daughter's home, ten months after burying his wife. The official cause of death was heart failure and tuberculosis.

His death, 55 years after the Declaration of Independence was signed, made him the third President to die on what would later become known as Independence Day. One other President that died on July 4th was John Adams. His last recorded words were, "Thomas Jefferson still survives." But that was not to be, as Jefferson also died on July 4, 1826, 50 years to the day of the country's birthday.

The *Niles' Weekly Register* published James Monroe's obituary on July 23. "The body having been brought by a guard of honor from the late residence of the deceased, accompanied by intimate relatives and friends, was deposited on the platform in front of City Hall. Immediately above it, a temporary stage, covered with a black cloth, had been erected."

The funeral was held at St. Paul's Episcopal Church and was conducted by Rev. Bishop Onderdonk and Rev. Dr. Wainwright.

"The body was carried on a hearse, covered with black cloth, fringed with gold," the obituary continued. "From the centre panels, the national flag hung reversed, and eight black feathers waved above the whole; the hearse was drawn by four black horses."

Even after his death, poverty still reared its ugly head and he was buried in New York City with financial assistance. He was interred at Marble Cemetery, but this was not his final resting place.

In 1858, Madison's coffin was exhumed and prepared for transport back to his home state of Virginia. After it was briefly on display at City Hall in New York City, it was loaded onto a barge in preparation for the trip. Unfortunately, the transport encountered several storms, including one which swept a member of the honor guard—Alexander Hamilton's grandson—overboard.

Finally, he was reinterred at the President's Circle at Hollywood Cemetery in Richmond, Virginia. The remains of his beloved wife were also exhumed and reinterred to rest eternally beside him at Hollywood Cemetery.

Conclusion

James Monroe, the fifth President of the United States, is often overlooked as a President. However, as one of the Founding Fathers, his steadfast desire to promote and preserve America's interests, was evident in his many deeds and accomplishments.

When Monroe left the White House, he had served the interests of the United States for more than 50 years, both domestically and internationally. His political elections are said to eclipse any other President for the number of appointments he was given.

James B. Murray, Jr. attended the College of William and Mary centuries after Monroe was a student before the Revolutionary War. In 1995, Murray paid tribute to Monroe's legacy at a Charter Day ceremony.

"While Monroe may not be credited as a creator of this nation, he should be credited with being a builder of this nation," Murray said in his speech. "We all revere the history of the College. We feel the pride of it in our bones, yet our appreciation for the roots of that pride is often episodic. Too often we overlook the greater glory of having educated one of America's greatest presidents."

Had Monroe not persevered in supporting the United States, the country may be vastly different now, he said. "Occasionally we need reminding that so much we take for granted about our nation today was far from assured during those early years. It took a nation-building president to assure this nation."

Here's another Captivating History book that you might be interested in

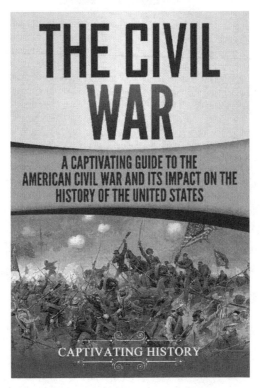

Sources

Richardson, James D. *A Compilation of the Messages and Papers of the Presidents / Volume 2: 1817-1833*. New York: Bureau of National Literature, 1897.

History, Hourly. *James Monroe: A Life From Beginning to End*. March 21, 2017.

https://www.whitehouse.gov/about-the-white-house/presidents/james-monroe/

http://www.ushistory.org/valleyforge/served/monroe.html

https://millercenter.org/president/monroe

https://www.britannica.com/biography/James-Monroe

https://www.biography.com/news/james-monroe-biography-facts

https://www.biography.com/people/james-monroe-9412098

http://bioguide.congress.gov/scripts/biodisplay.pl?index=m000858

http://www.potus.com/jmonroe.html

http://jamesmonroe.org/

https://www.loc.gov/collections/james-monroe-papers/about-this-collection/

http://academics.umw.edu/jamesmonroepapers/biography/

https://ead.lib.virginia.edu/vivaxtf/view?docId=lva/vi00868.xml

https://owlcation.com/humanities/James-Monroe-Biography-Fifth-President-of-the-United-States

https://www.revolvy.com/main/index.php?s=James+Monroe+Smith

https://history.state.gov/departmenthistory/people/monroe-james

http://www.sparknotes.com/biography/monroe/section5/

http://jamesmonroemuseum.umw.edu

http://highland.org/

---

https://hsp.org/calendar/spirit-people-james-monroes-1817-tour-northern-states

https://www.arcgis.com/home/item.html?id=5d91f9dadc3f4ff9ad2710d44af68824

https://catalog.hathitrust.org/Record/008650564

https://archive.org/details/tourofjamesmonro00wald

https://www.whitehousehistory.org/articles-of-the-best-kind

https://www.encyclopediavirginia.org

http://www.presidency.ucsb.edu/ws/index.php?pid=25808

https://www.loc.gov/rr/program/bib/inaugurations/monroe/index.html

https://www.cbsnews.com/htdocs/politics/inauguration/history.pdf

https://www.c-span.org/video/?425252-8/james-monroes-life-legacy

https://www.weather.gov/lwx/events_Inauguration

http://www.stateoftheunionhistory.com/2015/07/1819-james-monroe-purchase-of-florida.html

https://history.state.gov/departmenthistory/people/monroe-james

http://www.firstladies.org/biographies/firstladies.aspx?biography=5

http://firstladies.c-span.org/FirstLady/6/Elizabeth-Monroe.aspx

https://www.whitehousehistory.org/bios/elizabeth-monroe

http://www.womenhistoryblog.com/2011/03/elizabeth-kortright-monroe.html

http://www.presidential-power.org/us-first-ladies/elizabeth-monroe.htm

http://fortmonroe.org/lafayettes-visit-to-fort-monroe-in-1824-as-guest-of-the-nation/

http://rmc.library.cornell.edu/lafayette/exhibition/english/tour/

https://archive.org/details/lafayetteinamer01godmgoog

http://flathatnews.com/2015/05/02/making-monroe/

http://academics.umw.edu/jamesmonroepapers/

https://unclesamsnewyork.wordpress.com/2010/02/08/exhuming-president-james-monroe-1758-1831-5th-president-of-the-united-states-removed-from-nycs-marble-cemetery-in-1858/

https://www.varsitytutors.com/earlyamerica/world-early-america/famous-obits/obituary-james-monroe

http://bioguide.congress.gov/scripts/biodisplay.pl?index=m000858

https://www.thefamouspeople.com/profiles/james-monroe-1744.php

https://www.loc.gov/rr/program/bib/ourdocs/monroe.html

https://catalog.archives.gov/id/306420

https://www.ourdocuments.gov/doc.php?flash=false&doc=23

http://www.ushistory.org/documents/monroe.htm

http://www.blackpast.org/gah/monrovia-liberia-1821

http://www.stateoftheunionhistory.com/2015/07/1819-james-monroe-purchase-of-florida.html

https://www.ploddingthroughthepresidents.com/2016/04/james-monroe-famous-paintings.html

https://www.culturaltourismdc.org/portal/war-of-1812

https://study.com/academy/lesson/james-monroes-early-life-childhood.html

http://www.history.org/almanack/people/bios/biojmonroe.cfm

http://www.presidentprofiles.com/Washington-Johnson/James-Monroe-Final-years.html

Newton, Michael (2015) *Alexander Hamilton: The Formative Years*. Eletheria Publishing

Chernow, R. (2004) *Hamilton*. Penguin Books

Palmotto, M. (2014) *Combatting Human Trafficking: A Multidisciplinary Approach*. CRC Press

Clark, A., M.D. (2005) *Cipher/Code of Dishonor; Aaron Burr: An American Enigma*. AuthorHouse

Jenkinson, I. (2019) *Aaron Burr, His Personal and Political Relations with Thomas Jefferson and Alexander Hamilton*. Wentworth Press

Hamilton, A. "Hamilton, A. Letters," Retrieved from
https://founders.archives.gov/documents/Hamilton/01-25-02-0169

"Burr-Hamilton Duel," Retrieved from https://www.britannica.com/event/Burr-Hamilton-duel

"Aaron Burr," Retrieved from http://www.americaslibrary.gov/jb/nation/jb_nation_hamburr_1.html

"Election of 1800," Retrieved from https://lehrmaninstitute.org/history/1800.html#burr

"Biography of Aaron Burr," Retrieved from https://www.britannica.com/biography/Aaron-Burr

"Biography of Alexander Hamilton," Retrieved from https://www.britannica.com/biography/Aexander-Hamilton

"Bitterly Contested Presidential Election of 1800," Retrieved from https://constitutioncenter.org/blog/on-this-day-the-first-bitter-contested-presidential-election-takes-place

"Alexander Hamilton," Retrieved from https://history.howstuffworks.com/historical-figures/alexander-hamilton3.htm

Broadus, M. (1957) *Hamilton: Youth to Maturity 1755-1788.* The Free Press

Hamilton, A. "To the Royal Danish American Gazette," manuscript Library of Congress

Hamilton, A. "Report on Manufactures," manuscript Library of Congress

Randall, W. (2010) *Hamilton: A Life.* Harper Collins

Syrett, H. & Cooke, J., eds. (1987) *The Papers of Hamilton, 27 vols.* Columbia University Press

Berton, P. (1981) *Flames across the Border: 1813-1814.* London: McClellan & Stewart

Brookhiser, R. (2013) *James Madison.* New York: Basic Books

Clinton, J. D. and Meirowitz, A. (2004) "Testing Explanations of Strategic Voting Strategy in Legislatures: A re-examination of the Missouri Compromise of 1790," *American Journal of Political Science 48:4*

Elish, D. (2007) *James Madison.* London: Marshall Cavendish

Fritz, C. G. (2012) "Interposition and the Heresy of Nullification: James Madison and the Exercise of Sovereign Constitutional Powers." Retrieved from https://www.heritage.org/the-constitution/report/interposition-and-the-heresy-nullification-james-madison-and-the-exercise

Froner, E. and Garraty, J. (eds.) (1991) "The Missouri Compromise," *The Reader's Companion to American History.* New York: Houghton Mifflin Harcourt Publishing Co.

Furlong, P. J. and Sharkey, D. (1951) *A New Nation.* New York: Sadlier

Hammond, B. (2000) *Banks and Politics in America from the Revolution to the Civil War.* Princeton: Princeton University Press

Irwin, R.W. (1931) *The Diplomatic Relations of the United States with the Barbary Pirates: 1776-1816*. Chapel Hill: University of North Carolina Press

Ketcham, R. (1990) *James Madison: A Biography.* Charlottesville: University of Virginia Press

Klarman, M. J. (2011) "The Founding Revisited," *Harvard Law Review.* Retrieved from https://harvardlawreview.org/2011/12/the-founding-revisited/ 125:544

"James Madison Biography," (2017) Retrieved from https://www.biography.com/people/james-madison-9394965

"James and Dolley Madison House in Society Hill" Retrieved from https://philly.curbed.com/2016/5/9/11638828/james-dolley-madison-house-for-sale

"James and Dolley Madison at Montpelier," (2017) Retrieved from https://www.nps.gov/Nr/twhp/wwwlps/lessons/46montpelier/46facts3.htm

James Madison, (auth.), Hunt, G. (ed.) "The Writings of James Madison, Correspondence, 1819-1836" Vol. 9 Retrieved from http://oll.libertyfund.org/titles/madison-the-writings-vol-9-1819-1836#lf1356-09_footnote_nt_046

Jennings, P. (1799) "A Colored Man's Reminiscences of James Madison," Retrieved from https://docsouth.unc.edu/neh/jennings/jennings.html

"Law School Case Briefs: Marbury v. Madison," Retrieved from http://www.invispress.com/law/conlaw/marbury.html

"The Life of James Madison" (2017) Retrieved from https://www.montpelier.org/learn/the-life-of-james-madison

"The Origins of Freneau's National Gazette, July 1791," Retrieved from https://founders.archives.gov/documents/Madison/01-14-02-0046

Pickus, N. (2009) *True Faith and Allegiance: Immigration and American Civic Nationalism.* Princeton: Princeton University Press

Rutland, R. A. (1997) *James Madison: The Founding Father.* (Reprint) Kansas City: University of Missouri Press

"Virginia Landmarks Register" Retrieved from https://en.wikipedia.org/wiki/Montpelier_(Orange,_Virginia)#The_duPont_Family

Scofield, M. "Unraveling the Dolley Myths" Retrieved from https://www.whitehousehistory.org/unraveling-the-dolley-myths

Madison, D. (1886) *Memoirs and Letters of Dolly Madison: Wife of James Madison, President of the United States.* New York: Houghton Mifflin

"War of 1812" (2015) Retrieved from https://www.history.com/topics/war-of-1812

Wilder, H. B., Ludlum, R. P. and Brown, H. M. (1963) *This Is America's Story.* New York: Houghton Mifflin

Baird, C. W. (1871) *Chronicle of a Border Town: Rye, Westchester County, New York* Arson D.F. Randolph

Baird, J. (2010) *"John Jay and France,"* Retrieved from http://www.columbia.edu/cu/libraries/inside/dev/jay/jayandfrance.html by Columbia U.

Berton, P. (1981). "Ghent, August—December, 1814," From *Flames Across the Border: 1813– 1814.* McClelland & Stewart. pp. 418–9.

Brecher, F. W. (2003) *Securing American Independence: John Jay and the French Alliance*, Praeger

Casto, W. R. (2002) "The Early Supreme Court Justices' Most Significant Opinion," From *Foreign Affairs and the Constitution in the Age of Fighting Sail.* Ohio Northern University

Cowley, R. and Parker, G. (eds.) (1996) *The Reader's Companion to Military History.* Houghton Mifflin Harcourt Publishing Company

"Defending New York After the Revolution: The Governorship of John Jay," Gotham Center for New York History, Retrieved from https://www.gothamcenter.org/blog/defending-new-york-after-the-revolution-the-governorship-of-john-jay

"Democratic-Republican Party," Retrieved from http://law.jrank.org/pages/6058/Democratic-Republican-Party.html

Elkins, S. M. and McKitrick, E. (1994) *The Age of Federalism: The Early American Republic, 1788-1800* Oxford Paperbacks.

"Federalist 2: Concerning Dangers from Foreign Force and Influence," Retrieved from http://www.let.rug.nl/usa/documents/1786-1800/the-federalist-papers/the-federalist-2.php

"A Founding Father Confronts Multiple Disabilities," Retrieved from http://johnjayhomestead.org/wp-content/uploads/A-Founding-Family-Confronts-Multiple-Disabilities.pdf

"Federalist Party," Retrieved from https://www.history.com/topics/early-us/federalist-party

Flanders, H. (1855) *The Lives and Times of the Chief Justices of the Supreme Court of the United States.* Lippincott

Hulsebosch, D. J. (2006) *Constituting Empire: New York and the Transformation of Constitutionalism* University of North Carolina Press

Jay, J. "Correspondence and Public Papers of John Jay," Retrieved from https://oll.lIbertyfund.org/titles/jay-the-correspondence-and-public-papers-of-john-jay-vol-1-1763-1781

Jay, J. and Jay, S. L. and Freeman, Landa & North, Louise (eds.) (2010) *Selected Letters of John Jay and Sarah Livingston Jay: Correspondence by or to the First Chief Justice of the United States and His Wife.* McFarland.

"Jay and France: The Papers of John Jay," Retrieved from http://www.columbia.edu/cu/libraries/inside/dev/jay/jayandfrance.html

Jay, J. and Nuxoll, Elizabeth, Gallagher, Mary and Steenshorne, Jennifer (eds.) (2010) *The Selected Papers of John Jay 1760-1791* (Vol. 1) University of Virginia Press.

Jay, W. (1833) *The Life and Writings of John Jay,* Harper Row.

"John Jay: Land Ownership Rights," Retrieved from http://jayheritagecenter.org/land-ownership-residents/

"John Jay's Viewpoints," Retrieved from https://scholarship.law.upenn.edu/cgi/viewcontent.cgi?article=5005&context=penn_law_review

Johnson, H. A. (2006) *John Jay: Colonial Lawyer* (reprint) Beard Books

Johnson, H. A. "John Jay and the Supreme Court," From *New York History 2000* 81(1) pps. 59-90

Johnson, H. "John Jay: Lawyer in a Time of Transition, 1764-1775." Retrieved from https://scholarship.law.upenn.edu/cgi/viewcontent.cgi?article=5005&context=penn_law_review

Klein, M. M. (2000) "John Jay and the Revolution," From *New York History* 81(1): pps. 19-30

Littlefield, D. C. (2000) "John Jay, the Revolutionary Generation, and Slavery," From *New York History* 81(1): pps. 91-132

Lorigan, W. (2013) "The Supreme Court, the Establishment Clause, and the First Amendment," *Electronic Theses and Dissertations,* Paper 857 University of Louisville unpub. Master's Thesis

Marshall, J. (1980) "Journal of Libertarian Studies," Vol. IV, No. 3 (Summer, 1980) pps. 233-252

Morris, R. B. (1965) *The Peacemakers: The Great Powers and American Independence,* Harper Row

Morris, R. B. (1973) *Seven Who Shaped Our Destiny: The Founding Fathers as Revolutionaries,* Harper Row

Pellew, G. (1898) *John Jay* (Vol. 9) Houghton Mifflin.

Perkins, B. (1965) *The First Rapprochement; England and the United States: 1795-1805* University of Pennsylvania Press.

Pfister, J. M. (2016) *Charting an American Republic: The Origins and Writings of the Federalist Papers*, McFarland

"The 'Adam and Eve" letter, from Thomas Jefferson to William Short," (1996) *Thomas Jefferson: Radical and Racist.* (Reprint ed.) New York: The Atlantic Online

Bett, E. M., Bear Jr., J., eds. (1966) *Family Letters of Thomas Jefferson.* Columbia, MO: University of Missouri Press

Boyd, J.P., ed. (1950) *Commission as Lieutenant of Albemarie, 9 June 1770.* Princeton: University of Princeton Press

Boyd, J. P., ed. (1952) *The Papers of Thomas Jefferson, vol. 6, 21 May 1781-March 1784.* Princeton: Princeton University Press

Brodie, F. M. (1998) *Thomas Jefferson: An Intimate History.* New York: W.W. Norton

Chidsey, D.B. (1966) *The Siege of Boston: An on-the-scene Account of the Beginning of the American Revolution.* New York: Crown

Cook, D, (1996) *The Long Fuse: How England Lost the American Colonies, 1760-1785.* New York: Atlantic Monthly Press

The Declaration of Independence (Reprint ed.) (1999) Philadelphia: Independence Hall Association

DiIonna, M. (2000) *A Guide to New Jersey's Revolutionary War Trail.* New Brunswick: University of Rutgers Press

Elkins, S and McKitrick, E. (1993) *The Age of Federalism.* New York: Oxford University Press

Emerson, R.W. (1837) *Concord Hymn.* (Reprint ed.) Washington DC: National Park Service

Fresonke, K., Spence, M. D., eds. (2004) *Lewis & Clark: Legacies, Memories, and New Perspectives.* Berkeley, CA: University of California Press

Furlong, P. J., Margaret, S. S. H., Sharkey, D. (1951) *A New Nation.* New York: Sadlier, Inc.

Goesel, E. A., ed. (1993) *Wit and Wisdom of the 1700s, compiled from the Virginia Gazette.* Williamsburg, VA: Bicast Publishing Co.

Hitchens, C. (2009) *Thomas Jefferson: Author of America.* New York: Harper Row

Jefferson, T. A Summary (1774) *View of the Rights of British America.* Williamsburg: Clementine Rind

"Kentucky Resolutions of 1798," *The Papers of Thomas Jefferson, vol. 30: 1 January 1798-1799.* Princeton: Princeton University Press

Kilmeade, B. & Yaegar, D. (2016) *Thomas Jefferson and the Tripoli Pirates: The Forgotten War that Changed American History.* New York: Penguin Books

Knott, S. F. (2017) "America's Worst Secretary of State: Thomas Jefferson," *The National Interest,* New York: National Interest

Leicester Ford, P., ed. (1892) *The Writings of Thomas Jefferson.* New York: G.P. Putnam's Sons

Lewis, M., Clark, W., Moulton, G.E., eds. *The Definitive Journals of Lewis & Clark: Over The Rockies to St. Louis, vol 8.* Lincoln: University of Nebraska Press

Onuf, P. (2018) "Thomas Jefferson: Domestic Affairs," *U. S. Presidents.* Charlottesville, VA: University of Virginia Press

Paine, T., Kuklick B., ed. (1989) *Political Writings.* (Reprint Ed.) New York: Cambridge University Press

Peterson, M.D. (1986) *Thomas Jefferson and the New Nation: A Biography* New York: Oxford University Press

Peterson, M.D. and Vaughn, R.C., eds. (1988) *The Virginia Statute for Religious Freedom: Its Evolution and Consequences in American History.* Cambridge, N.Y.: Cambridge University Press

Randolph, T.J. (1829) *Memoirs, Correspondence and Private Papers of Thomas Jefferson, Late President of the United States.* Washington, DC: H. Coburn and R. Bentley

"The Rejection of Rumors Surrounding the Cowardice of Thomas Jefferson," *Journal of the House of Delegates of the Commonwealth of Virginia, December 12, 1781.* (Reprint ed.) (2016) Richmond, VA: Thomas A. White

Rowland, K. M. (1892) *The Life of George Mason, 1725-1792.* New York: G.P. Putnam's Sons

Schouler, J. (1999) *Americans of 1776, Daily Life in Revolutionary America.* Gansevoort, N.Y.: Corner House Historical Publications

Sloane, E. (1965) *Diary of an Early American Boy, Noah Blake 1805.* New York: Ballantine Books

Stockham, P. (1976) The Little Book of American Crafts & Trades. New York: Dover

Syrett, H. C., (ed.) (1979) *The Papers of Alexander Hamilton, vol 26, 1 May 1802-1803* New York: Columbia University Press

Thorpe, F.N., ed. (1909) *The Federal and State Constitutions Colonial Charters, and Other Organic Laws of the States, Territories, and Colonies Now or Heretofore Forming the United States of America.* Washington, DC: Government Printing Office

"Treaty of Alliance with France," (Reprint ed.) (2001) *Primary Documents in American History.* Washington DC: Library of Congress

Truell, T.S. (2009) *Presidents and Their Times: Thomas Jefferson.* New York: Marshall Cavendish, Times Publishing Group

US Congress (2011) *Journals of the Continental Congress, vol 1.* Washington, DC: Government Printing Office

U. S. Department of State (2001) "Treaty of Paris, 1783" (Reprint ed.) Washington DC: Government Printing Office

U. S. Department of State (2001) "John Jay's Treaty," (Reprint ed.) Washington DC: Government Printing Office

Wilder, H. B., Ludlam, R. P., Browne, H. M., (1963) *This Is America's Story.* New York: Houghton-Mifflin

Wilson, E. S. (2009) "The Battle over the Bank: Hamilton v. Jefferson," *History Now.* New York: The Gilder Lehrman Institute of American History

Adams, J. and Adams, C. (1851) *The Works of John Adams, Second President of the United States.* Little, Brown and Company

Adams, J. (author), Wroth, L and Zobel, H. (eds.) (1965) *The Legal Papers of John Adams*. Harvard University Press

"Adams Family Papers," Retrieved from http://www.masshist.org/adams/adams-family-papers

"Adams Campaigns and Election," Retrieved from https://millercenter.org/president/adams/campaigns-and-elections

Anderson, B. "John Adams: A Liberal Congregationalist and the American Revolution," Retrieved from https://allthingsliberty.com/2018/06/john-adams-a-liberal-congregationalist-and-the-american-revolution/

"Boston Tea Party," Retrieved from https://www.bostonteapartyship.com/john-adams-diplomat-france

Chinard, G. (1933) *Honest John Adams*. Little, Brown and Company

Diggins, J. (author) and Arthur M. Schlesinger, Jr. (ed.) (2003) *John Adams: The American Presidents Series: The 2nd President, 1797-1801*. Macmillan

"The Dutch Loan," Retrieved from https://www.johnadams.us/p/dutch-loan.html

Ferling, J. (1992) *John Adams: A Life*. University of Tennessee Press

Green, J. "The Discourses on Davila," Retrieved from https://presidentialfellows.wordpress.com/2012/03/20/john-adams-discourses-on-davila/ "The Center for the Study of the Presidency and Congress,"

Harmon, T. "How an Earlier Patriot Law Brought Down a President," Retrieved from https://www.bigeye.com/hartmann.htm

"Humphrey Ploughjogger to the Boston Gazette, 14 October 1765," Retrieved from https://founders.archives.gov/documents/Adams/06-01-02-0057

"John Adams and the Massachusetts Constitution," Retrieved from https://www.mass.gov/guides/john-adams-the-massachusetts-constitution

McCullough, D. (2001) *John Adams*. Simon Schuster

"Our Documents: The Judiciary," Retrieved from https://www.loc.gov/rr/program/bib/ourdocs/judiciary.html

Pollard, E. (1862) *The First Year of the War*. West & Johnson

"The Quasi-War, America's First Limited War," Retrieved from https://www.cnrs-scrn.org/northern_mariner/vol18/tnm_18_3-4_67-77.pdf

Ragsdale, B. "The Sedition Act Trials," Retrieved from https://www.fjc.gov/sites/default/files/trials/seditionacts.pdf

Ryerson et. al. (eds.) (1993) *Adams Family Correspondence, Vol 5.* The Belknap Press of Harvard University

Ryerson, R. (2016) *John Adams's Republic: The One, the Few, and the Many.* JHU Press

Smith P. (1962) *John Adams, Vols. 1 and II.* W.W. Norton

Wood, G. (2017) *Empire of Liberty: A History of the Early Republic.* Oxford University Press

Beck, G. (2012) The Indispensable Man as You've Never Seen Him. Simon and Schuster

"Did Slavery Make Economic Sense?" (2013) Retrieved from https://www.economist.com/free-exchange/2013/09/27/did-slavery-make-economic-sense

DiIonna, M. (2000) A Guide to New Jersey's Revolutionary War Trail. University of Rutgers Press

Ford, P. L. (1898) The True George Washington. J. B. Lippincott Co.

"From George Washington to James Madison," (1793) Washington Papers Retrieved from https://founders.archives.gov/documents/Washington/05-14-02-0146

Furlong, P. J., Margaret, S. S. H., Sharkey, D. (1951) A New Nation. Sadlier, Inc.

Goesel, E. A., ed. (1993) Wit and Wisdom of the 1700s, compiled from the Virginia Gazette. Bicast Publishing Co.

"Growth of Mount Vernon," (2018) Retrieved from https://www.mountvernon.org/library/digitalhistory/digital-encyclopedia/article/growth-of-mount-vernon/

"House of Burgesses," (2018) National Library for the Study of George Washington at Mount Vernon. Retrieved from https://www.mountvernon.org/library/digitalhistory/digital-encyclopedia/article/house-of-burgesses/

Irving, W. (1876) The American Revolution. J. P. Putnam Sons

Marshall, J. (1844) The Life of George Washington. James Crissey

McGuffey, W. H. (1836) The Eclectic Second Reader. Truman and Smith

"Nathaniel Greene," (2018) Retrieved from
https://www.mountvernon.org/library/digitalhistory/digital-encyclopedia/article/nathanael-greene/

"Parenting," (2018) Retrieved from https://www.mountvernon.org/library/digitalhistory/digital-encyclopedia/article/parenting/

Schouler, J. (1999) Americans of 1776, Daily Life in Revolutionary America. Corner House Historical Publications

Stefanelli, D., ed. (2017) "Visitors' Accounts of George Washington's Mount Vernon," Washington Papers. Retrieved from http://gwpapers.virginia.edu/visitors-accounts-george-washingtons-mount-vernon/

"Tribes of the Indian Nation," (1996) Jayhawk International

"Washington and the New Agriculture," (1843) George Washington Papers. Washington, D. C.: Library of Congress

Washington, G. (1848) *The Writings of George Washington: Part V.* (rep.) Harper and Row

Whipple, W. (1911) *The Story-life of Washington: A Life-history in Five Hundred True Stories.* John C Winston Co.

Wilder, H. B., Ludlum, R. P., Brown, H. (1963) This Is America's Story. Houghton Mifflin Co.

Adams, J., Taylor, R. (ed) "Papers of John Adams, Vol 2" Retrieved from
http://oll.libertyfund.org/titles/adams-the-works-of-john-adams-vol-5-defence-of-the-constitutions-vols-ii-and-iii

"Benjamin Franklin: Enlightenment Archetype" Retrieved from
https://atlassociety.org/commentary/commentary-blog/4934-benjamin-franklin-enlightenment-archetype

"Ben Franklin: His Autobiography 1706-1757" Retrieved from
http://www.let.rug.nl/usa/biographies/benjamin-franklin/

"Benjamin Franklin's Mission to London, 1757-1762," *Journal of the American Revolution.* Retrieved from https://allthingsliberty.com/2017/09/benjamin-franklins-mission-london-1757-1762/

"Colonists Respond to the Quartering Act of 1765," Making the Revolution: America 176-1791" Retrieved from
http://americainclass.org/sources/makingrevolution/crisis/text4/quarteringactresponse1766.pdf

Fleming, T. J. "A Touch of France/Taking Paris by Storm: Benjamin Franklin, Founding Father and First Ambassador to France," Retrieved from https://www.medicographia.com/2014/06/a-touch-of-france-taking-paris-by-storm-benjamin-franklin-american-founding-father-and-first-ambassador-to-france/

"Flashback: Lamps and Illuminants," *Collectors' Weekly.* Retrieved from https://www.collectorsweekly.com/articles/lamps-and-illuminants/

Ford, P. L. (1921) *The Many-Sided Franklin.* Century Company

Franklin, B. "Benjamin Franklin and the Stamp Act Crisis" Retrieved from http://www.digitalhistory.uh.edu/disp_textbook.cfm?smtID=3&psid=152

Franklin, R., Trent, W. P. (ed) (1906) *Benjamin Franklin: His Life* Ginn & Co.

Franklin, B., Bigelow, J. (ed) (1904) *Benjamin Franklin: Digital Version of the Autobiography, Vol. 5* G. P. Putnam

Franklin, B., Sparks, J. (ed.) (1882) *The Works of Benjamin Franklin: Containing Several Political and Historical Tracts Not Included in Any Former Edition and Many Letters, Official and Private, Vol. 4* Benjamin Franklin Stevens

"Franklin's Papers," *Packard Humanities Institute* Retrieved from http://franklinpapers.org/framedVolumes.jsp

"From Benjamin Franklin to Richard Jackson, 25 June 1764 Retrieved from https://founders.archives.gov/documents/Franklin/01-11-02-0064#BNFN-01-11-02-0064-fn-0002

"George Grenville" Retrieved from http://www.ouramericanrevolution.org/index.cfm/people/view/pp0012

Huth, E. J. (2006) Benjamin Franklin's Place in the History of Medicine," *The James Lind Library*. Retrieved from http://www.jameslindlibrary.org/articles/benjamin-franklins-1706-1790-place-in-the-history-of-medicine/

Kidd, T. S. (June 28, 201) "How Benjamin Franklin, a deist, and Became a Founding Father of a Unique Kind of American Faith," *The Washington Post*

Lapsansky-Werner, E., Talbott, T. (ed.) (2005) "At the End, an Abolitionist?" From *Benjamin Franklin in Search of a Better World*, pps. 273-296 Yale University Press

McClay, G. "A Long Road to Abolitionism: Benjamin Franklin's Transformation on Slavery," California State University (unpub. ms.) Retrieved from https://csueastbay-dspace.calstate.edu/bitstream/handle/10211.3/196230/Gregory.McClayThesis.pdf?sequence=1

Morgan, E. S. (2003) *Benjamin Franklin* Yale University Press

"Last Will and Testament of Benjamin Franklin" Retrieved from https://www.constitution.org/primarysources/lastwill.html

Ruppert, B. "Ben Franklin's Mission to London, 1757-1762" Retrieved from https://allthingsliberty.com/2017/09/benjamin-franklins-mission-london-1757-1762/

Scharf, J. T. (1884) *History of Philadelphia, 1609-1884, Vol. 3* L. H. Everts & Co.

Schultze, C. "Why Was Benjamin Franklin's Basement Filled with Skeletons?" *Smithsonian Magazine* Retrieved from https://www.smithsonianmag.com/smart-news/why-was-benjamin-franklins-basement-filled-with-skeletons-524521/

Waldstreicher, D. (2005) *Runaway America* Ferrar, Straus and Giroux

Weems, M. L. (1873) *The Life of Benjamin Franklin: With Many Choice Anecdotes and Admirable Sayings of this Great Man* Uriah Hunts & Sons

Whipple, W. (1916) *The Young Benjamin* Franklin Henry Altemus Co.

"William Pitt's Defense of the American Colonies," *Colonial Williamsburg.* Retrieved from http://www.history.org/almanack/life/politics/pitt.cfm

Wood, G.S. (2005) *The Americanization of Benjamin Franklin* Penguin

---

[i] Gouveneur" was Morris's first name.

[ii] In the courtroom, this is called "Taking the Fifth."

[iii] The U.S. Supreme Court has since ruled that money and/or property may be seized without a warrant if it may have been gained through the commission of crime.

[iv] These are often referred to as the "Miranda Rights." A statement to that effect is recited to anyone who is being arrested for an alleged crime, according to a 20th Century Supreme Court ruling.

[v] If a right is not specified in the U.S. Constitution, that cannot be construed to mean that a person doesn't have that right.

[vi] This means that the federal government only has the powers delineated in the Constitution. Any other powers can be decided by a state, for example levying a state income tax.